CECIL COUNTY, MARYLAND

MARRIAGE REFERENCES AND FAMILY RELATIONSHIPS

1825-1850

Henry C. Peden Jr.

Colonial Roots
Millsboro, DE
2015

Colonial Roots

Helping You Grow Your Family Tree

ISBN 978-1-68034-028-0

CONTENTS

INTRODUCTION

This volume is a comprehensive compilation of marriage references in Cecil County, Maryland from 1825 through 1850. Marriage information was gleaned from license books, newspapers (*Cecil Whig, Cecil Gazette, Cecil Republican, Cecil Democrat and Farmer's Journal, Elkton Press, Midland Journal, Cecil Courier, The Aegis, Easton Star, Kent News, Baltimore American, Baltimore Sun,* and *Delaware Gazette*), county court records, tombstone inscriptions, death records, church registers, bible records, census records, military records, selected family histories and other sources as cited within the text.

As with my other marriage books this volume is so much more than just a listing of names and dates. In many instances the reader may find years of birth and death, names of parents, children, siblings, other relationships, ministers, places of residence and migration, occupations, military ranks, subsequent marriages after 1850, places of burial, and more, including information about African Americans.

It should also be noted that in some instances herein the dates of marriages are exact dates while in other cases, due to the lack of actual marriage records, they are approximated dates. Some marriage references were found in records long after the marriage itself had taken place; therefore, the actual date could not be determined. Readers will also find in many instances the date the parties obtained a marriage license followed by the date they actually married. Over the years some researchers have mistaken the former for the latter. Many discrepancies were also found in different sources with respect to the dates of marriage and the spelling of names, especially with respect to the DAR books that were published in 1928 and 1955. Discrepancies have been noted and corrected where possible, but a few remain undetermined.

Marriages herein have been listed alphabetically by the surnames of the grooms while the names of the brides and other family members have been inserted within the text, also in alphabetical order, thus precluding the need for a separate index. And there is also an "Unknown" section for those persons whose names were either unknown or undetermined, and they were noted as such with a symbol (N) in the text.

A sincere thank you is extended to Gary L. Burns for his work in copying tombstone inscriptions over many years; to Gary A. Griffith for his work in abstracting information from the *Cecil Democrat* and creating a database of it; and, to Christopher T. Smithson and A. Amy Unverzagt for copying marriage records for me at the Maryland State Archives. A very special thanks goes to Jo Ann Gardner, volunteer extraordinaire at the Cecil County Historical Society, for reviewing microfilm, making copies of marriage announcements for my book from extant Cecil County newspapers and forwarding them to me via e-mail. It was always a pleasure to visit the society headquarters knowing that she would be there to help me out.

As it is with all of my genealogical reference books I trust that this latest work product will aid researchers who have Cecil County family lines as they search the paper trail for their elusive ancestors.

Henry C. Peden, Jr.
Bel Air, Maryland
January 21, 2015

CECIL COUNTY, MARYLAND MARRIAGE REFERENCES AND FAMILY RELATIONSHIPS, 1825-1850

ABBOTT

Abbott, Leonard, married Annesley Hyland circa 6 Oct 1842 (date of license) (Cecil County Marr. License Book; DAR transcript copied in 1955 misspelled her name as Myland)

Abbott, Lydia, see Joseph Scott

ABRAHAMS

Abrahams, Caroline F., see Theodore B. Knight

Abrahams, Catharine, see Arthur Alexander

Abrahams, Joseph W. (1808-1889, born Maryland) (merchant, Port Deposit), married Susan Marie Reynolds (1814-1862, born Maryland) circa 10 Feb 1834 (date of license) by Rev. Duke (Cecil County Marriage License Book; DAR transcript copied in 1928 spelled his name Abrams; Hopewell United Methodist Church Cemetery tombstone inscriptions; 1860 Cecil County Census listed his name as J. W. Abrams; *Cecil Whig*, 3 Oct 1863, reported that Susan Abrahams had died at Port Deposit in her 49th year)

Abrahams, Susan, see Joseph W. Abrahams

Abrahams, also see Abrams

ABRAMS

Abrams, John Rawlings (1812-1880, born Maryland) (farmer near Brick Meeting House), married 1st to Miss Maria Chandlee (1812-1856) on 29 Feb 1838, after obtaining a license on 24 Jan 1838, by Rev. Woolley, and married 2nd to Mary Ann White (1823-1906, born Maryland), widow of John White (1809-1855) and daughter of Isaac Brown and Elizabeth England, circa 19 Jan 1859 (date of license) (*Cecil Gazette*, 3 Mar 1838, mistakenly stated they married on "30" Feb 1838 and gave his name as Rawlings Abrams; Cecil County Marriage License Book; Zion Methodist Cemetery tombstone inscriptions; Rosebank Cemetery tombstone inscriptions; 1860 Cecil County Census; *Joseph England and his Descendants*, by C. Walter England, Ph.D., 1975, p. 194)

Abrams, Mary, see Joseph Tyson

Abrams, Richard, married Tilitha Alexander (1808-1895, born Maryland) circa 19 Mar 1827 (date of license) (Cecil County Marriage License Book; DAR transcript copied in 1928 misspelled her first name Letitha; Bethel Methodist Church Cemetery, at North East, tombstone inscription for Tilitha Abrams; 1860 Cecil County Census listed Tethilitha *(sic)* Abrams, aged about 50, head of household at Bay View)

Abrams, Thomas S. (born c1807, Maryland) (cooper at Principio), married Mary Owens (1815-1863, born Maryland) circa 13 Nov 1837 (date of license) by Rev. Duke (Cecil County Marriage License Book; DAR transcript copied in 1928 mistakenly listed his middle initial as P.; West Nottingham Cemetery tombstone inscription for Mary Abrams; 1860 Cecil County Census spelled his name Abrahams)

Abrams, William (born c1804, Maryland) (farmer near Bay View), married Amelia (N) (born c1813, Maryland) probably circa 1830; daughter Eliza born c1831 (1860 Cecil County Census)

Abrams, also see Abrahams

ADAMS

Adams, Evy S., married Nancy Sturdevant circa 3 Dec 1844 (date of license) (Cecil County Marriage License Book; DAR transcript copied in 1955 mistakenly spelled her name Sturdevenl)

Adams, Catherine, see Amos Hollis Hughes

Adams, James (1819-1881), married Barbara (N) (1822-1889) probably circa 1840 (Bethesda Methodist Cemetery, at Oakwood, tombstone inscriptions)

Adams, John C., of Talbot Co., MD, married Emily E. Bryan, daughter of Joseph Bryan, Esq., on 13 Feb 1843, after obtaining a license that same day, by Rev. Foulks in Cecil County at Bohemia Village (*Cecil Whig*, 18 Feb 1843; Cecil County Marriage License Book)

Adams, Louisa, see John Robinson

Adams, Mary Reed, see Adam Lambert

Adams, William, see Amos Hollis Hughes

Adams, William (1820-1897) (merchant), of Harford Co., MD, later of Cecil Co., MD and Knoxville, TN, married Miss Lewrenna E. Kerr (1824-1908) circa 3 Feb 1845 (date of license) (Cecil County Marriage License Book listed his county of residence and spelled her first name Leurena; DAR transcript copied in 1955 spelled her name Laurena, but did not list the county of residence; Hopewell United Methodist Church Cemetery, Cecil Co., Maryland, tombstone inscriptions; 1860 Cecil County Census spelled her first name Lurena)

AIKEN

Aiken, Elizabeth, see Ezekiel Thompson

Aiken, John Thomas (born c1822, Maryland) (farmer in 7th District), married Mary Ryan (1823-1888, born Maryland) circa 14 Oct 1850 (date of license) (Cecil County Marriage License Book; West Nottingham Cemetery tombstone inscription for Mary Aiken; 1860 Cecil County Census)

Aiken, Robert (1802-1855), married Mary Jackson (1812-1865) circa 4 Feb 1835 (date of license) by Rev. Griffith (Cecil County Marriage License Book; West Nottingham Cemetery tombstone inscriptions)

Aiken, Samuel (1806-1865), married Agnes Jackson (1806-1865) circa 28 Dec 1840 (date of license) (Cecil County Marriage License Book misspelled his name Aknes and the DAR transcript copied in 1955 correctly spelled it Aiken; West Nottingham Cemetery tombstone inscriptions)

Aiken, William C. (1804-1845), married Margaret Jackson (1804-1869) circa 27 Dec 1831 (date of license) by Rev. Magraw (Cecil County Marriage License Book; DAR transcript copied in 1928 listed his name without the middle initial; West Nottingham Cemetery tombstone inscriptions)

ALDEN

Alden, Ebenezer Jr., married Caroline Owens circa 31 Dec 1834 (date of license) by Rev. Duke (Cecil County Marr. License Book; DAR transcript copied in 1928 mistakenly listed his name without the Jr.)

Alden, George, married Hannah Matthias circa 10 Mar 1832 (date of license) by Rev. Duke (Cecil County Marriage License Book)

Alden, Margaret A., see Reuben Segers

Alden, Ruth Ann, see Silas H. Watson

ALDRICH, ALDRIDGE

Aldrich, Mary A., see Benjamin Wells

Aldridge, Ann Maria, see William Robinson

Aldridge, Fredus (born c1813, Pennsylvania) (tinner at Elkton), married Eliza or Elizabeth Jane Grant (born c1819, Maryland) circa 4 Apr 1839 (date of license) by Rev. Kennard; daughter Maggie A. Aldridge (1842-1870) married C. E. Harman and lived at Centreville, MD (Cecil County Marriage License Book; 1860 Cecil County Census; *Kent News*, 6 Aug 1870)

Aldridge, Harriet, see Andrew W. Alexander

Aldrich, Henry H. (1806-1872), married (N) probably circa 1828 and died at the home of his son William J. Aldrich in Elkton (*Cecil Whig*, 3 Aug 1872, stated he was late of Wilmington, DE)

Aldridge, John S. (1805-1885), married Ann Eliza Gottier (1807-1885) circa 10 Oct 1827 (date of license) (Cecil County Marriage License Book; Elkton Cemetery tombstone inscriptions)

Aldridge, Julia Ann, see William Robinson

Akdridge, Maggie A., see Fredus Aldridge

Aldridge, Sarah, see William C. Lewis

Aldrich, William, see Henry H. Aldrich

ALERTON

Alerton, Robert, married Mary Pogue circa 12 Nov 1827 (date of license) (Cecil Co. Marr. License Book)

ALEXANDER

Alexander, Amanda Ann, see Matthew Borland

Alexander, Andrew, see Andrew W. Alexander

Alexander, Andrew, of Elkton, married Ann J. (N) (1828-1864) probably circa 1848 (*Cecil Whig*, 23 Apr 1864, reported she was the wife of the late Andrew Alexander)

Alexander, Andrew W. (1811-1864) (blacksmith at Elkton), married Harriet Aldridge (1816-1860), of Elk Neck, circa 28 Apr 1836 (date of license) by Rev. Potts (Cecil County Marriage License Book; *Portrait and Biographical Record of Harford and Cecil Counties, Maryland* (1897, repr. 1989), p. 402, spelled her name Aldrich and listed their children as follows: John E. Alexander (born 14 Feb 1838), (N) Alexander (daughter, died at age 15) [namely, Rebecca M., 1842-1857], Louise McCauley [Louisa, born c1844], Andrew Alexander [born c1846], William Alexander (died young) [born 1849, died after 1860], and Harry Alexander (1850-1886) (1860 Cecil County Census; Elkton Methodist Church Cemetery tombstone inscriptions also list William Hyland Alexander (1840-1858), Anna Elizabeth Alexander (1854-1855) and Franklin Ross Alexander (1862-1863); *Cecil Whig*, 30 Jan 1864)

Alexander, Ann, see William Grant

Alexander, Anna, see Matthew Borland

Alexander, Anna Elizabeth, see Andrew W. Alexander

Alexander, Arthur, married Catharine Abrahams circa 6 May 1828 (date of license) (Cecil County Marriage License Book)

Alexander, Benjamin T., married Elizabeth Smith circa 23 Feb 1842 (date of license) (Cecil County Marriage License Book)

Alexander, Catherine J., see Arthur S. Edie

Alexander, Charles P., see John T. Alexander

Alexander, Cursey, see Reuben Alexander, Jr.

Alexander, Elisha, see William Alexander

Alexander, Elisha, married Sarah Steel circa 8 Sep 1846 (date of license) (Cecil Co. Marriage License Book)

Alexander, Eliza Jane, see John A. Johnson

Alexander, Elizabeth, see Samuel Hasson

Alexander, Emily, see Joseph Newsom and Thomas Logan

Alexander, Franklin Ross, see Andrew W. Alexander

Alexander, George (born c1822, Maryland) (farmer at North East), married Sarah (N) (born c1824, Maryland) probably circa 1842; daughter Elizabeth Alexander born c1843 (1860 Cecil County Census)

Alexander, George (born c1826, Maryland) (farmer, Elkton), married Susan (N) (born c1827, Pennsylvania) probably circa 1847; son Thomas Alexander born c1848 (1860 Cecil County Census)

Alexander, Hannah, see Thomas Fulton

Alexander, Harriet, see Norris Levis

Alexander, Harry, see Andrew W. Alexander

Alexander, Harvey E., see Reuben Alexander, Jr.

Alexander, Hetty Ann, see Jones Matthias

Alexander, Isabella, see Reuben Alexander, Jr.

Alexander, Israel, married Catharine McClure circa 26 Dec 1839 (date of license) by Rev. Barratt (Cecil County Marriage License Book)

Alexander, James, married Isabella Gay circa 12 Nov 1827 (date of license) (Cecil Co. Marr. License Book)

Alexander, James, married Amy Simpers circa 19 Apr 1831 (date of license) by Rev. Barratt (Cecil County Marriage License Book)

Alexander, James (born c1819, Maryland) (carpenter at North East), married Charlotte (N) (born c1816, Pennsylvania) probably circa 1839; son William born c1840, Maryland (1860 Cecil County Census)

Alexander, James W., married Louisa Jane Curtis circa 19 Feb 1845 (date of license) (Cecil County Marriage License Book)

Alexander, Jane, see Jonathan P. Burns

Alexander, Jane Ann, see Reuben Alexander, Jr.

Alexander, John, see James Wiley

Alexander, John E., see Andrew W. Alexander

Alexander, John G., see Reuben Alexander, Jr.

Alexander, John J., married Mary A. Rollings circa 19 Dec 1838 (date of license) by Rev. Burrows (Cecil County Marriage License Book)

Alexander, John T. (born c1817, Maryland) (blacksmith at North East), married Ann Eliza Thomas (born c1821, Maryland) circa 9 Dec 1838 (date of license); son Charles P. Alexander born c1839 (Cecil County Marriage License Book; 1860 Cecil County Census)

Alexander, John Washington (1810-1875), married Eliza Jane Benjamin (1816-1899), daughter of George Benjamin (1780-1864) and Sarah Taylor, circa 2 Mar 1836 (date of license) by Rev. Wilson, lived near Havre de Grace, Harford County, and was buried in Cecil County (Cecil County Marriage License Book; *Portrait and Biographical Record of Harford and Cecil Counties, Maryland* (1897, repr. 1989), p. 316; Bethel Methodist Church Cemetery, at North East, tombstone inscriptions)

Alexander, Joseph, see James Sweeny (Sweney) and Joseph Townsend Alexander

Alexander, Julia, see John Cleaves

Alexander, Julia Ann, see Moses Dean

Alexander, Justus, married Rebecca Reynolds circa 21 Apr 1837 (date of license) by Rev. Barratt (Cecil County Marriage License Book)

Alexander, Mabel Caroline, see Reuben Alexander, Jr.

Alexander, Margaret, see James Sweeny (Sweney)

Alexander, Marjery, see Reuben Alexander, Jr.

Alexander, Martha, see Edward Webb

Alexander, Mary Ann, see Joseph Townsend Alexander

Alexander, Mary S., see Reuben Alexander, Jr.

Alexander, Mary Sophia, see Benjamin Thompson

Alexander, Matthew, see Washington Alexander

Alexander, Rachel, see John H. Graham

Alexander, Rachel Catherine, see Reuben Alexander, Jr.

Alexander, Rachel Jane, see Reuben Alexander, Jr.

Alexander, Rebecca Jane, see Benjamin Wells

Alexander, Reuben Jr. (born 1821, Pennsylvania) (carpenter, 8th District), son of Reuben and Catherine Alexander (1791-1877), married Caroline H. Fulton (born 1830, Pennsylvania), daughter of Alexander (1794-1860) and Rachel Fulton (c1795-1877), on 28 Jun 1849 in Philadelphia, PA, by Rev. Demme, a Presbyterian minister (*Bible Records, Genealogical Society of Cecil County*, by Gary L. Burns (1990), pp. 2-3, stated that this family was from the Bald Friar area and listed the births of their ten children: John G., born 20 Jan 1850; Cursey, 1851-1855; Rachel Jane, 1853-1855; Jane Ann, born 18 Oct 1855; Marjery, no date [c1858]; Rachel Catherine, no date [c1861]; Isabella, no date [c1864]; Harvey E., born 2 May 1866; Mabel Caroline, born 21 May 1870; and, Mary S., born 29 Feb 1872; 1860 Cecil County Census)

Alexander, Robert P. (1820-1890) (wheelwright at Elkton), married Sarah Ann Miller (1819, Delaware – 1885, Maryland) circa 19 Aug 1840 (date of license) (Cecil County Marriage License Book; 1860 Cecil County Census; Elkton Cemetery tombstone inscriptions)

Alexander, Sarah, see George W. Moore and John W. Jackson

Alexander, Sarah Ann, see David Wherry

Alexander, Sarah Jane, see George Ferguson

Alexander, Susan, see John O. Ferry

Alexander, Thomas, see George Alexander

Alexander, Tilitha, see Richard Abrams

Alexander, Washington (born c1810, Maryland) (carpenter, Charlestown), married Eliza J. (N) (born c1817, Maryland) probably circa 1836; son Matthew born c1837 (1860 Cecil County Census)

Alexander, William, see Andrew W. Alexander, James Alexander and William V. Alexander

Alexander, William (1815-1857), married Miss Louisa M. Reynolds (1821-1842), daughter of William and Francina Reynolds, circa 19 Feb 1842 (date of license) (Cecil County Marriage License Book; Cherry Hill Methodist Church Cemetery tombstone inscriptions)

Alexander, William (born c1814) (laborer near Elkton), married Louretta (N) (born c1814) probably circa 1842; son Elisha Alexander born c1843 (1860 Cecil County Census)

Alexander, William, married Miss Anne Maria Atkinson on 23 Nov 1847, after obtaining a license that same day, by Rev. Milby (*Cecil Whig*, 4 Dec 1847; Cecil County Marriage License Book; DAR transcript copied in 1955 listed her name as Anna M. Atkinson)

Alexander, William Hyland, see Andrew W. Alexander

Alexander, William T. (born c1819) (shoemaker at Elkton), married Amanda (N) (1825-1873) circa 1843 (son William born c1844) and she died at Wilmington, DE, her husband having pre-deceased her (1860 Cecil County Census; *Cecil Whig*, 8 Feb 1873)

ALGARD

Algard, John (1806-1882, born Pennsylvania) (farmer near Brick Meeting House), married Elizabeth (N) (1808-1887, born Pennsylvania) probably circa 1828 (Zion Presbyterian Church Cemetery tombstone inscriptions; 1860 Cecil County Census)

ALLDERDICE

Allerdice, Abraham and Jane E., see David R. Sloan

ALLEN

Allen, Benjamin (born c1809, New Jersey) (farm hand at Cecilton), married Susan (N) (born 1824, Maryland) circa 1845; son Richard Allen born c1846, Maryland (1860 Cecil County Census)

Allen, Benjamin (born c1821, Maryland) (African American) (laborer, 7th District), married Jane (N) (born c1822, Maryland) probably circa 1844; son Otho Allen born c1845 (1860 Cecil County Census)

Allen, Hannah, see James Nickle

Allen, Mary, see Isaac M. Chesbrough

Allen, Matilda, see Passmore McCullough

Allen, Otho, see Benjamin Allen

Allen, Richard, see Benjamin Allen

ALLISON

Allison, Abner (born c1813, Maryland) (African American) (laborer, 8th District), married Harriet (N) (born c1823, Maryland) (African American) probably circa 1838; son Jacob Allison born c1839, Maryland, laborer (1860 Cecil County Census)

Allison, William F., married Miss Rebecca McClenahan, both of Port Deposit, on 6 Jan 1842, after obtaining a license on 5 Jan 1842, by Rev. Cunningham (Cecil County Marriage License Book; *Cecil Gazette*, 15 Jan 1842, spelled his name Alloson)

ALRICHS

Alrichs, Sarah E., see Edward Wilson Lockwood

ALTERSON

Alterson, Alice, see James Ruley

ANDERSON

Anderson, Abel, see Thomas Alexander

Anderson, Alexander (c1815-c1845), married Louisa Vansant (born c1815) circa 14 Feb 1837 (date of license) by Rev. Reed; daughter Sarah L. Anderson born c1840 and son John A. Anderson born c1842 (Cecil County Marriage License Book; 1850 and 1860 Cecil County Censuses listed Louisa Anderson as head of household in Cecilton)

Anderson, Allen, married Esther McCullough circa 25 Oct 1831 (date of license) by Rev. Magraw (Cecil County Marriage License Book)

Anderson, Ann J., see William Anderson

Anderson, Eliza J., see John N. Baldwin

Anderson, Emma Jane, see John Anderson

Anderson, James, married Maria Simpson circa 6 Oct 1827 (date of license) (Cecil Co. Marr. License Book)

Anderson, John, married Eliza Jane McGee circa 24 May 1827 (date of license) (Cecil County Marriage License Book; DAR transcript copied in 1928 spelled her name Megee)

Anderson, John (1800-1870), son of William and Lydia Anderson, married Jane Maria McVey (1813-1875), daughter of James McVey (1782-1858) and Martha Kidd (1791-1836), on 17 Nov 1842 after obtaining a license on 16 Nov 1842 (Cecil County Marriage License Book; *Bible Records, Genealogical Society of Cecil County*, by Gary L. Burns (1990), p. 53, stated the family was of Cecil Co., MD and Newark, DE, and listed the births of three children as follows: John Burke Anderson, born 13 Nov 1844; Emma Jane Anderson, born 14 Oct 1846, died 28 Sep 1876; and, Samuel Kidd Anderson, born 14 Mar 1849; Pedigree Chart prepared by Dolores K. Busker of Swarthmore, PA in 1991; Cecil Co. Will Book C, No. 10, p. 248)

Anderson, John (1813-1895), married Hannah J. (N) (1823-1886) probably circa 1841 (St. John's Church Cemetery, at Lewisville, tombstone inscriptions)

Anderson, John A., see Alexander Anderson

Anderson, John Burke, see John Anderson

Anderson, John C., married Sarah Watson circa 20 Dec 1826 (date of license) by Rev. Duke (Cecil County Marriage License Book)

Anderson, Lucian B. (1820-1864), married Rachel A. (N) (1818-1869) probably circa 1841 (Cherry Hill United Methodist Church Cemetery tombstone inscriptions)

Anderson, Lydia, see John Anderson

Anderson, Marion (born c1828) (tailor at Elkton), married Mary (N) (born c1827) probably circa 1849; son William Anderson born c1850 (1860 Cecil County Census)

Anderson, Mary, see James Bolton and William Anderson

Anderson, Patrick, see William Anderson

Anderson, Perry (African American), married Amy Buck (African American) circa 28 Jan 1845 (date of license) (Cecil County Marriage License Book)

Anderson, Prudence Jane, see John Thompson

Anderson, Rebecca, see William Anderson

Anderson, Robert, see William Anderson

Anderson, Samuel Kidd, see John Anderson

Anderson, Sarah, see John McCall

Anderson, Sarah A., see John W. Stradley

Anderson, Sarah L., see Alexander Anderson

Anderson, Thomas (born c1823, Maryland) (carpenter at Elkton), married Sarah (born c1826, Maryland) probably circa 1846; son Abel Anderson born c1847 (1860 Cecil County Census)

Anderson, William, see John Anderson, Marion Anderson and William Anderson

Anderson, William, married Ellen McKelvey, natives of Ireland, circa 1825 and had eleven children, of which eight reached adulthood, namely, Rebecca (died before 1897), Ann J., John (died before 1897), William, Elizabeth, Patrick (born 1838), Robert and Mary (*Portrait and Biographical Record of Harford and Cecil Counties, Maryland* (1897, repr. 1989), p. 334)

ANDREWS
Andrews, Caroline M., see John Wilson

Andrews, Catherine, see John Mackie

Andrews, Frances, see Joel Bryan

Andrews, Harriet C., see Timothy N. Terrell

Andrews, Joseph, married Miss Joannah Garrett, both of Chester Co., PA, on 6 Feb 1843 by Rev. Kennard (*Cecil Whig*, 15 Apr 1843)

Andrews, Margaret, see William Watts

Andrews, Sovreign, married Eliza Mumford circa 19 Sep 1839 (date of license) by Rev. Hagany (Cecil County Marriage License Book)

ARBUCKLE

Arbuckle, Daniel (1813-1891), married Mary S. (N) (1816-1905) on 2 Feb 1841 at Frankford, PA, a suburb of Philadelphia, PA (Cherry Hill United Methodist Church Cemetery tombstone inscriptions; *Midland Journal*, 6 Feb 1891, reported they celebrated their 50th anniversary at Andora; he was 77 and she was 75)

ARCHER

Archer, Catherine Cassandra, see Henry Dorsey Smithson

Archer, Harriet H., see L. J. Williams

Archer, Henry Wilson (1813-1887), son of Dr. John Archer (1777-1830) and Ann Stump, married Miss Mary Elizabeth Walker (1830-1908), daughter of John W. Walker and Elizabeth Constable, of Chestertown, Kent Co., MD on 7 Jun 1849 in Kent Co., MD by Rev. Jones and lived in Harford Co., MD (*Substantial Copy of Genealogical Record of the Stump Family of Maryland*, by Albert P. Silver and Henry W. Archer (1891), p. 3; *Descendants of the Signers of the Bush Declaration of March 22, 1775, Harford County, Maryland*, by Christopher T. Smithson and Henry C. Peden, Jr. (2010), p. 37; Archer Genealogy on file at the, Historical Society of Harford County; *Cecil Democrat and Farmer's Journal*, 16 Jun 1849)

Archer, John (1806-1889) (lieut., U. S. Army), of Cecil Co., later of Texas, son of Dr. Robert Harris Archer (1775-1857) and Mary Stump, of Harford Co., married Ann Dennison Savin (c1813-1879), daughter of Thomas L. Savin, Esq., and Sarah Dennison, of and at Port Deposit, MD, on 22 Oct 1833, after obtaining a license on 21 Oct 1833, by Rev. Goforth (Cecil County Marriage License Book; *Baltimore American and Commercial Daily Advertiser*, 2 Nov 1833; *Substantial Copy of Genealogical Record of the Stump Family of Maryland*, by Albert P. Silver and Henry W. Archer (1891), p. 18)

Archer, John, see Henry Dorsey Smithson

Archer, Robert Harris, see John Archer

ARCHIBALD

Archibald, David (1807-1871), married Elizabeth (N) (1813-1891) probably circa 1831 (West Nottingham Cemetery tombstone inscriptions)

Archibald, Robert, married Levina Trump circa 16 Oct 1827 (date of license) (Cecil County Marriage License Book)

ARMINGTON

Armington, Sarah E., see John S. Mahan

ARMOUR

Armour, Emma, see Hugh Armour

Armour, Hugh (1807-1871) (farmer at North East), married Mary E. (N) (1822-1897) probably circa 1848; daughter Emma born c1849 (Ebenezer Church Cem. tombstone inscriptions; 1860 Cecil County Census)

Armour, John (born c1815, Maryland) (mason, 6th District), married Ruth Ann Jenkins (born c1818, Maryland) circa 16 Feb 1839 (date of license) by Rev. Burrows (Cecil County Marriage License Book; DAR transcript copied in 1928 spelled her name Jenkings; 1860 Cecil County Census)

Armour, Mary B., see Stephen Armour

Armour, Stephen (born c1819, Maryland) (farmer near Bay View), married Mary B. Sproston (1817-1891, born Maryland) circa 23 Feb 1847 (date of license) (Cecil County Marriage License Book; 1860 Cecil County Census; Ebenezer Methodist Church Cemetery tombstone inscriptions for Mary B. Armour and her brother John T. Sproston, 1813-1891)

ARMSTRONG

Armstrong, Amanda, see Samuel Mackey

Armstrong, Catherine Ann, see William Holland

Armstrong, Frances A., see James A. Ruley

Armstrong, George H., married Mary Ann Clark circa 30 Jun 1835 (date of license) by Rev. Barratt (Cecil County Marriage License Book)

Armstrong, Henry, married Ellen Jane Fulton circa 7 Apr 1841 (date of license) (Cecil County Marriage License Book)

Armstrong, Hugh (born c1827, England) (watch maker at Chesapeake City), married Jane (N) (born c1825, England) probably circa 1849; son Joseph Armstrong born c1850, England (1860 Cecil County Census)

Armstrong, John, married Ann Jane Gallaher circa 27 Jun 1843 (date of license) (Cecil County Marriage License Book)

Armstrong, Joseph, see Hugh Armstrong

Armstrong, Louisa Jane, see Waldon Reed

Armstrong, Margaret, see Thomas Terry

Armstrong, Martha, see John Houston

Armstrong, Mary, see David Simpson, Jacob D. McConnell and William W. Rankin

Armstrong, Nancy, see William M. Armstrong

Armstrong, Robert, married Catharine Marshall circa 13 Aug 1827 (date of license) (Cecil County Marriage License Book)

Armstrong, Susan, see William S. Houston and Ferdinand Lungren

Armstrong, Walter, married Miss Emma Hall, both of Cecil Co., on 6 Dec 1848, after obtaining a license on 4 Dec 1848, by Rev. DeWitt at the residence of Levi Hall (Cecil County Marriage License Book; *Cecil Whig*, 15 Dec 1848; *Cecil Democrat and Farmer's Journal*, 23 Dec 1848)

Armstrong, William (born 1822) (stock and dairy farmer near Elkton), son of William Armstrong and Ann Booth, married Mary Jane Smith (born c1831), second daughter of William Smith, of Mechanicsville, PA, on 24 Dec 1849 by Rev. DeWitt (*Cecil Democrat and Farmer's Journal*, 5 Jan 1850; *Portrait and Biographical Record of Harford and Cecil Counties, Maryland* (1897, repr. 1989), pp. 393, 284-285, stated Mary Smith was of Delaware; 1860 Cecil County Census stated she was born in Pennsylvania)

Armstrong, William M. (born c1817) (farmer near Chesapeake City), married Sarah (N) (born c1818) probably circa 1848; daughter Nancy born c1849 (1860 Cecil County Census)

ARNEL

Arnel, Sarah Jane, see William Gorrell

ARRANTS

Arrants, Ann, see William Grace

Arrants, Elizabeth Melvina, see Norman W. Nowland

Arrants, Martha, see William Bristow

Arrants, Sarah Rebecca, see John James Moore

Arrants, Susan, see George M. Fillingame

Arrants, William (born c1816) (sailor at Cecilton), married Mary E. Mumford (born c1824) circa 10 Oct 1843 (date of license) (Cecil County Marriage License; 1860 Cecil County Census)

Arrants, William, married Mary Grace circa 11 Mar 1844 (date of license) (Cecil Co. Marr. License Book)

ARRISON

Arrison, John B. (1813-1895, born Pennsylvania) (farmer at North East), son of Jonathan (born c1793, Pennsylvania, died after 1860), married Abigail (N) (1814-1883, born Pennsylvania) probably circa 1835; daughter Sarah born c1836, Pennsylvania, son Howard S. (1841, Pennsylvania - 1909, Maryland), son John born c1846, Maryland, daughter Emily born c1850, Maryland, and daughter Mary born c1852, Maryland (Rosebank Cemetery, at Calvert, tombstone inscriptions; 1860 Cecil County Census)

ARTHUR, ARTHURS

Arthur, Catharine, see Daniel Harvey

Arthur, Mark, married Araminta Maulden circa 30 Jan 1832 (date of license) by Rev. Barratt (Cecil County Marriage License Book)

Arthurs, Robert H., married Mary E. Hickman circa 10 Nov 1843 (date of license) (Cecil County Marriage License Book)

ASAY

Asay, William, married Eliza S. Stidham circa 17 Jan 1842 (date of license) (Cecil Co. Marr. License Book)

ASH

Ash, Ann, see Thomas Howard, Jr.

Ash, John, married Ruth Ann Smythers circa 27 Sep 1825 (date of license) by Rev. Sharpley (Cecil County Marriage License Book)

Ash, Joseph Miles, married Mrs. Sarah Ann Dunbar (1809-1890) (neé Boulden, widow of Justus Dunbar), on 21 Apr 1844, after obtaining a license on 18 Apr 1844, by Rev. Shields (*Cecil Whig*, 27 Apr 1844; Cecil County Marriage License Book; Elkton Methodist Church Register, p. 140; Elkton Methodist Church Cemetery tombstone inscription for Sarah A. Ash, wife of Miles Ash)

Ash, Joshua, married Rebecca Wallace circa 18 Apr 1840 (date of license) by Rev. McIntire (Cecil County Marriage License Book)

Ash, Louisa, see John Kinkead

Ash, Miles, see Joseph Miles Ash

Ash, Rebecca, see Sylvester Williams

ASHEN

Ashen, Mary, see John Conegan

ASHBY, ASHLEY

Ashby or Ashley, Bayard B., married Miss Elizabeth Seth, both of Elk Mills, Cecil Co., on 15 Dec 1850 by Rev. Dr. Bissey at New London Cross Roads (*Cecil Whig*, 21 Dec 1850, spelled his surname Ashby and listed the minister's name as Rev. Mr. Bizzee; *Cecil Democrat and Farmer's Journal*, 21 Dec 1850, spelled his surname Ashley and listed the minister's name as Rev. Dr. Bissey)

ASKEW

Askew, Elizabeth, see David B. Trimble

Askew, Hannah, see Job Eldridge

Askew, Parkes, see Job Eldridge

Askew, Peter, see David B. Trimble

ASPRIL

Aspril, David T., married Miss Caroline Eliza Lightner, only daughter of George W. Lightner, Esq., of Cecil Co., on 15 Feb 1838, after obtaining a license on 14 Feb 1838, by the Rev. Brown (*Cecil Gazette*, 17 Feb 1838; Cecil County Marriage License Book; DAR transcript copied in 1928 misspelled her name Lighter)

ASTLE

Astle, John (1814-1893), married Mary (N) (1817-1886) probably circa 1840; buried beside daughter Rachel A. Astle, 1847-1934 (Rosebank Cemetery, at Calvert, tombstone inscriptions)

ASTON

Aston, Edwin W., of Lancaster Co., PA, married Margaret Taylor circa 8 Dec 1849 (date of license) (Cecil County Marriage License Book)

ATKINSON

Atkinson, Alexander, see Stephen Atkinson

Atkinson, Anne Maria, see William Alexander

Atkinson, Benjamin T., see Stephen Atkinson

Atkinson, Elisha (1807-1864, born Maryland) (farmer at South Milford), married Elizabeth Mahany (1815-1865, born Maryland) circa 12 Mar 1836 (date of license) by Rev. Wilson (Cecil County Marriage License Book; 1860 Cecil County Census; *Cecil Whig*, 14 Jan 1865 and 25 Feb 1865)

Atkinson, Francis "Frank" (born c1804, Maryland) (collier at North East), married Hester "Hetty" Logan (born c1806, Maryland) circa 27 Jun 1826 (date of license) by Rev. Barratt (Cecil County Marriage License Book; 1860 Cecil County Census)

Atkinson, Ida, see Stephen Atkinson

Atkinson, John A. (1821-1865, born Maryland) (laborer in the 7th District), married Miss Sarah E. Vannort (1829-1911, born Maryland) circa 8 May 1849 (date of license) (Cecil County Marriage License Book; Hopewell United Methodist Church Cemetery tombstone inscriptions; 1860 Cecil County Census)

Atkinson, Millard, see Stephen Atkinson

Atkinson, N. J., married Harriet N. (N) (1816-1872), of Cecil Co., later of New Brunswick, NJ, probably circa 1835 (*Cecil Whig*, 2 Mar 1872)

Atkinson, Norris M., see Stephen Atkinson

Atkinson, Stephen (1820-1897) (laborer at Bay View), son of Alexander Atkinson, of Ireland, later of Cecil Co., and Elizabeth Mahoney, married Hannah Maria Ramsey (1824-1903), daughter of William Ramsey, of Bay View, Cecil Co., on 23 Jun 1842 after obtaining a license on 21 Jun 1842 (Cecil County Marriage License Book; Bethel Methodist Church Cemetery, at North East, tombstone inscriptions; *Portrait and Biographical Record of Harford and Cecil Counties, Maryland* (1897, repr. 1989), p. 435, stated they had ten children of whom eight were living in 1897, namely, Theresa Logan [born c1844], William Atkinson [born c1848], Wesley Atkinson [born c1851], Martha Jane Barrett [born c1843], Norris M. Atkinson [born c1857], Benjamin T. Atkinson [born c1859], Ida Atkinson, Emma Corsett and Thompson R.; two children who died before 1897 were Stephen John Atkinson [born c1847] and Millard R. Atkinson [born c1855]; 1860 Cecil County Census mistakenly listed her name as Anna instead of Hannah)

Atkinson, Thompson R., see Stephen Atkinson

Atkinson, Wesley, see Stephen Atkinson

Atkinson, William, see Stephen Atkinson

ATWELL

Atwell, Deby, see John A. Roberts

AULDEN

Aulden, Elizabeth, see Thomas Garrett

AULDS

Aulds, Jane, see John Cannon

Aulds, Mary, see Isaac Lum

Aulds, Serena, see John T. Lee

AYRES, AYERS

Ayres, Rebecca S., see Alexander McConaughy

Ayres, Samuel P., married Miss Emeline Logan, both of New London Township, Chester Co., PA, on 28 Mar 1849 by Rev. Plummer at Mt. Olivet, New London Township, Chester Co., PA (*Cecil Democrat and Farmer's Journal*, 14 Apr 1849)

Ayers, William T. (1825-1895), married Sarah J. (N) (1830-1893) probably circa 1850 (St. John's Church, at Lewisville, tombstone inscriptions)

BAILEY

Bailey, Ann, see Joel T. Bailey

Bailey, Edward T. (c1804-1843), of Wilmington, DE, married Miss Mary Emma Woodland (c1810-1829) on 21 Mar 1825, after obtaining a license on 20 Mar 1825, by Rev. Duke in Elkton (Cecil County Marriage License Book; *Delaware Gazette*, 22 Mar 1825 and 3 Feb 1829 and 26 May 1843)

Bailey, Eliza, see James Boyd

Bailey, James, see Joel T. Bailey

Bailey, James, married Sarah M. Robinson circa 10 Sep 1838 (date of license) by Rev. Duke (Cecil County Marriage License Book)

Bailey, Joel T., son of James and Ann Bailey, both deceased, of West Marlborough Township, Chester Co., PA, married Elizabeth H. Pugh, daughter of Jesse and Elizabeth Pugh, the latter deceased, of East Nottingham Township, Chester Co., PA, on the 21st day of the 3rd month 1844 at a public Friends meeting at the home of Jesse Pugh (*Births, Deaths and Marriages of the Nottingham Quakers, 1680-1899*, by Alice L. Beard (1989), p. 226)

Bailey, John, married Joanna Jennings, both of Cecil Co., on 12 Dec 1844, after obtaining a license on 27 Nov 1844, by Rev. Goldsborough (Cecil County Marriage License Book; *Cecil Whig*, 14 Dec 1844, spelled his name Bayley and her name Jenkings)

Bailey, Lloyd, married Jerusha Harvey circa 10 Nov 1830 (date of license) by Rev. Hodgson (Cecil County Marriage License Book; DAR transcript copied in 1928 misspelled the minister's name as Hodson; Francis Hodgson was a Methodist Episcopal minister in Elkton at that time)

Bailey, Mary, see John Snowden

Bailey, Mary Ann, see James Burlin and William Orr

Bailey, Rebecca, see William Marshall

BAIRD

Baird, Joseph (1821-1879), married Jane (N) (1826-1918) probably circa 1845 (Hopewell United Methodist Church Cemetery tombstone inscriptions)

Baird, Robert, married Margaret A. Brookings circa 28 Dec 1849 (date of license) (Cecil County Marriage License Book)

BAKER

Baker, Caroline, see John A. Rankin

Baker, Christian (1812-1865, born Germany) (confectioner in Elkton), married Catherine Smith (1821-1888, born Maryland) probably circa 1841; daughter Elizabeth Baker born c1842, Maryland (Hopewell United Methodist Church Cemetery tombstone inscriptions; 1860 Cecil County Census abstract gave his first name as Christopher)

Baker, David, see John B. Baker

Baker, Elizabeth, see Christian Baker

Baker, Elizabeth Jane, see William Craig

Baker, Eugenia, see William Henry Baker

Baker, Hannah Gooding, see John Wilson

Baker, Henry, see William Craig

Baker, Henry Clay, see William Henry Baker

Baker, Janealiza, see William Henry Baker

Baker, Jeremiah, married Mary Campbell circa 25 Jan 1826 (date of license) by Rev. Magraw (Cecil County Marriage License Book)

Baker, John, see William Henry Baker

Baker, John, married Mrs. Catharine ----ton [page torn], both of Cecil Co., on 29 Apr 1847 by Rev. Th--- (N) [page torn] (*Cecil Whig*, 8 May 1847)

Baker, John B. (1812, Delaware - 1901, Maryland) (laborer, 6th District), married Letitia (N) (1822-1898, Maryland) probably circa 1846; son David Baker born c1847, Maryland (Hopewell United Methodist Church Cemetery tombstone inscriptions; 1860 Cecil County Census)

Baker, Lewis, see William Henry Baker

Baker, Lydia Ann, see William Lynch

Baker, Margaret A., see William Henry Baker

Baker, Mary, see Thomas Logan

Baker, Mary Ann, see James B. Herbert

Baker, Mary Louisa, see William Henry Baker

Baker, Philena, see John Cleaver

Baker, Robert H. (1820-1895, born Maryland) (farmer at St. Augustine), married Sarah A. (N) (1816-1885, born Maryland) probably circa 1844; daughter Sarah Baker born c1845 (St. Augustine Catholic Church Cemetery tombstone inscriptions; 1860 Cecil County Census)

Baker, Simon, married Maria Galloway circa 14 Mar 1834 (date of license) by Rev. Duke (Cecil County Marriage License Book; DAR transcript copied in 1928 misspelled her first name as Mana)

Baker, William Henry (born 1818) (laborer at Charlestown), married Eliza Jane Wilson (born c1818) circa 8 Jun 1844 (date of license) (Cecil County Marriage License Book; *Maryland Bible Records, Volume 4: Eastern Shore*, by Henry C. Peden, Jr. (2004), pp. 18-19, did not give their date of marriage, but listed these children: Henry Clay born 13 May 1845, Margaret A. born 9 Apr 1847, Janealiza born 2 Mar 1848, died 3 Feb 1849, and Mary Louisa born 7 Dec 1849; 1860 Cecil County Census also listed three more children: John born c1852, Lewis born c1854, and Eugenia born c1858)

BALDERSTON

Balderston, Annie, see Lloyd Balderston

Balderston, Emily, see William H. Balderston

Balderston, Lloyd (1818-1907, born Pennsylvania) (farmer, 6th District), married Catharine Canby (1819-1884, born Pennsylvania) probably circa 1843; daughter Annie born c1844, Maryland (Friends Cemetery, at Colora, tombstone inscriptions; 1860 Cecil County Census)

Balderston, William H. (1814-1886, born Maryland) (farmer in 6th District), married Rebecca J. (N) (1812-1894, born Pennsylvania) probably circa 1836; daughter Emily born c1842, Maryland (Friends Cemetery, at Colora, tombstone inscriptions; 1860 Cecil County Census)

BALDWIN

Baldwin, Jesse, married Ann Scott circa 6 Nov 1843 (date of license) (Cecil County Marriage License Book)

Baldwin, John N., married Eliza J. Anderson circa 12 Feb 1835 (date of license) by Rev. Duke (Cecil County Marriage License Book)

Baldwin, John, married Mary Ann Orr circa 23 Dec 1829 (date of license) by Rev. Ayres (Cecil County Marriage License Book)

BALL

Ball, Martha, see Samuel McCrea

Ball, Thomas, of New York, married Anna M. Giles (born 1794), daughter of Thomas Giles (1752-1812) and Ann Goodwin (1758-1800), of Birmingham, England, later of Cecil Co., MD, circa 8 Aug 1832 (date of license) in Elkton by Rev. Benson and probably removed to New York (Cecil County Marriage License

Book; *Thomas Giles, Born 1752 – Birmingham, England, Died 1812 – Elkton, Maryland, U. S. A.: A Genealogical History of His Descendants*, by Alexander W. Giles, Jr. (1986, updated 1996), pp. 9, 15)

BANKS
Banks, Thaddeus, married Delia Jane Reynolds circa 13 May 1841 (date of license) (Cecil County Marriage License Book; DAR transcript copied in 1955 misspelled his name as Beaks)

BAREN
Baren, Samuel (born c1820, Delaware) (bridge tender at Chesapeake City), married Lydia (N) (born c1823, Maryland) probably circa 1842; son Samuel born c1843, Maryland (1860 Cecil County Census)

BARKER
Barker, Ann, see James Milon

BARNABY
Barnaby, Elias P., married 1st to Don Maria Money circa 6 Feb 1840 (date of license) by Rev. Piggot, a Protestant Episcopal minister in North Sassafras, and married 2nd to Sarah E. Ruley circa 19 Jan 1843 (date of license) (Cecil County Marriage Book; 1840 Cecil County Census spelled his name Barnabas)

Barnaby, Joseph, married Rosanna Wilson, daughter of James Wilson, Esq., on 9 Feb 1845, after obtaining a license on 8 Feb 1845, by Rev. Goldsborough in Trinity Church (Cecil County Marriage License Book; *Cecil Whig*, 15 Feb 1845)

BARNARD
Barnard, Thomas P., married Henrietta Dobson, of Havre de Grace, on 12 Feb 1846, after obtaining a license in Harford Co. on 9 Feb 1846, by Rev. Blane (*Cecil Whig*, 21 Feb 1846; Harford County License Book)

BARNES
Barnes, Ann, see John Gamble

Barnes, Araminta H., see Steuart H. Gallaher

Barnes, Cordelia E., see James T. Trimble

Barnes, Edwin, see Alexander Williams

Barnes, Elizabeth, see Barney Mullen

Barnes, George Washington (1812-1880), of Havre de Grace, Harford Co., later of Carpenter's Point, Cecil Co., married 1st to Sarah Jane Morgan (son Perry K. Barnes, 1849-1919) and she died in 1857; he married 2nd to Rachel L. Kirby, daughter of Zebulon S. and Eliza Kirby, of Cecil Co., formerly of Talbot Co., in 1859; she died in 1893 (*Portrait and Biographical Record of Harford and Cecil Counties, Maryland* (1897, repr. 1989), p. 125; *Duck Hunters on the Susquehanna Flats, 1850-1930*, by Henry C. Peden, Jr. (2014), pp. 15, 16)

Barnes, Henry, see Benjamin F. Heath

Barnes, James (1798-1860), married Rhoda A. (N) (1804-1884) by 1835; buried beside son Thomas H. Barnes, 1836-1884 (Hopewell United Methodist Church Cemetery tombstone inscriptions)

Barnes, Jane, see John Moore

Barnes, John, married Jane Nickle circa 20 Jul 1835 (date of license) by Rev. Magraw (Cecil County Marriage License Book)

Barnes, Martha, see James Ewing

Barnes, Martha Ann, see Elijah J. Tyson

Barnes, Nathan C., married Elizabeth A. Grace circa 9 Dec 1840 (date of license) (Cecil County Marriage License Book)

Barnes, Perry K., see George Washington Barnes

Barnes, Rebecca, see John A. Keith

Barnes, Rebecca M., see Alexander Williams

Barnes, Sarah Rebecca, see Alexander Brown

Barnes, Thomas H., see James Barnes

Barnes, W. C., see Joseph R. Thomas

BARNETT

Barnett, Elizabeth, see Edward F. Keithley, Thomas Kiethley and William Keithley

Barnett, Emily, see Francis Keatly

Barnett, Jane, see Thomas Culbertson

Barnett, John, married Hannah Simpers circa 23 Sep 1837 (date of license) by Rev. Barratt (Cecil County Marriage License Book; DAR transcript copied in 1928 misspelled his surname as Barratt)

Barnett, Mary, see Thomas B. Gainor

Barnett, Richard, married Jane Hart circa 2 Feb 1836 (date of license) by Rev. Barratt (Cecil County Marriage License Book)

BARNWELL

Barnwell, Alice A., see Michael Hague

BARR

Barr, John (1804-1851), married Hannah (N) (1809-1892) probably circa 1830 (Hopewell United Methodist Church Cemetery tombstone inscriptions)

Barr, William S. (captain), of Cecil Co., married Miss Rose Ann Lee, of Baltimore, on 28 Jan 1835 by Rev. Reese in Baltimore (*Cecil Gazette*, 31 Jan 1835; *Baltimore American and Commercial Daily Advertiser*, 29 Jan 1835, misspelled his surname Bare)

BARRATT, BARRETT

Barratt, Amelia, see Samuel Smith

Barrett, Andrew, married Eliza Burns circa 5 Feb 1825 (date of license) by Rev. Griffith (Cecil County Marriage License Book; DAR transcript copied in 1928 listed her name as "Eliza Burris?")

Barratt, Andrew S., of near Principio, married Rosanna Lorritt (1801-1877) circa 11 Sep 1827 (date of license) (Cecil County Marriage License Book; DAR transcript copied in 1928 misspelled her name as Laritt; *Cecil Whig*, 13 Oct 1877, reported that Mrs. Rosanah Barratt died in her 77th year)

Barrett, Cornelius (1822-1888), married Julia A. (N) (1825-1896) by 1850; buried beside Willie A. Barrett, 1851-1852, Joseph H. Barrett, 1854-1855, and Mary E. Barrett, 1852-1922 (Rosebank Cemetery, at Calvert, tombstone inscriptions)

Barratt, Elmira, see Stearns Bullin

Barrett, Joseph H., see Cornelius Barrett

Barrett, Margaret, see Thomas C. McKinney

Barrett, Martha Jane, see Stephen Atkinson

Barrett, Mary E., see Cornelius Barrett

Barratt, Samuel (born c1820, Maryland) (laborer, 6th District), married Ellen (N) (born c1824, Maryland) probably circa 1845; daughter Virginia Barratt born c1846, Maryland (1860 Cecil County Census)

Barrett, Solomon (1763-1852) (War of 1812 veteran), of Cecil Co., married very late in life to Anna M. (N) (born 1819) on 1 Dec 1849 at Chestertown, Kent Co., and later moved to Baltimore (War of 1812 Bounty Land Warrant No. 55-160-91256; *Baltimore Sun*, 7 Jan 1852)

Barratt, Virginia, see Samuel Barratt

Barrett, Willie A., see Cornelius Barrett

BARROW

Barrow, John (born c1810, Maryland) (mason, 8th District), married Elizabeth (N) (born c1820, Maryland) probably circa 1836; son John Barrow, Jr. born c1837, Maryland, laborer (1860 Cecil County Census)

BARRY

Barry, John W., see George W. Thompson

Barry, William H., married Hannah L. (N) (1816-1907) probably by 1840; buried beside son E. Wilmer Barry, 1848-1870 (Elkton Methodist Church Cemetery tombstone inscriptions)

BARTLEY

Bartley, William, married Ann Davis circa 20 Feb 1837 (date of license) by Rev. Morris (Cecil County Marriage License Book)

BARTON

Barton, Sarah Ann, see Thomas Williams

BARWICK

Barwick, Alexander P., married Miss Rebecca H. Morton, both of New Castle Co., DE, on 3 Sep 1848 by Rev. McNamee (*Cecil Whig*, 9 Sep 1848)

Barwick, Anna Maria, see John Hanson, Jr.

Barwick, John R., married Emily Ann Hudson circa 17 May 1830 (date of license) by Rev. Duke (Cecil County Marriage License Book)

Barwick, Levina, see William Conlyn

Barwick, Mary Ann, see John Hanson, Jr.

Barwick, William, married Mary Ann Mears circa 29 Aug 1833 (date of license) by Rev. Duke (Cecil County Marriage License Book)

BASCOM

Bascom, H. B. (reverend) D. D., Professor of Moral Science and Belles Lettres, Augusta College, Kentucky) married Eliza Van Antwerp, daughter of the late Thomas Van Antwerp, of New York, on 14 Mar 1839 by Rev. Fitch Reed at the residence of James H. Ray in New York (*Cecil Gazette*, 16 Mar 1839)

BASKETTER

Basketter, (N), married Mary Ann (N) (1802-1875) probably circa 1825 and she died at the residence of her son-in-law John B. Dunbar in Elkton (*Cecil Whig*, 5 Jun 1875)

BATEMAN

Bateman, Benjamin, married Eliza (N) (1802-1868) probably circa 1825 (*Cecil Democrat and Farmer's Journal*, 22 Feb 1868, stated she was a member of the M. E. Church for 54 years)

BATES

Bates, Esther, see Aquilla Jones

BATTEN, BATTON

Batten, Mahlon, married Harriet Ann Mercer circa 20 Oct 1849 (date of license) (Cecil County Marriage License Book)

Batton, Sarah J., see Samuel Smith

Batton, William, see Samuel Smith

BAXTER

Baxter, Alexander, married Ellen Lutton circa 20 Feb 1844 (date of license) (Cecil Co. Marr. License Book)

BAYARD

Bayard, Andrew, see William Bayard

Bayard, Drusilla, see John W. McCullough

Bayard, Edwin, see Isaac Bayard

Bayard, Eliza, see Samuel Harris

Bayard, Francina, see John W. Wirt

Bayard, Hannah, see John Bouchelle

Bayard, Isaac (born c1820) (African American), married Martha (N) (born c1820) (African American) circa 1836; son Edwin Bayard (born c1837) (1860 Cecil County Census)

Bayard, Louise Jane, see William Richards

Bayard, Mary M., see Thomas Bouchelle

Bayard, Stephen, African American slave of Gen. Foreman, married Fanny Wilson, a free African American woman, on 14 Nov 1837 by Rev. Piggot (North Sassafras Parish, St. Stephen's P. E. Church Register)

Bayard, Susannah, see George W. Underwood

Bayard, Thomas J. (1800-1868), of St. Augustine, married Susan E. Bouchell circa 14 Jun 1841 (date of license) (Cecil County Marriage License Book spelled her name Bouchell; DAR transcript copied in 1955 spelled it Bouchelle; *Cecil Democrat and Farmer's Journal*, 25 Jan 1868)

Bayard, William (born c1826, Maryland) (African American) (laborer at Chesapeake City), married Mary (N) (born c1832, Maryland) (African American mulatto) probably circa 1847; son Andrew Bayard (African American black) born c1848 (1860 Cecil County Census)

BAYER

Bayer, William R. (born c1812, Maryland) (laborer at Chesapeake City), married Mary E. (N) (born c1822, Maryland) probably circa 1845; daughter Anna Bayer born c1846 (1860 Cecil County Census)

BAYLESS

Bayless, Phebe, see John F. McJilton

Bayless, Sydney Ann, see L. A. Wilmer

BEACH

Beach, Sheldon (1808-1887), married Miranda E. (N) (1810-1883) probably circa 1830 (West Nottingham Cemetery tombstone inscriptions)

BEARD

Beard, Hugh, see James McCauley

Beard, Jane Ann, see Samuel McCullough

Beard, Margaret, see Robert M. Walmsley

Beard, Rachel, see Daniel McCauley

Beard, Sarah, see James McCauley

BEASTON

Beaston, Andrew (1814-1886, born Delaware) (farmer at St. Augustine), married Sarah A. (N) (1818-1866, born Delaware) probably circa 1840; son Joseph Beaston born c1841, Delaware (1860 Cecil County Census; Bethel Church, at Chesapeake City, tombstone inscriptions)

Beaston, George J., married Susan Mitchell circa 16 Dec 1835 (date of license) by Rev. Coleman (Cecil County Marriage License Book)

Beaston, James M., of Kent Co., married Ann M. Piner, of Cecil Co., circa 24 Jan 1840 by Rev. Houston (Kent County Marriage License Book)

Beaston, Joseph, see Andrew Beaston

Beaston, Mary B., see Isaac B. Lum

BEATTY

Beatty, Anne E., see John E. Marsh

Beatty, Arthur, married Mary Davis circa 25 Oct 1832 (date of license) by Rev. Goforth (Cecil County Marriage License Book)

Beatty, Franklin, married Sarah Ann Wilson circa 25 Dec 1846 (date of license) (Cecil County Marriage License Book)

Beatty, Rebecca, see William Hyland and William G. Horner

Beatty, William, see John E. Marsh

Beatty, William (1804-1882, born Delaware) (druggist at North East), married 1st to Caroline Maffitt circa 3 Dec 1832 (date of license) by Rev. McCarrol, a Methodist Episcopal minister in Port Deposit, and married 2nd to Laura Maulden (born c1822) circa 8 Mar 1842 (date of license) (Cecil County Marriage License Book; 1860 Cecil County Census; *Cecil Democrat and Farmer's Journal*, 25 Mar 1882, stated William Beatty, "husband and father," died in his 78th year at North East)

BEAVEN

Beaven, John Sterrett, see Joseph Stebbing

Beaven, John Wood (1821-1895), married Mary Jane (N) (1819-1891) probably circa 1842 (Sterrett Family Cemetery tombstone inscriptions)

BEDWELL

Bedwell, Catharine, see John Bristow

Bedwell, John W., married Mary Ann Robinson circa 20 Mar 1843 (date of license) (Cecil County Marriage License Book)

Bedwell, Matilda, see Thomas Long

BEERS

Beers, Catherine, see Martin Meagher

Beers, Mary, see James Flemmer

Beers, Thomas, of Elkton, married Mrs. Mary Walsh, of Baltimore, on 12 Jul 1841 by Rev. Gildea (*Cecil Gazette*, 24 Jul 1841; *Baltimore Sun*, 21 Jul 1841)

BELL

Bell, Alfred (born c1822, Maryland) (African American) (laborer in the 7th District), married Jane (N) (born c1830, Maryland) (African American) probably circa 1847; daughter Laura Bell born c1848 (1860 Cecil County Census)

Bell, Elizabeth, see Samuel Whitelock

Bell, Emily, see William Bell

Bell, John, see Thomas Simpson

Bell, Laura, see Alfred Bell

Bell, Mary, see Ziba Moore

Bell, Mary Jane, see Hugh A. Thompson

Bell, Rachel, see Ziba Moore

Bell, Richard, see Ziba Moore

Bell, Robert M., married Mary Frances Broughton circa 1 Aug 1846 (date of license) (Cecil County Marriage License Book)

Bell, Sallie, see Thomas Simpson

Bell, William (born c1818, Delaware) (farmer at Cecilton), married Louisa (N) (born c1818) circa 1847; daughter Emily Bell born c1848, Delaware (1860 Cecil County Census)

BELLEVILLE

Belleville, Sarah, see Isaac Clark

BENEY, see Benny

BENJAMIN

Benjamin, A. Jefferson, see George W. Benjamin

Benjamin, Adeline J., see Hazlett Owens

Benjamin, Albert (1822-1903, born Maryland) (laborer, 9th District), married Sarah Catherine (N) (1828-1881, Maryland) probably circa 1850; daughter Ella Benjamin born c851 (Shelemiah Methodist Church tombstone inscriptions; 1860 Cecil County Census listed his wife's name as Catharine Benjamin)

Benjamin, Eliza Jane, see John Washington Alexander

Benjamin, Ella, see Albert Benjamin

Benjamin, Evan, son of George Benjamin (1780-1864) and Sarah Taylor, married Hannah Maria White (born 1825), daughter of John White and Jane Hall, on 20 Apr 1848 (*Maryland Bible Records, Volume 4: Eastern Shore*, by Henry C. Peden, Jr. (2004), p. 250)

Benjamin, George, see Evan Benjamin, Joseph Benjamin, Thomas T. Benjamin, William Benjamin and John W. Alexander

Benjamin, George W. (1818-1892, born Maryland) (shoemaker at Charles Town), married Frances (N) (1814-1900, born Pennsylvania) before 1842; son A. Jefferson Benjamin born c1843, Pennsylvania, and daughter Rosalie Benjamin born c1845, Maryland, as were their other children (Shelemiah Methodist Church Cemetery tombstone inscriptions; 1860 Cecil County Census)

Benjamin, Henry T., see William Benjamin

Benjamin, Jeremiah John, see William Benjamin

Benjamin, John, married Charlotte Owens circa 21 Dec 1832 (date of license) by Rev. Goforth (Cecil County Marriage License Book)

Benjamin, Joseph (born c1813, Maryland) (farmer near Bay View), son of George Benjamin (1780-1864) and Sarah Taylor, married Mary Ann Johnson (born c1821, Maryland), daughter of Jethro Johnson, on 15 Feb 1838, after obtaining a license on 12 Feb 1838, by Rev. Kennard at North East (*Cecil Gazette*, 10 Mar 1838; Cecil County Marriage License Book; *Portrait and Biographical Record of Harford and Cecil Counties, Maryland* (1897, repr. 1989), pp. 197, 316; 1860 Cecil County Census)

Benjamin, Joseph D., of Washington, D.C., married Miss Sarah M. Boulden, formerly of Elkton, on 21 Oct 1847, after obtaining a license on 20 Oct 1847, by Rev. Milby (*Cecil Whig*, 23 Oct 1847; Cecil County Marriage License Book)

Benjamin, Rebecca, see Richard Currier

Benjamin, Rosalie, see George W. Benjamin

Benjamin, Thomas T., son of George Benjamin (1780-1864) and Sarah Taylor, married Mary Ann Jackson circa 26 Mar 1838 (date of license) by Rev. Grace (Cecil County Marriage License Book; *Portrait and Biographical Record of Harford and Cecil Counties, Maryland* (1897, repr. 1989)

Benjamin, William (1826-1902), son of George Benjamin (1780-1864) and Sarah Taylor, married Sarah Jane Mahoney (1828-1904) on 12 Jan 1847 after obtaining a license on 9 Jan 1847 (Cecil County Marriage License Book spelled her name Mahony; DAR transcript copied in 1955 spelled it Mahoney; Shelemiah Methodist Church tombstone inscriptions; *Portrait and Biographical Record of Harford and Cecil Counties, Maryland* (1897, repr. 1989), p. 316, stated they had ten children of whom seven were still living in 1897, namely, Lavinia A. Campbell, Henry T. Benjamin, Deborah M. Tyson, William W. Benjamin, Martha E. Thompson, Winfield Scott Benjamin and Jeremiah John Benjamin)

Benjamin, William W., see William Benjamin

Benjamin, Winfield Scott, see William Benjamin

BENNETT

Bennett, Amelia F., see William C. Crow

Bennett, Ann, see William Hutton

Bennett, Elizabeth, see Cyrus Colmerry

Bennett, Hannah, see Samuel Logan

Bennett, Henry P., married Ellen J. Scott circa 24 Mar 1835 (date of license) by Rev. Duke (Cecil County Marriage License Book)

Bennett, John P. (born c1820, Pennsylvania) (pump maker and commercial fisherman), married Martha Scott (born c1821, Pennsylvania), daughter of Moses Scott, circa 27 Jun 1840 (date of license) (Cecil County Marriage License Book; *Portrait and Biographical Record of Harford and Cecil Counties, Maryland* (1897, repr. 1989), p. 450; 1860 Cecil County Census)

Bennett, Louisa, see William Calvert

Bennett, Lyda A., see William Hand

Bennett, Mary Elizabeth, see Levy Boulden

Bennett, Rudolph, of Elk Landing, married Sarah Jane Roach (1806-1877) circa 28 Apr 1829 (date of license) by Rev. Russell and she died in her 71st year, her husband having pre-deceased her (Cecil County Marriage License Book; *Cecil Whig*, 30 Jun 1877)

Bennett, Rudulph (born c1816, Pennsylvania), married Margery H. (N) (born c1813, Pennsylvania) before 1845; son William H. Bennett born c1846, Maryland (1860 Cecil County census)

Bennett, William, married Elizabeth McCall circa 30 Oct 1826 (date of license) by Rev. Barratt (Cecil County Marriage License Book)

BENNY

Benny, Charles W., of Talbot Co., married Caroline Amelia Elizabeth Nesbitt, eldest daughter of the late Samuel Nesbitt, Jr., Esq., on 22 Apr 1845, after obtaining a license that same day, by Rev. Mason at Port Deposit (*Cecil Whig*, 3 May 1845; Cecil County Marriage License Book spelled his name Benny; DAR transcript copied in 1955 listed it as "Benn(?)" and *Baltimore Sun*, 25 Apr 1845, misspelled his name Beney; 1850 Cecil County Census listed Charles Benny in the Elkton area)

BENSON

Benson, Amanda, see David Hurlock

Benson, Benjamin, married Ellen Conlyn circa 9 Oct 1843 (date of license) (Cecil County Marriage License Book spelled her name Conlyn; DAR transcript copied in 1955 misspelled it Conlgn)

Benson, Hebron, married Ann Price circa 24 Dec 1836 (date of license) by Rev. Reed (Cecil Co. Marriage License Book; DAR transcript copied in 1928 misspelled his name Bebron)

Benson, Hyland (born c1820) (farmer at Cecilton), married Laura (N) (born c1832) circa 1850; son John Benson born c1851 (1860 Cecil County Census)

Benson, James A., of New Castle Co., DE, married Miss Mary S. Severson, of Cecil Co., on 22 May 1849, after obtaining a license that same day, by Rev. Wiley (Cecil County Marriage License Book; *Cecil Whig*, 25 May 1849)

Benson, James H. (1804-1874) (merchant at Cecilton), married 1st to Louisa Rumford, daughter of John Rumford, of Wilmington, Delaware, on 18 Jun 1826 by Rev. McCoombs and married 2nd to Louisa Severson (1803-1886, born in Pennsylvania) circa 2 Nov 1833 (date of license) by Rev. Duke (Cecil County Marriage License Book; *Delaware Gazette*, 26 Jun 1826; 1860 Cecil County Census; St. Stephen's Protestant Episcopal Church Cemetery tombstone inscriptions)

Benson, John, see Hyland Benson

Benson, Joseph, married Mary Roberts circa 30 May 1838 (date of license) by Rev. Piggot (Cecil County Marriage License Book; DAR transcript copied in 1928 misspelled the minister's name Pickett; Robert Piggot was a Protestant Episcopal minister in North Sassafras at that time)

Benson, Rosetta H., see Gideon Lusby

BENTON

Benton, Joseph, married Araminta Walmsley circa 19 Aug 1846 (date of license) (Cecil County Marriage License Book)

BENTZ

Bentz, Franklin (born c1823, Maryland) (lawyer at Chesapeake City), married Sarah (N) (born c1825, Maryland) probably circa 1848; son Samuel born c1849 (1860 Cecil County Census)

BERBAGE

Berbage, Eliza J., see Emanuel Jester

BERNARD

Bernard, Parker, married Ann Carlisle circa 6 Oct 1836 (date of license) by Rev. Morris (Cecil County Marriage License Book)

BERRIKER

Berriker, Jacob (1804-1872), married Hester E. (N) (1824-1896) probably circa 1842-1845 (Zion Methodist Cemetery tombstone inscriptions)

BERRY

Berry, Ann, see Thomas Berry and Charles Boddy

Berry, Edward (born c1820, Delaware) (cabinet maker in the 7th District), married Margaret Strickland (born c1824, Pennsylvania) circa 8 Sep 1845 (date of license); son William Berry born c1847, Maryland (Cecil County Marriage License Book; 1860 Cecil County Census)

Berry, Elizabeth K., see Richard Hall

Berry, John (born c1813, Maryland) (African American) (laborer, 8th District), married Adeline (N) (born c1818, Maryland) probably circa 1839; daughter Josephine born c1840 (1860 Cecil County Census)

Berry, Josephine, see John Berry

Berry, Susanna, see Thomas Berry

Berry, Thomas (1820-1895, born Maryland) (constable, 7th District), married Catharine (N) (1817-1887, born Maryland) circa 1841; daughter Ann Berry born c1842; parents buried beside daughter Susanna Berry, 1844-1894 (Asbury Methodist Church Cemetery tombstone inscriptions; 1860 Cecil County Census)

Berry, William, see Edward Berry

Berry, William, married Hannah Lee circa 1 Apr 1847 (date of license) (Cecil County Marr. License Book)

BIDDLE

Biddle, Andrew (born c1825) (laborer at North East), married Elizabeth Marquiss (born c1826) circa 22 Mar 1843 (date of license) (Cecil County Marriage License Book; 1860 Cecil County Census)

Biddle, Ann, see George Reed and L. Biddle

Biddle, Ann Jemima, see William E. Howard

Biddle, Boulden N. (1814-1863), married Mary E. (N) (1822-1883) probably circa 1840 (Bethel Church, at Chesapeake City, tombstone inscriptions)

Biddle, David, married Elizabeth Ford circa 31 Oct 1840 (date of license) (Cecil Co. Marr. License Book)

Biddle, Edith Emeline, see Samuel Hayes

Biddle, Eliza, see Richard F. Biddle

Biddle, Elizabeth, see James Veal and Lewis Littaway

Biddle, Emily Ann, see Joseph P. Cantwell

Biddle, Frances, see John W. Biddle

Biddle, George, see Rensselaer Biddle

Biddle, George, married Rebecca Johnson circa 27 Nov 1828 (date of license) by Rev. Barratt (Cecil County Marriage License Book)

Biddle, George (1804-1859), son of Peregrine Biddle, married Frances A. Perkins (1815-1887), daughter of Dr. John D. Perkins of Queen Anne's Co., circa 1835; son George Biddle born 20 Aug 1836 (*Portrait and Biographical Record of Harford and Cecil Counties, Maryland* (1897, repr. 1989), p, 343; St. Stephen's Episcopal Church Cemetery tombstone inscriptions)

Biddle, Jacob, married Elizabeth Marcus circa 6 May 1835 (date of license) by Rev. Duke (Cecil County Marriage License Book)

Biddle, Jacob T., see Rensselaer Biddle

Biddle, James, see Joshua Biddle

Biddle, James (born c1818, Maryland) (laborer, Chesapeake City) married Mary (N) (born c1818, Maryland) circa 1840; son William Biddle born c1842 (1860 Cecil County Census)

Biddle, John W. (born c1811, Maryland) (laborer, Perryville), married Susan (N) (born c1830, Maryland) probably circa 1850; daughter Frances Biddle born c1851 (1860 Cecil County Census)

Biddle, Joshua (born c1820, Maryland) (farmer, St. Augustine) married Mary A. (N) (born c1822, Maryland) probably circa 1842; son James Biddle born c1843, Maryland (1860 Cecil County Census)

Biddle, Joshua F., married Rebecca W. Kennedy (1819-1847), daughter of James and Eliza Kennedy, circa 3 May 1841 (date of license) (Cecil County Marriage License Book did not list his middle initial; Bethel Church, at Chesapeake City, tombstone inscription for Rebecca Biddle)

Biddle, L. (born c1808, Maryland) (farmer near St. Augustine), married Amelia (N) (born c1813, Maryland) probably circa 1837; daughter Ann Biddle born c1838, Maryland (1860 Cecil County Census)

Biddle, Lambert W., married Ann T. Sluyter circa 13 Jan 1834 (date of license) by Rev. McKenney, a Protestant Episcopal minister in the North Sassafras area (Cecil County Marriage License Book; DAR transcript copied in 1928 listed her name as Slayter)

Biddle, Leonis S., see George R. Carpenter

Biddle, Louisa Ann, see George Boulden

Biddle, Margaret Savin, see William D. Mercer and John W. Wirt

Biddle, Mary, see Richard Fillingame

Biddle, Mary Amanda, see Alfred C. Nowland

Biddle, Mary Ann, see Nathaniel T. Biddle

Biddle, Millicent, see Eli Wright

Biddle, Nathaniel T., married Mary Ann Biddle circa 10 May 1848 (date of license) (Cecil County Marriage License Book gave his middle initial as T.; DAR transcript copied in 1955 listed it as S.)

Biddle, Noble (1804-1879), married Francina M. (N) (1805-1874) probably circa 1825 (Bethel Church, at Chesapeake City, tombstone inscriptions)

Biddle, Olivia A., see Lewis J. Cavendar

Biddle, Peregrine, see John W. Wirt and George Biddle

Biddle, Rensselaer (1809-1877) (miller and farmer), married Mary Egner (1811-1843) circa 9 Nov 1830 (date of license) by Rev. Hodgson (Cecil County Marriage License Book; DAR transcript copied in 1928 misspelled his first name Ranselen, her name Egnor and listed the minister's name as Hodson (Francis Hodgson was a Methodist Episcopal minister in Elton at that time); *Portrait and Biographical Record of Harford and Cecil Counties, Maryland* (1897, repr. 1989), p. 365, listed their three children as Jacob T. Biddle (born 1832), George Biddle (died before 1897) and Mary Devlin (living in 1897); Cherry Hill Methodist Church Cemetery tombstone inscriptions; *Cecil Whig*, 24 Nov 1877, obituary stated he helped build the Chesapeake and Delaware Canal)

Biddle, Rebecca, see John Haines and John J. Poole

Biddle, Richard F. (born c1814) (farmer at Elton), married Miss Margaret Jane Cleland (born c1822), of New Castle Co., DE, on 12 Jan 1843 by Rev.Wynkoop; daughter Eliza Biddle born c1844 in Maryland (*Delaware Gazette*, 13 Jan 1843; 1860 Cecil County Census)

Biddle, Sarah, see David Ward

Biddle, Stephen, married Deborah Compt circa 11 Mar 1837 (date of license) by Rev. Morris (Cecil County Marriage License Book)

Biddle, Susan A., see George W. Oldham

Biddle, Susanna, see John C. Williams

Biddle, Thomas A., married Jane L. Wolcott circa 15 Oct 1838 (date of license) by Rev. Young (Cecil County Marriage License Book)

Biddle, Thomas M., married Julia Ann Collasson circa 27 Nov 1849 (date of license) (Cecil County Marriage License Book)

Biddle, William, see James Biddle

Biddle, William, of Cecil Co., married Miss Armina Nichols, of Wilmington, DE, on 23 Jan 1839 by Rev. Gilbert in Wilmington (*Cecil Gazette*, 26 Jan 1839)

Biddle, William, married Margaret Riddle circa 7 Oct 1845 (date of license) (Cecil County Marriage License Book listed his name without a middle initial; DAR transcript copied in 1955 listed it as William N.)

Biddle, William R., married Ann Ruley circa 26 Dec 1838 (date of license) by Rev. Piggot, a Protestant Episcopal minister in North Sassafras (Cecil County Marriage License Book)

BIGGS

Biggs, Benjamin T. (1821-1893), married Mary Scott (1830-1914) probably circa 1850 (Bethel Methodist Church, at Chesapeake City, tombstone inscriptions)

Biggs, James (born c1816) (farm hand at Cecilton), married Mary (N) (born c1822) circa 1840; son Joseph Biggs born c1841 (1860 Cecil County Census)

Biggs, John H. (born c1820, Maryland) (laborer at Cecilton), married Hester Jane Truit (born c1831, Delaware) circa 24 Mar 1849 (date of license) (Cecil Co. Marriage License Book; 1860 Cecil Co. Census)

Biggs, Joseph (born c1813) (sailor at Cecilton), married Rebecca Pennington (born c1818) circa 30 May 1838 (date of license) by Rev. Piggot (Cecil County Marriage License Book; DAR transcript copied in 1928 mistakenly listed his name as Briggs and misspelled the minister's name Pickett (Robert Piggot was a Protestant Episcopal minister in North Sassafras); 1860 Cecil County Census)

Biggs, Joseph, see James Biggs

Biggs, Sarah, see Samuel Hessey

Biggs, William, married Ann Helens circa 4 Jan 1837 (date of license) by Rev. Smith (Cecil County Marriage License Book)

BILES

Biles, Ann Eliza, see John D. Wherry

Biles, John L. (1812-1873), of near Blue Ball, married Jane E. (N) (1812-1887) probably circa 1833 (Rosebank Cemetery, at Calvert, tombstone inscriptions; *Cecil Whig*, 8 Feb 1873)

BIRCH

Birch, Miles, married Miss Elizabeth Parkinson, of Newark, DE, on 4 May 1843, after obtaining a license on 29 Apr 1843, by Rev. Goldsborough at Trinity Church (*Cecil Whig*, 6 May 1843; Cecil County Marriage License Book)

BIRD

Bird, William, married Mrs. Naomi Husbands, both of New Castle Co., DE, on 24 Dec 1829 by Elder Peckworth (*Delaware Gazette*, 29 Dec 1829; *Elkton Press*, 2 Jan 1830, spelled her name Naomy)

BIRK, see Burk

BLACK

Black, Charles G., see B. F. Bussey

Black, Diedrich H., of Baltimore, married Miss Eliza Jane Tyson, of Cecil Co., on 14 May 1839, after obtaining a license that same day, by Rev. McIntire (*Cecil Gazette*, 25 May 1839; Cecil County Marriage License Book)

Black, Elizabeth, see Augustus Giles, George Black Giles, Thomas Giles, John Robert Giles, Jr., John C. Groome and Joseph Wallace

Black, George W., married Mary Price circa 26 Oct 1829 (date of license) by Rev. King (Cecil County Marriage License Book)

Black, James, see Alexander B. Hanson

Black, James R., see William S. Young

Black, John G., see Alexander B. Hanson

Black, Judge, see John C. Groome

Black, Maria A., see B. F. Bussey

Black, Martha Jane, see John Owens

Black, Mary, see John Wesley Taylor

Black, Mary Ann, see Robert H. Hays

Black, Rebecca Jane, see Benjamin Ferguson

Black, Sarah, see Edmund Physick

Black, Sarah S., see William S. Young

Black, Susan W., see Alexander B. Hanson

Black, William W. (1814-1887) (storekeeper and farmer in 7th District), married Miss Catharine P. Evans (1816-1897), both of Cecil Co., on 30 May 1848, after obtaining a license on 23 May 1848, by Rev. Bachus in Baltimore City (Cecil County Marriage License Book; *Portrait and Biographical Record of Harford and Cecil Counties, Maryland* (1897, repr. 1989), p. 163; West Nottingham Cemetery tombstone inscriptions; *Cecil Democrat and Farmer's Journal*, 3 Jun 1848; 1860 Cecil County Census)

BLACKISTON

Blackiston, Ann E., see James S. Naudain

Blackiston, William C., married Elizabeth Tomlinson circa 16 Jan 1838 (date of license) by Rev. Greenbank. a Methodist minister in Port Deposit (Cecil County Marriage License Book)

BLACKWAY

Blackway, Josiah (born c1822) (farmer at Cecilton), married Martha (N) (born c1825) circa 1849; daughter Hester Ann Blackway born c1850 (1860 Cecil County Census)

BLAIR

Blair, Rebecca, see Isaac Trimble

BLAKE

Blake, Catharine, see William Thompson

Blake, Hester Ann, see John McVey

Blake, Mary, see Solomon Blake

Blake, Rachel, see Thomas Janney

Blake, Solomon (c1795-1857) (War of 1812 veteran), married 1st to Martha Collins circa 2 Jul 1822 (date of license) and married 2nd to Mary Lynch on 25 Apr 1831, after obtaining a license that same day, by Rev. Griffith; widow Mary Blake died in 1885 (Cecil County Marriage License Book; War of 1812 Bounty Land Warrant No. 50-40-77541)

BLAKELEY

Blakeley, Mary Jane, see John Niblock

BLUMFIELD

Blumfield, Mary Ann, see Samuel Gay

BOARMAN

Boarman, Louisa Mary, see Otho Scott

BODDY

Boddy, Charles (born c1812, Maryland) (African American) (laborer, 8th District), married Ann Berry (born c1817, Maryland) (African American) probably circa 1839; son Gideon Boddy born c1840, Maryland; son John Boddy, 1844-1935; son George A. Boddy, 1846-1911 (1860 Cecil County Census; Family Family research by Michael Cain, of Aberdeen, Maryland, 2006; Cecil County death certificates of John Boddy, farmer, who lived near Colora, and George A. Boddy, day laborer, who lived at Conowingo)

Boddy, George (born c1820, Maryland) (African American mulatto) (farmhand, Rowlandville), married Nancy O. (N) (born c1826, Maryland) (African American) probably circa 1844; son William E. Boddy born c1845 (African American mulatto), Maryland (1860 Cecil County Census)

Boddy, George, see James Boddy

Boddy, George A., see George Boddy

Boddy, George J., see James Boddy

Boddy, Gideon, see Charles Boddy

Boddy, James (born c1819, Maryland) (African American) (laborer, 8th District), married Ann Coco Brown (born c1825, Philadelphia) (African American) probably c1839; son George Boddy born c1840, Maryland (1860 Cecil County Census; Cecil County death certificates of daughter Mrs. Mary Ann Peaco (1843-1923), of Rowlandville, son Rev. George J. Boddy (1840-1916), of Dublin, Harford Co., MD (listed his mother as Nancy Brown), and daughter Mrs. Adelaide Berry Haines (1841-1910), of Rowlandville)

Boddy, John, see Charles Boddy

Boddy, Mary Jane, see George Harris

Boddy, William E., see George Boddy

BOGGS

Boggs, Sewall (born c1816, Delaware) (farmer at Cecilton), married Mary M. (N) (born c1817, Delaware) circa 1837; son John Boggs born c1838, Delaware (1860 Cecil County Census)

BOIES

Boies (Bosee?), Henry, married Belinda Hamer circa 10 Dec 1839 (date of license) by Rev. Burrows (Cecil County Marriage License Book spelled his name Bosee; DAR transcript copied in 1928 listed his name as Bosie and mistakenly listed her name as Mlinda *(sic)* Hamer; Henry Bosee was not listed in the 1840 Maryland Census Index, but Jeremiah S. H. Boies (1796-1852) was in Cecil County in that Census and he later moved to Wilmington, DE; *Delaware Gazette*, 7 Jan 1853)

Boies, Jeremiah S. H., see Henry Boies

Boies, Martha, see Joseph Chick

BOLTON, BOULTON

Bolton, George, see (N) Money

Bolton, James, married Mary Anderson on 12 Oct 1843, after obtaining a license that same day, by Rev. Shields (Cecil County Marriage License Book; Elkton Methodist Church Register, p. 140)

Bolton, John H., married Catharine P. Ruley circa 2 Apr 1832 (date of license) by Rev. Duke (Cecil County Marriage License Book)

Boulton, William, married Mary Buchanan circa 16 Mar 1825 (date of license) by Rev. Chambers (Cecil County Marriage License Book; DAR transcript copied in 1928 spelled her name Buckhanan)

BOND

Bond, Edward (born c1827, Maryland) (African American) (laborer, 6th District), married Minty (N) (born c1832, Maryland) (African American) probably circa 1849; daughter Laura Bond born c1850 (1860 Cecil County Census)

Bond, Elizabeth, see Charles Willey

Bond, Ephraim, see Lloyd Bond

Bond, Freedom (born c1825, Maryland) (African American) (laborer, 7th District), married Elizabeth (N) (born c1826, Maryland) (African American) probably circa 1849; son John Bond born c1850 (1860 Cecil County Census)

Bond, James T. (born c1809, Maryland) (farmer, Warwick), married Mary Ann (N) (born c1809, Maryland) circa 1834; son Julius Bond born c1836 (1860 Cecil County Census)

Bond, John, see Freedom Bond

Bond, Laura, see Edward Bond

Bond, Lloyd (born c1824, Maryland) (African American) (laborer, 7th District), married Mary (N) (born c1830, Maryland) (African American) probably circa 1848; son Ephraim Bond born c1849 (1860 Cecil County Census)

Bond, Thomas (1800-1861), married Mary (N) (1805-1887) probably circa 1825 (Hopewell United Meth. Church Cemetery tombstone inscriptions)

BONSAL

Bonsal, Thomas L. (1801-1884), married Naomi P. (N) (1811-1869) probably circa 1830 (Friends Cemetery, at Harrisville, tombstone inscriptions)

BOON

Boon, James and Sally Eliza, see John W. Pierson

BOOTH

Booth, Ann, see William Armstrong

Booth, Anna, see Joseph Booth

Booth, George (born c1818, England) (farmer near Elkton), married Lydia (N) (born c1829, Maryland) probably circa 1848; son George born c1849, Maryland (1860 Cecil County Census)

Booth, Joseph (1811-1891, born England) (farmer near Elkton), married Barbara Ann "Barbary" (N) (1820-1884, born Pennsylvania) circa 1841; eldest daughter Anna Booth born c1842 in Pennsylvania; youngest son William Booth born c1854 in Maryland (1860 Cecil County Census; Elkton Presbyterian Church Cemetery tombstone inscriptions)

Booth, Samuel J. (born c1825, England) (farm hand, Cecilton), married Jane Ryland (born c1827, Maryland) circa 26 Apr 1849 (date of license) (Cecil County Marriage License Book spelled her name Ryland; DAR transcript copied in 1955 misspelled it as Byland; 1860 Cecil County Census)

Booth, William, see Joseph Booth

BOOTS

Boots, Sarah, see David Staats

BORCHAM

Borcham, Mary Ann, see William Hudson

BORLAND

Borland, Matthew (1817-1873) (blacksmith at Elkton), married Amanda Ann Alexander (born c1830) on 7 Dec 1848, after obtaining a license on 6 Dec 1848, by Rev. DeWitt at the home of Mrs. Anna Alexander near Rock Church (Cecil County Marriage License Book; *Cecil Democrat and Farmer's Journal*, 23 Dec 1848 *Cecil Whig*, 8 Mar 1873; 1860 Cecil County Census spelled his name Bourland)

Borland, Samuel, married Nancy Owens circa 29 Feb 1832 (date of license) by Rev. Magraw (Cecil County Marriage License Book; DAR transcript copied in 1928 spelled his name Boreland)

BORUM, BORAM

Borum (Boram), Josiah, married 1st to Amelia Robinson on 20 Jun 1839, after obtaining a license on 18 Jun 1839, by Rev. Hagany, and married 2nd to Ann Quinley on 31 Jul 1851, after obtaining a license that same day, by Rev. Fernley (Cecil County Marriage License Book; Elkton Methodist Church Register, p. 139)

Boram, Mary, see Samuel Johnson

Borum, Samuel, married Lydia Mitchell circa 2 Mar 1842 (date of license) (Cecil County Marriage License Book spelled his name Borum; DAR transcript compiled in 1928 spelled it Borem)

BOSIE, see Boies

BOSTICK

Bostick, Elizabeth, see Lewis Bristow

Bostick, George (African American), married Rachel Jane Ryder (African American) on 24 Jul 1844 by Rev. Shields (Elkton Methodist Church Register, p. 140; Cecil County Marriage License Book did not list it)

Bostick, Samuel, married Sarah Garrettson circa 4 Aug 1827 (date of license) (Cecil Co. Marr. Lic. Book)

BOUCHELL, BOUCHELLE

Bouchelle, John, married Hannah Bayard circa 5 Jan 1832 (date of license) by Rev. Rees (Cecil County Marriage License Book; DAR transcript copied in 1928 spelled his name Bouchell)

Bouchell, Hyland P., married Miss Elmira A. Martindale, both of Cecil Co., on 25 Apr 1848, after obtaining a license that same day, by Rev. Barrett (Cecil County Marriage License Book; *Cecil Whig*, 29 Apr 1848, spelled her name Almira)

Bouchell, Isaac C. (born c1811, Maryland) (farmer at St. Augustine), married Rebecca Plummer (born c1830, Maryland) circa 31 Mar 1849 (date of license); son Wilmer Bouchell born c1849 (Cecil County Marriage License Book; 1860 Cecil County Census listed him as Isaac Boshell)

Bouchell, Peter, married Miss Sarah Ellen Price, both of Cecil Co., on 16 Mar 1848, after obtaining a license on 14 Mar 1848, by Rev. McIntire (*Cecil Whig*, 18 Mar 1848; Cecil County Marriage License Book)

Bouchell, Susan E., see Thomas J. Bayard

Bouchelle, Thomas, married Mary M. Bayard circa 2 Mar 1829 (date of license) by Rev. Duke (Cecil County Marriage License Book)

Bouchell, Wilmer, see Isaac C. Bouchell

BOUCHER

Boucher, Richard (1806-1879, of Langford, Ireland), married Mary Susanne (N) (1802-1870, of Antrim, Ireland) probably circa 1828 (Ebenezer Church Cemetery tombstone inscriptions)

BOULDEN, BOULDIN

Boulden, Charles, of New Castle Co., DE, married Mary H. Thomas, of Cecil Co., MD, circa 6 Jan 1832 (date of license) by Rev. Rees (Cecil County Marriage License Book)

Boulden, Dorcas, see Richard B. Boulden

Boulden, Eleanor H., see David Fields

Boulden, Eliza, see John Boulden

Boulden, Eliza Margaret, see Caleb Edmundson, Jr.

Boulden, Elizabeth, see William Tyson

Boulden, Elizabeth S., see William Neal

Boulden, George, of New Castle Co., Delaware, married Miss Louisa Ann Biddle, of Cecil Co., on 9 Dec 1834, after obtaining a license on 6 Dec 1834, by Rev. Spry (Cecil County Marriage License Book; *Cecil Gazette*, 13 Dec 1834, spelled his surname Bouldin)

Boulden, Jacob (1814-1871), married Margaret J. (N), probably Margaret J. Wright, probably circa 1835; buried beside William Wright, 1790-1870 (Rosebank Cemetery, at Calvert, tombstone inscriptions; no dates on her marker)

Boulden, James, married Clarissa Jane Pearce circa 28 May 1844 (date of license) (Cecil County Marriage License Book; DAR transcript copied in 1955 mistakenly listed the license date as 29 May 1844)

Boulden, James A., see Levi Boulden

Boulden, Jesse, see Jacob Holden

Boulden, Jesse M. (or T.), of near Elkton, married Margaret Jane Johnson (1822-1864) circa 14 Jan 1846 (date of license) (Cecil County Marriage License Book listed his name as Jesse M. Boulden; *Cecil Whig*, 2 Apr 1864, listed her name as Margaret J. Boulden, aged about 42 years, consort of Jesse T. Boulden)

Boulden, John, married Rachel Simpers circa 25 Aug 1836 (date of license) by Rev. Wilson (Cecil County Marriage License Book)

Boulden, John, of New Castle Co., Delaware, married Eliza Boulden, of Cecil Co., circa 21 Mar 1831 (date of license) by Rev. Duke (Cecil County Marriage License Book)

Boulden, Levi, married Margaret S. Boulden circa 10 Oct 1831 (date of license) by Rev. Smith (Cecil County Marriage License Book)

Boulden, Levi, of Chesapeake City (collector for Chesapeake & Delaware Canal), married Mary Elizabeth Bennett circa 15 Oct 1836 (date of license) by Rev. Potts (Cecil County Marriage License Book; DAR transcript copied in 1928 misspelled his first name Levy and her last name Benneat; *Portrait and Biographical Record of Harford and Cecil Counties, Maryland* (1897, repr. 1989), p. 235, stated Levi died after a lengthy illness at the age of 47 and his son James A. Boulden was born 29 Dec 1837)

Boulden, Lewis, married Miss Mary Fulton, both of Cecil Co., on 19 Oct 1848, after obtaining a license that same day, by Rev. Goldsborough at Trinity Church (Cecil County Marriage License Book; *Cecil Democrat and Farmer's Journal*, 21 Oct 1848; *Cecil Whig*, 21 Oct 1848)

Boulden, Margaret, see Jacob Holden

Boulden, Margaret S., see Levi Boulden

Boulden, Mary, see John T. Simpers

Boulden, Mary Ann, see William Donaldson

Boulden, Matilda A., see Samuel McIntire

Boulden, Nancy, see Jacob Holden

Boulden, Nathan, see David Fields

Boulden, Rachel, see Joseph Merritt and Samuel R. Hogg

Boulden, Richard B. (died 1860) (War of 1812 veteran), married 1st to Dorcas Boulden in 1808 and married 2nd to Mary Ann Harrington (1805-1887) on 25 Jul 1825, after obtaining a license on 18 Jul 1825, by Rev. Chambers; buried in Bethel Cemetery near Chesapeake City (Cecil County Marriage License Book; DAR transcript copied in 1928 spelled her name Herrington; War of 1812 Bounty Land Warrant No. 55-160-114319 spelled her name Harrington)

Boulden, Richard, see Joseph Merritt

Boulden, Sarah Ann, see Justus Dunbar and Joseph Miles Ash

Boulden (Bouldin), Sarah Jane, see Charles Brown

Boulden, Sarah M., see Joseph D. Benjamin

Boulden, Thomas (born c1804, Delaware) (farmer at Elkton), married Ann Thomas (born c1803, Maryland) circa 13 Jan 1829 (date of license) by Rev. Woolford (Cecil County Marriage License Book; 1860 Cecil County Census)

Boulden, William W., married Jane S. Merritt, both of Cecil Co., circa 23 Jan 1847 (date of license) by Rev. Storks (Cecil County Marriage License Book; Elkton Methodist Church Register, p. 141, gave the year of marriage, but not the date, and spelled his name Bouldin)

Boulden, (N), married Rachel S. (N) (1820-1908) probably circa 1844; buried beside Henry S., Boulden, 1845-1872 (North East Methodist Church Cemetery tombstone inscriptions)

BOULEN, see Burlin

BOULTON, see Bolton.

BOWEN

Bowen, Harriet, see John Roberts

Bowen, Margaret, see Edward R. Gibbs

Bowen, Rachel, see Joseph Greer

Bowen, William, of Baltimore City, married Miss Sarah Ann Garrett, of Cecil Co., on 5 Jan 1843, after obtaining a license on 4 Jan 1843, by Rev. McIntire (Cecil County Marriage License Book; *Cecil Whig*, 7 Jan 1843)

BOWERHILL

Bowerhill, Robert F., of Edinburgh, Scotland, married Miss Elizabeth P. Haslett, of West Chester, PA, on 9 Mar 1837 by Rev. Graff in West Chester (*Cecil Gazette*, 18 Mar 1837)

BOWERS

Bowers, Mary Rebecca, see Benjamin Parrott

BOWMAN

Bowman, Caroline, see James Whitelock

BOWSER

Bowser, Henry (born c1810, Maryland) (African American) (laborer, 7th District), married Eliza (N) (born c1815, Maryland) (African American) probably circa 1838; son Abel Bowser born c1839 (1860 Cecil County Census)

BOYCE

Boyce, Araminta, see John T. West

Boyce, Mary, see Amos Slack

Boyce, Rachel, see Reuben Lake

BOYD

Boyd, Ann, see John Kidd

Boyd, Elizabeth, see William Parrott

Boyd, Enoch, married Catharine Ann Mahan circa 19 Jul 1831 (date of license) by Rev. Warburton (Cecil County Marriage License Book)

Boyd, Francis (1793-1869), married Sarah Patterson (1808-1893) circa 10 Feb 1827 (date of license) by Rev. Barratt (Cecil County Marriage License Book; West Nottingham Cemetery tombstone inscriptions)

Boyd, Grizzelda, see John Thomas Starr

Boyd, Harriet, see Aaron Parrott

Boyd, Hugh, married Margaret Fox circa 16 Mar 1826 (date of license) by Rev. Magraw (Cecil County Marriage License Book)

Boyd, Hugh (born c1817, Maryland) (laborer, 7th District) married Sarah Pennington (born c1828, Maryland) circa 26 Dec 1848 (date of license) (Cecil County Marriage License Book; 1860 Cecil County Census)

Boyd, James, married Eliza Bailey circa 22 Feb 1831 (date of license) by Rev. Goforth (Cecil County Marriage License Book)

Boyd, James (born c1817, Maryland) (laborer, 7th District), married Joanna (N) (born c1822, Maryland) probably circa 1845; daughter Josephine Boyd born c1846 (1860 Cecil County Census)

Boyd, John (born c1814, Maryland) (innkeeper, 7th District), married Ann (N) (born c1814, Maryland) by 1845; son William Boyd born c1846 (1860 Cecil County Census)

Boyd, John C., married Henrietta M. Chew circa 17 Nov 1841 (date of license) (Cecil County Marriage License Book)

Boyd, Josephine, see James Boyd

Boyd, Mary, see Andrew J. Lynch

Boyd, Sarah J., see James S. Nickel

Boyd, William, see John Boyd

Boyd, William, of Chester Co., PA, married Sarah Mahan, of Cecil Co., MD, circa 3 Apr 1832 (date of license) by Rev. Duke (Cecil County Marriage License Book)

Boyd, William C. (1802-1865), married Sarah A. White (1812-1879) circa 27 Sep 1837 (date of license) by Rev. Greenbank, a Methodist minister in Port Deposit (Cecil County Marriage License Book; DAR transcript copied in 1928 listed their names without middle initials; West Nottingham Cemetery tombstone inscriptions)

BOYDS

Boyds, John (born c1824, England), wool manufacturer at Bohemia Mills, married Mary (N) (born c1828, Pennsylvania) probably circa 1845 (all children were born in Pennsylvania: Sarah born c1846, Alice born c1848, Ann born c1851, Elizabeth born c1856, and Rebecca, born c1859) (1860 Cecil County Census)

BOYER

Boyer, Ann Eliza, see Thomas J. Britton

Boyer, Catherine, see George Harris

Boyer, Frisby (born c1815, Pennsylvania) (African American mulatto at Cecilton), married Sallie (N) (born c1820, Pennsylvania) (African American) circa 1841; son Helmsley born circa 1842 (African American) (1860 Cecil County Census)

Boyer, George, see John Boyer

Boyer, Helmsley, see Frisby Boyer

Boyer, Jane, see Richard Boyer

Boyer, John, see Robert Boyer

Boyer, John (born c1820, Maryland) (African American) (laborer in 8th District), married Hannah (N) (born c1825, Maryland) probably circa 1842; son George born c1843, Maryland (1860 Cecil County Census)

Boyer, Louisa, see Samuel Boyer

Boyer, Richard (born c1812, Maryland) (African American) (farmer at Cecilton), married (N) (born c1820) (African American) circa 1847; daughter Jane Boyer born c1848 (African American) (1860 Cecil County Census did not give his wife's first name, but listed her only as "Mrs. Boyer")

Boyer, Robert (born c1824, Maryland) (African American) (laborer near Elkton), married Mary Ann (N) (born c1825) (African American) probably circa 1846; son John born c1847 (1860 Cecil County Census)

Boyer, Samuel (born c1812, Maryland) (African American) (laborer near Elkton), married Mary (N) (born c1824) (African American) probably circa 1844; daughter Louisa born 1845 (1860 Cecil County Census)

BOYLE

Boyle, Patrick (1792-1873), married Hannah A. (N) (1811-1881) probably circa 1830s (St. Patrick's Catholic Church tombstone inscriptions)

Boyle, Roberta E., see Robert Rawlings

BOYNTON

Boynton, Austin H. (esquire), of Elmira, NY, married Miss Elizabeth B. Creswell, of Port Deposit, on 12 Nov 1850, after obtaining a license on 8 Nov 1850, by Rev. Lacy in Port Deposit (*Cecil Whig*, 16 Nov 1850; Cecil County Marriage License Book)

BRABSON

Brabson, Thomas (1820-1892), married Harriet Slicer (1817-1881) circa 10 Feb 1846 (date of license) (Cecil County Marriage License Book; Rosebank Cemetery, at Calvert, tombstone inscriptions)

BRADFORD

Bradford, Sidney George (1817-1849), of Middle Neck, Cecil Co., married 1st to Elizabeth Whitely (1821-1845), daughter of the late Col. Whitely, of Wilmington, DE, on 11 Oct 1842 by Rev. Work and married 2nd to Anna S. (N) in 1846 (only son William Crawford Bradford, 1847-1848) (*Delaware Gazette*, 14 Oct 1842, 1 Jul 1845, 11 Jul 1848 and 7 Sep 1849)

Bradford, William, married Mary Jane Price, both of Elkton, married in Baltimore on 20 Nov 1846 by Rev. McIntyre after obtaining a license in Elkton on 19 Nov 1846; their son Richard George Reese Bradford died of croup on 2 Jan 1850, aged 2 years and 3 months (Cecil County Marriage License Book; *Delaware Gazette*, 24 Nov 1846; *Cecil Democrat and Farmer's Journal*, 5 Jan 1850)

Bradford, Richard George Reese, see William Bradford

Bradford, William Crawford, see Sidney George Bradford

BRADLEY

Bradley, Edward (born c1815, Pennsylvania (wheelwright at Warwick), married Eliza (N) (born c1816, Maryland) circa 1840 (1860 Cecil County Census)

Bradley, Joshua, married Margaret Cameron circa 24 May 1838 (date of license) by Rev. Burrows (Cecil County Marriage License Book)

Bradley, Mary A. T., see Samuel Molten

BRADWAY

Bradway, Elizabeth H., Rachel and Thomas, see Lewis Brown

BRADY

Brady, Abigail Jane, see Nicholas Golden

BRANDRETH

Brandreth, Harriet, see Joseph H. Cameron

BRATTON

Bratton, Mary, see Samuel Stewart

BRAY

Bray, Ellen, see Edward Dougherty

BRICE

Brice, Amelia Ann Elizabeth, see John T. Brice

BRICKLEY

Brickley, Alem L., married Elizabeth Saunders circa 12 Dec 1845 (date of license) (Cecil County Marriage License Book)

Brickley, Andrew (1794-1870) (farmer and War of 1812 veteran), of Brickleytown, son of Joachim Brickley, of German origin, married Miss Mary Campbell (1794-1883), of Rising Sun, on 21 Aug 1828, after obtaining a license on 16 Aug 1828, at Farmington, MD, by Rev. Magraw (Cecil County Marriage License Book; *Elkton Press*, 30 Aug 1828; *Portrait and Biographical Record of Harford and Cecil Counties, Maryland* (1897, repr. 1989), pp. 427-428, stated they had one child, William Thomas Brickley, born 11 May 1829; Bounty Land Warrant 50-40-87285)

Brickley, Andrew James (1825-1873), of near Farmington, married Sarah J. (N) (1824-1877) probably circa 1846 (Friends Cemetery, at Harrisville, tombstone inscriptions; *Cecil Whig*, 5 Apr 1873 and 5 May 1877)

Brickley, Catherine, see William Maxwell

Brickley, Elam (1817-1846), married Elizabeth (N) (1825-1915) circa 1845 (Hopewell United Methodist Church Cemetery tombstone inscriptions)

Brickley, Everhart, see Nathaniel Brickley

Brickley, Joachim, see Andrew Brickley

Brickley, John, married Mary Thompson circa 10 Dec 1827 (date of license) (Cecil Co. Marr. License Book)

Brickley, Joseph, see William Brickley

Brickley, Mary Agnes, see Nevin W. McCormick

Brickley, Mary E., see William J. Dennis

Brickley, Nathaniel (born c1812, Maryland) (farmer in the 9th District), married Margaret (N) (born c1830, Maryland) probably circa 1847; son Everhart Brickley born c1848, Maryland (1860 Cecil County Census)

Brickley, Samuel (1802-1888), married Mary H. (N) (1805-1899) probably circa 1823 (Ebenezer Methodist Church Cemetery tombstone inscriptions)

Brickley, William (blacksmith), son of Joseph Brickley, of German descent, married 1st to Margaret McMullen circa 5 Apr 1831 (date of license) by Rev. Duke and married 2nd to Mrs. F. Lee (no date given) (Cecil County Marriage License Book; *Portrait and Biographical Record of Harford and Cecil Counties, Maryland* (1897, repr. 1989), p. 566)

Brickley, William (1807-1886) (farmer near Zion), married Pearl A. (N) (1819-1893) probably circa 1840 (Ebenezer Methodist Church Cemetery tombstone inscriptions; 1860 Cecil County Census)

Brickley, William Thomas, see Andrew Brickley

BRILEY

Briley, Ann, see John Deshane

Briley, Samuel, married Mary May circa 27 Jul 1825 (date of license) by Rev. Chambers (Cecil County Marriage License Book)

BRINTON

Brinton, James, married Mahala Ann McKinney circa 14 Feb 1843 (date of license) (Cecil County Marriage License Book)

BRINTS

Brints, Lewis (born c1800, Maryland) (waterman at Chesapeake City), married Elizabeth (N) (born c1810, Delaware) probably circa 1840l daughter Sarah born c1843 (1860 Cecil County Census)

Brints, William (born c1820, Maryland) (waterman at Chesapeake City), married Catharine (N) (born c1813, Maryland) probably circa 1846; daughter Sarah born c1847 (1860 Cecil County Census)

BRISBEE

Brisbee, John (born c1827, Maryland) (sailor at Chesapeake City), married Rebecca (N) (born c1830, Maryland) circa 1848; daughter Ann Brisbee born c1849 (1860 Cecil County Census)

BRISCOE

Briscoe, Henrietta W., see Joseph V. Smith

Briscoe, John, see Joseph V. Smith

Briscoe, John T., married Miss Amelia Ann Elizabeth Brice, of Kent Co., on 30 Sep 1834, after obtaining a license on 27 Sep 1834, by Rev. McKenney (Kent Co. Marr. License Book; *Cecil Gazette*, 11 Oct 1834)

Briscoe, Mary Rosetta, see Thomas S. Welch

BRISTOW

Bristow, Christia Ann, see Alexander Kirk

Bristow, John (born c1830, Maryland) (sailor at Chesapeake City), married Catharine Bedwell (born c1832, Maryland) circa 1 Nov 1847 (date of license); son Lewis Bristow born c1848 (Cecil County Marriage License Book; DAR transcript copied in 1955 misspelled his name Briston; 1860 Cecil County Census misspelled his name Bristo)

Bristow, John R., of Chesapeake City, married Elizabeth R. Hitchcock (1822-1866) circa 9 Aug 1848 (date of license) (Cecil County Marriage License Book; *Cecil Whig*, 15 Dec 1866)

Bristow, Lewis, see John Bristow

Bristow, Lewis, married Elizabeth Bostick circa 25 Oct 1825 (date of license) by Rev. Sharpley (Cecil County Marriage License Book)

Bristow, William, married Martha Arrants circa 9 May 1831 (date of license) by Rev. Barratt (Cecil County Marriage License Book)

Bristow, William Jr., married Catherine Ann Stoops, both of Cecil Co., circa 15 Oct 1846 (date of license) by Rev. Storks (Cecil County Marriage License Book; Elkton Methodist Church Register, p. 141, gave the year of marriage, but not the date)

Bristow, William D., married Sarah Webb circa 8 Aug 1849 (date of license) (Cecil County Marriage License Book)

BRITTON

Britton, Thomas J., married Ann Eliza Boyer circa 28 Jun 1847 (date of license) (Cecil County Marriage License Book; DAR transcript listed his middle initial as I.)

BROADWELL

Broadwell, William, married Susannah Q. Woolston circa 1 Jun 1834 (date of license) by Rev. Smith (Cecil County Marriage License Book; DAR transcript copied in 1928 listed her middle initial as J., but it was actually a Q, written in the shape of a large elongated 2, in the original marriage license book)

BROCK

Brock, Harriet, see Lambert G. Ford

Brock, Sophia, see Isaac J. Lort

BROGAN

Brogan, Morris (1823-1913, born Pennsylvania) (papermaker at Elkton), married Margaretta Carson (1821-1893, born Pennsylvania) probably circa 1850; daughter Mary Brogan born c1851, son William Brogan born c1854, and daughter Lucy Brogan born c1858, all in Maryland (Cherry Hill Methodist Church Cemetery tombstone inscriptions; 1860 Cecil County Census)

BROKAW

Brokaw, Caleb C. (1800-1875) (major), of Fair Hill, married Phebe (N) (1804-1875) probably circa 1825; buried beside daughter Julia L. T. Brokaw, 1832-1855 (Sharp's Cemetery tombstone inscriptions; *Cecil Whig*, 20 Mar 1875 and 6 Nov 1875)

BROMWELL

Bromwell, Beaulah H., see Alfred G. Ridgely

Bromwell, Maria Deborah, see George J. A. Coulson

BROOK

Brook, John, married Miss Ann Gorrell on 11 Sep 1834, after obtaining a license ion 8 Sep 1834, by Rev. Griffith (*Cecil Gazette*, 13 Sep 1834; Cecil County Marriage License Book misspelled her name Gorl; DAR transcript copied in 1928 misspelled her surname Gail)

BROOKINGS

Brookings, Charles, married Eliza Johnston circa 20 Oct 1828 (date of license) by Rev. Goforth (Cecil County Marriage License Book)

Brookings, Jane, see David Jenness

Brookings, Margaret A., see Robert Baird

Brookings, Richard (doctor), married Miss Mary Elizabeth Carter, youngest daughter of Robert Carter, Esq., all of Cecil Co., on 17 Feb 1846, after obtaining a license on 16 Feb 1846, by Rev. DeWitt (Cecil County Marriage License Book; *Cecil Whig*, 21 Feb 1846, noting that "The American Baltimore, U. S. Gazette Philadelphia, will please copy.")

BROOKS

Brooks, Anthony (born c1825) (African American), married Minta (N) (born c1830) (African American) circa 1845; son Jim born c1845 (1860 Cecil County Census)

Brooks, John (born c1824) (African American) (farmer at Cecilton), married Senia (N) (born c1837) circa 1849; son John Brooks born c1850 (African American mulatto) (1860 Cecil County Census)

Brooks, Joseph H. (born c1826, Virginia) (constable at Chesapeake City), married Miss Susanna Fillingame (born c1832, Maryland) circa 1 Oct 1849 (date of license); son Elliott Brooks born c1851, Maryland (Cecil County Marriage License Book spelled her name Fillingam; 1860 Cecil County Census misspelled his name Broocks)

Brooks, Sarah, see Ely Cameron

BROOMELL

Broomell, Elizabeth, see James Davis

BROSHERS

Broshers, Mary, see George Haines

BROUGHTON

Broughton, Henry B., married Isabella S. Evans circa 19 Dec 1825 (date of license) by Rev. Magraw (Cecil County Marriage License Book)

Broughton, Mary Frances, see Robert M. Bell

BROWN

Brown, Adelaide M., see Elisha Brown

Brown, Albina, see Isaac Moore

Brown, Alexander, married Mary Walker circa 29 Jan 1834 (date of license) by Rev. Goforth (Cecil County Marriage License Book)

Brown, Alexander (1810-1854), married Sarah Rebecca Barnes (1825-1880), both of Port Deposit, on 10 Mar 1846, after obtaining a license on 4 Mar 1846, by Rev. Townsend (*Cecil Whig*, 11Apr 1846; Cecil County Marriage License Book; Hopewell United Methodist Church Cemetery tombstone inscriptions)

Brown, Allen, see Samuel Brown

Brown, And. *(sic)* (born c1830) (African American) (farmer near Elkton), married Emaline (N) (born c1832) (African American) circa 1849; daughter Flora Brown born c1850 (1860 Cecil County Census)

Brown, Anderson, see Clemson Brown

Brown, Ann, see Henry Martin, John Brown, Lewis Brown, Thomas Kitchen and Benjamin Mason

Brown, Ann Coco, see James Boddy

Brown, Anna M., see Joseph Markee

Brown, Caleb, see Isaac Moore and Clemson Brown

Brown, Caroline, see Jacob Johnson and Edwin J. Brown

Brown, Catherine, see Amos Hollis Hughes

Brown, Charles (African American), married Sarah Jane Bouldin (African American) on 26 Dec 1844 by Rev. Shields (Elkton Methodist Church Register, p. 140; Cecil County Marr. License Book did not list it)

Brown, Charles H., of Cecil Co., married Mrs. Adeline Waters, of Baltimore City, on 7 Jan 1849 by Rev. Leakin (*Cecil Democrat and Farmer's Journal*, 13 Jan 1849; *Baltimore Sun*, 10 Jan 1849)

Brown, Charlotte Carter, see Frisby Tull and William Brown

Brown, Clemson (1818-1887, born Maryland) (farmer near Brick Meeting House), son of Caleb Brown (c1785-1860) and Elizabeth Clemson (1787-1848), of East Nottingham Township, Cecil Co., married Lydia Ann Griffith (1819-1899, born Maryland), daughter of Nathan and Mary Griffith, of the same place, on 21st day of the 2nd month 1844 at the public meeting of Friends at the home of Nathan Griffith. Among the witnesses were Caleb Brown, Elizabeth Brown, Lindley Brown (born 1820), Nathan Griffith, Mary Griffith, Alice Griffith, William H. Griffith, Job Griffith and Hannah C. Griffith. (*Births, Deaths and Marriages of the Nottingham Quakers, 1680-1899*, by Alice L. Beard (1989), pp. 21, 22, 225; 1860 Cecil County Census; Rosebank Cemetery, at Calvert, tombstone inscriptions; buried beside Anderson Brown (1850-1873), Mary Alice Brown (1855-1926) and Hannah Ann Brown (1859-1961)

Brown, Cornelia, see John Caulk

Brown, Daniel (1795-1865), son of Jesse and Rebecca Brown, married Lydia Pyle (1809-1862), daughter of Samuel and Rachel Pyle, probably circa 1830 (Rosebank Cemetery, at Calvert, tombstone inscriptions)

Brown, Edmund, married Martha Simpson circa 21 May 1829 (date of license) by Rev. Barratt (Cecil County Marriage License Book)

Brown, Edmund Jr. (merchant in Elkton), married Martha Jane Kennard, daughter of Rev. Edward Kennard, of Wilmington, DE, on 30 Apr 1850 by Rev. Storks in Wilmington (*Cecil Whig*, 4 May 1850; *Delaware Gazette*, 7 May 1850)

Brown, Edward, see Jesse Brown

Brown, Edwin J. (1816-1884), married Caroline H. (N) (1821-1885) probably circa 1840; buried beside daughter Caroline R. Brown, 1843-1875 (Rosebank Cemetery, at Calvert, tombstone inscriptions)

Brown, Elisha (1819-1893), married Elizabeth L. (N) (1820-1887) probably circa 1840 (Rosebank Cemetery, at Calvert, tombstone inscriptions)

Brown, Elisha (1815-1885, born Pennsylvania) (farmer near Brick Meeting House), son of Jehu Brown and Sarah England, married Sarah McFan (1818-1897, born Maryland) on 20 Sep 1838 in Chester Co., PA by Jesse Coulson, Justice of the Peace; buried beside daughters Vienna E. Brown, 1847-1923, and Adelaide M. Brown, 1859-1935 (Rosebank Cemetery, at Calvert, tombstone inscriptions and *Joseph England and his Descendants*, by C. Walter England, Ph.D., 1975, p. 154, gave his name as Elisha Brown, yet the 1860 Cecil County Census listed him as Elisha J. Brown)

Brown, Elisha, see Stephen John Brown

Brown, Eliza, see Hugh Brown

Brown, Eliza Jane, see Lewis Wright

Brown, Elizabeth, see Reuben Kirk, Eli Haines, Ellwood Brown, Clemson Brown, Isaac Reynolds and Robert Rawlings

Brown, Ellen J., see John Newton Harker

Brown, Ellwood, son of Samuel and Elizabeth Brown, of West Nottingham Hundred, Cecil Co., married Rachel Kirk, daughter of William and Elizabeth Kirk, of the same place, on the 23rd day of the 10th month 1845 at a public meeting of Friends at the home of William Kirk (*Births, Deaths and Marriages of the Nottingham Quakers, 1680-1899*, by Alice L. Beard (1989), p. 226)

Brown, Emeline, see Amor Cameron

Brown, Flora, see And. Brown

Brown, Granville T. (born c1820, Maryland) (farmer, 7th District), married Angeline K. Fisher (born c1826, Maryland) circa 6 May 1846 (date of license); eldest daughter Rebecca Brown born c1849 (Cecil County Marriage License Book; 1860 Cecil County Census)

Brown, Hannah, see Lewis Brown

Brown, Hannah Ann, see Clemson Brown

Brown, Hannah C., see Reuben Kirk

Brown, Harriet A. P., see Charles H. Wilcox

Brown, Henry A., married Sarah Ann McLaughlin circa 7 Sep 1841 (date of license) (Cecil County Marriage License Book spelled her name McLaughlin; DAR transcript copied in 1955 spelled it McLoughlin)

Brown, Hiram (1812-1875), of Rising Sun, married Sarah (N) (c1815-1899) probably circa 1834-1835 (Friends Cemetery, at Harrisville, tombstone inscriptions; *Cecil Whig*, 10 Apr 1875)

Brown, Hugh (War of 1812 veteran) (died 1864), married Eliza Manly on 23 Mar 1825 at North East (Bounty land Warrant 50-40-94735); Eliza Brown (died 1887) was subsequently pensioned as the mother of William T. Brown, Co. A, 5th MD Infantry, Civil War (MC-49358)

Brown, Hugh, see Amor Cameron

Brown, Huldah W., see Isaac Moore

Brown, Isaac, see Charles H. Wilcox, John Rawlings Abrams and John White

Brown, Jacob, see Lewis Brown

Brown, James, married Margaret Williams, daughter of John (died 1826) and Sarah Williams, circa 29 Mar 1830 (date of license) by Rev. Magraw (Cecil County Marriage License Book; Cecil County Will Book A, No. 8, p. 234)

Brown, James T., married Jane Jamar circa 17 Dec 1840 (date of license) (Cecil County Marriage License Book gave his middle initial as T.; DAR transcript copied in 1955 mistakenly listed it as P.; *Cecil Whig*, 9 Dec 1843, reported the death of a James T. Brown in Elkton on 3 Dec 1843, but his age was not given)

Brown, Jehu, see Elisha Brown and Levi Alexander Hill

Brown, Jeremiah, see Isaac Moore and Lewis Brown

Brown, Jeremiah, married Mary H. (N) (1809-1888) probably circa 1830 (Brick Meeting House, at Calvert, tombstone inscription for Mary H. Brown)

Brown, Jesse, see Daniel Brown

Brown, Jesse (born c1822, Pennsylvania) (carpenter at Port Herman), married Sarah (N) (born c1826, Pennsylvania) probably circa 1849; daughter Susannah born c1850, Pennsylvania, daughter Mary born c1857, Maryland and son Edward born c1859, Maryland (1860 Cecil County Census)

Brown, John, married Ann (N) (1807-1891) probably circa 1827 and she died at Mt. Pleasant (*Midland Journal*, 6 Feb 1891, stated Mrs. Ann Brown died in her 84th year and her seven sons and grandchildren were present at her funeral, but the name of the cemetery was not given; *Midland Journal*, 13 Feb 1891, stated only daughter Mary Kitchen was buried near her mother, but again the name of the cemetery was not given; *Cecil Whig*, 22 Dec 1849)

Brown, John, married Edith Foster circa 14 Aug 1830 (date of license) by Rev. Duke (Cecil County Marriage License Book)

Brown, John A., married Sarah Ann (N) (1811-1845) circa 1835; son William Freeman Brown, 1836-1838, and five other infants, buried next to Sarah Ann Brown)

Brown, John C., see Isaac Moore

Brown, John D. F., married Martha J. Humphries circa 21 Jan 1832 (date of license) by Rev. McCarrol, a Methodist Episcopal minister in Port Deposit (Cecil County Marriage License Book)

Brown, John E. (born c1809) (postmaster at Elkton), married Ann M. Robb (born c1813) circa 23 Nov 1836 (date of license) by Rev. Potts (Cecil County Marriage License Book; 1860 Cecil County Census)

Brown, John W. (1814-1884), married 1st to Catharine (N) (1818-1867) probably circa 1840 and married 2nd to Hannah E. (N) (1819-1883) after 1867 (Rosebank Cemetery, at Calvert, tombstone inscriptions)

Brown, Joseph, married Rachel Maria Tosh circa 14 Oct 1835 (date of license) by Rev. Duke (Cecil County Marriage License Book; DAR transcript copied in 1928 mistakenly listed his first name as John)

Brown, Joseph T. (1810-1865) (reverend), of Cherry Hill, married Millicent J. Simpers (1813-1873) circa 7 Apr 1835 (date of license) by Rev. Wolley (Cecil County Marriage License Book; Cherry Hill Methodist Church Cemetery tombstone inscriptions; *Cecil Whig*, 13 May 1865 and 17 Aug 1865)

Brown, Joshua, see James Wason

Brown, Lewis (1800-1848), son of Jacob and Hannah Brown, latter deceased, of East Nottingham Township, Chester Co., PA, married Rachel B. Rogers, daughter of Jeremiah and Ann Rogers, of East Nottingham Hundred, Cecil Co., on 19th day of 7th mo. 1827 at East Nottingham (*Births, Deaths and Marriages of the Nottingham Quakers, 1680-1899*, by Alice L. Beard (1989), pp. 22, 221, mistakenly listed him as Jacob)

Brown, Lewis, son of Jeremiah and Ann Brown, of Little Britain Township, Lancaster Co., PA, married Elizabeth H. Bradway, daughter of Thomas and Rachel Bradway, of East Nottingham Township, Chester Co., PA, on the 16th day of the 2nd month 1841 at East Nottingham (*Births, Deaths and Marriages of the Nottingham Quakers, 1680-1899*, by Alice L. Beard (1989), p. 224)

Brown, Lindley, see Clemson Brown

Brown, Lydia Ann, see Mark Brown

Brown, Mark (1804-1862), married Lydia Ann Brown (1809-1883) circa 22 Feb 1831 (date of license) by Rev. Griffith (Cecil County Marriage License Book; DAR transcript copied in 1928 mistakenly listed E. as her middle initial; Rosebank Cemetery, at Calvert, tombstone inscriptions)

Brown, Martha Jane, see Washington Snowden

Brown, Mary, see Jesse Brown, James Wason and Thomas Kitchen

Brown, Mary A., see Samuel Smith and James Wason

Brown, Mary Alice, see Clemson Brown

Brown, Mary Ann, see Levi Alexander Hill and John Rawlings Abrams

Brown, Mary E., see Robert Cantwell and George England

Brown, Mary H., see Jeremiah Brown

Brown, Millicent, see B. F. Maulden

Brown, Millicent Ann, see John William Hillyard

Brown, Montillion (1822-1908), married Martha J. (N) (1820-1880) prob. circa 1843 (Brick Meeting House, at Calvert, tombstone inscriptions)

Brown, Montillion (Montilion), see Benjamin Mason, Thomas Brown and Isaac Moore

Brown, Nathan, see George England

Brown, Phebe, see Isaac Moore

Brown, Rachel, see George England

Brown, Rebecca, see Daniel Brown, Granville Brown and Moses Rumsey

Brown, Rebecca H., see Isaac Moore

Brown, Robert, see William Brown

Brown, Ruth Ann, see William Sherer

Brown, Ruth Anna, see Benjamin Mason

Brown, Samuel, see Ellwood Brown

Brown, Samuel (1816-1891), son of Allen Brown, married Jane V. Gregg (1816-1896), daughter of Solomon Gregg, probably circa 1840; buried beside son Solomon C. Brown, 1847-1909 (Rosebank Cemetery, at Calvert, tombstone inscriptions)

Brown, Sarah, see James Evans Cooper, Levi Alexander Hill and Isaac Moore

Brown, Sarah Ann, see Stephen John Brown

Brown, Sarah H., see William Nelson

Brown, Stephen John (1821-1855) (coachmaker, 7th District), son of Elisha Brown and Nancy Gay, married Sarah Ann England (1828, near Brick Meeting House, Cecil Co. - 1898, Avon Park, Florida), daughter of Samuel John England and Esther Haines, circa 24 May 1848 (date of the license); Sarah Ann (England) Brown married 2nd to Charles Parker (1795-1879), widower, on 24 Jan 1857 and he died in Wilmington, DE (Cecil County Marriage License Book; *Joseph England and his Descendants*, by C. Walter England, Ph.D., 1975, p. 291)

Brown, Susannah, see Jesses Brown

Brown, Thomas, see Reuben Kirk

Brown, Thomas (1816-1882), son of Montilion Brown and Ann Rogers, married Elizabeth Amelia Kirk (1820-1879), daughter of William M. Kirk and Nancy Ann England, on the 31st day of the 12th month 1842; license dated 31 Dec 1842 (Cecil County Marriage License Book; Brick Meeting House, at Calvert, tombstone inscriptions; *Joseph England and his Descendants*, by C. Walter England, Ph.D., 1975, p. 145, stated burial was in East Nottingham Friends Cemetery)

Brown, Thomas W., of Philadelphia, PA, married Rebecca Price circa 17 Jul 1845 (date of license) (Cecil County Marriage License Book)

Brown, Timothy N. (1824-1868), married Hulden (Huldeh?) W. (N) (1822-1879) probably circa 1845 (Brick Meeting House, at Calvert, tombstone inscriptions)

Brown, Tom (born c1826) (African American) (farm hand at Cecilton), married Nancy (N) (born c1832) (African American) circa 1849 (1860 Cecil County Census listed son Henry Brown born c1850, mulatto, daughter Jane Brown born c1852, mulatto, and son George A. Brown born c1856, black)

Brown, Vienna E., see Elisha Brown

Brown, William, see Isaac Moore

Brown, William, married Mary Robinson circa 31 Mar 1827 (date of license) (Cecil Co. Marr. Lic. Book)

Brown, William, married Charlotte Carter (1817-1879) circa 11 Apr 1832 (date of license) by Rev. Duke and Charlotte Carter Brown married 2nd to Frisby Tull on 9 Jan 1838 (Cecil County Marriage License Book)

Brown, William (esquire), son of the late Gen. Robert Brown, of Pennsylvania, married Susan Ingels Conard, daughter of Judge Conard of Cecil Co., on 7 Nov 1843, after obtaining a license on 6 Nov 1843, by Rev. Happersen (*Cecil Whig*, 11 Nov 1843; Cecil County Marriage License Book)

Brown, William Freeman, see John A. Brown

Brown, William I. (African American), married Hannah Wallace (African American) on 21 Dec 1850 by Rev. Fernley (Elkton Methodist Church Register, p. 141; Cecil County Marr. License Book did not list it)

Brown, William J., married Ann M. Evans circa 3 Apr 1826 (date of license) by Rev. Russell (Cecil County Marriage License Book)

Brown, William T., see Hugh Brown

BROXSON

Broxson, Thomas, married Miss Temperance Ann King, both of Sassafras Neck, on 12 Oct 1848, after obtaining a license on 9 Oct 1848, by Rev. Wiley at St. Stephen's Church (*Cecil Whig*, 14 Oct 1848, spelled his name Broxson; Cecil County Marriage License Book spelled it Broxon; *Cecil Democrat and Farmer's Journal*, 14 Oct 1848, spelled it Brockson)

BRUCE

Bruce, Charles, married Mary Eliza Death circa 13 Apr 1830 (date of license) by Rev. Magraw (Cecil County Marriage License Book; DAR transcript copied in 1928 misspelled his name Charley)

Bruce, Elizabeth, see William Shelly

BRUMFIELD

Brumfield, Abraham (1814-1893), married Eliza A. (N) (1815-1903) probably circa 1835-1836 (St. Mark's Episcopal Church tombstone inscriptions)

Brumfield, Hannah, see Nathaniel K. Gilmore

Brumfield, Harriet, see Edward Jackson

Brumfield, John, married Ellen C. Gibson circa 12 Feb 1836 (date of license) by Rev. Potts (Cecil County Marriage License Book)

Brumfield, Joseph, married Jane Rutter circa 26 Aug 1836 (date of license) by Rev. Duke (Cecil County Marriage License Book)

Brumfield, Nathan, married Elizabeth Love circa 23 Oct 1833 (date of license) by Rev. Duke (Cecil County Marriage License Book; DAR transcript copied in 1928 listed her name as Lowe)

Brumfield, Sarah, see Victor Jackson

Brumfield, William, married Amelia Owens circa 8 Jun 1826 (date of license) by Rev. Magraw (Cecil County Marriage License Book)

BRYAN

Bryan, Eliza H., see Samuel Grace

Bryan, Emily E., see John C. Adams

Bryan, Joel, married Frances Andrews circa 18 Jun 1833 (date of license) by Rev. Rees (Cecil County Marriage License Book)

Bryan, Joseph, see John C. Adams

Bryan, Lydia, see Thompson Leonard

Bryan, Mary, see James H. Willard

Bryan, Thomas, married Leah Wallace circa 14 Feb 1825 (date of license) by Rev. Chambers (Cecil County Marriage License Book)

BRYSON

Bryson, Thomas (1823-1901) (laborer at Elkton), married Hester Ann Foreacre (1828-1890) circa 26 Nov 1845 (date of license); eldest son Robert Bryson born c1850 (Cecil County Marriage License Book; 1860 Cecil County Census; Wesley Methodist Church Cemetery tombstone inscriptions)

BUCHANAN

Buchanan, Christopher, see George R. Buchanan

Buchanan, Eliza, see Louis Buchanan

Buchanan, George, see Louis Buchanan

Buchanan, George R. (born c1815, Pennsylvania) (farmer at Elkton), married Ellen W. (N) (born c1818, Pennsylvania) circa 1844; son Christopher Buchanan born c1845 (1860 Cecil County Census)

Buchanan, John, see Louis Buchanan and John Buchanan

Buchanan, John B. (born c1823, Delaware) (blacksmith at Chesapeake City), married Susan (N) (born c1827, Delaware) probably circa 1844; son Franky(?) born c1845, Delaware, son John born c1853, Maryland, daughter Susan born c1856, Maryland (1860 Cecil County Census)

Buchanan, Louis, married Ellen Morgan circa 2 Mar 1842 (date of license) (Cecil County Marriage License Book spelled his name Buchannon; 1860 Cecil County Census listed them as Lewis Buckhannan, age 42, Elkton farmer, wife Eliza age 44, son John age 16, twins George and Mary age 14, son William age 10)

Buchanan, Margaret, see Isaac L. Crouch

Buchanan, Mary, see William Boulton and Louis Buchanan

Buchanan, Susan, see John B. Buchanan

Buchanan, William, see Louis Buchanan

BUCK

Buck, Amy, see Perry Anderson

BUCKLEY

Buckley, Alice J., see Jacob Heckendorn

Buckley, Charles (born c1816) (farmer at Elkton), married Elizabeth (N) (born c1818) circa 1837; son Thomas Buckley born c1838 (1860 Cecil County Census)

Buckley, Ida, see John W. Buckley

Buckley, John W. (born c1825, Maryland) (shoemaker, 7th District), married Isabella (N) (born c1830, Maryland) probably circa 1849; daughter Ida Buckley born c1850 (1860 Cecil County Census)

Buckley, Rebecca, see Jacob Heckendorn

Buckley, William J., see Jacob Heckendorn

BUCKWITH, BUCKWORTH

Buckwith, Ann, see John C. Cochran

Buckworth, Charles, married Elizabeth Orr circa 1 Feb 1835 (date of license) by Rev. Duke (Cecil County Marriage License Book)

Buckworth, John (born c1820, Maryland) (laborer at St. Augustine), married Eliza (N) (born c1822 *(sic)*, Maryland) and son John Buckworth, Jr. was born c1836 *(sic)*, Maryland (1860 Cecil County Census)

Buckwith, John Wesley, married Eliza Ann Robinson circa 10 Dec 1833 (date of license) by Rev. Duke (Cecil County Marriage License Book)

Buckwith, Samuel, married Miss Eliza Smith, both of Back Creek Neck, Cecil Co., on 8 Mar 1832, after obtaining a license on 6 Mar 1832, by Rev. Barnes (*Elkton Press*, 10 Mar 1832; Cecil County Marriage License Book)

BUDD

Budd, William (born c1825, Delaware) (trader at Warwick), married Catharine (N) (born c1832, Delaware) circa 1848; son James Budd born c1849 (1860 Cecil County Census)

BUENES

Buenes, Samuel, married Susan Taylor circa 13 Sep 1825 (date of license) by Rev. Sharpley (Cecil County Marriage License Book)

BUFFINGTON

Buffington, Ephraim, ----, of Penn Township, Chester Co., PA, married Miss Sarah ----, of New London Township, Chester Co., PA, on 12(?) Sep 1849 by Rev. Charles ---- at the residence of William ----, of East Nottingham Township, Chester Co., PA (*Cecil Democrat and Farmer's Journal*, 22 Sep 1849, newspaper poorly microfilmed, partially illegible)

BULLEN, BULLIN

Bullen, Harrison T. (c1810-1848), married Mary Price (1810-1849) on 11 Nov 1828, after obtaining a license that same day, by Rev. Barratt at Robert C. Lusby's in Elkton; Mrs. Mary Bullen, widow of the late H. T. Bullen, died of consumption in Newark, DE on 13 Apr 1849 in her 39th year, her death thought to have been hastened by the death of her husband seven months earlier (Cecil County Marriage License Book; *Elkton Press*, 18 Nov 1828; *Cecil Whig*, 21 Apr 1849, contains a memorial by "J. T. B." of Cherry Hill)

Bullin, James, see James Burlin

Bullen, Sarah, see John T. Cameron

Bullin, Stearns, married Elmira Barratt circa 2 Mar 1836 (date of license) by Rev. Barratt (Cecil County Marriage License Book spelled his name Bullins)

BULLOCK

Bullock, E. A., see William T. Reese

BURCHELL

Burchell, Jane, see Edward B. Lewis

BURDEN

Burden, Samuel, married Lydia Murphy circa 23 Aug 1827 (date of license) (Cecil County Marriage License Book; DAR transcript copied in 1928 misspelled her name Myrphey)

BURGOYNE

Burgoyne, Caleb K., married Elizabeth A. Lilley on 26 May 1838, after obtaining a license that same day, by Rev. Hagany (Cecil County Marriage License Book; DAR transcript copied in 1928 misspelled his name Burgoine and her name Lidley; Elkton Methodist Church Register, p. 139)

Burgoyne, Karon, see John A. Keith

Burgoyne, Mary, see John A. Keith

Burgoyne, Rebecca Jane, see Warner Reynolds Ramsey

BURK, BURKE

Burke, Elizabeth, see James Burke

Burke, Isabella, see James Burke

Burk, James M. (born c1815) (farmer near Elkton), married Letitia Veazey (born c1825) circa 28 Oct 1840 (date of license) (Cecil County Marriage License Book; DAR transcript copied in 1955 listed his name without a middle initial and spelled her name Veasey; 1860 Cecil County Census spelled his name Birk)

Burke, James (born c1830, Ireland) (laborer in the 7th District), married Rebecca (N) (born c1830, Ireland) probably circa 1849; son William born c1850, Ireland, daughter Margaret born c1852, Ireland, daughter Elizabeth born c1855, Maryland, daughter Isabella born c1857, Maryland, and daughter Rebecca born c1859, Maryland (1860 Cecil County Census)

Burk, John (War of 1812 veteran), married Mary Grace (born 1792) circa 16 Aug 1828 (date of license) by Rev. Barratt (Cecil County Marriage License Book; Bounty Land Warrant 55-120-5937 stated they married at Elk Neck on 9 Aug 1828 and had one child, John Burk, born 1 Sep 1832)

Burke, John (slave of Gen. Foreman), married Martha (N) (slave of William Lee) on 20 Feb 1825 by Rev. Epinette (*History of Saint Francis Xavier Church and Bohemia Plantation Now Known as Old Bohemia, Warwick, Maryland*, by Joseph C. Cann (1976), p. 47)

Burke, John (born c1824), married Rachel (N) (born c1821) circa 1849; daughter Martha Burke born c1850 (1860 Cecil County Census)

Burke, Margaret, see James Burke

Burke, Martha, see John Burke

Burke, Rachel, see Edward Pearce

Burke, Rebecca, see James Burke

Burke, William, see James Burke

BURLIN

Burlin, Frank (born c1815, Maryland) (innkeeper, Port Deposit), married Mary (N) (born c1825, Delaware) probably circa 1845 (1860 Cecil County Census)

Burlin, Henry, see James Burlin

Burlin, James, married Mary Ann Bailey on 25 Aug 1836 after obtaining a license that same day, by Rev. Duke (Cecil County Marriage License Book spelled his name Berlin; DAR transcript copied in 1928 listed his name as James Bulin; 1840 Cecil County Census listed his name as James Berlin; St. John's Episcopal Church, Havre de Grace Parish, Marriage Register, 1835-1858, in Harford County, stated they married in "Cecil at Mr. Bailey's" and mistakenly listed his name as Henry Boulen)

Burlin, Samuel L. (1808-1887, Maryland) (laborer, 7th District), married Ann (N) (1810-1880) probably circa 1830 (West Nottingham Cemetery tombstone inscriptions; 1860 Cecil County Census)

Burlin, William B. (1814-1892, born Maryland) (laborer, 7th District), married Rebecca Jones circa 9 Jun 1845 (date of license) (Cecil County Marriage License Book; West Nottingham Cemetery tombstone inscription; 1860 Cecil County Census)

BURNHAM

Burnham, Sophia, see Elisha Reynolds

BURNITE

Burnite, Elizabeth, see William Hassan

Burnite, Isabella, see Levi G. Smith

Burnite, James K. (born c1815), married Martha C. Hyland (1817-1866), daughter of Joshua and Margaret Hyland, circa 22 Mar 1838 (date of license) by Rev. McFarland (Cecil County Marriage License Book; DAR transcript copied in 1928 mistakenly listed the minister's name as Farland (James McFarland was a Methodist minister in Elkton at that time); Cherry Hill Methodist Church Cemetery tombstone inscription for Martha Burnite)

Burnite, Margaret, see Isaac McClay

Burnite, Mary Jane, see John Gamble

Burnite, Rachel S., see Samuel S. Kilvington

Burnite, Rebecca Ann, see James Getty

BURNS

Burns, Eliza, see Andrew Barrett

Burns, Henry (1804-1868, born Maryland) (farmer near North East), married Hannah McVey (born c1801, born Maryland) circa 11 Jun 1832 (date of license) by Rev. Duke (Cecil County Marriage License Book; DAR transcript copied in 1928 misspelled his name Burnes; Logan Family Cemetery tombstone inscription for Henry Burns; 1860 Cecil County Census)

Burns, Jonathan P., married Jane Alexander circa 26 Dec 1831 (date of license) by Rev. McKee (Cecil County Marriage License Book)

Burns, Samuel (1800-1892), married Rachel (N) (1820-1872) probably circa 1840 (Shelemiah Methodist Church Cemetery tombstone inscriptions)

BURRIS

Burris, Eliza, see Andrew Barrett

Burris, Elizabeth, see James Gillespie

BURROUGHS

Burroughs, Eli, married Martha C. Jackson circa 6 Feb 1849 (date of license) (Cecil County Marriage License Book)

Burroughs, George D., see John Burroughs

Burroughs, George R., of Cecil Co., married Miss Caroline Rumford, of Brandywine Hundred, on 25 Mar 1845 by Rev. Walker (*Delaware Gazette*, 28 Mar 1845)

Burroughs, John (1816-1897, born Maryland) (innkeeper, Perryville), married Jane E. (N) (1823-1887, born Maryland) probably circa 1843; son George D. Burroughs, 1844-1878 (St. Mark's Episcopal Church tombstone inscriptions; 1860 Cecil County Census misspelled his name Burrows)

BURROWES, BURROWS

Burrowes, George (reverend), married Helena R. (N) (1810-1848) probably circa 1835 (West Nottingham Cemetery tombstone inscription for Helena Burrowes)

Burrows, Mary Ann, see William Dennison

Burrows, also see Burroughs

BURTON

Burton, Miers and Sarah, see Gideon Waples

BUSH

Bush, George, married Anna E. Steele, daughter of the late Henry Steele, of Wilmington, DE, on 31 Oct 1837 by Rev. Gilbert in Wilmington (*Cecil Gazette*, 4 Nov 1837)

BUSSEY

Bussey, B. F. (doctor), married Maria A. Black, daughter of Charles G. Black, all of Cecil Co., on 6 May 1833 (*Baltimore American and Commercial Daily Advertiser*, 8 May 1833)

BUTCHER

Butcher, William H., of Frederick Co., MD, married Miss Elmira Cromwell, of Baltimore, on 9 Oct 1849 (*Cecil Democrat and Farmer's Journal*, 13 Oct 1849; *Baltimore Sun*, 11 Oct 1849)

BUTLER

Butler, Cassandra, see Robert E. Smith

Butler, Elizabeth, see Joseph T. Waite

Butler, Peter, see Robert Butler

Butler, Robert (born c1824) (African American) (farm hand at Cecilton), married Mary (N) (born c1832) (African American) circa 1849; son Peter born c1850 (African American) (1860 Cecil County Census)

BUTTERWORTH

Butterworth, Robert, married Harriet E. Darling circa 10 Jun 1846 (date of license) (Cecil County Marriage License Book)

BYE

Bye, Amos and Deborah, see Amos Pugh and Enoch Mortimer Bye

Bye, Enoch Mortimer (born 1818), son of Amos and Deborah Bye, of East Nottingham Township, Chester Co., PA, married Phebe Pusey Passmore (1821-1859), daughter of Andrew Moore Passmore (1800-1874) and Judith Wilson (1801-1885), of the same place, on the 23rd day of the 4th month 1843 at East Nottingham (*Births, Deaths and Marriages of the Nottingham Quakers, 1680-1899*, by Alice L. Beard (1989), pp. 23, 24, 70, 225; Brick Meeting House, at Calvert, tombstone inscriptions for Andrew M. and Judith Passmore, but no Bye markers)

Bye, Mary Ann, see Amos Pugh

Bye, Rachel, see Reuben Reynolds

CALDWELL

Caldwell, David (1795-1835) (War of 1812 veteran), married Rebecca Hanna (1803-1860) on 17 Mar 1825 by "Rev. Barton, pastor of a congregation called Old School Baptist" (Bounty Land Warrant; Rock Springs Old School Baptist Church Cemetery tombstone inscriptions)

Caldwell, James (born c1816, Maryland) (iron roller, 7th District), married Eliza (N) (born c1820, Maryland) probably circa 1843; daughter Sarah Caldwell born c1844 (1860 Cecil County Census)

Caldwell, John, married Rebecca Price circa 8 Mar 1826 (date of license) by Rev. Smith (Cecil County Marriage License Book)

Caldwell, Sarah, see James Caldwell

CALLENDAR

Callendar, Catherine, see Henry Hays

CALLICET

Callicet, Jemima, see Ephraim Thompson Mitchell

CALVERT

Calvert, Alice, see Samuel Thompson

Calvert, Jane, see William Richardson

Calvert, John Thomas, married Catharine J. Sturdevant circa 4 Jan 1850 (date of license) (Cecil County Marriage License Book; DAR transcript copied in 1955 misspelled his name as Calvertto)

Calvert, Mary Jane, see James Whitelock

Calvert, William, married Miss Louisa Bennett, both of Charles Town, Cecil Co., on 15 Feb 1838, after obtaining a license on 13 Feb 1838, by Rev. Kennard (*Cecil Gazette*, 10 Mar 1838; Cecil County Marriage License Book)

CALWELL

Calwell, J. (born c1821, Maryland) (collier near Charlestown), married Mary (N) (born c1821, Maryland) probably circa 1839; son John born c1840 (1860 Cecil County Census)

CAMBLIN

Camblin, Andrew, married Miss Leah Moody, both of Cecil Co., on 29 Mar 1838, after obtaining a license that same day, by Rev. McFarland (*Cecil Gazette*, 31 Mar 1838; Cecil County Marriage License Book; DAR transcript copied in 1928 mistakenly listed the minister's name as Farland (James McFarland was a Methodist minister in Elkton at that time); Elkton Methodist Church Register, p. 138)

CAMERON

Cameron, Amor (c1810-1885, born Maryland) (farmer near Bay View), son of Robert Cameron of Scotland, later of Cecil Co., married Emeline Brown (died 1850), daughter of Hugh Brown of Ireland, later of Cecil County, on 3 Sep 1834, after obtaining a license that same day, by Rev. Stork (Cecil County Marriage License Book; DAR transcript in 1928 misspelled his name as Amos; *Cecil Gazette*, 6 Sep 1834; *Portrait and Biographical Record of Harford and Cecil Counties, Maryland* (1897, repr. 1989), p. 318, listed their five children as Robert [born c1838], Hugh B. (died before 1897), James N. (born 10 Jul 1841), Alice [born c1843], ---- (Mrs. Jacob Minker of Delaware), and Margaret Elizabeth (died before 1897); 1860 Cecil County Census also listed children Christiana born c1853 and Melantier born c1856)

Cameron, Andrew M. (1817-1900), married Rachel Miller (1827-1911) probably circa 1847 (Rosebank Cemetery, at Calvert, tombstone inscriptions)

Cameron, Ann R., see James White

Cameron, Anna L., see William Craig

Cameron, Christiana, see Amor Cameron

Cameron, Deborah, see Reuben Lake

Cameron, Elizabeth, see David P. Maxwell and Thomas McVey

Cameron, Ellen, see Roberson Gallaher

Cameron, Eli, married Sarah Brooks circa 7 Feb 1831 (date of license) by Rev. Griffith (Cecil County Marriage License Book)

Cameron, Hugh B, see Amor Cameron

Cameron, James, see William Cameron and James Crothers

Cameron, James (1814-1895, born Maryland) (farmer, 6th District), married Rebecca Kirk (1819-1895, born Maryland) probably circa 1839; daughter Martha born c1840 (West Nottingham Cemetery tombstone inscriptions; 1860 Cecil County Census)

Cameron, James N., see Amor Cameron

Cameron, John, see Robert J. Cameron

Cameron, John, married Margaret Lynch circa 11 Jan 1826 (date of license) by Rev. Talley (Cecil County Marriage License Book)

Cameron, John (1808-1888), married Amelia Thompson (1825-1894) circa 19 Sep 1850 (date of license) (Cecil County Marriage License Book; West Nottingham Cemetery tombstone inscriptions)

Cameron, John C., see Robert J. Cameron

Cameron, John Thomas, married Sarah Bullen circa 6 Jul 1826 (date of license) by Rev. Magraw (Cecil County Marriage License Book)

Cameron, Joseph H. (born c1817, Maryland) (lumber inspector, 7th District), married Harriet Brandreth (born c1827, New Jersey) circa 27 Nov 1847 (date of license) (Cecil County Marriage License Book; 1860 Cecil County Census)

Cameron, Margaret, see Andrew Marnes and Joshua Bradley

Cameron, Margaret Elizabeth, see Amor Cameron

Cameron, Martha, see James Cameron

Cameron, Mary E., see George W. Oldham

Cameron, Melantier, see Amor Cameron

Cameron, Rachel, see James Crothers and Benjamin F. Kirk

Cameron, Robert, see Amor Cameron

Cameron, Robert J. (1824-1910), son of John C. Cameron (1803-1867) and Nancy A. (N) (1799-1824), married Margaretta (N) (1825-1912) by 1849; buried beside son John Cameron, 1850-1931 (Rosebank Cemetery, at Calvert, tombstone inscriptions)

Cameron, William (1806-1884, born Maryland) (farmer near Brick Meeting House), married Anna Maria Oldham (1810-1899, born Maryland) circa 7 Jan 1829 (date of license) by Rev. Duke (Cecil County Marriage License; Rosebank Cemetery, at Calvert, tombstone inscriptions; 1860 Cecil County Census)

Cameron, William (born c1811, Maryland) (farmer near Brick Meeting House), married Jane Maxwell (born c1815, Maryland) circa 7 Jun 1838 (date of license) by Rev. Burrows; son James Cameron born c1840 (Cecil County Marriage License Book; 1860 Cecil County Census)

Cameron, William (Professor of Languages in the Masonic College, Lexington, Missouri), married Martha E. Shewalter, daughter of Joseph Shewalter, Esq., formerly of Virginia, in 1850 [no date was given] at Hazlewood, near Lexington, by Rev. Bracken (*Cecil Democrat and Farmer's Journal*, 14 Sep 1850)

CAMPBELL

Campbell, Eliza Jane, see Caleb Edmondson

Campbell, Elizabeth, see Adam Little

Campbell, Ellender, see Absalom Jackson

Campbell, George, married Mary Ann DeValinger circa 2 Oct 1840 (date of license) (Cecil County Marriage License Book)

Campbell, James, married Elizabeth Clark circa 14 Jun 1837 (date of license) by Rev. Kennard (Cecil County Marriage License Book)

Campbell, John, married Temperance Pearson circa 14 Nov 1827 (date of license) (Cecil County Marriage License Book)

Campbell, John (1795-1878), married Eliza A. (N) (1813-1902) probably circa 1832 (Hopewell United Methodist Church Cemetery tombstone inscriptions)

Campbell, John B. (1805-1867), of North East, married Sarah McMullen circa 16 Feb 1825 (date of license) by Rev. Griffith (Cecil County Marriage License Book; *Cecil Democrat and Farmer's Journal*, 11 May 1867, stated he died in his 62nd year)

Campbell, Lavinia A., see William Benjamin

Campbell, Mary, see Andrew Brickley, Jeremiah Baker and Samuel Campbell

Campbell, Samuel (1815-1868) (farmer, 6th District), son of Samuel Campbell Sr. (1783-1846), married Mary E. M. Williams (1822-1895) circa 18 Mar 1844 (date of license) (Cecil County Marriage License Book listed her name as Mary E. M. Williams, but Ebenezer Methodist Church Cemetery tombstone inscriptions inscribed her married name as Mary A. M. Campbell; 1860 Cecil County Census)

Campbell, Samuel, married Sarah Ann Reynolds circa 2 Nov 1839 (date of license) by Rev. Hoopman (Cecil County Marriage License Book)

Campbell, William (1803-1874) (shoemaker at Elkton), married Jane B. Davidson (1805-1888), daughter of William Davidson, circa 2 Jan 1833 (date of license) by Rev. Wilson (Cecil County Marriage License Book; Leeds Methodist Church Cemetery tombstone inscriptions; 1860 Cecil County Census stated he was age 54 and she was age 45)

Campbell, William, married Nancy Weir circa 6 Mar 1826 (date of license) by Rev. Goforth (Cecil County Marriage License Book; *Ancestral Charts, Volume 3*, p. 149, Harford County Genealogical Society Publication, 1986)

CANBY

Canby, Catharine, see Lloyd Balderston

Canby, James (born c1820, Maryland) (carpenter, 7th District), married Rebecca (N) (born c1830, Maryland) probably circa 1846; son John Canby born c1847 (1860 Cecil County Census)

Canby, James Jr. (1807-1849), of Wilmington, DE, later of *Bay Side*, Kent Co., MD, married Matilda Price, daughter of Benjamin Price, Esq., of Kent Co., MD, on 23 Nov 1837 by Rev. Kemp at *Stoneton* in Kent County (*Cecil Gazette*, 2 Dec 1837; *Delaware Gazette*, 16 Mar 1849)

CANN

Cann, John (1824-1892) (reverend), married Sarah Ann (N) (1826-1899) probably circa 1846 (St. John's Church Cemetery, at Lewisville, tombstone inscriptions)

Cann, Mary, see Henry L. Peckard

Cann, Mary Ellen, see John Holt

Cann, Samuel (1822-1901), married Matilda E. (N) (1826-1899) probably circa 1846 (St. John's Church Cemetery, at Lewisville, tombstone inscriptions)

CANNON

Cannon, Edwin J., married Elizabeth King circa 29 Dec 1847 (date of license) (Cecil County Marriage License Book spelled his name Cannan)

Cannon, George W., married Sarah Reese circa 16 Dec 1833 (date of license) by Rev. Duke (Cecil County Marriage License Book)

Cannon, Jane, see Timothy Sullivan

Cannon, John, married Frances Kirk circa 11 Mar 1835 (date of license) by Rev. Griffith (Cecil County Marriage License Book; DAR transcript copied in 1928 misspelled her name as Francis)

Cannon, John, married Jane Aulds circa 2 Feb 1848 (date of license) (Cecil County Marriage License Book listed her name as All, but it was most likely Auld or Aulds)

Cannon, Mary E., see Lilburn Price

CANTWELL

Cantwell, John, married Mary Clark (1815-1858) circa 21 May 1827 (date of license) (Cecil County Marriage License Book; Elkton Methodist Church Cemetery tombstone inscription for Mary Cantwell)

Cantwell, Joseph P. (born c1816, Pennsylvania) (tinner and stove dealer in Elkton), married Emily Ann Biddle (born c1827, Pennsylvania) on 15 Nov 1842, after obtaining a license on 12 Nov 1842, by Rev. Janes (Cecil County Marriage License Book; DAR transcript copied in 1955 misspelled her name Beedle; 1860 Cecil County Census; *Cecil Whig*, 19 Nov 1842)

Cantwell, Matthew, married Miss Catharine L. "Kate" Estes (1822-1875) on 26 Nov 1848, after obtaining a license on 25 Nov 1848, by Rev. McIntire in Elkton; Kate Cantwell died at Rock Hall, Kent Co., MD (Cecil County Marriage License Book; *Cecil Democrat and Farmer's Journal*, 2 Dec 1848; *Cecil Whig*, 21 Aug 1875)

Cantwell, Robert, married Mary E. Brown circa 6 Dec 1836 (date of license) by Rev. Potts (Cecil County Marriage License Book)

Cantwell, Thomas, married Mary Ann Logan circa 5 Jul 1841 (date of license) (Cecil County Marriage License Book)

Cantwell, William, married Arena Hushebeck circa 17 Jan 1841 (date of license) (Cecil County Marriage License Book)

CARHART

Carhart, John (1804-1887), married Keziah Larason (1811-1881) probably circa 1830 (Zion Presbyterian Cemetery tombstone inscriptions)

Carhart, Samuel (1799-1852), married Fanny (N) (1807-1851) probably circa 1825 (Zion Presbyterian Cemetery tombstone inscriptions)

CARLISLE

Carlisle, Ann, see Parker Bernard

CARMAN

Carman, Henry, married Elizabeth Price circa 7 May 1833 (date of license) by Rev. Duke (Cecil County Marriage License Book)

Carman, Salina, see Lewis Price

CARNGY

Carngy, Peter (born c1815, Maryland) (blacksmith at Chesapeake City), married Isabella (N) (born c1823, Maryland) probably circa 1842; son Alexander born c1843 (1860 Cecil County Census)

CARPENTER

Carpenter, George R., married Miss Leonis S. Biddle, both of Cecil Co., on 20 Nov 1849, after obtaining a license that same day, by Rev. Elliott (Cecil County Marriage License Book; *Cecil Democrat and Farmer's Journal*, 24 Nov 1849; *Cecil Whig*, 1 Dec 1849, apparently mistakenly reported that George Carpenter and Miss Olivia Biddle, both of Cecil Co., were married on 13 Nov 1849 by Rev. Elliott)

Carpenter, Rachel Ann, see William Freeman

CARR

Carr, Robert, married Miss Eliza Jane Glenn, both of Cecil Co., on 10 Jan 1850, after obtaining a license on 8 Jan 1850, by Rev. Arthur at North East (Cecil County Marriage License Book; *Cecil Whig*, 19 Jan 1850; *Cecil Democrat and Farmer's Journal*, 19 Jan 1850)

CARROLL

Carroll. Frances, see William Stradley

Carroll, Hellen, see David Keilholtz

CARSON

Carson, Ann Ellen, see Amos F. Eves

Carson, John, see George W. Kidd

Carson, Margaretta, see Morris Brogan

Carson, Mary Jane, see George W. Kidd

CARTER

Carter, Amanda, see Amos Carter

Carter, Amos (born 1799), youngest son of Samuel (1740-1826) and Ruth Carter, the latter died before 1825, of West Nottingham Township, Chester Co., PA, married Sophia Haines, of West Nottingham Hundred, Cecil Co., MD, on the 21st day of 12th month 1825 at West Nottingham Meeting House (*Births, Deaths and Marriages of the Nottingham Quakers, 1680-1899*, by Alice L. Beard (1989), p. 221, misspelled his first name Amor and mistakenly listed his father's name as James; *Bible Records, Genealogical Society of Cecil County*, by Gary L. Burns (1990), p. 16, listed the births of their nine children in non-Quaker style: Caroline, born 28 Jan 1827; Jacob, born 6 Jun 1828; Jeremiah, born 21 Jan 1830; Amanda, born 13 Aug 1831; Hannah, born 4 Jun 1834; George, born 26 Mar 1838; Mary R., born 9 Aug 1839; Ruth Ann, born 15 Aug 1847; and, Samuel, born 18 Jun 1849)

Carter, Caroline, see Amos Carter

Carter, Charlotte, see William Brown and Frisby Tull

Carter, Cloud, see John W. Tyson

Carter, Eliza, see Norris Levis

Carter, Daniel (1820-1865), married (N) probably circa 1845 (Rock Springs Old School Baptist Church Cemetery tombstone inscription for "Father, Daniel Carter," but no marker for the mother)

Carter, Emily, see Thomas Smith

Carter, George, see Amos Carter

Carter, Georgeanna, see Nelson Carter

Carter, Hannah, see Amos Carter

Carter, Harriet, see Charles Parker

Carter, I. Day, see Frisby Tull

Carter, Jacob, see Amos Carter

Carter, James, see Amos Carter

Carter, James, married Sarah Owens circa 19 Sep 1832 (date of license) by Rev. Goforth (Cecil County Marriage License Book; *Cecil Democrat and Farmer's Journal*, 27 May 1882, reported a James C. Carter died at age 65 near Charlestown)

Carter, James P., married Frances Ann Parker circa 2 Jul 1840 (date of license) (Cecil County Marriage License Book)

Carter, Jeremiah, see Amos Carter

Carter, John D., married Mary Ann Love circa 5 Jan 1825 (date of license) by Rev. Sharpley (Cecil County Marriage License Book; DAR transcript copied in 1928 spelled her name Lowe)

Carter, Joseph (1808-1850), married Sarah Ann Reynolds (1813-1848), daughter of Elisha Reynolds, circa 18 Jan 1831 (date of license) by Rev. Duke (Cecil Co. Marriage License Book listed his name as Joseph C. Carter; Cherry Hill Methodist Church Cemetery tombstones; *Joseph England and his Descendants*, by C. Walter England, Ph.D., 1975, p. 66, stated Sarah was born in 1802, but her tombstone indicates 1813; *Cecil Whig*, 17 Jun 1848, stated Sarah died of typhoid fever at Cecil Paper Mills, but did not give her age; *Cecil Whig*, 9 Feb 1850, stated Joseph died of pulmonary consumption at his home at Cecil Paper Mills)

Carter, Joseph (1819-1874, born Pennsylvania) (potter at Elkton), married Elizabeth Harrigan (1820-1895, born Maryland) circa 13 Nov 1839 (date of license) by Rev. Wooley; daughter Mary Carter born c1841, Maryland (Cecil County Marriage License Book; Cherry Hill Methodist Church Cemetery tombstone inscriptions; 1860 Cecil County Census)

Carter, Lydia, see Frisby Tull

Carter, Lydia Ann, see William Snowden

Carter, Margaret, see Thomas Jefferson Potts

Carter, Margaret R., see John T. Miller

Carter, Mary, see Joseph Carter and Silas Evans Carter

Carter, Mary Elizabeth, see Richard Brookings

Carter, Mary R., see Amos Carter

Carter, Nelson (born c1830, Maryland) (African American) (laborer in the 8th District), married Margaret (N) (born c1830, Maryland (African American) probably circa 1848; daughter Georgeanna Carter born c1848, Maryland, and their other children were also born in Maryland (1860 Cecil County Census)

Carter, Richard C., married Miss Emeline Slaughter, of Caroline Co., on 17 Oct 1850 by Rev. Bell at Greensborough (*Cecil Democrat and Farmer's Journal*, 26 Oct 1850)

Carter, Robert, see William Snowden, Richard Brookings and Frisby Tull

Carter, Robert C. (1824-1886) (doctor near Elkton), married Martha J. M. Mearns (1825-1881) circa 23 Oct 1846 (date of license) (Cecil County Marriage License Book; Cherry Hill Methodist Church Cemetery tombstone inscriptions; 1860 Cecil County Census)

Carter, Ruth, see Amos Carter

Carter, Samuel, see Amos Carter

Carter, Sarah Jane, see John W. Tyson

Carter, Silas Evans (1823-1864) (farmer near Elkton), married Mary Janney (1820-1913), daughter of Jesse Janney (died 1865) and Maria Taylor (died 1863), circa 31 Dec 1845 (date of license) and Mary Carter was a widow who lived at Zion in Cecil Co. in 1897 (Cecil County Marriage License Book; *Portrait and Biographical Record of Harford and Cecil Counties, Maryland* (1897, repr. 1989), p. 192; Zion Methodist Cemetery tombstone inscriptions; 1860 Cecil County Census)

CARVER
Carver, Hannah, see Henry Harding Kimble

CASE
Case, Christian, see John Keithley

CASHO
Casho, Eliza, see William S. Mote

Casho, George A., son of Isaac Casho, of Cecil Co., whose family of French origin also lived in New Castle Co., Delaware, married Eliza Mote circa 1842; son James M. Casho born 16 Jan 1843 (*Portrait and Biographical Record of Harford and Cecil Counties, Maryland* (1897, repr. 1989), p. 407)

Casho, Isaac, see George A. Casho

Casho, Jacob, of Elkton, married 1st to Rachel (N) (1816-1850) probably circa 1836 and married 2nd to Miss Kuria Holgate (1823-1866), of Philadelphia, on 24 Dec 1850 by Rev. Fernley in Philadelphia (*Cecil Democrat and Farmer's Journal*, 28 Dec 1850, noting, "*Baltimore Sun* please copy," but they did not publish the marriage notice; Elkton Methodist Church Register, p. 141; Elkton Methodist Church Cemetery tombstone inscription for Kuria Casho; Cecil Whig, 28 Dec 1850)

CATES

Cates, Emory (born c1820) (African American) (farm hand at Cecilton), married Mary (N) (born c1822) (African American) circa 1844; daughter Mary Cates born c1845 (1860 Cecil County Census)

CATHER, CATHERS

Cathers, Anna Mary, see John B. Cathers

Cather, David (1813-1880, born Maryland) (laborer, 7th District), married Charlotte Cooley (1810-1892, born Maryland) circa 29 Apr 1835 (date of license) by Rev. Magraw (Cecil County Marriage License Book; West Nottingham Cemetery tombstone inscriptions; 1860 Cecil County Census)

Cathers, John B. (1818-1888, born Pennsylvania) (farmer near Zion), married Jane B. (N) (1822-1897, born Pennsylvania) circa 1845; buried beside daughter Anna Mary Cathers (1847-1919), born Pennsylvania (Zion Presbyterian Church Cemetery tombstone inscriptions; 1860 Cecil County Census)

Cather, Rebecca Ann, see Samuel Jenness

CATON

Caton, Thomas, married Mary Galloway circa 9 Mar 1831 (date of license) by Rev. Hodgson (Cecil County Marriage License Book; DAR transcript copied in 1928 misspelled the minister's name as Hodson; Francis Hodgson was a Methodist Episcopal minister in Elkton at that time)

CAULK

Caulk, Benjamin (esquire) (1798-1882), married Miss Jane W. Handy (1814-1887), both of Newark, DE, on 11 Jul 1850 by Rev. Stevens at the residence of Dr. Thomas W. Handy (*Cecil Democrat and Farmer's Journal*, 20 Jul 1850 and 27 Jul 1850; White Clay Creek Presbyterian Church, New Castle Co., DE, tombstone inscriptions)

Caulk, Jacob, see James R. Staats

Caulk, John, married Cornelia Brown circa 14 Dec 1836 (date of license) by Rev. Potts (Cecil County Marriage License Book)

Caulk, Lydia, see James L. Foard

Caulk, Mary A., see James R. Staats

CAVENDAR, CAVENDER

Cavendar, Catherine, see Patrick Murphy

Cavender, John (born c1814, Delaware) (farmer at Cecilton), married Emeline (N) (born c1820, Delaware) circa 1841; son John D. Cavender born c1842, Delaware (1860 Cecil County Census)

Cavendar, Lewis J., of Smyrna, New Castle Co., DE, married Miss Olivia Ann Biddle, of Chesapeake City, on 10 Apr 1850, after obtaining a license on 1 Apr 1850, by Rev. McIntire (Cecil County Marriage License Book spelled his name Cavendar; *Cecil Whig*, 13 Apr 1850, spelled his name Cavender)

CAZIER

Cazier, Araminta, see Thomas Maffitt

Cazier, C. Eugeine, see Samuel Dickey

Cazier, Henry, see Samuel Dickey

Cazier, John, see William M. Stucherst

Cazier, John F. married Ann Haines (c1807-1841) circa 6 Nov 1827 (date of license) (Cecil County Marriage License Book; *Cecil Gazette*, 5 Jun 1841)

Cazier, Martha Jane, see John McCracken

Cazier, Millicent A., see David White

Cazier, Olivia Ann, see William M. Stucherst

Cazier, Rebecca, see George Simcoe

Cazier, Thomas C., married Maria F. Ward circa 1 Aug 1837 (date of license) by Rev. McFarland (Cecil County Marriage License Book; DAR transcript copied in 1928 mistakenly listed her middle initial as L. and the minister's name as Farland; James McFarland was a Methodist minister in Elkton at that time; Elkton Methodist Church Register, p. 138, listed her middle initial as F.)

CHAMBERLAINE

Chamberlaine, Henry, see Richard Whittingham, Jr.

Chamberlaine, Rachel, see Benjamin F. Heath

Chamberlaine, Sarah Rebecca, see Richard Whittingham, Jr.

CHAMBERS

Chambers, Benjamin B., married 1st to Caroline J. Pearce circa 13 Mar 1827 (date of license) and married 2nd to Mrs. Mary Jane Fowler, all of Cecil Co., on 21 May 1839, after obtaining a license on 20 May 1839, by Rev. Pierson (Cecil County Marriage License Book; *Cecil Gazette*, 25 May 1839, noted, "With the above we received some appendages necessarily connected with the nuptial ceremony, for which we tender our acknowledgements.")

Chambers, Caroline, see George W. T. Perkins

Chambers, E. F., see George W. T. Perkins

Chambers, George (born c1807, Maryland) (African American) (laborer near Brick Meeting House), married Ann (N) (born c1811, Maryland) (African American) probably circa 1830 (1860 Cecil County Census)

Chambers, Phineas (born c1817, Delaware) (painter at Elkton), married Benjamina W. Crookham (born c1820, Delaware) circa 21 Dec 1841 (date of license) (Cecil County Marriage License Book; DAR transcript copied in 1955 mistakenly listed the marriage license date as 12 Dec 1841; 1860 Cecil County Census)

Chambers, Sarah, see Henry Reynolds

CHANDLEE

Chandlee, Ellis G. (1816-1879, Maryland) (merchant near Brick Meeting House), married Ann E. (N) (1816-1894, Maryland) probably circa 1839; son John B. Chandlee born c1840, Maryland, saddler (1860 Cecil County Census; Rosebank Cemetery, at Calvert, tombstone inscriptions)

Chandlee, John B., see Ellis G. Chandlee

Chandlee, Maria, see John Rawlings Abrams

CHANDLER

Chandler, Cornel, see Robert Cully

Chandler, George (born c1820, Maryland) (laborer, 9th District), married Ellen (N) (b0rn c1830, Maryland) probably circa 1840; daughter Mary Chandler, born c1851 (1860 Cecil County Census)

Chandler, John (born c1801, Maryland) (laborer at Chesapeake City), married Letitia (N) (born c1807, Maryland) probably circa 1825 (1860 Cecil County Census)

Chandler, Joshua, married Margaret Gibson circa 4 Mar 1848 (date of license) (Cecil County Marriage License Book)

Chandler, Maria J., see Robert Cully

Chandler, Mary, see George Chandler

Chandler, William Penn (editor of the *Delaware Gazette*), married Hannah S. Vaux, daughter of the late George Vaux, Esq., on 14 Jun 1848 by Rev. Miller at St. Philip's Church in Philadelphia (*Cecil Democrat and Farmer's Journal*, 17 Jun 1848; *Delaware Gazette*, 16 Jun 1848)

CHAPMAN

Chapman, Maria Louise, see George H. Joyce

Chapman, William H. (born c1828, Pennsylvania) (papermaker at Elkton), married Mary Gallaher (born c1832, Maryland) circa 8 Nov 1848 (date of license) (Cecil County Marriage License Book listed his name without the middle initial; 1860 Cecil County Census)

Chapman, (N), married Mary Ann (N) (1827-1909) probably by 1850 (Rosebank Cemetery, at Calvert, tombstone inscription for "Mother, Mary Ann Chapman," but no marker for her husband)

CHARSHEE

Charshee, Bennett (1821-1902) (lumberman), son of James Charshee and Annie Fletcher, married Catherine Virginia Cook (1830-1918), daughter of Thomas Cook and Susanna Sutor, of Elkton, later of Havre de Grace, by Rev. Robert L. Goldsborough in Havre de Grace on 11 Jan 1849 after obtaining a license on 9 Jan 1849 (Harford County marriage license listed his name as Bennet Charshe and her name mistakenly as Harriet Cook; *Cecil Whig*, 13 Jan 1849, and *Cecil Democrat and Farmer's Journal*, 13 Jan 1849, both spelled her name Cooke; Angel Hill Cemetery tombstone inscriptions; Harford County death certificates; *Men of Mark in Maryland*, by David H. Carroll and Thomas G. Boggs (1911), Volume III, pp. 209-212)

CHESBROUGH

Chesbrough, Isaac M., of Baltimore, MD, and Mary Jones, of Elkton, MD, obtained a license on 26 Nov 1831 (Cecil County Marriage License Book), but over a year later he married Mary Allen on 25 Dec 1832 (*Baltimore American and Commercial Daily Advertiser*, 1 Jan 1833)

CHEW

Chew, Henrietta M., see John C. Boyd

CHICK

Chick, Joseph (born c1815) (wheelwright at Chesapeake City), married Martha Boies circa 9 Nov 1839 (date of license) by Rev. Barratt; son John born 1840 (Cecil County Marriage License Book; 1860 Cecil County Census did not list a wife in his household so she apparently had died before 1860)

CHILDS

Childs, Sarah and John, see Edward H. Tarring

CHRISTIE

Christie, Anna M. K. (or R.), see John Sterrett Christie

Christie, Charles B., married Mary Orr circa 30 Dec 1844 (date of license) (Cecil Co. Marr. License Book)

Christie, Cornelia Eliza, see John Sterrett Christie

Christie, Fannie, see John Sterrett Christie

Christie, Frances, see James T. Kidd

Christie, Francis Steel, see John Sterrett Christie

Christie, George McCullough, see John Sterrett Christie

Christie, India Sophia, see John Sterrett Christie

Christie, James, see John Sterrett Christie

Christie, John Sterrett (1816-1869) (captain and miller at Rowlandville, son of James Christie, of Ireland, later of New York and Maryland, married Sophia McCullough Logan (1818-1877), daughter of Robert Logan, of Ireland, later of Maryland, on 8 Dec 1840 after obtaining a license on 3 Dec 1840 (Cecil County Marriage License Book; DAR transcript copied in 1955 mistakenly listed L. as his middle initial;

Bible Records, Genealogical Society of Cecil County, by Gary L. Burns (1990), p. 3, listed the births and deaths of their eight children: George McCullough, born 24 May 1844; Mary Jane, born 9 Jun 1846, died 15 May 1880; Robert Logan, born 16 Jul 1848; Anna M. K. (or M. R.), born 4 Sep 1850, died 18 Mar 1878; Francis Steel, born 10 Jan 1853; Fannie, born 19 Feb 1855; India Sophia, born 19 Sep 1857, died 4 Aug 1886; and, Cornelia Eliza, born 11 Feb 1860; *Portrait and Biographical Record of Harford and Cecil Counties, Maryland* (1897, repr. 1989), pp. 283-284; Hopewell United Methodist Church Cemetery tombstone inscriptions; 1860 Cecil County Census)

Christie, Mary Jane, see John Sterrett Christie

Christie, Robert Logan, see John Sterrett Christie

CHURCHMAN

Churchman, Amassa (1808-1865), married Ann (N) (1811-1894) probably circa 1830 (Rosebank Cemetery, at Calvert, tombstone inscriptions)

CLARK, CLARKE

Clark, Abraham, married Naomi Stewart circa 27 Sep 1832 (date of license) by Rev. Mahan (Cecil County Marriage License Book)

Clarke, Ann, see Edward Pearce

Clark, Ann Elizabeth, see James Shockley

Clark, Arthur, married Rachel Thackery circa 21 Apr 1828 (date of license) (Cecil Co. Marr. License Book)

Clark, Daniel, see E. P. Gaines

Clark, Edward, see Isaac Clark

Clark, Eliza, see John Little

Clark, Elizabeth, see James Campbell and James Simmons

Clark, Frances Abigail, see Joseph England Ramsey

Clark, Isaac, married Sarah Bellville circa 16 Apr 1835 (date of license) by Rev. Hammill (Cecil County Marriage License Book)

Clark, Isaac (born c1820, Maryland) (African American) (laborer in the 7th District), married Hannah (N) (born c1822, Maryland) (African American) probably circa 1850; son Edward Clark born c1851 (1860 Cecil County Census)

Clarke, James, married Kesiah Husfelt circa 4 Sep 1850 (date of license) (Cecil County Marriage License Book misspelled her name Hushefelt; DAR transcript copied in 1955 correctly spelled her name Husfelt)

Clark, John (born c1818) (sailing vessel captain), married Harriet R. Colmerry (born c1821) circa 14 May 1839 (date of license) by Rev. Foulks (Cecil County Marriage License Book; 1860 Cecil County Census)

Clark, Mary, see John Cantwell

Clarke, Mary, see Edward H. Hyland

Clark, Mary Ann, see George H. Armstrong

Clarke, Matthew J., married Miss Angelina Van Gesel, daughter of John Van Gesel, Esq., of Smyrna, DE, on 23 Dec 1850 (*Cecil Whig*, 11 Jan 1851; *Delaware Gazette*, 23 Dec 1850, listed his name as Matthew J. Clark and her name as Angeline Vangesil, and stated the minister was Rev. J. A. Roche)

Clark, Nicholas, married Margaret Ann Little circa 23 May 1831 (date of license) by Rev. Barratt (Cecil County Marriage License Book)

Clark, Samuel, married Catherine Hitselberger circa 25 Mar 1826 (date of license) by Rev. Magraw (Cecil County Marriage License Book)

Clark, Sarah, see Joseph George, William C. Clark and Thomas Pierce

Clark, Sarah E., see James B. Jester

Clark, Sarah Ellen, see Daniel Lilley

Clark, William C. (born c1823, Maryland) (laborer at Charlestown), married Ann Taylor (born c1817, Maryland) circa 22 Aug 1844 (date of license); daughter Sarah Clark born c1845, Maryland (Cecil County Marriage License Book; 1860 Cecil County Census)

CLAYLAND

Clayland, Samuel R., of Kent Co., married Mary Eliza McDonough, of Kent Co., circa 8 Oct 1829 (date of license) by Rev. Duke (Cecil County Marriage License Book)

CLAYPOOL

Claypool, David P., married Rachel Vance circa 17 Jan 1845 (date of license) (Cecil Co. Marr. Lic. Book)

CLAYTON

Clayton, James, see William H. Clayton

Clayton, Joshua (colonel), of Bohemia Manor, married 1st to Lydia A. Clayton, daughter of Richard Clayton, Esq., and she died on 23 Jan 1849 at Bohemia Manor, leaving three children (names not stated); Joshua married 2nd to Martha E. Lockwood, daughter of Richard Lockwood, of New Castle Co., DE, near Middletown, on 21 Feb 1850 by Rev. Harrolds (*Delaware Gazette*, 2 Feb 1849 and 26 Feb 1850; *Cecil Democrat and Farmer's Journal*, 23 Feb 1850, reported, "A bridal party, from Delaware, passed through here [Elkton] on Wednesday, on the way to Washington, where they will spend the honey-moon. On inquiry, we ascertained that the weddings had taken place that morning, at an early hour, and that the parties were Col. Joshua Clayton, to Miss Martha Lockwood; John Naudin *(sic)*, Esq., to Miss Mary Lockwood, both daughters of Richard Lockwood, Esq., near Middletown, and Mr. [John] McCrone, to Mrs. Elizabeth Norwood, sister of Mr. Naudin *(sic)*.")

Clayton, Lydia A., see Joshua Clayton

Clayton, Richard, see Joshua Clayton

Clayton, William H. (born c1825) (African American) (laborer at Elkton), married Emily (N) (born c1828) (African American) circa 1845; son James Clayton born c1846 (1860 Cecil County Census)

CLEAVER

Cleaver, John, married Philena Baker circa 9 Apr 1830 (date of license) by Rev. Griffith (Cecil County Marriage License Book)

CLEAVES

Cleaves, John B. (1820-1909) (carriage maker at Elkton), married Julia Alexander (1823-1901) circa 22 Jul 1846 (date of license) (Cecil County Marriage License Book; Cherry Hill Methodist Church Cemetery tombstone inscriptions; 1860 Cecil County Census spelled his name Cleaves and stated he was age 42)

CLELAND

Cleland, Margaret Jane, see Richard F. Biddle

CLEMENT, CLEMENTS

Clements, Ann, see William Clemson

Clements, Joel, of Long March, MD, married Margaret Lambdin, daughter of Daniel Lambdin, presiding elder of the Wilmington District of the Philadelphia Conference in Wilmington, in March 1848 by Rev. Thompson (date not given) (*Delaware Gazette*, 28 Mar 1848)

Clements, Rachel T., see William Clemson

Clements, Samuel, see William Clemson

Clement, Sarah, see Samuel Pusey

CLEMSON

Clemson, Elizabeth, see William Clemson

Clemson, Elizabeth N., see Henry Hess

Clemson, John, see William Clemson

Clemson, William, son of John and Elizabeth Clemson, of London Grove Township, Chester Co., PA, married Rachel T. Clements, daughter of Samuel and Ann Clements, of East Nottingham Hundred, Cecil

Co., on the 29th day of the 11th month 1838 at East Nottingham (*Births, Deaths and Marriages of the Nottingham Quakers, 1680-1899*, by Alice L. Beard (1989), p. 224; *Cecil Gazette*, 8 Dec 1838)

CLENDENIN

Clendenin, Arthur, married Susan Ricketts circa 3 Mar 1827 (date of license) (Cecil County Marriage License Book)

Clendenin, Daniel, married Rebecca Horton circa 28 Dec 1835 (date of license) by Rev. Finney (Cecil County Marriage License Book)

Clendenin, Deborah M., see John Thomas Janney

CLIFTON

Clifton, Mary Ann, see John Wright

CLINE

Cline, Helen, see Jacob Holden

Cline, William, married Lydia Ann Kirkpatrick circa 5 Oct 1850 (date of license) (Cecil County Marriage License Book)

CLOUD

Cloud, Caleb W., married Eliza Kean circa 26 Aug 1830 (date of license) by Rev. Duke (Cecil County Marriage License Book)

Cloud, Charles T. (F.?), married Julianna Pouder (or Ponder?), of Baltimore, MD, circa 30 Apr 1831 (date of license) by Rev. Duke (Cecil County Marriage License Book)

Cloud, E. (colonel), see William Voglesong and Albert M. Long

Cloud, Joseph C., of Elkton, MD, married Mary Stull, daughter of Judge Stull of Cumberland Co., NJ, on 2 Mar 1831 at Deerfield, NJ (*Baltimore American and Commercial Daily Advertiser*, 15 Mar 1831)

Cloud, Julia M., see Albert M. Long

Cloud, Margaret C., see William Voglesong

Cloud, Mary A., see Joseph Hopkins

CLUTE

Clute, Angelica, see Ezekiel Cooper

COALE

Coale, Ann, see George Coale and Nathan Hilles

Coale, Ellis P., son of Samuel and Lydia Coale, of Harford Co., married Ruthanna Moore, daughter of Joseph and Mercy Moore, the former deceased, of West Nottingham Hundred, Cecil Co., on the 2nd day of the 3rd month 1825 at the West Nottingham Meeting House. Among the witnesses were Margaret E. Coale, Samuel Coale, Jeremiah Coale, Samuel Coale, Jr., Rebecca Moore (listed twice), Mary Ann Moore, Anna Marie Moore, Joseph Moore, William Moore and Benjamin Moore. (*Births, Deaths and Marriages of the Nottingham Quakers, 1680-1899*, by Alice L. Beard (1989), p. 220)

Coale, Ellis P., see Joseph Moore

Coale, George (born c1820, Maryland) (African American) (laborer, 7th District), married Maria (N) (born c1826, Maryland) (African American) probably circa 1848; daughter Ann Coale born c1849 (1860 Cecil County Census)

Coale, Jeremiah, see Ellis P. Coale

Coale, Joseph, married Sarah Ann Watson circa 10 Jan 1835 (date of license) by Rev. Griffith (Cecil County Marriage License Book)

Coale, Lydia, see Ellis P. Coale and Joseph Moore

Coale, Margaret E., see Ellis P. Coale and John Y. Worthington

Coale, Maria R., see John Virtue

Coale, Rebecca, see Ellis P. Coale

Coale, Rose Ann S., see John B. Hays

Coale, Samuel, see Ellis P. Coale and Joseph Moore

Coale, Sarah S., see Nathan Hilles

Coale, Skipwith, see Nathan Hilles and John Y. Worthington

Coale, William (1819-1895) (farmer, 6th District), married Hannah E. (N) (1821-1904) probably circa 1840; son Louis born c1841 (Friends Cemetery, at Harrisville, tombstone inscriptions; 1860 Cecil Co. Census)

Coale, also see Cole

COATES

Coates, Abigail, see Merrick Coates

Coates, Merrick, son of Samuel and Abigail Coates, of Londonderry Township, Chester Co., PA, married Hannah Darlington, daughter of George and Lydia Darlington, of Lower Oxford Township, Chester Co., PA, on the 21st day of the 1st month 1847 at East Nottingham (*Births, Deaths and Marriages of the Nottingham Quakers, 1680-1899*, by Alice L. Beard (1989), p. 226)

Coates, Samuel, see Merrick Coates

COCHRAN

Cochran, Elizabeth, see Thomas L. Van Dyke

Cochran, Frances A., see William Lusby

Cochran, John, see William Cochran

Cochran, John C., married Ann Buckwith circa 11 Apr 1840 (date of license) by Rev. Foulks, a Methodist Protestant minister in the Kent Circuit (Cecil County Marriage License Book)

Cochran, Joseph (1808-1858), married Margaret (N) (1806-1883) probably circa 1832; son Dr. John H. Cochran was born 25 Jun 1833, Cecil Co., and died 10 Oct 1899, Harford Co. (Angel Hill Cemetery tombstone inscriptions, Havre de Grace; Harford County death certificate of Dr. John H. Cochran)

Cochran, Joseph W., married Eliza Robinson circa 27 Oct 1836 (date of license) by Rev. Potts (Cecil County Marriage License Book)

Cochran, Nancy, see Hugh Marnes

Cochran, Rachel, see Johnson Hyland

Cochran, Rebecca, see Samuel M. Magraw

Cochran, Thomas (esquire), married Miss Sophia Moody, both of Middletown, New Castle Co., Delaware, on 17 Apr 1849 by Rev. Haney (*Cecil Democrat and Farmer's Journal*, 14 Apr 1849)

Cochran, Thomas J., married Elizabeth Colmary on 16 Jan 1838, after obtaining a license on 15 Jan 1838; by Rev. McFarland (Cecil County Marriage License Book spelled her surname Colmerry; DAR transcript copied in 1928, and Elkton Methodist Church Register, p. 138, both spelled her name Colmary)

Cochran, William (born c1815, Maryland) (miller, 7th District), married Ann (N) (born c1812, Maryland) probably circa 1840; son John Cochran born c1843 (1860 Cecil County Census)

COE

Coe, Rouce, married Rachel Smith circa 14 Apr 1836 (date of license) by Rev. Morris (Cecil County Marriage License Book)

COFFIN

Coffin, Araminta, see Robert Price

COLE

Cole, Elenora, see John T. Veazey

Cole, George M., of Cecil Co., MD, married Ann Eliza Johnson, of Harford Co., MD, circa 7 Apr 1832 (date of license) by Rev. Webster (Cecil County Marriage License Book)

Cole, Hannah E., see William H. Reasin

Cole, William, married Hannah E. Cook circa 8 Feb 1841 (date of license) (Cecil County Marriage License Book)

Cole, also see Coale

COLEMAN

Coleman, John (born c1818, Maryland) (laborer at Cecilton), married Hannah A. (N) (born c1818, Delaware) circa 1845; son William Thomas Coleman born c1846, Maryland (1860 Cecil County Census)

COLLASSON

Collasson, Julia Ann, see Thomas M. Biddle

COLLINS

Collins, Daniel (1797-1861), married Caroline (N) (1807-1874) probably circa 1825-1828 (St. John's Church Cemetery, at Lewisville, tombstone inscriptions)

Collins, Martha, see Solomon Blake

COLMERRY, COLMARY

Colmerry, Cyrus, married Miss Elizabeth Bennett circa 16 Oct 1835 (date of license) by Rev. Barratt (Cecil County Marriage License Book; DAR transcript copied in 1928 misspelled his first name Cyprus)

Colmerry (Colmary), Elizabeth, see Thomas J. Cochran

Colmerry, Harriet R., see John Clark

Colmerry, Sarah M., see John Kent

Colmerry, William (c1790s - 1839) (War of 1812 veteran), married Rachel Oliver on 29 Nov 1826, after obtaining a license on 20 Nov 1826, by the Rev. Goforth, a Methodist minister (Cecil County Marriage License Book; War of 1812 Bounty Land Warrant No. 55-160-5366)

COMEGYS

Comegys, Edward M., married Georgia Ann Comegys circa 7 Feb 1845 (date of license) (Cecil County Marriage License Book)

Comegys, Georgia Ann, see Edward M. Comegys

Comegys, Sarah E. W., see Thomas Crookshanks

COMPT

Compt, Deborah, see Stephen Biddle

CONARD

Conard, Judge, see William Brown and Charles W. Owen

Conard, Laura W., see Charles W. Owen

Conard, Susan Ingels, see William Brown

CONAWAY

Conaway, Mary A. and Samuel, see James Denny

CONEKIN, CONEGAN

Conegan, John, married Mary Ashen circa 30 May 1827 (date of license) (Cecil County Marr. License Book)

Conekin, John, married Rebecca Henshaw circa 27 Feb 1834 (date of license) by Rev. Duke (Cecil County Marriage License Book; DAR transcript copied in 1928 spelled his name Conelkin)

Conekin, John, married Elizabeth Dinan or Duncan circa 19 Dec 1835 (date of license) by Rev. Houston (DAR Marriage License Transcript copied in 1928 listed her name as Duncan, but the original Cecil County Marriage License Book is unclear and the name looked more like Dinan or Denan than Duncan)

CONLYN

Conlyn, Deborah, see John H. Price

Conlyn, Ellen, see Benjamon Benson

Conlyn, James, married Ellen Cosden circa 27 Jan 1834 (date of license) by Rev. Duke (Cecil County Marriage License Book)

Conlyn, William, married Levina Barwick circa 15 Aug 1827 (date of license) (Cecil County Marriage License Book; DAR transcript copied in 1928 misspelled his name Conlin and her first name Lueina)

Conlyn, William, married Jane Rebecca Kimble circa 29 Jan 1833 (date of license) by Rev. Torbert (Cecil County Marriage License Book)

CONOLY, CONLEY

Conoly, David (1814-1871), married Sarah Ann (N) (1822-1907) probably circa 1840 (Rosebank Cemetery, at Calvert, tombstone inscriptions; *Cecil Whig*, 19 Aug 1871)

Conoly, Grace, see John R. Conoly

Conoly, John R. (1812-1865), married (N) (1824-1909) probably before 1849 (Rosebank Cemetery, at Calvert, tombstone inscription "Husband, John R. Conoly," but no mention of his wife, and he is buried beside Mary L. Conoly, 1850-1875, "Aunt, Grace Conoly," 1824-1909, and William Conoly, 1822-1864)

Conley, Patrick, married Maria Milligan on 25 Oct 1827 by Rev. Epinette (*History of Saint Francis Xavier Church and Bohemia Plantation Now Known as Old Bohemia, Warwick, Maryland*, by Joseph C. Cann (1976), p. 47, spelled her name Millegan; Cecil County Marriage License Book; DAR transcript copied in 1928 correctly spelled her name Milligan, but mistakenly listed his name as Onley and that they obtained a marriage license on 26 Oct 1827)

Conley, William, married Eliza Jane White circa 29 Sep 1834 (date of license) by Rev. McKenney, a Protestant Episcopal minister in North Sassafras (Cecil County Marriage License Book)

Conoly, William, see John R. Conoly

CONSTABLE

Constable, Elizabeth, see Henry Wilson Archer

CONWAY

Conway, Elizabeth Ann, see Firman Layman

Conway, John (born c1822, Maryland) (farmer at North East), married Jane (N) (born c1834, Maryland) probably circa 1850; daughter Sarah Conway born c1851 (1860 Cecil County Census)

Conway, Sarah, see John Conway

COOK

Cook, Alice, see Stephen Woodrow

Cook, Augusta, see Joseph N. Goldsborough

Cook, Catherine Virginia, see Bennett Charshee

Cook, Franklin, son of William and Susanna Cook, of Little Britain Township, Lancaster Co., PA, married Philena Preston, daughter of Jonas and Elizabeth Preston, of the same place, on the 28th day of the 2nd month 1839 at Octorara Meeting House (*Births, Deaths and Marriages of the Nottingham Quakers, 1680-1899*, by Alice L. Beard (1989), p. 224)

Cook, Hannah E., see William Cole

Cook, Helen, see Joseph Townsend England

Cook, Sarah A. A. M., see Joseph N. Goldsborough

Cook, Susanna, see Franklin Cook

Cook, Thomas, see Bennett Charshee and Joseph N. Goldsborough

Cook, William, see Franklin Cook

Cook, (N), married Hannah (N) (1815-1883) probably circa 1835 (Bethesda Cemetery, at Oakwood, tombstone inscription for "Mother, Hanna Cook" but no marker for her husband)

COOLEY

Cooley, Charlotte, see David Cather

Cooley, Corbin (1799-1876), of Harford Co., later of Cecil Co., son of John Cooley and wife Sarah Gilbert, married 1st to Jane Johnson (c1806-1832) circa 8 May 1826 (date of license) by Rev. Griffith in Cecil Co., married 2nd to Miss Mary Douglas Stephenson (1801-1837), daughter of James Stephenson and Priscilla Hopkins, on 10 Jan 1833, after obtaining a license in Harford Co. on 8 Jan 1833, by Rev. Stephenson, and married 3rd to Mary Shaw (1809-1892), probable daughter of Henry Shaw, on 19 Dec 1839 (Cecil County Marriage License Book; Harford County Marriage Licenses; *The Family History and Genealogy of John Cooley (1755-1807) of Harford & Cecil Counties, Maryland*, by Walter Lawson Cooley (2007), pp. 43-103, 200-202; *Portrait and Biographical Record of Harford and Cecil Counties, Maryland* (1897, repr. 1989), p. 275; West Nottingham Cemetery tombstone inscriptions; 1860 Cecil County Census indicated that Mary (Stephenson) Cooley was born in England)

Cooley, John, see Corbin Cooley

Cooley, Robert (1828-1906), formerly of Cecil Co., son of Corbin Cooley and Jane Johnson, married Miss Margaret H. Shermer (1829-1886), daughter of Jacob Shermer, Esq., of Philadelphia, on 19 Dec 1850 by Rev. Shermer. The Cooleys resided near Havre de Grace, Harford Co., before moving to Knox Co., NE in 1880. It appears some of his children disapproved of Robert's second marriage and that is probably why he moved to California. (*Cecil Democrat and Farmer's Journal*, 28 Dec 1850; *The Family History and Genealogy of John Cooley (1755-1807) of Harford & Cecil Counties, Maryland*, by Walter Lawson Cooley (2007), pp. 53-103)

Cooley, Sarah Jane, see Simon J. Temple

COOLING

Cooling, Benoni, of Charlestown, married Miss Mary Jane Cooper, daughter of John Cooper, Jr. (died 1844) and Jane Little (died 1861), circa 16 Oct 1847 (date of license) (Cecil County Marriage License Book; *Portrait and Biographical Record of Harford and Cecil Counties, Maryland* (1897, repr. 1989), p. 233)

COOMBE

Coombe, Pennell (reverend), married Elizabeth W. McCauley, both of Chesapeake City, MD, on 1 Oct 1850 by Rev. Gerry at Wilmington, DE (*Cecil Democrat and Farmer's Journal*, 19 Oct 1850)

COOPER

Cooper, Anna R., see Joseph Wells

Cooper, Elizabeth, see John B. Graham

Cooper, Ezekiel, of Philadelphia, married Miss Angelica Clute, of Delaware, on 25 Jun 1850 by Rev. Dr. Castle (*Cecil Democrat and Farmer's Journal*, 6 Jul 1850)

Cooper, Harriet Ann, see Benjamin Ferguson

Cooper, James Evans, married Sarah Brown circa 17 Feb 1831 (date of license) by Rev. Magraw (Cecil County Marriage License Book)

Cooper, James, married Phoebe Ann Thompson circa 13 Apr 1837 (date of license) by Rev. Barratt (Cecil County Marriage License Book)

Cooper, John Jr. (d. 1844), married Jane Little (died 1861) circa 8 Feb 1826 (date of license) by Rev. Magraw (Cecil County Marriage License Book; *Portrait and Biographical Record of Harford and Cecil Counties, Maryland* (1897, repr. 1989), p. 233, stated they had four children, but only two were living in 1897, namely, William Charles Cooper (born 12 Aug 1833) and Mary Jane Cooling)

Cooper, John T., married Sarah Heath circa 31 Dec 1850 (date of license) (Cecil Co. Marriage License Book)

Cooper, Mary Jane, see Benoni Cooling and John Cooper, Jr.

Cooper, Samuel, married Miss Sarah Harris on 7 Dec 1828 at Cantwell's Bridge, New Castle Co., DE, by Rev. Ryder (*Elkton Press*, 13 Dec 1828)

Cooper, William Charles, see John Cooper, Jr.

COPPER

Copper, Millicent, see James McKown

COPPIN

Coppin, John (born c1817) (African American mulatto) (laborer at Cecilton), married Jane (N) (born c1818) (African American mulatto) circa 1841; son Christopher born c1842 (African American) (1860 Cecil County Census)

CORDES

Cordes, Lepora (Zepora?), see James Knight

CORDRAY

Cordray, Isaac, married Ann M. Rickard circa 23 Mar 1835 (date of license) by Rev. Morris (Cecil County Marriage License Book)

CORMER

Cormer, James, married Sarah Ann Turner circa 19 Dec 1836 (date of license) by Rev. Barratt (Cecil County Marriage License Book)

CORNISH

Cornish, Ann, see Ephraim Cornish

Cornish, David (born c1810, Maryland) (African American) (laborer, 6th District), married Hannah (N) (born c1817, Maryland) (African American) probably circa 1837; son Robert Cornish born c1838, Maryland (1860 Cecil County Census)

Cornish, Elizabeth, see Elias Powell

Cornish, Ephraim (born c1811, Maryland) (African American) (laborer, 7th District), married Rachel (N) (born c1820, Maryland) (African American) probably circa 1843; daughter Ann Cornish born c1844, Maryland (1860 Cecil County Census)

Cornish, Henry, see William Cornish

Cornish, John, married Mary Ann McCreary, both of Cecil Co., on 6 Dec 1845, after obtaining a license on 19 Nov 1845, by Rev. Barton (Elkton Methodist Church Register, p. 141; Cecil County Marriage License Book; DAR transcript copied in 1955 mistakenly listed the marriage license date as 18 Nov 1845)

Cornish, Robert, see David Cornish

Cornish, William (born c1818, Maryland) (African American) (laborer, 7th District), married Margaret (N) (born c1821, Maryland) (African American) probably circa 1840; son Henry Cornish born c1841 (1860 Cecil County Census)

CORSETT

Corsett, Emma, see Stephen Atkinson

COSDEN

Cosden, Alexander C. (esquire), of Elkton, married Miss Amanda Jane Gray, of Philadelphia, on 4 Dec 1832 by Rev. Hodgson (*Cecil Republican*, 22 Dec 1832)

Cosden, Ann Elizabeth, see John H. Harris

Cosden, Ellen, see James Conlyn

Cosden, George, see John A. Cosden

Cosden, John A. (1821-1872) (bartender at Elkton), married Sarah Ann Donaldson (born c1825), of Bohemia Manor, on 18 Jun 1843, after obtaining a license on 17 Jun 1843, by Rev. James McIntire (Cecil County Marriage License Book; 1860 Cecil County Census misspelled his surname Causdin and listed their son George, age 16, who was a telegraph operator at that time; *Cecil Whig*, 24 Jun 1843 and 27 Jul 1872)

COSGROVE

Cosgrove, Ann, see Eli Cosgrove

Cosgrove, Eli (bon c1814, Maryland) (miller, Perryville), married Elizabeth (N) (born c1814, Pennsylvania) probably circa 1843; daughter Ann Cosgrove born c1844 (1860 Cecil County Census)

Cosgrove, William, married Catharine Thompson circa 10 Jan 1845 (date of license) (Cecil County Marriage License Book)

COSLETT

Coslett, Abraham (1813-1893), married Rachel (N) (1821-1881) probably circa 1840 (North East Methodist Church Cemetery tombstone inscriptions)

COSNER

Cosner, Elizabeth, see Charles Parker

COTTON

Cotton, George and Mary, see Henry Purnell

COULSON

Coulson, George J. A. (1819-1882), of Baltimore, married Maria Deborah Bromwell (1822-1897) circa 19 Oct 1844 (date of license) (Cecil Co. Marriage License Book; West Nottingham Cemetery tombstones)

Coulson, Jacob (1806-1844), married Sarah A. (N) (1807-1877) probably circa 1827 (Friends Cemetery, at Harrisville, tombstone inscriptions)

Coulson, James, married Elizabeth H. Tarring circa 15 Sep 1841 (date of license) (Cecil County Marriage License Book; DAR transcript copied in 1955 mistakenly spelled her name Carring and mistakenly listed the marriage license date as 16 Sep 1841)

Coulson, James A. (1818-1884) (carpenter, 6th District), married Esther A. Sidwell (1822-1885) circa 17 Apr 1843 (date of license) (Cecil County Marriage License Book listed her name as Esther, as did the Friends Cemetery, at Harrisville, tombstone inscriptions; 1860 Cecil County Census spelled her name Hester)

Coulson, Jesse R. (1820-1888), married Esther E. (N) (1822-1900) probably circa 1842 (Hopewell United Methodist Church Cemetery tombstone inscriptions)

Coulson, John, of West Nottingham, married Sophia Shaw, daughter of the late John Shaw, Esq., of Cecil Co., on 4 Jan 1844, after obtaining a license on 1 Jan 1844, by Rev. Burrowes (Cecil County Marriage License Book; *Cecil Whig*, 20 Jan 1844)

Coulson, John T. (born 1816), married Margaret Tosh (1818-1860) circa 16 1839 (date of license) by Rev. Wiggins (Cecil County Marriage License Book; *Midland Journal*, 27 Dec 1889, stated John T. Coulson, aged 73, resided in the 8th District; DAR transcript copied in 1928 mistakenly listed F. as his middle initial; West Nottingham Cemetery tombstone inscription for Margaret Coulson, wife of John T. Coulson)

Coulson, Joseph, married Deborah M. (N) (1830-1919), possibly Deborah M. Jenkins, probably circa 1850 (Rock Springs Old School Baptist Church Cemetery tombstone inscription for Deborah is inscribed "sister at rest, wife of Joseph Coulson" and she is buried next to Lydia R. Jenkins (1824-1911), "sister")

Coulson, Mary E., see Sylvester Coulson

Coulson, Rachel, see Hiram Hindman

Coulson, Susan Ann, see Richardson Plummer

Coulson, Sylvester (1810-1889), married Elizabeth (N) (1808-1893) circa 1826; buried beside Mary E. Coulson, 1827-1901 (Friends Cemetery, at Harrisville, tombstone inscriptions)

COULTER

Coulter, Peter M. (1818-1898, born New Jersey) (farmer at South Milford), married Isabella S. White (1819-1892, born Maryland) by 1849; daughter Mary Coulter born c1850 (Union Methodist Church Cemetery tombstone inscriptions; 1860 Cecil County Census)

COURTNEY
Courtney, Hollis, see John Keithley

COWAN, COWEN
Cowan, Benjamin C., married Miss Jane Taylor, both of Cecil Co., on 5 Apr 1838, after obtaining a license on 4 Apr 1838, by Rev. McFarland (*Cecil Gazette*, 11 Apr 1838; Cecil County Marriage License Book; Elkton Methodist Church Register, p. 138)

Cowan, Eliza, see Thomas Crawford

Cowan, Hannah Ann, see James Fury

Cowen, John K., see Washington Cowen

Cowan, Nancy, see Benjamin W. Jones

Cowen, Washington (1811-1891) (blacksmith), of Rising Sun, later of Mansfield, Ohio, married (N) probably circa 1832 and their son John K. Cowen was an attorney for the Baltimore & Ohio Railroad in Baltimore (*Midland Journal*, 2 Oct 1891)

Cowan, William, see Thomas Crawford and Benjamin W. Jones

COWHEY
Cowhey, John, married Joanna Fleming circa 25 Jun 1850 (date of license) (Cecil County Marriage License Book spelled her name Joanah Flemming)

COX
Cox, Benjamin, married Elizabeth Etherington circa 19 Dec 1829 (date of license) by Rev. King (Cecil County Marriage License Book)

Cox, Emaline, see George W. Gonce

Cox, Isaac H. R., married Elizabeth Lee circa 6 Jan 1838 (date of license) by Rev. Piggot, a Protestant Episcopal minister in North Sassafras (Cecil County Marriage License Book; DAR transcript copied in 1928 misspelled the minister's name as Pickett)

Cox, Jeremiah, married Susan Kirk circa 8 Jun 1837 (date of license) by Rev. Morris (Cecil County Marriage License Book is unclear as to his first name; the DAR transcript copied in 1928 transcribed it as Jeremiah)

Cox, Julia Ann, see Caleb Reed

Cox, Nathaniel (1816-1890, born in Ireland), married Ann Maria (N) (1819-1885, born in New York City) probably circa 1839 (St. Stephen's Episcopal Church Cemetery tombstone inscriptions)

COYLE
Coyle, Catharine, of Cecil Co., divorced from Terrence Coyle on 22 Mar 1836 (*Divorces and Names Changed in Maryland by Act of the Legislature, 1634-1867*, by Mary Keysor Meyer (1991), p. 20)

CRADDOCK
Craddock, Arrietta, see Joseph H. Stewart

Craddock, Benedict, see John M. Flintham

Craddock, Elizabeth A., see William P. Green

Craddock, Joseph, married Helena A. Green (1817-1854) circa 14 Jan 1839 (date of license) by Rev. King (Cecil County Marriage License Book; *Kent News*, 4 Mar 1854)

Craddock, Susan A., see John M. Flintham

Craddock, Thomas, married Margaret Shields circa 6 Oct 1841 (date of license) (Cecil County Marriage License Book)

CRAIG
Craig, Alexander, see Victor Craig and James Jackson

Craig, Ann, see Israel Snow and John Jackson

Craig, Anna Elizabeth, see David Scott

Craig, Christopher, see William Craig

Craig, David (1824-1891), married Sarah (N) (1824-1889) probably circa 1845 and he died at his home near Liberty Grove (West Nottingham Cemetery tombstone inscriptions; *Midland Journal*, 30 Oct 1891)

Craig, Edward L., see Victor Craig

Craig, Elizabeth, see James Gillespie

Craig, Ella M., see William Craig

Craig, Ellen, see Victor Craig

Craig, George W., married Ann Elizabeth Moore circa 30 Dec 1839 (date of license) by Rev. Piggot, a Protestant Episcopal minister in North Sassafras (Cecil County Marriage License Book)

Craig, George W., see William Craig

Craig, Grisella, see Victor Jackson

Craig, Henrietta C., see William Craig

Craig, James, see Victor Craig

Craig, James L., of Cecil Co., married Mary Ann Humes, daughter of Thomas Humes, Esq., on 16 Jun 1836 (*Baltimore American and Commercial Daily Advertiser*, 20 Jun 1836)

Craig, Jeremiah, see William Craig

Craig, John (1809-1871, born Maryland) (wheelwright, 7th District), married Catharine Jackson (1810-1866, born Maryland) circa 11 Mar 1834 (date of license) by Rev. Goforth (Cecil County Marriage License Book; St. Mark's Episcopal Church tombstone inscriptions; 1860 Cecil County Census)

Craig, Joseph, see Victor Craig

Craig, Lewis, see Victor Craig

Craig, Margaret, see James Jackson

Craig, Mary A., see Victor Craig

Craig, Mary Jane, see William T. Lynch

Craig, Merryman D., see William Craig

Craig, Millard F., see Victor Craig

Craig, Philip, married Ann A. Lee circa 13 May 1826 (date of license) by Rev. Duke (Cecil County Marriage License Book)

Craig, Philip, see William Craig

Craig, Sarah, see John McNeal

Craig, Victor (born c1808, Maryland) (farmer near Charlestown), married Margaret Elizabeth Gibson (born c1815, Maryland) circa 18 Mar 1839 (date of license) by Rev. Grace (Cecil County Marriage License Book; 1860 Cecil County Census; *Maryland Bible Records, Vol. 4: Eastern Shore*, by Henry C. Peden, Jr. (2004), pp. 60-61, lists the births of their nine children: James, born 14 Jan 1840; Ellen, born 11 May 1842; Lewis, born 12 Feb 1844; Mary A., born 11 Nov 1845; Victor, born 30 Oct 1847, died 21 Jun 1864; Alexander, born 11 Nov 1849; Joseph, born 12 Apr 1852; Edward L., born 27 Dec 1853; and, Millard F. Craig, born 8 Mar 1856)

Craig, William (1816-1894) (founder of the Green Hill Fire Brick Company), married Elizabeth Jane Baker (1819-1913), daughter of Henry Baker, circa 3 Jun 1845 (date of license) (Cecil County Marriage License Book; *Portrait and Biographical Record of Harford and Cecil Counties, Maryland* (1897, repr. 1989), pp. 217-218, stated they had five sons and three daughters and listed the seven children still living in 1897 as George W. Craig (born 22 Feb 1846), Anna L. Cameron, Ella M. Craig, Henrietta C. Craig, Philip Craig, Christopher Craig and Merryman D. Craig; St. Mark's Episcopal Church tombstone inscriptions included son Jeremiah Craig (1850-1881) and daughter Henrietta C. Craig (1854-1900) buried beside their parents; 1860 Cecil County Census listed William Craig's occupation simply as a farmer in the 7th District)

CRANDALL
Crandall, Julia Ann and Maria, see Levi Johnson

CRANMER

Cranmer, Joseph S., married Sarah Hamilton circa 3 Sep 1838 (date of license) by Rev. Duke (Cecil County Marriage License Book)

CRAWFORD

Crawford, J. H., see (N) Galbraith

Crawford, James, married Mary Ann McMullen circa 30 Dec 1845 (date of license) (Cecil County Marriage License Book)

Crawford, James S. (born c1827, Pennsylvania) (editor of the *Cecil Whig*), married Ann M. Pierson (born c1827, Maryland) circa 1 Aug 1848 (date of license) (Cecil County Marriage License Book; 1860 Cecil County Census)

Crawford, Mary A., see John W. Simpers

Crawford, Thomas, of New Castle Co., DE, married Eliza Cowan, youngest daughter of William Cowan, of and at Cowantown, Cecil Co., on 5 Jun 1834, after obtaining a license on 2 Jun 1834, by Rev. Russel (Cecil County Marriage License Book; *Delaware Gazette*, 10 Jun 1834)

CRAY

Cray, Samuel, married Ann Price circa 17 Jul 1828 (date of license) by Rev. Barratt (Cecil County Marriage License Book)

CRESWELL

Creswell, Caroline M., see Edward Heald

Creswell, Elizabeth B., see Austin H. Boynton

Creswell, John, see John Increase Creswell

Creswell, John G., married Elizabeth Rutter circa 16 Jul 1845 (date of license) (Cecil County Marriage License Book; DAR transcript copied in 1955 spelled his name Cresswell)

Creswell, John Increase (born 1818), son of John Creswell (1781-1824) and Tabitha Gatchell (1789-1847), married Hester Rutter on 22 Dec 1840 after obtaining a license on 21 Dec 1840 (date of license) (Cecil County Marriage License Book; *Maryland Bible Records, Volume 4: Eastern Shore*, by Henry C. Peden, Jr. (2004), pp. 66-67)

Creswell, Rebecca E., see Thomas L. Murphy

Creswell, Sidney A., see Joseph James Taylor

CRIPS

Crips, Isaac S. (1819-1851), married Sarah Ferguson (1819-1897) circa 9 Mar 1841 (date of license) (Cecil County Marriage License Book spelled his name Crips; DAR transcript copied in 1955 listed it as Crip; 1850 Cecil County Census Index listed Isaac Crips; Cherry Hill Methodist Church Cemetery tombstones)

CRISFIELD

Crisfield, Gilbert L. (born c1812, Delaware), of Chesapeake City, married Amelia (born c1812, Delaware) probably circa 1833 (1860 Cecil County Census)

CROCKETT

Crockett, Cluley, married Sarah Ann Jackson circa 8 Nov 1848 (date of license) (Cecil County Marriage License Book; 1850 Cecil County Census listed Cloud Crockett, but not Cluley Crockett)

CROMWELL

Cromwell, Elmira, see William H. Butcher

CROOKHAM

Crookham, Benjamina W., see Phineas Chambers

Crookham, William (born c1822, Maryland) (farmer, 6th District), married Hannah (N) (born c1823, Maryland) probably circa 1847; daughter Susan Crookham born c1848 (1860 Cecil County Census)

CROOKSHANKS

Crookshanks, Araminta, see Thomas C. Crookshanks

Crookshanks, Francis B. (1804-1877) (farmer at Cecilton), married Mary E. Mitchell (born c1815) circa 1 May 1834 (date of license) by Rev. McKenney (Cecil County Marriage License Book; *Cecil Whig*, 22 Sep 1877; St. Stephen's Episcopal Church Cemetery tombstone inscription spelled his name Cruikshank)

Crookshanks, Thomas, married Miss Sarah E. W. Comegys on 3 Oct 1834, after obtaining a license that same day, by Rev. Sharp (Cecil County Marriage License Book; *Cecil Gazette*, 18 Oct 1834)

Crookshanks, Thomas C. (born c1800) (farmer at Cecilton), married Elizabeth (N) (born c1817) circa 1835; daughter Araminta Crookshanks born c1836 (1860 Cecil County Census)

CROPPER

Cropper, A. P. (born c1814, Maryland) (steam boat captain at Chesapeake City), married Miss Rebecca B. Donoho (1816, Delaware – 1868, Nansemond Co., VA), of New Castle Co., DE, on 24 Oct 1841 by Rev. Maddux (1860 Cecil County Census; *Cecil Whig*, 27 Nov 1841; *Cecil Democrat and Farmer's Journal*, 14 Nov 1868, stated Rebecca Cropper died in her 53rd year, noting, Delaware papers please copy)

Cropper, Ebenezer, see John B. Yarnall

Cropper, Mary, see John B. Yarnall

Cropper, Mary Ann Maria, see John Tuffree (Puffree?)

Cropper, Sarah A., see James L. Schultz

CROSS

Cross, Andrew, see Joseph E. Trippe

Cross, David, married Miss Aceniah Sharp, both of Cecil Co., on 13 Jan 1829 in Wilmington, DE by Rev. Pardee (*Elkton Press*, 24 Jan 1829)

Cross, Sarah Patterson, see Joseph E. Trippe

CROSSMORE

Crossmore, John S. (1817-1882) (tailor at Cowantown), married Mary V. "Polly" (N) (1825-1873) probably circa 1842; son George Crossmore born c1843, Maryland, blacksmith (Cherry Hill Methodist Church Cemetery tombstone inscriptions; *Cecil Whig*, 8 Mar 1873, misspelled his name Crassmore; 1860 Cecil County Census misspelled it Crossman)

CROTHERS

Crothers, Alpheus (born c1820, Maryland) (miller in the 8th District), married Margaret (N) (born c1820, Maryland) probably circa 1844; son Ransom Crothers born c1845, Maryland (1860 Cecil County Census)

Crothers, Ann, see Benoni Nowland

Crothers, Caroline, see Lewis Crothers

Crothers, Elizabeth B., see Benjamin F. Kirk

Crothers, Isabella, see Samuel Thompson

Crothers, James (1799-1873), son of John Crothers, of Ireland, later of Cecil Co., married Rachel Cameron (c1800-1847), daughter of James Cameron, circa 13 Jan 1825 (date of license) by Rev. Magraw (Cecil County Marriage License Book; *Portrait and Biographical Record of Harford and Cecil Counties, Maryland* (1897, repr. 1989), p. 394)

Crothers, John, see James Crothers and Benjamin F. Kirk

Crothers, Jonathan L., see Benoni Nowland

Crothers, Lewis, married Caroline McElwee (born c1820, Maryland) circa 7 Jun 1841 (date of license) (Cecil County Marriage License Book; DAR transcript copied in 1928 listed him as "Leius(?)" and misspelled her name as Catherine McEliver; 1860 Cecil County Census listed Caroline Carothers as head of house)

Crothers, Mary, see Levi Hill

Crothers, Ransom, see Alpheus Crothers

CROUCER, CRONCER(?)

Croucer (Croncer?), Benjamin, married Rachel Stoops circa 6 Mar 1839 (date of license) by the Rev. Barratt (Cecil County Marriage License Book is unclear and his name could have been Croucer, but the DAR transcript copied in 1928 listed his name as Croncer)

CROUCH

Crouch, Charles H. (1809-1867), married Caroline May (1814-1850) circa 27 Feb 1834 (date of license) by Rev. Davis (Cecil County Marriage License Book; *Cecil Democrat and Farmer's Journal*, 23 Feb 1850, stated she died of brain fever, and 1 Jun 1867 stated he died in Richmond, Virginia)

Crouch, Cornelia, see Joseph Wells

Crouch, Elizabeth, see Enoch Crouch

Crouch, Elizabeth W., see Joshua Hyland

Crouch, Enoch (born c1814) (farmer at Elkton), married Christiana (N) (born c1816, Pennsylvania) circa 1840; daughter Rebecca born c1841, Pennsylvania, daughter Elizabeth born c1844, Maryland, and other children born in Maryland (1860 Cecil County Census)

Crouch, Hannah, see Nathaniel Simpers

Crouch, Isaac L., married Margaret Buchanan circa 24 Feb 1837 (date of license) by Rev. Potts (Cecil County Marriage License Book)

Crouch, James, married Mary Crouch circa 20 Sep 1831 (date of license) by Rev. Barratt (Cecil County Marriage License Book)

Crouch, John (born c1820) (laborer at North East), married Rebecca (N) (born c1828) probably circa 1847; daughter Mary Crouch born c1848 (1860 Cecil County Census)

Crouch, John F., married Mary Strong circa 6 Jun 1826 (date of license) by Rev. Barratt (Cecil County Marriage License Book)

Crouch, Mahala, see Samuel Decham (Dechain?)

Crouch, Mary, see James Crouch, John Crouch, James McCauley and Sampson Lum

Crouch, Mary E., see John McClure

Crouch, Milcha Ann, see Alexander Wilson

Crouch, Rachel, see Umphrey Riddle

Crouch, Rebecca, see Enoch Crouch

Crouch, Samuel, married Mary McKenney circa 12 Dec 1826 (date of license) by Rev. Barratt (Cecil County Marriage License Book)

CROW

Crow, Ann Maria, see James Crow

Crow, Emily E., see Lawrence Simmons, Jr.

Crow, James (born c1821, Maryland) (farmer at St. Augustine), married 1st to Ann Maria Crow circa 18 Jan 1843 (date of license) and married 2nd to Rachel Tridin (born c1839, Maryland) circa 1 Apr 1858 (Cecil County Marriage License Book; 1860 Cecil County Census)

Crow, William (c1795-1837, near New Castle, DE) (War of 1812 veteran), married Susan Rider circa 21 May 1834 (date of license) by Rev. Cropper (Cecil County Marriage License Book; Bounty Land Warrant No. 55-160-45271 stated they were married on 3 May 1833 by Rev. Craffred of the Episcopal Church)

Crow, William C., married 1st to Mary E. Hays circa 29 Jan 1850 (date of license) and married 2nd to Amelia F. Bennett circa 10 Mar 1859 (Cecil County Marriage License Book)

CRUIKSHANK, see Crookshanks

CULBERTSON

Culbertson, Ann, see John Keithley

Culbertson, Ann Eliza, see Samuel Haines

Culbertson, Margaret, see John Keithley

Culbertson, Rachel, see William Keithley

Culbertson, Thomas, see John Keithley

Culbertson, Thomas, married Jane Barnett circa 22 Jun 1842 (date of license) (Cecil County Marriage License Book)

CULLER

Culler, Chaulkley B. (born c1817, Maryland) (farmer in the 8th District), married Elizabeth (N) (born c1821, Pennsylvania) probably circa 1844; daughter Rebecca Culler born c1845, Maryland, and their other children were also born in Maryland (1860 Cecil County Census)

CULLEY, CULLY

Culley, Ann Elizabeth, see Samuel Redgraves

Culley, John, married Mary Ann Culley circa 14 Apr 1846 (date of license) (Cecil County Marriage License Book spelled his name Cully and her name Culley)

Culley, Lydia, see George Moore

Culley, Mary Ann, see John Culley

Cully, Robert, married Maria J. Chandler, daughter of Cornel Chandler, both of Havre de Grace, Harford Co., on 22 Jan 1835 by Rev. Goldsborough in Baltimore (*Cecil Gazette*, 31 Jan 1835)

CUMMINGS

Cummings, Amos, married Eliza Handlen circa 1 Sep 1836 (date of license) by Rev. Potts (Cecil County Marriage License Book)

Cummings, James (1814-1887) (tailor and farmer, 8th District), of Philadelphia and Pleasant Grove, PA and later of Pilot Town, Cecil Co., married Jane McColgan (born c1816), of Lancaster Co., PA, probably circa 1846; daughter Margaret Cummings born c1848, Maryland (*Portrait and Biographical Record of Harford and Cecil Counties, Maryland* (1897, repr. 1989), p. 287; 1860 Cecil County Census)

Cummings, James M. (esquire), of Lycoming Co., PA, married Miss Augusta H. Savin, daughter of Thomas L. Savin, Esq., formerly of Cecil Co., on 30 May 1849 by Rev. Heborn at Lock Haven in Lycoming Co. (*Cecil Democrat and Farmer's Journal*, 30 Jun 1849; *Cecil Whig*, 30 Jun 1849)

Cummings, Margaret, see James Cummings

Cummings, Morris (born c1826), of Philadelphia, later of Elkton (baker), married Miss Emily Elizabeth Johnson (born c1832), of Elkton, on 7 Nov 1849 by Rev. Donelan (*Baltimore Sun*, 20 Oct 1849; *Cecil Democrat and Farmer's Journal*, 17 Nov 1849, spelled his name Morros Cummins; 1860 Cecil County Census spelled his name Morris Cumins)

Cummings, Samuel, married Mary Perre(?) circa 11 Jan 1826 (date of their license) by Rev. Graham (Cecil County Marriage License Book spelled his name Cummins and the spelling of her name was not clear)

CUNNAY

Cunnay, Janetta, see Samuel Taylor

CUNNINGHAM

Cunningham, Ann (Anna), see Samuel Jackson

Cunningham, David, see Edward Kelly

Cunningham, Eleanor, see Bayard Tatman

Cunningham, Elizabeth, see William Johnson and Edward Kelly

66

Cunningham, Jacob (born c1833, Pennsylvania) (iron roller, 8th District), married Mary (N) (born c1830, Pennsylvania) probably circa 1850; daughter Mary Cunningham born c1851, Pennsylvania, son Theodore Cunningham born c1853, Maryland, and other children were born in Maryland (1860 Cecil Co. Census)

Cunningham, John, married Margaret Jackson circa 22 Jun 1839 (date of license) by Rev. Young (Cecil County Marriage License Book)

Cunningham, John, married Margaret Whitelock circa 26 Jun 1833 (date of license) by Rev. Goforth (Cecil County Marriage License Book)

Cunningham, Martha, see Alexander Curry and Henry Kimble

Cunningham, Mary, see Jacob Cunningham

Cunningham, Rebecca, see Edward Kelly

Cunningham, Sarah, see Lewis Littaway

Cunningham, Theodore, see Jacob Cunningham

Cunningham, Thomas, married Mary Ann Fulton, eldest daughter of George Fulton, all of Cecil Co., on 23 Jan 1838, after obtaining a license on 15 Jan 1838, by Rev. McFarland (*Cecil Gazette*, 3 Feb 1838; Cecil County Marriage License Book; DAR transcript copied in 1928 mistakenly listed the minister's name as Farland; James McFarland was a Methodist minister in Elkton)

CURRIER

Currier, Grizzell or Grizzy, see Jefferson M. White

Currier, Jonathan (1798-1863), of near Port Deposit, married Margaret E. (N) (1810-1877) probably circa 1828 (daughter Rosanna 1829-1845; son Matthew 1835-1865) (Asbury Cemetery tombstone inscriptions; *Cecil Whig*, 31 Mar 1877)

Currier, Leah Ann, see James H. Price

Currier, Mary, see Daniel Gillespie

Currier, Matthew, see Jonathan Currier

Currier, Rosanna, see Jonathan Currier

Currier, Richard, married Rebecca Benjamin circa 20 Jul 1831 (date of license) by Rev. Goforth (Cecil County Marriage License Book)

CURRY

Curry, Alexander, married Martha Cunningham circa 13 May 1829 (date of license) by Rev. Russell (Cecil County Marriage License Book)

Curry, Alexander (born c1808) (farmer near Elkton), married Miss Prudence Amelia Tyson (born c1825), youngest daughter of Matthias Tyson, Esq., all of Cecil Co., on 11 Aug 1842, after obtaining a license that same day, by Rev. McIntire (*Cecil Whig*, 13 Aug 1842; Cecil County Marriage License Book; 1860 Cecil County Census; DAR transcript copied in 1955 mistakenly listed the license date as 11 Sep 1842)

Curry, Charlotte, see William Curry

Curry, James, see John Curry

Curry, John (born c1820, Ireland) (laborer, 6th District), married Rosanna (N) (born c1822, Ireland) probably circa 1846; son James Curry born c1847, Maryland (1860 Cecil County Census)

Curry, Susan, see Isaac Johnson

Curry, William (born c1820, Maryland) (farmer near Elkton), married Mary (N) (born c1822, Delaware) probably circa 1841; daughter Charlotte Curry born c1842, Maryland (1860 Cecil County Census)

CURTIS

Curtis, Louisa Jane, see James W. Alexander

Curtis, William H., married Sarah E. Smyth circa 24 Nov 1847 (date of license) (Cecil County Marriage License Book)

CUTLER

Cutler, Mercey, see Joseph Thomas

DALSTER
Dalster, Sarah, see John J. Walmsley

DARLING
Darling, Harriet E., see Robert Butterworth

DARLINGTON
Darlington, George, see Merrick Coates
Darlington, Hannah, see Merrick Coates
Darlington, J. Lacy, married Jannetta Hazelett, daughter of the late William Hazelett, Esq., of Philadelphia, circa 1835; Jannetta Darlington died 13 Apr 1838, age 23, Westchester, PA (*Cecil Gazette*, 25 Apr 1838)
Darlington, Lydia, see Merrick Coates

DAUGHERTY
Daugherty, Elizabeth, see William H. Maffitt
Daugherty, Philip (1809-1892), married Helen Perry (1811-1891) on 1 Sep 1831 (St. John's Church Cemetery, at Lewisville, tombstone inscriptions)
Daugherty, also see Dougherty

DAVENPORT
Davenport, Robert (1816-1905), married Mary A. Jenkins (1813-1883) probably circa 1837 (Rock Springs Old School Baptist Church Cemetery tombstone inscriptions)

DAVIDS
Davids, James J. (dentist), of Elkton, married Elizabeth G. Turner, daughter of J. M. Turner, of Wilmington, DE, on 6 Sep 1847 by Rev. Castle (*Delaware Gazette*, 7 Sep 1847)

DAVIDSON
Davidson, Ann E., see Henry K. Reynolds
Davidson, Caroline, see John Huss Mahoney
Davidson, Deborah A., see John S. Strickland
Davidson, George, married Ann E. Haines (or Thomas?) circa 1 Jun 1825 (date of license) by Rev. Magraw (Cecil County Marriage License Book was unclearly written and her surname looked like either Thomas or Haines, and the DAR transcript copied in 1928 listed it as Haines)
Davidson, Hannah E., see Jonathan Harrigan
Davidson, Jane B., see William Campbell
Davidson, Mary Jane, see Alexander F. McFadden (McFadian)
Davidson, Mary P., see Robert Gregg
Davidson, Rebecca, see David Jenness
Davidson, Thomas J., married Martha Gallaher circa 1 Oct 1839 (date of license) by Rev. Wilson (Cecil County Marriage License Book)
Davidson, William, see William Campbell

DAVIS
Davis, Abel C., of Elkton, married Rachael Wallace, of Pearch Creek, on 18 Dec 1828 by Rev. Woolford (*Elkton Press*, 20 Dec 1828)
Davis, Abel J., married Miss Margaret A. Mahan, both of Cecil Co., on 26 Sep 1850, after obtaining a license on 24 Sep 1850, by Rev. McIntire (Cecil County Marriage License Book; *Cecil Democrat and Farmer's Journal*, 28 Sep 1850; *Cecil Whig*, 28 Sep 1850)
Davis, Amanda M., see James M. McClenahan

Davis, Ann, see William Bartley

Davis, Ann Elizabeth, see William G. Etherington

Davis, Caroline, see James Pennington and Thomas Tennant

Davis, Caroline C., see James Orr

Davis, David D. (born c1819) (farmer at Cecilton), married Mary (N) (born c1828) probably circa 1848; son Hamilton Davis born c1849 (1860 Cecil County Census)

Davis, Elizabeth, see George Hayes

Davis, George, see John Savin and Stephen Savin

Davis, George, married Mary Smith circa 27 Dec 1831 (date of license) by Rev. Duke (Cecil County Marriage License Book)

Davis, George, married Mary Young circa 26 Sep 1833 (date of license) by Rev. Barratt (Cecil County Marriage License Book)

Davis, George W. (1823-1900), married Susan (N) (1823-1898) probably circa 1844 (Elkton Cemetery tombstone inscriptions)

Davis, Hamilton, see David D. Davis

Davis, Howard (born c1819) (farmer near Elkton), married Eliza McCauley (born c1812) circa 14 Mar 1844 (date of license) (Cecil County Marriage License Book; 1860 Cecil County Census)

Davis, Isaac D., see John Newman Davis

Davis, Isabella, see John Newman Davis

Davis, James, married Rachel Davis circa 9 Jun 1831 (date of license) by Rev. Barratt (Cecil County Marriage License Book)

Davis, James, married Elizabeth Broomell on 24 Mar 1841 by a Justice of the Peace (name not given) and celebrated their 60th anniversary at their residence in Hopewell Borough, Chester Co., PA, having gone on horseback to the place the ceremony was performed (*Midland Journal*, 27 Mar 1891)

Davis, James (born c1821) (farmer near Elkton), married Miss Margaret Jane McCauley (born c1819), both of Cecil Co., on 7 Apr 1850, after obtaining a license on 30 Mar 1850, by Rev. McIntire (*Cecil Whig*, 20 Apr 1850; Cecil County Marriage License Book; 1860 Cecil County Census)

Davis, James A. (born c1820, Maryland) (merchant, Port Deposit), married 1st to Miss Margaret R. Smith, also of Port Deposit, on 17 Feb 1846, after obtaining a license on 13 Feb 1846, by Rev. Townsend, and married 2nd to Mary F. Reynolds circa 22 May 1855 (date of license) (*Cecil Whig*, 21 Feb 1846; Cecil County Marriage License Book; 1860 Cecil County Census)

Davis, James Sheridan, see Jehu Thomas Davis

Davis, Jehu Thomas (1803-1879), of Cooch's Bridge, DE, married Sarah Sheridan (1807-1890) on 16 Jun 1825; son James Sheridan Davis born 15 Mar 1829 at Port Deposit, Cecil Co., MD (*Ancestral Charts, Volume 4*, p. 152, Harford County Genealogical Society Publication, 1988)

Davis, John, married Rebecca Sample circa 6 Apr 1833 (date of license) by Rev. Benson (Cecil County Marriage License Book)

Davis, John E. (born c1815) (farmer near Elkton), married Margaret Wallis (born c1814) circa 23 Mar 1837 (date of license) by Rev. Potts (Cecil County Marriage License Book; DAR transcript copied in 1928 listed his name without the middle initial; 1860 Cecil County Census)

Davis, John Newman, of Red Bank, NJ, later of Cecil Co., son of Isaac Davis and Susanna Newman, married Rebecca Bolton in 1832 and their children were Mary, Isabella, Isaac D. (born 31 Dec 1841) and William (*Portrait and Biographical Record of Harford and Cecil Counties, Maryland* (1897, repr. 1989), p. 466, did not give the exact date of marriage)

Davis, John W. (born c1828, Maryland) (farmer at Warwick), married Mary E. Jones (born c1830, Maryland) circa 18 Dec 1847 (date of license) (Cecil Co. Marr. License Book; 1860 Cecil Co. Census)

Davis, Joshua, married Hannah Emory circa 9 Aug 1842 (date of license) (Cecil County Marr. License Book)

Davis, Margaret, see James Ford

Davis, Mary, see Arthur Beatty, John Newman Davis, Elijah Moore and Samuel McKowen

Davis, Mary Jane, see Samuel McDowell

Davis, Rachel, see James Davis and William Rider

Davis, Rebecca J., see William McCullough

Davis, Richard, see Thomas Tennant

Davis, Richard, married Martha Ann Mars circa 20 May 1835 (date of license) by Rev. Barratt (Cecil County Marriage License Book)

Davis, Samuel, married Eliza Vansant circa 8 Sep 1831 (date of license) by Rev. Duke (Cecil County Marriage License Book)

Davis, Stephen, married Caroline Smith circa 15 Mar 1825 (date of license) by Rev. Sharpley (Cecil County Marriage License Book)

Davis, William, see John Newman Davis

Davis, William H., married Margaret Worthington circa 9 Mar 1825 (date of license) by Rev. Waller (Cecil County Marriage License Book)

DAWSON

Dawson, Jacob (born c1830) (farmer near Elkton), married Melinda (N) (born c1832) probably circa 1847; son John Dawson born c1848 (1860 Cecil County Census)

Dawson, John, see Jacob Dawson

Dawson, Maria S., see Stephen H. Ford

DAY

Day, Isabella B., see James Dorsey

DEAL

Deal, George, married Mary Ann Tibbitt circa 10 Mar 1829 (date of license) by Rev. Duke (Cecil County Marriage License Book)

DEAN

Dean, Israel R., see Moses Dean

Dean, Jacob (born c1820, Maryland) (carpenter, 7th District), married Elizabeth (N) (born c1828, Maryland) probably circa 1848; son William Dean born c1849 (1860 Cecil County Census)

Dean, John, see Moses Dean

Dean, Moses (c1810-1865) (ironworker), of Cecil Co., MD and Lancaster Co., PA, son of John Dean, married Julia Ann Alexander (died 1869), of Cecil Co, by 1837 (son Israel R. Dean born 8 May 1838 in Lancaster Co., PA) (*Portrait and Biographical Record of Harford and Cecil Counties, Maryland* (1897, repr. 1989), p. 298)

Dean, Richard (1801-1872), married Sarah Morrow (1805-1875) circa 19 May 1828 (date of license) (Cecil County Marriage License Book is not clearly written, but the DAR transcript copied in 1928 stated her name was Morrow; Cherry Hill Methodist Church Cemetery tombstones; *Cecil Whig*, 14 Sep 1872)

Dean, William, see Jacob Dean

DEATH

Death, Julian, see Aaron Keech

Death, Mary Eliza, see Charles Bruce

DECHAM, DECHAIN

Decham (Dechain?), Samuel, of New Castle, DE, married Mahala Crouch, of New Castle, DE, circa 10 Jun 1830 (date of license) by Rev. Duke (Cecil County Marriage License Book)

DEHAVEN

DeHaven, Mary, see George I. Smith

DeHaven, Mary Jane, see William Falls

DENNIS

Dennis, Francina, see Francis Russum

Dennis, William J., married Mary E. Brickley circa 13 Dec 1841 (date of license) (Cecil County Marriage License Book; DAR transcript copied in 1955 mistakenly listed his name without the middle initial)

DENNISON

Dennison, Ann J., see Thomas L. Phillips

Dennison, Barbara H., see Clinton J. White

Dennison, Margaret Ann, see John T. Knight

Dennison, Martha, see Francis T. Reisling

Dennison, Sarah, see John Archer

Dennison, William, married Mary Ann Burrows circa 30 Dec 1828 (date of license) by Rev. Goforth (Cecil County Marriage License Book)

Dennison, William (born c1800, Maryland) (farmer near Bay View), married Sarah Logan (born c1808, Maryland) circa 19 Sep 1826 (date of license) by Rev. Barratt (Cecil County Marriage License Book; 1860 Cecil County Census)

DENNY

Denny, Ada, see Francis Denny

Denny, Araminta Matilda, see William Grant

Denny, Francis (born c1826, Delaware) (merchant at Elkton), married Mary (N) (born c1831, Delaware) circa 1850; daughter Ada Denny born c1851, Maryland (1860 Cecil County Census)

Denny, James (merchant), of Elkton, married Mary A. Conaway, daughter of Samuel Conaway, Esq., of Philadelphia, on 17 Dec 1850 by Rev. Clark (*Cecil Whig*, 21 Dec 1850' *Cecil Democrat and Farmer's Journal*, 21 Dec 1850)

Denny, John, married Mary Ann Pearce circa 7 Dec 1829 (date of license) by Rev. Rider (Cecil County Marriage License Book; DAR transcript copied in 1928 spelled his name Denney)

Denny, Timothy P., married Ann Merritt circa 7 Nov 1850 (date of license) (Cecil Co. Marr. License Book)

DEPUTY

Deputy, Elizabeth W., see Lewis Ellison, Jr.

Deputy, Joshua, see Lewis Ellison, Jr. and James M. Ellison

Deputy, Sarah J., see James M. Ellison

DESHANE

Deshane, John, married Ann Briley circa 29 Mar 1850 (date of license) (Cecil County Marr. License Book)

Deshane, Mary, see William Deshane

Deshane, William (born c1813, Delaware) (farmer at St. Augustine), married Rebecca (N) (born c1812, Maryland) probably circa 1837; daughter Mary born c1838, Delaware (1860 Cecil County Census)

DEVALINGER

DeValinger, Francis, married Martha Caroline Harris, daughter of Samuel Harris, all of Cecil Co., on 19 May 1844, after obtaining a license on 16 May 1844, "by the Parish Priest in Trinity Church" (Cecil County Marriage License Book; *Cecil Whig*, 25 May 1844: "We acknowledge the receipt from the happy couple a splendid piece of the wedding cake, and hope that their life may be one of perpetual sunshine and prosperity, and that they stand a chance for a full share of happiness, is rendered pretty certain by their attention to the *printer's fee*.")

DeValinger, Mary Ann, see George Campbell

DeValinger, Virginia, see Nathaniel Jaquett

DEVAULE, DUAULE(?)

Devaule (Duaule?), James Wesley, married Mary Richardson circa 3 Dec 1833 (date of license) by Rev. Barratt (Cecil County Marriage License is unclear; DAR transcript copied in 1928 spelled it "Duaule?")

DEVLIN

Devlin, Martha Ann, see William Missimer

Devlin, Mary, see Rensselaer Biddle

DEVOR, DEVON(?)

Devor (Devon?), Caroline N., see George Turner

DEWITT

DeWitt, Abraham (1798-1887) (reverend) (Pastor of Rock Church, 1841-1855), married Anna Terhune (1804-1888) probably circa 1825 (Sharp's Cemetery tombstone inscriptions)

DICK

Dick, William (born c1820, Maryland) (laborer at North East), married Sarah (N) (born c1825, Maryland) probably circa 1844; daughter Margaret Dick born c1845 (1860 Cecil County Census)

DICKEY

Dickey, Samuel (reverend), of Oxford, Chester Co., PA, married C. Eugeine Cazier, only daughter of Henry Cazier, Esq., on 8 Oct 1850 by Rev. Howell at the Cazier's home on Mount Vernon Farm in New Castle Co., DE (*Cecil Democrat and Farmer's Journal*, 26 Oct 1850)

DIFFENDERFER

Diffenderfer, John T., married Mrs. Harriet Watkins (neé McMullin), widow of Samuel Watkins, both of Port Deposit, on 13 Apr 1843, after obtaining a license that same day, by Rev. McIntire (*Cecil Whig*, 29 Apr 1843, spelled his name Diffenderfer; Cecil County Marriage License Book spelled it Diffendaffer; DAR transcript copied in 1955 spelled it Diffendeffer)

DILL

Dill, Ebenezer, of Cecil Co., married Louisa Phouns, of Kent Co., circa 11 Jan 1842 by Rev. Pearson (Kent County Marriage License Book)

DILLAHUNT

Dillahunt, John James, married Maria Greenwood circa 22 Jul 1836 (date of license) by Rev. Smith (Cecil County Marriage License Book)

DINAN

Dinan, Elizabeth, see John Conekin

DIXSON

Dixson, Thomas (born c1820, Delaware) (farmer at Elkton), married Hannah (N) (born c1822, Delaware) circa 1841 and moved to Cecil Co. by 1853 (1860 Cecil County Census)

DODD

Dodd, Abel, married Ann Miller circa 6 Feb 1843 (date of license) (Cecil County Marriage License Book)

DOLBY

Dolby, Nathan, married Isabella Maxwell circa 21 Mar 1833 (date of license) by Rev. Magraw (Cecil County Marriage License Book)

DONAHOO, DONOHO

Donahoo, James F., married Mary Jane Nail circa 28 Apr 1846 (date of license) (Cecil County Marriage License Book; DAR transcript copied in 1955 mistakenly listed his name without the middle initial)

Donahoo, Sarah, see Hugh Hamilton

Donahoo, William J. (1821-1890), married Emaline White (1823-1895) circa 3 Jul 1849 (date of license) (Cecil County Marriage License Book; St. Mark's Episcopal Church tombstone inscriptions)

Donoho, Rebecca B., see A. P. Cropper

DONALDSON

Donaldson, Julianna, see William B. Donaldson

Donaldson, R. (born c1824, Maryland) (waterman at North East), married Elizabeth (N) (born c1825, Maryland) probably circa 1849; son William Donaldson born c1850 (1860 Cecil County Census)

Donaldson, Sarah Ann, see John Cosden

Donaldson, William, see R. Donaldson

Donaldson, William, married Lydia Ann Fillingame circa 14 Feb 1849 (date of license) (Cecil County Marriage License Book misspelled her name Filingin)

Donaldson, William, married Mary Ann Boulden circa 2 May 1843 (date of license) (Cecil County Marriage License Book misspelled her name Balden)

Donaldson, William B., married Julianna Donaldson circa 23 Jan 1837 (date of license) by Rev. Smith (Cecil County Marriage License Book); however, Julianna Donaldson, of Cecil Co., had divorced from William B. Donaldson, on 28 Jan 1833, "neither to remarry," but they apparently did anyway (*Divorces and Names Changed in Maryland by Act of the Legislature, 1634-1867*, by Mary Keysor Meyer (1991), p. 26)

DORSEY

Dorsey, James, of Cecil Co., married Isabella B. Day on 6 Aug 1835 (*Baltimore American and Commercial Daily Advertiser*, 8 Aug 1835)

Dorsey, William (1823-1901), of Mount Pleasant, married Martha Ellen or Ellen Martha (N) (c1825-1866) probably circa 1845 (West Nottingham Cemetery tombstone inscriptions inscribed her name Ellen M. Dorsey; *Cecil Whig*, 8 Dec 1866, obituary gave her name as Martha E. Dorsey, wife of William)

DOUGHERTY

Dougherty, Ann, see Nicholas Smith

Dougherty, Edward, married Ellen Bray circa 27 Dec 1850 (date of license) (Cecil Co. Marr. License Book)

Dougherty, also see Daugherty

DOWLING

Dowling, Aramintha, see John Walmsley

DOWNEY

Downey, William, married Miss Sarah Jane Elseroad, both of Baltimore, on 3 Mar 1850 by Rev. Ryan (*Cecil Democrat and Farmer's Journal*, 9 Mar 1850; *Baltimore Sun*, 5 Mar 1850)

DRENNAN, DRENNEN

Drennan, Jonathan (1809-1880), married Ann (N) (1807-1885) probably circa 1830 (Elkton Presbyterian Church Cemetery tombstone inscriptions)

Drennen, Anna E., see Nicholas Manly

Drennen, Deborah, see George Evans

DREW
Drew, William (1822-1875), married Sarah E. (N) (1827-1894) probably circa 1845-1848 (Elkton Cemetery tombstone inscriptions)

DRUMMOND
Drummond, James H. Lemon (born c1810) (papermaker at Elkton), married Maria Spence (born c1810) circa 1 May 1833 (date of license) by Rev. Mahan (Cecil County Marriage License Book; 1860 Cecil County Census listed their names as Lemon and Maria Drumon)

Drummond, Matthew (born c1832) (papermaker at Elkton), married Hannah Scarborough (born c1826), daughter of Enos Scarborough, all of Cecil County, on 26 Aug 1847, after obtaining a license on 23 Aug 1847, by Rev. Goldsborough in Trinity Church (*Cecil Whig*, 28 Aug 1847; Cecil County Marriage License Book; 1860 Cecil County Census misspelled his name Drunnon)

Drummond, William (born c1812) (papermaker at Elkton), married Rachel (N) (born c1816) probably circa 1836; daughter Martha Drummond born c1837 (1860 Cecil County Census)

DUAULE, DEVAULE(?)
Duaule (Devaule?), James Wesley, married Mary Richardson circa 3 Dec 1833 (date of license) by Rev. Barratt (Cecil County Marriage License is unclear; DAR transcript copied in 1928 spelled it "Duaule?")

DUGAN
Dugan, Mary I. and Thomas E., see Edward Mansfield

DUHAMELL
Duhamell, Robert James (born c1808) (laborer at Cecilton), married Amelia Ann Patterson (born c1812) circa 13 Nov 1832 (date of license) by Rev. Duke (Cecil County Marriage License Book; 1860 Cecil County Census listed his name as R. J. Duhamel)

DULANEY
Dulaney, Cornelia A., see John J. Hyland

DUNBAR
Dunbar, John B., see (N) Basketter

Dunbar, Justus (cabinet maker), married Sarah Ann Boulden circa 4 Apr 1832 (date of license) by Rev. Barnes (Cecil County Marriage License Book; *Elkton Press*, 16 Aug 1828)

Dunbar, Sarah Ann, see Joseph Miles Ash

DUNCAN
Duncan, Eliza, see George Ross Veazey

Duncan, Elizabeth, see John Conekin

DUNN
Dunn, Eliza J., see William D. Spence

DUNOTT
Dunott, Justus (1804-1890) (doctor), married Emma B. (N) (1826-1896) probably circa 1846-1850 (Elkton Presbyterian Church Cemetery tombstone inscriptions)

DUPELLE, DUPELLEE
Dupelle, Ester, see John McClain

Dupellee, Antoine, married Ester Gibson circa 11 Sep 1827 (date of license) (Cecil Co. Marr. License Book)

DUPONT

DuPont, Charles J., of Brandywine, PA, married Ann Ridgely, daughter of Henry M. Ridgely, of Dover, DE, on 11 May 1841 by Rev. Bausman at Dover (*Cecil Gazette*, 29 May 1841)

DURBOROW

Durborow, Joshua (1817-1895), married Elizabeth (N) (1818-1889) probably circa 1838-1840 (Rosebank Cemetery, at Calvert, tombstone inscriptions)

DUVALL

Duvall, A. W., see Nathaniel Simpers

DUYCKINCK

Duyckinck, Horace H. (1819-1891, born New Jersey) (farmer near Brick Meeting House), son of Richard Bancker Duyckinck and Hannah Holden, married Emily Longstreet (1818-1903, born New Jersey), daughter of Aaron Longstreet, probably circa 1845; daughter Annie born c1846, New Jersey; daughter Magdalene was first child born in Maryland c1857 (Zion Presbyterian Cemetery tombstone inscriptions; 1860 Cecil County Census misspelled his name as Deykins; *Midland Journal*, 10 Apr and 17 Apr 1891)

DYKE, DYKES

Dyke (Dykes), Arthur, married Eliza Ann Walker circa 5 Jun 1837 (date of license) by Rev. Morris (Cecil County Marriage License Book; DAR transcript copied in 1928 spelled his name Dyke; 1840 Cecil County Census Index spelled his name Dykes)

EADES, EADER(?)

Eades (Eader?), Mary, see Samuel Green

EAGLE

Eagle, Dominick (merchant), of Columbia, PA, married Caroline W. Hessin, daughter of William Hessin, of Cecil Co., on 15 Jun 1831 (*Baltimore American and Commercial Daily Advertiser*, 16 Jun 1831)

EARLE

Earle, George (born c1822, Maryland) (attorney at Elkton), married Mary C. (N) (born c1822, Delaware) circa 1847; son B. Tilghman Earle born c1848, Maryland (1860 Cecil County Census)

EARLY

Early, Isabella, see Charles McLaughlin

EARNEST

Earnest, Fagan, married Martha Ann Mitchell circa 20 Sep 1836 (date of license) by Rev. Morrison (Cecil County Marriage License Book)

ECCLESTON

Eccleston, John C. (doctor), of Chestertown, married M. Almira Stevens, daughter of Col. John Stevens, of Easton, on 6 Jun 1850 by Rev. Dr. Johns in Baltimore at Christ Church (*Cecil Democrat and Farmer's Journal*, 22 Jun 1850; *Baltimore Sun*, 14 Jun 1850)

EDDY

Eddy, Jane Maria and O. T., see James Wingate

EDIE

Edie, Arthur S., married Catherine J. Alexander circa 27 Oct 1842 (date of license) (Cecil County Marriage License Book)

EDMONDSON, EDMUNDSON

Edmondson, Caleb, married Eliza Jane Campbell circa 25 Jan 1839 (date of license) by Rev. Hoffman (Cecil County Marriage License Book)

Edmundson, Caleb Jr., married Eliza Margaret Boulden circa 3 Feb 1836 (date of license) by Rev. Houston (Cecil County Marriage License Book)

Edmondson, Mary, see Absalom McVey

Edmondson, Sarah, see Green Williams

Edmondson, William, married Maria E. White circa 20 Dec 1826 (date of license) by Rev. Beem (Cecil County Marriage License Book)

Edmundson, Thomas, married Eliza Janney circa 3 Feb 1836 (date of license) by Rev. Houston (Cecil County Marriage License Book)

EDWARDS

Edwards, Perry, married Rebecca Hays, both of Cecil Co., on 29 Jan 1849, after obtaining a license that same day, by Rev. Gray (Cecil Co. Marr. License Book; *Cecil Democrat and Farmer's Journal*, 3 Feb 1849)

Edwards, Richard, married Margaret Ford circa 14 Sep 1840 (date of license) (Cecil Co. Marr. Lic. Book)

Edwards, William, married Miss Mary Reed, both of Kent Co., on 10 Feb 1829 by Rev. Smith (*Elkton Press*, 21 Feb 1829)

EGAN

Egan, James (c1805-1860), married Maria Elizabeth (N) (1807-1870) probably circa 1828 (West Nottingham Cemetery tombstone inscriptions)

Egan, John, married Elizabeth R. (N) (1810-1899) probably in the 1830s (Hopewell United Methodist Church Cemetery tombstone inscription for Elizabeth Egan)

EGNER

Egner, Elizabeth, see Andrew Huggins

Egner, John W. (born c1819, Delaware) (carpenter near Elkton), married Matilda (N) (born c1822, Maryland) probably circa 1840; son Robert Egner born c1841 (1860 Cecil County Census)

Egner, Margaret, see Thomas Holland

Egner, Mary, see Rensselaer Biddle

Egner, Robert, see John W. Egner

ELDERDICE

Elderdice, John (reverend), married Louisa (N) (1812-1875) probably circa 1835 (*Cecil Whig*, 1 May 1875)

ELIASON

Eliason, Jeremiah, married Ann Killen circa 9 Mar 1825 (date of license) by Rev. Chambers (Cecil County Marriage License Book)

Eliason, John A., married Ellinor M. Frazier circa 30 Oct 1847 (date of license) (Cecil County Marriage License Book; DAR transcript copied in 1955 spelled his name Elliason)

ELDRIDGE

Eldridge, Deborah, see Job Eldridge

Eldridge, Job, of Philadelphia, son of William and Deborah Eldridge, of New Jersey, married Mrs. Sarah A. Stubbs, daughter of Parkes and Hannah Askew, on the 23rd day of the 3rd month 1843 at East Nottingham (*Births, Deaths and Marriages of the Nottingham Quakers, 1680-1899*, by Alice L. Beard (1989), p. 225)

Eldridge, Joseph M. (c1810-1859), of the First District, Cecil Co., married 1st to Mary (N) (1811-1852) probably circa 1831 and married 2nd to Anna Tyson (1805-1882) of Philadelphia (St. Stephen's Episcopal Church Cemetery tombstone inscriptions; *Cecil Democrat and Farmer's Journal*, 22 Apr 1882)

Eldridge, William, see Job Eldridge

ELLIOTT

Elliott, Benjamin, married Mary Rock circa 1 Mar 1828 (date of license) (Cecil County Marr. License Book)

Elliott, James (born c1823, England) (machinist), married Elizabeth (N) (born c1822, Delaware) circa 1846; daughter Helen Elliott born c1847, Maryland (1860 Cecil County Census)

ELLIS

Ellis, Anna Eliza, see Washington Hyland

Ellis, Araminta, see Hezekiah Foard

Ellis, Francis Asbury (1806-1887, born Pennsylvania) (attorney at Elkton), married Eliza Ann Howard (1809-1861, born Maryland) on 2 Oct 1833, after obtaining a license that same day, by Rev. Hagany (Cecil County Marriage License Book; Elkton Methodist Church Register, p. 5; 1860 Cecil County Census; Elkton Cemetery tombstone inscriptions)

Ellis, Mary E., see James T. Walmsley

Ellis, Rowland, married Elizabeth Hyland circa 14 Nov 1831 (date of license) by Rev. Rees (Cecil County Marriage License Book)

ELLISON

Ellison, James M., of New Castle Co., DE, married Sarah J. Deputy, daughter of Joshua Deputy, Esq., of Kent Co., MD, on 6 Jun 1850 by Rev. M. E. Ellison of the N. J. Conference (*Cecil Whig*, 8 Jun 1850)

Ellison, Lewis P., married Miss Susan M. Stuckert (1821-1875), daughter of Dr. William Stuckert, of Philadelphia, probably circa 1840 and she died at Town Point, MD in 1875 (*Cecil Whig*, 16 Jan 1875)

Ellison, Lewis Jr., of New Castle Co., DE, married Miss Elizabeth W. Deputy, daughter of Joshua Deputy, of Cecil Co., on 12 Jun 1845, after obtaining a license in Kent Co., MD, on 9 Jun 1845, by Rev. M. Ellison of the New Jersey Conference (*Cecil Whig*, 28 Jun 1845; Kent County Marriage License Book spelled his name Louis and indicated that he was from Cecil County and she was from New Castle Co., Delaware)

ELSEROAD

Elseroad, Sarah Jane, see William Downey

EMERSON

Emerson, William H. (born c1816) (farmer at Cecilton), married 1st to (N) probably circa 1840 and married 2nd to Sophia Josephine Ruley (born c1831) circa 21 Feb 1849 (date of license) (Cecil County Marriage License Book; 1860 Cecil County Census listed his children as [by his 1st wife] Alexander, age 18, and Martha, age 15, and [by his 2nd wife] William, age 10, Isabella, age 7, and Samuel, age 2 months)

EMMONS

Emmons, Caleb, married Eleanor Ann Kyle circa 25 Oct 1832 (date of license) by Rev. Rees (Cecil County Marriage License Book; DAR transcript copied in 1955 misspelled the minister's name as Reese; William Henry Rees was a Protestant Episcopal minister in Elkton at that time)

Emmons, Edward J. (1800, Davenport, Delaware Co., NY - 1849, Philadelphia, PA) (lawyer, judge, and justice of the peace in Cecil County in 1829), married Mary Ann (N) probably circa 1825-1828 and they later resided in Port Deposit before removing to Philadelphia; daughter Indiana Cordelia Emmons born 19 Jul 1829; son (N) born c1831, died young; daughter Evalina Physick Emmons married Dr. Joseph Janvier Woodward II (1833-1883), of Philadelphia, on 18 Sep 1857 in Cecil County (license dated 14 Sep 1857); son Edward Emmons born c1832; daughter Harriet Ann Emmons born 14 Nov 1838 (Family research by Dana Dunbar King, of Richmond, Virginia, in 1999)

Emmons, Evalina Physick, see Edward J. Emmons

Emmons, Harriet Ann, see Edward J. Emmons

Emmons, Indiana Cordelia, see Edward J. Emmons

Emmons, John (born c1794, Maryland) (carpenter), married Mary (N) (born c1810, Maryland) probably circa 1829; son John Emmons, Jr. born c1830, Maryland, carpenter (1850 Cecil County Census)

Emmons, Mary E., see John H. Holland

EMORY

Emory, Hannah, see Joshua Davis

Emory, Frances Anne Hopper, see James Massey Seegar

Emory, John King Beck, see James Massey Seegar

Emory, Stephen, married Mary Ann Lucas circa 2 Aug 1841 (date of license) (Cecil County Marriage License Book)

ENALS

Enals, Levy (born c1830) (African American) (laborer at St. Augustine), married Jemima (N) (born c1822) (African American) probably circa 1846; son Joseph Enals born c1847 (1860 Cecil County Census)

ENDRESS

Endress, Jacob, of Elkton, married Miss Caroline Schwarz, of Philadelphia, on 10 Dec 1848 by Rev. Reichert in Philadelphia (*Cecil Democrat and Farmer's Journal*, 23 Dec 1848)

ENGLAND

England, Elisha, see John England, Samuel England, Elisha Hughes England and William Kirk

England, Elisha Hughes (1813-1869, born Maryland) (farmer near Brick Meeting House), son of Elisha England and Elizabeth Van Horn, married Anna Elizabeth Jones (1819-1906, born Maryland) on 7 Jan 1844 by Rev. Huloise (*Joseph England and his Descendants*, by C. Walter England, Ph.D., 1975, p. 199; Rosebank Cemetery, at Calvert, tombstone inscriptions; 1860 Cecil County Census)

England, Elizabeth, see John White and John Rawlings Abrams

England, George (1826-1850) (carpenter), son of Samuel John England and Esther Haines, married Mary E. Brown (c1826-1885, Lancaster Co., PA), daughter of Nathan and Rachel Brown, on 11 Feb 1847; Mary (Brown) England married 2nd to John Lake Gregg (blacksmith, Cecil Co.) on the 3rd day of the 11th month 1853 (*Joseph England and his Descendants*, by C. Walter England, Ph.D., 1975, p. 291, stated he died in Philadelphia, but the *Cecil Whig*, 31 Aug 1850, stated he died at Brick Meeting House in Cecil County)

England, George, see Charles Gamble, Haines England and Samuel John England

England, Haines (1830-1886) (carpenter and farmer in the 9th District), son of George England and Mary Kirk, married Annie E. (N) on 10 Apr 1850 and married 2nd to Elizabeth S. Fisher in 1872 (*Joseph England and his Descendants*, by C. Walter England, Ph.D., 1975, p. 176)

England, Hannah Brown, see William Kirk

England, Isaac, see Joseph Townsend England

England, Isaac H., see Joseph Townsend England

England, John (1800-1876, born Maryland) (farmer and undertaker near Brick Meeting House), son of Elisha England and Mary Kirk, married 1st to Mary Kirk (1805-1841), daughter of William Kirk and Elizabeth Howell, on the 22nd day of the 5th month 1826 and married 2nd to Sarah Gamble (born c1820, Maryland) on the 15th day of the 6th month 1843 (*Joseph England and his Descendants*, by C. Walter England, Ph.D., 1975, p. 147; 1860 Cecil County Census)

England, John (1822-1901) (carpenter), son of Samuel John England and Esther Haines, married Mary Sophia Young (c1825-1898), daughter of Peter and Sophia Young, of Philadelphia, on 7 Aug 1847 and died in Philadelphia (*Joseph England and his Descendants*, by C. Walter England, Ph.D., 1975, p. 291)

England, Joseph (born c1811, Maryland) (farmer near Brick Meeting House), married Ruth (N) (born c1819, Maryland) probably circa 1841; son Samuel England born c1842, Maryland (1860 Cecil County Census)

England, Joseph Townsend (1821-1900), of near Zion, son of Isaac England (1785-1877) and Maria Haines (1800-1882), married Mary Ann Alexander (1824-1909), of near Zion, daughter of Joseph Alexander, on 31 Jan 1850 in New London, PA and had three children, namely, Isaac H. England (1853-1909), Leroy England and Helen Cook (*Portrait and Biographical Record of Harford and Cecil Counties, Maryland* (1897, repr. 1989), p. 335; Rosebank Cemetery, at Calvert, tombstone inscriptions; *Joseph England and his Descendants*, by C. Walter England, Ph.D., 1975, p. 243)

England, Leroy, see Joseph Townsend England

England, Mary E., see George England

England, Nancy Ann, see Elisha England Kirk

England, Robert Haines (1824, near Brick Meeting House, Cecil Co. - 1903, Culpeper Co., VA) (carpenter and miller), son of Samuel John England and Esther Haines, married Sarah Ann Newton (1827-1915), daughter of Aaron B. and Zilpha Newton, on the 5th day of the 11th month 1846 (license dated 31 Oct 1846) (Cecil County Marriage License Book; DAR transcript copied in 1928 listed him without a middle name; *Joseph England and his Descendants*, by C. Walter England, Ph.D., 1975, p. 29)

England, Samuel, see Joseph England

England, Samuel (1816, Cecil Co. – 1847, Phillips, NE) (carpenter near Brick Meeting House), son of Elisha England and Elizabeth Van Horn, married Mary Jane Gregg (1822-1884, born Pennsylvania), daughter of John and Acentha Gregg, on 29 Aug 1843 at Brick Meeting House by S. Spear (*Joseph England and his Descendants*, by C. Walter England, Ph.D., 1975, p. 199; 1860 Cecil County Census)

England, Samuel John, see John England, Robert Haines England, George England, Stephen John Brown and Charles Parker

England, Sarah, see Elisha Brown and Levi Alexander Hill

England, Sarah A., see Stephen J. Brown

ENNIS
Ennis, Ellen, see John Radley

EPP
Epp, John, married Elizabeth Gritz or Gintz circa 15 Oct 1834 (date of license) by Rev. Goforth (Cecil County Marriage License Book)

ERSEMBREY
Ersembrey, Peter, of Kent Co., married Mrs. Catherine Preston, of Havre de Grace, Harford Co., on 21 Oct 1837 by Rev. Goldsborough in Havre de Grace (*Cecil Courier*, 4 Nov 1837)

ESTES
Estes, Catharine L., see Matthew Cantwell

Estes, Samuel (1800-1872), married Anna E. (N) (1804-1865) probably circa 1825 and was a resident of Elkton 30 years before his death (Elkton Presbyterian Church Cemetery tombstone inscriptions; *Cecil Whig*, 14 Oct 1865 and 16 Mar 1872, the latter misspelled his name Estus)

ETHERINGTON
Etherington, Ann E., see James Stanley

Etherington, Elizabeth, see Benjamin Cox

Etherington, James, see James Stanley

Etherington, Nelly, see Robert Hayes

Etherington, Sarah E., see James Stanley

Etherington, William G., married Ann Elizabeth Davis circa 27 Jan 1835 (date of license) by Rev. Duke (Cecil County Marriage License Book)

EVANS

Evans, Amos Standly, see John Patterson Evans

Evans, Ann M., see William J. Brown

Evans, Catharine P., see William W. Black

Evans, Edward, married Ellen Kimble circa 28 Jul 1834 (date of license) by Rev. Hammill (Cecil County Marriage License Book)

Ewing, Elisha R. (1822-1914), married Louisa (N) (1824-1904) probably circa 1844 (St. John's Church Cemetery, at Lewisville, tombstone inscriptions)

Evans, Eliza, see John Slack

Evans, Elizabeth A., see Elisha Foster

Evans, George, married Deborah Drennen circa 4 Jun 1828 (date of license) by Rev. Graham (Cecil County Marriage License Book)

Evans, Hannah M., see Laurence Sentman

Evans, Isaac, of Town Point, MD, married Hannah (N) (1807-1873) probably circa 1827 (*Cecil Whig*, 25 Jan 1873)

Evans, Isabella S., see Henry B. Broughton

Evans, James Hugh, see John Patterson Evans

Evans, James, married Jane Arbuckle Porter, fourth daughter of Col. James L. Porter, late of Cecil Co., on 13 Dec 1838 by Rev. Rutter of Lancaster Co., PA (*Cecil Gazette*, 22 Dec 1838)

Evans, Jane, see Ephraim Thompson Mitchell

Evans, Joel, married Margaret Scott circa 16 Aug 1831 (date of license) by Rev. Rees (Cecil County Marriage License Book)

Evans, John Patterson (1814-1892) (farmer, 6th District), son of James Evans and Mary Patterson, married Rebecca Steel (1809-1891), daughter of Hugh and Esther Steel, of Port Deposit, on 23 Nov 1843 after obtaining a license on 22 Nov 1843 (Cecil County Marriage License Book; DAR transcript copied in 1955 mistakenly listed their names as James P. Evans and Rebecca Steele; *Portrait and Biographical Record of Harford and Cecil Counties, Maryland* (1897, repr. 1989), pp. 126-128, listed their three sons: James Hugh Evans, born 1 Nov 1844; William Steel Evans, born 16 Dec 1846; and, Amos Standley Evans, born 5 Aug 1848) (West Nottingham Cemetery tombstone inscriptions; *Midland Journal*, 11 Sep 1891, stated that she died near Elkton; 1860 Cecil County Census)

Evans, Martha S., see James M. Steel

Evans, Mary, see William Stanton

Evans, Mary Ann, see Zadock Veach

Evans, Mary Eliza, see William Hollingsworth

Evans, Rebecca, see Gustavus Giles

Evans, Samuel, married Mary E. Phillips circa 11 Jan 1839 (date of license) by Rev. McIntire (Cecil County Marriage License Book)

Evans, Thomas, married Mary Hall circa 18 Feb 1826 (date of license) by Rev. Sharpley (Cecil County Marriage License Book)

Evans, William Steel, see John Patterson Evans

EVERETT

Everett, Clarissa, see Jeremiah Woodrow

EVERHAM

Everham, Sarah J., see John H. Krauss

EVERIST

Everist, John S., married 1st to (N) and married 2nd to Mary Patten (1807-1891), "daughter of the widow Patten," on 19 May 1842, after obtaining a license on 10 May 1842, by Rev. Burroughs (*Cecil Whig*, 28 May 1842; Cecil County Marriage License Book; *Midland Journal*, 25 Sep 1891, reported that Mary

Patten Everist, wife of John S. Everist, died at age 84 in the 6th District and her obituary also mentioned her daughter Mrs. Ellen M. Tosh and her stepchildren Francis S. Everist and Mrs. Mary E. Henderson)

EVES

Eves, Amos F., married Ann Ellen Carson circa 25 Jan 1847 (date of license) (Cecil Co. Marr. License Book)

Eves, Mary C., see Thomas J. Gillespie

EWELL

Ewell, Daniel F. (born c1815) (Methodist clergyman at Warwick), married (N) (born c1825, Maryland) circa 1849; daughter Mary J. Sewell born c1850 (1860 Cecil County Census listed them as Dr. and Mrs. Ewell; *Directory of Ministers and the Maryland Churches They Served, 1634-1990*, by Edna A. Kanely, p. 212)

EWING

Ewing, Amos (1793-1872), married Mary Steel (1801-1884) circa 11 Apr 1832 (date of license) by Rev. Magraw (Cecil County Marriage License Book; West Nottingham Cemetery tombstone inscriptions)

Ewing, Elizabeth, see Jonathan M. Lewis

Ewing, Elizabeth A., see John H. Jones

Ewing, George R., married Lydia Ward circa 22 Sep 1847 (date of license) (Cecil Co. Marr. License Book)

Ewing, James, married Martha Barnes circa 21 Feb 1832 (date of license) by Rev. Griffith (Cecil County Marriage License Book)

Ewing, James J. (1808-1879) (blacksmith, 6th District), married Agnes G. (N) (1805-1881) probably circa 1830 (Hopewell United Methodist Church Cemetery tombstone inscriptions; 1860 Cecil County Census)

Ewing, John, married Mary Jane Phillips circa 24 Dec 1833 (date of license) by Rev. Duke (Cecil County Marriage License Book)

Ewing, Rachel, see John Riddell

Ewing, William Penn (1822-1903) (farmer, 6th District), married Margaret Elizabeth Horton (1821-1856) circa 29 Mar 1849 (date of license) (Cecil County Marriage License Book; West Nottingham Cemetery tombstone inscriptions; 1860 Cecil County Census)

FAIRLAMB

Fairlamb, Henry V., married Jane Kee circa 7 Aug 1850 (date of license) (Cecil County Marr. License Book)

FALLS

Falls, Elijah (born c1808, Pennsylvania) (cooper and farmer near Principio), son of Hugh Falls (of Ireland, later of Pennsylvania and Cecil Co., died 1816), married Emily Riddle (c1811-1886, born Maryland) circa 13 Jun 1835 (date of license) by Rev. Cramer (Cecil County Marriage License Book; DAR transcript copied in 1928 mistakenly listed his name as Elmer; *Portrait and Biographical Record of Harford and Cecil Counties, Maryland* (1897, repr. 1989), p.296, stated their son J. Wesley Falls was born 31 May 1835 and the 1860 Cecil County Census stated son John Falls was aged 25)

Falls, Hugh, see Elijah Falls

Falls, John, see Elijah Falls

Falls, William (born c1819, Ireland) (innkeeper in Elkton), married Miss Mary Jane DeHaven (1821-1877, born Pennsylvania) on 5 Jan 1843, after obtaining a license on 4 Jan 1843, by Rev. McIntire and she died at Howard House in Elkton in 1877 (Cecil County Marriage License Book; Elkton Presbyterian Church Cemetery tombstone inscription; 1860 Cecil County Census; *Cecil Whig*, 7 Jan 1843 and 17 Nov 1877)

FARNLEY

Farnley, Lydia Ann, see Moses Gallaher

FARR

Farr, William, see Lyttleton Physick

FARRA

Farra, D. W. (born c1824, Delaware) (postmaster at Chesapeake City), married Mary (N) (born c1822, Delaware) probably circa 1848; son William Farra was born c1849, Delaware, daughter Sue Farra was born c1854, Maryland, and daughter Cary Farra was born c1859, Maryland (1860 Cecil County Census)

Farra, Harriet F. and John, see Francis Vincent

FARRAN

Farran, Elizabeth, see John Jordan

FARRELL

Farrell, Elizabeth, see Maurice Flinn

Farrell, Joseph (born c1818, Pennsylvania) (African American apprentice at Cecilton), married Sarah (N) (born c1825, Pennsylvania) (African American) circa 1845; son Lewis born c1846 (1860 Cecil Census)

FARROW

Farrow, Ann, see Edward L. Osborn

FAULKNER

Faulkner, Robert, married Elizabeth Price circa 24 Jan 1835 (date of license) by Rev. Duke (Cecil County Marriage License Book)

FAY

Fay, William (1817-1900), married Martha J. (N) (1822-1898) probably circa 1840 (St. John's Church Cemetery, at Lewisville, tombstone inscriptions)

FELL

Fell, Watson, married Lydia Ann Reynolds circa 6 Nov 1850 (date of license) (Cecil County Marriage License Book)

FERGUSON

Ferguson, Araminta, see Stephen Hodgson

Ferguson, Benjamin, married Harriet Ann Cooper circa 12 Sep 1832 (date of license) by Rev. Magraw (Cecil County Marriage License Book)

Ferguson, Benjamin (captain), married Rebecca Jane Black circa 27 Oct 1845 (date of license) (Cecil County Marriage License Book spelled his name Furguson; DAR transcript copied in 1955 spelled it Furgason, but did not indicate he was a captain)

Ferguson, Eliza, see Ebenezer Lutton

Ferguson, Elizabeth Jane, see John Huss Mahoney

Ferguson, Enoch M. (1815-1874), married Margaret J. (N) (1818-1869) circa 1840; buried beside Hugh T. Ferguson, 1847-1902, and Mary J. Ferguson, 1841-1889 (Rosebank Cemetery, at Calvert, tombstones)

Ferguson, George (born c1814, Maryland) (blacksmith in the 8th District), married Eliza (N) (born c1814, Delaware) probably circa 1838; daughter Pheby Ferguson born c1839, Maryland, and all their other children were also born in Maryland (1860 Cecil County Census)

Ferguson, George, married Miss Sarah Jane Alexander, both of Cecil Co., on 14 Feb 1850, after obtaining a license on 11 Feb 1850, by Rev. Elliott (Cecil County Marriage License Book; *Cecil Democrat and Farmer's Journal*, 23 Feb 1850; *Cecil Whig*, 23 Feb 1850)

Ferguson, Henrietta, see John E. Ferguson

Ferguson, Hugh T., see Enoch M. Ferguson

Ferguson, John, see William Ferguson

Ferguson, John (1822-1894), married Hannah Elizabeth McKinsey (1829-1864), eldest daughter of Tobias and Maria McKinsey, circa 2 Oct 1847 (date of license) (Cecil County Marriage License Book spelled his name Furguson; Cherry Hill Methodist Church Cemetery tombstones; *Cecil Whig*, 16 Jul 1864)

Ferguson, John E. (born c1828) (farmer at Cecilton), married Margaret Emma Jones (born c1830) circa 1 Feb 1850 (date of license); daughter Henrietta Ferguson born c1851 (Cecil County Marriage License Book spelled his name Forguson; 1860 Cecil County Census)

Ferguson, John Edward, see William Ferguson

Ferguson, Marshel H., married Miss Margaret Ann Jackson, both of Cecil Co., on 15 Jan 1846, after obtaining a license on 14 Jan 1846, by Rev. Humphries (Cecil County Marriage License Book spelled his name Marshel; DAR transcript copied in 1955 spelled it Marshall; *Cecil Whig*, 14 Feb 1846, listed his name as Marshel H. Furguson)

Ferguson, Mary J., see Enoch M. Ferguson

Ferguson, Pheby, see George Ferguson

Ferguson, Phoebe Ann, see Joseph Pennock

Ferguson, Sarah, see Isaac S. Crips

Ferguson, William, married Henrietta Mary Porter circa 31 Dec 1825 (date of license) by Rev. Davis (Cecil County Marriage License Book); Henrietta M. Ferguson, of Cecil Co., divorced from William Ferguson on 1 Mar 1832; son John mentioned in will of John Edward Ferguson, Sr., late of Cecil Co., and Henrietta was heir of Benjamin Porter, late of Cecil Co.; also, the divorce decree indicated that son John Ferguson would not be illegitimized (*Divorces and Names Changed in Maryland by Act of the Legislature, 1634-1867*, by Mary Keysor Meyer (1991), p. 31)

Ferguson, William, married Susan Thompson circa 26 Mar 1831 (date of license) by Rev. Magraw (Cecil County Marriage License Book)

Ferguson, William, married Maria Grant circa 1 Jun 1831 (date of license) by Rev. Barratt (Cecil County Marriage License Book)

FERRY

Ferry, John O., married Susan Alexander circa 28 Feb 1826 (date of license) by Rev. Duke (Cecil County Marriage License Book)

Ferry, (N), married Mary (N) (1819-1891) probably circa 1840 and she died in her 72nd year in Elkton (*Midland Journal*, 6 Mar 1891)

FIELDS

Fields, Bryan (1800-1883) (born England) (farmer at Bay View), married Mary (N) (1807-1893) (born Pennsylvania) probably circa 1825 (1860 Cecil County Census; Bethel Methodist Church, at North East, tombstone inscriptions)

Fields, David, married Eleanor H. Boulden, daughter of Nathan Boulden, Esq., both of New Castle Co., Delaware, on 10 May 1842 by Rev. McIntire (*Cecil Whig*, 14 May 1842)

FILLINGAME

Fillingame, Dorinda, see James C. Logue

Fillingame, Elizabeth, see Nicholas Vandegrift

Fillingame, George M., married Susan Arrants circa 8 Sep 1847 (date of license) (Cecil County Marriage License Book)

Fillingame, John W., married Miss Ann Irons, both of Cecil Co., on 14 Dec 1848, after obtaining a license on 30 Nov 1848, by Rev. Elliott (Cecil County Marriage License Book; *Cecil Democrat and Farmer's Journal*, 23 Dec 1848)

Fillingame, Lydia Ann, see William Donaldson

Fillingame, Richard, married Mary Biddle circa 31 Jan 1831 (date of license) by Rev. Smith (Cecil County Marriage License Book)

Fillingame, Susanna, see Joseph H. Brooks and John Martin

FINLEY

Finley, James B. (1794-1851, born at South Bend, Indiana) (doctor), married Mary E. M. (N) (1805-1888) probably circa 1825 (Elkton Cemetery tombstone inscriptions)

Finley, James H., of Port Carbon, PA, married Sarah Lydia Williamson, of Wilmington, DE, eldest daughter of the late James Williamson of Cecil Co., MD, on 30 Apr 1850 by the Mayor of Philadelphia (*Cecil Whig*, 4 May 1850)

FINNEGAN

Finnegan, Patricus, married Jane Gallaher circa 21 Sep 1830 (date of license) by Rev. Reece (Cecil County Marriage License Book)

FISH

Fish, Eliza, of Cecil Co., divorced from John Fish on 10 Feb 1825 (*Divorces and Names Changed in Maryland by Act of the Legislature, 1634-1867*, by Mary Keysor Meyer (1991), p. 31)

FISHER

Fisher, Andrew, married Caroline Yeamans circa 31 Oct 1837 (date of license) by Rev. Burrows (Cecil County Marriage License Book)

Fisher, Angeline K., see Granville T. Brown

Fisher, Clara, see James Caspard Maeder

Fisher, Elizabeth S., see Haines England

Fisher, Jane, see (N) Scott

Fisher, John (born c1830, Maryland) (farmhand in the 7th District), married Sarah E. Oldham (born c1830, Maryland) circa 15 Nov 1843 (date of license) (Cecil County Marriage License; 1860 Cecil Co. Census)

Fisher, Margaret, see (N) Scott

Fisher, Mary, see Thomas Rutter

Fisher, Rebecca, see Joseph Murphy

Fisher, Samuel, married Jane Scott circa 20 Oct 1830 (date of license) by Rev. Griffith (Cecil County Marriage License Book)

Fisher, Sarah, see (N) Scott

FLECK

Fleck, Jacob, married Miss Comfort Hudson, both of Cecil Co., on 6 Jan 1835, after obtaining a license on 1 Jan 1835, by Rev. Wilson (Cecil County Marriage License Book; DAR transcript copied in 1928 misspelled her first name Cumford; *Cecil Gazette*, 10 Jan 1835)

FLEHEARTY

Flehearty, Catherine, see Thomas McMullen

FLEMMER

Flemmer, James, married Mary Beers circa 3 Apr 1850 (date of license) (Cecil County Marriage License Book; DAR transcript copied in 1955 misspelled his name as Fleminer)

FLEMING

Fleming, Henry, see Jeremiah B. Haines

Fleming, Joanna, see John Cowhey

FLETCHER

Fletcher, Annie, see Bennett Charshee

FLINN

Flinn, Maurice, married Elizabeth Farrell on 22 May 1825, after obtaining a license that same day, by Rev. Epinette (Cecil County Marriage License Book; DAR transcript copied in 1928 listed their names as Morris Flinn and Elizabeth Farral; *History of Saint Francis Xavier Church and Bohemia Plantation Now Known as Old Bohemia, Warwick, Maryland*, by Joseph C. Cann (1976), p. 47)

FLINTHAM

Flintham, George, of Cecil Co., married Miss Sarah Ann Stanert or Stewart, of New Castle Co., DE, on board the steamboat *Kent* on her passage to Philadelphia on 25 Mar 1846 by Rev. Mason (*Cecil Whig*, 4 Apr 1845, spelled her name Stanert; *Delaware Gazette*, 31 Mar 1846, spelled it Stewart)

Flintham, John M. (c1792-1867) (War of 1812 veteran), married Mrs. Susan A. Craddock, both of Cecil Co., widow of Benedict Craddock (War of 1812 veteran who married Susan A. Hessey on 5 Jun 1835 in Wilmington, DE and died at Warwick in 1845), on 5 Jun 1849, after obtaining a license on 2 Jun 1849, by the Rev. Clark (Cecil County Marriage License Book; *Cecil Whig*, 9 Jun 1849, spelled her name Craddick; in 1855 the War of 1812 Bounty Land Application of Benedict's widow Susan stated she married second to John M. Flintham on 7 Jun 1849; *Cecil Democrat*, 13 Jul 1867)

Flintham, Sarah, see George B. Pennington

FLOUNDERS

Flounders, Sarah, see John W. Miller

FOARD

Foard, Edward B., married Sarah Severson circa 13 Sep 1826 (date of license) by Rev. Smith (Cecil County Marriage License Book)

Foard, Edward L. (1813-1865) (merchant), of Elkton, married Mary Ann Henry, daughter of Capt. James Henry, of New Castle Co., DE, on 26 Nov 1837 by Rev. Walker at Marcus Hook, PA (*Cecil Gazette*, 30 Dec 1837; *Cecil Whig*, 8 Apr 1865)

Foard, Emelie L., see James M. Mulford

Foard, Hezekiah, married Miss Araminta Ellis, both of Elkton, on 21 Feb 1843, after obtaining a license that same day, by Rev. McIntire (*Cecil Whig*, 25 Feb 1843; Cecil County Marriage License Book spelled his name Ford)

Foard, Hezekiah Jr., married Mary Ann Hyland circa 5 Nov 1828 (date of license) by Rev. Barratt (Cecil County Marriage License Book)

Foard, J. L., see James M. Mulford

Foard, James L. (born c1816) (farmer near Elkton), son of Dr. Josiah Foard and Lydia Caulk, of Elkton, married Martha Rebecca Hyland (born c1822), daughter of Stephen Hyland and Maria Kankey, of Elk Neck, on 11 Apr 1843, after obtaining a license that same day, by Rev. Barrett (*Cecil Whig*, 15 Apr 1843; Cecil County Marriage License Book spelled his name Foard; DAR transcript copied in 1955 listed it as Ford; *Portrait and Biographical Record of Harford and Cecil Counties, Maryland* (1897, repr. 1989), p. 504; 1860 Cecil County Census)

Foard, Jeremiah (born c1814, Maryland) (stove and tin manufacturer, 7th District), married Sophia Maulden (born c1819, Maryland), daughter of John Maulden, Esq., all of Cecil Co., on 8 Mar 1838, after obtaining a license on 5 Mar 1838, by Rev. Kennard (Cecil County Marriage License Book; *Cecil Gazette*, 17 Mar 1838, spelled his name Ford and her name Mauldin; 1860 Cecil County Census spelled his name Ford)

Foard, Josiah, see James L. Foard

Foard, Millicent, see Joseph T. Stout

Foard, Richard J., of Cecil Co., married Miss Susan Jefferson, of New Castle Co., DE, on 16 Sep 1834 by Rev. Hagany (*Cecil Gazette*, 27 Sep 1834)

Foard, also see Ford

FOLEY

Foley, Ann, see John McEnestry

FOOT

Foot, Harriet, see William E. Moore

FORD

Ford, Alfred, see John Ford

Ford, Ann Eliza, see William Hackett

Ford, Ann Maria, see Lambert D. Nowland

Ford, Ann Rebecca, see Reuben D. Jamar

Ford, Arabella V., see James Ford

Ford, Caroline, see John B. Hagany

Ford, Charles, see John Ford

Ford, Cornelia, see Benjamin Walmsley

Ford, Edwin, see John Ford

Ford, Edward B., married Rosetta H. Lusby circa 18 Apr 1835 (date of license) by Rev. Duke (Cecil County Marriage License Book; DAR transcript copied in 1928 mistakenly listed his name as Edwin D. Ford)

Ford, Elizabeth, see David Biddle

Ford, Elmira, see Josiah Hall

Ford, Frederick A., see George A. Ford

Ford, George A. (born c1819) (merchant at Cecilton), married Laura E. (N) (born c1825) circa 1849; son Frederick A. Ford born c1850 (1860 Cecil County Census)

Ford, Isaac Henry, see John Ford

Ford, James, married Margaret Davis circa 1 Mar 1830 (date of license) by Rev. Duke (Cecil County Marriage License Book)

Ford, James (born c1805), married Temperance E. Myers (born c1816) circa 26 Jan 1833 (date of license) by Rev. Duke; daughter Arabella V. Ford born c1839 (Cecil County Marriage License Book; 1860 Cecil County Census)

Ford, James S., see Stephen H. Ford

Ford, John (1805-1891) (farmer and preacher at North East), married Elizabeth Simpers (1807-1876) circa 19 Dec 1827 (date of license) and lived at Oldfield Point (Cecil County Marriage License Book; DAR transcript copied in 1928 listed his name as Foard; North East Methodist Church Cemetery tombstone inscriptions; *Portrait and Biographical Record of Harford and Cecil Counties, Maryland* (1897, repr. 1989), p. 504, spelled his name Ford and stated they had eleven children and seven were living in 1897, namely, Charles, John Fletcher, Samuel (captain) [and merchant, born c1832], Margaret (unmarried) [born c1837], Alfred [born c1850, brick manufacturer at North East in 1871], I. [Isaac] Henry (born 21 Oct 1845) and Sarah M. (unmarried) [born c1851]; 1860 Cecil County Census listed three other children: Thomas (carpenter, born c1833), Edwin (born c1839) and Wilkeford (born c1841, farmhand); *Cecil Whig*, 17 Jun 1871; *Midland Journal*, 23 Oct 1891)

Ford, John Fletcher, see John Ford

Ford, Lambert G. (captain) (born c1822, Maryland) (tailor near Elkton), married Miss Harriet Brock (born c1828, Pennsylvania), both of Elk Neck, on 20 Mar 1844, after obtaining a license that same day, by Rev. Goentner (*Cecil Whig*, 30 Mar 1844; Cecil County Marriage License Book; 1860 Cecil County Census)

Ford, Margaret, see Richard Edwards and John Ford

Ford, Millicent, see Joseph T. Stout

Ford, Samuel, see John Ford

Ford, Sarah M., see John Ford

Ford, Stephen H., married Miss Maria S. Dawson, both of Cecil Co., on 16 Dec 1834, after obtaining a license on 15 Dec 1834, by Rev. Duke (Cecil County Marriage License Book; *Cecil Gazette*, 20 Dec

1834; 1860 Cecil County Census listed Maria S. Ford, age 59, as head of household in Cecilton, with James S. Ford, age 24, and Stephen H. Ford, age 22)

Ford, Thomas, see John Ford

Ford, Thomas (born c1821, Maryland) (farmer at Warwick), married Helen M. Wheeler (born c1821, Maryland) circa 30 Sep 1845 (date of license) (Cecil County Marriage License Book; 1860 Census)

Ford, Wilkeford, see John Ford

Ford, also see Foard

FOREACRE

Foreacre, Hester Ann, see Thomas Bryson

Foreacre, Robert, married Martha M. Short, daughter of Jeremiah Short, on 19 Jun 1849, after obtaining a license that same day, by Rev. Goldsborough in Trinity Church (*Cecil Democrat and Farmer's Journal*, 23 Jun 1849; Cecil County Marriage License Book spelled his name Foracre)

FORMAN, FOREMAN

Forman (Foreman), Francis E. (esquire), of Baltimore City, married Eliza Jane Miller, daughter of Samuel Miller, Esq., of Cecil Co., on 13 Jun 1850, after obtaining a license that same day, by Rev. Mann (Cecil County Marriage License Book spelled his name Forman; *Cecil Democrat and Farmer's Journal*, 15 Jun 1850, spelled it Foreman)

Forman (Foreman), General, see John Burke and Stephen Bayard

Forman, James, see James Tarman (Tarnan)

FORTNIER, FORTINER

Fortnier (Fortiner), Charles C., married Rebecca Ann Hance circa 14 Jan 1846 (date of license) (Cecil County Marriage License Book; 1850 Cecil County Census Index listed his name as Fortner)

FOSTER

Foster, Ann, see Ebenezer Mayberry and Washington Holt

Foster, Catharine, see William H. Wilson

Foster, Charles T. Ford (1812-1871), married Elizabeth Robinson (1811-1887) circa 24 Jun 1841 (date of license) (Cecil County Marriage License Book listed his name as Charles T. F. Foster; DAR Typescript copied in 1955 listed his name as Charles P. F. Foster; North East Methodist Church Cemetery tombstone inscriptions inscribed his name as Charles Ford Foster; *Cecil Whig*, 23 Sep 1871)

Foster, Edith, see John Brown

Foster, Elisha, married Elizabeth A. Evans circa 25 Jan 1839 (date of license) by Rev. Barratt (Cecil County Marriage License Book)

Foster, Elisha, married Eliza Lane circa 25 Mar 1847 (date of license) (Cecil County Marr. License Book)

Foster, Elizabeth, see Eli Pearson and Jacob Holden

Foster, Francis A. (born c1818) (cabinet maker at North East), married Caroline R. Onion (born c1826), of Baltimore County, circa 7 Oct 1844 (date of license) (Cecil County Marriage License Book; 1860 Cecil County Census)

Foster, Frederick (born c1822, Maryland) (laborer at Chesapeake City), married Sarah (N) (born c1831) probably circa 1849l daughter Laura Foster born c1850, Maryland (1860 Cecil County Census)

Foster, Harman, married Frances Jay (or Joy?) circa 5 Jan 1829 (date of license) by Rev. Barratt (Cecil County Marriage License Book)

Foster, James, see Robert P. Hays

Foster, Jesse, see Washington Holt

Foster, John J. (1817-1895, born Maryland) (farmer, 6th District), married Frances S. Hall (1826-1892, born Maryland) circa 7 Feb 1849 (date of license) (Cecil County Marriage License Book; Hopewell United Methodist Church Cemetery tombstone inscriptions; 1860 Cecil County Census)

Foster, Laura, see Frederick Foster

Foster, Margaret Jane, see Joseph McKinney

Foster, Marjory, see Levi Lottman

Foster, Martha Jane, see John S. Inskip

Foster, Samuel (1819-1875, born Maryland) (farmer, 6th District, near Woodlawn), married Sarah J. Kelly (1820-1877, born Maryland) circa 6 Mar 1848 (date of license) (Cecil County Marriage License Book; Hopewell United Methodist Church Cemetery tombstone inscriptions; 1860 Cecil County Census; *Cecil Whig*, 21 Apr 1877)

Foster, Sarah Ann, see Robert P. Hays

Foster, Thomas J. (born c1805, Pennsylvania), later of Elkton, married Miss Rebecca Slagle (born c1811, Maryland) circa 27 Aug 1828 (date of license) by Rev. Barratt (Cecil County Marriage License Book; 1860 Cecil County Census)

Foster, William W., of New Castle, DE, married Elizabeth Ward, daughter of William Ward, of Cecil Co., on 29 Jun 1843, after obtaining a license that same day, by Rev. McIntire (Cecil County Marriage License Book; *Cecil Whig*, 15 Jul 1843)

FOUCHS

Fouchs, George (born c1818, Maryland) (carpenter at Chesapeake City), married Sarah (born c1829, Maryland) probably circa 1847; son Joseph born c1848 (1860 Cecil County Census)

FOUNDS

Founds, Joseph, married Hannah E. (N) (1815-1886) probably circa 1835 (Bethesda Cemetery, at Oakwood, tombstone inscription for Hannah E. Founds)

Founds, also see Phouns

FOWLER

Fowler, Benjamin P., married Mary Jane Maffitt circa 14 Sep 1835 (date of license) by Rev. Hammill (Cecil County Marriage License Book)

Fowler, Mary Jane, see Benjamin B. Chambers

Fowler, Rachel A., see Charles W. Maxwell

FOX

Fox, Justus, married Eliza Jane Gordon circa 20 Dec 1842 (date of license) (Cecil Co. Marr. License Book)

Fox, Margaret, see Hugh Boyd

FRANKLIN

Franklin, Evelina, see Lyttleton Physick

FRAZIER, FRAZER

Frazier, Ellinor M., see John A. Eliason

Frazier, John Jr., married Sarah E. Spencer (1829-1882) circa 6 Aug 1845 (date of license) (Cecil County Marriage License Book; *Cecil Democrat and Farmer's Journal*, 4 Feb 1882. obituary stated Sarah E. Frazier, relict of John Frazier, Jr., formerly of Kent Co., MD, died in her 53rd year in Philadelphia)

Frazer, James (1807-1872, born Delaware) (farmer at Elkton), married Emily (N) (1818-1895) probably circa 1836 and moved to Cecil Co. by 1851 (1860 Cecil County Census; Elkton Cemetery tombstone inscriptions; *Cecil Whig*, 6 Apr 1872)

FREDERICK

Frederick, Louisa, see August Raisin

FREEMAN

Freeman, Isaac (African American), married Hannah Young (African American) on 19 Sep 1844 by Rev. Shields (Elkton Methodist Church Register, p. 140; Cecil County Marriage License Book did not list it)

Freeman, John Wesley (born c1810) (carpenter at Elkton), married Araminta Johnson (born c1808) circa 28 Jun 1836 (date of license) by Rev. Potts (Cecil County Marr. License Book; 1860 Cecil County Census)

Freeman, Samuel H., married Harriet Thomas circa 24 Dec 1834 (date of license) by Rev. Morris (Cecil County Marriage License Book; DAR transcript copied in 1928 misspelled his first name as Damuel)

Freeman, William, married Rachel Ann Carpenter circa 23 Jan 1844 (date of license) (Cecil County Marriage License Book)

FRIEZE

Frieze, Noah, married Rebecca Thompson circa 26 Nov 1825 (date of license) by Rev. Talley (Cecil County Marriage License Book)

FRIST

Frist, Abraham B., married Miss Elizabeth C. Patterson on 12 Jun 1845, after obtaining a license on 11 Jun 1845, by Rev. Townsend near Perryville (*Cecil Whig*, 21 Jun 1845; Cecil County Marriage License Book; DAR transcript copied in 1955 listed his name without the middle initial; Patterson Family Cemetery tombstones for Martha Jane Frist (24 Oct 1849 - 5 Apr 1857) and Harlin L. Frist (7 Nov 1851 - 21 Oct 1855), children of "Abram and Elizzie Frist," but no markers found here for Abraham and Elizabeth)

FULTON

Fulton, Agatha R., see David Scott

Fulton, Alexander, see Thomas Fulton and Reuben Alexander, Jr.

Fulton, Caroline H., see Reuben Alexander, Jr.

Fulton, David, married Mary A. Wickworth circa 10 Jun 1842 (date of license) (Cecil County Marriage License Book)

Fulton, Eliza Ann, see William J. Fulton

Fulton, Elizabeth, see James Fulton and Jesse H. Simpers

Fulton, Ellen Jane, see Henry Armstrong

Fulton, George, see Thomas Cunningham

Fulton, Harriet, see Michael Sentman

Fulton, Jacob, see Jesse H. Simpers

Fulton, Jacob (born c1813) (farmer near Elkton), married Eveline (N) (born c1813) probably circa 1840; daughter Missouri Fulton born c1842 (1860 Cecil County Census)

Fulton, James (born c1824) (saddler at Elkton), married Menamy (N) (born c1830) probably circa 1849; daughter Elizabeth Fulton born c1850 (1860 Cecil County Census)

Fulton, John, see Minshall W. Fulton

Fulton, Maria, see Isaac J. Fulton

Fulton, Mary, see Lewis Boulden

Fulton, Mary Ann, see Thomas Cunningham

Fulton, Minshall W. (born c1823, Maryland) (merchant, 8th District), married Oscella (N) (born c1828, Maryland) probably circa 1850; son John Fulton born c1851, Maryland (1860 Cecil County Census)

Fulton, Missouri, see Jacob Fulton

Fulton, Rachel, see Reuben Alexander, Jr.

Fulton, Ruth Amelia, see William Oliver

Fulton, Sarah, see Samuel H. Weaver

Fulton, Thomas (born c1816) (laborer near Elkton), married Hannah Alexander (born c1821) circa 30 Jun 1843 (date of license) (Cecil County Marriage License Book; 1860 Cecil County Census)

Fulton, Thomas, married Catherine Porter circa 7 Apr 1846 (date of license) (Cecil Co. Marr. License Book)

Fulton, Thomas (born c1826, Maryland) (farmer in the, 8th District), married Amelia (N) (born c1824, Pennsylvania) probably circa 1847; son Alexander Fulton born c1848, Maryland, and their other children were also born in Maryland (1860 Cecil County Census)

Fulton, William J., married Eliza Ann Fulton circa 17 Dec 1845 (date of license) (Cecil County Marriage License Book; DAR transcript copied in 1955 listed his name without the middle initial)

FURNESS
Furness, Gardner, see James Gillespie

FURY
Fury, James, married Hannah Ann Cowan circa 1 Aug 1832 (date of license) by Rev. Duke (Cecil County Marriage License Book)

FUZZLE
Fuzzle, Sally, see John Miles

GAILY
Gaily, Jane, see Andrew J. Galbraith

GAINES
Gaines, E. P. (maj. gen., U. S. Army), married Mrs. Myra Clark Whitney, only daughter of the late Daniel Clark, Esq., of New Orleans, on 17 Apr 1839 by Rev. Clapp in New Orleans (*Cecil Gazette*, 4 May 1839)

GAINOR
Gainor, Thomas B. (1816-1890) (captain and sailor at North East), married Mary Barnett (1817-1892) circa 13 Dec 1836 (date of license) by Rev. Duke (Cecil County Marriage License Book; Hart's Methodist Church Cemetery tombstone inscriptions; 1860 Cecil County Census)

GALBRAITH
Galbraith, Andrew J., married Jane Gaily circa 24 Aug 1833 (date of license) by Rev. Goforth (Cecil County Marriage License Book; DAR transcript copied in 1928 spelled his name Gilbreath)

Galbraith, George H., married Maria M. Reynolds circa 24 May 1844 (date of license) (Cecil County Marriage License Book)

Galbraith, Isabella, see Nevin Orr

Galbraith, Sarah M., see William M. Townsend

Galbraith, (N), married Rosanna (N) (1814-1876) probably circa 1834; she died at the residence of J. H. Crawford in Wilmington, DE and was buried in Charlestown M. E. Cemetery (*Cecil Whig*, 3 Jun 1876)

GALE
Gale, Anna Maria, see Cornelius McClean, Jr.

Gale, George, see Cornelius McClean, Jr.

Gale, Georgeanna E., see Cornelius McClean, Jr.

Gale, Henrietta Elizabeth, see Richard Whittingham, Jr.

Gale, Mary W., see John Ward Morgan

GALLAGHER
Gallagher, Elizabeth, see John McCleary

Gallagher, Frances, see William J. Grant

Gallagher, Martha Jane, see Andrew Sisco

GALLAHAN

Gallahan, John W., married Maria Joice on 9 Nov 1837, after obtaining a license on 7 Nov 1837, by Rev. McFarland (Cecil County Marriage License Book; DAR transcript copied in 1928 misspelled her name as Boice and mistakenly listed the minister's name as Farland; James McFarland was a Methodist minister in Elkton at that time; Elkton Methodist Church Register, p. 138)

GALLAHER

Gallaher, Alice, see William J. Gallaher

Gallaher, Ann Jane, see John Armstrong

Gallaher, Anna M., see Isaac H. McKaig

Gallaher, Annie, see William J. Gallaher

Gallaher, Elizabeth, see John Weston Holt

Gallaher, Ellen, see William J. Gallaher

Gallaher, Enoch (1814-1886), married Mary (N) (1805-1872) probably circa 1835-1836 (Friends Cemetery, at Harrisville, tombstone inscriptions)

Gallaher, Francis, married Agnes McCullough circa 25 Oct 1826 (date of license) by Rev. Goforth (Cecil County Marriage License Book; DAR transcript copied in 1928 misspelled his name Goleober)

Gallaher, Jane, see Patricus Finnegan

Gallaher, John, see John Weston Holt

Gallaher, John, married Susan Logan circa 3 May 1828 (date of license) (Cecil County Marr. License Book)

Gallaher, John T. (1813-1891) (blacksmith at Elkton), married 1st to Sarah Morrison (1813-1841) on 1 Oct 1838, after obtaining a license that same day, by Rev. Hagany, and married 2nd to Hannah Amelia Hayes (1824-1899) circa 3 Nov 1844 (date of license) (Cecil County Marriage License Book; DAR transcript copied in 1955 misspelled his name as Gallalier; Elkton Methodist Church Register, p. 139; Leeds Methodist Church Cemetery tombstone inscriptions; *Midland Journal*, 31 Jul 1891, reported he died at his residence near Child's Station, B&O Railroad; 1860 Cecil Co. Census misspelled his name Gallagher)

Gallaher, Martha, see Thomas J. Davidson and John Weston Holt

Gallaher, Martha Ann, see William P. Strickland

Gallaher, Mary, see John Lowry, William J. Gallaher and William H. Chapman

Gallaher, Moses (born c1812) (coach maker at Elkton), married Lydia Ann Farnley (born c1816) circa 16 Apr 1834 (date of license) by Rev. Wilson (Cecil County Marr. License Book; 1860 Cecil Co. Census)

Gallaher, Nancy, see Richard Lee

Gallaher, Roberson, married Ellen Cameron circa 12 Sep 1842 (date of license) (Cecil County Marriage License Book spelled his first name Roberson; 1850 Cecil County Census spelled it Robinson)

Gallaher, Stewart H. (born c1815) (carpenter near Elkton), married Miss Araminta H. Barnes (born c1823), both of Cecil Co., on 6 Jul 1841, after obtaining a license on 5 Jul 1841, by Rev. Maddux (*Cecil Gazette*, 10 Jul 1841; Cecil County Marriage License Book; 1860 Cecil County Census)

Gallaher, William J. (born c1821, Maryland) (blacksmith at Elkton), married Mary E. McCrea (born c1825, Maryland) circa 26 Jun 1844 (date of license); daughter Annie Gallaher born c1850, Virginia, daughter Mary Gallaher born c1852, Virginia, daughter Ellen Gallaher born c1855, Virginia, and daughter Alice Gallaher born 1860, Maryland (Cecil County Marriage License Book; 1860 Cecil County Census)

GALLOWAY

Galloway, Amos P., see Amos Pierson

Galloway, John, married Margaret Ann Gashore circa 24 Feb 1825 (date of license) by Rev. Sharpley (Cecil County Marriage License Book)

Galloway, John L., see Amos Pierson

Galloway, Maria (Mana?), see Simon Baker

Galloway, Mary, see Thomas Caton

GALT
Galt, Henrietta, see Jacob Smeltzer

GAMBLE
Gamble, Charles (c1820-1869, born Maryland) (farmer, Brick Meeting House), married 1st to Rachel Ann England (1822-1863, born Maryland), daughter of George England and Mary Kirk, probably circa 1840 (daughter Laura Gamble born c1841, Maryland) and married 2nd to Emma J. (N) probably circa 1864 (*Joseph England and his Descendants*, by C. Walter England, Ph.D., 1975, p. 175; Rosebank Cemetery tombstones for Rachel A. Gamble and son Levin Gamble (1844-1862), but no marker for Charles)

Gamble, John, married Ann Barnes circa 8 Aug 1827 (date of license) (Cecil County Marr. License Book)

Gamble, John (born c1815, Pennsylvania) (shoemaker at Elkton), married Mary Jane Burnite (born c1815, Maryland) circa 29 Oct 1840 (date of license) (Cecil County Marr. License Book; 1860 Cecil Co. Census)

Gamble, Laura, see Charles Gamble

Gamble, Levin, see Charles Gamble

Gamble, Margaret, see Upton Terry

Gamble, Sarah, see John England

GAMISON, see Jamison

GARDENER
Gardener, John (born c1833, Maryland) (laborer, 9th District), married Frances (N) (born c1829, Maryland) probably circa 1850; son Joshua Gardener born c1851 (1860 Cecil County Census)

GARRETT
Garrett, David, of Cecil Co., married Miss Catharine Wilson, of New Castle Co., DE, on 8 Aug 1850 by Rev. Plummer (*Cecil Democrat and Farmer's Journal*, 17 Aug 1850; and again in the *Cecil Democrat and Farmer's Journal*, 26 Oct 1850, and *Delaware Gazette*, 22 Oct 1850, both spelled his name Garret)

Garrett, Elizabeth M., see Reese Mahan

Garrett, Joannah, see Joseph Andrews

Garrett, John T. (1818-1883), married Miss Ruth Ann Spence (1819-1896), both of Cecil Co., on 10 Oct 1844, after obtaining a license on 9 Oct 1844, by Rev. David Shields (Cecil County Marriage License Book; Elkton Methodist Church Register, p. 140; Cherry Hill Methodist Church Cemetery tombstone inscriptions; *Cecil Whig*, 12 Oct 1844; 1860 Cecil County Census)

Garrett, Mary, see James Scott

Garrett, Sarah Ann, see Nathan Wilkinson and William Bowen

Garrett, Thomas, married Elizabeth Aulden circa 4 Apr 1828 (date of license) (Cecil County Marriage License Book)

Garrett, William, see Nathan Wilkinson

Garrett, (N), married Julia A. (N) (1818-1874) probably circa 1840 (Cherry Hill Methodist Church Cemetery tombstone inscription inscribed "Mother" but no marker for her husband)

GARRETTSON
Garrettson, Mary B., see James Mansfield

Garrettson, Sarah, see Samuel Bostic

GASHORE
Gashore, Margaret Ann, see John Galloway

GATCHELL
Gatchell David (1802-1852), married Rebecca V. (N) (1819-1855) probably circa 1840 (Rosebank Cemetery, at Calvert, tombstone inscriptions)

Gatchell, Eleanor, see Samuel Harlan

Gatchell, Henry E. (1804-1885) (cooper at Elkton), married Elizabeth Simpson (1807-1885) circa 3 May 1828 (date of license) (Cecil County Marriage License Book; Cherry Hill Methodist Church Cemetery tombstone inscriptions; 1860 Cecil County Census)

Gatchell, Jeremiah (born c1822, Maryland) (carpenter, 6th District), married Eliza (N) (born c1824, Maryland) probably circa 1843; daughter Martha born c1844 (1860 Cecil County Census)

Gatchell, Job (born c1818, Pennsylvania) (farmer, 6th District), married Elizabeth (N) (born c1815, Maryland) probably circa 1843; son Nathaniel born c1845, Maryland (1860 Cecil County Census)

Gatchell, Joshua L. (1819, Chester Co., PA – 1870, Washington, DC) (carpenter in the Elkton District), married Susan Ann (N) (1824-1873, born Pennsylvania), possibly Susan Ann Rivers, probably circa 1841; daughter Malissa Gatchell was born circa 1842, Maryland (Cherry Hill Methodist Church Cemetery tombstone inscriptions; 1860 Cecil County Census listed his name as Josya L. Gatchell and living in their household at that time was Deborah Rivers, age 77; *Cecil Whig*, 14 Jan 1871)

Gatchell, Malissa, see Joshua L. Gatchell

Gatchell, Martha, see Jeremiah Gatchell

Gatchell, Nathaniel, see Job Gatchell

Gatchell, Tabitha, see John Increase Creswell

GAW

Gaw, Henry L., married Millicent Wingate on 7 Jan 1834, after obtaining a license that same day, by Rev. Hagany (Cecil County Marriage License Book; Elkton Methodist Church Register, p. 5)

GAY

Gay, Isabella, see James Alexander

Gay, Nancy, see Stephen John Brown

Gay, Samuel (1807-1881), married Mary Ann Blumfield (1805-1883) circa 26 Dec 1839 (date of license) by Rev. Burrows (Cecil County Marriage License Book; DAR transcript copied in 1928 listed him as Jr.; West Nottingham Cemetery tombstone inscriptions)

GELBACH

Gelbach, Christian and Sophia, see Matthew Shaw

GEORGE

George, Henrietta, see Lewis W. Neal

George, James H., married Harriett Ann Hyland circa 29 Mar 1837 (date of license) by Rev. Barratt (Cecil County Marriage License Book)

George, Joseph, married Sarah Clark circa 24 May 1825 (date of license) by Rev. Wilson (Cecil County Marriage License Book)

George, Margaret E., see Nicholas H. Johnson

George, Mathias, see Lewis W. Neal

George, Nicholas, married Millicent Wingate circa 2 Jan 1830 (date of license) by Rev. Barratt (Cecil County Marriage License Book)

George, Nicholas, married Araminta Hyland circa 28 Jan 1833 (date of license) by Rev. Duke (Cecil County Marriage License Book)

GERRY

Gerry, Mary Jane, see William Richardson

Gerry, Robert, married Hannah E. Reynolds circa 11 Jul 1829 (date of license) by Rev. Ayres (Cecil County Marriage License Book)

GETTY

Getty, James (1791-1856), married Rebecca Ann Burnite (1816-1886) circa 25 Jun 1838 (date of license) by Rev. Kennard (Cecil County Marriage License Book; Cherry Hill Methodist Church Cemetery tombstone inscriptions; 1860 Cecil County Census)

GIBBONS

Gibbons, Catherine, see David Thomas

GIBBS

Gibbs, Edward R., married Margaret Bowen circa 5 Sep 1825 (date of license) by Rev. Smith (Cecil County Marriage License Book)

GIBERSON

Giberson, Susan, see Samuel Perry

GIBSON

Gibson, Ellen C., see John Brumfield

Gibson, Ester, see Antoine Dupellee

Gibson, Hugh, married Mary E. Gillespie circa 3 Jul 1843 (date of license) (Cecil Co. Marr. License Book)

Gibson, Joseph, married Jane E. Knight circa 8 Jul 1828 (date of license) by Rev. Goforth (Cecil County Marriage License Book)

Gibson, Margaret, see Joshua Chandler

Gibson, Margaret Elizabeth, see Victor Craig

Gibson, Martha, see Evan Morgan

Gibson, Mary A., see William Warden and William J. Grant

Gibson, Samuel, of Jefferson Co., VA, married Ellen A. Maffitt, of Cecil Co., circa 31 Dec 1840 (date of license) (Cecil County Marriage License Book)

Gibson, William, married Catherine Hughes circa 20 Dec 1826 (date of license) by Rev. Graham (Cecil County Marriage License Book)

Gibson, William, married Elizabeth E. Owens circa 8 Jun 1841 (date of license) (Cecil County Marriage License Book)

Gibson, William (1817-1884), married Dinah (N) (1823-1909) probably circa 1843 (West Nottingham Cemetery tombstone inscriptions)

GIFFORD

Gifford, Benjamin (1814-1880), married Susan Watson (1819-1892) probably circa 1840 (Hopewell United Methodist Church Cemetery tombstone inscriptions)

Gifford, Samuel (1818-1901), married Sarah A. (N) (1825-1882) circa 1846; buried beside their eldest son John J. Gifford, 1848-1869 (Zion Presbyterian Church Cemetery tombstone inscriptions)

GILBERT

Gilbert, Clara, see Hiram Gilbert

Gilbert, Elizabeth, see Hiram Gilbert

Gilbert, Hiram (born c1815, Pennsylvania) (farmhand near Elkton), married Elizabeth (N) (born c1826, Pennsylvania) probably circa 1841; daughter Elizabeth Gilbert born c1842, Pennsylvania, daughter Clara Gilbert born c1854, Pennsylvania, son Robert Gilbert born c1857, Maryland (1860 Cecil County Census)

Gilbert, Jacob (born c1827) (laborer at North East), married Ann V. Worth (born c1830) circa 15 Mar 1848 (date of license) (Cecil County Marriage License Book; 1860 Cecil County Census)

Gilbert, Mahala, see Thomas Keithley

Gilbert, Michael, see Thomas Keithley

Gilbert, Robert, see Hiram Gilbert

Gilbert, Sarah, see Corbin Cooley

Gilbert, Stephen (1802-1877), married Ann R. (N) (1801-1865) probably circa 1825 (Rosebank Cemetery, at Calvert, tombstone inscriptions)

GILES

Giles, Amelia, see Walter Elias Harding and Samuel Reeve Williams

Giles, Anna M., see Thomas Ball

Giles, George Black (1808-1888) (miller), of Elkton, later of Chester, PA, son of John R. Giles and Elizabeth Black, married 1st to Sarah (N) (1803-1853) circa 1833 (eldest daughter Hannah born 1834) and married 2nd to Sarah Jane Porter (1833-1897), of Blackbird, New Castle Co., DE, on 30 Jan 1855, after obtaining a license on 29 Jan 1855, by Rev. J. T. Brown at Cherry Hill Methodist Church (Cecil County Marriage License Book; *Thomas Giles, Born 1752 – Birmingham, England, Died 1812 – Elkton, Maryland, U.S.A., A Genealogical History of His Descendants*, by Alexander W. Giles, Jr. (1986, updated 1996), pp. 17-20)

Giles, Gustavus (1816-1876) (carpenter), of Elkton, later of Baltimore, youngest child of John R. Giles and Elizabeth Black, married Rebecca Evans (born 1820), of Baltimore, on 29 or 30 Sep 1838 in Baltimore City (*Thomas Giles, Born 1752 – Birmingham, England, Died 1812 – Elkton, Maryland, U. S. A.: A Genealogical History of His Descendants*, by Alexander W. Giles, Jr. (1986, updated 1996), p. 21, stated they were married on 29 Sep 1838, but *Baltimore Sun*, 5 Oct 1838, stated they married on 30 Sep 1838; *Baltimore Sun*, 22 Aug 1876, stated Gustavus B. Giles died on 21 Jul 1876, aged 60 years)

Giles, Hannah, see George Black Giles

Giles, John R., see Thomas Giles, George Black Giles, Augustus Giles and John Robert Giles, Jr.

Giles, John Robert Jr. (1813-1861) (hotel owner), of Elkton, later of Baltimore, son of John R. Giles and Elizabeth Black, of Elkton, married Arrietta Myers (1812-1861), of Baltimore, in 1837 (*Thomas Giles, Born 1752 – Birmingham, England, Died 1812 – Elkton, Maryland, U.S.A.: A Genealogical History of His Descendants*, by Alexander W. Giles, Jr. (1986, updated 1996), p. 21; *Baltimore Sun*, 6 Mar 1861, reported John died on 5 Mar 1861; *Baltimore Sun*, 9 Mar 1861, reported Arrietta died on 8 Mar 1861)

Giles, Sarah D., see William Roney

Giles, Thomas, see William B. Giles and Thomas Ball

Giles, Thomas (1810-c1870s) (miller), of Caroline Co., later of Elkton, second son of John R. Giles and Elizabeth Black, married Mary Hemphill (born 1815) circa 2 Feb 1832 (date of license) by Rev. Barratt and they separated sometime between 1843 and 1850 (Cecil County Marriage License Book; *Thomas Giles, Born 1752 – Birmingham, England, Died 1812 – Elkton, Maryland, U.S A.: A Genealogical History of His Descendants*, by Alexander W. Giles, Jr. (1986, updated 1996), p. 20)

Giles, William B. (born 1798) (restaurant owner and store keeper in Elkton), son of Thomas Giles (1752-1812) and Ann Goodwin (1758-1800), of Birmingham, England, later of Elkton, married Mrs. Mary Wells (1790-1865), widow of Orin Wells, on 30 Dec 1833, after obtaining a license that same day, by Rev. Goforth at Port Deposit (Cecil County Marriage License Book; *Thomas Giles, Born 1752 – Birmingham, England, Died 1812 – Elkton, Maryland, U.S.A.: A Genealogical History of His Descendants*, by Alexander W. Giles, Jr. (1986, updated 1996), pp. 9, 15; *Cecil Whig*, 16 Sep 1865)

GILL

Gill, Martha, see George C. Weaver

GILLASPY

Gillaspy, George (major), married Mrs. Sarah Hanna, both of the vicinity of Newport, DE, on 15 Mar 1829 (*Elkton Press*, 21 Mar 1829, spelled her surname Hannah)

GILLESPIE

Gillespie, Daniel, married Mary Currier circa 20 Dec 1827 (date of license) (Cecil Co. Marr. License Book)

Gillespie, James (1801-1874), married Mary E. (N) (1812-1850) circa 1829; buried beside son John W. Gillespie (1830-1864) and other children (West Nottingham Cemetery tombstone inscriptions)

Gillespie, James, married Miss Eliza McEllary, both of Cecil Co., on 13 Jan 1829 by Gardner Furness, Esq. (*Elkton Press*, 31 Jan 1829)

Gillespie, James, married Elizabeth Craig circa 30 Dec 1834 (date of license) by Rev. Griffith (Cecil County Marriage License Book)

Gillespie, James, married Elizabeth Burris, both of Cecil Co., on 12 Jan 1849, after obtaining a license that same day, by Rev. Arthur (Cecil County Marriage License Book; *Cecil Democrat and Farmer's Journal*, 3 Feb 1849)

Gillespie, John W., see James Gillespie

Gillespie, Jonathan, married Mary Ann Sturgeon circa 18 Mar 1829 (date of license) by Rev. Goforth (Cecil County Marriage License Book)

Gillespie, Mary E., see Hugh Gibson

Gillespie, Nicholas H. (1820-1896), married Mary Y. (N) (1824-1878) probably circa 1845 (West Nottingham Cemetery tombstone inscriptions)

Gillespie, Robert B. (1803-1856), married Margaret Nesbitt (1803-1878) circa 19 Dec 1826 (date of license) by Rev. Magraw (Cecil County Marr. License Book; West Nottingham Cemetery tombstone inscriptions)

Gillespie, Samuel (born c1812, Maryland) (innkeeper at Warwick), married Ellen (N) (born c1818, Maryland) circa 1837 (1860 Cecil County Census)

Gillespie, Samuel, married Mary McVey circa 5 Feb 1840 (date of license) by Rev. Burrows (Cecil County Marriage License Book)

Gillespie, Samuel (born c1804, Maryland) (carpenter, 7th District), married Susan Shroff (1808-1890, born Maryland) circa 26 Sep 1828 (date of license) by Rev. Goforth (Cecil County Marriage License Book; 1860 Cecil County Census; *Midland Journal*, 2 May 1890, stated Mrs. Susan Gillespie died in her 81st year at Liberty Grove)

Gillespie, Samuel E., married Margaret (N) (1803-1880) probably circa 1825 (West Nottingham Cemetery tombstone inscriptions)

Gillespie, Thomas J. (1807-1887, born Delaware) (farmer, 6th District), married Mary C. Eves (1812-1873, born Delaware) probably circa 1832 (West Nottingham Cemetery tombstone inscriptions; 1860 Cecil County Census)

Gillespie, William, married Emeline Lomans circa 30 Mar 1830 (date of license) by Rev. Griffith (Cecil County Marriage License Book)

Gillespie, William J. (1815-1870), married Margaret H. (N) (1829-1890) probably circa 1848-1850 (West Nottingham Cemetery tombstone inscriptions)

GILMORE, GILMOUR

Gilmore, Adaline, see John Wilson

Gilmore, Angelina, see John J. Heckart

Gilmore, David, married Sarah Irvin circa 10 Jan 1825 (date of license) by Rev. Magraw (Cecil County Marriage License Book)

Gilmore, David, married Elizabeth White circa 28 Feb 1828 (date of license) (Cecil County Marriage License Book)

Gilmore, Eliza, see John H. Gilmore

Gilmore, Eliza T., see John T. Scarborough

Gilmore, John H. (1813-1855) (captain), married Eliza Jenkins (1818-1886) circa 30 Jun 1840 (date of license) and Eliza Gilmore married 2nd to John Wilson in 1858 (Cecil County Marriage License Books; Hopewell United Methodist Church Cemetery tombstone inscriptions)

Gilmore, Joseph C., married Elmira C. White circa 24 Aug 1842 (date of license) (Cecil County Marriage License Book)

Gilmore, Mary Horton, see Thomas Keithley

Gilmore, Nancy A., see Ebenezer Smith

Gilmore, Nathaniel K. (born c1811, Maryland) (sea captain, 7th District), married Hannah Brumfield (born c1812, Maryland) circa 30 Jan 1839 (date of license) by Rev. Greenbank (Cecil County Marriage License Book; 1860 Cecil County Census)

Gilmore, Robert, married Miss Louisa Tagart, both of Cecil Co., on 22 Jun 1843, after obtaining a license on 17 Jun 1843, by Rev. Shields in Elkton (Cecil County Marriage License Book, spelled her name Tagert; *Cecil Whig*, 24 Jun 1843, and Elkton Methodist Church Register, p. 140, both spelled her name Tagart)

Gilmore, Robert M., married Adaline White circa 29 Apr 1836 (date of license) by Rev. Hickey (Cecil County Marriage License Book; DAR transcript copied in 1928 transcribed W. as his middle initial)

Gilmour, William (1822-1856), married Mary Jane Shockley (1825-1877) circa 15 Jan 1846 (date of license) (Cecil County Marriage License Book misspelled his name as Gilmore; Cherry Hill Methodist Church Cemetery tombstone inscriptions; *Cecil Whig*, 19 May 1877, reported that she died at the residence of her son, name not given, in Newark, DE, in her 53rd year)

GILPIN

Gilpin, Hannah James, see George Jenkins

Gilpin, Henry H., married Margaret Ricketts circa 14 Feb 1833 (date of license) by Rev. Duke (Cecil County Marriage License Book)

Gilpin, Isaiah H., married Martha T. Moffitt circa 5 Apr 1825 (date of license) by Rev. Duke (Cecil County Marriage License Book)

Gilpin, James, see George Jenkins

Gilpin, Jane, see William Spence

Gilpin, John, see William H. Gilpin

Gilpin, Margaret Ann, see William H. Gilpin

Gilpin, Samuel S., see George Jenkins

Gilpin, Sarah L., see George Jenkins

Gilpin, William H. (c1810-1884), son of John Gilpin and Mary Hollingsworth, of Elkton, married Margaret Ann Price (1811-1895), daughter of David E. Price and Rachel Smith, of Harford Co., on 23 Apr 1833, after obtaining a license on 19 Apr 1833, by Rev. Stephenson at the residence of Mr. Wilson in Harford Co.; Margaret Ann Gilpin married 2nd to William Wilson late in life (Harford County Marriage License Book; *Cecil Republican*, 27 Apr 1833; *Substantial Copy of Genealogical Record of the Stump Family of Maryland*, by Albert P. Silver and Henry W. Archer (1891), p. 26; *Heirs & Legatees of Harford County, Maryland, 1802-1846*, by Henry C. Peden, Jr. (1988), p. 41; *History of Cecil County*, by George Johnston (1881, repr. 1989), p. 513)

GINN

Ginn, Moses, married Lucretia Myers circa 23 Feb 1847 (date of license) (Cecil County Marr. License Book)

GINNA

Ginna, Hannah, see John Ramsey

GINTZ

Gintz, Elizabeth, see John Epp

GIRVIN

Girvin, James, married Ann Taylor on 19 Sep 1838, after obtaining a licenses that same day, by Rev. Hagany (Cecil County Marriage License Book) James Girvin divorced Ann Girvin on 7 Mar 1850 (*Divorces and Names Changed in Maryland by Act of the Legislature, 1634-1867*, by Mary Keysor Meyer (1991), p. 35; Elkton Methodist Church Register, p. 139, mistakenly listed his name as John)

Girvin, Mary, see Richard James Marcus

Girvin, William, married Mary Ann Richardson circa 21 Dec 1840 (date of license) (Cecil County Marriage License Book)

GLANDEN

Glanden, Sarah M., see William H. Walmsley

GLEAVES

Gleaves, George E., see George T. Megee

GLENN

Glenn, Elias B., married Rachael Ann Taylor circa 3 Dec 1825 (date of license) by Rev. Sharpley (Cecil County Marriage License Book)

Glenn, Eliza Jane, see Robert Carr

Glenn, John, married Pheby Knight circa 19 Dec 1825 (date of license) by Rev. Sharpley (Cecil County Marriage License Book)

Glenn, Samuel, see William Glenn

Glenn, William (born c1814, Ireland) (farmer near Brick Meeting House), married Martha (N) (born c1825, Ireland) probably circa 1843; son Samuel Glenn born c1844, Maryland (1860 Cecil County Census)

Glenn, William C., married Martha E. Sewall circa 19 May 1835 (date of license) by Rev. Johns (Cecil County Marriage License Book)

GOFORTH

Goforth, Ann, see Samuel Grace

GOLDEN

Golden, Nicholas, married Abigail Jane Brady circa 3 Oct 1836 (date of license) by Rev. Williams (Cecil County Marriage License Book; DAR transcript copied in 1928 misspelled her first name Abrigail)

GOLDSBOROUGH

Goldsborough, Henrietta, see Philemon B. Hopper

Goldsborough, Joseph N., married Augusta Cook, youngest daughter of the late Thomas B. Cook, all of Queen Anne's Co., on 7 Feb 1850, after obtaining a license that same day, by Rev. Sumption (*Cecil Democrat and Farmer's Journal*, 2 Mar 1850; Queen Anne's County Marriage License Book listed her name as Sarah A. A. M. Cook and mistakenly listed his name as James N. Goldsborough)

Goldsborough, Robert, see Philemon B. Hopper

GONCE

Gonce, George W., married Emaline Cox circa 2 Jan 1850 (date of license) (Cecil Co. Marr. License Book)

Gonce, Margaret Ann, see George Moore

GOODING

Gooding, William, of Kent Co., MD, married Lydia Ann Miller, daughter of Samuel Miller, Esq., of Cecil Co., on 14 Jun 1849, after obtaining a license on 11 Jun 1849, by Rev. Elliott (Cecil County Marriage License Book; *Cecil Democrat and Farmer's Journal*, 14 Jul 1849, and her death notice in that paper on 28 Jan 1882 stated Lydia A. Gooding died at Newark, Worcester Co., MD, wife of William Gooding and daughter of the late Samuel Miller, of Cecil Co., but it did not give her age or place of burial)

GOODWIN

Goodwin, Ann, see William B. Giles, William Roney and Thomas Ball

GORDON

Gordon, Eliza Jane, see Justus Fox

Gordon, Francis, married Hetty Reynolds circa 30 Sep 1830 (date of license) by Rev. Griffith (Cecil County Marriage License Book)

Gordon, Jane Ella, see Stephen Smith

Gordon, Lydia, see Silas Gordon

Gordon, Mary Ann, see Silas Townsend

Gordon, Silas (born c1822) (African American) (laborer at Elkton), married Rebecca (N) (born c1830) (African American) circa 1848; daughter Lydia Gordon born c1849 (1860 Cecil County Census)

GORRELL

Gorrell, Ann, see John Brook, Henry Jackson and James Whitelock

Gorrell Ann (Agnes) Hamilton, see John Charles Whitelock, Jr.

Gorrell, Elizabeth, see David Taylor

Gorrell, Georgiana, see Charles W. Jackson

Gorrell, Harriet, see Samuel Tyson

Gorrell, James, married Ann Woodden circa 6 Feb 1848 (date of license) (Cecil County Marr. License Book)

Gorrell, John, married Mary Jackson circa 20 Dec 1842(date of license) (Cecil County Marr. License Book)

Gorrell, Martha, see Thomas Simpers

Gorrell, Nancy, see Henry Jackson

Gorrell, William (born c1815, Delaware) (laborer at North East), married Miss Sarah Jane Arnel (born c1823, Maryland), both of Cecil Co., on 23 Mar 1845, after obtaining a license on 22 Mar 1845, by Rev. Humphries (*Cecil Whig*, 5 Apr 1845; Cecil County Marriage License Book spelled his name Gorrel; 1860 Cecil County Census spelled his name Gorell)

GOTTIER

Gottier, Ann Eliza, see John S. Aldridge

Gottier, Francis B. (1800-1889), married 1st to Rebecca Wingate circa 28 Mar 1826 (date of license) by Rev. Duke and married 2nd to Miss Alicia Moore (1805-1897), both of Cecil Co., on 17 Jan 1838, after obtaining a license on 15 Jan 1838, by Rev. Kennard (Cecil County Marriage License Book; *Cecil Gazette*, 3 Feb 1838; Elkton Cemetery tombstone inscriptions)

Gottier, Margaret A. L., see Edward B. Lewis

GOVEN

Goven, Richard (born c1825, Maryland) (African American) (laborer, 7th District), married Hester (N) (born c1829, Maryland) (African American) probably circa 1849; son Henry born c1850 (1860 Cecil Census)

GOVER

Gover, Gerard, married Cassandra G. Smithson (1824-1920), daughter of William Smithson, Jr. and Margaret Hall Lee, circa 12 Jan 1850 (date of license) and lived in Harford County (Cecil County Marriage License Book; DAR transcript copied in 1955 misspelled his name as Cover; *Thomas Smithson (1675-1732) of Baltimore County, Maryland and His Descendants*, by Diane Dieterle (1993), p. 88)

GRACE

Grace, Elizabeth A., see Nathan C. Barnes

Grace, Ephraim P., married 1st to Miss Mary Ann Manly, both of Cecil Co., on 20 Mar 1845, after obtaining a license on 19 Mar 1845, by Rev. Shields, and married 2nd to Sarah J. Rutter circa 18 Mar 1854 (date of license) (Elkton Methodist Church Register, p. 140; Cecil County Marriage License Book spelled her name Manley; *Cecil Whig*, 22 Mar 1845)

Grace, John, married Rebecca Murphy, both of Cecil Co., on 19 May 1850, after obtaining a license on 16 May 1850 in Cecil Co., by Rev. William H. Trapnell at Havre de Grace in Harford Co. (St. John's Episcopal Church, Havre de Grace Parish, Marriage Register, 1835-1858; Cecil County Marriage License Book spelled her surname Murphey)

Grace, Mary, see John Burk and William Arrants

Grace, Samuel, married Ann Goforth circa 16 Feb 1838 (date of license) by Rev. Wooley (Cecil County Marriage License Book)

Grace, Samuel (reverend), of Chesapeake City, married Eliza H. Bryan (1799-1875) circa 5 Jan 1843 (date of license) (Cecil County Marriage License Book; *Cecil Whig*, 10 Apr 1875)

Grace, William, married Jane Roach circa 11 Oct 1827 (date of license) (Cecil County Marr. License Book)

Grace, William, married Ann Arrants circa 6 Jun 1844 (date of license) (Cecil County Marr. License Book)

GRACY

Gracy, Joseph (1825-1885), married Esther (N) (1826-1909) by 1849; buried beside son Charles T. Gracy, 1850-1894 (St. John's Church Cemetery, at Lewisville, tombstone inscriptions)

GRADY

Grady, George, married Judyth "Judy" Parcell on 22 Jan 1828, after obtaining a license on 19 Jan 1828, by Rev. Epinette (Cecil County Marriage License Book is unclear and the DAR transcript copied in 1928 listed her name as "Judy Precall (Pascall?);" *History of Saint Francis Xavier Church and Bohemia Plantation Now Known as Old Bohemia, Warwick, Maryland*, by Joseph C. Cann (1976), p. 47, listed her name as Judyth Parcell)

GRAHAM

Graham, James (born c1818, Maryland) (mason, 7th District), married Mary (N) (born c1823, Maryland) probably circa 1846; daughter Sarah Graham born c1847 (1860 Cecil County Census)

Graham, John, married Elizabeth Love circa 25 Mar 1833 (date of license) by Rev. Magraw (Cecil County Marriage License Book)

Graham, John B. (born 1822) (cabinet maker and boat and bridge builder), son of Zachariah Butcher Graham (died 1854) and Rebecca Lewis (died 1848), married 1st to Miss Elizabeth Cooper, both of Charlestown, on 25 Jun 1844, after obtaining a license on 21 Jun 1844, by Rev. Shields, and married 2nd to Caroline M. Richardson, daughter of Henry Richardson, circa 3 Mar 1851 (date of license) (Cecil County Marriage License Book; Elkton Methodist Church Register, p. 140; *Portrait and Biographical Record of Harford and Cecil Counties, Maryland* (1897, repr. 1989), pp. 210-211, stated he had one child John C. Graham by his first wife and two children by his second wife, namely, Helen Matting and William H. Graham; *Cecil Whig*, 29 Jun 1844)

Graham, John C., see John B. Graham

Graham, John H., married Rachel Alexander circa 9 Feb 1830 (date of license) by Rev. Miller (Cecil County Marriage License Book)

Graham, Mary, see David Rea

Graham, Mary Ann, see Thomas Thompson

Graham, Sarah, see James Graham and Benjamin B. Thompson

Graham, Robert, see David Rea

Graham, William E. G., married Mary Ann Lewis circa 5 Sep 1831 (date of license) by Rev. Barratt (Cecil County Marriage License Book)

Graham, William H., see John B. Graham

Graham, Zachariah Butcher, see John B. Graham

GRANT

Grant, Eliza Jane, see Fredus Aldridge

Grant, George, married Hannah Ann Whann circa 26 May 1828 (date of license) by Rev. Barratt (Cecil County Marriage License Book)

Grant, George, married Sophia Lowery circa 1 Sep 1829 (date of license) by Rev. Barratt (Cecil County Marriage License Book)

Grant, John E., married Emily J. Woodden circa 4 Feb 1848 (date of license) (Cecil County Marriage License Book)

Grant, Joseph, see William T. Grant

Grant, Joseph M., married Miss Mary Elizabeth Holt, both of Cecil Co., on 31 Jul 1850, after obtaining a license on 30 Jul 1850, by Rev. Crouch in Newark, DE (Cecil County Marriage License Book; *Cecil Democrat and Farmer's Journal*, 24 Aug 1850; *Cecil Whig*, 24 Aug 1850)

Grant, Louisa, see Thomas Smith

Grant, Margaret, see Joseph Worth

Grant, Maria, see William Ferguson

Grant, Mary, see John Yeamans

Grant, Mary A., see John McMullen

Grant, Sarah, see Seborn Grant and John Short

Grant, Sarah Jane, see Richard Miller

Grant, Seborn (1798-1867), of Charlestown, married Sarah Worth (1801-1877) circa 16 May 1825 (date of license) by Rev. Rider (Cecil County Marriage License Book; *Cecil Democrat and Farmer's Journal*, 15 Jun 1867, stated he died in his 69th year; *Cecil Whig*, 10 Feb 1877, stated Sarah died at Westamwell Mills)

Grant, William, married Ann Alexander circa 24 Sep 1825 (date of license) by Rev. Duke (Cecil County Marriage License Book)

Grant, William (1806-1871) (shoemaker at Charlestown), married Araminta Matilda Denny (1811-1890) circa 8 Nov 1830 (date of license) by Rev. Barratt (Cecil County Marriage License Book; Charlestown Cemetery tombstone inscriptions; 1860 Cecil County Census listed her by her middle name Matilda)

Grant, William J. (born c1824) (cabinet maker at Elkton), married 1st to Frances Gallagher circa 23 Dec 1843 (date of license) and married 2nd to Mary A. Gibson (born c1834) circa 12 Dec 1854 (date of license) (Cecil County Marriage License Book; 1860 Cecil County Census)

Grant, William T. (born c1821) (merchant at North East), married Matilda (N) (born c1821) probably circa 1845; son Joseph Grant born c1847 (1860 Cecil County Census)

Grant, Zachariah, see William Grant

GRASON

Grason, Elizabeth, see Otho Scott

GRAY

Gray, Amanda Jane, see Alexander C. Cosden

Gray, Ann, see William Henry Pryor

Gray, Elizabeth, see Levi Kirk

Gray, Mary, see Robert Lewis

Gray, Rutha, see John W. Prior

Gray, Susan or Susanna, see Andrew Wilson

Gray, also see Grey

GREEN

Green, B. Franklin (professor), of Troy, NY, married Miss Mary E. Wickes, eldest daughter of Col. Joseph Wickes, of Chestertown, MD, on 11 Apr 1848, after obtaining a license on 10 Apr 1848, by Rev. C. F. Jones (*Cecil Whig*, 22 Apr 1848; Kent County Marriage License Book)

Green, Helena A., see Joseph Craddock

Green, John, of Chester Co., PA, married Harriet (N) (c1810-1864) probably circa 1830 and she died in her 54th year (*Cecil Whig*, 25 Jun 1864)

Green, Joshua (1804-1881), married Harriet (N) (1804-1883) probably circa 1825; buried beside son Joshua Green, Jr., 1830-1910 (Sharp's Cemetery tombstone inscriptions)

Green, Lavinia, see James Wilson

Green, Levi (born c1820, Maryland) (farmhand, 8th District), married Rebecca (N) (born c1830, Maryland) probably circa 1845; daughter Margaret Green born c1846, Maryland (1860 Cecil County Census)

Green, Margaret, see Levi Green and Elihu Hargan

Green, Millicent, see Henry Jamar

Green, Prudence, see Elihu Hargan

Green, Samuel, married Mary Eades (or Eader?) circa 8 Jun 1837 (date of license) by Rev. Morris (Cecil County Marriage License Book is unclear as to the last letter of her last name)

Green, Susan, see Joseph Lambson

Green, William P., married Elizabeth A. Craddock circa 25 Sep 1839 (date of license) by Rev. King (Cecil County Marriage License Book)

Green, William, married Eliza Taylor circa 28 Feb 1828 (date of license) (Cecil County Marr. License Book)

GREENWOOD

Greenwood, Alexander, married Catharine Purnell circa 7 Jan 1834 (date of license) by Rev. Duke (Cecil County Marriage License Book)

Greenwood, Margaret B., see Thomas W. Skirven

Greenwood, Maria, see John James Dillahunt

Greenwood, Mary, see Andrew Thompson

GREER

Greer, Joseph, married Rachel Bowen circa 17 Dec 1828 (date of license) by Rev. Barratt (Cecil County Marriage License Book)

GREGG

Gregg, Acentha, see Samuel England

Gregg, Eliza Jane, see Richard Kennedy Whitcraft

Gregg, Jane V., see Samuel Brown

Gregg, John (1819-1905), married Mary (N) (1830-1908) prob. circa 1850 (Sharp's Cemetery tombstones)

Gregg, John, see Samuel England

Gregg, John Lake, see George England

Gregg, Mary Jane, see James Smith and Samuel England

Gregg, Robert, of Baltimore Co., married Miss Mary P. Davidson, of Cecil Co., on 20 Sep 1849, after obtaining a license on 19 Sep 1849, by Rev. Goldsborough in Trinity Church (Cecil County Marriage License Book; *Cecil Democrat and Farmer's Journal*, 22 Sep 1849, stated he was of Baltimore County; *Cecil Whig*, 22 Sep 1849, misspelled his surname Graig and stated they were all of Cecil County)

Gregg, Solomon, see Samuel Brown

GREY

Grey, Adley (born c1819, Pennsylvania) (iron roller in the 7th District), married Rebecca (N) (born c1821, Pennsylvania) probably circa 1843; daughter Mary born c1844, Maryland (1860 Cecil County Census)

Grey, James (born c1824, Maryland) (iron roller in the 7th District), married Jane (N) (born c1829, Maryland) probably circa 1849; daughter Mary Grey born c1850 (1860 Cecil County Census)

Grey, John (born c1818, Pennsylvania) (forgeman, 8th District), married Lydia (N) (b. c1819, Pennsylvania) probably circa 1839; son James Grey born c1840, Pennsylvania, son Samuel Grey born c1843, Maryland, and their other children were also born in Maryland (1860 Cecil County Census)

Grey, Mary, see Adley Grey and James Grey

Grey, Nancy, see William Grey

Grey, Samuel, see John Grey

Grey, William (born c1834, Maryland) (farmhand, 8th District), married Susan (N) (born 1822, Maryland) probably circa 1847; daughter Nancy Grey born c1848 (1860 Cecil County Census)

Grey, also see Gray

GRIEST

Griest, (N), married Rebecca (N) (1808-1842) probably circa 1828 (Rock Springs Old School Baptist Church Cemetery tombstone inscription for "Our Mother, Rebecca Griest," but no marker for their father)

GRIFFEE

Griffee, Mary, see James Smith

Griffee, Rachel M., see William Tammany

Griffee, Richard (1801-1870), married Mary Smith (1800-1893) circa 10 Feb 1830 (date of license) by Rev. Magraw (Cecil County Marr. License Book; Hopewell U. M. Church Cemetery tombstone inscriptions)

Griffee, William (1800-1870), son of William Griffee (1779-1812) and Mary (N) (1778-1860), married Mary A. (N) (1807-1875) probably circa 1827 (West Nottingham Cemetery tombstone inscriptions)

GRIFFITH

Griffith, Anson, married Merium N. (N) (1812-1870) probably circa 1830 and they resided in the 2nd District (*Cecil Whig*, 24 Dec 1870)

Griffith family, see Clemson Brown

GRITZ

Gritz, Elizabeth, see John Epp

GROOME

Groome, Eliza Jeannette, see Matthew Carroll Pearce

Groome, John, see Matthew Carroll Pearce and John C. Groome

Groome, John C. (1800-1866) (colonel and attorney), of Elkton, son of Dr. John Groome and wife Elizabeth (Black) Wallace, married Elizabeth R. Black (1810-1902, born Delaware), second daughter of Judge Black, of and at New Castle, DE, on 6 Dec 1836 (*Baltimore American and Commercial Daily Advertiser*, 10 Dec 1836; *Portrait and Biographical Record of Harford and Cecil Counties, Maryland* (1897, repr. 1989), p. 237; 1860 Cecil County Census; Elkton Presbyterian Church Cemetery tombstone inscriptions; *Cecil Whig*, 8 Dec 1866)

GROVES

Groves, Melvinia, see (N) Groves

Groves, Rebecca, see John Henderson and (N) Groves

Groves, Richard, married Ann Henderson circa 9 Jan 1833 (date of license) by Rev. Duke (Cecil County Marriage License Book)

Groves, (N) (c1812-c1852), married Mary J. (N) (born c1815) circa 1837; daughter Rebecca Groves born c1838, son William Groves born c1848 and daughter Melvinia Groves born c1851 (1860 Cecil County Census listed Mary as head of household in Chesapeake City)

Groves, William, see (N) Groves

GRUBB

Grubb, Sarah Ann, see John B. Wilson

GURLIE

Gurlie, Joseph, married Emily Taylor circa 17 Apr 1834 (date of license) by Rev. Magraw (Cecil County Marriage License Book)

GUTHRIE

Guthrie, Sarah Ann, see Joseph W. Smith

GWINN

Gwinn, Jacob (1801-1856), married Sarah (N) (1805-1868) probably circa 1825 (Hopewell United Methodist Church Cemetery tombstone inscriptions)

Gwinn, Mary Ann, see Joel H. Hays

HAARHANS

Haarhans, Otto, married Elizabeth A. (N) (1819-1869) probably circa 1838-1840 (Elkton Methodist Church Cemetery tombstone inscription for Elizabeth A. Haarhans)

HACKETT

Hackett, Edward, formerly of Cecil Co., married Miss Mary Ann Reilly, of Baltimore Co., on 15 Jun 1848 by Rev. Cook (*Cecil Democrat and Farmer's Journal*, 24 Jun 1848)

Hackett, John, of Cecil Co., married Ann Thompson, of Kent Co., circa 6 Mar 1837 by Rev. Rawley (Kent County Marriage License Book)

Hackett, Joseph, married Henrietta Pennington circa 16 Nov 1831 (date of license) by Rev. Duke (Cecil County Marriage License Book)

Hackett, Lydia Ann, see George B. Hollace

Hackett, William, married Ann Eliza Ford circa 29 Sep 1832 (date of license) by Rev. Duke (Cecil County Marriage License Book)

Hackett, William D., married Martha Ann Morgan circa 7 Nov 1832 (date of license) by Rev. Duke (Cecil County Marriage License Book)

HADDEN

Hadden, John L., married Sally Ann Hedgick, daughter of the late John Hedgick, of Wilmington, DE, on 31 Oct 1837 by Rev. Gilbert in Wilmington (*Cecil Gazette*, 4 Nov 1837)

HADDOCK

Haddock, Samuel (1821-1896, born Pennsylvania) (farmer near Zion), married Louisa A. (N) (1824-1895, born Maryland) probably circa 1846; son James Haddock born c1847, Maryland (Rosebank Cemetery, at Calvert, tombstone inscriptions; 1860 Cecil County Census)

HADEN

Haden, George (born c1825, Pennsylvania) (African American) (laborer at Elkton), married Eliza (N) (born c1828, Pennsylvania) (African American) circa 1841; daughter Emaline Haden born c1842 (1860 Cecil County Census)

HAGAN

Hagan, David, married Milcah Lowe circa 23 Jan 1839 (date of their license) by Rev. King (Cecil County Marriage License Book)

HAGANY

Hagany, John B. (reverend doctor), married Caroline S. Ford circa 25 Mar 1835 (date of license) by Rev. Smith; she died in Brooklyn, NY in 1877 (Cecil County Marr. License Book; *Cecil Whig*, 11 Aug 1877)

HAGUE, HAUGE

Hague, John L., married Ann H. Stevens, both of Cecil Co., circa 14 Aug 1834 by Rev. Smith (Kent County Marriage License Book spelled his name Hauge)

Hague, Michael, married Alice A. Barnwell circa 1 Jun 1840 (date of license) by Rev. Piggot (Cecil County Marriage License Book; DAR transcript copied in 1928 listed his name as Michail Hauge)

Hague, William, married Rachel Lurtz circa 2 Jan 1839 (date of license) by Rev. Smith (Cecil County Marriage License Book)

HAINES

Haines, Ann, see John Foard Cazier

Haines, Ann E., see George Davidson

Haines, Bazil (born c1811, Maryland) (farmer in the 6th District), married Lydia (N) (born c1818, Maryland) probably circa 1838; son George Haines born c1839 (1860 Cecil County Census)

Haines, Charles H., see Joseph Haines

Haines, E. Henry, see Samuel Haines

Haines, E. W. (dentist), married Sarah E. (N) (1822-1890) probably circa 1845 (*Midland Journal*, 19 Dec 1890, stated Sarah E. Haines died in her 68th year at Newark, DE)

Haines Edwin, see Job Haines

Haines, Eli (1811-1855) (pottery owner), of Rising Sun, later of North East, Cecil Co., son of Joseph Haines, married Hannah Marshall, of Chester Co., PA, daughter of Humphrey Marshall, by 1840 (son L. Marshall Haines, born 10 Dec 1846, was one of seven children) (*Portrait and Biographical Record of Harford and Cecil Counties, Maryland* (1897, repr. 1989), pp. 314-315)

Haines, Eli, see Isaac Reynolds and Samuel Haines

Haines, Eliza, see A. Roman

Haines, Elizabeth, see Isaac Reynolds, Henry Reynolds and Reuben Reynolds

Haines, Esther, see John E. Powley, John England, Robert Haines England, George England, Stephen John Brown and Charles Parker

Haines, Frank, see Samuel Haines

Haines, George (1808-1877) (blacksmith, Port Deposit), married 1st to Jane Jones (1810-1851), daughter of William and Mary Jones, circa 29 Feb 1832 (date of license) by Rev. Griffith and married 2nd to Mary Broshers (1821-1888) circa 7 Jun 1853 (date of license) (Cecil County Marr. License Book; 1860 Cecil County Census; Hopewell United Methodist Church Cemetery tombstones; *Cecil Whig*, 17 Mar 1877)

Haines, George, see Bazil Haines and Samuel Haines

Haines, Jefferson, see Samuel Haines

Haines, Jeremiah B., of Little Britain, Lancaster Co., PA, married Sarah H. Thomas, of Cecil Co., on 8 Jul 1841 by Henry Fleming, Esq., at West Chester, PA (*Cecil Gazette*, 17 Jul 1841)

Haines, Job (born c1821, Maryland) (merchant near Elkton), married Elizabeth (N) (born c1820, Delaware) probably circa 1845; son Edwin Haines born c1846, Maryland (1860 Cecil County Census)

Haines, John, married Rebecca Biddle circa 26 Jul 1838 (date of license) by Rev. Kennard (Cecil County Marriage License Book)

Haines, Joseph, see Eli Haines

Haines, Joseph (1798-1866), married Harriet (N) (1803-1858) circa 1825; eldest son Charles H. Haines (1826-1866) was Clerk of the Circuit Court (Rosebank Cemetery, at Calvert, tombstone inscriptions; *Cecil Whig*, 27 Jan 1866)

Haines, Joseph H. (born c1825, Maryland) (farmer in the 6th District), married Rebecca (N) (born c1828, Maryland) probably circa 1846; son John L. Haines born c1847 (1860 Cecil County Census)

Haines, L. Marshall, see Eli Haines

Haines, Lucy, see William M. McCullough

Haines, Margaret E., see William Radley

Haines, Maria, see Joseph Townsend England

Haines, Mira, see Isaac Reynolds

Haines, Samuel (1801-1891), son of Eli Haines and Elizabeth Brown, both deceased, of West Nottingham Hundred, Cecil Co., married Mary Eliza Reynolds (1811-1849), daughter of Jonathan Reynolds and Elizabeth Haines, of the same place, on the 21st day of the 12th month 1831 (*Joseph England and his Descendants*, by C. Walter England, Ph.D., 1975, pp. 91-92; *Births, Deaths and Marriages of the Nottingham Quakers, 1680-1899*, by Alice L. Beard (1989), pp. 44, 222, stated the marriage information was illegible; Friends Cemetery, at Harrisville, tombstone inscriptions; *Midland Journal*, 16 Oct 1891, obituary mentioned sons Jefferson Haines of Cecil Co., MD and E. Henry Haines of Lancaster Co., PA)

Haines, Samuel (died 1880), of Port Deposit, Cecil Co., married Mary Jane Rockhold (died 1885), of Harford Co., circa 11 Jul 1833 (date of Harford Co. license) by Rev. Donohay (*Portrait and Biographical Record of Harford and Cecil Counties, Maryland* (1897, repr. 1989), pp. 234-235, stated Mary Jane's maiden name was Rockwell and stated they had 11 children, but only 5 were living in 1897: William H. Haines (born 19 Jun 1834), George Haines, Ann Eliza Culbertson, James Haines and Frank Haines)

Haines, Sophia, see Amos Carter

Haines, William H., see Samuel Haines

HALL

Hall, Charles (1819-1892) (lawyer), of Harford Co., later of Baltimore, son of Washington Hall, of Cecil Co., married Catherine Maria "Kate" Norris (b. c1826), daughter of Capt. Otho Norris and Cornelia Wright, on 24 Nov 1846 in Baltimore and died in San Francisco, CA in June 1892 at which time his wife and children were still living *(Baltimore Sun*, 2 Dec 1846; *The Aegis and Intelligencer*, 1 Jul 1892; *The Norris Family of Maryland and Virginia*, by Harry Alexander Davis (1941), p. 615)

Hall, Charles (born c1826) (African American), married Elizabeth (N) (born c1819) (African American) circa 1844; daughter Mary A. Hall born c1845 (1860 Cecil County Census)

Hall, Christiana J., see Edward L. Osborn

Hall, Elias, married Eliza Simmons circa 24 Apr 1848 (date of license) (Cecil County Marr. License Book)

Hall, Eliza M., see James McDowell

Hall, Emma, see William A. Hall and Walter Armstrong

Hall, Frances S., see John J. Foster

Hall, Francis J., see James Hall

Hall, Hannah E., see James Lofland

Hall, Ida, see William A. Hall

Hall, Isabella, see John Mousley

Hall, James (born c1815, Maryland) (cooper, Bay View), married Ellen J. (born c1828, Maryland) probably circa 1849; son Francis J. Hall born c1850, Maryland (1860 Cecil County Census)

Hall, James A. (1807-1883), married Eliza J. (N) (1825-1898) probably circa 1843-1845 (Zion Methodist Cemetery tombstone inscriptions)

Hall, Jane, see David Steel and Evan Benjamin

Hall, Joseph, married Charity Scarborough circa 21 Dec 1825 (date of license) by Rev. Sharpley (Cecil County Marriage License Book)

Hall, Josiah (1810-1868), of Cecilton, married Elmira Ford circa 24 Dec 1834 (date of license) by Rev. Sharp (Cecil County Marriage License Book; *Cecil Democrat and Farmer's Journal*, 15 Feb 1868)

Hall, Martha, see William G. Hall

Hall, Mary, see Thomas Evans

Hall, Mary A., see Charles Hall

Hall, Mary Elizabeth, see Albanus L. Saxton

Hall, Richard, married Elizabeth K. Berry circa 29 Oct 1834 (date of license) by Rev. Griffith (Cecil County Marriage License Book)

Hall, Samuel, married Eliza Tyson circa 26 Dec 1827 (date of license) (Cecil County Marr. License Book)

Hall, Samuel, married Mary E. Price, daughter of Lewis Price, Esq., of Cecil Co., on 29 Nov 1849, after obtaining a license on 23 Nov 1849, by Rev. Prettyman (Cecil County Marriage License Book; *Cecil Democrat and Farmer's Journal*, 8 Dec 1849)

Hall, Washington, see Charles Hall

Hall, William, see William A. Hall

Hall, William A. (born c1824, Maryland) (carpenter, 7th District), married Elizabeth M. Mackinson (born c1825, Pennsylvania) circa 20 Dec 1847 (date of license); daughter Emma born c1851, Pennsylvania, son William born c1854, Maryland, and daughter Ida born c1856, Maryland (Cecil County Marriage License Book; 1860 Cecil County Census)

Hall, William G. (1820-1879, born Maryland) (floater, 7th District), married Elizabeth E. (N) (1823-1905, born Maryland) probably circa 1848; daughter Martha Hall born c1850 (Hopewell United Methodist Church Cemetery tombstone inscriptions; 1860 Cecil County Census)

HALMAN, HALMON
Halman, John (born c1823, Delaware), miller at North East, married Ann (N) (born c1826, Maryland) probably circa 1844; son John born c1845, Maryland (1860 Cecil County Census)

Halmon, James (born c1825, Delaware), millwright at North East, married Mary (N) (born c1825, Maryland) probably circa 1848; daughter Elizabeth born c1849, Maryland (1860 Cecil County Census)

HAM, HAMM
Ham, Abbey Francina, see John G. Walker

Ham, James (born c1815, Maryland) (African American) (laborer at Elkton), married Jane (N) (Born c1822, Maryland) (African American) probably circa 1840; son John born c1841 (1860 Cecil County Census)

Ham, John, see James Ham

Hamm, Susan B., see James S. Purnell

HAMBLETON
Hambleton, Hugh S., see Philemon F. Hemsley

Hambleton, Joseph (1809-1892), married Mary (N) (1800-1896) by 1835 (son James Hambleton, 1836-1847 (Brick Meeting House, at Calvert, tombstone inscriptions)

Hambleton, Mary E., see Philemon F. Hemsley

HAMER
Hamer, Belinda, see Henry Boies

Hamer, Patterson, married Miss Phebe Ann Hamer, both of Kennett Township, Chester Co., PA, on 1 May 1839 at Hamerton by Rev. Lamborn (*Cecil Gazette*, 4 May 1839)

Hamer, Phebe Ann, see Patterson Hamer

HAMILL
Hamill, Hannah and Jane, see Thomas Mackey

HAMILTON
Hamilton, Hugh, married Sarah Donahoo circa 19 May 1835 (date of license) by Rev. Cramer (Cecil County Marriage License Book)

Hamilton, Philip, married Rebecca Wells McLane circa 27 Dec 1842 (date of license) (Cecil Co. Marriage License Book)

Hamilton, Sarah, see Joseph S. Cranmer

HAMMERSMITH
Hammersmith, Adriann, see David E. Lockard

Hammersmith, John (born c1812, Maryland) (farmer, 6th District), married Elizabeth (N) (born c1811, Maryland), probably circa 1833 (1860 Cecil County Census did not list any children)

HANCE
Hance, Rebecca Ann, see Charles C. Fortnier (Fortiner)

HAND
Hand, William (born c1827, Delaware) (tailor at Charlestown), married Lydia A. Bennett (born c1828, Maryland) circa 20 Oct 1846 (date of license); son William born c1849, Maryland (Cecil County Marriage License Book; 1860 Cecil County Census)

HANDLEN

Handlen, Eliza, see Amos Cummings

HANDY

Handy, Benjamin R., of Newark, DE, married Miss Martha R. Price, of Cecil Co., on 22 May 1850 by the mayor of Philadelphia (*Delaware Gazette*, 31 May 1850; *Cecil Democrat*, 8 Jun 1850)

Handy, Jane W., see Benjamin Caulk

Handy, Thomas W., see Benjamin Caulk

HANNA

Hanna, James, see Elisha England Kirk

Hanna, John G. (1813-1896), married (N) probably circa 1835 (Rock Springs Old School Baptist Church Cemetery tombstone inscription for "Our Father, John G. Hanna," but no marker for their mother)

Hanna, Joseph (1800-1869), married Jane Marshall (1815-1905) circa 7 Mar 1835 (date of license) by Rev. Magraw (Cecil County Marriage License Book; DAR transcript copied in 1928 misspelled his surname Hannah; Rock Springs Old School Baptist Church Cemetery tombstone inscriptions)

Hanna, Rebecca, see David Caldwell

Hanna, Rebecca A,, see Elisha England Kirk

Hanna, Sarah, see George Gillaspy

Hanna, Sarah Jane, see Jethro McCauley

HANSHAW

Hanshaw, Adaline G., see Francis Marion Rawlings

HANSON

Hanson, Alexander B. (captain), married Susan W. Black, only daughter of the late Dr. James Black, all of Kent Co., MD, on 22 Dec 1829 by Rev. Piggot at the residence of John G. Black (*Elkton Press*, 2 Jan 1830; *Delaware Gazette*, 29 Dec 1829)

Hanson, John Jr., of Cecil Co., married Anna Maria Barwick, of New Castle Co., DE, on 26 Sep 1850, after obtaining a license that same day, by Rev. Howell (Cecil County Marriage License Book listed her name as Anna Maria Barwick; *Cecil Democrat and Farmer's Journal*, 28 Sep 1850, listed her name as Miss Mary Ann Barwick, of Delaware)

HARDEN

Harden, Nicholes L., married Sarah Patterson (1822-1855), daughter of Jesse Patterson (born 1796) and Kitturah "Kitty" Jordan (1798-1872), on 28 Jan 1846 (*Maryland Bible Records, Volume 4: Eastern Shore*, by Henry C. Peden, Jr. (2004), pp. 174-175)

HARDGRAVES

Hardgraves, Holland (born c1813, England) (blacksmith at Elkton), married Catherine (N) (born c1825, Maryland) probably circa 1845; son Holland born c1846 (1860 Cecil County Census)

HARDING

Harding, Philip, see Walter Elias Harding and Samuel Reeve Williams

Harding, Sarah, see Samuel Reeve Williams

Harding, Sarah Ann, see John Markee

Harding, Walter Elias (1816-1858), of Elkton, later of Philadelphia, son of Philip Harding (1797-1825) and Amelia Giles (1787-1864), married Mary Woelper, of Baltimore, probably circa 1837 (*Thomas Giles, Born 1752 – Birmingham, England, Died 1812 – Elkton, Maryland, U.S.A., A Genealogical History of His Descendants*, by Alexander W. Giles, Jr. (1986, updated 1996), p. 14)

HARGAN

Hargan, Elihu (1815-1868?) (wheelwright, 6th District), married Prudence (N) (1821, Pennsylvania - 1898, Maryland), probably Prudence Green, circa 1840; son Randolph Hargan born c1846 (Friends Cemetery, at Harrisville, tombstone inscriptions; marker somewhat illegible; 1860 Cecil County Census spelled his name Harigan and listed Margaret Green, age 65, born Pennsylvania, in their household)

Hargan, John Sr. (1825-1910), married Sarah A. (N) (1820-1896) probably by 1850 (Rosebank Cemetery, at Calvert, tombstone inscriptions)

HARKER

Harker, John Newton (1808-1851) (editor of the *Delaware Gazette*) married Miss Ellen J. Brown, both of Wilmington, DE, on 27 Feb 1844 by Rev. J. H. Kennard at Wilmington, DE (*Cecil Whig*, 2 Mar 1844; *Delaware Gazette*, 31 Oct 1851)

HARLAN

Harlan, Hester, see Edward Thompson

Harlan, Joseph, married Margaret Scott circa 17 Mar 1828 (date of license) (Cecil Co. Marr. License Book)

Harlan, M., see Isaac R. Taylor

Harlan, Mary, see Stephen Harlan

Harlan, Mary E., see Andrew Nickle

Harlan, Rebecca M., see Abraham Whitaker

Harlan, Samuel (1783-1859) (miller and grocer), of Chester Co., PA, later of Baltimore, married Eleanor Gatchell (1794-1872), of Cecil Co., on 19 Mar 1829 in Baltimore (*Ancestral Charts, Volume 4*, pp. 178-179, Harford County Genealogical Society Publication, 1988)

Harlan, Stephen (born c1825, Maryland) (farmer, 8th District), married Sarah (N) (born c1826, Pennsylvania) probably circa 1846; daughter Mary born c1847, Maryland (1860 Census spelled his surname Harland)

HARMAN

Harman, C. E., see Fredus Aldridge

HARRAGAN, HARRIGAN

Harragan, Elihu, see William Shroff

Harrigan, Elizabeth, see Joseph Carter

Harrigan, Emma, see John W. Harrigan

Harrigan, John W. (born c1826, Maryland) (farm laborer near Blue Ball), married Sarah (N) (born c1822, Maryland) probably circa 1849; daughter Emma Harrigan born c1850 (1860 Cecil County Census)

Harragan, Jonathan, married Hannah E. Davidson circa 5 Dec 1850 (date of license) (Cecil County Marriage License Book)

Harrigan, also see Hargan

HARRINGTON

Harrington, Mary Ann, see Richard B. Boulden

Harrington, Rebecca, see Benjamin Reed

HARRIS

Harris, Ada, see Samuel Harris

Harris, Alexander, see John H. Harris

Harris, Amanda, see William Harris

Harris, Catharine Marion, see Solomon Sharpe

Harris, Charles (c1808-1875), married Lydia C. (N) (1809-1883) prob. circa 1829-1830 (Friends Cemetery, at Harrisville, tombstone inscriptions)

Harris, Elisha (born c1816, Maryland) (farmer, 7th District), married Ellen (N) (born c1816) probably by 1840; daughter Margaret Harris born c1844 (1860 Cecil County Census)

Harris, George (born c1820, Maryland) (African American) (laborer, 6th District), married Catherine Boyer (born c1821, Maryland) (African American) probably circa 1840; daughter Margaret Harris born c1841; daughter Mrs. Mary Jane Boddy, c1846-1931 (1860 Cecil County Census states Catherine was born in Maryland; Cecil Co. death certificate of daughter Mary Jane states her mother was born in Pennsylvania)

Harris, Harman (born c1822, Maryland) (tanner, 7th District), married Elizabeth (N) (born c1821, Delaware) probably circa 1844; daughter Rebecca Harris born c1845, Maryland (1860 Cecil County Census)

Harris, John H. (born c1825, Delaware) (ferryman at Cecilton), married Ann Elizabeth Cosden (born c1812, Maryland) circa 25 Jun 1849 (date of license); son Alexander Harris born 1850 (Cecil County Marriage License Book; 1860 Cecil County Census)

Harris, Margaret, see Elisha Harris, George Harris and James Todd

Harris, Martha Caroline, see Francis DeValinger

Harris, Rebecca, see Harman Harris

Harris, Samuel, married Maria Hudson circa 17 Mar 1826 (date of license) (Cecil Co. Marr. License Book)

Harris, Samuel, married Eliza Bayard circa 10 Jan 1844 (date of license) (Cecil County Marr. License Book)

Harris, Samuel, married Sarah Jane Plummer circa 16 May 1844 (date of license) (Cecil County Marriage License Book)

Harris, Samuel (born c1820) (African American) (farmer at Cecilton), married Maria (N) (born c1825) (African American) circa 1848; daughter Ada Harris born c1849 (1860 Cecil County Census)

Harris, Samuel, see Francis DeValinger

Harris, Sarah, see Samuel Cooper

Harris, Wilder (1802-1884, born Maryland) (shoemaker, 7th District), married Alice McMullin (1808-1869, born Maryland) circa 2 Feb 1835 (date of license) by Rev. Smith (Cecil County Marriage License Book; Hopewell United Methodist Church Cemetery tombstone inscriptions; 1860 Cecil County Census)

Harris, William (born c1808, Maryland) (blacksmith, 7th District), married Ann (N) (born c1818, Maryland), probably circa 1840; daughter Amanda Harris born c1841 (1860 Cecil County Census)

HART

Hart, Jane, see Richard Barnett

Hart, Phebe, see William I. (J.?) Merritt

Hart, Robert (born c1815, Maryland) (farmer near North East on Elk Neck), married Julia Ann (Wilson) Moore (1811-1877), widow of George H. Moore, on 15 Mar 1842 after obtaining a license on 10 Mar 1842 (Cecil Co. Marriage License Book; 1860 Cecil Co. Census; *Cecil Whig*, 4 Aug and 11 Aug 1877)

HARVEY

Harvey, Andrew (1791-1868) (War of 1812 veteran), married 1st to Lydia McCauley (1796-1837) circa 3 Feb 1817 (date of license which spelled her name Elydia) and married 2nd to Lydia Quarll (1810-1886) on 27 Oct 1842, after obtaining a license on 25 Oct 1842, by Rev. McQue, a Presbyterian minister (Cecil County Marriage License Book; War of 1812 Bounty Land Warrant and Pension Claim No. WC-16797; Leeds Methodist Church Cemetery tombstone inscriptions; *Cecil Democrat*, 19 Sep 1868)

Harvey, Daniel, married Miss Catharine Arthur, both of Baltimore City, on 18 Apr 1850 by Rev. Duncan (*Cecil Democrat and Farmer's Journal*, 27 Apr 1850; *Baltimore Sun*, 23 Apr 1850)

Harvey, George, see William G. Harvey

Harvey, Jerusha, see Lloyd Bailey

Harvey, John (1798-1859), married Abigail Janney (1810-1888) circa 9 Apr 1830 (date of license) by Rev. Smith (Cecil County Marriage License Book; Leeds Methodist Church Cemetery tombstone inscriptions)

Harvey, William G. (born c1810, Maryland) (laborer, North East), married Mary (N) (born c1818, Maryland) probably circa 1826; son George Harvey, potter, born c1827 (1860 Cecil County Census)

HASLETT

Haslett, Elizabeth P., see Robert F. Bowerhill

HASSON

Hasson, Anne E., see James Hasson

Hasson, George Washington (1812-1890), married Mary Ann Whitaker (1817-1898) circa 2 Aug 1839 (date of license) by Rev. Grace (Cecil County Marriage License Book; Hopewell United Methodist Church Cemetery tombstone inscriptions showed their names as Washington and Mary Ann Hasson)

Hasson, James (1803-1861) (Assistant Marshall at Elkton), married Louisa (N) (1807-1851) circa 1828; daughter Anne E. Hasson born c1829 (West Nottingham Cemetery tombstone inscriptions; 1860 Census)

Hasson, Samuel (1801-1883), married Elizabeth Alexander (1797-1875) circa 6 Jan 1830 (date of license) by Rev. Magraw (Cecil County Marriage License Book; West Nottingham Cemetery tombstone inscriptions)

Hasson, Washington, see George Washington Hasson

Hasson, William (1817-1872) (farmer near Elkton), married Elizabeth Burnite (1819-1895) circa 5 Sep 1837 (date of license) by Rev. Kennard (Cecil County Marriage License Book; DAR transcript copied in 1928 spelled his name Hassan and her name Burnight; Cherry Hill Methodist Church Cemetery tombstone inscriptions; 1860 Cecil County Census)

HASWELL

Haswell, Jessie, see Thomas K. Spencer

HATHAWAY

Hathaway, Henry, married Martha (N) (1825-1885) probably circa 1843-1845 (Hopewell United Methodist Church Cemetery tombstone inscription for Martha Hathaway)

HAUGE, see Hague

HAWAY

Haway(?), Amelia, see Michael Rieley

HAWKINS

Hawkins, Alexander, see James Hawkins

Hawkins, Eliza, see John W. McCall

Hawkins, James (born c1826) (African American) (laborer at St. Augustine), married Ischell (N) (born c1830) (African American) probably circa 1848; son Alexander born c1849 (1860 Cecil County Census)

HAYDEN

Hayden, James T., married Ann Mayson circa 1 Nov 1832 (date of license) by Rev. Duke (Cecil County Marriage License Book)

HAYES, HAYS

Hayes, Eleanor, see Robert H. Hayes

Hayes, Hannah Amelia, see John T. Gallaher

Hayes, George (born 1806), of Elkton, Cecil Co., married Margaret D. Silver (1809-1876), daughter of William Silver (1778-1837) and Elizabeth Davis (1782-1848), on 11 Sep 1828 after obtaining a license on 6 Sep 1828 (Harford County marriage license; Harford Methodist Circuit, Register of Births; *The Whiteford Genealogy*, by Hazel Whiteford Baldwin (1992), pp. 322-323; *Our Silver Heritage*, by Benjamin Stump Silver and Frances Aylette (Bowen) Silver (1976), pp. 3151, 3156)

Hays, Henry, married Catherine Callendar circa 20 Jul 1842 (date of license) (Cecil County Marriage License Book; DAR transcript copied in 1955 mistakenly listed the marriage license date as 20 Jun 1842)

Hays, Henry M. (born c1815, Maryland) (laborer at Cecilton), married Mary E. Satterfield (born c1825, Maryland) circa 9 Mar 1841 (date of license); son Robert H. Hayes born c1842 (Cecil County Marriage License Book; 1860 Cecil County Census)

Hayes, Jedediah, married Hannah Knight circa 7 Aug 1832 (date of license) by Rev. Duke (Cecil County Marriage License Book)

Hays, Joel H., married Miss Mary Ann Gwinn, both of Cecil Co., on 12 Dec 1848, after obtaining a license that same day, by Rev. Taft (Cecil County Marriage License Book; *Cecil Democrat and Farmer's Journal*, 23 Dec 1848)

Hays, John, married Sarah Ann Money circa 16 Nov 1831 (date of license) by Rev. Duke (Cecil County Marriage License Book)

Hays, John B., married Rose Ann S. Coale circa 7 Apr 1842 (date of license) (Cecil County Marriage License Book; DAR Typescript copied in 1955 spelled his name Hayes and her name Coal)

Hayes, Louisa, see William S. Hessey

Hays, Mary Ann, see Thomas Lake

Hays, Mary E., see William C. Crow

Hayes, R. M. (1808-1889), married Eliza J. (N) (1814-1874) probably circa 1832-1834 (Elkton Presbyterian Church Cemetery tombstone inscriptions)

Hays, Rebecca, see Perry Edwards

Hayes, Rebecca Ann, see James W. Morgan

Hayes, Robert Jr., married Alethea Money circa 13 May 1835 (date of license) by Rev. Coleman (Cecil County Marriage License Book)

Hayes, Robert H., see Henry M. Hayes

Hayes, Robert H., married Eleanor "Nelly" Etherington circa 22 May 1828 (date of license) (Cecil County Marriage License Book) and Robert H. Hayes, of Cecil Co., divorced from Eleanor Hayes on 5 Mar 1834, "neither to remarry" (*Divorces and Names Changed in Maryland by Act of the Legislature, 1634-1867*, by Mary Keysor Meyer (1991), p. 42; *Midland Journal*, 3 Jan 1890, reported a Robert Hayes died in his 82nd year in the 4th District at Barksdale)

Hays, Robert H., married Mary Ann Black circa 19 Mar 1850 (date of license) (Cecil County Marriage License Book)

Hays, Robert P., of New Castle Co., Delaware, married Sarah Ann Foster, daughter of Capt. James Foster, of Cecil Co., on 25 Jun 1849 by Rev. Cooper (*Cecil Democrat and Farmer's Journal*, 7 Jul 1849, noting that "The happy pair will receive our acknowledgements for the cake which accompanied the above notice." The paper had also requested, "*Baltimore Sun* please copy," but it was not published in that newspaper.)

Hays, Samuel, married Edith Emeline Biddle circa 27 Mar 1826 (date of license) by Rev. Smith (Cecil County Marriage License Book misspelled her first name as Edieth)

Hays, Stephen T. (born c1822) (plasterer at Elkton), married Miss Cenah B. Mitchell (born c1826), both of Cecil Co., on 23 Nov 1848, after obtaining a license on 16 Nov 1848, by Rev. McIntire (Cecil County Marriage License Book; 1860 Cecil County Census; *Cecil Democrat and Farmer's Journal*, 2 Dec 1848)

Hayes, Thomas, married Rebecca Smith circa 8 Jun 1830 (date of license) by Rev. Mahan (Cecil County Marriage License Book)

HAYNES
Haynes, Adriana, see Lyttleton Physick

HAZELETT
Hazelett, Jannetta and William, see J. Lacy Darlington

HEADLEY
Headley, Hulda, see Thomas Jones

HEALD

Heald, Edward, of Baltimore City, married Caroline M. Creswell, of Cecil Co., circa 14 Nov 1846 (date of license) (Cecil County Marriage License Book)

HEATH

Heath, Benjamin F. (1812-1881) (merchant), of Lapidum, Harford Co., married 1st to Rachel Chamberlaine circa 29 Dec 1842 (date of license) and married 2nd to Hester Ann Murphy (1826-1911, former wife of John B. Murphy [married in 1843 and divorced in 1859; he then moved to Kentucky], daughter of Henry Barnes and Sarah B. Whitaker, in 1866; both marriages took place in Cecil County (Cecil County Marriage License Book; Angel Hill Cemetery tombstone inscriptions; Harford County death certificate of Hester Ann Heath in 1911; Harford County Equity Case 1303 (complaint filed by her on 2 Jun 1858 and divorce granted on 28 Apr 1859); Murphy family research by Kathy Franke, of St. Louis, MO, in 2014)

Heath, Catharine, see Andrew Pearce

Heath, Catherine A., see William T. Jones

Heath, Hester Ann, see Benjamin F. Heath

Heath, John, married Susanna Moore circa 2 Jan 1826 (date of license) by Rev. Goforth (Cecil County Marriage License Book)

Heath, John T. (born c1820) (farmer, Cecilton), married Mary (N) (born c1818) circa 1845; son Washington born c1836 (1860 Cecil County Census)

Heath, Martha Jane, see John Thomas McCleary

Heath, Sarah, see John T. Cooper

Heath, Washington, see John T. Heath

HEAVELO

Heavelo, James, married Elizabeth Hofecker circa 30 Jul 1849 (date of license) (Cecil County Marriage License Book)

HECKART

Heckart, John J. (1804-1872, born Pennsylvania) (lumber merchant, Port Deposit), married Miss Angelina Gilmore (1818-1908, born Maryland) circa 8 Feb 1837 (date of license) by Rev. Potts (Cecil County Marriage License Book; 1860 Cecil County Census; West Nottingham Cemetery tombstone inscriptions; *Cecil Whig*, 6 Jul 1872)

HECKENDORN

Heckendorn, Jacob (born c1818, Pennsylvania (machinist at Elkton), married Miss Alice J. Buckley (born c1828, Pennsylvania), of Cecil Co., on 8 Nov 1849 at New London, Chester Co., PA, by Rev. Dubois; son Henry Heckendorn born c1850, Maryland, and daughter Lynda Heckendorn born c1852, Maryland (*Cecil Whig*, 10 Nov 1849, and *Cecil Democrat and Farmer's Journal*, 19 Nov 1849, both acknowledged the "excellent and ample supply of cake" which accompanied the notice; 1860 Cecil County Census stated William J. Buckley, age 30, and Rebecca Buckley, age 18, both born in Maryland, lived with them)

HEDGES

Hedges, Hannah F. and John, see James Stroud

HEDGICK

Hedgick, John and Sally Ann, see John L. Hadden

HEDNEY

Hedney, Rebecca, see James Proctor

HEDRICK

Hedrick, Joseph, married Miss Amanda Vance, both of Cecil Co., on 21 Nov 1849 by Rev. Elliott (Cecil County Marriage License Book stated they obtained a license on 26 Nov 1849, but *Cecil Democrat and Farmer's Journal*, 1 Dec 1849, and *Cecil Whig*, 1 Dec 1849, both reported they married on 21 Nov 1849)

HELENS

Helens, Ann, see William Biggs

HELLINGER

Hellinger, Joseph, near Bay View, married Eliza (N) (1809-1875) and she is buried in Shelemiah Cemetery (*Cecil Whig*, 18 Sep 1875)

HEMPFIELD, HEMPHILL

Hempfield, Evans, see Hyland Marcus

Hemphill, James (born c1823) (blacksmith at Chesapeake City), married Harriett Slack (born c1822), both of Cecil Co., on 3 Jul 1845, after obtaining a license that same day, by Rev. Barton (Cecil County Marriage License Book; Elkton Methodist Church Register, p. 141; 1860 Cecil County Census)

Hemphill, Joseph (born c1818) (laborer at Elkton), married 1st to Ellen Kirkpatrick circa 16 Dec 1846 (date of license) and married 2nd to Priscilla J. Jackson (born c1835) circa 21 Mar 1855 (date of license) (Cecil County Marriage License Book; 1860 Cecil County Census spelled his name Hempfield)

Hempfield (Hemphill), Margaret, see John P. Sanders

Hemphill, Mary, see Benjamin Taylor and Thomas Giles

Hempfield, Thomas (born c1825) (farmer at Elkton), married Mary (N) (born c1826, Maryland), possibly Mary Pluck, circa 1850; daughter Mary Hempfield born c1851 (1860 Cecil County Census listed them with Rebecca Pluck, head of household, age 64, born Delaware)

HEMSLEY

Hemsley, Philemon F., married Mary E. Hambleton, eldest daughter of late Hugh S. Hambleton, on 29 May 1850 by Rev. Dr. Mason at Christ Church in Easton (*Cecil Democrat and Farmer's Journal*, 1 Jun 1850)

HENDERSON

Henderson, Ann, see Richard Groves

Henderson, John (c1792-1854) (War of 1812 veteran), married Rebecca Groves (born 1808) on 2 Mar 1830, after obtaining a license on 1 Mar 1830, by Rev. Ryder, a Methodist minister (Cecil County Marriage License Book; War of 1812 Bounty Land Warrant No. 55-rej-24343; *Cecil Democrat*, 18 Mar 1854)

Henderson, Mary E., see John S. Everist

HENDRICKSON

Hendrickson, Peregrine (c1788-1851), married 1st to Rebecca Pearce circa 28 Dec 1811 (date of license) and married 2nd to Sophia Sappington, of Kent Co., circa 26 Dec 1825 (date of license) by Rev. Jackson (Cecil County Marriage License Book in 1811; Kent County Marriage License Book in 1825; *Delaware Gazette*, 27 May 1851, stated he died at home near Middletown, DE)

Hendrickson, Peregrine (born 1820, Maryland) (farmer at Bohemian Mills), married 1st to Margaret Hill, both of New Castle Co., DE, circa 16 Dec 1843 (date of license) and married 2nd to Margaret N. Roberts (born 1824, Maryland) circa 2 Apr 1850 (date of license) (Cecil County Marriage License Book; 1860 Cecil County Census listed his name as P. Hendreckson)

Hendrickson, William H., married Miss Ann Maria Vernon, of Wilmington, DE, on 20 Sep 1849 by Rev. Dubose at New London, Chester Co., PA (*Cecil Democrat and Farmer's Journal*, 22 Sep 1849; *Delaware Gazette*, 25 Sep 1849; *Cecil Whig*, 22 Sep 1849)

HENRY

Henry, James, see Edward L. Foard

Henry, Jane, see Joseph Taylor

Henry, Mary, see Hugh McConkey, Jr.

Henry, Mary Ann, see Edward L. Foard

Henry, Mary D., see Robert Marshbank

HENSHAW

Henshaw, Rebecca, see John Conekin

HEPBRON

Hepbron, James, married Sarah Jane Morgan circa 23 Feb 1833 (date of license) by Rev. Duke (Cecil County Marriage License Book)

HERBERT

Herbert, James B., married Mary Ann Baker circa 5 Jul 1825 (date of license) by Rev. Duke (Cecil County Marriage License Book)

HESS

Hess, Henry (born 1819), of Lancaster Co., PA, later of Cecil Co., married Elizabeth N. Clemson, of Lancaster Co., in 1849 (*Portrait and Biographical Record of Harford and Cecil Counties, Maryland* (1897, repr. 1989), pp. 244-245)

HESSEY

Hessey, Ellen H., see James Price

Hessey, John H. (1819-1906, born Ohio), married Laura E. Morgan (1829-1902), daughter of William and Jane Morgan, of Maryland, circa 1847; daughter Laura Hessey born c1848, Maryland (St. Stephen's Episcopal Church Cemetery tombstone inscriptions; 1860 Cecil County Census)

Hessey, Laura, see John H. Hessey

Hessey, Samuel, married Sarah Biggs circa 7 Mar 1837 (date of license) by Rev. Smith (Cecil County Marriage License Book spelled his name Hessy)

Hessey, Susan A., see John M. Flintham

Hessey, William S. (1811-1867), of Sassafras Neck, married Louisa Hayes, both of Cecil Co., on 31 Oct 1837, after obtaining a license on 28 Oct 1837, by Rev. Piggot (Cecil County Marriage License Book; DAR transcript copied in 1928 misspelled his name Hesse and the minister's name Pickett; Rev. Robert Piggot was a Protestant Episcopal minister in North Sassafras; St. Stephen's P. E. Church Register; *Cecil Democrat and Farmer's Journal*, 8 Jun 1867, stated William died in his 56th year)

HESSIN

Hessin, Caroline W. and William, see Dominick Eagle

HICKEY

Hickey, James L. (born c1810, Pennsylvania) (house painter at Elkton), married Ann S. (N) (born c1815, Maryland) circa 1833; daughter Ellen born c1834, Pennsylvania (1860 Cecil County Census)

HICKMAN

Hickman, Mary Ann, see Oliver A. Reese

Hickman, Mary E., see Robert H. Arthur

Hickman, T., see Oliver A. Reese

HILAMAN

Hilaman, John Smith (1818-1885), son of Jacob and Martha D. Hilaman, married Margaret (N) (1826-1899) probably circa 1845 (Rosebank Cemetery, at Calvert, tombstone inscriptions)

HILL

Hill, Alexander (1817-1894, born Maryland) (farmer near Elkton), married Elizabeth "Eliza" Sentman (1816-1873, born Pennsylvania) circa 12 Oct 1842 (date of license) (Cecil County Marriage License Book; Sharp's Cemetery tombstone inscriptions; 1860 Cecil County Census)

Hill, Amos, see James Hill

Hill, Edwin, see Washington Hill

Hill, Elijah, see Levi Alexander Hill

Hill, Isaac (1809-1874, born Maryland) (cooper in the 8th District), married Hannah (N) (1815-1889, born Pennsylvania) probably circa 1833; son Levi Hill was born c1834, Maryland (Rock Springs Old School Baptist Church Cemetery tombstone inscriptions; 1860 Cecil County Census)

Hill, James (born c1805, Maryland) (teamster near Blue Ball), married Mary (N) (born c1820, Maryland) probably circa 1835; son Amos Hill born c1835, Maryland (1860 Cecil County Census)

Hill, Lavinia Ann, see William Vincinger

Hill, Levi, see Isaac Hill

Hill, Levi, married Mary Crothers circa 13 Jan 1825 (date of license) by Rev. Griffith (Cecil County Marriage License Book)

Hill, Levi Alexander (born 1823), son of Elijah Hill (1788-1857) and Mary Ann Brown (1788-1846), of Cecil Co., married Sarah Brown (born 1823 near Brick Meeting House), daughter of Jehu Brown and Sarah England, of Cecil Co., probably circa 1844 and lived in Chester Co., PA (*Joseph England and his Descendants*, by C. Walter England, Ph.D., 1975, p. 154; Sharp's Cemetery tombstone inscriptions)

Hill, Margaret, see Peregrine Hendrickson

Hill, Maria H., see Lawrence Sentman

Hill, Washington (born c1820, Maryland) (farmer, 8th District), married Amanda (N) (bon c1824, Maryland) probably circa 1845; son Edwin Hill born c1846, Maryland (1860 Cecil County Census)

HILLES

Hilles, David and Dinah, see Nathan Hilles

Hilles, Nathan, son of David and Dinah Hilles, latter deceased, of London Grove Township, Chester Co., PA, married Miss Sarah S. Coale, daughter of Skipwith and Ann Coale, former deceased, of West Nottingham Hundred, Cecil Co., on the 19th day of the 10th month 1824 at West Nottingham Meeting House (*Births, Deaths and Marriages of the Nottingham Quakers, 1680-1899*, by Alice L. Beard (1989), p. 220)

HILLYARD

Hillyard, John William, formerly of Fredericksburg, VA, married Miss Millicent Ann Brown, of Cecil Co., on 5 Dec 1850 by Rev. Heffner in Baltimore (*Cecil Democrat and Farmer's Journal*, 14 Dec 1850; *Baltimore Sun*, 13 Dec 1850)

HINDMAN

Hindman, Elinor, see Robert Nesbitt Jr.

Hindman, Eliza, see James Tosh

Hindman, Hiram, married Rachel Coulson before 1845 (son John Coulson Hindman born 28 Oct 1845) (*Portrait and Biographical Record of Harford and Cecil Counties, Maryland* (1897, repr. 1989), p. 396)

Hindman, John Coulson, see Hiram Hindman

Hindman, Margaret, see Henry Woodrow

Hindman, Robert N. (1815-1893) (farmer, 6th District), married Rachel Maria Swisher (1815-1881) circa 24 Jan 1837 (date of license) by Rev. Burris (Cecil County Marriage License Book; West Nottingham Cemetery tombstone inscriptions; 1860 Cecil County Census)

Hindman, Samuel (1808-1870), married Prudence Woodrow (1810-1871) probably circa 1828-1830 (West Nottingham Cemetery tombstone inscriptions)

Hindman, Samuel, married Jane Eleanor Tosh circa 5 Jan 1833 (date of license) by Rev. Magraw (Cecil County Marriage License Book)

HINES

Hines, Isaac, of Kent Co., MD, married Miss Ann Knock, of Queen Anne's Co., MD, on 11 Nov 1828 by Rev. Ryder (*Elkton Press*, 18 Nov 1828)

Hines, Joseph (born c1818, Maryland) (blacksmith, 7th District), married 1st to Sarah Jackson circa 20 Dec 1843 (date of license) and married 2nd to Mary A. Simpers (born c1833, Maryland) circa 12 Jun 1855 (date of license) (Cecil County Marriage License Book; 1860 Cecil County Census

Hines, Rachel, see Richard L. Simpers

Hines, Samuel (born c1809, Maryland) (farmer, 7th District), married Mary (N) (born c1810, Maryland) probably circa 1833; son William Hines born c1834 (1860 Cecil County Census)

Hines, Thomas, married Mary Bennett circa 5 Jun 1839 (date of license) by Rev. Barratt (Cecil County Marriage License Book)

Hines, William, married Rachel Kirkpatrick circa 27 Feb 1837 (date of license) by Rev. Barratt; Mrs. Rachel Hines married 2nd to Richard Simpers, both of Cecil Co., on 12 Mar 1846 by Rev. Barratt (Cecil County Marriage License Book spelled his name Hinds in 1837; *Cecil Whig*, 4 Apr 1846)

Hines, William, see Samuel Hines

HINSON

Hinson, James A., of Elkton, married Sarah Jane (N) (1823-1877) circa 1843 (*Cecil Whig*, 23 Jun 1877)

HIRONS

Hirons, Lydia Gilpin, see George Clinton Veazey

Hirons, Mary M., see John W. Lynch

HITCHCOCK

Hitchcock, Elisha, married Margaret White circa 18 Aug 1846 (date of license) (Cecil Co. Marr. Lic. Book)

Hitchcock, Eliza Ann, see William Stalcup

Hitchcock, Elizabeth R., see John R. Bristow

Hitchcock, Samuel, married Harriet B. White, both of Cecil Co., on 7 Aug 1849 by Rev. Lemmon (*Cecil Democrat and Farmer's Journal*, 18 Aug 1849; no marriage license was found in Cecil County)

HITSELBERGER

Hitselberger, Catherine, see Samuel Clark

HODGE

Hodge, Mary, see Joseph Whitelock

HODGSON

Hodgson, Stephen, married Araminta Ferguson circa 5 Jun 1833 (date of license) by Rev. Wilson (Cecil County Marriage License Book)

HOFECKER

Hofecker, Elizabeth, see James Heavelo

HOGAN

Hogan, (N) (African American), married Matilda (N) (born c1821) (African American) probably circa 1841 (1860 Cecil County Census listed daughters Susanna born c1842, Indiana, born c1847, Georgianna, born c1850, and Victoria, born c1858)

HOGG

Hogg, Emma L., see John R. Hogg

Hogg, John R. (1805-1888, born Delaware) (baggage agent at Elkton), married Ann B. (N) (born c1804, Delaware) circa 1830; daughter Martha B. Hogg born c1837, Delaware; son John Hogg born c1804, Maryland; daughter Mary A. Hogg born c1842, Maryland; and, daughter Emma L. Hogg born c1846 (1860 Cecil County Census; *Easton Star*, 5 Jun 1888)

Hogg, Martha B., see John R. Hogg

Hogg, Mary, see William T. Richardson

Hogg, Mary A., see John R. Hogg

Hogg, Robert E., married Caroline Purnell circa 9 Apr 1829 (date of license) by Rev. Duke (Cecil County Marriage License Book)

Hogg, Samuel R., married Rachel Boulden circa 14 Jun 1825 (date of license) by Rev. Gilbert (Cecil County Marriage License Book)

Hogg, William, married Jane Moffitt circa 23 May 1826 (date of license) by Rev. Graham (Cecil County Marriage License Book; *Cecil Democrat and Farmer's Journal*, 21 Dec 1867, reported that a William Hogg died in his 65th year in Baltimore)

HOHN

Hohn, Anton (1808-1880), married Elizabeth (N) (1800-1860) probably circa 1829-1830 (Hopewell United Methodist Church Cemetery tombstone inscriptions)

HOLDEN

Holden, Hannah, see Horace H. Duyckinck

Holden, Jacob (1795-1859), son of William and Elizabeth Holden, married Margaret Boulden (1808-1881), daughter of Jesse and Nancy Boulden, on 5 Oct 1830, after obtaining a license that same day, by Rev. Hodgson (Cecil County Marriage License Book; DAR transcript copied in 1928 spelled her surname Boulding and misspelled the minister's name as Hodson; Francis Hodgson was a Methodist Episcopal minister in Elkton at that time; *Bible Records, Genealogical Society of Cecil County*, by Gary L. Burns (1990), p. 8, stated this family was from the Union Church area and listed the births of four children: Mary Ann, born 18 May 1831; Sarah Elizabeth, born 25 Nov 1832; William Wesley, born 7 May 1835; and, Wabb(?), born – Mar 1843, while the 1860 Cecil County Census listed Margarett Halden, age 52, Jacob, age 20, Martha, age 12 and Alexana, age 10, residing in South Milford, and *Portrait and Biographical Record of Harford and Cecil Counties, Maryland* (1897, repr. 1989), p. 156, listed their surviving children in 1897 as Mary Ann Potts, Elizabeth Foster, Helen Cline, Jacob Holden, Mitchell Holden, and William W. Holden (born 7 May 1835)

HOLGATE

Holgate, Kuria, see Jacob Casho

HOLLACE

Hollace, George B., married Lydia Ann Hackett circa 8 Jan 1831 (date of license) by Rev. Duke (Cecil County Marriage License Book)

HOLLAND

Holland, John H., married Mary E. Emmons circa 19 Mar 1849 (date of license) (Cecil County Marriage License Book)

Holland, Thomas, married Margaret Egner circa 16 Jan 1826 (date of license) by Rev. Woolford (Cecil County Marriage License Book)

Holland, William (born c1815, New Jersey) (wheelwright near Elkton), married Catherine Ann Armstrong (born c 1815, Maryland) circa 6 Apr 1837 (date of license) by Rev. Jordan (Cecil County Marriage License Book; 1860 Cecil County Census)

HOLLINGSWORTH

Hollingsworth, Hannah, see Lewis Kirk

Hollingsworth, Jane, see Lewis Kirk

Hollingsworth, John, see Lewis Kirk

Hollingsworth, Joshua, see Lewis Kirk

Hollingsworth, Mary, see William H. Gilpin

Hollingsworth, Robert, see William Hollingsworth

Hollingsworth, William (1780-1844) (War of 1812 veteran), married Mary Eliza Evans (1803-1871) on 9 Oct 1827, after obtaining a license on 8 Oct 1827, by Rev. Magraw, a Presbyterian minister; son Dr. Robert Hollingsworth, 1826-1860 (Cecil County Marr. License Book; War of 1812 Bounty Land Warrant 55-160-23889; Elkton Presbyterian Church Cemetery tombstone inscriptions; *Cecil Whig*, 25 Mar 1871)

HOLLY

Holly, George W., of Cecil Co., later of Havre de Grace, Harford Co., married Martha Ann Nesbitt on 9 Jan 1850 after obtaining a license on 7 Jan 1850 (Cecil County Marriage License Book; *Bible Records, Genealogical Society of Cecil County*, by Gary L. Burns (1990), p. 78, spelled her name Nasbitt and listed the births of their seven children: William W., born 21 Jan 1851; Joseph G., born 25 Sep 1853; Mary E., born 4 Apr 1861; George J., born 22 Sep 1863. died 5 May 1932; Anna S., born 21 Aug 1865; Martha E., born 11 Apr 1869; and, John B., born 19 Jan 1872)

HOLLOWELL

Hollowell, Sarah A., see Frederick McNamee

HOLMES

Holmes, Abner, married Mary Milburn circa 11 Aug 1841 (date of license) (Cecil Co. Marr. License Book)

HOLT

Holt, Andrew, see Washington Holt

Holt, Isaac, see John Weston Holt

Holt, Isaac Lumsdon, see Washington Holt

Holt, John, married Mary Ellen Cann circa 21 Oct 1843 (date of license) (Cecil County Marr. License Book)

Holt, John Weston (1807-1876) (farmer near Elkton), son of Isaac Holt, married Elizabeth Gallaher (1808-1892), daughter of John and Martha Gallaher, circa 12 Jan 1831 (date of license) by Rev. Duke (Cecil County Marriage License Book; Union Methodist Church Cemetery tombstone inscriptions; *Cecil Whig*, 15 Jan 1876, reported he died after being thrown from his wagon; 1860 Cecil County Census)

Holt, Lizzie, see Washington Holt

Holt, Martha A., see Thomas M. Touchstone

Holt, Mary Elizabeth, see Joseph M. Grant

Holt, May, see Washington Holt

Holt, Washington (1817-1901, born Maryland) (laborer at North East), son of Andrew Holt, and of Welsh descent, married Ann Foster (1821-1907), daughter of Jesse Foster, circa 1842 and had six children, four of whom were living in 1897: Andrew W. (born 28 Aug 1844), Isaac Lumsdon, Elizabeth "Lizzie" and May (*Portrait and Biographical Record of Harford and Cecil Counties, Maryland* (1897, repr. 1989), p. 163; Wesley Methodist Church Cemetery tombstone inscriptions; 1860 Cecil County Census also listed children Thomas, born c1846, and Charles, born c1855)

HOOPER

Hooper, Mary, see John Stump and James T. McCullough

HOPKINS

Hopkins, Ann, see Henry S. Magraw

Hopkins, Cassandra Morgan, see William Latham Rowland

Hopkins, Emily W., see Henry S. Magraw

Hopkins, George G., see Joseph Hopkins

Hopkins, George R., see Henry S. Magraw

Hopkins, Henry (born c1822, Maryland) (African American) (laborer, 7th District), married Charlotte (N) (born c1829, Maryland) probably circa 1844; daughter Rebecca born c1845 (1860 Cecil County Census)

Hopkins, John, see Thomas C. Hopkins and William Latham Rowland

Hopkins, John (born c1824, Maryland) (African American) (laborer, 8th District), married Nehetta (N) (born c1824, Maryland) (African American) probably circa 1843; son John Hopkins, Jr. born c1844, Maryland, and their other children were also born in Maryland (1860 Cecil County Census)

Hopkins, Joseph (born c1823, Maryland) (doctor near Brick Meeting House), married Mary A. Cloud (born c1826, Pennsylvania) circa 24 May 1848 (date of license); son Joseph Jr. born c1850 and son George G. born c1855, both in Maryland (Cecil County Marriage License Book; 1860 Cecil County Census)

Hopkins, Philip, married Sarah Marshbank circa 25 Oct 1843 (date of license) (Cecil County Marriage License Book spelled her name Marshbanks)

Hopkins, Priscilla, see Corbin Cooley and Robert Stephenson

Hopkins, Rebecca, see Henry Hopkins

Hopkins, Samuel (born c1824, Maryland) (carpenter, 7th District), married Mary (N) (born c1821, Maryland) probably circa 1846; daughter Susanna Hopkins born c1847 (1860 Cecil County Census)

Hopkins, Susanna, see Samuel Hopkins

Hopkins, Thomas C. (1819-1885, born Maryland) (farmer, 6th District), married Hannah E. (N) (1822-1911, born Maryland) probably circa 1845; son John Hopkins was born c1846 (Friends Cemetery, at Colora, tombstone inscriptions; 1860 Cecil County Census)

HOPPER

Hopper, Levi, see Samuel Pusey

Hopper, Philemon B. Jr. (esquire), married Henrietta Goldsborough, daughter of Dr. Robert Goldsborough, all of Centreville, on 14 Mar 1850 by Rev. Brown in Centreville, Queen Anne's Co. (*Cecil Democrat and Farmer's Journal*, 30 Mar 1850)

Hopper, Rachel, see Samuel Pusey

Hopper, Samuel W. T., of the firm of Richardson & Hopper, married Emeline Virginia Webb, youngest daughter of Abner Webb, Esq., all of Baltimore, on 22 Nov 1849 by Rev. Webster in Baltimore (*Cecil Democrat and Farmer's Journal*, 24 Nov 1849)

HORNER

Horner, Henry (1819-1882), married Sophia C. (N) (1812-1897) probably circa 1830 (Bethesda Cemetery, at Oakwood, tombstone inscriptions)

Horner, William G., married Rebecca Beatty circa 4 May 1850 (date of license) (Cecil County Marriage License Book)

HORTON

Horton, Margaret Elizabeth, see William Penn Ewing

Horton, Rebecca, see Daniel Clendenin

HOTCHKISS

Hotchkiss, William A., married Sophia Winchester circa 18 Oct 1848 (date of license) (Cecil County Marriage License Book; DAR transcript copied in 1955 misspelled his name Hochkiss)

HOUSE

House, Mary E., see William H. Kirk

House, Samuel, of Little Britain, PA, married Miss Amanda M. Schuck, of Cecil Co., on 5 Apr 1838 at Lancaster, PA (*Cecil Gazette*, 25 Apr 1838)

HOUSTON, HUSTON

Houston, James L. (reverend), of Lancaster, PA, married Adaline Price, daughter of Mr. Benjamin Price, of Staunton Farm, Kent Co., MD, on 10 Apr 1838, after obtaining a license on 7 Apr 1838, by Rev. Benjamin Price at Staunton Farm (*Cecil Gazette*, 11 Apr 1838; Kent County Marriage License Book)

Houston, John, of Chester Co., PA, married Martha Armstrong circa 17 Feb 1841 (date of license) (Cecil County Marriage License Book)

Houston (Huston), William S., married Susan Armstrong circa 2 Jan 1849 (date of license) by Rev. DeWitt (Cecil County Marriage License Book spelled his surname Houston; DAR transcript copied in 1955 spelled it Huston; *Cecil Democrat and Farmer's Journal*, 6 Jan 1849, and on 3 Feb 1849 the paper announced the marriage again and spelled his name Huston, but did not give the marriage date)

HOWARD

Howard, Eliza Ann, see Francis Asbury Ellis

Howard, Jacob C. (1800-1868), of Elkton, married Araminta Hyland (c1807-1888) circa 26 Apr 1827 (date of license) (Cecil County Marriage License Book; Elkton Presbyterian Church Cemetery tombstone inscriptions; *Cecil Democrat and Farmer's Journal*, 18 Jul and 25 Jul 1868, stated he died at the residence of his son-in-law A. G. Tuite); see Aaron G. Tuite, *q.v.*

Howard, Mary Elizabeth, see Aaron G. Tuite

Howard, Rachel, see Charles K. Manly

Howard, Samuel, married Esther Ann Webb circa 5 Jun 1828 (date of license) by Rev. Sharp (Cecil County Marriage License Book)

Howard, Spencer, married Miss Ann Macklan, both of the vicinity of Newark, DE, on 16 Mar 1829 by Rev. Hagany (*Elkton Press*, 21 Mar 1829)

Howard, Thomas Jr. (1808-1863), married Ann Ash (1812-1866) circa 21 Feb 1837 (date of license) by Rev. Hammill (Cecil County Marriage License Book; Elkton Presbyterian Church Cemetery tombstone inscriptions; *Cecil Whig*, 22 Nov 1866)

Howard, William E., of Elkton, married Ann Jemima Biddle, daughter of John H. Biddle, both of Cecil Co., on 20 Sep 1848, after obtaining a license on 19 Sep 1848, by Rev. McIntire in Elkton (*Cecil Whig*, 23 Sep 1848; Cecil County Marriage License Book spelled her name Annjamima; DAR transcript copied in 1955 mistakenly listed her name as Araminta; *Cecil Democrat and Farmer's Journal*, 23 Sep 1848, noted, "The happy couple will receive our acknowledgements for a supply of delicious cake.")

Howard, William Frederick (1818-1893, born Hampton Gay, Oxfordshire, England), married Ann Pier (1816-1909, born London, England) probably circa 1840 (Leeds Methodist Church Cemetery tombstones)

HOWELL

Howell family, see Jacob James Howell

Howell, Charlotte, see William Moore

Howell, Elizabeth, see John England

Howell, Jacob James (1804-1860) (farmer at Elkton), son of James Howell (1773-1821) and Sarah "Sary" Standley (born 1771), married Rebecca Price (1809-1895) on 11 Oct 1825 (*Maryland Bible Records, Volume 4: Eastern Shore*, by Henry C. Peden, Jr. (2004), pp. 110-112, listed the births of their ten children: James P., born 19 Oct 1826; George, born 11 Jan 1829; Emily Ann, born 3 Jan 1832; John F., born 6 Jul 1834; Sarah, born – Sep 1836 at Cox Point on Bohemia Manor; William Thomas, born 15 Jun 1838; Sarah Terreasa, born 20 Jan 1842; Augusta N., born 6 Feb 1844; Alice Jane, born 14 Feb 1847; and, Henrietta, born 5 Dec 1849; 1860 Cecil County Census mistakenly stated he was age 63)

Howell, William, see William Moore

HOWITT
Howitt, William (born c1804, Maryland) (farm hand at Cecilton), married Mary (N) (born c1814, Maryland) circa 1834; son Benjamin Howitt born c1835 (1860 Cecil County Census)

HUDSON
Hudson, Caroline, see John Mears

Hudson, Comfort, see Jacob Fleck

Hudson, Eliza, see John Mears

Hudson, Emily Ann, see John R. Barwick

Hudson, Lemuel, married Hannah Porter circa 27 Dec 1840 (date of license) (Cecil Co. Marr. License Book)

Hudson, Maria, see Samuel Harris

Hudson, Mary Ann, see Ebenezer Neal

Hudson, Richard, married Letitia Mills circa 6 Jun 1831 (date of license) by Rev. Barnes (Cecil County Marriage License Book)

Hudson, William, married Mary Ann Borcham circa 8 Feb 1831 (date of license) by Rev. Duke (Cecil County Marriage License Book)

HUFF
Huff, Elizabeth, see Elijah Moore

HUGGINS
Huggins, Andrew, married Elizabeth Egner circa 13 Aug 1828 (date of license) by Rev. Woolford (Cecil County Marriage License Book)

Huggins, Elizabeth, see Robert McCleary

Huggins, John Thomas, married Sarah Oldham circa 14 Jun 1837 (date of license) by Rev. Barratt (Cecil County Marriage License Book)

HUGHES
Hughes, Amos Hollis (1812-1892), son of John Hall Hughes, Jr. and Charlotte Mitchell, of Harford County, married Hannah Catherine Adams (1821-1911), daughter of William Adams, of England, and Catherine Brown. of Cecil Co., on 25 Feb 1841, after obtaining a license on 23 Feb 1841 (Harford County marriage license; John Hughes Family Bible; *Biographical Record of Harford and Cecil Counties, Maryland* (1897), p. 176; *Heirs & Legatees of Harford Co., Maryland, 1802-1846*, by Henry C. Peden, Jr. (1988), p. 51; *Hughes Genealogy, 1636-1953*, by Joseph L. Hughes (1953), pp. 78-90, 102; *The Aegis*, 7 Oct 1892)

Hughes, Catherine, see William Gibson

Hughes, John Hall Jr., see Amos Hollis Hughes

Hughes, Mary, see John McCaffery

HUGHLETT
Hughlett, Tamsey A. and William, see Levi R. Reese

HUKILL
Hukill, Henry T. (born c1825, Delaware) (hotel man at Chesapeake City), married Sarah (N) (born c1822, Delaware) probably circa 1845-1846; son William born c1847, Delaware, daughter Edith born c1851, Delaware, daughter Laura born c1854, Maryland (1860 Cecil County Census)

HUMES

Humes, Mary Ann and Thomas, see James L. Craig

HUMPHREYS, HUMPHRIES

Humphreys, Elizabeth, see Edward Kelly

Humphreys, Hetty Ann, see Benjamin B. Sweet

Humphries, Martha J., see John D. F. Brown

HUNT

Hunt, Marshall (born c1812, Maryland) (farmer, 6th District), married Elmira (N) (born c1824, Maryland) probably circa 1844; daughter Margaret Hunt born c1845 (1860 Cecil County Census)

HUNTER

Hunter, Amelia S., see Philip F. Jackson

Hunter, Elizabeth A., see Alexander H. McFadden (McFadian)

Hunter, John C. L., married Amelia Sophia Owens circa 30 Oct 1841 (date of license) (Cecil County Marriage License Book)

Hunter, Mary Ann, see Horatio N. Sherwood

HUNTINGTON

Huntington, Cyrus, married Henrietta Mary (N) (1802-1879), of Cecil Co., later of Dover, DE, probably circa 1825 (West Nottingham Cemetery tombstone inscriptions)

HURFORD

Hurford, Eli, of Brick Meeting House, married Elizabeth B. (N) (1804-1872) probably circa 1825 (Rosebank Cemetery, at Calvert, tombstone inscription for Elizabeth B. Hurford; *Cecil Whig*, 13 Jan 1872)

HURLOCK

Hurlock, David, married Amanda Benson circa 5 Aug 1848 (date of license) (Cecil Co. Marr. License Book)

HUSBANDS

Husbands, Naomi, see William Bird

HUSFELT

Husfelt, Charles (1810-1890), married Kesiah (N) (1809-1852) probably circa 1830 (St. Stephen's Episcopal Church Cemetery tombstone inscriptions)

Husfelt, Daniel, see William Timms

Husfelt, John (1805-1872, born Pennsylvania) (farmer near Cecilton on Sassafras Neck), married Ann (N) (1810-1872, born New Jersey) probably circa 1830 (St. Stephen's Episcopal Church Cemetery tombstone inscriptions; 1860 Cecil County Census; *Cecil Whig*, 16 Mar 1872 and 30 Nov 1872)

Husfelt, Kesiah, see James Clarke

HUSHEBECK

Hushebeck, Arena, see William Cantwell

HUTCHINSON

Hutchinson, Joseph (born c1827, Delaware) (farmer at Warwick), married Catharine (N) (born c1830, Delaware) circa 1849; son John Hutchinson born c1850 (1860 Cecil County Census)

Hutchinson, William, of Huntingdon Co., PA, married Elizabeth Wallace, youngest daughter of the late Thomas Wallace, Esq., of Cecil Co., MD, on 10 Jun 1833 (*Baltimore American and Commercial Daily Advertiser*, 14 Jun 1833)

HUTSON

Hutson, William, married Mariah Robinson circa 11 Jul 1826 (date of license) by Rev. Duke (Cecil County Marriage License Book)

HUTTON

Hutton, Elizabeth, see George W. Wells

Hutton, Hannah, see Allen Maxwell

Hutton, Mary E., see George W. Walker

Hutton, William, married Ann Bennett circa 5 Dec 1836 (date of license) by Rev. Morris (Cecil County Marriage License Book; DAR transcript copied in 1928 misspelled his name Hulton)

HYLAND

Hyland, Annesley, see Leonard Abbott

Hyland, Araminta, see Jacob C. Howard and Nicholas George

Hyland, Edward H. (born c1812, Maryland) (farmer at North East), married Mary Clarke (born c1817, Ireland) circa 21 Nov 1836 (date of license) by Rev. Potts (Cecil County Marriage License Book; 1860 Cecil County Census)

Hyland, Elizabeth, see Rowland Ellis

Hyland, Elizabeth Jane, see Stephen Hyland, of N.

Hyland, George W. (born c1823, Maryland) (carpenter at North East), married Sarah E. Thompson (born c1825) circa 23 Dec 1846 (date of license) (Cecil Co. Marr. License Book; 1860 Cecil County Census)

Hyland, Harriett Ann, see James H. George

Hyland, Jacob (esq.), married Miss Hanna R. Thompson, both of North East, Cecil Co., on 26 Aug 1850 by Rev. Dorsey in Baltimore (*Cecil Whig*, 7 Sep 1850; *Cecil Democrat and Farmer's Journal*, 7 Sep 1850)

Hyland, John J., married Cornelia A. Dulaney circa 5 Dec 1850 (date of license) (Cecil County Marriage License Book)

Hyland, Johnson, married Rachel Cochran circa 12 Feb 1834 (date of license) by Rev. Barratt (Cecil County Marriage License Book)

Hyland, Joshua, married Elizabeth W. Crouch circa 28 Nov 1832 (date of license) by Rev. Torbert (Cecil County Marriage License Book)

Hyland, Martha C., see James K. Burnite

Hyland, Martha Rebecca, see James L. Foard

Hyland, Mary Ann, see Hezekiah Foard, Jr.

Hyland, Mary L., see Edward H. Hyland

Hyland, Millicent, see Thomas Wingate

Hyland, Stephen, see James L. Foard

Hyland, Stephen, of Stephen, married Mary Jane Maulden circa 22 Jan 1833 (date of license) by Rev. Duke (Cecil County Marriage License Book)

Hyland, Stephen, of N., married Elizabeth Jane Hyland circa 20 Apr 1830 (date of license) by Rev. Duke (Cecil County Marriage License Book; DAR transcript copied in 1928 listed him as "Stephen, of W.")

Hyland, Washington (1808-1868), married Anna Eliza Ellis (1822-1888) circa 1 Dec 1842 (date of license) (Cecil County Marriage License Book; Hart's Methodist Church Cemetery tombstone inscriptions)

Hyland, William, married Mrs. Araminta Little, widow of John Little, on 16 May 1850, after obtaining a license that same day, by Rev. Barrett (*Cecil Whig*, 18 May 1850; Cecil County Marriage License Book; DAR transcript copied in 1955 mistakenly listed her name as Rebecca Beatty and mistakenly listed the marriage license date as 4 May 1850; Rebecca Beatty actually married William G. Horner, not William Hyland, in 1850)

Hyland, William, see William G. Horner

HYNSON

Hynson, Mary Ann, see George B. Westcott

ILER

Iler, Mary, see Isaac Robinson

INSKIP

Inskip, John S., married Martha Jane Foster circa 30 Oct 1836 (date of license) by Rev. Potts (Cecil County Marriage License Book)

IRONS

Irons, Ann, see John W. Fillingame

IRVIN

Irvin, Mary A., see John S. Wilson

Irvin, Sarah, see David Gilmore

IRWIN

Irwin, James H., married Mary Reynolds (born 1805), daughter of Elisha Reynolds, on 7 Nov 1826 (*Joseph England and his Descendants*, by C. Walter England, Ph.D., 1975, p. 66)

Irwin, James T. (born c1827, Maryland) (cooper), married Rachel (N) (born c1828, Pennsylvania) probably circa 1845 and lived at Principio; daughter Georgiann born c1846, Maryland (1860 Cecil County Census)

Irwin, Rebecca Ann, see John Williams

Irwin, Samuel B. (doctor), of Chester Co., PA, married Emeline Whitaker, daughter of Francis A. Whitaker, Esq., of Elk Iron Works, on 14 May 1845, after obtaining a license on 9 May 1845, by Rev. Campbell (Cecil County Marriage License Book; *Cecil Whig*, 17 May 1845)

IVORY

Ivory, William (born c1825) (African American), married Mintey (N) (born c1822) (African American) circa 1839; eldest daughter Hester Ivory born c1840 (1860 Cecil County Census)

JACKSON

Jackson, Absalom (1822-1893, born Maryland) (farmer in 7th District), married Ellender "Ellen" Campbell (1830-1901, born Pennsylvania) circa 27 Nov 1847 (date of license); daughter Mary Jackson born c1848, Maryland, and their other children were also born in Maryland (Cecil County Marriage License Book; Principio Cemetery tombstone inscriptions; 1860 Cecil County Census spelled her name "Elnor")

Jackson, Agnes, see John Washington Richardson and Samuel Aiken

Jackson, Alexander (born c1813, Maryland) (painter in the 7th District), married Mary (N) (born c1820, born Maryland) probably circa 1837; son John Jackson born c1838 (1860 Cecil County Census)

Jackson, Asael (born c 1820, Maryland) (farmhand, 6th District), married Mary (N) (born c1830, Maryland), probably circa 1845; son William Jackson born c1846 (1860 Cecil County Census)

Jackson, Catharine, see John Craig

Jackson, Charles W. (c1815-c1858), married Georgiana Gorl, probably Gorrell (born c1815, Maryland) circa 26 Dec 1839 (date of license) by Rev. Grace (Cecil County Marriage License Book; 1860 Cecil County Census listed Georgeanna Jackson as head of household in the 7th District)

Jackson, Edward (born c1813, Maryland) (carpenter, 7th District), married Caroline Watson (born c1815, Maryland) circa 25 Jan 1842 (date of license); daughter Elenora Jackson born c1843 (Cecil County Marriage License Book; 1860 Cecil County Census)

Jackson, Edward (1819-1878), married Harriet Brumfield (1830-1906) probably circa 1848-1850 (Hopewell United Methodist Church Cemetery tombstone inscriptions)

Jackson, Elenora, see Edward Jackson

Jackson, Elizabeth, see Richard Rutter, John Rutter, Jr. and Robert Murphy

Jackson, Emeline, see James Jackson

Jackson, Eugenia, see John Jackson

Jackson, Georgeanna, see Chares W. Jackson

Jackson, Grace, see Henry Whitelock

Jackson, Harriet, see Caleb Veazey

Jackson, Henry (born c1811, Maryland) (farmhand in the 7th District), married Nancy "Ann" Gorrell (born c1815, Maryland) circa 14 Oct 1833 (date of license) by Rev. Goforth (Cecil County Marriage License Book; DAR transcript copied in 1928 gave her name as Ann, as did the *Cecil Republican*, 19 Oct 1833, which listed their marriage, but did not give the date; 1860 Cecil County Census gave her name as Nancy)

Jackson, James, married Margaret Craig, daughter of Alexander Craig, on 12 Dec 1833 at *Ellersly*, after obtaining a license on 10 Dec 1833, by Rev. Goforth (Cecil County Marriage License Book; *Cecil Republican*, 14 Dec 1833)

Jackson, James (born c1816, Maryland) (painter in the 7th District), married Martha Whitelock (born c1820, Maryland) circa 21 Sep 1847 (date of license); daughter Emeline born in 1848 (Cecil County Marriage License Book; 1860 Cecil County Census)

Jackson, James Henry, see John Jackson

Jackson, John, see Victor Jackson

Jackson, John, married Ann Craig circa 31 Mar 1827 (date of license) (Cecil County Marriage License Book)

Jackson, John (1812-1898) (farmer on Stump's Neck near Perryville), married Mary Elizabeth Little (1830-1893), of Poplar Point, on 10 Feb 1848, after obtaining a license on 7 Feb 1848, at Greenbank (date of license) (Cecil County Marriage License Book; *Maryland Bible Records, Volume 4: Eastern Shore*, by Henry C. Peden, Jr. (2004), pp. 115-116, listed the births of their four children: James Henry, born 15 Mar 1849; Winfield Scott, born 31 Aug 1832; Eugenia, born 19 Oct 1855; and, John Jerome, born 23 Mar 1860 (the author also inadvertently typed the father John's birth year as 1912 instead of 1812); St. Mark's Episcopal Church tombstone inscriptions; 1860 Cecil County Census)

Jackson, John Jerome, see John Jackson

Jackson, John W. (born c1825, Maryland) (painter in the 7th District), married Sarah Alexander (born c1828, Maryland) circa 2 May 1835 (date of license) by Rev. Crane (Cecil County Marriage License Book; 1860 Cecil County Census)

Jackson, Margaret, see John Cunningham, Robert Jackson and William Aiken

Jackson, Margaret Ann, see Marshel H. Ferguson

Jackson, Maria, see James Kennedy

Jackson, Martha C., see Eli Burroughs

Jackson, Mary, see John Gorrell, Absalom Jackson and Robert Aiken

Jackson, Mary A., see Philip Jackson

Jackson, Mary Ann, see Thomas T. Benjamin

Jackson, Mary Elizabeth, see John Thomas Owens

Jackson, Philip (1804-1868), married Mary A. Jackson (1807-1849) circa 7 Jan 1833 (date of license) by Rev. Goforth (Cecil County Marr. License Book; St. Mark's Episcopal Church tombstone inscriptions)

Jackson, Philip F., married Amelia S. Hunter circa 20 Mar 1848 (date of license) (Cecil County Marriage License Book)

Jackson, Priscilla J., see Joseph Hemphill

Jackson, Robert (born c1823, Maryland) (mason, 6th District), married Ann (N) (born c1825, Maryland) probably circa 1845; daughter Margaret Jackson born c1846 (1860 Cecil County Census)

Jackson, Samuel (1800-1856), married Ann or Anna Cunningham (1806-1852) circa 24 Jan 1831 (date of license) by Rev. Goforth (Cecil Co. Marriage License Book; St. Mark's Episcopal Church tombstones)

Jackson, Sarah, see Joseph Hines

Jackson, Sarah Ann, see Cluley Crockett

Jackson, Victor (1806-1882, born Maryland) (laborer, 7th District), son of John Jackson (1770-1824) and Grisella Craig (1777-1856), of Jackson Station, Cecil Co., married Sarah Brumfield (c1816-1883, born

Maryland) circa 4 Jan 1834 (date of license) by Rev. Goforth (Cecil County Marriage License Book; *Ancestral Charts, Volume 1*, Harford County Genealogical Society (1986), p. 35; 1860 Cecil Co. Census)

Jackson, William (born c1830) (shoemaker near Elkton), married Isabella (N) (born c1833) probably circa 1849; son William Jackson born c1850 (1860 Cecil County Census)

Jackson, William, married Annjaline Stubbins circa 7 Oct 1850 (date of license) (Cecil County Marriage License Book)

Jackson, William, see Asael Jackson

Jackson, Winfield Scott, see John Jackson

Jackson, (N), married Joanna Richards (1822-1855) probably in 1840s (Friends Cemetery, at Harrisville, tombstone inscription; Joanna Richards Jackson is buried beside Thomas Richards, 1787-1868, who was probably her father, but there is no marker for her husband)

Jackson, (N), married Miss Caroline Taylor on 20 Sep 1849 at Wilmington, Delaware (*Cecil Democrat and Farmer's Journal*, 22 Sep 1849)

JACOBS

Jacobs, Cyrus H., married Jane W. Mackall circa 16 Dec 1833 (date of license) by Rev. Duke (Cecil County Marriage License Book; *Cecil Gazette*, 17 Feb 1838, reported Mrs. Jane W. Jacobs, relict of the late Rev. Cyrus H. Jacobs, and only daughter of Benjamin F. Mackall, Esq., of Cecil Co., died on 10 Feb 1838)

JAMAR

Jamar, Ann Rebecca, see David F. Karsner

Jamar, Hannah, see John D. McCauley

Jamar, Henry (blacksmith), married Miss Caroline Shipley circa 5 Jul 1827 (date of license) (Cecil County Marriage License Book; DAR transcript copied in 1928 spelled her name Shiplie; *Elkton Press*, 1 Nov 1828, reported that Henry Jamar's blacksmithing business needed an apprentice)

Jamar, Henry, of Cecil Co., married Millicent Green, of Kent Co., circa 26 Nov 1834 by Rev. Bain (Kent County Marriage License Book)

Jamar, James H. (Register of Wills), married Vilotta R. Scott on 9 Nov 1837, after obtaining a license that same day, by Rev. McFarland (Cecil County Marriage License Book; DAR transcript copied in 1928 mistakenly listed the minister's name as Farland; James McFarland was a Methodist minister in Elkton at that time; Elkton Methodist Church Register, p. 138; *Kent News*, 22 Feb 1856)

Jamar, Jane, see James T. Brown

Jamar, Reuben D. (1815-1878) (Register of Wills), married Ann Rebecca Ford (1818-1898), daughter of the late John H. Ford, Esq., all of Cecil Co., on 8 Mar 1838, after obtaining a license on 6 Mar 1838, by Rev. McFarland (*Cecil Gazette*, 17 Mar 1838; Cecil County Marriage License Book; DAR transcript copied in 1928 mistakenly listed the minister's name as Farland; James McFarland was a Methodist minister in Elkton at that time; Elkton Methodist Church Register, p. 138; 1860 Cecil County Census listed their names as R. B. Jamar, age 44, railroad conductor, and Anna Jamar, age 40; Elkton Cemetery tombstone inscriptions; *Easton Star*, 10 Dec 1878)

JAMES

James, Ann, see Elihu Jefferson

JAMISON

Jamison, Edward L. (born c1820, New Jersey) (steam mill manager at Chesapeake City), married Lavinia (N) (born c1820, Delaware) circa 1840; daughter Fanney born c1841, New Jersey, and daughter Ella born c1845, Delaware (1860 Cecil County Census spelled his name Gamison)

Jamison, John S. (born c1825) (wheelwright at Elkton), married Miss Caroline Shockley (born c1830) on 9 Nov 1848, after obtaining a license on 4 Nov 1848, by Rev. Elliott (Cecil County Marriage License Book; 1860 Cecil County Census; *Cecil Whig*, 2 Dec 1848, spelled his name Jamaison)

Jamison, Rebecca, see Joseph McCrea

JANES

Janes, Thomas C., married Catharine Karr circa 4 Apr 1850 (date of license) (Cecil Co. Marr. License Book)

JANNEY

Janney, Abigail, see John Harvey

Janney, Eliza, see Thomas Edmundson

Janney, George W. (born c1824, Maryland) (cooper near Bay View), married Elizabeth A. (N) (born c1830, Maryland) probably circa 1850; son Wilbur Janney born c1851, Maryland (1860 Cecil County Census)

Janney, Jesse, see Silas Evans Carter

Janney, John Thomas (born c1823, Maryland) (farmer, 9th District), married Miss Deborah M. Clendenin (born c1845, Maryland) on 22 Aug 1844, after obtaining a license on 20 Aug 1844, by Rev. Barton (Cecil County Marriage License Book; DAR transcript copied in 1955 mistakenly listed the marriage license date as 21 Aug 1844; *Cecil Whig*, 31 Aug 1844; 1860 Cecil County Census)

Janney, Mary, see Silas Evans Carter

Janney, Thomas, married Rachel Blake circa 19 Mar 1834 (date of license) by Rev. Duke (Cecil County Marriage License Book)

Janney, Thomas J. (1821-1863), married Anna H. (N) (1830-1885) prob. circa 1848-1850 (Zion Methodist Cemetery tombstone inscriptions)

Janney, Wilbur, see George W. Janney

JANVIER

Janvier, Elizabeth DeH., see Thomas J. Meredith

JAQUETT

Jaquett, Nathaniel, married Virginia DeValinger circa 6 Oct 1846 (date of license) (Cecil County Marriage License Book spelled her name DeVallinger; Cecil County Burial Permit for Virginia L. Jaquette, 1830-1912, state she died at the Alms House and was buried in Elkton Cemetery)

JAY

Jay, Frances, see Harman Foster

JEANES

Jeanes, Rebecca, see Joseph Williams

JEFFERSON

Jefferson, Elihu (esquire), married Miss Ann James, both of New Castle Co., DE, on 17 May 1829 at Elkton, Cecil Co., by Rev. Rider (*Delaware Gazette*, 26 May 1829)

JEFFRIES

Jeffries, William, married Miss Harriet Jones, both of Cecil Co., on 20 Sep 1841, after obtaining a license that same day. By Rev. Janes (*Cecil Gazette*, 25 Sep 1841; Cecil County Marriage License Book; Elkton Methodist Church Register)

JENKINS

Jenkins, David (1794-1857), married Hannah J. Runner (1808-1873) probably circa 1826; among those buried nearby is Joseph Jenkins (1827-1920) and his wife Mary (1833-1918) (Rock Springs Old School Baptist Church Cemetery tombstone inscriptions)

Jenkins, Deborah M., see Joseph Coulson

Jenkins, Eliza, see John H. Gilmore

Jenkins, Francis, see George Jenkins

Jenkins, George, of Philadelphia, son of Francis and Phebe Jenkins, the former deceased, of Hudson, NY, married Hannah James Gilpin, of Wilmington, DE, daughter of James and Sarah L. Gilpin, both deceased, on the 19th day of the 2nd month 1825 at the Octorara Meeting House in Cecil County. Among the witnesses were Judith B. Jenkins, Matthew C. Jenkins, John L. Gilpin and Samuel S. Gilpin. (*Births, Deaths and Marriages of the Nottingham Quakers, 1680-1899*, by Alice L. Beard (1989), p. 219)

Jenkins, George (1817-1891), married Susan Jane Thomas (1821-1889) circa 28 Jun 1841 (date of license) (Cecil County Marriage License Book; Rock Springs Old School Baptist Church Cemetery tombstone inscriptions; *Midland Journal*, 6 Feb 1891, stated a George Jenkins, farmer in Lancaster Co., died in his 70th year at Wrightsville)

Jenkins, Joseph, see David Jenkins

Jenkins, Judith B., see George Jenkins

Jenkins, Lydia R., see Joseph Coulson

Jenkins, Margaret, see Levi M. McVey

Jenkins, Mary, see David Jenkins

Jenkins, Mary A., see Robert Davenport

Jenkins, Matthew C., see George Jenkins

Jenkins, Phebe, see George Jenkins

Jenkins, Ruth Ann, see John Armour

JENNESS

Jenness, David, married Rebecca Davidson circa 29 Mar 1825 (date of license) Rev. Sharpley (Cecil County Marriage License Book; DAR transcript copied in 1928 spelled his name Jennis)

Jenness, David, married Jane Brookings circa 5 Jan 1837 (date of license) by Rev. Rider (Cecil County Marriage License Book)

Jenness, Hannah, see Samuel Jenness

Jenness, John G., married Ann (N) (1804-1858) probably circa 1825 (Hopewell United Methodist Church Cemetery tombstone inscription for Ann Jenness)

Jenness, Samuel (born c1825, Maryland) (miller, 7th District), married Rebecca Ann Cather (born c1827, Maryland) circa 30 May 1846 (date of license); daughter Hannah born c1849 (Cecil County Marriage License Book; 1860 Cecil County Census)

JENNINGS

Jennings, Jacob F., married Margaret Jane McFann circa 19 Jun 1841 (date of license) (Cecil County Marriage License Book; DAR transcript copied in 1955 mistakenly listed the names as Jacob H. Jennings and Margaret J. McHam)

Jennings, Joanna, see John Bailey

JESTER

Jester, Emanuel, married Eliza J. Berbage circa 15 Feb 1843 (date of their license) (Cecil County Marriage License Book)

Jester, Isaac B., married Rebecca Stradley circa 5 Oct 1832 (date of license) by Rev. Duke (Cecil County Marriage License Book)

Jester, James B. (born c1822, Delaware) (farmer near Chesapeake City), married Sarah E. Clark (born c1825, Maryland) circa 14 Oct 1846 (date of license) (Cecil County Marriage License Book; 1860 Cecil Census)

Jester, Jane F., see William Robinson

Jester, John, married Hannah Updegrove circa 22 Mar 1837 (date of license) by Rev. Potts (Cecil County Marriage License Book; *Cecil Whig*, 21 Feb 1846, reported that a Mr. John Jester, of Delaware, died on 19 Feb 1846 in the 32nd year of his age)

Jester, Mary, see John McKinzey

Jester, Philip R., married Henrietta Severson circa 13 Dec 1843 (date of license) (Cecil County Marriage License Book; DAR transcript copied in 1955 mistakenly listed her name as Stevenson)

JOHNSON

Johnson, Alsey, see Benjamin Reynolds

Johnson, Andrew, see David Johnson

Johnson, Ann, see (N) Tyson

Johnson, Ann Eliza, see George M. Cole

Johnson, Araminta, see John Wesley Freeman

Johnson, Benjamin F. (farmer and miller), son of Charles Johnson, married Miss Mary McCullough circa 1 Mar 1830 (date of their license) by Rev. Magraw (Cecil County Marriage License Book; *Portrait and Biographical Record of Harford and Cecil Counties, Maryland* (1897, repr. 1989), p. 429, listed their three children as Joseph, Charles L. and Samuel M. Johnson (born 25 Mar 1836) and spelled Mary's maiden name as McCollough)

Johnson, Caleb Parker (esquire and editor of the *Delaware Gazette*), married 1st to Ann Eliza "Annie" Young (1826-1849), daughter of Thomas Young, Esq., of Wilmington, DE, on 7 Sep 1848 by the Rev. Mr. Cole in Wilmington and married 2nd to Martha B. Young, daughter of Thomas Young, Esq., on 28 Jul 1853 by Rev. Carrow in Wilmington (*Cecil Whig*, 16 Sep 1848 and 2 Jun 1849; *Delaware Gazette*, 2 Aug 1853)

Johnson, Catherine, see William Johnson

Johnson, Charles, see (N) Tyson, Richard L. Thomas and Benjamin F. Johnson

Johnson, David (born c1813) (African American) (laborer at North East), married Elizabeth (N) (born c1814) (African American) probably circa 1840; son Andrew Johnson born c1841 (1860 Cecil County Census abstract did not give their places of birth)

Johnson, Deborah L., see John B. Russell

Johnson, Eliza, see William Johnson

Johnson, Elizabeth, see James Merritt

Johnson, Ellen, see Jacob Scott

Johnson, Emma. See Joshua Johnson

Johnson, Emily Elizabeth, see Morris Cummings

Johnson, Enoch (1805-1882), married Miss Mary Ann Sturgeon (1819-1898), both of Cecil Co., on 14 Nov 1843, after obtaining a license on 3 Oct 1843, by Rev. Goentner at North East (Cecil County Marriage License Book; *Cecil Whig*, 9 Dec 1843l Ebenezer Church Cemetery tombstone inscriptions)

Johnson, Garrett (1821-1899), married Rachel A. (N) (1822-1912) probably circa 1842 (Rosebank Cemetery, at Calvert, tombstone inscriptions)

Johnson, Hannah, see Seth Stewart

Johnson, Helen, see Richard Severson

Johnson, Isaac, married Susan Curry circa 11 Jan 1826 (date of their license) by Rev. Barratt (Cecil County Marriage License Book)

Johnson, Jacob (born c1810) (hotel keeper at Elkton), married Caroline Brown (born c1815) on 6 Feb 1840, after obtaining a license on 4 Feb 1840, by Rev. Hagany (Cecil County Marriage License Book; Elkton Methodist Church Register, p. 139; 1860 Cecil County Census)

Johnson, Jane, see Corbin Cooley and Robert Cooley

Johnson, Jethro, see Joseph Benjamin and Jethro Johnson McCullough

Johnson, Jethro, married Hannah Willix circa 8 Dec 1849 (date of license) (Cecil Co. Marr. License Book)

Johnson, John A., married Sarah Wallace circa 6 Jan 1831 (date of license) by Rev. Barratt (Cecil County Marriage License Book)

Johnson, John A. (1807-1868), of near Elkton, married Eliza Jane Alexander (1808-1895) circa 22 Oct 1840 (date of license) (Cecil County Marriage License Book; Elkton Cemetery tombstone inscriptions; *Cecil Democrat and Farmer's Journal*, 29 Feb 1868)

Johnson, Joseph, see Benjamin F. Johnson

Johnson, Joseph, married Susan Green on 31 Dec 1839, after obtaining a license on 30 Dec 1839, by Rev. Hagany (Cecil County Marriage License Book; DAR transcript copied in 1928 mistakenly listed his name as Joseph Lambson; Elkton Methodist Church Register, p. 139, listed his name as Joseph Johnson)

Johnson, Joshua, married Sarah (N) before 1846; son Robert Worrell Johnson died on 10 Oct 1847, aged 8 months and 2 days (*Cecil Whig*, 23 Oct 1847, with a poem by his mother)

Johnson, Joshua (born c1815) (African American) (laborer at Bohemian Mills), married Elizabeth (N) (born c1825) (African American) probably circa 1835; daughter Emma born c1846 (1860 Cecil County Census)

Johnson, Levi (1819-1893) (laborer, 6th District), married Miss Julia Ann Crandall (1822-1889) circa 9 Apr 1847 (date of license); buried beside Maria Crandall (1800-1866) (Cecil County Marriage License Book spelled her name Crandle; Hopewell United Methodist Church Cemetery tombstone inscriptions; 1860 Cecil County Census)

Johnson, Lewis (1818-1912), married Mary H. Johnson (1820-1884) probably circa 1840 (Rosebank Cemetery, at Calvert, tombstone inscriptions transcribed his marker once as Lewis Johnson and once as Levi S. Johnson and her name once as Mary Johsnon and once as Mary H. Johnson)

Johnson, Margaret Jane, see Jesse M. Boulden

Johnson, Mary, see (N) Tyson, Richard L. Thomas and Henry H. Robinson

Johnson, Mary Ann, see Joseph Benjamin

Johnson, Mary E., see David G. Orr

Johnson, Mary Jane, see Frederick Slagle

Johnson, Nicholas F. (1818-1883), married Margaret E. George (1824-1898) circa 24 Oct 1844 (date of license) (Cecil County Marriage License Book; DAR transcript copied in 1955 mistakenly listed H. as his middle initial; Elkton Cemetery tombstone inscriptions)

Johnson, Rachel, see Hasson Lynch

Johnson, Rebecca, see George Biddle

Johnson, Richard C., married Agnes R. Malsburgher circa 30 Nov 1846 (date of license) (Cecil County Marriage License Book)

Johnson, Robert Worrell, see Joshua Johnson

Johnson, Samuel, married Mary Boram circa 26 Aug 1844 (date of license) (Cecil Co. Marr. License Book)

Johnson, Samuel M., see Benjamin F. Johnson

Johnson, Sarah, see Richard L. Thomas

Johnson, Stephen (1818-1886), married Letitia A. (N) (1820-1893) probably circa 1840 (Leeds Methodist Church Cemetery tombstone inscriptions)

Johnson, Victorine, see Samuel Moffitt

Johnson, William, married Millicent Watson circa 15 May 1830 (date of license) by Rev. Griffith (Cecil County Marriage License Book)

Johnson, William, married Elizabeth Cunningham circa 3 Aug 1840 (date of license) (Cecil County Marriage License Book)

Johnson, William (born c1825, Ireland) (laborer, 7th District), married Catherine (N) (born c1826, Ireland) probably circa 1849; daughter Catherine Johnson born c1850, Ireland, son William Johnson born c1857, Maryland, and daughter Eliza Johnson born c1859, Maryland (1860 Cecil County Census)

JOHNSTON

Johnston, Eliza, see Charles Brookings

Johnston, George, married Deborah (N) (1816-1877) probably circa 1836 and she died near Mechanicsville, Delaware, her husband having pre-deceased her (*Cecil Whig*, 17 Feb 1877)

Johnston, Mary, see James Pritchard

JOICE

Joice, Maria, see John W. Gallahan

Joice, also see Joyce

JONES

Jones, Amelia, see Edward J. Thompson

Jones, Ann, see Robert Jones

Jones, Ann Elizabeth, see Elisha Hughes England

Jones, Ann Maria, see James Whitaker, Jr.

Jones, Aquilla, married Miss Esther Bates circa 23 Feb 1832 (date of license) by Rev. Magraw (Cecil County Marriage License Book)

Jones, Benjamin W., of Chester Co., PA, married Nancy Cowan, daughter of William Cowan, Esq., of Cowantown, Cecil Co., on 23 Dec 1834, after obtaining a license on 22 Dec 1834, by Rev. Russel (Cecil County Marriage License Book; *Cecil Gazette*, 27 Dec 1834)

Jones, Charles B., see Thomas P. Jones

Jones, Commodore, see Abraham Kennard and Henry Nindson

Jones, Daniel (1800-1866), married Lydia M. (N) (1812-1884) probably circa 1830-1832 (Elkton Cemetery tombstone inscription for Lydia M. Jones)

Jones, Deborah, see Edward Wilkins

Jones, Deborah Ann, see John Tignor

Jones, Ellis, married Miss Mary W. Price, both of Elkton, on 22 Dec 1828 in Wilmington, Delaware by Rev. Higgins (*Elkton Press*, 27 Dec 1828, spelled her name Pryce)

Jones, Frances, see Hanson Jones

Jones, George, of Elkton, married Miss Joanna Naff, of Wilmington, DE, on 15 Oct 1829 by Rev. Pardee (*Delaware Gazette*, 16 Oct 1829)

Jones, Hanson (born c1820, Maryland) (African American) (laborer, 7th District), married Jane (N) (born c1830, Maryland) (African American) probably circa 1846; daughter Frances Jones born c1847 (1860 Cecil County Census)

Jones, Harriet, see William Jeffries

Jones, Isabella, see Thomas Logan

Jones, James (1811-1877), of near Bay View, married Ann McDowell circa 30 Aug 1836 (date of license) by Rev. Lane (Cecil County Marriage License Book; *Cecil Whig*, 30 Jun 1877)

Jones, James, see Robert Jones

Jones, James L., see John H. Jones

Jones, Jane, see George Haines

Jones, John (born c1819, Maryland) (plasterer, 8th District), married Elizabeth (N) (born c1822, Maryland) probably circa 1842; son William Jones born c1843, Maryland, blacksmith (1860 Cecil County Census)

Jones, John H. (1818-1893), married Elizabeth A. Ewing (1822-1906) before 1845; buried beside James L. Jones, 1846-1915 (Bethesda Cemetery, at Oakwood, tombstone inscriptions)

Jones, John T. (born c1820, Maryland) ("call agent" at Elkton), married Mary (N) (born c1822, Maryland) circa 1848; son John Jones born c1849 (1860 Cecil County Census)

Jones, Letitia W., see Isaac Wilson

Jones, Lewis, married Ann Patton circa 22 Aug 1837 (date of license) by Rev. Parks (Cecil County Marriage License Book)

Jones, Lieutenant, see Abraham Kennard

Jones, Margaret Emma, see John E. Ferguson

Jones, Martha, see Stansbury Moffett

Jones, Mary, see Robert Jones, Isaac M. Chesbrough, George Haines and Richard Barnett Keithley

Jones, Mary E., see John W. Davis

Jones, Matilda, see John E. Thomas

Jones, Rebecca, see William B. Burlin

Jones, Robert (1820-1873), married (N) probably circa 1845 (Elkton Methodist Church Cemetery tombstone inscription for "Father" Robert Jones; 1860 Cecil County Census listed an R. Jones, age 38, laborer, wife Mary, age 26, son James, age 10, and daughters Ann, age 6, and Mary, age 2, living at North East)

Jones, Sarah E., see John R. Russell

Jones, Thomas, married Hulda Headley (1827-1902) probably circa 1848 (West Nottingham Friends Cemetery tombstone inscription for "Hulda Headley, wife of Thomas Jones," but no marker for him)

Jones, Thomas J., married Elizabeth S. (N) (1815-1882) probably circa 1835 (*Cecil Democrat and Farmer's Journal*, 25 Feb 1882, obituary stated she died in her 58th year in Baltimore, formerly of Cecil Co.)

Jones, Thomas P. (born c1822) (farmer at Cecilton), married Ann C. (born c1813) circa 1842; son Charles B. Jones born c1843 (1860 Cecil County Census)

Jones, William, see George Haines and John Jones

Jones, William, married Lydia Maria McKinsey circa 22 Apr 1828 (date of license) (Cecil County Marriage License Book)

Jones, William (born c1819) (carpenter at Cecilton), married Miss Hannah M. Knock (born c1822) on 11 Jul 1850, after obtaining a license that same day, by Rev. Howell (*Cecil Whig*, 13 Jul 1850; Cecil County Marriage License Book; 1860 Cecil County Census)

Jones, William T. (1819-1900), married Catherine A. Heath (1822-1885) on 15 Dec 1842, after obtaining a license on 14 Dec 1842, by Rev. Janes (Cecil County Marriage License Book misspelled her name Heah; Elkton Methodist Church Register; Elkton Cemetery tombstone inscriptions; *Cecil Whig*, 17 Dec 1842)

JORDAN

Jordan, John, married Elizabeth Farran circa 22 Mar 1825 (date of license) by Rev. Sharpley (Cecil County Marriage License Book)

Jordan, Kitturah, see Nicholes L. Harden

JOY

Joy, Frances, see Harman Foster

JOYCE

Joyce, George H., married Maria Louise Chapman circa 2 Feb 1836 (date of license) by Rev. Williams (Cecil County Marriage License Book)

Joyce, Owen (born c1814, Maryland (sailor, 7th District), married Rebecca (N) (born c1825, Pennsylvania) probably circa 1845; son James R. Joyce born c1846, Maryland (1860 Cecil County Census)

KANKEY

Kankey, Maria, see James L. Foard

KARR

Karr, Catharine, see Thomas C. Janes

KARSNER

Karsner, David F. (born c1819, Pennsylvania) (merchant at Chesapeake City), probable son of Daniel (born c1785, Maryland) and Eleanor F. Karsner (born c1795, Maryland), married Miss Ann Rebecca Jamar (born c1822, Pennsylvania), of Elkton, on 20 Aug 1843 by Rev. McIntire (no marriage license found in Cecil County); son George H. Karsner born c1844, Maryland (*Cecil Whig*, 26 Aug 1843; 1860 Cecil County Census abstract mistakenly spelled his name as Karmer)

KEAN

Kean, Eliza, see Caleb W. Cloud

Kean, Susan, see John McCord

KEATLEY, KEATLY, KEETLEY

Keatly, Catharine, see John Rutter

Keatley, Edwin, see Thomas Keatley

Keatly, Francis, married Emily Barnett circa 5 Nov 1838 (date of license) by Rev. Barratt (Cecil County Marriage License Book; DAR transcript copied in 1928 misspelled his first name Frances)

Keatley, Jane, see Isaac N. Sidwell

Keatly, John, married Elizabeth Lewis on 24 Mar 1842 after obtaining a license on 21 Mar 1842 (Cecil County Marriage License Book; Elkton Methodist Church Register)

Keetley, Joseph, of North East, married Catharine White (c1807-1872) circa 1 Feb 1827 (date of license) by Rev. Barratt (Cecil County Marriage License Book; *Cecil Whig*, 23 Mar 1872)

Keatley, Thomas (1815-1877) (waterman at North East), married Araminta (N) (1828-1899) probably circa 1848; son Edwin Keatley born c1849 (Hart's Methodist Church Cemetery tombstone inscriptions; 1860 Cecil County Census listed him as Capt. T. Keathly)

Keathly, William (1803-1873), of near Octoraro, married Mary Pennington circa 14 Aug 1827 (date of license) (Cecil County Marriage License Book; DAR transcript copied in 1928 spelled his name Keetley; *Cecil Whig*, 1 Feb 1873)

Keatley, also see Keithley

KEE
Kee, Jane, see Henry V. Fairlamb

KEECH
Keech, Aaron, married 1st to Mary Ellen Thompson circa 23 Jan 1828 (date of license) and married 2nd to Julian Death circa 27 Jan 1834 (date of license) by Rev. Goforth (Cecil County Marriage License Book)

KEELER
Keeler, Richard, married Sarah Maxwell circa 26 Jan 1829 (date of license) by Rev. Magraw (Cecil County Marriage License Book)

KEETLEY, see Keatley and Keithley

KEILHOLTZ
Keilholtz, David, of Baltimore, MD, married Hellen Carroll, of York, PA, on 23 May 1848 by Rev. Lochman in York, PA (*Cecil Democrat and Farmer's Journal*, 10 Jun 1848)

Keilholtz, John (1821-1909) (cooper and farmer), of Baltimore City, later of Cecil Co., married 1st to Sarah Massey (1823-1869) circa 9 May 1843 (date of license) and married 2nd to Miss Martha E. Kirk (1836-1927) in 1872 (Cecil County Marriage License Book; *Portrait and Biographical Record of Harford and Cecil Counties, Maryland* (1897, repr. 1989), pp. 342-343, misspelled Sarah's name as Mossey; Hopewell United Methodist Church Cemetery tombstone inscriptions; 1860 Cecil County Census)

KEITH
Keith, John A. (1805-1879), of Cecil Co., later of Harford Co., married Mary M. Burgoyne (1812-1903), of Cecil Co., daughter of Karon Burgoyne of France and Rebecca Barnes of Delaware, circa 22 May 1828 (date of license) (Cecil County Marriage License Book spelled their names Keath and Bergoin; Emory United Methodist Church tombstone inscriptions; Harford County death certificate of Mary M. Keith)

KEITHLEY
Keithley, Agnes C., see John Keithley

Keithley Ann Elizabeth, see John Keithley

Keithley, Edward Francis (1814-1862), son of Richard Keithley (1778-c1851) and Elizabeth Barnett (1773-1834), married Emily Barnett (1809-1860) on 5 Nov 1838 (Family research by Mary K. Walker, of Bel Air, MD, 1989; West Nottingham Cemetery tombstone inscriptions)

Keithley, John (1803-c1866), son of Richard Keithley (1778-c1851) and Elizabeth Barnett (1773-1834), married Margaret Culbertson (1806-1835?), daughter of Thomas (1780-1874) and Ann Culbertson, circa 2 Feb 1830 (date of license) by Rev. Barratt and he may have married 2nd to Helen Taylor (c1804-1887), sister of John Taylor, of Perryman, and half-sister of Hollis Courtney, of Havre de Grace, circa 11 May 1846 (date of license) in Harford County; Helen Keithley, married 2nd to Christian Case in 1874 in Havre de Grace, she being his third wife (Cecil County Marriage License Book; DAR transcript copied in 1928 misspelled his name Keatly and her name Culberson; McKenney Family Cemetery tombstone inscription for Margaret Culbertson Keithley; Harford County marriage licenses; *Bel Air Times*, 25 Mar 1887)

Keithley, John (1821-1885), married Elizabeth Barnett (1822-1898) circa 1842; buried beside daughters Ann Elizabeth Keithley (1843-1913) and Agnes C. Keithley (1846-1936) (Hopewell United Methodist Church Cemetery tombstone inscriptions)

Keithley, Richard, see Edward Francis Keithley, Thomas Keithley and William Keithley

Keithley, Richard Barnett (1812-1879) (collier, Elkton), son of Richard Keithley (1778-c1851) and Elizabeth Barnett (1773-1834), married Mary Jones (1815-1871) circa 2 Jan 1840 (date of license) by Rev. Pierson (Cecil County Marriage License Book spelled his name Keatley; DAR transcript copied in 1928 misspelled the minister's name as Purson (John W. Pierson was a Methodist Protestant minister on the Kent Circuit); 1860 Cecil County Census misspelled his name Keetly; North East Methodist Church Cemetery tombstone inscriptions; *Cecil Whig*, 5 Aug 1871; Family research by Mary K. Walker, of Bel Air, Maryland, in 1989)

Keithley, Richard T., see William Keithley

Keithley, Thomas (1805-1865), of Cecil Co., later of Harford Co., son of Richard Keithley (1778-c1851) and Elizabeth Barnett (1778-1839), married Mahala Gilbert (1809-1885), daughter of Michael Gilbert (1764-1828) and Mary Horton Gilmore (c1762-1826), of Harford Co., circa 21 Apr 1831 (date of license and marriage authorization certificate issued to Rev. Webster on file at the Historical Society of Harford County; Gilbert-Keithley family research by Esther G. Hannon, of Bloomington, IL in 1988 and Mary K. Walker, of Bel Air, MD, in 1989; West Nottingham Cemetery tombstone inscriptions in Cecil County)

Keithley, William (1808-1890), son of Richard Keithley (1778-1851) and Elizabeth Barnett (1773-1834), of Cecil Co., married Rachel Culbertson (1808-1887), of Delaware, circa 18 Jan 1832 (date of license) by Rev. Barratt; buried beside son Richard T. Keithley, 1832-1835 (West Nottingham Cemetery tombstone inscriptions; Cecil County Marriage License Book; DAR transcript copied in 1928 spelled his name Keatly; Family research by Mary K. Walker, of Bel Air, MD, 1989)

Keithley, also see Keatley

KELLY

Kelly, Catherine, see John Kelly

Kelly, Edward, see Thomas R. McMullen and Edward Kelly

Kelly, Edward (c1807-1878), son of Edward and Mary Kelly, of Woodlawn, Cecil Co., married 1st to Rebecca Cunningham (1813-1842), daughter of David and Elizabeth Cunningham, circa 3 Sep 1835 (date of license) by Rev. Potts, married 2nd to Elizabeth Humphreys circa 5 Dec 1843 (date of license) and married 3rd to Hester Creswell (Cecil County Marriage License Book; *Ancestral Charts, Volume 3*, p. 149, Harford County Genealogical Society Publication, 1986)

Kelly, Hugh, married Sarah White on 8 Jun 1828, after obtaining a license on 3 Jun 1828, by Rev. Epinette (Cecil County Marriage License Book; *History of Saint Francis Xavier Church and Bohemia Plantation Now Known as Old Bohemia, Warwick, Maryland*, by Joseph C. Cann (1976), p. 47)

Kelly, Jane, see Thomas R. McMullen

Kelly, John (born c1814, Maryland) (shoemaker, 6th District), married Elizabeth (N) (born c1823, Maryland) probably circa 1842; daughter Catherine born c1843 (1860 Cecil County Census)

Kelly, Mary, see Edward Kelly and Thomas R. McMullen

Kelly, Robert S. (1816-1892), married Mary A. (N) (c1816-1879) circa 1837 and died at the home of his son R. Anderson Kelly at Priestford Bridge, Harford Co.; buried in Bethesda Cemetery at Oakwood, Cecil Co. (*The Aegis and Intelligencer*, 12 Aug 1892; Oakwood Cemetery tombstone inscriptions)

Kelly, Sarah J., see Samuel Foster

Kelly, Thomas, married Sarah Rutter circa 29 Mar 1834 (date of license) by Rev. Duke (Cecil County Marriage License Book)

KEMP

Kemp, Frederick Caesar, of Baltimore, married Hannah Rebecca Ringgold, daughter of Rev. Samuel Ringgold, of Kent Island, on 18 May 1850 in Baltimore by Rev. Larkin (*Cecil Democrat and Farmer's Journal*, 1 Jun 1850; *Baltimore Sun*, 30 May 1850)

KENNARD

Kennard, Abraham, slave of John H. Lusby, married Rachel Moore, a free African American woman, on 8 Jul 1837 by Rev Piggot in the presence of Commodore Jones and Lady, and Lieutenant Jones and Lady (North Sassafras Parish, St. Stephen's P. E. Church Register spelled his name Kinnard)

Kennard, Edward, see Edmund Brown, Jr.

Kennard, Frances, see James Massey Seegar

Kennard, Martha Jane, see Edmund Brown, Jr.

Kennard, Thomas (1817-1892, born Maryland) (shoemaker, 6th District), married Elizabeth Riker (1815-1890, born Pennsylvania) circa 31 Oct 1837 (date of license) by Rev. Burrows (Cecil County Marriage License Book; West Nottingham Cemetery tombstone inscriptions; 1860 Cecil County Census)

KENNEDY

Kennedy, Eliza, see Joshua F. Biddle

Kennedy, James, see Joshua F. Biddle

Kennedy, James, married Miss Maria Jackson, both of Cecil Co., on 18 Mar 1845, after obtaining a license that same day, by Rev. Humphries (Cecil County Marriage License Book, and *Cecil Whig*, 5 Apr 1845, both spelled his name Kennady)

Kennedy, Rebecca W., see Joshua F. Biddle

KENT

Kent, John, married Sarah M. Colmerry circa 13 Dec 1841 (date of license) (Cecil Co. Marr. License Book)

KERNAN

Kernan, Edward (born c1822) (pumpmaker at Cecilton), married Elizabeth (N) (born c1832) circa 1848; son William Francis Kernan born c1849 (1860 Cecil County Census)

KERR

Kerr, Agnes M., see Robert Stephenson

Kerr, Edward, see Thomas Maxwell

Kerr, Elizabeth G., see Thomas Maxwell

Kerr, Francina, see Joseph Stebbing

Kerr, John Bozman (honorable), married Lucy Hamilton Stephens, only daughter of John Stephens, Esq., of Talbot County, on 25 Oct 1849 in Christ Church in Easton by Rev. Mason (*Cecil Democrat and Farmer's Journal*, 3 Nov 1849)

Kerr, Lewrenna E., see William Adams

KERSHAW

Kershaw, James (born c1829, England) (weaver at Elkton), married Miss Amelia Jane Simpers (born c1831, Maryland), both of Cecil Co., on 2 May 1850, after obtaining a license on 20 Apr 1850, by Rev. Fernley at the Elkton M. E. Parsonage; son James born in 1851 (*Cecil Whig*, 4 May 1850; Cecil County Marriage License Book; Elkton Methodist Church Register, p. 141; 1860 Cecil County Census abstract misspelled his name Kenshaw and listed her name as Jane)

Kershaw, William (1817-1890) (reverend), married Marian (N) (1817-1884) probably circa 1840 (Cherry Hill Methodist Church Cemetery tombstone inscriptions)

KIBLER

Kibler, Anne, see John Kibler

Kibler, Henry, married Francina B. Wirt, daughter of the late Capt. John T. Wirt, both of Cecil Co., on 4 May 1848 by Rev. Hard, of St. Paul's Ch., Chester, PA (*Cecil Whig*, 13 May 1848: "The printer acknowledges the receipt of a slice of cake and wishes the happy couple a life filled with all earthly bliss.")

Kibler, John (born c1810, Pennsylvania) (farmer near Chesapeake City), married Miss Matilda Marinor (born c1821), of New York City, on 30 May 1850 by Rev. Coombe in Wilmington, DE; daughter Anne born 1851, Maryland (*Cecil Whig*, 8 Jun 1850; 1860 Census indicated Matilda was born in Maryland)

KIDD

Kidd, Andrew, married Sarah Ring circa 4 Dec 1827 (date of license) (Cecil County Marriage License Book)

Kidd, George W., married Mary Jane Carson (1821-1849), eldest daughter of John Carson, Esq., on 11 Jan 1844, after obtaining a license on 10 Jan 1844, by Rev. Finney near Port Deposit; Mary Jane Kidd, wife of G. W. Kidd, of Wilmington, DE, died on 25 Sep 1849 at Port Deposit, MD (Cecil County Marriage License Book; *Delaware Gazette*, 28 Sep 1849; West Nottingham Cemetery tombstone inscription for Mary Jane Kidd; *Cecil Whig*, 27 Jan 1844)

Kidd, Jacob (1827-1891), married Margaret (N) (1817-1900) probably by 1850 (Rosebank Cemetery, at Calvert, tombstone inscriptions; *Midland Journal*, 23 Jan 1891, stated Jacob H. Kidd died in his 65th year near Lombard and was buried in Rosebank Cemetery)

Kidd, James T., married Frances Christie circa 28 Jun 1828 (date of license) by Rev. Goforth (Cecil County Marriage License Book)

Kidd, John, married Ann Boyd circa 21 Aug 1833 (date of license) by Rev. Goforth (Cecil County Marriage License Book)

Kidd, Mary Jane, see George W. Kidd

KILLEN

Killen, Ann, see Jeremiah Chambers

KILLINGSWORTH

Killingsworth, Oliver Perry (1817-1884) (merchant at North East), married Elizabeth A. Waters (1820-1878) circa 27 Sep 1838 (date of license) by the Rev. Greenbank (Cecil County Marriage License Book; DAR transcript copied in 1928 misspelled his name as Killingtonworth; Hopewell United Methodist Church Cemetery tombstone inscriptions; 1860 Cecil County Census)

KILPATRICK

Kilpatrick, Mary, see Joseph Sumption

KILVINGTON

Kilvington, Samuel S. (born c1816, Delaware) (farmer near Elkton), married Miss Rachel S. Burnite (born c1825, Maryland), both now of Cecil Co., on 2 Mar 1843, after obtaining a license that same day, by Rev. Kennard (*Cecil Whig*, 15 Apr 1843, mistakenly stated they married 2 Feb 1843; Cecil County Marriage License Book misspelled her name as Burnight; 1860 Cecil County Census spelled his name Kelvington)

KIMBLE

Kimble, Ellen, see Edward Evans

Kimble, Henry, married Miss Martha Cunningham, both of Cecil Co., on 23 May 1833, after obtaining a license on 22 May 1833, by Rev. Hagany (Cecil County Marriage License Book; Elkton Methodist Church Register, p. 5; *Cecil Republican*, 25 May 1833, spelled his name Kemble)

Kimble, Henry Harding (1824-1887) (farmer, merchant, teacher), of Bucks Co., PA, later of Fair Hill, Cecil Co., son of John Kimble and Hannah Carver, married Mary Titus, eldest daughter of Seruch Titus, in

November 1847 (*Portrait and Biographical Record of Harford and Cecil Counties, Maryland* (1897, repr. 1989), pp. 484, 487)

Kimble, Jane Rebecca, see William Conlyn

Kimble, John, see Henry Harding Kimble

Kimble, Mary Jane, see Peter Tome

KING

King, Agnes, see John King

King, Alfred, see Thomas P. King

King, Amos, see John King

King, Ann, see John King and Thomas P. King

King, Eleanor, see John Nichols

King, Elizabeth, see Edwin J. Cannon and Samuel King

King, Francis, married Deborah Mears circa 9 Dec 1837 (date of license) by Rev. Greenbank, a Methodist minister in Port Deposit (Cecil County Marriage License Book)

King, Francis, married Mary S. Pantry circa 10 Oct 1846 (date of license) (Cecil Co. Marr. License Book)

King, George, see Samuel King

King, John, see Samuel King

King, John, son of James and Phebe King, the former deceased, of Little Britain Township, Lancaster Co., PA, married Mary Reynolds, daughter of Joshua and Rachel Reynolds, the former deceased, of West Nottingham Hundred, Cecil Co., on the 25th day of the 5th month 1825 at West Nottingham Meeting House. Among the witnesses were Thomas King, Amos King, Lewis King, Ann King, Rachel King, Agnes King, Sarah King, Esther Reynolds, Jacob Reynolds, Elisha B. Reynolds and Elizabeth Reynolds. (*Births, Deaths and Marriages of the Nottingham Quakers, 1680-1899*, by Alice L. Beard (1989), p. 220)

King, Joshua, see Thomas P. King

King, Lewis, see John King and Thomas P. King

King, Mary, see Samuel King

King, Rachel, see John King

King, Samuel (born c1815, England) (brick maker at Elkton), married Mary (N) (born c1829, England) circa 1848; daughter Mary King born c1849, Pennsylvania, son George King, born c1851, Pennsylvania, son Thomas King born c1853, Maryland, daughter Elizabeth King, born c1855, son Samuel King born c1857, Maryland, and son John King born c1859, Maryland (1860 Cecil County Census)

King, Sarah, see John King

King, Temperance, see William Price and Thomas Broxson

King, Thomas, see John King and Samuel King

King, Thomas P., son of Lewis and Sarah King, the latter deceased, of Fulton Township, Lancaster Co., PA, married Phebe H. Preston, daughter of Joseph and Rebecca Preston, of Octorara Hundred, Cecil Co., on the 25th day of the 11th month 1847 at Octorara Meeting House. Among the witnesses were Joshua King, Lewis King, Edith King, Ann King, William King, Alfred King, Ruth Hannah Preston, Elizabeth Preston, Joseph B. Preston, Esther R. Preston, Deborah C. Preston, Lydia R. Preston, Rebecca R. Preston, Josephelina Preston and William F. Preston. (*Births, Deaths and Marriages of the Nottingham Quakers, 1680-1899*, by Alice L. Beard (1989), p. 227)

KINKEAD

Kinkead, Anna Maria, see James Owens

Kinkead, George, formerly of Elkton, married Miss Lydia A. Windle, of Wilmington, DE, on 26 Mar 1846 by Rev. Hogarth in Wilmington (*Cecil Whig*, 4 Apr 1846; *Delaware Gazette*, 3 Apr 1846)

Kinkead, John, married Louisa Ash circa 17 Dec 1827 (date of license) (Cecil County Marr. License Book)

Kinkead, Margaret, see John McCrea

KINNEY

Kinney, Mary, see Andrew McCue

KIRBY

Kirby, Rachel L. and Zebulon S., see George Washington Barnes

KIRK

Kirk, Abner, see William Kirk

Kirk, Alexander, married Christia Ann Bristow circa 18 Mar 1829 (date of license) by Rev. Barratt (Cecil County Marriage License Book, DAR transcript copied in 1928)

Kirk, Alexander (born c1802, Maryland) (plasterer at Chesapeake City), married Eliza Ann Madden (born c1830, Maryland), both of Cecil Co., on 12 Jan 1850, after obtaining a license that same day, by Rev. Goldsborough at Trinity Church; daughter Sarah Kirk born c1851 and son Alexander Kirk born c1859 (Cecil County Marriage License Book; *Cecil Democrat and Farmer's Journal*, 19 Jan 1850; *Cecil Whig*, 19 Jan 1850; 1860 Cecil County Census)

Kirk, Alexander, married Adrianna Reynolds, daughter of Jacob Reynolds (1791-1869) and Annie Moore (1793-1874), probably by 1850 (*Portrait and Biographical Record of Harford and Cecil Counties, Maryland* (1897, repr. 1989), p. 261)

Kirk, Alphonso, married Miss Elmirah Kirk, both of Cecil Co., on 19 Mar 1849 at Friends Meeting (*Cecil Democrat and Farmer's Journal*, 14 Apr 1849)

Kirk, Benjamin F. (1817-1886), son of Elisha Kirk and Martha McCullough, married Elizabeth B. Crothers (1826-1906), daughter of James Crothers and Rachel Cameron, circa 11 Mar 1846 (date of license) (Cecil County Marriage License Book; *Portrait and Biographical Record of Harford and Cecil Counties, Maryland* (1897, repr. 1989), pp. 394, 471-472; West Nottingham Cemetery tombstone inscriptions)

Kirk, Elijah (1820-1860), married Martha J. (N) (1823-1852) probably circa 1843 (West Nottingham Cemetery tombstone inscriptions)

Kirk, Elisha, see Benjamin F. Kirk and Elisha England Kirk

Kirk, Elisha England (1819-1901) (farmer, of Chester Co., PA, later near Blue Ball), son of William M. Kirk and Nancy Ann England, married 1st to Rebecca A. Hanna (c1823-1875), daughter of James Hanna, of Lancaster Co., PA, on the 17th day of the 10th month 1843 and married 2nd to Isabelle Taylor, daughter of James Taylor, of Cecil Co., in 1875; buried in Rosebank Cemetery (*Portrait and Biographical Record of Harford and Cecil Counties, Maryland* (1897, repr. 1989), p. 208; *Cecil Whig*, 18 Dec 1875, reported that Mrs. Elisha Kirk died near Brick Meeting House, no age given; *Joseph England and his Descendants*, by C. Walter England, Ph.D., 1975, p. 145; 1860 Cecil County Census)

Kirk, Eliza, see Norris Levis

Kirk, Elizabeth, see Ellwood Brown, John Kirk, Job H. Kirk and Reuben Kirk

Kirk, Elizabeth Amelia, see Thomas Brown

Kirk, Ellis P. (1813-1891), married Sarah A. (N) (1816-1908) probably circa 1836 and lived at East Nottingham (Rosebank Cemetery, at Calvert, tombstone inscriptions; *Midland Journal*, 3 Jul 1891)

Kirk, Elmirah, see Alphonso Kirk

Kirk, Esther E., see John Kirk

Kirk, Frances, see John Cannon and William Manly

Kirk, Jesse B. (1820-1886), married Sabina W. (N) (1815-1880) probably circa 1842 (Rosebank Cemetery, at Calvert, tombstone inscriptions)

Kirk, Job H. (1809-1888) (farmer near Brick Meeting House), son of William and Elizabeth Kirk, of Cecil Co., married Lydia Wilson (1809-1875), daughter of Samuel and Phebe Wilson, of East Nottingham Township, Chester Co., PA, in 1833 (*Cecil Whig*, 14 Aug 1875; *Births, Deaths and Marriages of the Nottingham Quakers, 1680-1899*, by Alice L. Beard (1989), p. 60, listed his name as Job Kirk and p. 222 mistakenly listed it as Job C. Kirk, but the Brick Meeting House, at Calvert, tombstone inscription states his name was Job H. Kirk; wife Lydia Kirk is buried at East Nottingham; 1860 Cecil County Census)

Kirk, John (1801-1882), married Mary (N) probably circa 1825 (Friends Cemetery, at Harrisville, tombstone inscription for him, but unable to read her marker)

Kirk, John (born c1801, Maryland) (merchant, 6th District), son of William and Elizabeth Kirk, the latter deceased, of West Nottingham Hundred, Cecil Co., married Esther E. Kirk (born c1816, Maryland), daughter of William and Elizabeth Kirk, of East Nottingham Hundred, Cecil Co., on the 21st day of the 1st month 1847 at East Nottingham (*Births, Deaths and Marriages of the Nottingham Quakers, 1680-1899*, by Alice L. Beard (1989), p. 226; 1860 Cecil County Census)

Kirk, Levi, married Elizabeth Gray circa 13 Jan 1829 (date of their license) by Rev. Barratt (Cecil County Marriage License Book)

Kirk, Lewis (1807-1847), married Miss Jane Hollingsworth, daughter of Joshua (or John?) and Hannah Hollingsworth, of East Nottingham Township, Chester Co., PA, on the 23rd day of the – month 1836 at Little Elk (*Births, Deaths and Marriages of the Nottingham Quakers, 1680-1899*, by Alice L. Beard (1989), p. 61 listed her father's name as Joshua, but on p. 223 it listed her father's name as John)

Kirk, Lydia, see Job H. Kirk

Kirk, Martha E., see John Keilholtz

Kirk, Mary, see Charles Gamble, John England and Haines England

Kirk, Mary A., see Howard Morris

Kirk, Mary Ann, see William R. Marnes

Kirk, Mary J., see Azariah Rittenhouse

Kirk, P. T. (born c1817, Maryland) (merchant, 6th District), married Elizabeth (N) (born c1826, Maryland) probably circa 1846; daughter Rachel Kirk born c1847 (1860 Cecil County Census)

Kirk, Rachel, see P. T. Kirk and Ellwood Brown

Kirk, Rachel Ann, see Daniel Stubbs

Kirk, Rebecca, see James Cameron

Kirk, Reuben (1814-1899, born Maryland) (farmer near Brick Meeting House), son of William and Elizabeth Kirk, of West Nottingham Hundred, married Hannah C. Brown (1821-1868, born Maryland), daughter of Thomas and Elizabeth Brown, of East Nottingham Hundred, on the 22nd day of the 4th month 1841 at East Nottingham (*Births, Deaths and Marriages of the Nottingham Quakers, 1680-1899*, by Alice L. Beard (1989), p. 225; Brick Meeting House, at Calvert, tombstone inscriptions; 1860 Cecil County Census)

Kirk, Sarah, see Alexander Kirk and John Roberts

Kirk, Susan, see Jeremiah Cox

Kirk, William, see Ellwood Brown, John England John Kirk, Job H. Kirk and Reuben Kirk

Kirk, William, married Jane Williams circa 26 Feb 1835 (date of license) by Rev. Griffith (Cecil County Marriage License Book)

Kirk, William (1817-1903, born Maryland) (farmer, carpenter, cabinet maker and undertaker near Brick Meeting House), son of Abner Kirk and Mary McCrea, married Hannah Brown England (1820-1892, born Maryland), daughter of Elisha England and Elizabeth Van Horn, on the 17th day of the 2nd month 1842 (*Joseph England and his Descendants*, by C. Walter England, Ph.D., 1975, p. 229; Rosebank Cemetery, at Calvert, tombstone inscriptions; 1860 Cecil County Census)

Kirk, William H., of Cecil Co., married Miss Mary E. House, of Chester Co., PA, on 5 Dec 1850 by Rev. Timlow (*Cecil Democrat and Farmer's Journal*, 21 Dec 1850)

Kirk, William M., see Elisha England Kirk

KIRKPATRICK

Kirkpatrick, Ellen, see Joseph Hemphill

Kirkpatrick, James, married Martha Owens circa 16 Apr 1834 (date of license) by Rev. Hammill (Cecil County Marriage License Book)

Kirkpatrick, Lydia Ann, see William Cline

Kirkpatrick, Rachel, see William Hinds

KIRKWOOD

Kirkwood, Elizabeth, see Frederick McNamee

KITCHEN

Kitchen, Anna, see Thomas Kitchen

Kitchen, Mary, see (N) Brown

Kitchen, Thomas (born c1820, Pennsylvania) (shoemaker near Elkton), married Miss Mary Brown (c1830, Delaware - 1891, Maryland), daughter of John and Ann Brown, on 20 Dec 1849, after obtaining a license on 18 Dec 1849, by Rev. Shauck; daughter Anna Kitchen born c1850, Maryland (Cecil County Marriage License Book; 1860 Cecil County Census; *Midland Journal*, 13 Feb 1891; *Cecil Whig*, 22 Dec 1849, stated Thomas was of Harrisville, Cecil Co., and Mary lived near the same place); see John Brown, *q.v.*

KNAPP

Knapp, Ambrose, married Rachel Touchstone circa 13 Jul 1831 (date of license) by Rev. Duke (Cecil County Marriage License Book)

KNIGHT

Knight, Catharine, see William Knight

Knight, Cornelius, see Theodore Knight

Knight, Hannah, see Jedediah Hayes

Knight, James, married Lepora (Zepora?) Cordes circa 26 Jan 1833 (date of license) by Rev. Smith (Cecil County Marriage License Book)

Knight, Jane E., see Joseph Gibson

Knight, John B. (born c1827, Pennsylvania) (laborer, 7th District), married Elizabeth (N) (born c1820, Pennsylvania) probably circa 1845; daughter Sarah born c1846, Maryland (1860 Cecil County Census)

Knight, John F., married Mary E. Shannon circa 24 Jun 1847 (date of license) (Cecil County Marriage License Book)

Knight, John T., married Margaret Ann Dennison circa 29 Sep 1830 (date of license) by Rev. Goforth (Cecil County Marriage License Book spelled her name Denison)

Knight, Pheby, see John Glenn

Knight, Sarah, see John B. Knight

Knight, Sarah Ann, see John Taylor

Knight, Theodore (born c1811, Maryland) (merchant in the 7th District), married Rachel (N) (born c1815, Pennsylvania) probably circa 1836; eldest son Cornelius Knight born c1837, Maryland, was a physician by 1860 (Cecil County Census)

Knight, Theodore B., married Caroline F. Abrahams circa 7 Jun 1842 (date of their license) (Cecil County Marriage License Book)

Knight, William (born c1813) (farmer, Cecilton), married Arabella A. (N) (born c1820) circa 1843; daughter Catharine Knight born c1844 (1860 Cecil County Census)

KNOCK

Knock, Ann, see Isaac Hines

Knock, Hannah M., see William Jones

KNOTTS

Knotts, Jonathan, married Mary Ann Wallace on 14 Sep 1841 after obtaining a license that same day (Cecil County Marriage License Book spelled his name Knots; Elkton Methodist Church Register)

Knotts, Sarah Ann, see Robert H. Thackery

Knotts, Thomas, married Elizabeth Patterson on 22 Nov 1838, after obtaining a license that same day, by Rev. Hagany (Cecil County Marriage License Book; DAR transcript copied in 1928 spelled her name Pattison; Elkton Methodist Church Register, p. 139)

KRAUSS

Krauss, Bernard G. (1826-1870, born Maryland) (shoemaker, 6th District), married Mary Ann Morrison (1829-1870, born Maryland) circa 22 Jun 1850 (date of license) (Cecil County Marriage License Book; West Nottingham Cemetery tombstone inscriptions; 1860 Cecil County Census)

Krauss, Charlotte A., see Thomas M. Krauss

Krauss, Elizabeth, see George W. Wells

Krauss, Ellan and Emma, see Thomas M. Krauss

Krauss, Henry (born c1813, Maryland) (carpenter, 6th District), married Martha (N) (born c1815, Maryland) probably circa 1838; son Henry Krauss, Jr. born c1839, Maryland (1860 Cecil County Census)

Krauss, Jacob (1808-1870), married Rebecca (N) (1803-1885) probably circa 1829-1830 (Friends Cemetery, at Harrisville, tombstone inscriptions)

Krauss, John H. (1820-1868, born Maryland) (bricklayer, 6th District), married 1st to Abigail (N) (1812-1856) probably circa 1845 (son Jonathan born c1846, Maryland) and married 2nd to Sarah J. "Sallie" Everham (1833-1862), of New Jersey, circa 14 Mar 1859 (date of license) (Cecil County Marriage License Book; Krauss Family Cemetery tombstone inscriptions; 1860 Cecil County Census)

Krauss, Thomas M. (1823-1883, born Maryland) (bricklayer, 6th District), married 1st to Catharine (N) (1829-1855) probably circa 1848, daughters Charlotte A. Krauss (1849-1905) and Emma Krauss born 1855, and married 2nd to Caroline (N) (born c1827, Maryland) circa 1858 and Ellan Krauss born circa 1859 (Krauss Family Cemetery tombstone inscriptions; 1860 Cecil County Census)

KREWSON

Krewson, Samuel (1818-1903), married Eliza (N) (1814-1897) probably circa 1839-1840 (Friends Cemetery, at Harrisville, tombstone inscriptions)

KYLE

Kyle, Eleanor Ann, see Caleb Emmons

Kyle, Robert, married Frances Nowland circa 20 May 1845 (date of license) (Cecil County Marriage License Book; DAR transcript copied in 1955 mistakenly listed the marriage license date as 30 May 1845)

LACKLAND

Lackland, Rachel S., see William Thompson

Lackland, Thomas, married Anna M. (N) (1827-1862) probably c1845-1850 (Ebenezer Church Cemetery tombstone inscription for Anna M. Lackland)

LAIR

Lair, Benjamin R. (1820-1901), married Mary J. (N) (1831-1906) circa 1850; son Azariah Lair, 1851-1861 (Zion Presbyterian Cemetery tombstone inscriptions)

LAKE

Lake, Patty, see Richard Roach

Lake, Placida, see Jonas Sea

Lake, Reuben, married Deborah Cameron circa 8 Mar 1826 (date of license) by Rev. Tally (Cecil County Marriage License Book)

Lake, Reuben, married Rachel Boyce circa 6 Apr 1830 (date of license) by Rev. Barratt (Cecil County Marriage License Book; DAR transcript copied in 1928 spelled her name Boice)

Lake, Thomas (born c1810, Maryland) (farmer, North East), married Mary Ann Hays circa 8 Jan 1834 (date of license) by Rev. Barratt (Cecil Co. Marr. Lic. Book; 1860 Cecil Co. Census listed him but not his wife)

LAMBDIN

Lambdin, Daniel and Margaret, see Joel Clements

LAMBERT

Lambert, Adam (1816-1900), married Mary Reed Adams (1819-1900) circa 28 Sep 1842 (date of license) (Cecil County Marriage License Book; North East Methodist Church Cemetery tombstone inscriptions)

Lambert, James (born c1823, England) (laborer near Elkton), married Lydia (N) (1822, England – 1882, Maryland) circa 1847 (1860 Cecil County Census listed these children: Sarah born c1848, England; John born c1850, England; James born c1852, Delaware; Robert born c1856, Delaware; Thomas born c1858, Maryland; and, George born 1860, Maryland; *Cecil Democrat and Farmer's Journal*, 4 Feb 1882, stated Lydia Lambert, wife of James Lambert, died at age 60 near Elkton)

LAMM

Lamm, John (1820-1882, born Germany) (shoemaker in Pennsylvania, later in Elkton), married Caroline (N) (1825-1892, born Maryland) probably circa 1846; eldest son John Lamm, Jr. born c1847 in Pennsylvania (West Nottingham Cemetery tombstone inscriptions; 1860 Cecil County Census)

LANCASTER

Lancaster, John, married Mary Lum circa 24 Oct 1829 (date of license) by Rev. Rider (Cecil County Marriage License Book)

LANDERS

Landers, George, married Margaret Price circa 17 Sep 1827 (date of license) (Cecil Co. Marr. License Book)

Landers, Robert A., married Mary Russell circa 24 Jan 1838 (date of license) by Rev. Goldsborough (Cecil County Marriage License Book)

LANE

Lane, Eliza, see Elisha Foster

Lane, Jane, see John Murphy

Lane, Mary, see Thomas Lane

Lane, Thomas (born c1827, Delaware) (livery stable at Chesapeake City), married Sarah (N) (born c1829, Delaware) probably circa 1848; daughter Mary Lane born c1849, Maryland (1860 Cecil County Census)

LANGDON

Langdon, Benjamin F., married Miss Rebecca Ellen Maxwell, both of West Nottingham Hundred, Cecil Co., on 5 Sep 1843, after obtaining a license on 31 Aug 1843, by Rev. Burrows (Cecil County Marriage License Book; *Cecil Whig*, 9 Sep 1843)

Langdon, Franklin (1821-1888), married Rebecca E. (N) (1822-1894) probably circa 1843 (West Nottingham Cemetery tombstone inscriptions)

Langdon, William, married Miss Almira Shauck, both of Maryland, on 28 Feb 1839 by Rev. Dickey (*Cecil Gazette*, 16 Mar 1839)

LARASON

Larason, Keziah, see John Carhart

LARUE

Larue, Thomas (born c1805, Maryland) (African American) (laborer, 7th District), married Caroline (N) (born c1812, Maryland) (African American) probably circa 1840; daughter Hetty Larue born c1844 and son Ceasar Augustus Larue born c1851, married Jane Miller in 1869 (1860 Cecil County Census spelled his name Lerou; Family Research by Michael Cain, of Aberdeen, Maryland, 2006)

LAURENSON

Laurenson, Mary, see George Lewis

LAW

Law, Ann Maria, see Joseph T. Stoops

LAWRENCE

Lawrence, Isaiah (1817-1869, born Pennsylvania) (stone cutter, 7th District), married Sarah J. (N) (1819-1885, born Delaware) probably circa 1838; daughter Indiana Lawrence born c1839, Maryland (Hopewell United Methodist Church Cemetery tombstone inscriptions; 1860 Cecil County Census)

LAYMAN

Layman, Firman, married Elizabeth Ann Conway circa 11 Jul 1837 (date of license) by Rev. Morris (Cecil County Marriage License Book)

LAYTON

Layton, Rachel, see Benjamin F. Thornton

LEE

Lee, Ann, see Samuel Lee

Lee, Ann A., see Philip Craig

Lee, Ann Jane, see William P. Morgan

Lee, Elizabeth, see Isaac H. R. Cox

Lee, F. (Mrs.), see William Brickley

Lee, Hannah, see William Berry

Lee, John T., married Miss Serena Aulds, both of Cecil Co., on 31 May 1849, after obtaining a license on 30 May 1849, by Rev. McIntire (Cecil County Marriage License Book misspelled her name as Alls; *Cecil Democrat and Farmer's Journal*, 2 Jun 1849; *Cecil Whig*, 2 Jun 1849)

Lee, Letitia, see Abraham Watson

Lee, Margaret Hall, see Gerard Gover and Henry Dorsey Smithson

Lee, Richard, married Nancy Gallaher circa 31 May 1839 (date of license) by Rev. Wiggin (Cecil County Marriage License Book)

Lee, Rose Ann, see William S. Barr

Lee, Samuel (born c1800, Maryland) (African American) (laborer at Elkton), married Pheby (N) (African American) (born c1816, Maryland) probably circa 1839; daughter Ann born c1840 (1860 Cecil Census)

Lee, Washington, married Sarah Ringold on 5 Oct 1842 (Elkton Methodist Church Register; Cecil County Marriage License Book did not list this marriage)

Lee, William, see John Burke

LEONARD

Leonard, Thompson (1807-1884), married 1st to Lydia Bryan circa 26 Mar 1831 (date of license) by Rev. Duke and married 2nd to Rebecca (N) (1823-1891) by 1851; daughter Mary D. Leonard, 1852-1933, buried beside Thompson and Rebecca Leonard (Cecil Co. Marriage License Book; Rosebank Cemetery, at Calvert, tombstone inscriptions)

LEPAIRE

Lepaire, Marguerite, see Prosper Siebra

LEVIS

Levis, Joseph K., see Norris Levis

Levis, Norris (1796-1875) (paper manufacturer and flour miller), of Delaware Co., PA, later of Cecil Co., married Eliza Kirk circa 23 Mar 1831 (date of license) by Rev. Duke (Cecil County Marriage License Book; *Portrait and Biographical Record of Harford and Cecil Counties, Maryland* (1897, repr. 1989), page 446; p. 352 stated they had 9 children and 6 were living in 1897, namely, Joseph K. Levis (born 28 Aug 1833), Eliza Carter, Amelia E. Russell, Robert C. Levis (born in 1840), Harriet Alexander, and Mary Mitchell; *Cecil Whig*, 13 Mar 1875, reported that he died at his residence *Walnut Valley*)

Levis, Rebecca P., see Arthur W. Milby

Levis, Robert C., see Norris Levis

Levis, Samuel, see Arthur W. Milby

Levis, William, married Ann Maria Lorritt circa 30 Sep 1830 (date of their license) by Rev. Goforth (Cecil County Marriage License Book spelled his name Leavis and her name Loritt)

Levis, (N), married Sarah P. (N) (1807-1877) probably circa 1825-1830 (St. John's Church Cemetery, at Lewisville, tombstone inscription for "Mother" Sarah P. Levis)

LEWIS

Lewis, Edward B. (doctor in Elkton), married 1st to Margaret A. L. Gottier circa 2 Jul 1836 (date of license) by Rev. Duke and married 2nd to Mrs. Jane Burchell, of Baltimore Co., on 25 Jan 1849, after obtaining a license on 24 Jan 1849, by Rev. Elliott (Cecil County Marriage License Book; *Cecil Democrat and Farmer's Journal*, 27 Jan 1849, marriage notice acknowledged "the delicious cake which accompanied their announcement")

Lewis, Elizabeth, see John Keatley

Lewis, Elizabeth Ann, see William H. Stalcup

Lewis, George, married Mary Laurenson circa 10 Jan 1826 (date of license) by Rev. Sharpley (Cecil County Marriage License Book)

Lewis, Jonathan M., married Elizabeth Ewing circa 27 Jan 1846 (date of license) (Cecil County Marriage License Book)

Lewis, Mary Ann, see William E. G. Graham

Lewis, Rebecca, see John B. Graham

Lewis, Robert, married Mary Gray circa 13 Feb 1833 (date of license) by Rev. Duke (Cecil County Marriage License Book)

Lewis, William C. (1804-1881), married Sarah Aldridge (1811-1895) circa 19 May 1831 (date of license) by Rev. Barratt (Cecil County Marriage License Book; Elkton Cemetery tombstone inscriptions)

LIGHTNER

Lightner, Caroline E. and George W., see David T. Aspril

LILLEY

Lilley, Daniel, married Sarah Ellen Clark circa 11 Dec 1833 (date of license) by Rev. Barratt (Cecil County Marriage License Book spelled his name Lilly; DAR transcript copied in 1928 misspelled his name Killy)

Lilley, Elizabeth A., see Caleb K. Burgoyne

Lilley, John (born c1811, Maryland) (papermaker in Elkton), married Elizabeth (N) (born c1815, Maryland) probably circa 1838, daughter Susan Lilley born c1839 (1860 Cecil County Census)

Lilley, William (1810-1864) (pumpmaker in Elkton), married Eliza A. (N) (1812-1883) probably circa 1835 (Cherry Hill Methodist Church Cemetery tombstone inscriptions; 1860 Cecil County Census)

LINDSEY

Lindsey, Henry, see William Lindsey

Lindsey, Susan, see John H. Thomas

Lindsey, William (born c1822, Delaware) (lumber inspector at Chesapeake City), married Anna (N) (born c1825, Delaware) probably circa 1843; son Henry born c1844, Maryland (1860 Cecil County Census)

LINTON

Linton, Francis (born c1823, Maryland) (blacksmith, 7th District), married Susan (N) (born c1830, Delaware) probably circa 1850; son John Linton born c1851, Maryland (1860 Cecil County Census)

Linton, John, see Francis Linton
Linton, Martha, see William R. Moore

LISTER
Lister, Mary, see Robert Walmsley

LITTLE
Little, Adam, married Elizabeth Campbell circa 29 Sep 1829 (date of license) by Rev. Magraw (Cecil County Marriage License Book)
Little, Araminta, see William Hyland
Little, Christopher, see George Thomas
Little, Christopher, married Ann Moffitt circa 22 Feb 1827 (date of license) by Rev. Magraw (Cecil County Marriage License Book)
Little, Christopher, married Isabella B. Moore circa 18 Jan 1848 (date of license) (Cecil County Marriage License Book)
Little, Jane, see John Cooper and Benoni Cooling
Little, John, married Araminta Manly circa 29 Dec 1840 (date of license) and died by 1849; Mrs. Araminta Little married 2nd to William Hyland on 16 May 1850 (Cecil County Marriage License Book; *Cecil Whig*, 18 May 1850)
Little, John, married Eliza Clark circa 13 Jul 1831 (date of license) by Rev. Barratt (Cecil County Marriage License Book)
Little, Louisa, see George Thomas
Little, Margaret Ann, see Nicholas Clark
Little, Mary Ann, see Joseph S. Wingate
Little, Mary Elizabeth, see John Jackson
Little, William (1795-1876), married 1st to Hannah Simcoe (1795-1842) circa 14 Mar 1825 (date of license) by Rev. Magraw and married 2nd to Miss Mary Maxwell (1812-1880) on 24 Sep 1844, after obtaining a license that day, by Rev. Burrows (Cecil County Marriage License Book; West Nottingham Cemetery tombstone inscriptions; *Cecil Whig*, 12 Oct 1844)

LITTAWAY, LITWAY
Littaway, Lewis (born c1790, Amsterdam) (saddler at Chesapeake City), married 1st to Sarah Cunningham circa 1 Jan 1838 (date of license; spelled his name Littaway) by Rev. Morris and married 2nd to Elizabeth Biddle (born c1810, Maryland) circa 24 Dec 1848 (date of license; spelled his name Litway); daughter Caroline born c1831, son Edward born c1839 and son John born c1842 (Cecil County Marriage License Book; 1840 Cecil County Census spelled his name Littoway and 1860 Census spelled his name Litway)

LLOYD
Lloyd, Nicholas, married Catharine Stephens circa 19 Jan 1839 (date of license) by Rev. Smith (Cecil County Marriage License Book; 1860 Cecil County Census listed Catherine F. Stephens (born c1819) as head of household in Cecilton with children Mary age 16, Nicholas age 12, Louisa age 9, Hamilton age 6, and Anna age 2)
Lloyd, Peregrine F., married 1st to Letitia Smith circa 26 Mar 1828 (date of license) and married 2nd to Rebecca Price circa 13 Feb 1833 (date of license) by Rev. McKenney (Cecil Co. Marriage License Book)
Lloyd, Philemon, married Martha J. Robinson circa 10 Feb 1849 (date of license) (Cecil County Marriage License Book)

LOCKARD
Lockard, David E., married 1st to Adriann Hammersmith circa 25 Mar 1831 (date of license) by Rev. Magraw and married 2nd to Rachel Prior circa 4 Jan 1842 (date of license) (Cecil County Marriage

License Book; DAR transcript copied in 1928 did not include his middle initial and spelled his name Lockart in 1831)

Lockard, John, married Dollie Ann Tyson circa 9 Jan 1828 (date of license) (Cecil Co. Marr. License Book)

Lockard, John P., married Ann McKinney circa 28 Oct 1835 (date of license) by Rev. Barratt (Cecil County Marriage License Book)

LOCKWOOD

Lockwood, Edward Wilson (born c1822, Delaware) (lumber merchant at Cecilton), married Sarah E. Alrichs (born c1824, Delaware) circa 1846; son George W. Lockwood was born 18 Feb 1847 on the Meadows Farm in Cecil Co. (*Portrait and Biographical Record of Harford and Cecil Counties, Maryland* (1897, repr. 1989), p. 181; 1860 Cecil County Census)

Lockwood, George W., see Edward Wilson Lockwood

Lockwood, J. P. (born c1812, Delaware) (laborer at North East), married Ann (N) (born c1817, Maryland) probably circa 1836; daughter Margaret Lockwood born c1837 (1860 Cecil County Census)

Lockwood, Margaret, see J. P. Lockwood

Lockwood, Martha E., see Joshua Clayton, John Naudain and John McCrone

Lockwood, Mary, see John Naudain, Joshua Clayton and John McCrone

Lockwood, Richard, see John Naudain, Joshua Clayton and John McCrone

LOFLAND

Lofland, Henry J. (1823-1905), married Isabella M. (N) (1828-1907) probably circa 1848-1850 (West Nottingham Cemetery tombstone inscriptions)

Lofland, James, married Hannah E. Hall circa 14 Mar 1849 (date of license) (Cecil Co. Marr. License Book)

Lofland, Rachel, see John McIntyre

Lofland, Stephen (born c1815, Delaware) (farmer at Cecilton), married Mary (N) (born c1818, Maryland) circa 1842; son William Lofland born c1843 (1860 Cecil County Census spelled his name Loffland)

Lofland, William, see Stephen Lofland

LOFTIS

Loftis, Elizabeth, see Samuel Whitlock

LOGAN

Logan, Ann, see Isaac Wardell

Logan, Emeline, see Samuel P. Ayres

Logan, Hannah, see Samuel Logan

Logan, Hazlet, married Ann Murphy circa 30 Jan 1838 (date of license) (Cecil County Marr. License Book)

Logan, Henrietta, see Samuel Logan

Logan, Hester or Hetty see Francis Atkinson

Logan, Hiram, see Samuel Logan

Logan, Immanuel, see Samuel Logan

Logan, Jane, see John Richardson

Logan, Jane, see Nathan McVey

Logan, John Thomas, see Samuel Logan

Logan, Laura, see Samuel Logan

Logan, Lydia Ann, see Samuel Logan

Logan, Lydia Jane, see Philip Smeltzer

Logan, Mary Ann, see Thomas Cantwell

Logan, Mary Elizabeth, see Samuel Logan

Logan, Samuel, married Margaret McCall circa 12 Jul 1825 (date of license) by Rev. Magraw (Cecil County Marriage License Book)

Logan, Samuel (born c1815) (blacksmith at Charlestown), married Sarah Reed (born c1814) circa 26 Jan 1836 (date of license) by Rev. Megready (Cecil County Marriage License Book; 1860 Cecil Co. Census)

Logan, Samuel (born c1830, Maryland) (laborer at North East), married Hannah Bennett (born c1825, Maryland) on 26 Aug 1841 after obtaining a license on 25 Aug 1841 (Cecil County Marriage License Book; 1860 Cecil County Census; *Bible Records, Genealogical Society of Cecil County*, by Gary L. Burns (1990), p. 1, listed the births of their eleven children: John Thomas, born 1 Jun 1842; Immanuel, 1843-1847; Hannah, born 1845; Sarah Katherine, born 23 Mar 1848; Lydia Ann, born 7 Oct 1849; Henrietta, 1850-1853; (N), 1853-1853; Laura, born 13 Dec 1855; Walter Bennett, born 15 Jan 1857; Mary Elizabeth, born 20 Apr 1859; and, Hiram, 1861-1909)

Logan, Sarah, see William Dennison

Logan, Sarah Katherine, see Samuel Logan

Logan, Sophia, see James M. Wilson

Logan, Sophia McCullough, see John Sterrett Christie

Logan, Susan, see John Gallaher

Logan, Theresa, see Stephen Atkinson

Logan, Thomas, married Isabella Jones circa 20 Dec 1838 (date of license) by Rev. Inskip (Cecil County Marriage License Book)

Logan, Thomas, married Mary Baker circa 21 Sep 1839 (date of license) by Rev. Grace (Cecil County Marriage License Book)

Logan, Thomas (born c1820, Maryland) (laborer at North East), married Emily Alexander (born c1822, Maryland) circa 27 Aug 1840 (date of license) (Cecil Co. Marr. License Book; 1860 Cecil Co. Census)

Logan, Walter Bennett, see Samuel Logan

Logan, William (born c1803, Maryland) (constable at Charlestown), married Harriett Rutter (born c1812, Maryland) circa 11 Feb 1830 (date of license) by Rev. Goforth (Cecil County Marriage License Book; 1860 Cecil County Census)

LOGIE
Logie, John and Mary J., see Bryan M. Thomas

LOGUE
Logue, James C., of Cecil Co., married Dorinda Fillingame, of Kent Co., circa 22 Aug 1826 by Rev. Smith (Kent County Marriage License Book)

Logue, William, married Margaret Ann Simmons circa 24 Jan 1837 (date of license) by Rev. Smith (Cecil County Marriage License Book)

LOMANS
Lomans, Emeline, see William Gillespie

LONG
Long, Albert M., married Julia M. Cloud, daughter of Col. E. Cloud, on 23 May 1850 by Rev. Hitchcock at the Second Presbyterian Church (*Cecil Democrat and Farmer's Journal*, 8 Jun 1850, reported a double wedding ceremony with her sister Margaret C. Cloud who married William Voglesong)

Long, Thomas, married Matilda Bedwell circa 23 Dec 1844 (date of license) (Cecil Co. Marr. License Book)

LONGSTREET
Longstreet, Aaron and Emily, see Horace H. Duyckinck

LORRITT
Lorritt, Ann Maria, see William Levis

Lorritt, Rosanna, see Andrew S. Barratt

Lorritt, Sarah B., see John Rutter

LORT

Lort, Franklin W. (1826-1871), married Elizabeth T. Merry circa 7 Mar 1848 (date of license) (Cecil County Marriage License Book; *Cecil Whig*, 25 Nov 1871)

Lort, Isaac J. (1818-1862, Maryland) (sailor and bay captain), married Sophia Brock (1824, New Jersey – 1867, Maryland), residents of Elk Neck, Cecil Co., on 7 Dec 1848, after obtaining a license on 6 Dec 1848, by Rev. Arthur (Cecil County Marriage License Book; 1860 Cecil County Census; *Cecil Democrat and Farmer's Journal*, 23 Dec 1848 and 19 Oct 1867; Elkton Cemetery tombstone inscriptions)

Lort, Joseph Jr., son of Capt. Joseph Lort (1783-1850) of Elk Neck, married Ann Maulden circa 2 Feb 1841 (date of license) (Cecil County Marr. License Book; *Cecil Democrat and Farmer's Journal*, 20 Jul 1850)

Lort, Millicent Amanda, see George W. Merry

LOTTMAN

Lottman, Levi, married 1st to Mary Rutter circa 22 Sep 1830 (date of license) by Rev. Goforth and married 2nd to Marjory Foster circa 29 Mar 1836 (date of license) by Rev. Wilson (Cecil Marriage License Book)

Lottman, Nicholas, married 1st to Ann Rutter circa 14 Nov 1827 (date of license) and married 2nd to Elizabeth Yeager circa 2 Mar 1843 (date of license) (Cecil County Marriage License Book)

LOUMIER

Loumier, Benjamin, married Miss Mary R. Pluck, both of Cecil Co., on 2 Jan 1845, after obtaining a license that same day, by Rev. Shields (Cecil County Marriage License Book; Elkton Methodist Church Register, page 140; *Cecil Whig*, 4 Jan 1845)

LOVE

Love, Catharine A., see John Tosh

Love, Elizabeth, see John Graham and Nathan Brumfield

Love, Mary Ann, see John D. Carter

Love, Robert (1813-1895), married Agnes Ann "Abbie" Todd (1824-1884) circa 16 May 1843 (date of license) and died at Castleton in Harford County (*The Aegis and Intelligencer*, 5 Apr 1895; Cecil County Marriage License Book; West Nottingham Cemetery tombstone inscriptions)

Love, (N), married Eliza (N) (1808-1876), of Harrisville, probably circa 1828 (*Cecil Whig*, 30 Sep 1876)

LOWE

Lowe, Elizabeth, see Nathan Brumfield

Lowe, Ephraim P. (1808-1880), of North East, married Martha Jane Roach (1816-1877) circa 11 Nov 1834 (date of license) by Rev. Barratt (Cecil County Marriage License Book listed her maiden name only as Jane Roach; North East Methodist Church Cemetery tombstone inscriptions; *Cecil Whig*, 16 Jun 1877)

Lowe, Milcah, see David Hagan

LOWERY, LOWRY

Lowery, James, married Mary Simpers circa 26 Jul 1826 (date of license) by Rev. Page (Cecil County Marriage License Book)

Lowry, John, of Cherry Hill, married Mary Gallaher (1806-1872) circa 11 Apr 1842 (date of license) (Cecil County Marriage License Book; *Cecil Whig*, 3 Aug 1872)

Lowery, Sophia, see George Grant

Lowery, William, married Rachel Richardson (1804-1875) circa 27 May 1826 (date of license) by Rev. Duke and she died at Charlestown (Cecil County Marriage License Book; DAR transcript copied in 1928 misspelled his name as Lowey; *Cecil Whig*, 25 Sep 1875, noting "Baltimore papers please copy," but no obituary was published in the *Baltimore Sun* for Rachel Lowery)

LOWMAN

Lowman, Charles (born c1819, Delaware) (shoemaker, Elkton), married Eliza J. (N) (born c1819, Delaware) circa 1843; son Mathis Lowman born c1844 (1860 Cecil County Census)

LUCAS

Lucas, Mary Ann, see Stephen Emory

Lucas, Sarah Amanda, see Lawrence Miller

LUKENS

Lukens, (N), married Eliza J. (N) (1821-1888) probably circa 1840-1842 (Rosebank Cemetery, at Calvert, tombstone inscription for "Mother, Eliza J. Lukens," but no marker for her husband)

LUM

Lum, Frances Ann, see Lewis W. Thomas

Lum, Isaac, married Mary D. Aulds circa 16 Oct 1844 (date of license) (Cecil County Marriage License Book; DAR transcript copied in 1955 listed her name without the middle initial)

Lum, Isaac A., married Mary B. Beaston circa 2 Jun 1834 (date of license) by Rev. Morris (Cecil County Marriage License Book)

Lum, J. (born c1815, Maryland) (farmer near St. Augustine), married Debora (N) (born c1823, Maryland) probably circa 1845; son John born c1846, Maryland (1860 Cecil County Census spelled his name Lumb)

Lum, Jane, see John Thompson

Lum, John, see J. Lum

Lum, Martha, see John W. Mercer

Lum, Mary, see John Lancaster

Lum, Millicent Ann, see James N. Mercer

Lum, Nicholas, married Miss Ann Zane, both of North East, Cecil Co., on 4 Jan 1838, after obtaining a license on 2 Jan 1838, by Rev. Kennard (Cecil County Marr. License Book; *Cecil Gazette*, 3 Feb 1838)

Lum, Rebecca K., see James C. Oldham

Lum, Sampson, married Mary Crouch circa 20 Mar 1838 (date of license) by Rev. Barratt (Cecil County Marriage License Book)

LUNGREN

Lungren, Ferdinand (1801-1882), married Susan Armstrong (1810-1880) probably circa 1828 (St. John's Church Cemetery, at Lewisville, tombstone inscriptions)

LURTZ

Lurtz, Rachel, see William Hague

LUSBY

Lusby, Gideon (1800-1833), married Rosetta H. Benson circa 16 Feb 1827 (date of license) by Rev. Higgins and Rosetta H. Lusby married 2nd to Edward B. Ford circa 18 Apr 1835 (date of license) (Cecil County Marr. License Book; St. Stephen's Episcopal Church Cemetery tombstone inscription for Gideon Lusby)

Lusby, John H., see Abraham Kennard

Lusby, Mary E., see Thomas Lusby

Lusby, Rebecca, see James Noble and William Reed

Lusby, Robert C., see John R. Price and Harrison S. Bullen

Lusby, Rosetta H., see Edward B. Ford and Gideon Lusby

Lusby, Thomas (born c1817, Maryland) (farmer, Warwick), married Mary E. Lusby (born c1819, Maryland) circa 11 Dec 1838 (date of their license) by Rev. King (Cecil County Marriage License Book; 1860 Cecil County Census)

Lusby, Virginia H., see Charles E. Roberts

Lusby, William, married Frances A. Cochran circa 6 Feb 1827 (date of their license) by Rev. Wilson (Cecil County Marriage License Book; DAR transcript copied in 1928 misspelled her name as Francis)

LUTTON

Lutton, Ebenezer, married Miss Eliza Ferguson, both of Cecil County, on 4 Aug 1827 by Rev. Peckworth (*Delaware Gazette*, 10 Aug 1827, spelled his name Luton)

Lutton, Ellen, see Alexander Baxter

Lutton, John (born c1817, Maryland) (cooper at Elkton), married Ann Jane McCrea (born c1820, Maryland) circa 17 Aug 1840 (date of license); son William Lutton born c1841 (Cecil County Marriage License Book misspelled her name as McCray; 1860 Cecil County Census)

Lutton, Robert, married Miss Margaret Ramsey on 16 Oct 1834, after obtaining a license that same day, by Rev. Hammill (Cecil County Marriage License Book; *Cecil Gazette*, 18 Oct 1834)

Lutton, William, see John Lutton

LYLE

Lyle, Ann, see Robert Marshbank

LYNCH

Lynch, Andrew J., married Mary Boyd circa 13 Jun 1850 (date of license) (Cecil Co. Marr. License Book)

Lynch, Eliza A., see Robert Marshbank

Lynch, Grizzella, see David Tucker

Lynch, Hannah, see William D. Terbit

Lynch, Hasson (born c1804, Maryland) (farmer near Principio), married 1st to Hannah McElwee circa 23 Jun 1828 (date of license) by Rev. Barratt and married 2nd to Rachel Johnson (born c1810, Maryland) circa 11 Oct 1836 (date of license) by Rev. Wilson (Cecil Co. Marr. License Book; 1860 Cecil County Census)

Lynch, James, of Cecil Co., divorced from Mary Ann Lynch on 22 Jan 1838 (*Divorces and Names Changed in Maryland by Act of the Legislature, 1634-1867*, by Mary Keysor Meyer (1991), p. 57)

Lynch, John W., married Mary M. Hirons circa 22 Dec 1838 (date of license) by Rev. Piggot, a Protestant Episcopal minister in North Sassafras (Cecil County Marriage License Book)

Lynch, L. (born c1818, Maryland) (laborer near Charlestown), married Lydia (N) (born c1821, Maryland) probably circa 1843; daughter Margaret Lynch born c1844 (1860 Cecil County Census)

Lynch, Margaret, see L. Lynch and John Cameron

Lynch, Mary, see Solomon Blake

Lynch, Mary Ann, see James Lynch

Lynch, Rachel, see Hugh Ramsey

Lynch, William (born c1803, Maryland) (laborer near Bay View), married Lydia Ann Baker (born c1814, Maryland) circa 1 Feb 1831 (date of the license) by Rev. Goforth (Cecil County Marriage License Book; 1860 Cecil County Census)

Lynch, William T., married Mary Jane Craig, daughter of James Craig, of Elk Neck, on 31 Oct 1850, after obtaining a license on 30 Oct 1850, by Rev. Goldsborough at Trinity Church (Cecil County Marriage License Book; *Cecil Democrat and Farmer's Journal*, 2 Nov 1850; *Cecil Whig*, 2 Nov 1850)

LYNN

Lynn, Margaret S., see Benjamin Vandiver

LYON

Lyon, James, married Maria Taylor circa 1 Apr 1834 (date of license) by Rev. Goforth (Cecil County Marriage License Book)

MACKALL

Mackall, Henry C. (1820-1864), married Mary E. (N) (1820-1885) probably circa 1841 (Elkton Presbyterian Church Cemetery tombstone inscriptions)

Mackall, Jane W., see Cyrus H. Jacobs

MACKEY

Mackey, Alfred Wilson, see Thomas Mackey

Mackey, Charles H., see David Mackey

Mackey, Clara, see Thomas Mackey

Mackey, David (1805-1854), married Catherine (N) (1807-1884) probably circa 1827 (St. John's Church Cemetery, at Lewisville, tombstone inscriptions)

Mackey, David (c1815-1863), married 1st to Emeline Perry (c1818-1843) on 7 Aug 1837 and married 2nd to Jane McCleary (1809-1881) on 26 Nov 1844 (*Bible Records, Genealogical Society of Cecil County*, by Gary L. Burns (1990), p. 11, stated they were originally from New London, PA and listed David's five children: [by his 1st wife] John B., born 19 Dec 1838, and Mary E., born 28 Oct 1842; and, [by his 2nd wife] Charles H., born 11 Jan 1846, George J., born 21 Jun 1848, and David W., born 14 Feb 1850)

Mackey, David W., see David Mackey

Mackey, Edwin, see Thomas Mackey

Mackey, Elisha Hamill, see Thomas Mackey

Mackey, Eliza, see John B. Pitt

Mackey, Emma Jane, see Thomas Mackey

Mackey, George J., see David Mackey

Mackey, George Thomas, see Thomas Mackey

Mackey, James, see Thomas Mackey

Mackey, John B., see David Mackey

Mackey, Lorean A., see Thomas Mackey

Mackey, Mary, see John Miller

Mackey, Mary E., see David Mackey

Mackey, Robert Alison, see Thomas Mackey

Mackey, Samuel, married Amanda Armstrong, both of Cecil Co., on 29 Jan 1849, after obtaining a license that same day, by Rev. DeWitt (Cecil County Marriage License Book; *Cecil Democrat and Farmer's Journal*, 3 Feb 1849)

Mackey, Thomas (1810-1888), married Hannah Hamill (1813-1874), daughter of (N) and Jane Hamill (1789-1869), on 6 Dec 1832 (*Bible Records, Genealogical Society of Cecil County*, by Gary L. Burns (1990), p. 10, stated they were originally of Chester Co., PA and listed the births and deaths of their eleven children: William, born 29 Sep 1833, died – Sep 1843(?); James, born 21 Jun 1836; Elisha Hamill and Robert Alison (twins), born 1838 (Robert died 28 Jul 1874); Emma Jane, born 10 Apr 1841; William Stewart, born 6 Dec 1843; George Thomas, born 31 May 1846, died 21 Jun 1900; Clara, born 28 Oct 1848, died 12 Nov 1868; Edwin, born 25 Sep 1850; Lorean A., born 24 Nov 1852, died 14 Jul 1868; and, Alfred Wilson, born 18 Feb 1855)

Mackey, William, see Thomas Mackey

MACKIE

Mackie, Albert, see James Mackie

Mackie, J. Alfred, see John Mackie

Mackie, James (born c1817, Pennsylvania) (auger maker at Elkton), married Sarah (N) (born c1819, Pennsylvania) probably circa 1840; eldest son Albert born c1844, Maryland (1860 Cecil County Census)

Mackie, John (born c1812, Maryland) (tanner at Elkton), married Catherine Andrews, of Natchez, MS, circa 1837; eldest son J. Alfred Mackie was born in Maryland in 1838 (*Portrait and Biographical Record of Harford and Cecil Counties, Maryland* (1897, repr. 1989), p. 274; 1860 Cecil County Census stated she was born in Louisiana)

MACKINSON

Mackinson, Elizabeth M., see William A. Hall

Mackinson, also see Makinson

MACKLAN

Macklan, Ann, see Spencer Howard

MADDEN

Madden, Eliza Ann, see Alexander Kirk

MAEDER

Maeder, James Caspard, married Miss Clara Fisher, of the Theatre, on 3 Jan 1835 by Rev. Dr. Wainwright at Trinity Church in Boston (*Cecil Gazette*, 10 Jan 1835)

MAFFITT

Maffitt, Caroline, see William Beatty

Maffitt, Clayton S., see Samuel S. Maffitt

Maffitt, Ellen A., see Samuel Gibson

Maffitt, Jane, see John Marnes

Maffitt, Mary Jane, see Benjamin P. Fowler

Maffitt, Mary S., see James Warburton

Maffitt, Samuel S. (1819-1864) (esquire and farmer near Elkton), married A. C. (N) (born c1823) circa 1844; son Clayton S. Maffitt born c1845 (1860 Cecil County Census; *Cecil Whig*, 28 May 1864, reported that he was the late Comptroller of Maryland and was buried in Elkton Presbyterian Church Cemetery)

Maffitt, Sarah, see William Pannell

Maffitt, Thomas (1802-1837), married Araminta Cazier (1804-1946) circa 19 Sep 1826 (date of license) by Rev. Wallace (Cecil County Marriage License Book; DAR transcript copied in 1928 misspelled his name Moffitt and her name Cozier; North East Methodist Church Cemetery tombstone inscription spelled his name Maffitt)

Maffitt, William H., married Elizabeth Daugherty circa 4 Oct 1825 (date of license) by Rev. Duke (Cecil County Marriage License Book)

Maffitt, William R. (esquire), of Cecil Co., married Miss Martha A. Walling, of Frederick Co., on 12 Dec 1848 by Rev. Spangler in Baltimore (*Cecil Democrat and Farmer's Journal*, 16 Dec 1848; *Baltimore Sun*, 14 Dec 1848; both newspapers spelled his name Maffit)

Maffitt, also see Moffitt

MAGAW

Magaw, James (1800-1877), married Nancy (N) (1803-1885) probably circa 1825 (Rosebank Cemetery, at Calvert, tombstone inscriptions)

MAGEE

Magee, John, of Newark, DE, married Miss Eliza Jane Moore, eldest daughter of John Moore, of White Clay Creek Hundred, DE, on 1 Jan 1835 (*Cecil Gazette*, 3 Jan 1835)

MAGENS

Magens, William, of Kirkwood, DE, married Sally A. (N) (1810-1877) probably circa 1830 and died at the residence of Edmond Brown in Elkton; buried in Brandywine Cemetery (*Cecil Whig*, 3 Nov 1877, noting, Baltimore papers please copy; however, it did not appear in the *Baltimore Sun*)

MAGRAW

Magraw, Henry S. (1815-1867), married Emily W. Hopkins (1818-1870), daughter of George R. and Ann Hopkins, probably circa 1840 (West Nottingham Cemetery tombstone inscriptions)

Magraw, Samuel M. (1809-1871), son of Rev. Samuel Magraw and Rebecca Cochran, married Mary Ann S. Maxwell (1807-1888), daughter of Robert Maxwell, of Lancaster Co., PA, on 6 Mar 1838 by Rev. Dr. Ashbel Green in Philadelphia (West Nottingham Cemetery tombstones; *Cecil Gazette*, 17 Mar 1838)

MAHAN, MAHON

Mahan, Angeline, see George Rozean

Mahan, Ann, see William P. Mahan

Mahan, Catharine Ann, see Enoch Boyd

Mahan, Elizabeth, see Robert Ross and George Mahan

Mahan, George (1791-1856) (War of 1812 veteran), of Cecil Co., married 1st to Lydia Wells circa 5 Jul 1821 (date of license) in Cecil Co., married 2nd to Elizabeth Wood on 17 Jul 1830 in Pike Co., PA, and died in Milford, DE; widow Elizabeth Mahan died in 1886 in Philadelphia (Bounty Land Warrant 50-40-20877; Cecil County Marriage License Book)

Mahan, Hannah, see David M. Wells

Mahan (Mahon), John S., married Sarah E. Armington circa 31 May 1849 (date of license) (Cecil County Marriage License Book)

Mahan, Margaret A., see Abel J. Davis

Mahan, Reese (born c1818, Maryland) (shoemaker, 6th District), married Elizabeth Garrett (born c1822, Maryland) circa 5 May 1840 (date of license) by Rev. Warburton (Cecil County Marriage License Book and 1860 Cecil County Census did not include a middle initial for her, yet the DAR transcript copied in 1928 listed her name as Elizabeth M. Garret)

Mahan, Sarah, see William Boyd

Mahan, William P. (1812-1843), of Elkton District, married Ann Spence (1815-1895) circa 7 Mar 1835 (date of license) by Rev. Wilson; buried beside son William T. Mahan, 1842-1880 (Cecil County Marriage License Book; Cherry Hill Methodist Church Cemetery tombstone inscriptions; 1860 Cecil County Census stated Ann Mahan, aged 42, was born in Maryland and head of household)

MAHER

Maher, John (born c1824, Ireland) (furnace keeper at Charlestown), married Ann (N) (born c1824, Ireland) probably circa 1849; daughter Mary Maher born c1850, Maryland (1860 Cecil County Census)

MAHONEY, MAHANEY, MAHANY

Mahoney, Caroline, see James R. Smith

Mahoney, Dennis (1810-1892), of Queenstown, County Cork, Ireland, later of Cecil Co., married Margaret (N) (1816-1901) probably circa 1835 (St. Patrick's Catholic Church tombstone inscriptions)

Mahoney, Edward, see John H. Mahoney

Mahoney (Mahany), Elisha (born c1813) (farmer at North East), married Miss Rebecca Ann Weaver (born c1820) on 1 Mar 1838, after obtaining a license on 28 Feb 1838, by Rev. Parkins (*Cecil Gazette*, 10 Mar 1838, spelled his name Mahany; 1860 Cecil County Census spelled his name Mahoney; Cecil County Marriage License Book spelled his name Mahanny)

Mahoney, Elisha (born c1823) (cooper at Elkton), married Maria Mahoney (born c1821) circa 3 Dec 1845 (date of license) (Cecil County Marriage License Book; 1860 Cecil County Census)

Mahoney (Mahany), Elizabeth, see Elisha Atkinson and Stephen Atkinson

Mahoney, Harriet, see William R. Mahoney

Mahoney, Jeremiah, married Miss Emily Reed, both of Cecil Co., on 2 Jan 1845, after obtaining a license on 31 Dec 1844, by Rev. Shields (Cecil County Marriage License Book; Elkton Methodist Church Register, page 140; *Cecil Whig*, 4 Jan 1845)

Mahoney, John Huss (born c1825) (cooper at Elkton), married 1st to Elizabeth Jane Ferguson circa 26 Sep 1840 (date of license), married 2nd to Maria Mahoney (born c1821), daughter of Jeremiah Mahoney, all of Cecil Co., on 30 Sep 1847, after obtaining a license on 29 Sep 1847, by Rev. Goldsborough in Trinity Church, and married 3rd to Caroline Davidson circa 16 Dec 1854 (date of license) (*Cecil Whig*, 2 Oct 1847; Cecil County Marriage License Book spelled Maria's name Mahaney; DAR transcript copied in 1955 spelled John's name Mahoney and in the 1840 license did not include Elizabeth's middle name; 1860 Cecil County Census spelled his name Mahoney)

Mahoney, Joseph R. (born c1824, Maryland) (laborer at Charlestown), married Miss Sarah Jane Moore (born c1828, Maryland) circa 22 Dec 1846 (date of license) by Rev. Alderdice (Cecil County Marriage License Book and 1860 Cecil County Census both spelled his name Mahony)

Mahoney, Martha J., see James T. Simpson

Mahoney, Patty, see William Ramsey

Mahoney, Sarah Jane, see William Benjamin

Mahoney, William R. (1816-1898), married Harriet Mahoney (1822-1880) circa 19 Sep 1838 (date of license) by Rev. Budd (Cecil County Marriage License Book; DAR transcript copied in 1928 misspelled their surname Mahanny; Union Methodist Church Cemetery tombstone inscriptions)

MAKINSON

Makinson, John (1799-1861), married Susan (N) (1805-1897) probably circa 1823-1825 (Hopewell United Methodist Church Cemetery tombstone inscriptions)

Makinson, also see Mackinson

MALONEY, MALLONY

Maloney, Catherine, see Martin Maloney

Maloney, Francis (1815-1868), near Elkton, married Mary (N) (1828-1889) probably circa 1850 (Immaculate Conception Catholic Church Cemetery tombstones; *Cecil Democrat and Farmer's Journal*, 10 Oct 1868)

Maloney, Martin (born c1822, Ireland) (farmhand, 6th District), married Bridget (N) (born c1824, Ireland) probably circa 1850; daughter Catherine Maloney born c1851, Maryland (1860 Cecil County Census)

Mallony, Henry, married Julia O'Donald on 21 Feb 1828 by Rev. Epinette (*History of Saint Francis Xavier Church and Bohemia Plantation Now Known as Old Bohemia, Warwick, Maryland*, by Joseph C. Cann (1976), p. 47)

MALSBURGHER

Malsburgher, Agnes R., see Richard C. Johnson

MANLOVE

Manlove, James (born c1823, Maryland) (farmer at Cecilton), married Sarah (N) (born c1827, Maryland) circa 1843; son Julius Manlove born c1844 (1860 Cecil County Census)

Manlove, Julius, see James Manlove

Manlove, Mark (born c1816, Maryland) (wagoner at Warwick), married Emma (N) (born c1831) circa 1848; son William Manlove born c1849 (1860 Cecil County Census)

Manlove, William, see Mark Manlove

MANLY, MANLEY

Manly, Araminta, see John Little

Manly, Charles K., married Rachel Howard on 2 Oct 1833, after obtaining a license that same day, Rev. Hagany (Cecil County Marriage License Book; Elkton Methodist Church Register, p. 5)

Manly, Margaret S., see Joseph W. Veazey

Manly, Mary Ann, see Ephraim P. Grace

Manly, Nicholas (1795-1864) (sea captain), Elk Neck, Cecil Co., married Sarah W. Highland (c1800-1856), daughter of John Highland, of Chestertown, Kent Co., MD, on 10 May 1831 (*Portrait and Biographical*

Record of Harford and Cecil Counties, Maryland (1897, repr. 1989), pp. 419-420, listed their two children in 1897 as Nicholas P. Manley (born 16 Apr 1834) and Anna E. Drennen)

Manly, Nicholas P., see Nicholas Manly

Manly, Rachel, see Benjamin F. May

Manly, William, married Frances Kirk circa 9 Jan 1839 (date of license) by Rev. Barratt (Cecil County Marriage License Book)

Manly, William (1799-1873) (captain), married Deborah Ann Roach (1812-1880) circa 14 Feb 1849 (date of license) (Cecil County Marriage License Book spelled his name Manley; North East Methodist Church Cemetery tombstone inscriptions inscribed his name Manly; *Cecil Whig*, 15 Mar 1873)

MANSFIELD

Mansfield, Edward (editor of the *Kent News*), married Mary I. Dugan, daughter of the late Thomas E. Dugan, all of Kent Co., on 28 Nov 1849 by Rev. McFaden (*Cecil Democrat and Farmer's Journal*, 8 Dec 1849)

Mansfield, James, married Mrs. Mary B. Garrettson circa 22 Jun 1837 (date of license) by Rev. Peck (Cecil County Marriage License Book; DAR transcript copied in 1928 spelled her name Garritson)

MARCUS

Marcus, Elizabeth, see Jacob Biddle

Marcus, Hyland, see James Marcus

Marcus, Hyland L. (born c1820) (farmer near Elkton), married Anne "Annie" C. (N) (c1816/1824-1875) circa 1842 (1860 Cecil County Census stated she was age 36 and did not list any children, but an Evans Hempfield, born c1845, was listed with them; *Cecil Whig*, 31 Jul 1875, obituary stated she was age 59)

Marcus, James (born c1819) (laborer at Elkton), married Mary A. (N) (born c1812) circa 1838; son Hyland Marcus born c1839 (1860 Cecil County Census)

Marcus, Richard James, married Mary Girvin circa 27 Oct 1836 (date of license) by Rev. Potts (Cecil County Marriage License Book)

MARINER, MARINOR

Mariner, Peter, married Ann McGerr or McGear on 23 Jan 1840, after obtaining a license on 22 Jan 1840, by Rev. Hagany (Cecil County Marriage License Book spelled her name McGerr; Elkton Methodist Church Register, p. 139, spelled it McGear; 1860 Cecil County Census listed a Peter Mariner, born c1811, Maryland, steamer captain at Chesapeake City, with wife Catharine, born c1825, daughter Catherine, born c1844, daughter Julia born c1848, and son Edward, born c1852, all born in Delaware)

Marinor, Matilda, see John Kibler

MARKEE

Markee, Jacob (born c1812) (miller near Cherry Hill), married Deborah Taylor (1816-1876), both of Cecil Co., circa 26 Jan 1847 (date of license) by Rev. Storks (Cecil County Marriage License Book; Elkton Methodist Church Register, p. 141, gave the year of marriage, but not the day and month; 1860 Cecil County Census abstract misspelled his name as Marker; *Cecil Whig*, 22 Jan 1876)

Markee, John (c1809-1871, born Switzerland) (farmer near Elkton), married 1st to Sarah Ann Harding circa 16 Jul 1832 (license date) by Rev. Duke and married 2nd to Margaret Ann Pluck (born c1814, Maryland) circa 5 Apr 1837 (license date) by Rev. Potts (Cecil County Marriage License Book; 1860 Cecil County Census stated he was aged 51 and spelled his name Markey; *Cecil Whig*, 8 Apr 1871)

Markee, Joseph, married Anna M. Brown circa 23 Oct 1827 (date of license) (Cecil County Marriage License Book; DAR transcript copied in 1928 listed his name as Jos. Marrcee)

MARNES

Marnes, Andrew, married Margaret Cameron circa 5 Jun 1827 (date of license) (Cecil County Marriage License Book)

Marnes, Hugh, married Nancy Cochran circa 25 Mar 1826 (date of license) by Rev. Graham (Cecil County Marriage License Book)

Marnes, John, married Jane Maffitt circa 13 Apr 1835 (date of license) by Rev. Duke (Cecil County Marriage License Book)

Marnes, William R. (born c1821) (farmer at North East), married 1st to Mary Ann Kirk circa 1 May 1844 (date of license) and married 2nd to Jane (N) (born c1822) probably circa 1850 (Cecil County Marriage License Book; 1860 Cecil County Census)

Marnes, also see Mearns

MARQUISS

Marquiss, Elizabeth, see Andrew Biddle

MARS

Mars, Margaret E., see John Schritz

Mars, Martha Ann, see Richard Davis

MARSH

Marsh, John E. (doctor), of Kent Co., MD, married Anne E. Beatty, daughter of William Beatty, Esq., of North East, Cecil Co., on 13 Nov 1849, after obtaining a license on 11 Nov 1849, by Rev. Arthur (Cecil County Marriage License Book; *Cecil Democrat and Farmer's Journal*, 24 Nov 1849)

MARSHALL

Marshall, Catharine, see Robert Armstrong

Marshall, Deborah, see Samuel Marshall

Marshall, Francis, see Samuel Marshall and Wilson Marshall

Marshall, Hannah, see Eli Haines

Marshall, Humphrey, see Eli Haines

Marshall, James, see Samuel Marshall

Marshall, Jane, see Joseph Hanna

Marshall, John, see Samuel Marshall

Marshall, John, married Margaret McKinley circa 4 Dec 1827 (date of license) (Cecil County Marriage License Book)

Marshall, John (1806-1894), married Ruth (N) (1805-1891) probably circa 1827 (Brick Meeting House, at Calvert, tombstone inscriptions)

Marshall, Mary, see Samuel Marshall

Marshall, Priscilla, see Samuel Marshall

Marshall, Ruth, see Samuel Marshall

Marshall, Samuel (born 1823), son of William and Sarah Marshall, of East Nottingham Hundred, Cecil Co., married Asenath Smith (born 1827), daughter of Francis P. and Deborah Smith, of Octorara Hundred, Cecil Co., on the 18th day of the 10th month 1848 at a public meeting of Friends at the home of Francis P. Smith and among the witnesses were Francis Marshall, James Marshall, Priscilla Marshall, William Marshall, Sarah Marshall, John Marshall, Ruth Marshall, Clarissa Smith, John G. Smith, Mary Smith, Francis P. Smith and Deborah Smith (*Births, Deaths and Marriages of the Nottingham Quakers, 1680-1899*, by Alice L. Beard (1989), p. 63, stated his parents were William and Mary Marshall, of England, but p. 227 stated his parents were William and Sarah Marshall, of Cecil County)

Marshall, Sarah, see Samuel Marshall

Marshall, William, see Samuel Marshall

Marshall, William (captain), married Miss Rebecca Bailey, both of Cecil Co., on 8 Feb 1838, after obtaining a license on 30 Jan 1838, by Rev. Greenbank, a Methodist minister in Port Deposit (Cecil County Marriage License Book spelled her name Bayley; *Cecil Gazette*, 10 Feb 1838)

Marshall, Wilson (born c1814, Pennsylvania) (farmer near Brick Meeting House), married Mary (N) (born c1815, Pennsylvania) probably circa 1835; son Francis born c1836, Maryland (1860 Cecil Co. Census)

MARSHBANK

Marshbank, Francina, see William J. Marshbank

Marshbank, Mary A., see William J. Marshbank

Marshbank, Robert (1821-1897) (cabinet maker, undertaker and vice president of the Mutual Building Association), of Chester Co., PA, later of Baltimore and Elkton, son of Robert Marshbank and Ann Lyle, married 1st to Eliza Jane Short circa 10 Mar 1846 (date of license), married 2nd to Eliza A. Lynch (1822-1877) circa 10 May 1852 (date of license) and married 3rd to Mary D. Henry in 1884 (Cecil County Marriage License Book spelled his name once as Marshbanks; *Portrait and Biographical Record of Harford and Cecil Counties, Maryland* (1897, repr. 1989), pp. 452-453; 1860 Cecil County Census; *Cecil Whig*, 4 Aug 1877)

Marshbank, Rachel A., see William J. Marshbank

Marshbank, Sarah, see Philip Hopkins

Marshbank, Susanna, see William J. Marshbank

Marshbank, William J. (born c1826, Pennsylvania) (coachmaker near Brick Meeting House), married Esther (N) (born c1831, Maryland) probably circa 1849; daughter Rachel A. born c1850, Pennsylvania, daughter Francina born c1851, Pennsylvania, daughter Mary A. born c1856, Maryland, and daughter Susanna born 1860, Maryland (1860 Cecil County Census)

MARTIN

Martin, Henry, married Ann Brown on 9 Jan 1828, after obtaining a license on 3 Jan 1828, by Rev. Epinette (Cecil County Marriage License Book; *History of Saint Francis Xavier Church and Bohemia Plantation Now Known as Old Bohemia, Warwick, Maryland*, by Joseph C. Cann (1976), p. 47)

Martin, John, married Rosanna Silk circa 14 Oct 1835 (date of license) by Rev. Duke (Cecil County Marriage License Book)

Martin, John, married Susanna Fillingame circa 22 Jan 1842 (date of license) by Rev. Polks (Cecil County Marriage License Book)

Martin, Sarah, see Charles S. Nowland

MARTINDALE

Martindale, Charles H., see Peter Tome

Martindale, Elmira A., see Hyland P. Bouchell

MARVEL

Marvel, Philip, of Wilmington, DE, married Miss Alice McCartney, of Elkton, Cecil Co., on 22 Mar 1849 in Philadelphia by Rev. Gerry (*Delaware Gazette*, 27 Mar 1849; *Cecil Democrat and Farmer's Journal*, 31 Mar 1849)

MASON, MAYSON

Mason, Benjamin (1811-1888), son of George and Tabitha Mason, of East Nottingham, Chester County, PA, married Ruth Anna Brown (1818-1897), daughter of Montillion and Ann Brown, of Cecil Co., on the 26th day of the 5th month 1836 at East Nottingham (*Births, Deaths and Marriages of the Nottingham Quakers, 1680-1899*, by Alice Beard (1989), pp. 64, 223; Brick Meeting House, at Calvert, tombstone inscriptions)

Mayson, Ann, see James T. Hayden

MASSEY

Massey, James A., married Ann P. (N) (1811-1876) probably circa 1830 (*Cecil Whig*, 2 Dec 1876, reported she was the mother of Mrs. Virginia C. Phoebus, of Elkton, Cecil Co., and died at the residence of her son-in-law John W. Phoebus in Somerset Co., MD; buried in Easton, MD)

Massey, Louisa, see William Stevens
Massey, Major J., see William Stevens
Massey, Sarah, see John Keilholtz

MATTHEWS

Matthews, James, married Leah Moody circa 18 Jan 1838 (date of license) by Rev. McFarland (Cecil County Marriage License Book; DAR transcript copied in 1928 mistakenly listed the minister's name as Farland; James McFarland was a Methodist minister in Elkton at that time)

Matthews, James, married Miss Mary Weaver on 22 Mar 1838, after obtaining a license on 20 Mar 1838, by Rev. McFarland (*Cecil Gazette*, 31 Mar 1838; Cecil County Marriage License Book; DAR transcript copied in 1928 mistakenly listed the minister's name as Farland; James McFarland was a Methodist minister in Elkton at that time; Elkton Methodist Church Register, p. 138)

Matthews, Rebecca, see James Stalcup
Matthews, Sarah, see Thomas Thackery

MATTHIAS

Matthias, Hannah, see George Alden

Matthias, Jones (born c1799, Pennsylvania) (farmer near Elkton), married Hetty Ann Alexander (born c1799, Maryland) circa 7 Nov 1831 (date of license) by Rev. Duke; son John J. Matthias born c1832, Maryland (Cecil County Marriage License Book; *Cecil Democrat and Farmer's Journal*, 29 Apr 1882, obituary reported Hetty A. Mathias, wife of Jones Mathias, died "at an advanced age" near Flint Hill; 1860 Cecil County Census spelled his name Methias)

MATTING

Matting, Helen, see John B. Graham

MATTIX

Mattix, John (1808-1853), married Martha (N) (1811-1886) probably circa 1830 (Elkton Methodist Church Cemetery tombstone inscriptions)

MAULDIN, MAULDEN

Mauldin, Ann, see Joseph Lort, Jr.
Maulden, Araminta, see Mark Arthur
Maulden, B. F., married Millicent Brown circa 1 May 1845 (date of license) (Cecil Co. Marr. License Book)
Mauldin, Benjamin, see Thomas R. Sewall
Mauldin, Catharine, see Alexander Wilson
Maulden, John, see Jeremiah Foard
Mauldin, John, married Sophia T. Simpers circa 29 Jan 1834 (date of license) by Rev. Wolley (Cecil County Marriage License Book)
Maulden, Laura, see William Beatty
Maulden, Mary Jane, see Stephen Hyland
Mauldin, Rebecca, see Thomas R. Sewall
Maulden, Sophia, see Jeremiah Foard
Maulden, Zebulon K., married Sarah B. Simpers circa 14 Oct 1847 (date of license) (Cecil County Marriage License Book)

MAULSBY

Maulsby, I. D. and Sarah Jane, see John Yellott

MAXWELL

Maxwell, Allen, married Hannah Hutton circa 27 Feb 1827 (date of license) (Cecil Co. Marr. License Book)

Maxwell, Charles W., married Miss Rachel A. Fowler, both of Elkton, on 29 Aug 1850 by Rev. Barton (*Cecil Whig*, 31Aug 1850; *Cecil Democrat and Farmer's Journal*, 31 Aug 1850, which noted, "Our acknowledgements are due the happy pair for an ample slice of cake, which accompanied the above.")

Maxwell, David P., married Elizabeth Cameron circa 29 Nov 1841 (date of license) (Cecil County Marriage License Book)

Maxwell, Isabella, see Nathan Dolby

Maxwell, James Leiper (1800-1878), married Jane Meek McCullough (1806-1845) circa 21 Nov 1832 (date of license) by Rev. Magraw (Cecil County Marriage License Book; West Nottingham Cemetery tombstone inscriptions; *Cecil Whig*, 21 Jun 1845, reported that Jane Maxwell died at Port Deposit, "and left a disconsolate and affectionate husband and five small children to mourn their irreparable loss.")

Maxwell, Jane, see William Cameron

Maxwell, Mary, see William Little

Maxwell, Mary Ann, see Samuel M. Magraw

Maxwell, Mary E., see Thomas Maxwell

Maxwell, Rebecca Ellen, see Benjamin F. Langdon

Maxwell, Robert, see Samuel M. Magraw

Maxwell, Samuel (born c1797) (farmer near Elkton), married Eliza Russell (born c1808) circa 30 Aug 1826 (date of license) by Rev. Duke (Cecil County Marriage License Book; 1860 Cecil County Census)

Maxwell, Sarah, see Richard Keeler

Maxwell, Thomas (1802-1874), of Cecil Co., married Elizabeth G. Kerr (1822-1869), eldest daughter of Edward Kerr, Esq., late of Harford Co., on 25 May 1841, after obtaining a license on 22 May 1841, by Rev. Park; buried beside daughter Mary E. Maxwell (1842-1863) (*Cecil Gazette*, 5 Jun 1841; Harford County Marriage License Book; West Nottingham Cemetery tombstone inscriptions)

Maxwell, William, married Catherine Brickley circa 6 Jul 1842 (date of license) (Cecil County Marriage License Book)

Maxwell, William M. A. S. (doctor), married Anna Maria Price, of Kent Co., circa 26 Nov 1845 (date of license) (Cecil County Marriage License Book)

MAY

May, Benjamin F. (born c1812, Delaware) (merchant at Elkton), married Mrs. Rachel Manly (1811-1861, born Maryland) on 29 Jul 1841, after obtaining a license on 28 Jul 1841, by Rev. McIntyre (Cecil County Marriage License Book; *Cecil Gazette*, 31 Jul 1841; 1860 Cecil County Census; Elkton Presbyterian Church Cemetery tombstone inscription for Rachel May)

May, Caroline, see Charles H. Crouch

May, James, of Kent Co., married Caroline Rhoads circa 7 Jan 1847 (date of license) (Cecil County Marriage License Book)

May, Mary, see Samuel Briley

MAYBERRY

Mayberry, Ebenezer, married Ann Foster circa 29 Aug 1832 (date of license) by Rev. Goforth (Cecil County Marriage License Book)

MAYNER

Mayner, Roger, married Ann Veach circa 1 Feb 1831 (date of license) by Rev. Hodgson (Cecil County Marriage License Book; DAR transcript copied in 1928 misspelled the minister's name as Hodson; Francis Hodgson was a Methodist Episcopal minister in Elkton at that time)

McALLISTER

McAllister, John A., (1827-1899), married Mary E. (N) (1829-1903) probably circa 1848-1850 (Moore's Methodist Church Cemetery tombstone inscriptions)

McCAFFERY
McCaffery, John, married Mary Hughes circa 14 Aug 1840 (date of license) (Cecil Co. Marr. License Book)

McCAFFERTY
McCafferty, John (born c1811, Ireland) (farmer at Cecilton), married Catharina P. (N) (born c1820, Ireland) circa 1841; daughter Mary McCafferty born c1842, Pennsylvania, daughter Anna McCafferty born c1843, Maryland, and son Burnet (Barnet?) McCafferty born c1844, Maryland (1860 Cecil County Census)

McCALL
McCall, Annie M. W., see Henry C. McCall

McCall, Elizabeth, see William Bennett

McCall, Henry C. (born c1821) (lawyer in Elkton), married Mary E. (N) (born c1821) probably circa 1844; daughter Annie M. W. McCall born c1845 (1860 Cecil County Census)

McCall, James (1813-1896), married Elizabeth (N) (1812-1892) probably circa 1834-1835 (Hopewell United Methodist Church Cemetery tombstone inscriptions)

McCall, John, married Sarah Anderson circa 20 Mar 1839 (date of license) by Rev. Barratt (Cecil County Marriage License Book)

McCall, John W., married Eliza Hawkins circa 3 Apr 1828 (date of license) (Cecil Co. Marr. License Book)

McCall, Margaret, see Samuel Logan

McCall, Mary, see Nicholas Murphy

McCANE
McCane, James (born c1820, Ireland) (farmer near Elkton), married Hester (N) (born c1826, Maryland) probably circa 1845; son William McCane born c1846, Maryland (1860 Cecil County Census also listed James McCane, weaver, aged 83, and wife Mary, aged 70, both born in Ireland, who lived nearby)

McCARTNEY
McCartney, Alice, see Philip Marvel

McCartney, John H., married Eliza Woodrow circa 27 Sep 1833 (date of their license) by Rev. Guiber (Cecil County Marriage License Book)

McCAULEY
McCauley, Absalom (1807-1884), of Cecil Co., married Miss Olivia Ann Tyrrel (1822-1856), of New Castle Co., DE, on 19 Feb 1846 by Rev. Hare; they had twins Amanda J. McCauley (1850-1869) and Francis L. McCauley (1850-1872) (*Cecil Whig*, 28 Mar 1846; *Delaware Gazette*, 31 Mar 1846; Union Methodist Church Cemetery tombstone inscriptions)

McCauley, Amanda J., see Absalom McCauley

McCauley, Ann, see John E. Simpers

McCauley, Daniel (1803-1877), married Rachel Beard (1808-1883) circa 20 Dec 1825 (date of license) by Rev. Wilson (Cecil County Marriage License Book. DAR transcript copied in 1928 misspelled his name Daniel M. McCauley, Jr.; Elkton Presbyterian Church Cemetery tombstones were inscribed Daniel and Rachel McCauley)

McCauley, Daniel H., see Jethro McCauley

McCauley, Daniel J., married Sarah Miller circa 21 Feb 1835 (date of license) by Rev. Reed (Cecil County Marriage License Book)

McCauley, Eliza, see Howard Davis

McCauley, Elizabeth, see William T. Warburton and Pennell Coombe

McCauley, Francina, see Enos D. Wood

McCauley, Francis L., see Absalom McCauley

McCauley, Hattie S., see James McCauley

McCauley, Helen A., see James McCauley

McCauley, Henry B. (1822-1882), of New Leeds, married Miss Martha J. Touchstone (1825-1872), also of Cecil Co., on 15 Apr 1847, after obtaining a license on 9 Apr 1847, by Rev. Kennard (*Cecil Whig*, 17 Apr 1847; Cecil County Marriage License Book; DAR transcript copied in 1955 misspelled her name as Martha I. Touchlon; Union Methodist Church Cemetery tombstone inscriptions; *Cecil Whig*, 4 May 1872)

McCauley, James (1809-1897) (surveyor, cooper, register of wills, state legislator, and orphans court judge), married 1st to Sarah Beard (c1810-1846), youngest daughter of the late Hugh Beard, Esq., all of Cecil Co., on 27 Nov 1834, after obtaining a license on 26 Nov 1834, by Rev. Wilson, and married 2nd to Miss Millicent R. Price (born c1817), daughter of Jacob Price, all of New Leeds, Cecil Co., on 30 Aug 1849, after obtaining a license that same day, also by Rev. Wilson (Cecil County Marriage License Book; *Cecil Gazette*, 13 Dec 1834; *Cecil Whig*, 29 Sep 1849; *Portrait and Biographical Record of Harford and Cecil Counties, Maryland* (1897, repr. 1989), pp. 409-410, listed his eight children in 1897 (five by his first wife and three by his second wife), namely, Elizabeth Reese [born c1836], Mary Crouch, John McCauley [born c1839], Rachel McCauley [born c1841], Hannah Louise Yates [born c1844], Helen A. McCauley ["Ella" born c1851], James J. McCauley [born c1854] and Hattie S. McCauley [born c1858]; 1860 Cecil County Census)

McCauley, James J., see James McCauley

McCauley, Jethro (born c1810) (cooper at Elkton), married Sarah Jane Hanna (born c1825) circa 21 Dec 1847 (date of license); son Daniel H. McCauley born c1848 (Cecil County Marriage License Book spelled her surname Hannah; 1860 Cecil County Census)

McCauley, John, see James McCauley and William T. Warburton

McCauley, John (1817-1896), married Esther J. (N) (1830-1913) probably circa 1850 (Moore's Methodist Church Cemetery tombstone inscriptions)

McCauley, John D., married Hannah Jamar (1818-1876) on 12 Oct 1843 by Rev. Shields (Elkton Methodist Church Register, p. 140; Cecil Co. Marr. Lic. book did not list this marriage; *Cecil Whig*, 18 Mar 1876)

McCauley, John H., married Rachel S. Simpers circa 12 Jul 1847 (date of license) (Cecil County Marriage License Book)

McCauley, Louise (Louisa), see Andrew W. Alexander

McCauley, Lydia, see Andrew Harvey

McCauley, Lydia Ann, see Joseph T. Terrell

McCauley, Margaret J., see James Davis

McCauley, Mary Jane, see Thomas W. Tyson

McCauley, Rachel, see James McCauley

McCLAIN

McClain, John, married Ester Dupelle circa 28 May 1833 (date of license) by Rev. Duke (Cecil County Marriage License Book)

McCLAY

McClay, Isaac, married Margaret Burnite circa 18 Jul 1825 (date of license) by Rev. Sharpley (Cecil County Marriage License Book)

McClay, William (c1810-1856), married Lydia Peterson (born c1813, Pennsylvania) circa 3 May 1832 (date of license) by Rev. Duke (Cecil County Marriage License Book; 1860 Cecil County Census listed Lydia McClay as head of household with William, age 17, Martha, age 9, and John, age 8; Administration Account for William McClay, deceased, 1856)

McCLEAN

McClean, Cornelius Jr. (1807-1861), of Baltimore Co., married Georgeanna E. Gale (1803-1856), daughter of George and Anna Maria Gale, of Cecil Co., circa 26 May 1832 (date of license) by Rev. Higby (Cecil County Marriage License Book spelled his name McLean; St. Mark's Episcopal Church tombstone inscriptions spelled the name McClean)

McCLELLAND

McClelland, William, of Newark, Delaware, married Miss Margaret Stuart, of Elkton, on 17 Apr 1849 by Rev. Barton (*Cecil Whig*, 21 Apr 1849)

McCLEARY

McCleary, Jane, see David Mackey

McCleary, John (1816-1905, born Ireland) (shoemaker and farmer at Fair Hill), son of John McCleary of Ireland and Ann Robinson, later of Delaware and Cecil Co., married Miss Elizabeth Gallagher (1819-1902, born Maryland) on 1 Oct 1839 (*Portrait and Biographical Record of Harford and Cecil Counties, Maryland* (1897, repr. 1989), p. 354; Sharp's Cemetery tombstone inscriptions; 1860 Cecil Co. Census)

McCleary, John Thomas, married Martha Jane Heath circa 16 Dec 1845 (date of license) (Cecil County Marriage License Book)

McCleary, Robert (1811-1885), married Elizabeth Huggins (1812-1883) probably circa 1832-1834 (Sharp's Cemetery tombstone inscriptions)

McCLENAHAN, McCLENEHAN

McClenahan, Ebenezer Dickey (1806-1896, born Maryland) (farmer in the 7th District), married Margaretta J. Megredy (1808-1877, born Maryland) circa 1 Mar 1833 (date of license) by Rev. Thomas McCarrol, a Methodist minister (Cecil County Marriage License Book; Hopewell United Methodist Church Cemetery tombstone inscriptions; 1860 Cecil County Census)

McClenahan, James M., married Amanda M. Davis on 24 Apr 1842 after obtaining a license on 14 Apr 1842 (Cecil County Marriage License Book spelled his name McClanehan; Elkton Methodist Church Register spelled his name McClenhan)

McClenehan, John (born c1831, Maryland) (laborer in the 7th District), married Susanna (N) (born c1830, Pennsylvania) probably circa 1849; son Josiah born c1850, Maryland (1860 Cecil County Census)

McClenahan, Josiah, married Margaret Walker circa 20 May 1840 (date of license) by Rev. Grace (Cecil County Marriage License Book)

McClenahan, Maria, see William Watson

McClenehan, Rebecca, see William F. Allison

McCLENAN

McClenan, Lawson (born c1832, Maryland) (laborer in the 6th District), married Peggy (N) (born c1830, Maryland) probably circa 1849; daughter Sarah born c1850 (1860 Cecil County Census)

McClenan, William (born c1827, Delaware) (merchant at Elkton), married Margaret (N) (born c1825, Delaware) probably circa 1849; son Samuel born c1850, Delaware, son William born c1851, Delaware, daughter Ann born c1855, Pennsylvania, daughter Laura born c1857, Maryland, and son Evans born c1859, Maryland (1860 Cecil County Census)

McCLINTOCK

McClintock, James (born c1824, Pennsylvania) (farmer in the 7th District), married Mary (N) (born c1828, Maryland) probably circa 1849; daughter Elizabeth McClintock born c1850, and their other children were also born in Maryland (1860 Cecil County Census)

McCLURE

McClure, Catharine, see Israel Alexander

McClure, German (b. c1800) (blacksmith), married 1st to Miss Charity Quinlan (1805-1830) on 11 Feb 1829, after obtaining a license on 4 Feb 1829, by Rev. O'Brien in Harford Co. (St. Ignatius Catholic Church, Marriage Register, 1817-1854, p. 10, mistakenly stated they were married in January 1829); married 2nd to Ann Maria Garrison circa 25 Oct 1836 (Harford County Marriage License Book; *Elkton Press*, 21 Feb 1829; St. Ignatius Catholic Church tombstone inscription for Charity McClure; *Under the Spreading Chestnut Tree ... Blacksmithing in America*, by Henry C. Peden, Jr. and Jack L. Shagena, Jr. (2007), p.

265). It should be noted that German McClure was charged with having begotten an illegitimate male child (no name given) on the body of Elizabeth McFaddon, said child born on 28 Apr 1833 (Harford County Court Minutes, 1830-1839, p. 121)

McClure, John, married Mary E. Crouch circa 8 Jan 1840 (date of license) by Rev. Barratt (Cecil County Marriage License Book)

McCOLGAN

McColgan, Jane, see James Cummings

McCONAUGHY

McConaughy, Alexander, married Rebecca S. Ayres, daughter of Rev. J. B. Ayres, all of Delaware City, DE, on 20 Jun 1850 by Rev. Long (*Cecil Whig*, 29 Jun 1850; *Cecil Democrat and Farmer's Journal*, 29 Jun 1850, misspelled their surnames McConaugy and Ayars)

McCONKEY

McConkey, Hugh Jr., of Lancaster, Pennsylvania, married Mary Henry, of Cecil Co., circa 16 Jul 1831 (date of license) by Rev. Duke (Cecil County Marriage License Book)

McCONNELL

McConnell, Jacob D. (1808-1884), of Chester Co., Pennsylvania, married Mary Armstrong (1817-1898) circa 17 Jan 1842 (date of license) (Cecil County Marriage License Book; Sharp's Cemetery tombstones)

McCORD

McCord, John, married Susan Kean circa 29 Aug 1826 (date of license) by Rev. Woolford (Cecil County Marriage License Book)

McCORMICK

McCormick, Frank, see James O. McCormick

McCormick, James O. (1813-1889), married Ann (N) (1813-1850) circa 1844; buried beside son Frank O. McCormick (1845-1876) (West Nottingham Cemetery tombstone inscriptions)

McCormick, James, see Nevin W. McCormick

McCormick, Jemima, see John Tosh

McCormick, Joseph L. Brickley, see Nevin W. McCormick

McCormick, Lewis (esquire), of New Castle Co., DE, married Miss Rebecca Ellen Pass, daughter of Isaac Pass, Esq., of London Brittain Township, Chester Co., PA, on 31 May 1849 by Rev. Plummer (*Cecil Democrat and Farmer's Journal*, 16 Jun 1849)

McCormick, Margaret J., see Absalom B. McVey

McCormick, Nevin W. (1817-1861, born Maryland) (farmer, 6th District), married Mary Agnes Robinson (1824-1903, born Pennsylvania), possibly Mary Agnes Brickley, circa 8 Sep 1846 (date of license); buried beside Joseph L. Brickley McCormick (1847-1849); son James McCormick born c1849 (Cecil County Marriage License Book mistakenly listed Nevin's middle initial as O.; 1860 Cecil County Census; West Nottingham Cemetery tombstone inscriptions)

McCOWAN

McCowan, James (born c1817) (farmer at North East), married Malissa (N) (born c 1832) probably circa 1847; daughter Mary McCowan born c1848 (1860 Cecil County Census)

McCowan, also see McKowen

McCOY

McCoy, Robert (1803-1870), married (N) probably circa 1825 and he died at the residence of his son Nathan H. McCoy at Sassafras (*Cecil Whig*, 26 Nov 1870)

McCRACKEN

McCracken, John, see Richard L. Thomas

McCracken, John (1805-1863) (farmer at Elk Neck), son of William McCracken, of Ireland, later of Cecil Co., and Ruth Richardson, married Martha Jane Cazier (1808-1873), daughter of Thomas Cazier, circa 16 Feb 1829 (date of the license) by Rev. Sharp (Cecil County Marriage License Book; *Portrait and Biographical Record of Harford and Cecil Counties, Maryland* (1897, repr. 1989), pp. 398-399; 1860 Cecil County Census; *Cecil Whig*, 26 Sep 1863)

McCracken, Mary Jane, see Richard L. Thomas

McCracken, Ruth Ann, see Richard L. Thomas

McCracken, William, see John McCracken

McCREA

McCrea, Ann Jane, see John Lutton

McCrea, David A., married Ann Taylor, daughter of Joseph Taylor of the Washington Hotel, all of Elkton, on 11 Jun 1848, after obtaining a license on 10 Jun 1848, by Rev. Elliott (Cecil County Marriage License Book; DAR transcript copied in 1955 misspelled his name as McCred; *Cecil Democrat and Farmer's Journal*, 17 Jun 1848; *Cecil Whig*, 17 Jun 1848)

McCrea, John, married Margaret Kinkead circa 22 Mar 1825 (date of license) by Rev. Duke (Cecil County Marriage License Book)

McCrea, Joseph (1811-1890), married Rebecca Jamison (1811-1891) on 6 Oct 1838, after obtaining a license that same day, by Rev. Hagany (Cecil County Marriage License Book; Elkton Methodist Church Register, p. 139; Sharp's Cemetery tombstone inscriptions)

McCrea, Mary, see William Kirk

McCrea, Mary E., see William J. Gallaher

McCrea, Samuel (1822-1884) (mason at Elkton), of Cecil Co., married Miss Martha Ball (1819-1896), of New Castle Co., DE, on 12 Dec 1848 by Rev. Kennard (*Cecil Democrat and Farmer's Journal*, 23 Dec 1848; *Delaware Gazette*, 22 Dec 1848; Sharp's Cemetery tombstone inscriptions; 1860 Cecil County Census misspelled his name McCrey)

McCrea, William, married Mary Slack circa 24 Jul 1833 (date of license) by Rev. Duke (Cecil County Marriage License Book; DAR transcript copied in 1928 misspelled his name McOrea)

McCREARY, McCRERY

McCreary, John D. (born c1817) (wheelwright at Elkton), married Hannah (N) (born c1818) circa 1845; son John C. McCreary born c1846 (1860 Cecil County Census)

McCrery, John (1804-1880), married Sophia Perry (1807-1855) circa 23 Nov 1830 (date of license) by Rev. Graham (Cecil County Marriage License Book spelled his name McCreary; *Portrait and Biographical Record of Harford and Cecil Counties, Maryland* (1897, repr. 1989), p. 304, spelled his name McCrery; mistakenly stated Sophia died in 1853, aged 40, and listed their six children: John T. (1834-1872); James (born 6 Aug 1836); Sarah (1838-1864); William (1840-1893); Harriet (born 31 Dec 1842); and, Albert (born 8 Dec 1845); Sharp's Cemetery tombstone inscriptions spelled his name McCrery)

McCreary, Mary Ann, see John Cornish

McCrery, Thomas (a slave hunter before the Civil War), married Mary (N) (1804-1891) probably circa 1825 and she died at the residence of her son-in-law Henry Ward near Elkton, her husband having pre-deceased her (*Midland Journal*, 6 Mar 1891)

McCRONE

McCrone, John, married Mrs. Elizabeth Norwood, both of Appoquinnick Hundred, DE, on 21 Feb 1850 near Middletown, DE, by Rev. Hamilton (*Delaware Gazette*, 1 Mar 1850; *Cecil Democrat and Farmer's Journal*, 23 Feb 1850, reported, "A bridal party, from Delaware, passed through here [Elkton] on Wednesday, on the way to Washington, where they will spend the honey-moon. On inquiry, we ascertained that the weddings had taken place that morning, at an early hour, and that the parties were Col. Joshua Clayton, to Miss Martha Lockwood; John Naudin *(sic)*, Esq., to Miss Mary Lockwood, both daughters of Richard Lockwood, Esq., near Middletown, and Mr. [John] McCrone, to Mrs. Elizabeth Norwood, sister of Mr. Naudin *(sic)*.")

McCUE
McCue, Andrew, married Mary Kinney circa 5 Dec 1826 (date of license) by Rev. Magraw (Cecil County Marriage License Book; DAR transcript copied in 1928, spelled her name Kiney)

McCULLOUGH
McCullough, Agnes, see Francis Gallaher

McCullough, Ann, see Thomas West

McCullough, Catharine, see Jehu Montgomery

McCullough, Charles, see Jethro Johnson McCullough

McCullough, Delia, see James T. McCullough

McCullough, Delphina, see Jethro Johnson McCullough

McCullough, Enoch, see Jethro Johnson McCullough

McCullough, George, married Sybilla A. Miller circa 12 Apr 1847 (date of license) (Cecil County Marriage License Book)

McCullough, George, see Jethro Johnson McCullough

McCullough, Hiram (1813-1885) (attorney), married Sarah Jane Ricketts (1817-1855), youngest daughter of the late Capt. William Ricketts, all of Cecil Co., on 11 Jan 1842, after obtaining a license on 10 Jan 1842, by Rev. McIntyre at *Belle Hill* (Cecil County Marriage License Book; Elkton Presbyterian Church Cemetery tombstone inscriptions; *Cecil Gazette*, 15 Jan 1842, noted, "Accompanying the above we received a very liberal share of the wedding cake, in return for which the happy couple have our best wishes for their future prosperity and happiness.")

McCullough, Isaac, see Jethro Johnson McCullough

McCullough, James (born c1811, Maryland) (laborer, 6th District), and Ruth (N) (born 1817, Maryland, died 1891 at the residence of son James McCullough at Hopewell) probably married circa 1837; son Robert born c1838 (1860 Cecil County Census; *Midland Journal*, 6 Feb 1891)

McCullough, James H. (1816-1882) (cooper, 6th District), of Cherry Hill, married Mary (N) (1802-1887) probably circa 1837 (Hopewell United Methodist Church Cemetery tombstone inscriptions; 1860 Cecil County Census; *Cecil Democrat and Farmer's Journal*, 20 May 1882)

McCullough, James T. (1816-1888) (attorney), of New Castle Co., DE, later of Elkton, married Catharine W. Mitchell (1821-1899, born Maryland), daughter of Col. George Edward Mitchell and Mary Hooper, of Elkton, on 19 Jun 1845, after obtaining a license on 18 Jun 1845, by Rev. McIntire; Catharine and James' eldest daughter Delia McCullough was born circa 1850 in Missouri and their other children were born in Maryland (Cecil County Marriage License Book; *Portrait and Biographical Record of Harford and Cecil Counties, Maryland* (1897, repr. 1989), p. 557; 1860 Cecil County Census; Elkton Presbyterian Church Cemetery tombstone inscriptions; *Easton Star*, 24 Jan 1888; *History of Cecil County*, by George Johnston (1881, repr. 1989), p. 507; *Cecil Whig*, 21 Jun 1845)

McCullough, Jane Meek, see James Leiper Maxwell

McCullough, Jethro, see Jethro Johnson McCullough

McCullough, Jethro Johnson (1810-1878, born Pennsylvania) (iron manufacturer at North East), son of Enoch McCullough, of White Clay Hundred, New Castle Co., DE, later of Cecil Co., was named after Jethro Johnson, a Baptist minister, and married Elizabeth Tull (1811-1885), daughter of John Tull, of Cecil Co., on 2 Jan 1834 (*Portrait and Biographical Record of Harford and Cecil Counties, Maryland* (1897, repr. 1989), pp. 515-516, stated they had ten children of whom only four were living in 1897, namely, Enoch, George [born c1840], John [born c1845] and Samuel D. (born 29 Aug 1855); North East Methodist Church Cemetery tombstone inscriptions; *Cecil Whig*, 22 Sep 1877 (image and biography spelled his middle name Johnston) and 1 Jun 1878; 1860 Cecil County Census listed these other children: Jethro born c1842, Isaac born c1847, Charles born c1849, and Delphina born c1852)

McCullough, John, see Jethro Johnson McCullough

McCullough, John, married Elizabeth McVey circa 10 Nov 1828 (date of license) by Rev. Graham (Cecil County Marriage License Book)

McCullough, John (born c1818, Maryland) (shoemaker in the 8th District), married Anna (N) (born c1830, Maryland) probably circa 1847; daughter Mary McCullough born c1848 (1860 Cecil County Census)

McCullough, John W., of Cecil Co., married Miss Drusilla Bayard, of Havre de Grace, Harford Co., on 30 Jun 1850, after obtaining a license on 28 Jun 1850 in Cecil Co., by Rev. Dr. Nathan S. Buckingham (1821-1884), Methodist Episcopal minister in Havre de Grace, 1849-1851 (*Cecil Democrat and Farmer's Journal*, 6 Jul 1850; *Baltimore Sun*, 3 Jul 1850; *Directory of Ministers and the Maryland Churches They Served, 1634-1990*, by Edna Agatha Kanely (1991), p. 87; Cecil County Marriage License Book)

McCullough, Martha, see Benjamin F. Kirk and Joseph Richardson

McCullough, Martha Ankrim, see William McCullough

McCullough, Mary, see John McCullough and Benjamin F. Johnson

McCullough, Passmore, formerly of Cecil Co., married Miss Matilda Allen, of Anne Arundel Co., MD, on 10 Jun 1841, after obtaining a license on 9 Jun 1814, by Rev. Furlong (*Cecil Gazette*, 26 Jun 1841; Anne Arundel County Marriage License Book spelled her name Allein)

McCullough, Robert, see James McCullough

McCullough, Samuel, married Jane Ann Beard circa 31 Jan 1833 (date of license) by Rev. Wilson (Cecil County Marriage License Book)

McCullough, Samuel D., see Jethro Johnson McCullough

McCullough, Sanders, married Sarah Maria Rowland circa 6 May 1840 (date of license) by Rev. Burroughs (Cecil County Marriage License Book)

McCullough, Sarah Jane, see William T. Miller

McCullough, William (1806-1862), married Martha Ankrim McCullough (1811-1881) circa 27 Nov 1833 (date of license) by Rev. Magraw (Cecil County Marriage License Book; West Nottingham Cemetery tombstone inscriptions)

McCullough, William, married Rebecca Jane Davis circa 18 Jan 1848 (date of license) (Cecil County Marriage License Book)

McCullough, William M. (1805-1862) (farmer. 6th District), married Miss Lucy Haines (1809-1870), both of Cecil Co., on 12 Dec 1833, after obtaining a license on 10 Dec 1833, by Rev. Dickey (Cecil County Marriage License Book; West Nottingham Cemetery tombstone inscriptions; *Cecil Republican*, 14 Dec 1833, mistakenly spelled his first name Williams; 1860 Cecil County Census)

McDANIEL

McDaniel, James, see Samuel McDaniel

McDaniel, Julia, see Henry Wallen

McDaniel (McDannell), Samuel (1812-1881) (miller at Elkton), married Mary (N) (1801-1882) probably circa 1832; son James born circa 1833 (Cherry Hill Methodist Church Cemetery tombstone inscriptions spelled his surname McDannell; 1860 Cecil County Census spelled it McDaniel)

McDaniel, William, married Mrs. Milcah Wilkins, both of Chestertown, Kent Co., MD, on 31 Mar 1829 by Rev. Smith (*Elkton Press*, 4 Apr 1829)

McDOLE

McDole, Alexander (born c1808, Maryland) (laborer in the 7th District), married Harriet (N) (born c1817, Maryland) probably circa 1840; daughter Amanda McDole born c1845 (1860 Cecil County Census)

McDONOUGH

McDonough, Mary Eliza, see Samuel R. Clayland

McDowell, Ann, see James Jones

McDOWELL

McDowell, Alonzo, see Nelson McDowell

McDowell, James (born c1820, Maryland) (laborer at North East), married Miss Margaret Milburn or Milbourne (born c1827, Maryland) on 3 Apr 1845, after obtaining a license on 2 Apr 1845, by Rev. Goldsborough in Trinity Church (Cecil County Marriage License Book spelled her name Milburn; *Cecil Whig*, 5 Apr 1845, spelled her name Milbourne; 1860 Cecil County Census)

McDowell, James, married Eliza M. Hall circa 26 Nov 1849 (date of license) (Cecil Co. Marr. License Book)

McDowell, James, see Francis Thomas

McDowell, Mary, see John Tyson

McDowell, Nelson (born c1820, Maryland) (mason in the 6th District), married Margaret (N) (born c1822, Maryland) probably circa 1845; son Alonzo McDowell born c1846 (1860 Cecil County Census)

McDowell, Sally, see Francis Thomas

McDowell, Samuel, married Mary Jane Davis on 15 Jan 1849, after obtaining a license that same day, by Rev. Hanes (Cecil County Marriage License Book; *Cecil Democrat and Farmer's Journal*, 3 Feb 1849)

McDowell, William, married Rachel Milburn circa 1 Oct 1845 (date of license) (Cecil County Marriage License Book)

McELLARY

McEllary, Eliza, see James Gillespie

McELWEE

McElwee (McIlvee?, McWee?), Benjamin, married Mary Ann Riker circa 20 Nov 1832 (date of license) by Rev. Thomas McCarrol, a Methodist minister (Cecil County Marriage License Book)

McElwee, Caroline, see Lewis Crothers

McElwee, Hannah, see Hasson Lynch

McENESTRY

McEnestry, John, married Ann Foley on 31 Jul 1825 by Rev. Epinette (*History of Saint Francis Xavier Church and Bohemia Plantation Now Known as Old Bohemia, Warwick, Maryland*, by Joseph C. Cann (1976), p. 47)

McFADDEN, McFADIEN

McFadden (McFadien), Alexander F., married Mary Jane Davidson (1823-1848) on 12 Oct 1843, after obtaining a license on 4 Oct 1843, by Rev. Shields (Cecil County Marriage License Book; Elkton Methodist Church Register, p. 140; Cherry Hill Methodist Church Cemetery tombstone inscription)

McFadden (McFadien), Alexander H. (1829-1900), married Elizabeth A. Hunter (1819-1892) circa 4 Mar 1850 (date of license) (Cecil County Marriage License Book; Cherry Hill Methodist Church Cemetery tombstone inscriptions)

McFAN, McFANN

McFan, Sarah, see Elisha Brown

McFann, Margaret Jane, see Jacob F. Jennings

McFARLOVE

McFarlove, John (born c1800, Ireland) (laborer at Elkton), married Isabella (N) (born c1810, Ireland) circa 1826; oldest child William born c1827 and youngest child Margaret born c1850; they and all children in between were born in Ireland; immigrated to America after 1850 (1860 Cecil County Census)

McGAUGHLIN

McGaughlin, Jane, see Thomas Rogers

McGEE

McGee, Ann Elizabeth, see Reece Merritt

McGee, Eliza Jane, see John Anderson

McGee, John, married Mary Stewart circa 5 Dec 1825 (date of license) (Cecil County Marr. License Book)

McGee, Sylvester, married Catharine Welch circa 26 Mar 1828 (date of license) (Cecil Co. Marr. Lic. Book)

McGee, also see Magee

McGERR, McGEAR

McGerr (McGear), Ann, see Peter Mariner

McGILL, MEGILL

McGill (Megill), Joseph (born c1814, Scotland) (farmer at Cecilton), married Josephine (N) (born c1816, Pennsylvania) circa 1837 (1860 Cecil Co. Census listed oldest son William, age 22, born Pennsylvania, second son George, age 20, born New Jersey, and youngest son Samuel, age 6, born Maryland)

McINTIRE, McINTYRE

McIntire, Mary Eliza, see Samuel Jefferson Smith

McIntyre, James (reverend), married Mrs. Mary Ann Richardson, both of the Elkton vicinity, on 4 May 1843, after obtaining a license on 3 May 1843, by Rev. Work (*Cecil Whig*, 6 May 1843; Cecil County Marriage License Book; DAR transcript copied in 1955 mistakenly listed her name as Margaret Ann)

McIntyre, John, married Honor Money on 22 Jan 1828, after obtaining a license on 15 Jan 1828, by Rev. Epinette (Cecil County Marriage License Book is unclear, but looks like Honor Muney; DAR transcript copied in 1928 listed her name as Hannah Murrey; *History of Saint Francis Xavier Church and Bohemia Plantation Now Known as Old Bohemia, Warwick, Maryland*, by Joseph C. Cann (1976), p. 47, listed her name as Honored Money)

McIntyre, John, married Rachel Lofland circa 3 Apr 1848 (date of license) (Cecil Co. Marr. License Book)

McIntire, Samuel (c1820-1883), of Cecil Co., married Miss Matilda A. Boulden (1820-1880), of New Castle Co., DE, on 7 Mar 1844 by Rev. McIntire (*Cecil Whig*, 9 Mar 1844; *Delaware Gazette*, 12 Mar 1844; Elkton Presbyterian Church Cemetery tombstone inscriptions)

McJILTON

McJilton, Daniel, married Amelia Tyson circa 27 Dec 1831 (date of license) by Rev. Griffith (Cecil County Marriage License Book; DAR transcript coped in 1928 mistakenly listed him as Daniel M. Jilton)

McJilton, Elizabeth Ann, see David Thompson

McJilton, John F., married Phebe Bayless circa 16 Jul 1828 (date of license) by Rev. Magraw (Cecil County Marriage License Book misspelled his name as McGilton)

McKAIG

McKaig, Isaac H., married Miss Anna M. Gallaher, both of Cecil Co., on 10 Aug 1841, after obtaining a license on 9 Aug 1841, by Rev. Janes (*Cecil Gazette*, 14 Aug 1841; Elkton Methodist Church Register; Cecil County Marriage License Book)

McKELVEY

McKelvey, Ellen, see William Anderson

McKENNEY

McKenney, Mary, see Samuel Crouch

McKenney, also see McKinney

McKEY

McKey, Lewis, married Rachel Woolston circa 18 Aug 1828 (date of license) by Rev. Smith (Cecil County Marriage License Book; 1830 Maryland Census lists Lewis McKee in Baltimore City)

McKINNEY

McKinney, Ann, see John P. Lockard

McKinney, Elizabeth M., see James Wason

McKinney, Jane, see Passmore McVey

McKinney, John S., see James Wason

McKinney, Joseph (born c1815) (farmer at North East), married Margaret Jane Foster (born c1817) circa 21 Oct 1840 (date of license) (Cecil County Marriage License Book; 1860 Cecil County Census)

McKinney, Mahala Ann, see James Brinton

McKinney, Margaret Elizabeth, see James Wason

McKinney, Thomas C. (born c1821, Maryland) (laborer at North East), married Margaret Barrett (born c1822, Maryland (circa 18 Feb 1843 (date of license) (Cecil County Marriage License Book; 1860 Cecil County Census listed him as T. C. McKiny)

McKinney, Thomas G. (1820-1902), married Margaret Ann Weaver (1822-1864) circa 10 Sep 1842 (date of license) (Cecil County Marr. License Book; Hart's Methodist Church Cemetery tombstone inscriptions)

McKINSEY, McKINZEY

McKinsey, Elizabeth A., see Alfred W. Plattenburgh

McKinsey, Hannah Elizabeth, see John Ferguson

McKinsey, James (1818-1893), married Catherine N. (N) (1827-1918) probably circa 1845 (Elkton Cemetery tombstone inscriptions)

McKinzey, John, of Elkton, married Miss Mary Jester, of New Castle Co., Delaware, on 21 May 1843, after obtaining a license on 20 May 1843, by Rev. McIntire near Elkton (Cecil County Marriage License Book; *Delaware Gazette*, 26 May 1843)

McKinsey, Lydia Maria, see William Jones

McKinsey, Maria, see John Ferguson

McKinsey, Tobias, see John Ferguson

McKOWEN

McKowen, James, married Miss Sophia Jane Snowden, both of Charlestown, on 28 Jan 1844, after obtaining a license on 25 Jan 1844, by Rev. Goentner (*Cecil Whig*, 30 Mar 1844; Cecil County Marriage License Book spelled his name McKown)

McKowen, James, married Millicent Cooper circa 11 Sep 1848 (date of license) (Cecil County Marriage License Book spelled his name McKowen and the 1850 Cecil County Census listed Millicent McCowan as head of household)

McKowen, Samuel, married Mary Davis circa 15 Sep 1848 (date of license) (Cecil County Marriage License Book spelled his name McKown; *Cecil Whig*, 30 Mar 1844 spelled it McKowen and the 1850 Cecil County Census Index spelled it McCowan)

McKowen, also see McCowan

McLANE

McLane, Allan, see Thomas V. Ward

McLane, Louis, see Henry Tiffany

McLane, Mary, see Thomas V. Ward

McLane, Rebecca Wells, see Philip Hamilton

McLane, Sally Jones, see Henry Tiffany

McLAUGHLIN

McLaughlin, Charles, married Isabella Early circa 6 Jul 1849 (date of license) (Cecil County Marriage License Book)

McLaughlin, Sarah Ann, see Henry A. Brown

McMULLEN, McMULLIN

McMullin, Alice, see Wilder Harris

McMullin, Harriet, see Samuel Watkins and John T. Diffenderfer

McMullin, John (1818-1854), married Mary A. Grant circa 18 Jan 1847 (date of license) (Cecil Co. Marriage License Book; DAR transcript copied in 1955 spelled his name McMullen and mistakenly listed the marriage license date as 8 Jan 1847; Hopewell United Methodist Church Cemetery tombstone inscription)

McMullen, Joseph, married Sarah Ann Owens circa 28 Jun 1839 (date of license) by Rev. Hagany (Cecil County Marriage License Book)

McMullen, Margaret, see William Brickley

McMullen, Mary Ann, see James Crawford

McMullen, Robert, see Thomas R. McMullen

McMullen, Robert (1805-1878), married Deborah Williams (1809-1890) circa 6 Jun 1826 (date of license) by Rev. Magraw (Cecil County Marriage License Book spelled his name McMullin; Rosebank Cemetery, at Calvert, tombstones inscribed Robert and Deborah McMullen)

McMullen, Sarah, see John B. Campbell

McMullen, Thomas (born c1816, Maryland) (laborer, 7th District), married Catherine Flehearty (born c1828, Maryland) circa 28 Aug 1841 (date of license) (Cecil County Marriage License; 1860 Cecil Co. Census)

McMullen, Thomas R. (c1810-1879) (blacksmith), son of Robert McMullen and Margaret Read, married Jane Kelly (c1804-1864), daughter of Edward and Mary Kelly, circa 9 Oct 1843 (date of license) (Cecil County Marriage License Book; *Ancestral Charts, Volume 4*, pp. 178-179, Harford County Genealogical Society Publication, 1988)

McNAMEE

McNamee, Frederick (1811-1877) (shoemaker and farmer), son of Francis McNamee of Ireland, later of Cecil Co., and Elizabeth (N) (1789-1867), married Sarah A. Hollowell (1814-1894), of Chester Co., PA, circa 1835 and had five children: Merritt S. McNamee (born 8 Sep 1836, died 1910); William A. McNamee; Stephen D. McNamee; Elizabeth Kirkwood; and, Cornelia J. McNamee (1857-1916) (*Portrait and Biographical Record of Harford and Cecil Counties, Maryland* (1897, repr. 1989), p. 327; Friends Cemetery, at Harrisville, tombstone inscriptions; *Cecil Whig*, 24 Nov 1877)

McNamee, William (1807-1885), married Eliza C. (N) (1812-1894) probably circa 1830 (Elkton Cemetery tombstone inscriptions)

McNEAL

McNeal, John, married Sarah Craig circa 26 Apr 1826 (date of license) by Rev. Woolford (Cecil County Marriage License Book)

McNeal, Thomas (1804-1874), of Bell Hill near Elkton, married Hannah (N) (1805-1872) probably circa 1825 (Elkton Methodist Church Cemetery tombstone inscription for "Father" Thomas McNeal; *Cecil Whig*, 4 May 1872 and 17 Oct 1872)

McNIT

McNit, James, married Martha Tamblin circa 3 May 1825 (date of license) by Rev. Chambers (Cecil County Marriage License Book)

McNUTT

McNutt, Martha, see James Van Winkle

McVEY

McVey, Absalom, married Mary Edmondson circa 21 Feb 1825 (date of license) by Rev. Griffith (Cecil County Marriage License Book spelled his first name Absalum)

McVey, Absalom B. (1810-1885, born Maryland) (farmer near Zion), married Margaret J. McCormick (1821-1880, born Maryland) circa 18 Mar 1845 (date of their license) (Cecil County Marriage License Book; Zion Presbyterian Cemetery tombstone inscriptions; 1860 Cecil County Census)

McVey, Amy, see William Reed

McVey, Andrew J. (1825-1898), married Mary T. (N) (1823-1896) probably circa 1846 (West Nottingham Cemetery tombstone inscriptions)

McVey, Elizabeth, see John McCullough

McVey, George S., see James K. McVey

McVey, Hannah, see Henry Burns

McVey, James, see John Anderson

McVey, James, married Elizabeth Shockley circa 17 Aug 1831 (date of license) by Rev. Barnes (Cecil County Marriage License Book)

McVey, James K. (1809-1891), married Catharine (N) (1814-1889) before 1840; buried beside Martha K. McVey, 1841-1863 (Rosebank Cemetery, at Calvert, tombstone inscriptions; *Midland Journal*, 13 Feb 1891, reported that he died in his 82nd year at the residence of his son George S. McVey near Zion)

McVey, Jane Maria, see John Anderson

McVey, John, married Hester Ann Blake circa 15 Oct 1836 (date of license) by Rev. Davis (Cecil County Marriage License Book)

McVey, Jonathan, married Frances Taylor circa 17 Apr 1832 (date of license) by Rev. Magraw (Cecil County Marriage License Book)

McVey, Levi (born c1812, Maryland) (carpenter, Port Deposit), married Miss Margaret Jenkins (1816-1867) on 9 Jan 1842, after obtaining a license on 5 Jan 1842, by Rev. Cunningham (Cecil County Marriage License Book; *Cecil Gazette*, 15 Jan 1842; Hopewell United Methodist Church Cemetery tombstone inscription; 1860 Cecil County Census)

McVey, Martha, see John Anderson and Nicholas Milburn

McVey, Martha K., see James K. McVey

McVey, Mary, see Samuel Gillespie and Robert Rawlings

McVey, Mary Ann, see Robert White

McVey, Nathan, married Jane Logan circa 9 Jul 1834 (date of their license) by Rev. Griffith (Cecil County Marriage License Book)

McVey, Nathan (born c1806, Maryland) (wheelwright, 6th District), married Elizabeth (N) (born c1825, Maryland) probably circa 1848; son Woolford McVey born c1849 (1860 Cecil County Census)

McVey, Passmore, married Jane McKinney circa 26 Apr 1832 (date of the license) by Rev. Barratt (Cecil County Marriage License Book)

McVey, Rebecca, see Samuel Williams

McVey, Thomas, married Elizabeth Cameron circa 24 Jul 1844 (date of the license) (Cecil County Marriage License Book)

McVey, Woolford, see Nathan McVey

MEAGHER

Meagher, Martin, married Catherine Beers circa 18 Feb 1843 (date of the license) (Cecil County Marriage License Book)

MEARNS

Mearns, Elizabeth, see Israel Reynolds

Mearns, James (1804-1877, born Maryland) (farmer near Zion), married Lavenia (N) (1806-1884, born Maryland) probably circa 1826 (Rosebank Cemetery tombstone inscriptions; 1860 Cecil County Census)

Mearns, James A., see Levi R. Mearns

Mearns, John, of Cecil Co., married Mary Waugh, daughter of Robert Waugh, of Chester Co., PA, on 14 May 1839 by Rev. Duboies (*Cecil Gazette*, 25 May 1839)

Mearns, Levi R. (born c1825, Maryland) (farmer near Brick Meeting House), married Miss Amanda F. Tilaman (born c1828), of Chester Co., Pennsylvania, on 20 Jun 1850 by Rev. Dickey; son James A. Mearns born c1851, Pennsylvania (*Cecil Democrat and Farmer's Journal*, 22 Jun 1850; 1860 Cecil County Census indicated Levi and Amanda were born in Maryland)

Mearns, Martha S. M., see Robert C. Carter

Mearns, also see Marnes

MEARS

Mears, Deborah, see Francis King

Mears, John, married Caroline Hudson circa 6 Sep 1842 (date of license) (Cecil County Marr. License Book)

Mears, John, married Eliza Hudson circa 15 Mar 1838 (date of license) by Rev. Morris (Cecil Co. Marriage License Book)

Mears, Mary Ann, see William Barwick

MEDFORD

Medford, Susan, see Stephen Savin

MEGEE

Megee, George T., married Mary E. Townsend circa 20 Mar 1843 (date of license); daughter Margaret Megee (1846-1899), of Cecil Co., married George E. Gleaves of Shenandoah, VA (Cecil County Marriage License Book; *Centreville Record*, 23 Jul 1899)

MEGINNIS

Meginnis, Benjamin R., of Kent Co., married Martha E. Murphy, of Cecil Co., circa 19 Oct 1843 by Rev. Sutton (Kent County Marriage License Book)

MEGREDY

Megredy, Daniel, see Edwin Wilmer

Megredy, Hannah E., see Edwin Wilmer

Megredy, Margaretta J., see Ebenezer Dickey McClenahan

Megredy, Mary, see Greenberry Purnell

Megredy, Sarah, see Eli White

MENDENHALL

Mendenhall, Annie, see Eli Mendenhall

Mendenhall, Eli (born c1822, Delaware) (cabinet maker in Elkton), married Elizabeth (N) (born c1823, Maryland) probably circa 1845; daughter Annie born circa 1847, Delaware (1860 Cecil County Census)

Mendenhall, Hannah, see James Trimble

Mendenhall, Sarah, see James Trimble

MERCER

Mercer, Ann, see John B. Pennington

Mercer, Benjamin, married Cassandra White circa 3 Mar 1825 (date of license) by Rev. Stephenson (Cecil County Marriage License Book)

Mercer, Cassy, see James H. Reily

Mercer, Eliza Ann, see William Veazey

Mercer, Harriet Ann, see Mahlon Batten

Mercer, James, married Ann Catherine (N) (1821-1850) probably circa 1840 and she died on 9 Aug 1850, aged 29 years (*Cecil Whig*, 24 Aug 1850)

Mercer, James N., married Millicent Ann Lum circa 8 Oct 1829 (date of license) by Rev. Barratt (Cecil County Marriage License Book)

Mercer, Jane, see Peregrine F. Lloyd

Mercer, John W., married Martha Lum circa 3 Apr 1841 (date of license) (Cecil County Marr. License Book)

Mercer, Joshua (born c1820) (African American) (laborer at St. Augustine), married Louisa (N) (born c1819) (African American) probably circa 1842l son Stephen born c1843 (1860 Cecil County Census)

Mercer, Margaret Savin Biddle, see William D. Mercer and John W. Wirt

Mercer, Mary L., see Launcelot Moffitt

Mercer, Stephen, see Joshua Mercer

Mercer, William D., married Margaret Savin Biddle circa 12 Nov 1838 (date of license) by Rev. Piggot, a Protestant Episcopal minister in North Sassafras; Mrs. Margaret Savin Biddle Mercer married 2nd to Dr. John W. Wirt in 1848 (Cecil Co. Marr. License Book; *Cecil Whig*, 12 Aug 1848); see John W. Wirt, *q.v.*

MEREDITH

Meredith, John (1823-1909), married Rachel Pope circa 9 Feb 1850 (date of license) (Cecil County Marriage License Book; Cecil County Burial Permit states he was buried in Cecilton Cemetery)

Meredith, Thomas J., of Baltimore Co., married Elizabeth DeH. Janvier circa 23 Jun 1846 (date of license) (Cecil County Marriage License Book; DAR transcript copied in 1955 misspelled her name Janview)

MERRITT

Merritt, Ann, see Timothy P. Denny

Merritt, Charles F. (born c1815, Maryland) (blacksmith at South Milford), married Mary Ellen Terry (born c1829, Maryland) circa 25 Nov 1847 (date of license) (Cecil County Marriage License Book; DAR transcript mistakenly listed H. as his middle initial; 1860 Cecil Co. Census did not list a middle initial)

Merritt, James, married Catherine Price on 7 Sep 1841, after obtaining a license on 24 Aug 1841, by Rev. Jones (Cecil County Marriage License Book; DAR transcript copied in 1955 mistakenly listed her name as Catherine White; Elkton Methodist Church Register spelled his name Merit)

Merritt, James, of New Castle Co., Delaware, married Miss Elizabeth Johnson, of Elkton, on 20 Dec 1832, after obtaining a license that same day, by Rev. Benson (Cecil County Marriage License Book; *Cecil Republican*, 22 Dec 1832)

Merritt, James, see Joseph Merritt

Merritt, Jane S., see William W. Boulden

Merritt, Joseph (born c1820, Delaware) (farmer at Bohemian Mills), married Rachel Boulden (born c1819, Maryland), daughter of Richard Boulden, circa 5 Jun 1847 (date of license); son James Merritt born c1848, Maryland (Cecil County Marriage License Book; *Portrait and Biographical Record of Harford and Cecil Counties, Maryland* (1897, repr. 1989), pp. 453-454; 1860 Cecil County Census)

Merritt, Joseph, of Baltimore City, married Miss Margaretta E. Walton, of Elkton, Cecil Co., on 1 Aug 1848 at the Seminary in Baltimore by Rev. Elder (*Cecil Democrat and Farmer's Journal*, 5 Aug 1848; *Baltimore Sun*, 3 Aug 1848)

Merritt, Reece, married Ann Elizabeth McGee circa 5 Apr 1831 (date of license) by Rev. Duke (Cecil County Marriage License Book)

Merritt, William I. (J.?), married Phebe Hart circa 5 Jun 1847 (date of license) (Cecil Co. Marr, Lic. Book)

MERRY, MERREY

Merry, Elizabeth T., see Franklin W. Lort

Merry, George W., married Miss Millicent Amanda Lort, both of Cecil Co., on 23 Nov 1848, after obtaining a license that same day, by Rev. Barrett (Cecil County Marriage License Book spelled his name Merrey; *Cecil Democrat and Farmer's Journal*, 2 Dec 1848)

Merry, James (born c1826, Pennsylvania) (boot and shoe maker at Elkton), married Araminta R. Rutter (born c1829, Maryland) circa 7 Mar 1848 (date of license) (Cecil County Marriage License Book; 1860 Cecil County Census)

MILES

Miles, John, a Revolutionary soldier (age 86), married Mrs. Sally Fuzzle (aged 82), of Fuzzle's Creek, all of Rankin Co., MS, on 5 May 1843 (*Cecil Whig*, 6 May 1843, noted "None but the brave deserves the fair.")

MICHAEL

Michael, Frederick H., married Mary Watkins circa 29 Feb 1836 (date of license) by Rev. Potts (Cecil County Marriage License Book; DAR transcript copied in 1928 mistakenly listed his name as Mitchell and her name as Walkins)

MILBURN

Milburn, Catharine, see William Howard Rutter

Milburn (Milbourne), Margaret, see James McDowell

Milburn, Mary, see Abner Holmes

Milburn, Nicholas (1817-1893) (farmer at North East), married Amy Ann Ramsey (born c1828), daughter of William Ramsey and Martha McVey, on 7 Jan 1847 after obtaining a license on 6 Jan 1847 (Cecil County Marriage License Book; *Portrait and Biographical Record of Harford and Cecil Counties, Maryland* (1897, repr. 1989), pp. 371-372, misspelled her mother's name as Mevay; 1860 Cecil County Census)

Milburn, Rachel, see William McDowell

Milburn (Millburn), R. J. (born c1820, Pennsylvania) (farmer at Cecilton), married Elizabeth H. (N) (born c1824, Delaware) circa 1846 (1860 Cecil County Census listed son Samuel C. Millburn born c1837, Delaware, and son Richard J. Millburn born c1851, Pennsylvania)

MILBY

Milby, Arthur W. (reverend), of the Philadelphia Conference, married Rebecca P. Levis, daughter of Samuel Levis, Esq., of Delaware Co., Pennsylvania, on 11 Nov 1847 by Rev. Dr. Scott (*Cecil Whig*, 4 Dec 1847)

MILLER

Miller, Ann, see Abel Dodd

Miller, Benjamin, married Lydia M. Simpson circa 11 Mar 1835 (date of license) by Rev. Duke (Cecil County Marriage License Book)

Miller, Eliza Jane, see Francis E. Forman

Miller, Jane, see Jesse H. Simpers

Miller, John, of Newark, DE, married Mary Mackey, of Elkton, on 14 May 1833, after obtaining a license that same day, by Rev. Hagany (Cecil County Marriage License Book; Elkton Methodist Church Register, p. 5; *Cecil Republican*, 18 May 1833)

Miller, John D., of Chester Co., PA, married Miss Martha Wright, of Cecil Co., on 10 Sep 1850 by Rev. Atwood (*Cecil Democrat and Farmer's Journal*, 21 Sep 1850)

Miller, John T. (1823-1871) (farmer near Elkton), married Margaret R. Carter (born c1828), daughter of ---- Carter, Esq., of Cherry Hill, on 14 Dec 1848, after obtaining a license on 11 Dec 1848, by Rev. Ayres (Cecil County Marriage License Book; *Cecil Democrat and Farmer's Journal*, 23 Dec 1848; 1860 Cecil County Census; *Kent News*, 11 Mar 1871)

Miller, John W. (born c1820, Maryland) (farmer near Elkton), married Sarah Flounders (born c1825, Pennsylvania) circa 8 Jan 1845 (date of license); daughter Margaret Miller born c1846, Maryland (Cecil County Marriage License Book; 1860 Cecil County Census)

Miller, Joseph (1809-1882) (reverend), of Cherry Hill, married 1st to Margaret Warburton (1807-1865) circa 13 Nov 1830 (date of license) by Rev. Mahan and married 2nd to Rebecca L. Simpson (1814-1889) in 1867 (Cecil County Marriage License Book; Cherry Hill Methodist Church Cemetery tombstone inscriptions; *Cecil Whig*, 8 Jul 1865)

Miller, Joseph W., married Martha Whann circa 17 Mar 1825 (date of license) by Rev. Sharpley (Cecil County Marriage License Book; *Cecil Whig*, 5 Apr 1873, reported a Joseph W. Miller, age 72, formerly of Cecil Co., died in Ohio)

Miller, Lancy or Laney, see Jesse Updegrove

Miller, Lawrence, married Sarah Amanda Lucas circa 13 Aug 1846 (date of license) (Cecil County Marriage License Book)

Miller, Lydia Ann, see William Gooding

Miller, Margaret, see John W. Miller and Benoni Nowland

Miller, Rachel, see Andrew M. Cameron

Miller, Richard, married Sarah Jane Grant circa 7 Jun 1838 (date of license) by Rev. Barratt (Cecil County Marriage License Book)

Miller, Samuel, see William Gooding and Francis E. Forman

Miller, Sarah, see Daniel J. McCauley and John Charles Whitelock, Jr.

Miller, Sarah Ann, see Robert P. Alexander

Miller, Sybilla A., see George McCullough

Miller, Thomas, see Jesse H. Simpers and William T. Miller

Miller, William T. (born 1821) (carpenter and farmer near Elkton), son of Thomas Miller and Ann Simpers, married 1st to Miss Sarah Jane McCullough (born c1825) circa 20 Jan 1847 (date of license) and married 2nd to Miss Annie Whitson (no date given) after his first wife died (Cecil County Marriage License Book; *Portrait and Biographical Record of Harford and Cecil Counties, Maryland* (1897, repr. 1989), p. 355; 1860 Cecil County Census)

MILLIGAN

Milligan, Maria, see Patrick Conley

MILLS

Mills, Letitia, see Richard Hudson

MILON

Milon, James, see Ann Barker

MINGLING

Mingling, Susan, see Thomas Wilson

MINKER

Minker, Alice, see Amor Cameron

Minker, William (born c1803, Pennsylvania) (forgeman at Charlestown), married Lydia (N) (born c1812, Pennsylvania) probably circa 1834; son Robert born c1835, Pennsylvania, and son Adam born c1841, Maryland, plus eight other children all born before 1860 in Maryland (1860 Cecil County Census)

MISSIMER

Missimer, William, of London Brittain Township, Chester Co., PA, married Miss Martha Ann Devlin, of Cecil Co., on Thanksgiving Day, 29 Nov 1849, by Rev. Plummer (*Cecil Democrat and Farmer's Journal*, 15 Dec 1849)

MITCHELL

Mitchell, Abraham David, see Ephraim Thompson Mitchell

Mitchell, Catharine W., see James T. McCullough

Mitchell, Cenah B., see Stephen T. Hays

Mitchell, Charlotte, see Amos Hollis Hughes

Mitchell, Ephraim Thompson (1819-1864), eldest son of Abraham David Mitchell and Jane Evans, of Fair Hill, Cecil Co., married Jemima Callicet circa 13 Sep 1843 (date of license) and died at Devall's Bluff on the White River in Arkansas (Cecil County Marriage License Book; *Cecil Whig*, 28 May 1864; *History of Cecil County*, by George Johnston (1881, repr. 1989), p. 497)

Mitchell, George Edward, see John Stump and James T. McCullough

Mitchell, Jane, see John Pennington

Mitchell, John T., married Margaret White circa 3 May 1843 (date of their license) (Cecil County Marriage License Book)

Mitchell, Lydia, see Samuel Borum

Mitchell, Martha Ann, see Fagan Earnest

Mitchell, Mary, see Norris Levis

Mitchell, Mary Alicia, see John Stump

Mitchell, Mary E., see Francis B. Crookshanks

Mitchell, Susan, see George J. Beaston

MOARN, MOURN

Moarn (Mourn), William, married Mrs. Margaret Waterson, both of Cecil Co., on 18 May 1841, after obtaining a license that same day, by Rev. Maddux (*Cecil Gazette*, 29 May 1841, spelled his name Moarn; Cecil County Marriage License Book spelled his name Mourn)

MOFFITT, MOFFETT

Moffitt, Ann, see Christopher Little

Moffitt, Jane, see William Hogg

Moffitt, Lancelot, married Mary L. Mercer circa 24 Jun 1846 (date of license) (Cecil County Marriage License Book; DAR transcript copied in 1955 spelled his name Launcelot Moffett)

Moffitt, Martha T., see Isaiah H. Gilpin

Moffitt, Samuel, married Miss Victorine Johnson on 18 Dec 1838, after obtaining a license on 17 Dec 1838, by Rev. Hagany (Cecil County Marriage License Book; Elkton Methodist Church Register, p. 139; *Cecil Gazette*, 22 Dec 1838, misspelled his name Mofford)

Moffitt, Samuel D. (1815-1891), married Ann H. (N) (1816-1900) probably circa 1840 (Rosebank Cemetery, at Calvert, tombstone inscriptions)

Moffett, Stansbury, of Kent Co., married Martha Jones, of Cecil Co., circa 4 Apr 1846 by Rev. Pearson (Kent County Marriage License Book)

Moffitt, also see Maffitt

MOLTEN

Molten, Samuel, married Mary A. T. Bradley circa 21 Oct 1845 (date of license) (Cecil County Marriage License Book)

MONEY

Money, Alethea, see Robert Hayes, Jr.

Money, Benjamin M. (born c1823) (farmer at Cecilton), married Susan Elizabeth Newnam (born c1832), of Cecil Co., on 16 Jan 1849, after obtaining a license that same day, by Rev. Wiley; son William Money born c1850 (Cecil County Marriage License Book; DAR transcript copied in 1928 misspelled her name as Newman; 1860 Cecil County Census; *Cecil Democrat and Farmer's Journal*, 3 Feb 1849)

Money, Don Maria, see Elias P. Barnaby

Money, Honor, see John McIntire

Money, Mary, see Mills M. Rickard

Money, Sarah Ann, see John Hayes

Money, William, see Benjamin M. Money

Money, (N), married Sarah E. (1812-1891) probably circa 1830 and she died in her 79th year at the residence of her son-in-law George Bolton in Sassafras Neck (*Midland Journal*, 6 Mar 1891)

MONTGOMERY

Montgomery, Charlotte, see James S. Nickel

Montgomery, Jehu, of Harford Co., married Miss Catharine McCullough, of Cecil Co., on 21 Jan 1830 by Rev. Jacob Job (*Independent Citizen*, 28 Jan 1830)

MOODY

Moody, Leah, see Andrew Camblin and James Matthews

Moody, Sophia, see Thomas Cochran

MOON

Moon, David (1816-1892), married Rachel Williams (1815-1900) circa 31 Mar 1846 (date of license) (Cecil County Marriage License Book; Union Methodist Church Cemetery tombstone inscriptions)

MOORE

Moore, Adrianna, see Joseph Moore and Joseph Thomas

Moore, Alicia, see Francis B. Gottier

Moore, Amanda, see James Moore

Moore, Amos, see William H. Way

Moore, Amos (1808-1889) (farmer, 6th District), married Eliza C. (N) (1812-1881) prob. circa 1830-1834; daughter Martha Moore born c1835 (Friends Cemetery, at Harrisville, tombstone inscriptions; 1860 Cecil County Census)

Moore, Ann Elizabeth, see George W. Craig

Moore, Anna Marie, see Ellis P. Coale

Moore, Annie, see Alexander Kirk

Moore, Benjamin, see Ellis P. Coale and Joseph Moore

Moore, Catherine, see John Moore

Moore, Charlotte, see Henry Reynolds

Moore, David, see Ezekiel Moore, Henry Reynolds and Ziba Moore

Moore, Elijah, married Mary Davis circa 15 Dec 1830 (date of license) by Rev. Griffith (Cecil County Marriage License Book)

Moore, Elijah, married Elizabeth Huff circa 30 Jul 1836 (date of license) by Rev. Stephenson (Cecil County Marriage License Book)

Moore, Eliza Jane, see John Magee

Moore, Eliza P., see Henry Reynolds

Moore, Elizabeth, see George W. Moore

Moore, Ezekiel, son of David Moore, deceased, of Chester Co., PA, married (N) Trump, of West Nottingham Hundred, Cecil Co., in 1829 at West Nottingham (*Births, Deaths and Marriages of the Nottingham Quakers, 1680-1899*, by Alice L. Beard (1989), p. 221)

Moore, Gabriel (1804-1875) (reverend), married Sarah (N) (1817-1877) probably circa 1838 (Moore's Methodist Church Cemetery tombstone inscriptions)

Moore, George, married Lydia Culley circa 22 Dec 1841 (date of license) (Cecil Co. Marr. License Book)

Moore, George, married Margaret Ann Gonce circa 7 Jan 1846 (date of license) (Cecil County Marriage License Book)

Moore, George, married Miss Elizabeth Phillips, both of North East, on 13 Jun 1849, after obtaining a license on 12 Jun 1849, at North East by Rev. Arthur (Cecil County Marriage License Book; *Cecil Democrat and Farmer's Journal*, 16 Jun 1849; *Cecil Whig*, 16 Jun 1849)

Moore, George H., married Julia Ann Wilson (1811-1877) on 25 Oct 1827 after obtaining a license on 20 Oct 1827 and died in 1839; Julia Ann Moore married 2nd to Robert Hart on 15 Mar 1842 (Cecil County Marriage License Book; *Cecil Whig*, 4 Aug and 11 Aug 1877)

Moore, George W. (esquire), married 1st to Miss Elizabeth Simmons (c1819-1842), both of Elkton, on 2 May 1839, after obtaining a license that same day, by Rev. McIntire and married 2nd to Miss Sarah Alexander, both of Elkton, on 18 Jan 1844, after obtaining a license that same day, by Rev. McIntire (*Cecil Gazette*, 4 May 1839, spelled her name Simmonds; Cecil County Marriage License Book; *Cecil Whig*, 29 Oct 1842, reported Mrs. Elizabeth Moore, wife of George W., died after a long illness; *Cecil Whig*, 20 Jan 1844)

Moore, Hannah, see Joseph Moore

Moore, Isabella B., see Christopher Little

Moore, James (born c1821, Maryland) (laborer at Port Herman), married Elizabeth Motts (born c1821, Maryland) circa 14 Dec 1840 (date of license); son Samuel Moore born c1842 (Cecil County Marriage License Book; 1860 Cecil County Census)

Moore, James (born c1818, Maryland) (African American) (laborer at Elkton), married Sarah (N) (born c1820, Maryland) (African American) probably circa 1840; daughter Amanda Moore born c1841 (1860 Cecil County Census)

Moore, James H., see John Moore

Moore, Jane, see James R. Reynolds, William Moore and Joseph Moore

Moore, John, see John Magee

Moore, John (1812-1881), married Albinah (N) (1812-1896) probably circa 1832-1833 (St. John's Church Cemetery, at Lewisville, tombstone inscriptions)

Moore, John (1797-1867), married Jane Barnes (1806-1854) probably circa 1825-1826 (West Nottingham Cemetery tombstone inscriptions)

Moore, John, married Catherine (N) (1822-1884) probably circa 1844 (Bethesda Cemetery, at Oakwood, tombstone inscription for Catherine Moore; buried nearby is James H. Moore, 1845-1847)

Moore, John, married Rebecca Walmsley circa 1 Aug 1846 (date of license) (Cecil Co. Marr. License Book)

Moore, John James (1807-1888), married Sarah Rebecca Arrants (1817-1900) circa 20 Jan 1836 (date of license) by Rev. Barratt (Cecil County Marriage License Book listed James as a middle name for John, but his Hopewell United Methodist Church Cemetery tombstone inscription did not)

Moore, Joseph, see William H. Way, Ellis P. Coale, William Moore and Joseph Thomas

Moore, Joseph, son of Joseph and Jane Moore, both deceased, of Chester Co., PA, married Ann Coale, widow of Skipwith Coale and daughter of George and Sarah Matthews, of Baltimore, on the 13th day of the 11th month 1825 at West Nottingham Meeting House in Cecil County. Among the witnesses were Adrianna Moore, Hannah Moore, Benjamin Moore, Samuel Coale, Lydia Coale, Samuel Coale (a minor) and Ellis P. Coale. (*Births, Deaths and Marriages of the Nottingham Quakers, 1680-1899*, by Alice L. Beard (1989), pp. 220-221)

Moore, Julia Ann, see George H. Moore and Robert Hart

Moore, Martha, see Amos Moore and Ziba Moore

Moore, Mary, see Henry Reynolds

Moore, Mary Ann, see Ellis P. Coale and Henry Reynolds

Moore, Mary Elena, see Henry Reynolds

Moore, Mary Elma, see William H. Way

Moore, May, see Henry Richardson

Moore, Mercy, see William W. Moore and Ellis P. Coale

Moore, Rachel, see Abraham Kennard

Moore, Rachel Jane, see Joshua Pennington

Moore, Rebecca, see Isaac Trimble and Ellis P. Coale

Moore, Richard, married Ann Phillips circa 14 Nov 1827 (date of license) (Cecil Co. Marr. License Book)

Moore, Richard B., see William H. Way

Moore, Ruthanna, see Ellis P. Coale

Moore, Samuel, see James Moore

Moore, Sarah, see Samuel Tippett, Henry Reynolds and Isaac Moore

Moore, Sarah Jane, see Joseph R. Mahoney and Henry Reynolds

Moore, Sophia, see George Parks

Moore, Susanna, see John Heath

Moore, Timothy, see William H. Way

Moore, Walter (doctor), married Eliza Ann White circa 15 Oct 1844 (date of license) (Cecil County Marriage License Book listed his name "Doctor Walter Moore")

Moore, William, see Ellis P. Coale and Henry Reynolds

Moore, William, married Margaret Steele circa 10 Mar 1828 (date of license) (Cecil Co. Marr. Lic. Book)

Moore, William, son of Joseph and Jane Moore, both deceased, of West Nottingham Hundred, Cecil Co., married Charlotte Howell (born 1803), daughter of William Howell and Hannah Pugh, of the same place, on the – day of the 3rd month 1829 at West Nottingham (*Births, Deaths and Marriages of the Nottingham Quakers, 1680-1899*, by Alice L. Beard (1989), pp. 49, 222)

Moore, William, married Mary Ann Thornton circa 24 Jul 1838 (date of license) by Rev. Grason (Cecil County Marriage License Book)

Moore, William C. (1815-1881), married Anna B. (N) (1819-1901) probably circa 1840 (West Nottingham Cemetery tombstone inscriptions)

Moore, William E., married Miss Harriet Foot, both of Newark, DE, on 13 Sep 1850 by Rev. George Foot (*Cecil Whig*, 28 Sep 1850)

Moore, William R., married Martha Linton circa 28 Dec 1829 (date of license) by Rev. Ayres (Cecil County Marriage License Book)

Moore, William W. (1817-1904, born Maryland) (farmer, 6th District), married Hannah H. (N) (1819-1901, born Maryland) probably circa 1841; daughter Mercy Moore born c1842 (West Nottingham Cemetery tombstone inscriptions; 1860 Cecil County Census)

Moore, Ziba, son of David and Martha Moore, the former deceased, of London Grove Township, Chester Co., PA, married Mary Bell, daughter of Richard and Rachel Bell, the former deceased, of West Nottingham Hundred, Cecil Co., on 21st day of 12th month 1831 at the West Nottingham Meeting House (*Births, Deaths and Marriages of the Nottingham Quakers, 1680-1899*, by Alice L. Beard (1989), p. 222)

MORGAN

Morgan, Araminta M., see John Wroth

Morgan, Charles H. (born c1820) (laborer at Chesapeake City), married Rebecca Robinson (born c1822) circa 13 Jun 1843 (date of license) (Cecil County Marriage License Book; 1860 Cecil County Census)

Morgan, Eleanor, see William Latham Rowland

Morgan, Ellen, see Louis Buchanan

Morgan, Emily, see Joseph Veach

Morgan, Evan, married 1st to Martha Gibson circa 5 May 1830 (date of license) by Rev. Goforth and married 2nd to Miss Ann Strawbridge on 7 Oct 1834, after obtaining a license that same day, by Rev. Stork (Cecil County Marriage License Book; *Cecil Gazette*, 18 Oct 1834)

Morgan, Henrietta E., see Noble Pennington

Morgan, Isabella, see Andrew Orr

Morgan, James H., of Elkton, married Miss Elizabeth W. Watson, of Wilmington, DE, on 27 Oct 1850 in Philadelphia by Rev. Mason, St. Paul's M. E. Ch. (*Cecil Democrat and Farmer's Journal*, 2 Nov 1850)

Morgan, James W. (born c1818) (farmer at Cecilton), married Rebecca Ann Hayes (born c1819) circa 1 Jan 1839 (date of license) by Rev. Piggot, a Protestant Episcopal minister in North Sassafras; son William R. Morgan born 1840 (Cecil County Marriage License Book; 1860 Cecil County Census)

Morgan, John H. (born c1823, Delaware) (house painted at Cecilton) married Mary (N) (born c1828, Delaware) circa 1848; daughter Mary Morgan born c1849) (1860 Cecil County Census)

Morgan, John T. (born c1810) (laborer at Elkton), married Ann (N) (born c1811) circa 1840; twin sons William and Joseph Morgan born c1842 (1860 Cecil County Census)

Morgan, John Ward (1809-1871) (farmer at Cecilton), married Mary W. Gale (1812-1886) circa 19 Dec 1829 (date of license) by Rev. King (Cecil County Marriage License Book; 1860 Cecil County Census; St. Stephen's Episcopal Church Cemetery tombstone inscriptions)

Morgan, Joseph, see John T. Morgan

Morgan, Laura E., see John H. Hessey

Morgan, Martha Ann, see William D. Hackett

Morgan, Mary, see John H. Morgan

Morgan, Millaminty, see William H. Pearce

Morgan, Sarah Jane, see James Hepbron and George Washington Barnes

Morgan, William, see John T. Morgan

Morgan, William P. (1811-1874) (farmer at Elkton), married Ann Jane Lee (1812-1867) circa 8 Jun 1836 (date of license) by Rev. Potts (Cecil County Marriage License Book; 1860 Cecil County Census; Elkton Presbyterian Church Cemetery tombstones; *Cecil Democrat and Farmer's Journal*, 23 Feb 186 (poem)

Morgan, William R., see James W. Morgan

MORRIS

Morris, Burton P. (born c1816, Delaware) (trader in Elkton), married Mary Matilda (N) (c1820-1874, Maryland) probably circa 1845 and she died in Wilmington, DE; son John Morris born c1847, Maryland (*Cecil Whig*, 3 Oct 1874, reported Mary was the wife of Burton P. Morris and she died at age 53; *Cecil Whig*, 10 Oct 1874, reported Mary was the wife of Burton T. Morris and she died in her 55th year; 1860 Cecil County Census listed his name as Burton P. Morris)

Morris, Howard, married Mary A. Kirk circa 18 Jun 1834 (date of license) by Rev. Barratt (Cecil County Marriage License Book)

Morris, James (born c1810) (wheelwright at Cecilton), married Elizabeth (N) (born c1811) circa 1840; daughter Mary A. E. Morris born c1842 (1860 Cecil County Census)

Morris, John, see Burton P. Morris

Morris, Mahala, see Thomas S. Reed

Morris, Mary A. E., see James Morris

Morris, William D. (born c1819, Delaware) (laborer at Cecilton), married Mary (N) (born c1825, Maryland) circa 1844; daughter Laura Morris born c1845 (1860 Cecil County Census)

MORRISON

Morrison, Arthur (born 1803), married Susan Pennington circa 5 Mar 1834 (date of license) by Rev. Duke (Cecil County Marriage License Book; *Cecil County, Maryland Indentures, 1777-1814*, by Jerry M. Hynson (2002), p. 36)

Morrison, Granville, see Jacob Morrison

Morrison, Hamilton (born c1817, Maryland) (quarrier in the 7th District), married Elizabeth (N) (born c1830, Delaware) probably circa 1842; son William born c1843, Maryland (1860 Cecil County Census)

Morrison, Jacob (born c1814, Maryland) (iron roller in the 7th District), married Elizabeth (N) (born c1822, Pennsylvania) probably circa 1843; son Granville born c1844 (1860 Cecil County Census)

Morrison, James, see Matthew Morrison

Morrison, Mary A., see Bernard G. Krauss

Morrison, Matthew (1808-1885, born Maryland) (farmer, 6th District), married Martha Jane (N) (1811-1900, born Maryland) probably circa 1835; son James Morrison born circa 1838 (West Nottingham Cemetery tombstone inscriptions; 1860 Cecil County Census)

Morrison, Sarah, see John T. Gallaher

Morrison, William, see Hamilton Morrison

MORROW

Morrow, James, married Sophia Thompson circa 26 Jul 1827 (date of license) (Cecil County Marriage License Book)

Morrow, James L., formerly of Elkton, married Anna E. Robinson, daughter of Edward P. Robinson, Esq., all of Wilmington, DE, on 30 May 1850 by Rev. Atwood in Wilmington (*Cecil Whig*, 1 Jun 1850; *Cecil Democrat and Farmer's Journal*, 8 Jun 1850; *Delaware Gazette*, 4 Jun 1850)

Morrow, Sarah, see Richard Dean

Morrow, William (1818-1871), married Jane (N) (1816-1878) probably circa 1838-1840 (West Nottingham Cemetery tombstone inscriptions)

MORTON

Morton, Hamilton (born c1820, Maryland) (farmer, Warwick), married Mary J. (N) (born c1826, Maryland) circa 1844; daughter Adelaide born c1845 (1860 Cecil County Census)

Morton, Moor, of Baltimore, married Miss Eliza Reynolds, of Cecil Co., on 6 Jun 1850 by Rev. Sargent in Baltimore (*Cecil Democrat and Farmer's Journal*, 15 Jun 1850; *Baltimore Sun*, 8 Jun 1850)

Morton, Rebecca H., see Alexander P. Barwick

MOSS

Moss, William, married Joannah Jennings circa 9 Apr 1835 (date of license) by Rev. Barratt (Cecil County Marriage License Book)

MOTE

Mote, Eliza, see George A. Casho

Mote, Margaret A., see Gideon B. Scott

Mote, William S., married Eliza Casho circa 7 Apr 1846 (date of license) (Cecil County Marr. License Book)

MOTTS

Motts, Elizabeth, see James Moore

MOUSELY, MOUSLEY

Mousely, Catharine E., see William Walter

Mousley, John, married 1st to Rachel Simpson (date unknown and she divorced him on 9 Mar 1850) and he married 2nd to Isabella Hall circa 15 Jun 1850 (date of license) (Cecil Co. Marr. License Book; *Divorces and Names Changed in Maryland by Act of the Legislature, 1634-1867*, by Mary K. Meyer (1991), p. 65)

MULFORD

Mulford, Claressa, see Joseph T. Stout

Mulford, James M. (esquire), of Philadelphia, married Miss Emelie L. Foard, daughter of Dr. J. L. Foard, of Elkton, on 22 Jun 1848 by Ald. J. A. Elkinton in Philadelphia (*Cecil Whig*, 1 Jul 1848)

MULHOLLAND

Mulholland, James, married Margaret Veazey circa 10 Jun 1826 (date of license) by Rev. Page (Cecil County Marriage License Book; DAR transcript copied in 1928 spelled her name Veasey)

Mulholland, Mary Ann, see David K. Price

MULLEN

Mullen, Barney, of Elkton, married Elizabeth Barnes circa 1 Aug 1826 (date of license) by Rev. Goforth (Cecil County Marriage License Book; *Elkton Press*, 12 Sep 1829)

Mullen, William C. (1827-1891), of Rock Springs, Cecil Co., married (N) probably circa 1850 and was buried in East Nottingham, PA, his wife (N) having survived him (*Midland Journal*, 25 Dec 1891)

MUMFORD

Mumford, Eliza, see Sovreign Andrews

Mumford, Mary E., see William Arrants

Mumford, Mary, see T. B. Mumford

Mumford, T. B. (born c1820, Maryland) (laborer at St. Augustine), married Sina (N) (born c1830, Maryland) probably circa 1845; daughter Mary Mumford born c1846, Maryland (1860 Cecil County Census)

MURPHY, MURPHEY

Murphy, Ann, see Hazlet Logan

Murphy, Hester Ann, see Benjamin F. Heath

Murphy, John, married Jane Lane circa 19 Oct 1837 (date of license) by Rev. Kennard (Cecil County Marriage License Book)

Murphy, John (born c1815, Maryland) (tailor at Charlestown), married Mary (N) (born c1828, Maryland) probably circa 1839; son William born c1840 (1860 Cecil County Census)

Murphy, John B., see Benjamin F. Heath

Murphy, Joseph, married Rebecca Fisher circa 23 Dec 1840 (date of license) (Cecil County Marriage License Book spelled his name Murphey)

Murphy, Lydia, see Samuel Burden

Murphy, Martha E., see Benjamin R. Meginnis

Murphy, Mary, see Andrew Weir

Murphy, Mary E., see William H. Wilson

Murphy, Nicholas, married Mary McCall circa 26 Sep 1828 (date of license) by Rev. Barratt (Cecil County Marriage License Book)

Murphy, Patrick, married Catherine Cavendar on 24 Jul 1825, after obtaining a license on 20 Jul 1825, by Rev. Epinette (Cecil County Marriage License Book; *History of Saint Francis Xavier Church and Bohemia Plantation Now Known as Old Bohemia, Warwick, Maryland*, by Joseph C. Cann (1976), p. 47)

Murphy, Rebecca, see John Grace and Joseph Ricketts

Murphy, Robert, married Elizabeth Jackson circa 14 Jan 1832 (date of license) by Rev. Goforth (Cecil County Marriage License Book)

Murphy, Thomas L. (doctor), of Baltimore, married Miss Rebecca E. Creswell, of Port Deposit, on 10 Nov 1850, after obtaining a license on 8 Nov 1850, by Rev. Lacy in Port Deposit (*Cecil Whig*, 16 Nov 1850; Cecil County Marriage License Book spelled his name Murphey)

Murphy, William, see John Murphy

MURRAY, MURREY

Murrey, Hannah, see John McIntire

Murray, James (c1810-1890), married Mary A. (N) (1813-1885) probably circa 1833 (St. Patrick's Catholic Church tombstone inscriptions)

Murray, John C. (1824-1904), married (N) probably circa 1845-1847 (Zion Presbyterian Church Cemetery tombstone inscription for "Father" John C. Murray, but no marker for his wife)

Murray, Rebecca, see (N) Scott

Murray, William, married Ann Simmons circa 27 Aug 1847 (date of their license) (Cecil County Marriage License Book spelled his name Murry)

MUSGROVE

Musgrove, William A. (dentist), of Elkton, later of Camden, NJ, married N. J. Elizabeth (N) (1807-1890) probably circa 1828 (*Midland Journal*, 19 Dec 1890, stated she died a widow in her 84th year and was the mother of Dr. Thomas H. Musgrove)

MYERS

Myers, Arrietta, see John Robert Giles, Jr.

Myers, Lucretia, see Moses Ginn

Myers, Mary Jane, see Thomas Rasin

Myers, Temperance E., see James Ford

NAFF
Naff, Joanna, see George Jones

NAIL
Nail, Mary Jane, see James Donahoo

NAUDAIN
Naudain, James S. (doctor), of New Castle Co., Delaware, married Ann E. Blackiston, of Cecil Co., circa 3 Sep 1832 (date of license) by Rev. Duke (Cecil County Marriage License Book)

Naudain, John (esquire), married Miss Mary Lockwood, daughter of Richard Lockwood, near Middletown, DE on 20 Feb 1850 (*Cecil Democrat and Farmer's Journal*, 23 Feb 1850, reported, "A bridal party, from Delaware, passed through here [Elkton] on Wednesday, on the way to Washington, where they will spend the honey-moon. On inquiry, we ascertained that the weddings had taken place that morning, at an early hour, and that the parties were Col. Joshua Clayton, to Miss Martha Lockwood; John Naudin *(sic)*, Esq., to Miss Mary Lockwood, both daughters of Richard Lockwood, Esq., near Middletown, and Mr. McCrone, to Mrs. Elizabeth Norwood, sister of Mr. Naudin *(sic)*.")

NAVY
Navy, Eleanor, see John Taylor

NEAL
Neal, Anselm W. (esquire), of Georgetown, DE, married Louisa C. W. Powell, of Talbot Co., MD, on 7 Feb 1850 by Rev. McKim (*Cecil Democrat and Farmer's Journal*, 2 Mar 1850)

Neal, Ebenezer, of Cecil Co., married Mary Ann Hudson, of Kent Co., circa 26 Apr 1849 by Rev. Wright (Kent County Marriage License Book)

Neal, Lewis W., of Talbot Co., married Henrietta George, daughter of Mathias George, Esq., of Queen Anne's Co., on 6 Jun 1850, after obtaining a license on 5 Jun 1850, by Rev. Sutherland (*Cecil Democrat and Farmer's Journal*, 15 Jun 1850; Queen Anne's County Marriage License Book, 1817-1858, listed their names as Louis W. Neel and Henrietta M. E. George and spelled the minister's name Southerland)

Neal, Thomas, married Catherine Tomlinson (c1818-1854), daughter of John Tomlinson, circa 10 Aug 1838 (date of license) by Rev. Greenbank (Cecil County Marriage License Book; *Kent News*, 19 Aug 1854)

Neal, William, married Miss Elizabeth S. Boulden, both of Cecil Co., on 19 May 1842, after obtaining a license on 18 May 1842, by Rev. Janes (Cecil County Marriage License Book; Elkton Methodist Church Register; *Cecil Whig*, 28 May 1842)

NELSON
Nelson, Henry (born c1810, Maryland) (African American) (laborer, 7th District), married Mary (N) (born c1823, Maryland) (African American) probably circa 1843; son Charles Nelson born c1844 (1860 Cecil County Census)

Nelson, William, married Sarah H. Brown, both of Harford Co., circa 17 Dec 1845 (date of license) (Cecil County Marriage License Book)

NESBITT
Nesbitt, Caroline Amelia Elizabeth, see Charles W. Benny
Nesbitt, Elizabeth M., see Samuel F. Way
Nesbitt, Henrietta Maria, see James Wilson
Nesbitt, Margaret, see Robert B. Gillespie
Nesbitt, Martha Ann, see George W. Holly
Nesbitt, Moses (1813-1895, born Maryland) (farmer in 6th District), married Mary J. (N) (1817-1890, born Maryland) probably circa 1837 (West Nottingham Cemetery tombstones; 1860 Cecil County Census)

Nesbitt, Robert Jr., married Elinor Hindman circa 20 Jun 1825 (date of license) by Rev. Magraw (Cecil County Marriage License Book)

Nesbitt, Samuel Jr., see Charles W. Benny and James Wilson

NEVILL

Nevill, Thomas, married Miss Sarah Sophia Pearce on 22 Sep 1834 by Rev. Morris. On 21 Mar 1837 Sarah Sophia Neville *(sic)*, of Cecil Co., divorced from Thomas Neville *(sic)* and she was to have custody of any children. On 26 Oct 1837 Thomas Nevill and Sarah Sophia Nevill, both of Kent Co., MD, were remarried by Rev. Humphreys. (*Cecil Gazette*, 27 Sep 1834; *Divorces and Names Changed in Maryland by Act of the Legislature, 1634-1867*, by Mary Keysor Meyer (1991), p. 66; *Cecil Courier*, 4 Nov 1837)

NEWNAM

Newnam, Susan Elizabeth, see Benjamin M. Money

NEWSOM

Newsom, Joseph, married Emily Alexander circa 4 Jun 1836 (date of license) by Rev. Potts (Cecil County Marriage License Book; DAR transcript copied in 1928 transcribed his name as Mewson)

NEWTON

Newton, Aaron B., see Robert Haines England

Newton, Arad B. (1803-1873), near Brick Meeting House, married Eliza J. (N) (1810-1881) by 1833; buried beside son Howard M. Newton, 1834-1866 (Zion Presbyterian Church Cemetery tombstone inscriptions; *Cecil Whig*, 18 Jan 1873)

Newton, Howard M., see Arad B. Newton

Newton, Sarah Ann, see Robert Haines England

Newton, Zilpha, see Robert Haines England

NIBLOCK

Niblock, John (born c1808, Maryland) (farmer in the 7th District), married Mary Jane Blakeley (born c1812, Maryland) circa 27 May 1827 (date of license) (Cecil Co. Marr. License Book; 1860 Cecil Co. Census)

Niblock, John Webb (1809-1894), married Mary T. (N) (1811-1868) probably circa 1830 (Zion Presbyterian Church Cemetery tombstone inscriptions; *Cecil Democrat and Farmer's Journal*, 1 Feb 1868)

NICHOLS

Nichols, Armina, see William Biddle

Nichols, Henry M., married Ann S. Richardson circa 1 Mar 1847 (date of license) (Cecil County Marriage License Book)

Nichols, John, married Eleanor King circa 10 Jun 1842 (date of license) (Cecil County Marr. License Book)

NICKLE, NICKEL, NICKELL

Nickle, Andrew (born c1810, Maryland) (cooper in the 8th District), married Mary E. Harlan (born c1813, Maryland) circa 12 Mar 1830 (date of license) by Rev. Magraw (Cecil County Marriage License Book spelled his name Nickle; 1860 Cecil County Census spelled his name Nickell)

Nickel, Cooley, see John Nickel

Nickel, Isabella E., see Gilbert S. Toyer

Nickel, James, married Hannah Allen circa 20 Dec 1834 (date of license) by Rev. Magraw (Cecil County Marriage License Book)

Nickel, James S. (1820-1888), married 1st to Miss Charlotte Montgomery (c1825-1852) on 8 Dec 1845 and married 2nd to Miss Sarah J. Boyd (1834-1918) on 31 May 1855; both marriages were performed in Philadelphia (*Bible Records, Genealogical Society of Cecil County*, by Gary L. Burns (1990), p. 54)

Nickle, Jane, see John Barnes

Nickel, John (born c1810, Maryland) (carpenter, 6th District), married Mary (N) (born c1825, Maryland) probably circa 1849; son Cooley Nickel born c1850 (1860 Cecil County Census spelled name Nickell)

Nickle, Samuel, married Catharine M. Porter circa 2 Apr 1828 (date of license) (Cecil County Marriage License Book)

Nickel, William, see Gilbert S. Toyer

NINDSON

Nindson, Henry, slave of Commodore Jacob Jones, married Ann (N), slave of Thomas Brockus Veazey, Esq. (1792-1844), of Sassafras Neck, on 28 Dec 1837 by Rev. Piggot (North Sassafras Parish, St. Stephen's Protestant Episcopal Church Register; *Cecil Democrat*, 13 Mar 1844)

NOBLE

Noble, Eliza, see John Walker

Noble, James, married Rebecca Lusby circa 10 Jun 1846 (date of license) (Cecil Co. Marr. License Book)

NORMAN

Norman, Stephen P. (born 1811, Lower Marion Township, Montgomery Co., PA – died 1871, Wilmington, DE), married Lydia (N) (1809-1884) probably circa 1830; buried next to Thomas E. Norman (1810-1867), Charles H. Norman (1841-1861, 8th Maryland Regiment, killed in Civil War at Laurel Hill, VA) and Howard Norman (1842-1861) (Ebenezer Methodist Church Cemetery tombstone inscriptions)

NORRIS

Norris, Catherine Maria, see Charles Hall

Norris, David U. (born c1810, Maryland) (laborer, 7th District), married Rachel A. (N) (1817-1878, born Maryland) probably circa 1838; daughter Mary Norris born c1839 (Hopewell United Methodist Church Cemetery tombstone inscriptions; 1860 Cecil County Census; *Cecil Whig*, 15 Jun 1878, stated that Mrs. Rachel Norris, aged over 60 years, died at the residence of her son-in-law John Vannort)

Norris, Mary, see David U. Norris

Norris, Otho, see Charles Hall

Norris, William, married Louisa Whitelock circa 1 Mar 1825 (date of license) by Rev. Smith (Cecil County Marriage License Book; DAR transcript copied in 1928 misspelled her name Whitlock)

NORWOOD

Norwood, Elizabeth, see John McCrone, Joshua Clayton and John Naudain

NOWLAND

Nowland, Alfred C., married 1st to Phebe Pennington circa 4 Feb 1826 (date of license) and married 2nd to Mary Amanda Biddle circa 22 Feb 1830 (date of license), both marriages were performed by Rev. Duke (Cecil County Marriage License Book)

Nowland, Ann, see John V. Price and Benoni Nowland

Nowland, Benoni (born c1805, Maryland) (farmer, Bay View), married 1st to Margaret "Peggy" Miller circa 10 Feb 1829 (date of license), by Rev. Barratt, and married 2nd to Ann (N) (1815-1891), probably Ann Crothers; Ann Nowland died 14 Jan 1891, her husband having pre-deceased her (Cecil County Marriage License Book; Rosebank Cemetery, at Calvert, tombstone inscription states "Ann, wife of Benonia *(sic)* Nowland," but there is no marker for him; *Midland Journal*, 23 Jan 1891, stated Ann C. Nowland, widow of Benoni, died in her 76th year at the home of Jonathan L. Crothers near Zion; 1860 Cecil Co. Census)

Nowland, Charles S., married Sarah Martin circa 24 Aug 1827 (date of license) (Cecil County Marriage License Book; DAR transcript copied in 1928 misspelled his name Newland)

Nowland, Ebenezer W., married Phebe Ann Smith circa 13 Feb 1840 (date of license) by Rev. Burrows (Cecil County Marriage License Book)

Nowland, Frances, see Robert Kyle

Nowland, John, married Mary Warburton circa 11 Feb 1827 (date of license) by Rev. Beem (Cecil County Marriage License Book misspelled her name as Warbutton)

Nowland, Lambert D. (merchant), married Miss Ann Maria Ford, both of Cecil Co., on 16 Dec 1830, after obtaining a license that day, by Rev. McGee (Cecil Co. Marr. License Book; *Elkton Press*, 25 Dec 1830)

Nowland, Louisa H., see Samuel W. Staples

Nowland, Alfred C., see Stephen Savin

Nowland, Norman W. (born c1823, Pennsylvania) (carpenter, 7th District), married Miss Elizabeth Melvina Arrants (born c1830, Maryland) on 28 Dec 1848, after obtaining a license on 27 Dec 1848, by Rev. Taft (Cecil County Marriage License Book; *Cecil Democrat and Farmer's Journal*, 6 Jan 1849; *Baltimore Sun*, 4 Jan 1849, listed names as Norman W. Noland and Melvina E. Arrants; 1860 Cecil County Census)

Nowland, Otho (1800-1874, born Maryland) (hotelkeeper and farmer near Brick Meeting House), married Eliza Warburton (1815-1894, born Maryland) circa 27 Nov 1834 (date of license) by Rev. Sorin (Cecil County Marriage License Book; DAR transcript copied in 1928 misspelled his first name as Otto; St. Mary Anne's Episcopal Church Cemetery tombstone inscriptions; 1860 Cecil County Census)

Nowland, William H., married Eliza Stephens circa 30 Jun 1835 (date of license) by Rev. Morrison (Cecil County Marriage License Book)

NUNNS
Nunns, Mary, see Samuel A. Smith

NUNVILLE
Nunville, Isaac, married Lydia A. Rutter circa 6 May 1841 (date of license) (Cecil Co. Marr. License Book)

OBERLANDER
Oberlander, Mary Jane, see Peter Tome

O'BRIEN
O'Brien, Sophia, see Francis Owens

O'DANIEL
O'Daniel, Ann E., see Joseph Scarborough

O'DONALD
O'Donald, Alice, see Alfred B. Thomas
O'Donald, Julia, see Henry Mallony

OLDHAM
Oldham, Absolom, married Henrietta M. White circa 20 Mar 1833 (date of license) by Rev. McCarrol, a Methodist Episcopal minister in Port Deposit (Cecil County Marriage License Book)

Oldham, Anna Maria, see William Cameron

Oldham, Biddle, see George W. Oldham

Oldham, Edward, married Elizabeth Semans circa 22 Dec 1845 (date of the license) (Cecil County Marriage License Book)

Oldham, Eliza, see Joseph Strawbridge

Oldham, George W., married Susan A. Biddle circa 29 Aug 1826 (date of license) by Rev. Duke (Cecil County Marriage License Book; *Cecil Democrat and Farmer's Journal*, 26 Oct 1850, reported their daughter Victoria, age 12, and Biddle, age 20, both died on 19 Oct 1850 of scarlet fever)

Oldham, George W. (1815-1884, born Maryland) (farmer at Zion), married Mary E. Cameron (1825-1910, born Maryland) circa 20 May 1846 (date of license) (Cecil County Marriage License Book; 1860 Cecil County Census; Zion Presbyterian Church Cemetery tombstone inscriptions)

Oldham, James C. (born c1818) (county sheriff), married Rebecca K. Lum (born c1821), of North East, on 11 May 1843, after obtaining a license on 10 May 1843, by Rev. Goentner (Cecil County Marriage License Book; 1860 Cecil County Census; *Cecil Whig*, 13 May 1843)

Oldham, John W. (born c1824, Maryland), married Mary A. E. Taylor (born c1825, Pennsylvania) circa 21 May 1847 (date of license) (Cecil County Marriage License Book; 1860 Cecil County Census)

Oldham, Mary Ann, see William Pannell

Oldham, Robert E. (born c1813, Maryland) (farmer near Principio), married Sarah A. C. White (born c1823, Maryland), daughter of Thomas White, on 1 Jun 1841, after obtaining a license on 31 May 1841, by Rev. Grace (*Cecil Gazette*, 12 Jun 1841; Cecil County Marriage License Book; DAR transcript copied in 1955 misspelled her name Whyte; 1860 Cecil County Census)

Oldham, Sarah, see John Thomas Huggins

Oldham, Sarah E., see John Fisher

Oldham, Victoria, see George W. Oldham

OLIVER

Oliver, Rachel, see William Colmerry

Oliver, Thomas Vinton (1819-1882), of Vermont, later of Elkton and Baltimore, married Caroline Sewall (born c1821, Maryland) circa 2 Nov 1846 (date of license) (Cecil County Marriage License Book; 1860 Cecil County Census; *Cecil Democrat and Farmer's Journal*, 25 Feb 1882)

Oliver, William, married Ruth Amelia Fulton circa 11 Aug 1849 (date of license) (Cecil County Marriage License Book)

O'NEAL

O'Neal, Charles, married Emily Robinson circa 6 Apr 1841 (date of license) (Cecil Co. Marr. License Book)

ONION

Onion, Caroline R., see Francis A. Foster

O'ROURKE

O'Rourke, Timothy (1820-1891), of County Tipperary, Ireland, married Alice (N) (1830-1893), of County Tipperary, Ireland, probably circa 1848-1850 (Immaculate Conception Catholic Church Cemetery, at Elkton, tombstone inscriptions)

ORR

Orr, Andrew, married Isabella Morgan circa 7 Oct 1833 (date of license) by Rev. Goforth (Cecil County Marriage License Book)

Orr, David G., married Miss Mary E. Johnson, both of Port Deposit, on 29 Nov 1849, after obtaining a license on 27 Nov 1849, by Rev. Lacey (Cecil County Marriage License Book; *Cecil Whig*, 1 Dec 1849)

Orr, Elizabeth, see Charles Buckworth

Orr, James (1819-1892, born Maryland) (plasterer, 7th District), married Caroline C. Davis (1818-1890, born Maryland) circa 23 Sep 1839 (date of license) by Rev. Wiggins; daughter Mary born c1841 (Cecil County Marriage License Book; Hopewell United Methodist Church Cemetery tombstone inscriptions; 1860 Cecil County Census)

Orr, Jane, see Robert Thompson

Orr, Mary, see James Orr and Charles B. Christie

Orr, Mary Ann, see John Baldwin

Orr, Nevin, married Isabella Galbraith circa 8 Feb 1833 (date of license) by Rev. Goforth (Cecil County Marriage License Book)

Orr, William, married Mary Ann Bailey circa 20 Mar 1848 (date of license) (Cecil Co. Marr. License Book)

OSBORN, OSBORNE

Osborn, Edward L., of Kent Co., married 1st to Ann Farrow, of Kent Co., circa 30 Nov 1840 by Rev. Pierson and married 2nd to Christiana J. Hall, of Cecil Co., circa 2 Sep 1844 by Rev. Price (Kent County Marriage License Book)

Osborne, Theodore, married Adaliza White circa 4 Aug 1836 (date of license) by Rev. Megredy (Cecil County Marriage License Book; DAR transcript copied in 1928 mistakenly listed his name as Thos. Osborne and questionably listed her name as "Adalina? White")

OWEN

Owen, Charles W. (doctor), of Baltimore, married Laura W. Conard, daughter of Judge Conard, on 5 Jun 1849, after obtaining a license on 2 Jun 1849, by Rev. McIntire (Cecil County Marriage License Book; *Cecil Whig*, 9 Jun 1849)

Owen, Jane G., see John Wesley Tomlinson

Own, Thomas G., see John Wesley Tomlinson

OWENS

Owens, Ambrose B. (born c1820, Maryland) (farmer near Brick Meeting House), married Margaret (N) (born c1822, Maryland) probably circa 1843; daughter Jane born c1844 (1860 Cecil County Census)

Owens, Amelia, see William Brumfield

Owens, Amelia Sophia, see John C. L. Hunter

Owens, Annet, see Robert Richie

Owens, Caroline, see Ebenezer Alden, Jr.

Owens, Charlotte, see John Benjamin

Owens, Elizabeth E., see William Gibson

Owens, Francis, married Sophia O'Brien circa 3 Jun 1826 (date of license) by Rev. Reynolds (Cecil County Marriage License Book)

Owens, Hazlett, married Adeline J. Benjamin circa 29 Jul 1833 (date of license) by Rev. Griffith (Cecil County Marriage License Book)

Owens, James, married Anna Maria Kinkead circa 1 May 1849 (date of license) (Cecil County Marriage License Book)

Owens, Jane, see Ambrose B. Owens

Owens, John (1809-1878) (Justice of the Peace at Elkton), married Martha Jane Black (1816-1865) circa 25 Nov 1835 (date of license) by Rev. Finney (Cecil County Marriage License Book; West Nottingham Cemetery tombstone inscriptions; 1860 Cecil County Census mistakenly stated he was age 47 and she was age 35; *Cecil Whig*, 2 Feb 1878, stated a John Owens, son of the late Capt. Jonas Owens, of Cecil Co., died in his 66th year at this residence in Baltimore)

Owens, John Thomas (born c1827) (railroad manager near Charlestown), married Mary E. Jackson (born c1830) circa 23 Dec 1850 (date of license); daughter Octavia Owens born 1851 (Cecil County Marriage License Book; 1860 Cecil County Census)

Owens, Jonas, see John Owens

Owens, Martha, see James Kirkpatrick

Owens, Mary, see Thomas S. Abrams

Owens, Nancy, see Samuel Boreland

Owens, Octavia, see John Thomas Owens

Owens, Sarah Ann, see Joseph McMullen

Owens, Sarah, see James Carter

OWL

Owl, Leven (born c1820) (African American) (laborer in the 7th District), married Harriet (N) (born c1822) (African American) probably circa 1844; daughter Maria Owl born c1845 (1860 Cecil County Census)

PACKER

Packer, William L. (1822-1888), married Annie A. (N) (1824-1900) probably circa 1845 (Zion Methodist Cemetery tombstone inscriptions)

PANNELL

Pannell, William, married Mary Ann Oldham circa 29 Nov 1827 (date of license) (Cecil County Marriage License Book)

Pannell, William, married Sarah Maffitt circa 21 Dec 1831 (date of license) by Rev. Barratt (Cecil County Marriage License Book)

PANTRY

Pantry, John, married Mary Jane Patterson circa 30 Jan 1830 (date of license) by Rev. King (Cecil County Marriage License Book)

Pantry, Mary S., see Francis King

PARADEE

Paradee, C. (born c1825, Delaware) (farmer at Port Herman), married Harriet (N) (born c1823, Delaware) probably circa 1847; daughter Ann born c1848, Maryland, son William born c1849, Delaware, daughter Clara born c1856, Maryland, and daughter Kate born c1859, Maryland (1860 Cecil County Census)

PARCELL

Parcell, Judyth, see George Grady

PARKER

Parker, Charles (1811-1893), married Elizabeth Cosner (1810-1856) probably circa 1833; buried beside Henry S. Parker, 1835-1867 (Zion Presbyterian Cemetery tombstone inscriptions)

Parker, Charles (1809-1869), married Harriet Carter (1805-1892) circa 18 Jun 1828 (date of license) by Rev. Barratt (Cecil County Marriage License Book; Cherry Hill Methodist Church Cemetery tombstone inscriptions)

Parker, Charles, see Stephen John Brown

Parker, Frances Ann, see James P. Carter

Parker, Henry S., see Charles Parker

Parker, William (1814-1896), married Lydia A. (N) (1814-1850) probably circa 1835 (Hopewell United Methodist Church Cemetery tombstone inscriptions)

PARKINSON

Parkinson, Elizabeth, see Miles Birch

PARKS

Parks, George, married Sophia Moore circa 3 Nov 1846 (date of license) (Cecil County Marr. License Book)

PARROTT

Parrott, Aaron, married Harriet Boyd circa 8 Jun 1848 (date of license) (Cecil County Marr. License Book)

Parrott, Benjamin, married Miss Mary Rebecca Bowers, both of Kent Co., MD, on 18 Dec 1832, after obtaining a license on 10 Dec 1832, by Rev. Jones (*Cecil Republican*, 22 Dec 1832; Kent County Marriage License Book)

Parrott, William, married Miss Elizabeth Boyd, both of Cecil Co., on 10 Jan 1850, after obtaining a license that same day, by Rev. Arthur at North East (*Cecil Whig*, 19 Jan 1850; Cecil County Marriage License Book; DAR transcript copied in 1955 mistakenly listed the marriage license date as 10 Jan 1852; *Cecil Democrat and Farmer's Journal*, 19 Jan 1850)

PARTRIDGE

Partridge, John (1810-1898), married Mary (N) (1808-1890) probably circa 1831-1833 (Elkton Cemetery tombstone inscriptions)

PASS

Pass, Isaac (1803-1882, born Pennsylvania) (wheelwright at Elkton), of Cecil Co., later of Wilmington, DE, married Anna Maria (N) (1808-1908, born Maryland) probably circa 1830 (St. John's Church Cemetery, at Lewisville, tombstone inscriptions; *Cecil Democrat and Farmer's Journal*, 25 Mar 1882, obituary stated he died Wilmington in his 79th year; 1860 Cecil County Census); see Lewis McCormick, *q.v.*

Pass, Rebecca Ellen, see Lewis McCormick

PASSMORE

Passmore, Andrew Moore, see Enoch Mortimer Bye

Passmore, Phebe, see Daniel Stubbs

Passmore, Phebe Pusey, see Enoch Mortimer Bye

PATTERSON

Patterson, Alexander (born c1825) (laborer at Cecilton), married Sophia Walmsley (born c1823), daughter of (N) and Ann Walmsley (born c1797) circa 22 Dec 1846 (date of license); daughter Ann Patterson born c1851 (Cecil County Marriage License Book)

Patterson, Amelia Ann, see Robert James Duhamell

Patterson, Ann, see Alexander Patterson

Patterson, Callendar (1801-1863), married Leah (N) (c1809-1865) probably circa 1830 (Patterson Family Cemetery tombstone inscriptions)

Patterson, Elizabeth, see Thomas Knotts

Patterson, Elizabeth C., see Abraham Frist

Patterson, Jesse, see Nicholes L. Harden

Patterson, Mary Jane, see John Pantry

Patterson, Sarah, see Nicholes L. Harden and Francis Boyd

PATTON, PATTEN

Patton, Ann, see Lewis Jones

Patton, Eleanor, see Madison Rowland

Patten, John P. (1806-1884), married Esther (N) (1805-1866) circa 1826; they are buried beside their son William Thompson Patten, Lt., USN (1827-1861), daughter Martha Jane Patten (1833-1907), son Thomas Hugh Patten (1840-1921), and daughter Mary Elizabeth Patten (1842-1864) (West Nottingham Cemetery tombstone inscriptions)

Patten, Mary, see John S. Everist

Patton, Sarah, see John Steel

PAXSON

Paxson, Isaac and Maria J., see Reuben Reynolds

PAYNTER

Paynter, Rebecca, see John Wilkins

PEACH

Peach, John Jr., of Bohemia Manor, son of John and Margaret Peach (1770-1853), of Mill Creek Hundred, New Castle Co., DE, married Eliza Y. (N) (1816-1849) probably circa 1835 (*Delaware Gazette*, 27 Apr 1849 and 19 Apr 1853)

PEACO

Peaco, Mary Ann, see James Boddy

PEACOCK

Peacock, Mr., see Samuel Perry

PEARCE

Pearce, Amelia Margaret, see John D. Turner

Pearce, Andrew, married Catharine Heath circa 24 May 1845 (date of license) (Cecil Co. Marr. Lic. Book)

Pearce, Caroline J., see Benjamin B. Chambers

Pearce, Charles H. (born c1823, Delaware) (laborer at Bohemian Mills), married Sarah (N) (born c1822, Delaware) probably circa 1844; daughter Sarah born c1845, Maryland (1860 Cecil County Census)

Pearce, Charlotte, see Joseph Williams

Pearce, Clarissa Jane, see James Boulden

Pearce, Davidson D., married Eliza M. (N) (1809-1887) probably circa 1830 (Elkton Cemetery tombstone inscription)

Pearce, Edward, married Rachel Burke circa 21 Dec 1829 (date of license) by Rev. Barratt (Cecil County Marriage License Book)

Pearce, Edward, married Ann Clarke circa 9 Dec 1843 (date of license) (Cecil County Marr. License Book)

Pearce, Emma J., see Eugene D. K. Richardson

Pearce, George D., see George R. Pearce

Pearce, George R., see Eugene D. K. Richardson

Pearce, George R., married Julia Ann Ward circa 17 Oct 1829 (date of license) by Rev. Sitgreaves, a Protestant Episcopal minister in Sassafras Parish (Cecil County Marriage License Book)

Pearce, George R. (born c1816, Delaware) (farmer at Cecilton), married Elizabeth (N) (born c1819, Delaware) circa 1844; son George D. Pearce born c1845 (1860 Cecil County Census)

Pearce, Henry, see Joshua B. Pearce and Thomas Pearce

Pearce, John H., married Miss Elizabeth Stapleford, both of Cecil Co., on 1 Aug 1843, after obtaining a license on 31 Jul 1843, by Rev. Shields in Elkton (Cecil County Marriage License Book; Elkton Methodist Church Register, p. 140; *Cecil Whig*, 5 Aug 1843)

Pearce, Joshua B. (born c1821) (farmer near Chesapeake City), married Mary (N) (born c1826) probably circa 1847; son Henry born c1848 (1860 Cecil County Census)

Pearce, Mary Ann, see John Denny

Pearce, Mary L., see Abraham Taylor

Pearce, Matthew Carroll (1805-1881) (captain), son of Matthew Pearce and Mary Reed, married Eliza Jeannette Groome (1805-1866), daughter of the late Dr. John Groome and Elizabeth (Black) Wallace, of Elkton, at the residence of Col. Thomas W. Veazey on 13 Dec 1831, after obtaining a license on 12 Dec 1831, by Rev. Rees (*Baltimore American and Commercial Daily Advertiser*, 3 Jan 1832; Cecil County Marriage License Book listed her name as Eliza Jane; *Portrait and Biographical Record of Harford and Cecil Counties, Maryland* (1897, repr. 1989), p. 237, listed her name as Eliza Jeannette; St. Stephen's Episcopal Church Cemetery tombstone inscriptions spelled her name Elizabeth Jennett; *Cecil Whig*, 8 Sep 1866, obituary listed her name as Eliza J. Pearce, wife of Capt. M. C. Pearce)

Pearce, Rebecca, see Peregrine Hendrickson

Pearce, Sarah, see Charles H. Pearce

Pearce, Sarah Sophia, see Thomas Nevill

Pearce, Thomas (born c1829) (butcher at Cecilton), married Augusta (N) (born c1830) circa 1849; son Henry C. Pearce born c1850 (1860 Cecil County Census)

Pearce, also see Peirce

192

PEARSON

Pearson, Eli, married Elizabeth Foster circa 25 Oct 1837 (date of license) by Rev. Barratt (Cecil County Marriage License Book)

Pearson, Peter, married Rebecca Simpers circa 28 Dec 1831 (date of license) by Rev. Griffith (Cecil County Marriage License Book)

Pearson, Temperance, see John Campbell

Pearson, also see Pierson

PECKARD

Peckard, Henry L., married Miss Mary Cann, both of Christiana Bridge, DE, on 20 Jan 1829 by Rev. Gilbert (*Elkton Press*, 7 Feb 1829)

PENNINGTON

Pennington, Abraham F., married Elizabeth Reed on 28 May 1825, after obtaining a license on 27 May 1825, by Rev. Epinette (Cecil County Marriage License Book; *History of Saint Francis Xavier Church and Bohemia Plantation Now Known as Old Bohemia, Warwick, Maryland*, by Joseph C. Cann (1976), p. 47)

Pennington, Amelia, see William Simmons Wood

Pennington, Daniel (born c1821) (farmer at Cecilton), married Elizabeth (N) (born c1817) circa 1846; daughter Mary Pennington born c1847 (1860 Cecil County Census)

Pennington, Edward H., formerly of Cecil Co., married Ann E. Riley, of Baltimore, on 18 Jan 1849 at North Point by Rev. Bend (*Cecil Democrat and Farmer's Journal*, 27 Jan 1849; *Baltimore Sun*, 20 Jan 1849)

Pennington, George B. (1813-1878), of Middle Neck, married Sarah Flintham (born c1810) circa 10 Dec 1836 (date of license) by Rev. Duke; son William C. Pennington born c1838 (Cecil County Marriage License Book; 1860 Cecil County Census; *Cecil Whig*, 16 Feb 1878)

Pennington, Henrietta, see Joseph Hackett

Pennington, James, married Caroline Davis circa 26 Feb 1826 (date of license) by Rev. Smith (Cecil County Marriage License Book)

Pennington, John, married Jane Mitchell circa 2 Mar 1835 (date of license) by Rev. Spry (Cecil County Marriage License Book)

Pennington, John B., married Ann Mercer on 2 Oct 1838, after obtaining a license that same day, by Rev. Hagany (Cecil County Marriage License Book; Elkton Methodist Church Register, p. 139)

Pennington, Joshua, of Cecil Co., married Rachel Jane Moore, of Kent Co., circa 4 Jan 1844 by Rev. Foulks (Kent County Marriage License Book spelled her name More)

Pennington, Letitia A., see Thomas Pryor

Pennington, Mary, see William Keathly and Daniel Pennington

Pennington, Noble (1802-1858), married Henrietta E. Morgan (1810-1852) circa 11 Jan 1831 (date of their license) by Rev. Duke (Cecil County Marriage License Book; St. Stephen's Episcopal Church Cemetery tombstone inscriptions)

Pennington, Perry (born c1817, Maryland) (farmer at Cecilton), married Sarah A. (N) (born c1817, Delaware) circa 1840 (1860 Cecil County Census did not list any Pennington children)

Pennington, Phebe, see Alfred C. Nowland

Pennington, Rebecca, see Joseph Biggs

Pennington, Robert, married Mary Seagers circa 14 Feb 1833 (date of license) by Rev. Benson (Cecil County Marriage License Book)

Pennington, Sarah, see Hugh Boyd

Pennington, Sarah Jane, see William Rutter

Pennington, Susan, see Arthur Morrison

Pennington, William C., see George B. Pennington

PENNOCK

Pennock, Ann, see Elisha H. Rogers

Pennock, Joseph, married Phoebe Ann Ferguson circa 14 Mar 1839 (date of license) by Rev. Miller (Cecil County Marriage License Book)

PENSEL
Pensel, Frederick, married Catharine M. (N) (c1814-1864) probably circa 1834 and she died by drowning in her 50th year (*Cecil Whig*, 11 Jun 1864)

PEOPLES
Peoples, Hannah M., see Robert Rawlings

Peoples, William (1820-1881), married Martha (N) (1824-1882) probably circa 1845 (West Nottingham Cemetery tombstone inscriptions)

PEREGOY
Peregoy, Louisa H., of Cecil Co., divorced from Nathan W. Peregoy on 6 Mar 1847 and she was to have custody of their child (*Divorces and Names Changed in Maryland by Act of the Legislature, 1634-1867*, by Mary Keysor Meyer (1991), p. 69)

PERKINS
Perkins, Frances A., see George Biddle

Perkins, George W. T., married Caroline Chambers, youngest daughter of E. F. Chambers, of Chestertown, MD, on 28 Aug 1849 by Rev. Jones at Chestertown (*Cecil Democrat and Farmer's Journal*, 1 Sep 1849)

Perkins, John D., see George Biddle

Perkins, Phoenix (born c1820) (African American) (farmer at Cecilton), married Sarah A. (N) (born c1832) (African American) circa 1843; daughter Eliza Perkins born c1844 (1860 Cecil County Census)

Perkins, William C., of Delaware, married Susannah A. Price circa 28 Oct 1850 (date of license) (Cecil County Marriage License Book)

PERRE
Perre, Mary, see Samuel Cummings

PERRY
Perry, Ebenezer (1800-1858), married Margaret (N) (1810-1853) probably circa 1830 (Cherry Hill Methodist Church Cemetery tombstone inscriptions)

Perry, Emeline, see David Mackey

Perry, Emily, see Christopher Price

Perry, Helen, see Philip Daugherty

Perry, Isabella, see John Perry

Perry, John (1796-1866) (carriage maker at Elkton), married Jane (N) (1804-1872) probably circa 1825; daughter Isabella Perry born c1830 (St. John's Church Cemetery, at Lewisville, tombstone inscriptions; 1860 Cecil County Census stated he was aged 62 and she was aged 50, both born in Maryland)

Perry, Melinda, see William Rock

Perry, S. Cloud (1818-1884), married Sarah (N) (1820-1901) probably circa 1839-1840 (St. John's Church Cemetery, at Lewisville, tombstone inscriptions)

Perry, Samuel, married Miss Susan Giberson, both of Cecil Co., on 2 Nov 1830, after obtaining a license that same day, by Rev. Hodgson at Mr. Peacock's in Elkton (*Elkton Press*, 6 Nov 1830; Cecil County Marriage License Book; DAR transcript copied in 1928 misspelled the minister's name as Hodson; Francis Hodgson was a Methodist Episcopal minister in Elkton at that time)

Perry, Sophia, see John McCrery

PETERMAN

Peterman, Benjamin F. (1803-1884), married Mary M. (N) (1808-1879) probably circa 1826-1830 (Leeds Methodist Church Cemetery tombstone inscriptions)

PETERS

Peters, Harry (born c1822, Pennsylvania) (African American) (laborer, 8th District), married Susan (N) (born c1820, Maryland) (African American) probably circa 1843; eldest daughter Hannah Peters born c1844, Maryland, and their other children were also born in Maryland (1860 Cecil County Census)

PETERSON

Peterson, George H. (1810-1891, born Delaware) (farmer near Fair Hill), married Delia A. (N) (1821-1891, born Delaware) probably circa 1842-1843; daughter Sarah born c1844, Maryland (Cherry Hill Methodist Church Cemetery tombstone inscriptions; *Midland Journal*, 13 Feb 1891; 1860 Cecil County Census)

Peterson, Lydia, see Tobias Peterson and William McClay

Peterson, Tobias (born c1814, Maryland) (farmer near Elkton), married Sarah (N) (born c1816, Maryland) probably circa 1839; daughter Lydia Peterson born c1840 (1860 Cecil County Census)

PHILLIPS

Phillips, Ann, see Richard Moore

Phillips, Elizabeth, see George Moore

Phillips, Ellis C. (1820-1862, born Pennsylvania) (blacksmith, 6th District), married Nancy S. (N) (1820-1862, born Maryland) probably circa 1843; daughter Nancy born c1844, Maryland (Ebenezer Church Cemetery tombstone inscriptions; 1860 Cecil County Census)

Phillips, Isaac J., married Miss Maria Fulton, both being of Cecil Co., on 3 May 1827 by Rev. Peckworth (*Delaware Gazette*, 8 May 1827, spelled his name Philips)

Phillips, Mary E., see Samuel Evans

Phillips, Mary Jane, see John Ewing

Phillips, Nancy, see Ellis C. Phillips

Phillips, Rachel, see John White

Phillips, Samuel, married Susan Thomas circa 8 Nov 1837 (date of license) by Rev. Barratt (Cecil County Marriage License Book)

Phillips, Thomas L., married Ann Jane Dennison circa 26 Sep 1849 (date of license) (Cecil County Marriage License Book; DAR transcript copied in 1955 mistakenly gave the marriage license date as 6 Sep 1849)

Philips, William, married Mary Smith circa 4 Apr 1833 (date of license) by Rev. Magraw (Cecil County Marriage License Book)

PHOEBUS

Phoebus, John W. and Virginia C., see James A. Massey

PHOUNS

Phouns, Louisa, see Ebenezer Dill

PHYSICK

Physick, Adriana, see Lyttleton Physick

Physick, Ann Elizabeth, see Lyttleton Physick

Physick, Edmund, married Miss Sarah Black circa 24 Mar 1837 (date of license) by Rev. Potts (Cecil County Marriage License Book)

Physick, Henry Lyttleton, see Lyttleton Physick

Physick, Henry White, see Lyttleton Physick

Physick, Lyttleton (c1815-1844), son of Henry White Physick and Adriana Haynes (whose families had Philadelphia and Delaware and Cecil County connections), married Evelina Franklin (c1820-1878, born

Alabama) probably circa 1837; daughter Ann Elizabeth Physick (c1838-1864), son Henry Lyttleton Physick (1839-1883), and daughter Adriana "Addie" Physick (c1844-1891), were all born in Maryland (St. Mark's Episcopal Church tombstone inscriptions; 1860 Cecil County Census also listed Hannah Physick, age 70, born Pennsylvania, and Adrianna Physick, age 58, born Maryland, in the household of "Mrs. Eveline Physic," age 40, born Alabama, plus a William Farr, age 18, who was born in Ireland)

Physick, William, married Rebecca Whitelock circa 13 May 1837 (date of license) by Rev. Grace (Cecil County Marriage License Book)

PICKERING

Pickering, Benjamin F. (1818-1853), married Elinor M. (N) (1824-1893) probably circa 1842; buried next to Charles W. Pickering, 1825-1894 (Rosebank Cemetery, at Calvert, tombstone inscriptions)

PIER

Pier, Ann, see William Frederick Howard

PIERCE

Pierce, John (born c1822, Delaware) (pumpmaker at Cecilton), married Mary J. (N) (born c1824, Delaware) circa 1848; daughter Mary F. Pierce born c1849, Delaware (1860 Cecil County Census)

Pierce, Mary, see John Pierce

Pierce, Thomas, of Cecil Co., married Miss Sarah Ann Clark, of Elm Grove near New Castle, DE, on 4 Mar 1828 by Rev. Prestman at Elm Grove (*Delaware Gazette*, 7 Mar 1828)

Pierce, William H. (born c1820) (tailor at Cecilton), married Millaminty Morgan (born c 1826) circa 23 Oct 1843 (date of license); daughter Mary Jane born c1847 (Cecil County Marriage License Book; 1860 Cecil County Census listed their names as Wm. H. Pearce and Mille Minta Pearce)

Pierce, also see Pearce

PIERSON

Pierson, Adaline J., see Joseph Pierson

Pierson, Amos (1806-1850), married Ruhana E. (N) (1810-1879) by 1832; buried beside daughter Elizabeth W. Pierson (1833-1856) who married John L. Galloway and their son Amos P. Galloway died at age 5 months, no dates given (Rosebank Cemetery, at Calvert, tombstone inscriptions)

Pierson, Cloud (1819-1907, born Delaware) (blacksmith near Brick Meeting House), married Rebecca (N) (1818-1890, born Delaware) probably circa 1840s and moved to Cecil County between 1856 and 1860 (Rosebank Cemetery, at Calvert, tombstone inscriptions; 1860 Cecil County Census)

Pierson, Elizabeth W., see Amos Pierson

Pierson, Ann M., see James S. Crawford

Pierson, Jesse (born c1813) (plasterer in Elkton), married Beulah Ann Tyson (born c1823), both of Cecil Co., on 5 Jun 1845, after obtaining a license on 4 Jun 1845, by Rev. McIntire (*Cecil Whig*, 14 Jun 1845; Cecil County Marriage License Book listed her as Bulia Ann Tyson; 1860 Cecil County Census spelled her name Bula A. Pierson)

Pierson, John W. (reverend), of the Philadelphia Annual Conference, married Sally Eliza Boon, daughter of James Boon, of Kent Co., MD, on 11 Apr 1839 by Rev. Scott in Philadelphia at Ebenezer Church (*Cecil Gazette*, 20 Apr 1839)

Pierson, Joseph (1796-1871), married Ruth (N) (1805-1882) before 1830; buried beside their daughters Sarah C. Pierson, 1831-1853, and Adaline J. Pierson, 1840-1853 (Rosebank Cemetery, at Calvert, tombstone inscriptions)

Pierson, Moses R. (born c1820, Maryland) (farmer, 6th District), married Mary (N) (born c1824, Maryland) probably circa 1841; daughter Sarah born c1842 (1860 Cecil County Census)

Pierson, Sarah, see Moses R. Pierson

Pierson, Sarah C., see Joseph Pierson

Pierson, also see Pearson

PINER

Piner, Ann M., see James M. Beaston

Piner, Louisa H., see Joseph Price

PINKNEY

Pinkney, Anna Maria and William, see James Morsell Sewall

PITT

Pitt, John B., married Eliza Mackey circa 9 Nov 1826 (date of license) by Rev. Graham (Cecil County Marriage License Book)

PLATTENBURGH

Plattenburgh, Alfred W., of Wheeling, [West] Virginia, married Miss Elizabeth A. McKinsey, formerly of Elkton, on 10 Sep 1846 by Rev. Kenney (*Cecil Whig*, 10 Oct 1846)

PLUCK

Pluck, Margaret A., see John Markee

Pluck, Mary, see Thomas Hempfield

Pluck, Mary R., see Benjamin Loumier

Pluck, Rebecca, see Thomas Hempfield

Pluck, Stephen, married Mary Ann Scott circa 2 Oct 1845 (date of license) (Cecil County Marriage License Book)

PLUMMER

Plummer, John T., married Rosette Simmons circa 26 Mar 1847 (date of license) (Cecil County Marriage License Book)

Plummer, Philip C. (born c1810, Delaware) (farmer near Chesapeake City), married Mary E. Robinson (1811-1878, born Maryland) circa 12 Feb 1835 (date of license) by Rev. Morris (Cecil County Marriage License Book; Elkton Cemetery tombstone inscription; 1860 Cecil County Census)

Plummer, Rebecca, see Isaac C. Bouchell

Plummer, Rebecca T., see Elias Rhodes

Plummer, Richardson, married Susan Ann Coulson circa 12 Mar 1834 (date of license) by Rev. Duke (Cecil County Marriage License Book)

Plummer, Sarah Jane, see Samuel Harris

Plummer, Susan Ann, see Peter R. Wright

POE

Poe, Eliza, see William Tyson

Poe, Rebecca, see Thomas Poe

Poe, Thomas (born c1826, Maryland) (miller at North East), married Miss Ann Eliza Thomas (born c1832, Maryland) circa 8 Sep 1847 (date of license); daughter Rebecca Poe born c1849 (Cecil County Marriage License Book; 1860 Cecil County Census)

POGUE

Pogue, Mary, see Robert Alerton

POINSETT

Poinsett, Elizabeth, see George Simcoe

PONDER

Ponder (Pouder?), Julianna, see Charles T. (F.?) Cloud

POOLE

Poole, John J., married Rebecca Biddle circa 23 Jun 1840 (date of license) (Cecil Co. Marr. License Book)

POPE

Pope, Rachel, see John Meredith

POPLAR

Poplar, Georgeanna, see Joseph Stebbing

PORTER

Porter, Benjamin, see William Ferguson
Porter, Catharine (Catherine), see Samuel Nickle and Thomas Fulton
Porter, Hannah, see Lemuel Hudson
Porter, Henrietta Mary, see William Ferguson
Porter, James L., see James Evans
Porter, Jane Arbuckle, see James Evans
Porter, Sarah Jane, see George Black Giles

POSTILL

Postill, James, married Miss Sarah Savin, both of Cecil Co., on 22 Aug 1843, after obtaining a license that same day, by Rev. McIntire (Cecil County Marriage License Book; *Cecil Whig*, 26 Aug 1843)

POTTER

Potter, Edward, married Elizabeth Reynolds (1803-1885), daughter of Elisha Reynolds, on 11 Sep 1832 (*Joseph England and his Descendants*, by C. Walter England, Ph.D., 1975, p. 66)
Potter, Zebdial W. (c1825-1855) (colonel), of Caroline Co., married Miss Caroline "Carrie" Stephens, only daughter of Samuel H. Stephens, Esq., of Cecil Co., at *Oakland Hall* on 2 May 1848, after obtaining a license on 29 Apr 1848, by Rev. Bell (*Cecil Whig*, 13 May 1848; Cecil County Marriage License Book; DAR transcript copied in 1955 mistakenly listed his name with no middle initial; *Kent News*, 7 Apr 1855)

POTTS

Potts, Adam L., see W. W. Potts
Potts, Emma, see W. W. Potts
Potts, Jacob, see W. W. Potts
Potts, James, see Thomas Jefferson Potts
Potts, Margaret, see W. W. Potts
Potts, Mary Ann, see Jacob Holden
Potts, Thomas Jefferson (1798-1877), youngest son of Major James Potts and Sarah Wesselly of Philadelphia Co., PA, married Margaret Carter (1813-1874) in 1835 and resided in Highland Township, Chester Co., PA (*Cecil Whig*, 21 Nov 1874 and 3 Nov 1877)
Potts, W. W. (born c1827, Pennsylvania) (carpenter at South Milford), married Mary (N) (born c1832, Maryland) circa 1849; son Jacob born c1850, Pennsylvania, son William born c1851 Pennsylvania, son Adam L. born c1855, Maryland, daughter Margaret born circa 1857, Maryland, and daughter Emma born c1859, Maryland (1860 Cecil County Census)
Potts, William, see W. W. Potts

POUDER

Pouder (Ponder?), Julianna, see Charles T. (F.?) Cloud

198

POWELL

Powell, Elias, married Elizabeth Cornish circa 12 Dec 1846 (date of license) (Cecil Co. Marr. License Book)

Powell, Louisa C. W., see Anselm W. Neal

Powell, Mary, see Samuel Powell

Powell, Samuel (born c1822, New Brunswick) (engineer at Chesapeake City), married Mary (N) (born c1830, Massachusetts) probably circa 1848-1849; daughter Mary Powell was born circa 1850, Maryland (1860 Cecil County Census)

POWLEY

Powley, John E., married Esther Haines circa 19 Mar 1830 (date of license) by Rev. Ayres (Cecil County Marriage License Book)

PRESTON

Preston, Amos (1810-1875), of near Colora, married Ruth Hannah (N) (1817-1909) probably circa 1835 (Friends Cemetery, at Harrisville, tombstone inscriptions; *Cecil Whig*, 4 Sep 1875)

Preston, Catherine, see Peter Ersembrey

Preston, Elizabeth, see Franklin Cook

Preston family, see Thomas P. King

Preston, Jonas, see Franklin Cook

Preston, Philena, see Franklin Cook

PRICE

Price, Adaline, see James L. Houston

Price, Alexander, see William H. Price

Price, Ann, see Andrew Jackson Vandegrift, Hebron Benson, Samuel Cray and Thomas Reese

Price, Anna Maria, see William M. A. S. Maxwell

Price, Anna W., see Jeremiah C. Price

Price, Benjamin, see James L. Houston and James Canby, Jr.

Price, Benjamin B. (1819-1901, born Maryland), married Matilda Soulnier (1816-1877, born Pennsylvania) circa 11 Jan 1841 (date of license); son Fredus Price born c1842, Maryland (Cecil County Marriage License Book spelled her name Sollenair; 1860 Cecil County Census; St. Stephen's Episcopal Church Cemetery tombstone inscriptions spelled her name Soulnier)

Price, Catherine, see James Merritt

Price, Christopher, married Emily Perry circa 22 Dec 1836 (date of license) by Rev. Wooley (Cecil County Marriage License Book)

Price, David E., see William H. Gilpin

Price, David K., married Miss Mary Ann Mulholland on 21 Sep 1848, after obtaining a license on 20 Sep 1848, on Sassafras Neck (Cecil County Marriage License Book; *Cecil Democrat and Farmer's Journal*, 23 Sep 1848)

Price, Edward, see Levy Price

Price, Eliza Ann, see William W. Wilson

Price, Elizabeth, see Henry Carman and Robert Faulkner

Price, Ellen E., see Jeremiah C. Price

Price, Eugene, see Jeremiah C. Price

Price, Fredus, see Benjamin B. Price

Price, Fredus A., see Jeremiah C. Price

Price, George, see William H. Price

Price, Hannah, see David Staats

Price, Henrietta E., see Samuel Severson

Price, Hyland, see John Savin

Price, Jacob, see James McCauley

Price, Jacob, married Martha Wilson circa 15 Jun 1831 (date of license) by Rev. Duke (Cecil County Marriage License Book)

Price, James, see William H. Price

Price, James (born c1822) (merchant at Cecilton), married Ellen H. Hessey (born c1829) circa 1 May 1850 (date of license) (Cecil County Marriage License Book; 1860 Cecil County Census)

Price, James H., married Miss Leah Ann Currier, both of Cecil Co., on 19 Jun 1845 by Rev. James Reid in Baltimore (*Cecil Whig*, 21 Jun 1845, *Baltimore Sun*, 20 Jun 1845)

Price, Jeremiah C. (born c1821) (farmer at Cecilton), married Ellen E. Price (c1826-1864) circa 11 Jan 1845 (date of license) and she died at Sassafras Neck in her 38th year (Cecil County Marriage License Book; *Cecil Whig*, 27 Aug 1864; *Portrait and Biographical Record of Harford and Cecil Counties, Maryland* (1897, repr. 1989), p. 362, stated they had ten children, but only four were living in 1897, namely, Eugene, Anna W., Fredus A., and Jeremiah C. Price, Jr. (born 7 May 1852); 1860 Cecil County Census listed his name as J. R. C. Price)

Price, John, see Thomas Price

Price, John, of Christiana, DE, married Miss Jane Underwood, of Cecil Co., on 27 Apr 1826 in Wilmington (*Delaware Gazette*, 9 May 1826)

Price, John H. (1804-1884), married Deborah Conlyn (1808-1888) circa 31 Mar 1828 (date of license) (Cecil County Marriage License Book; DAR transcript copied in 1928 misspelled her name Canlyn; St. Stephen's Episcopal Church Cemetery tombstone inscriptions)

Price, John N., see John V. Price

Price, John R., married Miss Rachel R. Walmsley on 11 Nov 1828, after obtaining a license that same day, by Rev. Barratt at Robert C. Lusby's in Elkton (Cecil County Marriage License Book; *Elkton Press*, 18 Nov 1828)

Price, John V., married Ann K. Nowland on 15 Feb 1825, after obtaining a license on 14 Feb 1825, by Rev. Epinette (Cecil County Marriage License Book; *Portrait and Biographical Record of Harford and Cecil Counties, Maryland* (1897, repr. 1989), p. 347, listed their children as Thomas, Susanna, Margaret C. (born 10 Mar 1839) and John N. Price (died before 1897; *History of Saint Francis Xavier Church and Bohemia Plantation Now Known as Old Bohemia, Warwick, Maryland*, by Joseph C. Cann (1976), p. 47)

Price, John V. (born c1820) (farmer at Cecilton), married Mary A. (N) (born c1813) circa 1841; son George H. Price born c1842 (1860 Cecil County Census)

Price, Joseph (born c1817, Maryland) (farmer near Bohemian Mills), married Louisa H. Piner (c1818-1877), of Kent Co., circa 20 Feb 1844 by Rev. Price (Kent County Marriage License Book; 1860 Cecil County Census listed no children; *Cecil Whig*, 29 Dec 1877, reported Louisa died at Warwick, aged about 60)

Price, Levy (born c1821) (African American) (laborer at Chesapeake City), married Elizabeth (N) (born c1825) (African American) probably circa 1845; son Edward born c1846 (1860 Cecil County Census)

Price, Lewis, married Salina Carman circa 22 Sep 1829 (date of license) by Rev. King (Cecil County Marriage License Book; see Samuel Hall, *q.v.*)

Price, Lilburn, married Mary E. Cannon circa 19 Nov 1834 (date of license) by Rev. Davis (Cecil County Marriage License Book; DAR transcript copied in 1928 mistakenly spelled his name Albun)

Price, Margaret, see George Landers

Price, Margaret Ann, see Thomas Price and William H. Gilpin

Price, Margaret C., see John V. Price

Price, Martha R., see Benjamin R. Handy

Price, Mary, see George W. Black and Harrison S. Bullen

Price, Mary E., see Samuel Hall

Price, Mary Jane, see William Bradford

Price, Mary V., see William H. Price

Price, Mary W., see Ellis Jones

Price, Matilda, see James Canby, Jr.

Price, Millicent R., see James McCauley

Price, Morgan, married Harriet Veazey circa 19 May 1828 (date of license) (Cecil Co. Marr. License Book)

Price, Rebecca, see John Caldwell, Peregrine F. Lloyd, Jacob J. Howell and Thomas W. Brown

Price, Robert, married Araminta Coffin circa 24 Jan 1831 (date of license) by Rev. Duke (Cecil County Marriage License Book)

Price, Sarah Ellen, see Peter Bouchell

Price, Susan, see James Whitelock

Price, Susanna, see John V. Price

Price, Susannah A., see William C. Perkins

Price, Thomas, see John V. Price

Price, Thomas (born c1804, Delaware) (laborer at Chesapeake City), married Margaret Ann Price (born c1813, Delaware) circa 28 Dec 1833 (date of license) by Rev. Duke (Cecil County Marriage License Book; 1860 Cecil County Census)

Price, Thomas (born c1824, Maryland) (farmer at Cecilton), married Sarah (N) (born c1826, Delaware) circa 1846; son John Price born c1847 (1860 Cecil County Census)

Price, William, married Temperance King circa 10 Dec 1832 (date of license) by Rev. Duke (Cecil County Marriage License Book)

Price, William B., married Elizabeth Stephens, both of Cecil Co., circa 10 Feb 1834 by Rev. Jones (Kent County Marriage License Book)

Price, William H. (born c1823, Maryland) (farmer at Cecilton), married Mary (N) (born c1833, England) circa 1850; son Alexander Price born c1851, Kansas, son James Price born c1853, Mexico, son George Price born c1747, Mexico, and daughter Mary V. Price, born 1859, Maryland (1860 Cecil Co. Census)

PRITCHARD

Pritchard, James, married Frances R. Simpson circa 13 Apr 1846 (date of license) (Cecil County Marriage License Book)

Pritchard, James, married Mary Johnston circa 4 Dec 1827 (date of license) (Cecil Co. Marr. License Book)

PROCTOR

Proctor, James, married Rebecca Hedney circa 14 Feb 1826 (date of license) by Rev. Duke (Cecil County Marriage License Book)

PRYOR, PRIOR

Pryor, Elizabeth, see William Simpers

Prior, John W. (born c1820, Maryland) (laborer at North East), married Rutha Gray (born c1819, Maryland) circa 30 Dec 1840 (date of license) (Cecil County Marriage License Book; 1860 Cecil County Census spelled their names John and Ruth Pryor)

Prior, Rachel, see David E. Lockard

Pryor, Thomas, married Letitia A. Pennington circa 24 Dec 1847 (date of license) (Cecil County Marriage License Book)

Pryor, William Henry, married Ann Gray circa 13 Jan 1830 (date of license) by Rev. Barratt (Cecil County Marriage License Book)

PUFFREE

Puffree (Tuffree?), John, married Mary Ann Maria Cropper circa 26 Sep 1835 (date of license) by Rev. Wilson (Cecil County Marriage License Book)

Puffree (Tuffree?), Joseph, married Mary Ann Woolston circa 4 Jul 1835 (date of license) by Rev. Smith (Cecil County Marriage License Book)

PUGH

Pugh, Amos (1798-1885), son of Jesse and Elizabeth Pugh, the latter deceased, of East Nottingham Township, Chester Co., PA, married 1st to Elizabeth Sidwell (1801-1838), daughter of Job and Sarah

Sidwell, of the same place, on the 21st day of the 10th month 1825 at East Nottingham Meeting House and married 2nd to Mary Ann Bye (born 1809), daughter of Amos and Deborah Bye, of East Nottingham Township, Chester Co., PA, on the 19th day of the 4th month 1843 at Little Elk Meeting House (*Births, Deaths and Marriages of the Nottingham Quakers, 1680-1899*, by Alice L. Beard (1989), pp. 23, 74, 75, 99, 221, 225)

Pugh, Elizabeth, see Amos Pugh and Joel T. Bailey

Pugh, Hannah, see William Moore

Pugh, James (born c1821, Maryland) (captain at North East), married Mary Ann Slagle (born c1822, Maryland) circa 9 Jan 1846 (date of license) (Cecil County Marriage License Book; 1860 Cecil County Census spelled his name Pue)

Pugh, Jesse, see Amos Pugh and Joel T. Bailey

PURNELL

Purnell, Caroline, see Robert E. Hogg

Purnell, Catharine, see Alexander Greenwood

Purnell, Greenberry, married Mary Megredy circa 22 Dec 1835 (date of license) by Rev. Houston (Cecil County Marriage License Book; DAR transcript copied in 1928 misspelled his name Gueensberry)

Purnell, Henry (born c1822) (African American) (laborer at Chesapeake City), married Fanny (N) (born c1825) (African American) probably circa 1850 and in 1860 Laura White, born c1851, Mary Cotton, born c1820, and George Cotton, born c1850 (all African Americans) were enumerated in his household (1860 Cecil County Census)

Purnell, James S., of Elkton, married Miss Susan B. Hamm, of Kent Co., DE, on 29 Sep 1835 by Rev. Durborah (*Delaware Gazette*, 6 Oct 1835)

Purnell, L. H. (born c1820, Maryland) (Justice of the Peace at Elkton), married Harriet (N) (born c1827, New Jersey) circa 1846; son William K. Purnell born c1847, Pennsylvania (1860 Cecil County Census)

Purnell, William K., see L. H. Purnell

PUSEY

Pusey, Samuel, of Drumore Township, Lancaster Co., PA, son of Joshua and Mary Pusey, of London Grove, Chester Co., PA, married Mrs. Sarah Clement (died 1873), of East Nottingham Hundred, Cecil Co., MD, later of Wilmington, DE, widow of Thomas Clement and daughter of Levi and Rachel Hopper, of Deptford Township, Gloucester Co., NJ, on the 5th day of the 2nd month 1841 at East Nottingham (*Births, Deaths and Marriages of the Nottingham Quakers, 1680-1899*, by Alice L. Beard (1989), pp. 29, 225)

PYLE

Pyle, Joseph H. (1803-1878, born Pennsylvania) (miller near Brick Meeting House), married Miss Milcah E. "Milkey" (N) (1812-1896, born Maryland) probably circa 1833 (daughter Sophia Pyle born 8th day of the 10th month 1834) (Brick Meeting House, at Calvert, tombstone inscriptions; 1860 Cecil County Census; *Cecil Whig*, 16 Mar 1878)

Pyle, Priscilla Ann, see Samuel Slicer

Pyle, Rachel, see Daniel Brown

Pyle, Samuel, see Daniel Brown

Pyle, Sophia, see Joseph H. Pyle

QUARLL

Quarll, Lydia, see Andrew Harvey

QUEIN

Quein, Robert (1820-1904, born Pennsylvania) (shoemaker at Elkton), married Emeline (N) (1824-1876, born Pennsylvania) probably circa 1843; son Amos Quein born c1844 (Sharp's Cemetery tombstone inscriptions; *Cecil Whig*, 12 Feb 1876; 1860 Cecil County Census spelled his name Queen)

QUINLAN

Quinlan, Charity, see German McClure

RADLEY

Radley, William, married Margaret E. Haines circa 25 Jul 1842 (date of license) (Cecil County Marriage License Book)

RAFE

Rafe, Margaret E., see Samuel Woodrow

RAFFERTY

Rafferty, John, married Ellen Ennis circa 29 Dec 1849 (date of license) (Cecil County Marr. License Book)

RAISIN

Raisin, August, married Louisa Frederick circa 16 Mar 1848 (date of license) (Cecil County Marriage License Book)

Raisin, James, married Mary Jane Robinson circa 13 Oct 1835 (date of license) by Rev. Morrison (Cecil County Marriage License Book)

Raisin, also see Rasin

RALSTON

Ralston, Carlotta, see John Wright

RAMSEY

Ramsey, Amy Ann, see Nicholas Milburn

Ramsey, Andrew, married Mary Thompson circa 29 Dec 1825 (date of license) by Rev. Magraw (Cecil County Marriage License Book)

Ramsey, Hannah M., see Stephen Atkinson

Ramsey, Harriet, see William W. Tipton

Ramsey, Hugh, of Chester Co., PA, married Miss Rachel Lynch, of Cecil Co., on 8 Feb 1838 by Rev. ---- [blank space] (*Cecil Gazette*, 17 Feb 1838)

Ramsey, John, married Hannah Ginna circa 12 Feb 1834 (date of license) by Rev. Magraw (Cecil County Marriage License Book)

Ramsey, Jefferson (born c1810, Virginia) (farmer, 7th District), married Marion (N) (born c1820, Maryland) probably circa 1836; daughter Marion Ramsey born c1837 (1860 Cecil County Census)

Ramsey, Joseph England (born 1816, Maryland) (carpenter, 6th District), son of William Ramsey and Sarah Reynolds, of West Nottingham, married Miss Frances Abigail Clark (born c1825, Maryland), also of Cecil Co., on 25 Nov 1841, after obtaining a license that same day, by Rev. Goldsborough (*Cecil Whig*, 27 Nov 1841; Cecil County Marriage License Book; 1860 Cecil County Census; *Joseph England and his Descendants*, by C. Walter England, Ph.D., 1975, p. 67)

Ramsey, Margaret, see Robert Lutton

Ramsey, Marion, see Jefferson Ramsey

Ramsey, Rebecca Jane, see Warner Reynolds Ramsey

Ramsey, Warner Reynolds, son of William Ramsey and Sarah Reynolds, of West Nottingham, married Rebecca Jane Burgoyne circa 12 Aug 1848 (date of license) (Cecil County Marriage License Book; *Joseph England and his Descendants*, by C. Walter England, Ph.D., 1975, p. 67, states they married on the 12th day of the 8th month 1848) Rebecca Jane Ramsey was named in the will of Thomas Richardson in 1861, but no relationship was given (Cecil County Will Book C, No. 10, p. 521)

Ramsey, William, see Nicholas Milburn, Joseph England Ramsey, William Thomas Ramsey, Warner Reynolds Ramsey and Stephen Atkinson

Ramsey, William Thomas (born 1818), son of William Ramsey and Sarah Reynolds, of West Nottingham, married Patty Mahanny or Mahoney circa 17 Mar 1841 (date of license) (Cecil County Marriage License Book spelled her name Mahanny; *Joseph England and his Descendants*, by C. Walter England, Ph.D., 1975, p. 67, gave her name as Betty Mahaney)

RANKIN

Rankin, John A. (1802-1897), married Caroline Baker (1808-1891) probably circa 1826 and she died at Elkton in her 83rd year (Elkton Presbyterian Church Cemetery tombstone inscriptions; *Midland Journal*, 24 Apr 1891)

Rankin, William W., married Mary Armstrong circa 23 May 1844 (date of license) (Cecil County Marriage License Book)

RARICK

Rarick, John, married Margery Wilson circa 1 May 1828 (date of license) (Cecil Co. Marr. License Book)

RASIN

Rasin, Edward F. (doctor), of Millington, Kent Co., MD, married Janette R. Turner (c1810-1842), of Baltimore, on 10 Apr 1839 by J. Roach, Esq., Mayor of Philadelphia (*Cecil Gazette*, 20 Apr 1839, spelled her name Jannet R. Turner; *Baltimore Sun*, 11 Jul 1842, spelled her name Janette T. Raisin)

Rasin, Thomas, of Kent Co., married Mary Jane Myers, of Cecil Co., circa 17 Sep 1842 by Rev. Houston (Kent County Marriage License Book)

Rasin, also see Raisin

RAWLINGS

Rawlings, Francis Marion (1819-1900), married Adaline G. Hanshaw (1824-1904) probably circa 1844 (Hopewell United Methodist Church Cemetery tombstone inscriptions)

Rawlings, John M., see Robert Rawlings

Rawlings, Robert (farmer), son of John Rawlings, married Mary McVey circa 1840 and had five children, all were living in 1897, namely, Elizabeth Brown, John M. Rawlings (born 1844), Z. Taylor Rawlings (born 1848), Hannah M. Peoples and Roberta E. Boyle (*Portrait and Biographical Record of Harford and Cecil Counties, Maryland* (1897, repr. 1989), pp. 303, 455)

Rawlings, Z. Taylor, see Robert Rawlings

REA

Rea, David (1809-1885) (slater and farmer), of Bangor, County Down, Ireland, later of New York City, New Orleans and Cecil Co., married Miss Mary Graham (1822-1904), daughter of Robert Graham of Scotland and later of New York City, in 1838 (*Portrait and Biographical Record of Harford and Cecil Counties, Maryland* (1897, repr. 1989), p. 469, did not give the exact date of marriage; West Nottingham Cemetery tombstone inscriptions)

Rea, Edwin, see James S. Rea

Rea, James S. (1817-1896, born Maryland) (mason in the 6th District), married Emma K. (N) (1826-1919, born Pennsylvania) probably circa 1842; son Edwin Rea born c1843, Pennsylvania (West Nottingham Cemetery tombstone inscriptions; 1860 Cecil County Census misspelled the surname as Ray)

READ

Read, Margaret, see Thomas R. McMullen

Read, also see Reed

REARDON

Reardon, Helen J. and Lambert, see William C. Scott

REASIN

Reasin, William H., of Baltimore, married Miss Hannah E. Cole, of Harford Co., on 11 Jun 1850 by Rev. Brindal in Cambridge, Dorchester Co. (*Cecil Democrat and Farmer's Journal*, 22 Jun 1850; *Baltimore Sun*, 14 Jun 1850)

REBEN

Reben, Joseph (born c1815, Maryland) (African American mulatto), of Chesapeake City, married Eliza (N) (born c1820, Maryland) (African American mulatto) probably circa 1837; son Joseph Reben, Jr. born c1838 (African American black) (1860 Cecil County Census)

REDGRAVES

Redgraves, Martha Ann, see Thomas Sturgeon

Redgraves, Samuel, married Ann Elizabeth Colley (or Culley?) circa 19 Jan 1839 (date of license) by Rev. Smith (Cecil County Marriage License Book spelled her name Colley; DAR transcript copied in 1928 misspelled his name Reagraves and her name Colley)

REED

Reed, Benjamin, married Rebecca Harrington circa 31 Jan 1838 (date of license) by Rev. Piggot, a Protestant Episcopal minister in North Sassafras (Cecil County Marriage License Book)

Reed, Caleb, of Kent Co., MD, married Julia Ann Cox, of Cecil Co., MD, circa 20 Jun 1832 (date of license) by Rev. Duke (Cecil County Marriage License Book)

Reed, Elizabeth, see Abraham F. Pennington

Reed, Emily, see Jeremiah Mahoney

Reed, George, married Ann Biddle circa 2 Dec 1828 (date of license) by Rev. Hodskie (Cecil County Marriage License Book)

Reed, Joseph Taggard (1821-1902), married Isabella Ann Russell (1826-1918) circa 26 Mar 1849 (date of license) (Cecil Co. Marr. License Book; Shelemiah Methodist Church Cemetery tombstone inscriptions)

Reed, Mary, see William Edwards and Matthew Carroll Pearce

Reed, Samuel (born c1811, Pennsylvania) (carpenter in the 6th District), married Louisa (N) (born c1812, Pennsylvania) probably circa 1835; daughter Susan born c1846, Maryland (1860 Cecil County Census)

Reed, Sarah, see Samuel Logan

Reed, Sarah Ann, see Isaac Walker

Reed, Susan, see Samuel Reed

Reed, Thomas S. (born c1802, Delaware) (laborer at Elkton), married Mahala Morris (born c1807, Maryland) circa 8 Jul 1833 (date of license) by Rev. Barratt (Cecil County Marriage License Book; 1860 Cecil County Census)

Reed, Waldon (c1825-1864), of near South Milford, married Miss Louisa Jane Armstrong (1829-1864), on 8 Jun 1848, after obtaining a license that same day, by Rev. Elliott in Elkton (Cecil County Marriage License Book; DAR transcript copied in 1955 mistakenly listed his name as Haldon Read; Cecil County Will Book D, No. 11, page 135; *Cecil Democrat and Farmer's Journal*, 10 Jun 1848, spelled his name Walden Read; *Cecil Whig*, 16 Apr 1864, 7 May 1864, reported he died about three weeks after his wife)

Reed, William, married Mary White circa 26 Nov 1830 (date of license) by Rev. Duke (Cecil County Marriage License Book)

Reed, William, married Rebecca Lusby circa 28 Dec 1835 (date of license) by Rev. Morrison (Cecil County Marriage License Book)

Reed, William, married Amy McVey circa 12 Sep 1836 (date of license) by Rev. Lane (Cecil County Marriage License Book)

REEDER

Reeder, Christian V. (1817-1880), married Martha C. (N) (1815-1880) probably circa 1840 (Rosebank Cemetery, at Calvert, tombstone inscriptions)

Reeder, Josiah (1819-1898), married Elizabeth J. (N) (1815-1903) probably circa 1837 (daughter Sarah E. Reeder, 1838-1890) (Rosebank Cemetery, at Calvert, tombstone inscriptions)

Reeder, Morris, see William H. Reeder

Reeder, William H. (born c1822, Pennsylvania) (farmer, Bay View), married Margaret E. (N) (born c1830, Maryland) probably circa 1850; son Morris Reeder born c1851, Maryland (1860 Cecil County Census)

REES

Rees, John R., of Pennsylvania, later of Cecil Co., married Anna E. Sevil circa 1838 and had three children, namely, Thomas A. (born 25 Sep 1839), John R. (died before 1897), and William (*Portrait and Biographical Record of Harford and Cecil Counties, Maryland* (1897, repr. 1989), pp. 306-307)

REESE

Reese, Elizabeth, see James McCauley

Reese, Levi R. (reverend), of the Maryland Conference of the Methodist Protestant Church, married Miss Tamsey A. Hughlett, eldest daughter of the late Col. William Hughlett, of Talbot Co., on 6 Nov 1849 at Easton by Rev. McLean (*Cecil Democrat and Farmer's Journal*, 10 Nov 1849)

Reese, Oliver A., married Mary Ann Hickman, daughter of T. Hickman, Esq., all of Chester Co., PA, on 15 Mar 1849, after obtaining a license that same day, by Rev. Goldsborough in Trinity Church (Cecil County Marriage License Book; *Cecil Whig*, 17 Mar 1849; *Cecil Democrat and Farmer's Journal*, 17 Mar 1849)

Reese, Rosetta, see William T. Reese

Reese, Sarah, see George W. Cannon

Reese, Thomas, married Ann Price circa 20 Aug 1828 (date of license) by Rev. Duke (Cecil County Marriage License Book)

Reese, William T. (born c1815, Delaware) (farmer near Chesapeake City), married Miss E. A. Bullock (born 1832, Pennsylvania), later of Wilmington, DE, on 19 Feb 1848 by Rev. Billop, of New Castle Co., DE; daughter Rosetta born c1850, Maryland (*Cecil Whig*, 11 Mar 1848; *Delaware Gazette*, 14 Mar 1848; 1860 Cecil County Census listed her name as Hester, but most probably it could have been Esther)

REGISTER

Register, Walter (Wharton?) (born c1812, Delaware) (laborer at Cecilton), married Susan Ann Spence (born c1817, Maryland) circa 11 Feb 1839 (date of license) by Rev. Piggot, a Protestant Episcopal minister in North Sassafras (Cecil County Marriage License Book is unclear, but the DAR transcript copied in 1928 spelled his first name Wharton; 1860 Cecil County Census listed Walter Register as head of household)

REILY, REILLY

Reily, James H., married Cassy Mercer circa 14 Sep 1833 (date of license) by Rev. McKenney, a Protestant Episcopal minister in North Sassafras (Cecil County Marriage License Book)

Reilly, Mary Ann, see Edward Hackett

REISLING

Reisling, Francis T., married Martha Dennison circa 9 Sep 1845 (date of license) (Cecil County Marriage License Book)

REYNOLDS

Reynolds, Adrianna, see Alexander Kirk

Reynolds, Ann C., see Henry Reynolds

Reynolds, Benjamin, see John D. Thompson

Reynolds, Benjamin, married Alsey Johnson circa 8 Feb 1826 (date of license) by Rev. Sharpley (Cecil County Marriage License Book)

Reynolds, Benjamin F., married Elizabeth H. Slagle circa 7 Jan 1850 (date of license) (Cecil County Marriage License Book)

Reynolds, Caleb, married Mary Simpson circa 25 Jun 1833 (date of license) by Rev. Duke (Cecil County Marriage License Book)

Reynolds, Catherine, see John D. Thompson

Reynolds, David, see Haines Reynolds

Reynolds, Delia Jane, see Thaddeus Beaks

Reynolds, Edith, see Henry Reynolds

Reynolds, Elisha (1783-1843), of Rising Sun, later of Union Co., OH, married 1st to Mary Witter (1781-1828) circa 1801 and married 2nd to Sophia Burnham in 1829 (*Joseph England and his Descendants*, by C. Walter England, Ph.D., 1975, p. 66); see Joseph Carter, James H. Irwin and Edward Potter, *q.v.*

Reynolds, Elisha B., see John King

Reynolds, Eliza, see Moor Morton

Reynolds, Elizabeth, see John King, Henry Reynolds, Edward Potter and Samuel Haines

Reynolds, Elmira S., see William O. Towson

Reynolds, Esther, see John King and John Reynolds

Reynolds, Francina, see William Alexander

Reynolds, Haines (born c1801, Maryland) (miller, 6th District), married Pheby (N) (born c1812, Maryland), probably circa 1831; son David Reynolds born c1832 (1860 Cecil County Census); see Henry Reynolds

Reynolds, Hannah E., see Robert Gerry

Reynolds, Henry (1813-1889) (farmer near Rising Sun), son of Jonathan Reynolds and Elizabeth Haines, the latter deceased, of West Nottingham Hundred, Cecil Co., married Eliza P. Moore (1815-1885), daughter of David Moore and Sarah Chambers, of Rowlandsville, Octorara Hundred, Cecil Co., on the 18th day of the 4th month 1839 at Octorara Meeting House. Among the witnesses were John C. Reynolds, Edith Reynolds, Henry J. Reynolds, Anna C. Reynolds, Jane Reynolds, Jonathan Reynolds, Mary P. Reynolds, Haines Reynolds, Phebe Reynolds, William H. Reynolds, Samuel L. Reynolds, Isaac S. Reynolds, Mary Elena Moore, William Moore, Mary Moore, Sarah Moore, Mary Ann Moore, Sarah Jane Moore and Charlotte Moore. (*Births, Deaths and Marriages of the Nottingham Quakers, 1680-1899*, by Alice L. Beard (1989), pp. 88, 224; Friends Cemetery, at Harrisville, tombstone inscriptions; *Joseph England and his Descendants*, by C. Walter England, Ph.D., 1975, p. 92; 1860 Cecil County Census)

Reynolds, Henry J., see Henry Reynolds

Reynolds, Henry K., married Ann E. Davidson circa 8 Oct 1838 (date of license) by Rev. Kennard (Cecil County Marriage License Book)

Reynolds, Hetty, see Francis Gordon

Reynolds, Isaac (1799-1882) (farmer and cattle dealer near Rising Sun), son of Jonathan Reynolds and Elizabeth Haines, married Mira Haines (1805-1870), daughter of Eli Haines and Elizabeth Brown, on 2nd day of 4th month 1826 (*Joseph England and his Descendants*, by C. Walter England, Ph.D., 1975, p. 91)

Reynolds, Isaac G., married Sarah Ann Tredaway circa 16 Sep 1841 (date of license) (Cecil County Marriage License Book)

Reynolds, Isaac S., see Henry Reynolds

Reynolds, Isabella, see George W. Smith

Reynolds, Israel (1809-1891) (farmer near Elkton), married Miss Elizabeth Mearns (1822-1868), both of Cecil Co., on 30 May 1844, after obtaining a license on 29 May 1844, by Rev. DeWitt (*Cecil Whig*, 8 Jun 1844; Cecil County Marriage License Book; Rosebank Cemetery, at Calvert, tombstone inscriptions; *Cecil Democrat and Farmer's Journal*, 21 Mar 1868; *Midland Journal*, 6 Mar 1891, stated he died at the residence of his son Taylor T. Reynolds at Blue Ball; 1860 Cecil County Census)

Reynolds, Jacob, see Alexander Kirk, John King and John Reynolds

Reynolds, James R., married Jane Moore circa 28 May 1832 (date of license) by Rev. Duke (Cecil County Marriage License Book)

Reynolds, Jane, see Henry Reynolds

Reynolds, Joel, married Eliza (N) (1819-1855), possibly Eliza Taylor, probably circa 1840 (Taylor Family Cemetery tombstone inscription at *Taylor's Venture* for Eliza Reynolds)

Reynolds, John, son of Jacob and Esther Reynolds, married Margaret Woods, daughter of Thomas and Elizabeth Woods, on 29 Oct 1832 (*Bible Records, Genealogical Society of Cecil County*, by Gary L. Burns (1990), p. 70, states they were Quakers)

Reynolds, John C., see Henry Reynolds

Reynolds, John T. (1826-1900), married Elizabeth W. (N) (1826-1906) probably circa 1847-1850 (West Nottingham Cemetery tombstone inscriptions)

Reynolds, Jonathan, see Samuel Haines, Isaac Reynolds, Reuben Reynolds and Henry Reynolds

Reynolds, Joseph J., see (N) Reynolds

Reynolds, Leonard, see William O. Towson

Reynolds, Louisa M., see William Alexander

Reynolds, Lydia Ann, see Watson Fell

Reynolds, Maria M., see George H. Galbraith

Reynolds, Mary, see James H. Irwin

Reynolds, Mary Ann, see Levi Todd

Reynolds, Mary Eliza, see Samuel Haines

Reynolds, Mary P., see Henry Reynolds

Reynolds, Phebe (Pheby), see Henry Reynolds and Samuel Reynolds

Reynolds, Rachel, see John King and William Reynolds

Reynolds, Rebecca, see (N) Reynolds and Justus Alexander

Reynolds, Reuben (1805-1875) (farmer near Rising Sun), son of Jonathan Reynolds and Elizabeth Haines, married 1st to Amelia (N) probably circa 1830 (Thomas Reynolds, 1832-1857, son of Reuben and Amelia Reynolds, is buried in Rosebank Cemetery, at Calvert) and Reuben married 2nd to Maria J. Paxson (1812-1890), daughter of Isaac Paxson and Rachel Bye, on 28 Mar 1850 (Friends Cemetery, at Harrisville, tombstone inscriptions; *Cecil Whig*, 13 Feb 1875; *Joseph England and his Descendants*, by C. Walter England, Ph.D., 1975, p. 91)

Reynolds, Samuel (1815-1890, born Maryland) (laborer, 6th District), married Susan (N) (1821-1901, born Maryland) before 1849; daughter Pheby Reynolds born c1850 (Mount Pleasant United Methodist Church Cemetery tombstone inscriptions; 1860 Cecil County Census)

Reynolds, Samuel L., see Henry Reynolds

Reynolds, Sarah, see Joseph England Ramsey, Warner Reynolds Ramsey and William Thomas Ramsey

Reynolds, Sarah Ann, see Joseph Carter and Samuel Campbell

Reynolds, Stephen (1798-1872), son of Jacob and Esther Reynolds, married Mary Love (1806-1890), daughter of Samuel and Catherine Love, on 7 Jun 1842 (*Bible Records, Genealogical Society of Cecil County*, by Gary L. Burns (1990), p. 71, stated the Reynolds were Quakers)

Reynolds, Susan Marie, see Joseph W. Abrahams

Reynolds, Taylor T., see Israel Reynolds

Reynolds, Thomas, see Reuben Reynolds

Reynolds, William, see William Alexander

Reynolds, William (born Maryland, waterman at North East), married Martha Jane Slagle (born Maryland) circa 23 Jul 1845 (date of license) (Cecil County Marriage License Book; 1860 Cecil County Census stated they were both age 30, thus they were married at age 15; daughter Rachel was born in 1846)

Reynolds, William B., married Phebe Ann (N) probably circa 1845; their daughter Ann Louisa Reynolds died at Cochranville on 18 Apr 1850, aged 3 years and 5 months (*Cecil Democrat and Farmer's Journal*, 27 Apr 1850)

Reynolds, (N), married Rebecca (N) probably circa 1830 (*Midland Journal*, 25 Apr 1890, stated Rebecca Reynolds, over age 80, died at the residence of her son Joseph J. Reynolds on Stone Run near Rising Sun)

RHOADS, RHODES

Rhoads, Caroline, see James May

Rhodes, Elias, married Rebecca T. Plummer circa 18 Feb 1847 (date of license) by Rev. Storks (Cecil County Marriage License Book; Elkton Methodist Church Register, p. 141, gave the year of marriage, but not the date; *Cecil Whig*, 18 Mar 1876, reported Elias Rhoades died at Chesapeake City, no age given)

RIALE

Riale, Joseph S. (1811-1875, born Pennsylvania) (hotelkeeper near Brick Meeting House), married Hannah J. (N) (1807-1885, born Pennsylvania) probably circa 1835 and moved to Cecil County between 1850 and 1860; daughter Margaret Riale born c1836 (1860 Cecil County Census; Rosebank Cemetery, at Calvert, tombstone inscriptions state "Mother" and "Father" and they are buried next to their daughter Phoebe C. Riale (1850-1875), whose marker is inscribed "Sister")

RICHARDS

Richards, Joanna, see (N) Jackson

Richards, John (born c1813, Delaware) (Cecilton innkeeper), married Martha A. (N) (born c1817, Maryland) circa 1840; son Henry born c1841 (1860 Cecil County Census)

Richards, Stephen (born c1820, Maryland) (farmer in the 6th District), married Rebecca (N) (born c1825, Pennsylvania) probably circa 1845; son Vincent Richards born c1846, Maryland (1860 Cecil Co. Census)

Richards, Thomas, see (N) Jackson

Richards, Vincent, see Stephen Richards

Richards, William, married Louise Jane Bayard circa 13 Nov 1834 (date of license) by Rev. Duke (Cecil County Marriage License Book)

RICHARDSON

Richardson, Ann S., see Henry M. Nichols

Richardson, Armstrong (1812-1872), married Rachel M. (N) (1818-1860) probably circa 1840 (Harmony Chapel tombstone inscriptions)

Richardson, Caroline M., see John B. Graham

Richardson, Eugene D. K. (esquire), of Denton, MD, married Emma J. Pearce, daughter of the late Dr. George R. Pearce, of Sassafras Neck, Cecil Co., on 22 May 1849, after obtaining a license on 14 May 1849, by Rev. Wiley (Cecil County Marriage License Book listed her name as Miss Emma J. Pierce; *Cecil Whig*, 9 Jun 1849; *Cecil Democrat and Farmer's Journal*, 9 Jun 1849)

Richardson, Henry, see John B. Graham

Richardson, Henry, married May Moore circa 4 Jul 1835 (date of license) by Rev. Magraw (Cecil County Marriage License Book; DAR transcript copied in 1928 mistakenly listed his name as Henry Richards)

Richardson, John, see Wakeman Richardson

Richardson, John, married Jane Logan circa 14 Jan 1834 (date of license) by Rev. Duke (Cecil County Marriage License Book)

Richardson, John Washington, married Agnes Jackson circa 2 Sep 1839 (date of license) by Rev. Grace (Cecil County Marriage License Book; DAR transcript copied in 1928 mistakenly listed his name as George Wash. Richardson)

Richardson, Joseph (born c1824) (carpenter in the 6th District), married Margaret McCullough (born c1827) circa 1850; son Davis H. Richardson born in 1851 (*Portrait and Biographical Record of Harford and Cecil Counties, Maryland* (1897, repr. 1989), p. 574; 1860 Cecil County Census)

Richardson, Joshua, married Mary Ann Scott circa 1 May 1832 (date of license) by Rev. Duke (Cecil County Marriage License Book)

Richardson, Mary, see James Wesley Devaule (Duaule?) and John Ward

Richardson, Mary Ann, see William Girvin and James McIntyre

Richardson, Rachel, see William Lowery

Richardson, Thomas, see Warner Reynolds Ramsey

Richardson, Wakeman (born c1827, Maryland) (laborer in the 6th District), married Louisa (N) (born c1829, Maryland) probably circa 1849; son John Richardson born c1850, Maryland (1860 Cecil County Census)

Richardson, William (1813-1882), married Mary Jane Gerry (1815-1902) probably circa 1835 (West Nottingham Cemetery tombstone inscriptions)

Richardson, William, married Jane Calvert circa 24 Jul 1838 (date of license) by Rev. Kennard (Cecil County Marriage License Book)

Richardson, William T. (1821-1909, born Maryland) (merchant at Charlestown), married Mary Hogg (1820-1858), both of Cecil Co., on 8 Feb 1846, after obtaining a license on 28 Jan 1846, by Rev. Humphries (*Cecil Whig*, 14 Feb 1846; Cecil County Marriage License Book; Charlestown Cemetery tombstone inscriptions; 1860 Cecil County Census abstract mistakenly listed his name as W. F. Richardson)

Richardson, (N), married Augustena (N) (1800-1878) probably circa 1820-1825 (*Cecil Whig*, 23 Feb 1878, stated Mrs. Augustena Richardson died in her 78th year at North East)

RICHIE

Richie, Robert, married Annet Owens circa 29 Nov 1831 (date of license) by Rev. Magraw (Cecil County Marriage License Book; DAR transcript copied in 1928 mistakenly stated he was of New York State, but that information applied to the preceding marriage in the license book)

RICKARD

Rickard, Ann M., see Isaac Cordray

Rickard, Mills M., married Mary Money circa 5 Mar 1835 (date of license) by Rev. Duke (Cecil County Marriage License Book; DAR transcript copied in 1928 mistakenly listed her name as Stoney)

RICKETTS

Ricketts, John T. (esquire), of Fairfax Co., VA, married Susan L. Watson, daughter of Thomas Watson, Esq., of Philadelphia, on 7 May 1833 by Rev. Brantley in Philadelphia (*Cecil Republican*, 18 May 1833)

Ricketts, Joseph, married Rebecca Murphy circa 31 May 1831 (date of license) by Rev. Smith (Cecil County Marriage License Book)

Ricketts, Margaret, see Henry H. Gilpin

Ricketts, Mills M., married Frances Ruley circa 14 Feb 1844 (date of license) (Cecil Co. Marr. Lic. Book)

Ricketts, Rebecca, see Thomas H. Young

Ricketts, Sarah Jane, see Hiram McCullough

Ricketts, Susan, see Arthur Clendenin

Ricketts, William, see Hiram McCullough

Ricketts, William H., see Thomas H. Young

RIDDELL

Riddell, Anna E., see George I. Smith

Riddell, John, of William, married Rachel Ewing circa 14 May 1839 by Rev. Hoopman (Cecil County Marriage License Book)

RIDDLE

Riddle, Emily, see Elijah Falls

Riddle, John, see Levy Riddle

Riddle, John, married Eliza Jane Todd circa 19 Mar 1841 (date of license) (Cecil Co. Marr. License Book)

Riddle, Levy (born c1810, Maryland) (laborer at Bay View), married Mary (N) (born c1820, Maryland) probably circa 1845; son John Riddle born c1846 (1860 Cecil County Census)

Riddle, Margaret, see William Biddle

Riddle, Susanna, see John C. Williams

Riddle, Umphrey, married Rachel Crouch circa 29 Mar 1827 (date of license) (Cecil County Marriage License Book)

Riddle, Uphrey, married Mary Thompson circa 1 Jan 1825 (date of license) by Rev. Griffith (Cecil County Marriage License Book; DAR transcript copied in 1928 misspelled his name Umphres Biddle)

RIDER

Rider (Ryder), Rachel Jane, see George Bostick

Rider, Susan, see William Crow

Rider, William, married Rachel Davis circa 13 Oct 1828 (date of license) by Rev. Goforth (Cecil County Marriage License Book)

RIDGELY

Ridgely, Alfred G., of Washington, DC, married Beaulah H. Bromwell, of Cecil Co., on 10 Apr 1849, after obtaining a license on 7 Apr 1849, by Rev. Burrowes (Cecil County Marriage License Book spelled his name Ridgley and misspelled her name as Bullah H. Broomwell; *Cecil Democrat and Farmer's Journal*, 14 Apr 1849)

Ridgely, Ann, see Charles J. DuPont

Ridgely, Henry M., see Charles J. DuPont

RIELEY

Rieley, Michael, married Amelia Haway(?) circa 31 May 1827 (date of license) (Cecil County Marriage License Book was unclear as to the spelling of her last name and there appears to have been a first name (with the middle name being Amelia) for her as well, but it is also illegible)

RIKER

Riker, Elizabeth, see Thomas Kennard

Riker, Mary Ann, see Benjamin McElwee (McIlvee?, McWee?)

RILEY

Riley, Ann E., see Edward H. Pennington

RING

Ring, Sarah, see Andrew Kidd

RINGOLD, RINGGOLD

Ringold, Georgeanna, see Thomas Ringold

Ringgold, Hannah Rebecca, see Frederick Caesar Kemp

Ringgold, Martha, see Robert Rose

Ringgold, Samuel, see Frederick Caesar Kemp

Ringold, Sarah, see Washington Lee

Ringold, Thomas (born c1815) (African American) (laborer, 7th District), married Mary (N) (born c1829, Maryland) (African American) probably circa 1849; daughter Georgeanna Ringold born c1850 (1860 Cecil County Census)

RITCHIE

Ritchie, Charles (born c1822, Maryland) (laborer in the 8th District), married Elizabeth (N) (born c1824, Maryland) probably circa 1842; daughter Mary born c1843, Maryland (1860 Cecil County Census)

RITTENHOUSE

Rittenhouse, Azariah (1818, New Jersey - 1871, Maryland) (merchant at Rising Sun, 6th District), married Mary J. Kirk (1824, Pennsylvania –1908, Maryland) probably circa 1843 (daughter Susanna born c1844, Pennsylvania) and moved to Cecil County between 1855 and 1860; they are buried beside son Thomas Rittenhouse, 1850-1892 (Brookview Cemetery tombstone inscriptions; 1860 Cecil County Census; *Cecil Whig*, 15 Apr 1871)

Rittenhouse, Jeremiah (1807-1889, born New Jersey) (farmer, 9th District), married Sarah (N) (1818-1901, born New Jersey) probably circa 1838 (Zion Presbyterian Church Cemetery tombstone inscriptions; 1860 Cecil County Census)

RIVERS
Rivers, Deborah and Susan Ann, see Joshua L. Gatchell

ROACH
Roach, Deborah Ann, see William Manly

Roach, Jane, see William Grace

Roach, Martha Jane, see Ephraim P. Lowe

Roach, Mary, see Thestty (Westly?) Roach and John Slacum

Roach, Rebecca, see Robert Virtue

Roach, Richard, married Patty(?), Sophy(?), or Raphy(?) Lake circa 26 Mar 1836 (date of license) by Rev. Barratt (Cecil County Marriage License Book is unclear regarding her first name, but it looked like Sophy, perhaps even Raphy, and the DAR transcript copied in 1928 questionably transcribed it as Patty)

Roach, Sarah Jane, see Rudolph Bennett

Roach, Thestty (Westly?) (born c1812, Delaware) (blacksmith at Elkton), married Caroline (N) (born c1821, Maryland) before 1846; daughter Mary Roach born c1847 (1860 Cecil County Census)

ROBB
Robb, Ann M., see John E. Brown

ROBERSON
Roberson, Elijah H. (1811-1889) (doctor at Rising Sun), married Gertrude (N) (1804-1873) probably circa 1834 (Zion Presbyterian Church Cemetery tombstone inscriptions; *Cecil Whig*, 8 Feb 1873; *Midland Journal*, 3 Jan 1889, contains his obituary, and 10 Jan 1889, contains a memorial)

ROBERTS
Roberts, Charles E., married Miss Virginia H. Lusby, both of Cecil Co., on 30 Mar 1848 by Rev. Rheese of Wilmington, DE (*Cecil Whig*, 1 Apr 1848)

Roberts, David A. (born c1824, Maryland) (farmer at Port Herman), married Elizabeth (N) (born c1833, Maryland) probably circa 1849; son David Roberts born c1850, Maryland (1860 Cecil County Census)

Roberts, John A., married Deby Atwell circa 16 Jun 1845 (date of license) (Cecil Co. Marr. License Book)

Roberts, John, married Harriet Bowen circa 16 Dec 1830 (date of license) by Rev. Duke (Cecil County Marriage License Book)

Roberts, John, married Sarah A. Kirk circa 23 Aug 1849 (date of license) (Cecil County Marr. License Book)

Roberts, Joseph H. (born c1822, Delaware) (laborer at Elkton), married Ellen (N) (born c1823, Maryland) probably circa 1845; son Samuel Roberts born c1846, Maryland (1860 Cecil County Census)

Roberts, Margaret N., see Peregrine Hendrickson

Roberts, Mary, see Joseph Benson

Roberts, Samuel, see Joseph H. Roberts

Roberts, Thomas A., married Augusts Veazey circa 22 Jan 1828 (date of license) (Cecil County Marriage License Book)

Roberts, William, married Sina Russem circa 14 Nov 1846 (date of license) (Cecil Co. Marr. License Book)

ROBERTSON
Robertson, Robert, married Ann Eliza Williams circa 5 Jan 1826 (date of license) by Rev. Davis (Cecil County Marriage License Book)

ROBINSON

Robinson, Amelia, see Josiah Borum

Robinson, Ann, see John McCleary

Robinson, Anna E., see James L. Morrow

Robinson, Edward P., see James L. Morrow

Robinson, Eliza, see Joseph W. Cochran

Robinson, Eliza Ann, see John Wesley Buckwith

Robinson, Elizabeth, see Charles T. Ford Foster

Robinson, Emily, see Charles O'Neal

Robinson, Henry H. (born c1815, Maryland) (chair maker at Chesapeake City), most likely the son of John Robinson (born c1792, Maryland), married Mary Johnson (born c1823, Pennsylvania) circa 29 Dec 1842 (date of license) (Cecil County Marriage License Book; 1860 Cecil County Census)

Robinson, Isaac, married Mary Iler circa 12 Apr 1826 (date of license) by Rev. Wyatt (Cecil County Marriage License Book)

Robinson, John, married Louisa Adams circa 24 May 1841 (date of license) (Cecil Co. Marr. License Book)

Robinson, John, see Henry H. Robinson

Robinson, Margery H., see Thomas Williams

Robinson, Martha J., see Philemon Lloyd

Robinson, Mary, see William Brown

Robinson, Mary Agnes, see Nevin W. McCormick

Robinson, Mary Ann, see John W. Bedwell

Robinson, Mary E., see Philip C. Plummer

Robinson, Mary Jane, see James Raisin

Robinson, Rebecca, see Charles H. Morgan

Robinson, Sarah, see Richard Wingate

Robinson, Sarah M., see James Bailey

Robinson, William, married Ann Maria Aldridge circa 12 Jun 1828 (date of license) by Rev. Barratt (Cecil County Marriage License Book)

Robinson, William (1804-1866) (captain), of Elkton, married Julia Ann Aldridge (born 1809) circa 3 Feb 1829 (date of license) by Rev. Barratt (Cecil County Marriage License Book; Wesley Methodist Church Cemetery tombstone inscriptions; *Cecil Whig*, 2 Jun 1866)

Robinson, William, married Eliza Satterfield circa 9 Mar 1833 (date of license) by Rev. McKenney (Cecil County Marriage License Book)

Robinson, William (born c1807) (farmer at Cecilton), married Jane F. Jester (born c1816) circa 8 Sep 1842 (date of license) (Cecil County Marriage License Book; 1860 Cecil County Census)

ROCK

Rock, Francis (c1794-1844) (War of 1812 veteran), married Ann Smith (born c1800) on 15 Mar 1827, after obtaining a license on 13 Mar 1827, by Rev. Barrett (Cecil County Marriage License Book; DAR transcript copied in 1928 misspelled his name Roch; War of 1812 Bounty Land Warrant 55-160-57435)

Rock, Mary, see Benjamin Elliott

Rock, William, married Melinda Perry circa 11 Mar 1835 (date of license) by Rev. Griffith (Cecil County Marriage License Book)

ROE

Roe, Mary Jane, see William Roe

Roe, William, married Mary Jane Roe circ 6 Jun 1836 (date of license) by Rev. Morrison (Cecil County Marriage License Book)

ROGERS

Rogers, Abner (1798-1881), married Sarah A. (N) (1819-1882) probably circa 1840 (Brick Meeting House, at Calvert, tombstone inscriptions)

Rogers, Ann, see Lewis Brown and Thomas Brown

Rogers, Elisha H., married Ann Pennock circa 1 Sep 1841 (date of license) (Cecil Co. Marr. License Book)

Rogers, Jeremiah, see Lewis Brown

Rogers, Rachel B., see Lewis Brown

Rogers, Thomas, married Jane McGaughlin circa 17 Aug 1833 (date of license) by Rev. Mahan (Cecil County Marriage License Book)

ROHALSKI

Rohalski, T. (born c1820, Poland) (farmer near St. Augustine), married Julia (N) (born c1830, Maryland) probably circa 1846; daughter Florian Rohalski born c1847, Maryland (1860 Cecil County Census)

ROLLINGS

Rollings, Mary A., see John J. Alexander

ROMAN

Roman, A. (1801-1872), married Eliza Haines (1811-1844) probably circa 1829-1830 (Friends Cemetery, at Harrisville, tombstone inscriptions)

Roman, Joseph Jr., of Cecil Co., married Rebecca T. West, daughter of Mahlon H. and Mary T. West, of Harford Co., on 6 Oct 1836 (*Heirs & Legatees of Harford County, Maryland, 1802-1846*, by Henry C. Peden, Jr. (1988), p. 48; *Baltimore American and Commercial Daily Advertiser*, 10 Oct 1836)

RONEY

Roney, William, married Sarah D. Giles, both of Philadelphia, later of Cincinnati, OH, daughter of Thomas Giles (1752-1812) and Ann Goodwin (1758-1800), of Cecil Co., on 4 Jan 1838 by Rev. Thomas Hunt in Philadelphia (*Cecil Gazette*, 27 Jan 1838; *Thomas Giles, Born 1752 – Birmingham, England, Died 1812 – Elkton, Maryland, U. S.A., A Genealogical History of His Descendants*, by Alexander W. Giles, Jr. (1986, updated 1996), p. 15, inadvertently stated they married on 27 Jan 1838; they moved to Cincinnati, OH in 1838; she died on 13 Feb 1861; her body was returned to Philadelphia and buried in the Harding family mausoleum in Monument Cemetery; the cemetery and its monuments no longer exist and the land is now part of Temple University; all remains were re-interred in a common grave in Lawnview Cemetery)

ROSE

Rose, Robert, married Martha Ringgold (1819-1904) probably circa 1838-1840 (Hart's Methodist Church Cemetery tombstone inscription for Martha Ringgold Rose)

ROSS

Ross, Peter, married Elizabeth Wiley circa 24 Dec 1832 (date of license) by Rev. Magraw (Cecil County Marriage License Book)

Ross, Robert, married Elizabeth Mahan circa 17 Sep 1835 (date of license) by Rev. Warburton (Cecil County Marriage License Book)

ROWLAND

Rowland, Hannah Jane, see Hugh Steel

Rowland, Jonathan M., of Newark, DE, married Miss Elizabeth Wicks, of Cecil Co., on 9 Apr 1846, after obtaining a license on 8 Apr 1846, by Rev. Kennard (*Cecil Whig*, 11 Apr 1846; Cecil County Marriage License Book)

Rowland, Madison (1805-1882), married Eleanor "Ellen" Patton (1803-1897) circa 1 Oct 1842 (date of license) (Cecil County Marriage License Book; West Nottingham Cemetery tombstone inscriptions)

Rowland, Sarah Maria, see Sanders McCullough

Rowland, William Latham (1799-1863, born Maryland) (doctor), of Cecil Co., married Cassandra Morgan Hopkins (c1816-1846, born Pennsylvania), daughter of John Hopkins and Eleanor Morgan, on 4 Feb 1836 after obtaining a license in Harford County on 3 Feb 1836 (*Descendants of the Signers of the Bush Declaration of March 22, 1775, Harford County, Maryland*, by Christopher T. Smithson and Henry C. Peden, Jr. (2010), pp. 230, 233; *Hopkins Family, 1690 to 1890*, by Harlin D. Bagley and Lora V. Bagley (1996), p. 292; 1860 Cecil County Census)

ROZEAN

Rozean, George, married Angeline Mahan circa 29 Jan 1845 (date of license) (Cecil Co. Marr. Lic. Book)

RULEY

Ruley, Ann, see William R. Biddle

Ruley, Benjamin M., married Sarah E. Severson on 26 Sep 1839, after obtaining a license that same day, by Rev. Hagany (Cecil County Marriage License Book; Elkton Methodist Church Register, p. 139)

Ruley, Catharine P., see John H. Bolton

Ruley, Frances, see Mills M. Ricketts

Ruley, James, married Alice Alterson circa 16 Dec 1830 (date of license) by Rev. Duke (Cecil County Marriage License Book)

Ruley, James, married Elizabeth Whitelock circa 9 Sep 1835 (date of license) by Rev. Houston (Cecil County Marriage License Book)

Ruley, James A., married Frances A. Armstrong circa 7 Dec 1846 (date of license) (Cecil County Marriage License Book)

Ruley, Penina or Penanah, see Thomas Stradley

Ruley, Sarah E., see Elias P. Barnaby

Ruley, Sophia Josephine, see William H. Emerson

RUMFORD

Rumford, Caroline, see George R. Burroughs

Rumford, John, see James H. Benson

Rumford, Louisa, see James H. Benson

RUMSEY

Rumsey, Moses, married Rebecca Brown circa 27 Oct 1825 (date of license) by Rev. Goforth (Cecil County Marriage License Book)

RUNNER

Runner, Hannah J., see David Jenkins

RUSSELL

Russell, Amelia E., see Norris Levis

Russell, Eliza, see Samuel Maxwell

Russell, Isabella Ann, see Joseph Taggard Reed

Russell, John B. (born c1819, Maryland) (farmer and fisherman at North East), married Deborah L. Johnson (born c1824, Maryland) on 13 Jun 1843, after obtaining a license on 13 Jun 1843, by Rev. Goentner at North East (Cecil County Marriage License Book; *Cecil Whig*, 17 Jun 1843; 1860 Cecil County Census)

Russell, John R., married Sarah E. Jones circa 25 Dec 1850 (date of license) (Cecil Co. Marr. License Book)

Russell, Mary, see Robert A. Landers and Robert R. Vandiver

Russell, Mary Ann, see Edward Wilkins

Russell, R. M., of Savannah, GA, married Miss Laura O. Smith, daughter of Col. Smith of New Orleans, LA, on 14 Feb 1849 by Rev. Father Twiney at New Orleans (*Cecil Whig*, 24 Feb 1849; *Cecil Democrat and Farmer's Journal*, 24 Feb 1849)

RUSSEM, RUSSUM

Russem, Sina, see William Roberts

Russum, Francis, married Francina Dennis circa 18 Dec 1835 (date of license) by Rev. Coleman (Cecil County Marriage License Book)

RUTTER

Rutter, Ann, see Nicholas Lottman

Rutter, Araminta R., see James Merry

Rutter, Catherine, see William Rutter

Rutter, Elizabeth, see John G. Creswell

Rutter, Ellen, see George Shannon

Rutter, Harriett, see William Logan

Rutter, Hester, see John Increase Creswell

Rutter, James W., married Margery Wilson circa 8 Feb 1830 (date of license) by Rev. Barratt (Cecil County Marriage License Book)

Rutter, Jane, see Joseph Brumfield

Rutter, John (1803-1844), married Sarah B. Lorritt (1807-1893) circa 27 Dec 1826 (date of license) by Rev. Barratt (Cecil County Marr. License Book; Wesley Methodist Church Cemetery tombstone inscriptions)

Rutter, John, married Catharine Keatly circa 8 Nov 1834 (date of license) by Rev. Griffith (Cecil County Marriage License Book)

Rutter, John Jr., married Elizabeth Jackson circa 3 Dec 1834 (date of license) by Rev. Griffith (Cecil County Marriage License Book; DAR transcript copied in 1928 mistakenly listed his name without the Jr.)

Rutter, Lydia A., see Isaac Nunville

Rutter, Martha, see John Weir

Rutter, Mary, see Levi Lottman

Rutter, Richard (born c1810, Maryland) (cooper, 7th District), married Elizabeth Jackson (born c1807, Maryland) circa 7 Feb 1832 (date of license) by Rev. Magraw (Cecil County Marriage License Book; 1860 Cecil County Census)

Rutter, Sarah, see Thomas Kelly

Rutter, Sarah J., see Ephraim P. Rutter

Rutter, Sophia, see Edward White

Rutter, Thomas, married Mary Fisher circa 16 Feb 1825 (date of license) by Rev. Duke (Cecil County Marriage License Book)

Rutter, William (born c1816, Maryland) (farmer in the 7th District), married Ann Maria Whittall (born c1816, Maryland) circa 25 Feb 1839 (date of license) by Rev. Grace (Cecil County Marriage License Book; 1860 Cecil County Census also listed Catherine Rutter, age 72, born Maryland, living in their household)

Rutter, William, married Sarah Jane Pennington circa 9 May 1832 (date of license) by Rev. Barratt (Cecil County Marriage License Book)

Rutter, William Howard, married Catharine Milburn circa 9 May 1849 (date of license) (Cecil County Marriage License Book)

RYAN

Ryan, Delilah, see Thomas Watson

Ryan, Mary, see John Thomas Aiken

RYLAND

Ryland, Jane, see Samuel J. Booth

SAMPLE

Sample, Rebecca, see John Davis

SANDERS

Sanders, John P., of Wilmington, DE, married Miss Margaret Hempfield, of Elkton, on 18 Feb 1849 at Marcus Hook, PA by Rev. Joseph Walker (*Cecil Democrat and Farmer's Journal*, 3 Mar 1849, spelled her name Hempfield; *Delaware Gazette*, 2 Mar 1849, spelled it Hemphill and listed his name as John F.)

SAPPINGTON

Sappington, Sophia, see Peregrine Hendrickson

SATTERFIELD

Satterfield, Eliza, see William Robinson

Satterfield, Mary E., see Henry M. Hays

SAUNDERS

Saunders, Elizabeth, see Alem L. Brickley

Saunders, Rachel, see John Waring

SAUTER

Sauter, Philip (1810-1870), married Rebecca (N) (1816-1890) probably circa 1834-1836 (West Nottingham Cemetery tombstone inscriptions)

SAVIN

Savin, Ann Dennison, see John Archer

Savin, Augusta H., see James M. Cunnings

Savin, Eliza Margueritte, see William F. Savin

Savin, John, slave of George Davis, Esq., married Jane Wilson, slave of Hyland Price, on 3 Jun 1837 by Rev. Piggot (North Sassafras Parish, St. Stephen's P. E. Church Register)

Savin, Richard, see Thomas Savin

Savin, Sarah, see James Postill

Savin, Stephen, slave of George Davis, Esq., married Susan Medford, slave of Alfred C. Nowland, on 12 Aug 1837 by Rev. Piggot (North Sassafras Parish, St. Stephen's P. E. Church Register)

Savin, Thomas (born c1810) (African American), married Elizabeth (N) (born c1810) (African American) circa 1837; son Richard Savin born c1838 (1860 Cecil County Census)

Savin, Thomas L., see John Archer, James M. Cummings and William F. Savin

Savin, William F., married Eliza Margueritte Savin, eldest daughter of Thomas L. Savin, Esq., all of Elkton, at Hygent Mount in Cecil Co. on 16 Oct 1832, after obtaining a license on 15 Oct 1832, by Rev. Goforth (*Baltimore American and Commercial Daily Advertiser*, 19 Oct 1832; Cecil County Marriage License Book listed her only as Eliza Margaretta with no last name)

SAW

Saw, Margaret, see Thomas Taylor

SAXTON

Saxton, Albanus L. (born c1827, Pennsylvania) (machinist near Elkton), married Miss Mary Elizabeth Hall (born c183), Maryland), both now of Cecil Co., on 19 Aug 1847, after obtaining a license on 14 Aug 1847, by Rev. Milby at Elkton (*Cecil Whig*, 21 Aug 1847; Cecil County Marriage License Book; 1860 Cecil County Census spelled his surname Saxon and listed her name as Elizabeth Saxon)

SCANLIN

Scanlin, James and Mary, see William Axon Stokes

SCARBOROUGH

Scarborough, Charity, see Joseph Hall

Scarborough, Enos, see Matthew Drummond

Scarborough, Enos T. (1824-1886) (papermaker at Elkton), married Elizabeth E. Spence (1828-1913) circa 17 Mar 1847 (date of license) (Cecil County Marriage License Book; Cherry Hill Methodist Church Cemetery tombstone inscriptions; 1860 Cecil County Census)

Scarborough, George W., see Sutton Scarborough

Scarborough, Hannah, see Matthew Drummond

Scarborough, Hugh F., married Miss Frances S. Spence on 10 Aug 1848, after obtaining a license on 5 Aug 1848, by Rev. Kennard at Cherry Hill (Cecil County Marriage License Book; *Cecil Whig*, 26 Aug 1848)

Scarborough, John T., married Eliza T. Gilmore, both of Cecil Co., on 13 Mar 1845, after obtaining a license on 11 Mar 1845, by Rev. Kennard (Cecil County Marriage License Book; DAR transcript copied in 1955 misspelled her name Gilmour; *Cecil Whig*, 22 Mar 1845)

Scarborough, Joseph (1793-1848) (War of 1812 veteran), of Bucks Co., PA, later of Cecil Co., married 1st to Rebecca Boyd (1800-1829), of Port Deposit, circa 20 Dec 1823 (date of license) and married 2nd to Sarah Williams (1798-1878), daughter of John (died 1826) and Sarah Williams, circa 20 Feb 1839 (date of license) by Rev. Wilson; buried in Leeds Methodist Church Cemetery (Cecil County Marriage License Book; Cecil County Will Book A, No. 8, p. 234; *Portrait and Biographical Record of Harford and Cecil Counties, Maryland* (1897, repr. 1989), p. 186, stated the four children (no names given) by his first wife all died before 1897 and of the seven children by his second wife only three were living in 1897, namely, Ann E. O'Daniel and Mary S. Wright, both of Oxford, PA, and Joseph S. Scarborough, of Cecil County)

Scarborough, Joseph S., see Joseph Scarborough

Scarborough, Sutton (1805-1893), married Rebecca (N) (1803-1882) probably circa 1829 and they are buried beside George W. Scarborough, 1830-1877, and Elizabeth T. Scarborough Smith, 1836-1815 (Rosebank Cemetery, at Calvert, tombstone inscriptions)

Scarborough, Watson (1801-1876) (cooper at Elkton), married Jane Wright (1806-1888) circa 7 Oct 1828 (date of their license) by Rev. Barratt (Cecil County Marriage License Book; Leeds Methodist Church Cemetery tombstone inscriptions; 1860 Cecil County Census)

SCHOFIELD

Schofield, John (born c1802, Maryland) (sailor at Cecilton), married Susan (N) (born c1808, Delaware) circa 1834; son Gustavus born c1835 Maryland (1860 Cecil County Census)

SCHRITZ, SCHRITZE

Schritz, John (1796-1855), of Germany, later of Port Deposit, Cecil Co., and Havre de Grace, Harford Co. (buried at Hopewell in Cecil Co.), married Margaret E. Mars (1804-1880) on 19 Sep 1827 in Florstat, Germany (*Bible Records, Genealogical Society of Cecil County*, by Gary L. Burns (1990), pp. 72-73, listed the births of their sixteen children and also spelled their surname Schritze: John Conrad, born 14 Aug 1828; Catharine, born 24 Aug 1829; Dorathy, born 21 Sep 1830; Margaret, born 25 Dec 1831; Christopher, born 29 Sep 1833; Elizabeth, born 28 Aug 1836; Louisa, born 4 Jul 1837 and (N), twin sister, born dead; Susannah, born 30 Sep 1839; John Archer, born 20 Dec 1841; Henry, born 20 Aug 1842; Theodore, born 17 Dec 1843; Hannah Mary, born 20 May 1845; Emma Rasin, born 20 Sep 1847; Anna Augusta, born 16 Jan 1849; and, Caroline Amanda, born 15 Feb 1851; Hopewell United Methodist Church Cemetery tombstone inscriptions spelled the name Schritz)

SCHUCK

Schuck, Amanda M., see Samuel House

SCHULTZ

Schultz, James L., of New York, married Sarah A. Cropper circa 24 Mar 1843 (date of their license) (Cecil County Marriage License Book)

SCHWARZ

Schwarz, Caroline, see Jacob Endress

SCOTT

Scott, Alexander (born c1821, Maryland), married Elizabeth A. Tweed (born c1830, Delaware) circa 13 Mar 1850 (date of license) (Cecil County Marriage License Book; 1860 Cecil County Census)

Scott, Ann, see Jesse Baldwin

Scott, Benjamin, married Miss Jane Spence, both of Cecil Co., on 30 Mar 1848, after obtaining a license on 29 Mar 1848, by Rev. McIntire (*Cecil Whig*, 1 Apr 1848; Cecil County Marriage License Book)

Scott, Daniel, see Otho Scott

Scott, David (born c1818) (farmer near Elkton), married Miss Agatha R. Fulton (born c1815), both of Cecil Co., on 4 Jul 1844, after obtaining a license on 3 Jul 1844, by Rev. Work (Cecil County Marriage License Book; *Cecil Whig*, 13 Jul 1844; 1860 Cecil County Census)

Scott, David (1824-1879) (Clerk of the Cecil County Court, 1867-1873, and State Weigher in Baltimore, 1875-1879), married 1st to Mary Jane Wilson (1826-1858) probably by 1850 (no marriage license found in Cecil County) and married 2nd to Anna "Annie" Elizabeth Craig (1830-1914) in 1866 (*Portrait and Biographical Record of Harford and Cecil Counties, Maryland* (1897, repr. 1989), p. 297; Cecil County Marriage License Book; Elkton Presbyterian Church Cemetery tombstone inscriptions)

Scott, Ellen J., see Henry P. Bennett

Scott, George (born c1820, Maryland) (African American) (farmer, 6th District), married Levenia (N) (born c1832, Maryland) (African American) probably circa 1847; daughter Mary Scott born c1848 (African American) (1860 Cecil County Census)

Scott, Gideon B., married Miss Margaret V. Mote, both of Cecil Co., circa 20 Jun 1849 (date of license) (Cecil County Marriage License Book misspelled her name Moat; *Cecil Democrat and Farmer's Journal*, 30 Jun 1849, requested "Baltimore and Wilmington papers please copy," but the marriage was not published in the *Baltimore Sun* nor in the *Delaware Gazette*)

Scott, Jacob, married Ellen Johnson circa 30 Jan 1834 (date of license) by Rev. Hammill (Cecil County Marriage License Book)

Scott, James (1812-1863), married Mary Garrett (1814-1887) circa 13 Jul 1835 (date of license) by Rev. Hammill (Cecil County Marriage License Book; St. John's Church Cemetery, at Lewisville, tombstones)

Scott, Jane, see Samuel Fisher

Scott, John, married Ellen Sutton circa 12 Feb 1846 (date of license) (Cecil County Marriage License Book)

Scott, John, married Ann Sutton circa 11 Mar 1847 (date of license) (Cecil County Marriage License Book)

Scott, John (1811-1882), married Martha R. (N) (1825-1911) probably circa 1845 (Rock Springs Old School Baptist Church Cemetery tombstone inscriptions)

Scott, Joseph, married Lydia Abbott circa 14 Dec 1835 (date of license) by Rev. Houston (Cecil County Marriage License Book)

Scott, Margaret, see Joel Evans and Joseph Harlan

Scott, Margaret E., see Palmer C. Strickland

Scott, Martha, see John P. Bennett

Scott, Mary, see George Scott

Scott, Mary Ann, see Stephen Pluck

Scott, Moses, see John P. Bennett

Scott, Otho (1797-1864) (attorney), of Harford Co., son of Daniel Scott and Margaret Short, married 1st to Louisa Mary Boarman (1800-1864) circa 29 Oct 1823 and married 2nd to Elizabeth Grason (1815-1862), eldest daughter of ex-Governor Grason, on 29 Apr 1843 by Rev. Brown at the residence of her father in

Queen Anne's County (*Cecil Whig*, 6 May 1843; *Harford County, Maryland Marriage References and Family Relationships, 1825-1850*, by Henry C. Peden, Jr., 2014, p. 230; *The Aegis*, 18 Mar 1864)

Scott, Robert, married Violet Scott circa 21 Dec 1848 (date of license) (Cecil County Marr. License Book)

Scott, Sophia C., see Levi Todd

Scott, Vilotta R., see James H. Jamar

Scott, Violet, see Robert Scott

Scott, William, married Mary Short circa 3 Jan 1833 (date of license) by Rev. Benson (Cecil County Marriage License Book)

Scott, William C. (esquire), of Cecil Co., married Helen J. Reardon, daughter of Lambert Reardon, on 25 May 1835 (*Baltimore American and Commercial Daily Advertiser*, 29 May 1835)

Scott, (N), married Sarah Fisher (born 1809) probably circa 1830; her sisters were Jane Fisher (1807-1891) of Cecil Co., Margaret Fisher (born 1807) and Rebecca Murray (born 1811) (*Easton Star*, 2 Jun 1891)

SCOTTEN

Scotten, William (1815-1884), married Martha Spence (1818-1880) circa 20 May 1839 (date of license) by Rev. Miller (Cecil County Marriage License Book; Cherry Hill Methodist Church Cemetery tombstone inscriptions)

SEA

Sea, Jonas, married Miss Placida Lake on 22 Feb 1838 in Lee Co., Virginia, by Rev. Smith (*Cecil Gazette*, 17 Mar 1838, included this short verse: "Hymen did here commit a sad mistake, Tho' it was done midst sportive glee, Or else he'd not have chang'd *A. Placid Lake*, Into a rude tempestuous *Sea*.")

SEEGAR, SEAGERS, SEGARS, SEGERS

Seegar, Emily Ann, see Philip Thomas, Jr.

Seegar, James Massey (1820-1872) (esquire), of Queen Anne's Co., married Miss Frances Anne Hopper Emory, daughter of Dr. John King Beck Emory (1800-1873) and Frances Kennard (1805-1840), of Elkton, Cecil Co., and Queen Anne's Co., on 20 Dec 1848 in Baltimore City by Rev. Murray (*Cecil Democrat and Farmer's Journal*, 23 Dec 1848; *Baltimore Sun*, 25 Dec 1848, Sons of the American Revolution Application of Dr. John King Beck Emory Seegar, Jr., National No. 83491, approved 1957)

Seagers, Mary, see Robert Pennington

Segars, Mary, see James Willis

Segers, Reuben, married Margaret A. Alden circa 16 Dec 1829 (date of license) by Rev. Duke (Cecil County Marriage License Book)

SEMANS

Semans, Elizabeth, see Edward Oldham

SENTMAN

Sentman, David, see Michael Sentman

Sentman, Elijah, see Lawrence Sentman

Sentman, Elizabeth, see Alexander Hill

Sentman, Jonathan (1820-1909) (farmer near Elkton), married Mary Ellen Sentman (1823-1897) circa 15 Dec 1845 (date of license) (Cecil County Marriage License Book; *Portrait and Biographical Record of Harford and Cecil Counties, Maryland* (1897, repr. 1989), p. 434; St. John's Church Cemetery, at Lewisville, tombstone inscriptions; 1860 Cecil County Census misspelled his name Centman)

Sentman, Laurence, married Miss Hannah M. Evans, both of Cecil Co., on 29 Dec 1847 by Rev. Rockwell in Wilmington, DE (*Cecil Whig*, 1 Jan 1848)

Sentman, Lawrence (born c1825, Pennsylvania) (carpenter at Elkton), married Maria H. Hill (born c1825, Maryland), both now of Cecil Co., on 11 Dec 1848, after obtaining a license on 9 Dec 1848, by Rev.

DeWitt; son Elijah Sentman born c1850 (Cecil County Marriage License Book; *Cecil Democrat and Farmer's Journal*, 23 Dec 1848; 1860 Cecil County Census misspelled his name Centman)

Sentman, Mary Ellen, see Jonathan Sentman

Sentman, Michael (born c1820, Pennsylvania) (carpenter at Elkton), married Miss Harriet Fulton (born c1817, New York), both now of Cecil Co., on 29 Dec 1842, after obtaining a license on 24 Dec 1842, by Rev. DeWitt; son David Sentman born c1846, Maryland (Cecil County Marriage License Book; *Cecil Whig*, 7 Jan 1843; 1860 Cecil County Census misspelled his name Centman)

SETH
Seth, Elizabeth, see Bayard B. Ashby or Ashley

SEVERSON
Severson, Henrietta, see Philip R. Jester

Severson, Louisa, see James H. Benson

Severson, Mary S., see James A. Benson

Severson, Richard, married Helen Johnson circa 21 Feb 1837 (date of license) by Rev. Barratt (Cecil County Marriage License Book; DAR transcript copied in 1928 misspelled his name Leverson)

Severson, Samuel, married Henrietta E. Price circa 20 Aug 1827 (date of license) (Cecil County Marriage License Book)

Severson, Sarah, see Edward B. Foard

Severson, Sarah E., see Benjamin M. Ruley

SEVIL
Sevil, Anna E., see John R. Rees

SEWALL
Sewall, Caroline, see Thomas V. Oliver

Sewall, George, see Perry Sewall

Sewall, Jacob (free African American), married Nancy Yorkman (free African American) on 28 Dec 1837 by Rev. Piggot (North Sassafras Parish, St. Stephen's Protestant Episcopal Church Register)

Sewall, James Morsell, of Elkton, married Anna Maria Pinkney, daughter of Col. William Pinkney, of Baltimore, on 11 Feb 1845 by Rev. Goldsborough in Trinity Church at Elkton (*Cecil Whig*, 15 Feb 1845)

Sewall, Perry (born c1813) (African American) (farmer at Cecilton), married Louisa (N) (born c1825) (African American) circa 1849; son George Sewall born c1850 (1860 Cecil County Census)

Sewall, Thomas R. (doctor), married Rebecca Mauldin (born 1821), daughter of Benjamin Mauldin and Sarah Thomas, circa 15 Apr 1845 (date of license) (Cecil County Marriage License Book; *Maryland Bible Records, Volume 4: Eastern Shore*, by Henry C. Peden, Jr. (2004), pp. 145-146)

Sewall, Martha E., see William C. Glenn

SHAFER
Shafer, John (born c1820), married Caroline Spence (born c1822) circa 11 Apr 1833 (date of license) by Rev. Barratt (Cecil County Marriage License Book; 1860 Cecil County Census)

SHANNON
Shannon, George, married Ellen Rutter (1809-1884) circa 25 Mar 1828 (date of license) (Cecil County Marriage License Book; West Nottingham Cemetery tombstone inscription for Ellen Shannon)

Shannon, Mary E., see John F. Knight

SHARP, SHARPE
Sharp, Aceniah, see David Cross

Sharp, Rebecca R., see George A. Steele

Sharpe, Solomon (doctor), of Christiana, DE, married Miss Catharine Marion Harris, of Cecil Co., on 27 Nov 1828 by Rev. Dunn in Philadelphia (*Delaware Gazette*, 9 Dec 1828; *Elkton Press*, 13 Dec 1828)

SHARPLESS
Sharpless, David W. (1817-1868), married Mary (N) (1821-1900) probably circa 1840 (Friends Cemetery, at Harrisville, tombstone inscriptions)

SHAUCK
Shauck, Almira, see William Langdon

SHAW
Shaw, Henry, see Corbin Cooley

Shaw, James, see Matthew Shaw

Shaw, John, see John Coulson and Matthew Shaw

Shaw, Mary, see Corbin Cooley

Shaw, Matthew (1800-1885), of Cecil Co., later of Baltimore, married Sophia Gelbach (1812-1867), eldest daughter of Christian Gelbach, a merchant in Baltimore City, on 20 Sep 1832 (*Baltimore American and Commercial Daily Advertiser*, 24 Sep 1832; *Cecil Democrat and Farmer's Journal*, 14 Sep 1867, stated Sophia G. Shaw, wife of Matthew Shaw, died in her 55th year at the residence of her brothers-in-law John and James Shaw; *Baltimore Sun*, 7 Sep 1867 and 21 Sep 1885)

Shaw, Sophia, see John Coulson

SHELLEY, SHELLY
Shelley, John (1812-1890), married Martha (N) (1820-1895) probably circa 1838-1840 (Friends Cemetery, at Harrisville, tombstone inscriptions)

Shelly, William, married Elizabeth Bruce circa 26 Jul 1837 (date of license) by Rev. Grace (Cecil County Marriage License Book)

SHEPPARD
Sheppard, (N), married Sarah Ann (N) (1809-1891) probably circa 1830 (Rosebank Cemetery, at Calvert, tombstone inscription for "Mother, Sara Ann Sheppard," but no marker for her husband)

SHERER
Sherer, David M. (1797-1863), married Mary Smith (1817-1867) circa 22 Dec 1841 (date of license) (Cecil County Marriage License Book; Union Methodist Church Cemetery tombstone inscriptions)

Sherer, William, married Ruth Ann Brown circa 2 Jan 1833 (date of license) by Rev. Graham (Cecil County Marriage License Book; "Ruth A. Sherrier" (1808-1881) is buried in the Rosebank Cemetery, at Calvert, but there is no marker for her husband William)

SHERIDAN
Sheridan, John (born c1820, Ireland) (farmer, 7th District), married Eliza (N) (born c1825, Ireland) probably circa 1850; son John Sheridan, Jr. born c1851, Maryland (1860 Cecil County Census)

Sheridan, Sarah, see Jehu Thomas Davis

SHERMAN
Sherman, Mary Jane, see Henry G. Simpers

SHERMER
Shermer, Jacob and Margaret H., see Robert Cooley

SHERWOOD

Sherwood, Horatio N., married Mary Ann Hunter circa 6 Oct 1836 (date of license) by Rev. Wilson (Cecil County Marriage License Book; DAR transcript copied in 1928 misspelled his first name Horatic)

SHEWALTER

Shewalter, Joseph and Martha E., see William Cameron

SHIELDS

Shields, Jane A., see Alfred B. Thomas

Shields, Margaret, see Thomas Craddock

SHIFFLEY

Shiffley, Suzanne, see James Warter

SHIPLEY

Shipley, Caroline, see Henry Jamar

SHIVERY

Shivery, Temperance Ann, see Thomas Wood

SHOCKLEY

Shockley, Ann R., see John S. Strickland

Shockley, Caroline, see John S. Jamison

Shockley, Elizabeth, see James McVey

Shockley, James, married Ann Elizabeth Clark circa 28 Dec 1837 (date of license) by Rev. Morrison (Cecil County Marriage License Book)

Shockley, Mary Jane, see William Gilmour

SHORT

Short, Eliza Jane, see Robert Marshbanks

Short, Jeremiah, see Robert Foreacre

Short, John, married Sarah Grant circa 9 Feb 1826 (date of license) by Rev. Sharpley (Cecil County Marriage License Book)

Short, Margaret, see Otho Scott

Short, Martha M., see Robert Foreacre

Short, Mary Ann, see James Spence

SHROFF

Shroff, Susan, see Samuel Gillespie

Shroff, William (1810-1877) (reverend), of Wilmington M. E. Conference,, married Eleanor (N) (1808-1874) probably circa 1831 and he died at the residence of Elihu Harragan near Colora (Hopewell United Methodist Church Cemetery tombstone inscriptions; *Cecil Whig*, 12 May 1877, included a memorial)

SHURE

Shure, John (1806-1881), of Dauphin Co., PA, later of Rowlandsville, Cecil Co., son of John Shure, married Catharine (N) (1810-1895) circa 1832 (son John P. Shure born 1833, died 1903) and are buried in Harford County (Southern Methodist Cemetery tombstone inscriptions; *The Aegis*, 4 Feb 1881)

SIDWELL

Sidwell, Elizabeth, see Amos Pugh

Sidwell, Esther A., see James A. Coulson

Sidwell, H., see W. Sidwell

Sidwell, Isaac N., married Jane Keatley circa 4 Dec 1830 (date of license) by Rev. Griffith (Cecil County Marriage License Book)

Sidwell, Job, see Amos Pugh

Sidwell, Sarah, see Amos Pugh

Sidwell, Thomas E. (1820-1898), married Rebecca J. (N) (1829-1902) probably circa 1848-1850 (Friends Cemetery, at Harrisville, tombstone inscriptions)

Sidwell, W. (1803-1864), son of H. Sidwell (1780-1877), married Levinia (N) (1808-1893) probably circa 1828 (Friends Cemetery, at Harrisville, tombstone inscriptions)

SIEBRA

Siebra, Prosper, married Marguerite Lepaire circa 11 Dec 1847 (date of license) (Cecil Co, Marr. Lic. Book)

SILCOX

Silcox, Elizabeth, see James Townsend

SILK

Silk, Rosanna, see John Martin

SILLS

Sills, Samuel (born c1820), married Sophia (N) (born c1825) probably circa 1849; son George Sills was born circa 1850 (1860 Cecil County Census)

SILVER

Silver, Adeline Matilda, see William Torbert

Silver, Margaret D., see George Hayes

Silver, William, see William Torbert and George Hayes

SIMCOE

Simcoe, George (1822-1905, born Maryland) (lumber merchant at North East), son of William Simcoe and Rebecca Cazier, married Miss Elizabeth Poinsett (1821-1910, born New Jersey) probably circa 1847; son William born circa 1848 in Maryland (*Portrait and Biographical Record of Harford and Cecil Counties, Maryland* (1897, repr. 1989), p. 383, stated that he married "while still quite young," but he was actually about 25; North East Methodist Church Cemetery tombstone inscriptions; 1860 Cecil County Census)

Simcoe, Hannah, see William Little

Simcoe, William, see George Simcoe

SIMMERS

Simmers, Joseph (born c1824, Maryland) (carpenter, 8th District), married Mary (N) (born c1824, Maryland) probably circa 1847; daughter Mary Simmers born c1848, Maryland (1860 Cecil County Census)

SIMMONS

Simmons, Ann, see William Murray

Simmons, Eliza, see Elias Hall

Simmons, Elizabeth, see George W. Moore

Simmons, James, married Elizabeth Clark circa 19 Jul 1831 (date of license) by Rev. Barnes (Cecil County Marriage License Book)

Simmons, Lawrence Jr. (born c1825, Delaware) of Chesapeake City, married Emily E. Crow (born c1818) circa 9 May 1842 (date of license) (Cecil County Marriage License Book; 1860 Cecil County Census)

Simmons, Margaret Ann, see William Logue

Simmons, Mary, see Peregrine Vandegrift

Simmons, Rosette, see John T. Plummer

Simmons, Thomas W., married Miss Julia Woodford, both of Elkton, on 8 May 1844, after obtaining a license that same day, by Rev. McIntire (*Cecil Whig*, 11 May 1844; Cecil County Marr. License Book)

SIMPERS

Simpers, Amelia Jane, see James Kershaw

Simpers, Amy, see James Alexander

Simpers, Ann, see Henry G. Simpers and William T. Miller

Simpers, Elizabeth, see John Foard

Simpers, Hannah, see John Barnett

Simpers, Henry, married Laney Simpson circa 14 Jul 1841 (date of license) (Cecil County Marriage License Book; DAR transcript copied in 1955 mistakenly listed her first name as Laura and the marriage license date as 14 Jun 1841)

Simpers, Henry G. (born c1820) (teacher at North East), married 1st to Ann Simpers circa 10 Apr 1828 (date of license) and married 2nd to Miss Mary Jane Sherman (born c1830), also of North East, on 19 Mar 1846, after obtaining a license on 18 Mar 1846, by Rev. Humphries (*Cecil Whig*, 28 Mar 1846; Cecil County Marriage License Book; 1860 Cecil County Census)

Simpers, Henry Thomas, see John E. Simpers

Simpers, Jesse, married Mary Ann Simpers circa 15 Oct 1835 (date of license) by Rev. Morrison (Cecil County Marriage License Book)

Simpers, Jesse H. (1797-1878) (farmer, fisherman and cooper), son of William Simpers, married 1st to Jane Miller (1801-1845), daughter of Rev. Thomas Miller, circa 26 Mar 1821 (date of license) and married 2nd to Elizabeth Fulton (1821-1883), daughter of Jacob Fulton, on 9 Nov 1848, after obtaining a license on 7 Nov 1848, by Rev. Bayne (*Portrait and Biographical Record of Harford and Cecil Counties, Maryland* (1897, repr. 1989), p. 156; *Cecil Whig*, 18 Nov 1848; Cecil County Marriage License Book; Union Methodist Church Cemetery tombstone inscriptions; *Cecil Whig*, 27 Apr 1878, stated he died in his 81st year at Westamwell near Union Methodist Episcopal Church)

Simpers, John E. (c1795-1845) (War of 1812 veteran), married Ann McCauley circa 15 Mar 1830 (date of license) by Rev. Griffith and she pre-deceased him (Cecil County Marriage License Book; War of 1812 Bounty Land Warrant No. 55-160-43127 listed their children as Sarah Maria, born 1 Oct 1834, John Goforth, born 14 Aug 1836, and Henry Thomas, born 27 Apr 1839)

Simpers, John Goforth, see John E. Simpers

Simpers, John T., married Mary Boulden circa 22 Oct 1832 (date of license) by Rev. Mahan (Cecil County Marriage License Book)

Simpers, John W., married Mary A. Crawford circa 21 Jan 1847 (date of license) (Cecil County Marriage License Book)

Simpers, Johnson, see Joseph T. Stout

Simpers, Martha C., see Samuel A. West

Simpers, Mary, see James Lowery

Simpers, Mary A., see Joseph Hines

Simpers, Mary Ann, see Jesse Simpers and Benjamin Stoops

Simpers, Mary Mauldin, see Joseph T. Stout

Simpers, Millicent, see Joseph T. Stout

Simpers, Millicent J., see Joseph T. Brown

Simpers, Nathaniel, married Hannah Crouch circa 22 Aug 1825 (date of license) by Rev. Miller (Cecil County Marriage License Book)

Simpers, Nathaniel (1810-1878), of North East, married Rebecca Slagle (1810-1871) circa 10 May 1843 (date of license) (Cecil County Marriage License Book; *Cecil Whig*, 20 May 1871; *Cecil Whig*, 4 May 1878, stated he died in Philadelphia and mentioned his son-in-law Dr. A. W. Duvall)

Simpers, Rachel, see John Boulden and John Mousley

Simpers, Rachel S., see John H. McCauley

Simpers, Rebecca, see Peter Pearson

Simpers, Richard L., married 1st to Rachel Wood on 12 Mar 1840, after obtaining a license on 11 Mar 1840, by Rev. Hagany, and married 2nd to Mrs. Rachel Hines, widow of William Hines, on 17 Mar 1846, after obtaining a license on 11 Mar 1846, by Rev. Barratt (Cecil County Marriage License Book; Elkton Methodist Church Register, p. 139; *Cecil Whig*, 4 Apr 1846)

Simpers, Sarah B., see Zebulon K. Maulden

Simpers, Sarah Maria, see John E. Simpers

Simpers, Sophia T., see John Mauldin

Simpers, Thomas, married Mary Slagle circa 16 Dec 1835 (date of license) by Rev. Barratt (Cecil County Marriage License Book; DAR transcript copied in 1928 questionably listed her name as "Moyle?")

Simpers, Thomas (born c1826) (carpenter at North East), married Martha Gorrell (born c1821) circa 8 Sep 1845 (date of license) (Cecil County Marriage License Book listed his name as Thomas M. Simpers; 1860 Cecil County Census listed it as T. S. Simpers)

Simpers, William, see Jesse H. Simpers

Simpers, William, married Elizabeth Pryor circa 28 Dec 1829 (date of license) by Rev. Barratt (Cecil County Marriage License Book)

Simpers, (N), married Polly (N) (1806-1864) probably circa 1825 (*Cecil Whig*, 23 Apr 1864, reported that "Mrs. Polly Simpers" had died at Elkton, but the name of her husband was not given)

SIMPSON

Simpson, David, married Mary Armstrong circa 8 Oct 1829 (date of license) by Rev. Barratt (Cecil County Marriage License Book; DAR transcript copied in 1928 mistakenly listed his name as Simpers)

Simpson, Elizabeth, see Henry E. Gatchell

Simpson, Frances R., see James Pritchard

Simpson, James (born c1816, Maryland) (African American) (laborer, 7th District), married Jane (N) (born c1820, Maryland) (African American) probably circa 1843; son Robert Simpson born c1844 (1860 Cecil County Census)

Simpson, James T. (1818-1886), married Martha J. Mahoney (1825-1892) circa 9 Nov 1847 (date of license) (Cecil County Marriage License Book; Union Methodist Church Cemetery tombstone inscriptions)

Simpson, Laney, see Henry Simpers

Simpson, Lydia M., see Benjamin Miller

Simpson, Maria, see James Anderson

Simpson, Martha, see Edmund Brown

Simpson, Mary, see Caleb Reynolds

Simpson, Rebecca L., see Joseph Miller

Simpson, Robert, see James Simpson

Simpson, Thomas, of Millington, Kent Co., MD, married Miss Sallie Bell, daughter of John Bell, of Elkton, on 11 Jul 1848 (*Cecil Democrat and Farmer's Journal*, 22 Jul 1848)

SINGLETON

Singleton, Sarah Angelica, see Abraham Van Buren

SISCO

Sisco, Andrew, married Miss Martha Jane Gallagher, both of Cecil Co., on 29 Sep 1850 by Rev. Tongue (*Cecil Democrat and Farmer's Journal*, 5 Oct 1850)

SKIRVEN

Skirven, Thomas W., married Margaret B. Greenwood circa 13 Jan 1829 (date of license) by Rev. Smith (Cecil County Marriage License Book)

SLACK

Slack, Amos, married Mary Boyce circa 1 Jun 1826 (date of license) by Rev. Barratt (Cecil County Marriage License Book)

Slack, Emma and Hannah, see William H. Slack

Slack, Harriett, see James Hemphill

Slack, John, of Baltimore, MD, married Eliza Evans, of New Castle, DE, circa 20 Mar 1830 (date of license) by Rev. Duke (Cecil County Marriage License Book)

Slack, Mary, see William H. Slack and William McCrea

Slack, William H. (born c1820, Pennsylvania) (laborer at Zion 9th District), married Ann (N) (born c1822, Pennsylvania) probably circa 1841; their eldest daughter Mary E. Slack was born c1842, Pennsylvania; youngest children (twins) Emma and Hannah Slack born 1859, Maryland (1860 Cecil County Census)

SLACUM

Slacum, John, of Wilmington, DE, married Miss Mary Roach, of North East, Cecil Co., on 18 Apr 1847, after obtaining a license on 10 Apr 1847, by Rev. Cox (*Delaware Gazette*, 20 Apr 1847, listed his name as John W. E. Slacum, the Cecil County Marriage License Book listed his name as John W. H. Slacum and mistakenly recorded the license date as 10 Apr 1846, and the *Cecil Whig*, 17 Apr 1847, listed his name as John J. K. Slacum and noted "Wilmington papers please copy.")

SLAGLE

Slagle, Elizabeth H., see Benjamin F. Reynolds

Slagle, Frederick, married Mary Jane Johnson circa 12 Jul 1837 (date of license) by Rev. Barratt (Cecil County Marriage License Book)

Slagle, Mary Ann, see James Pugh

Slagle, Rebecca, see Nathaniel Simpers and Thomas J. Foster

Slagle, William, married Rebecca Ann Smith circa 27 Sep 1826 (date of license) by Rev. Barratt (Cecil County Marr. License Book spelled his name Slagel; DAR transcript copied in 1928 misspelled it Steigal)

SLAUGHTER

Slaughter, Emeline, see Richard C. Carter

SLAVEN

Slaven, Eleanor, see James Tarman (Tarnan)

SLICER

Slicer, Harriet, see Thomas Brabson

Slicer, Mary, see Roswell Wakeman

Slicer, Samuel, married Miss Priscilla Ann. Pyle, both of Cecil Co., on 17 Jan 1850, after obtaining a license on 10 Jan 1850, by Rev. Arthur at North East (*Cecil Whig*, 19 Jan 1850; Cecil County Marriage License Book; *Cecil Democrat and Farmer's Journal*, 19 Jan 1850)

Slice, Sarah Ann, see William Wilson

SLOAN

Sloan, David R., of Baltimore, married Jane E. Allderdice, eldest daughter of Abraham, of Wilmington, DE, on 22 May 1849 by Rev. Reese in Wilmington (*Cecil Whig*, 2 Jun 1849; *Baltimore Sun*, 31 May 1849)

SLUYTER

Sluyter, Ann T., see Lambert W. Biddle

SMELTZER

Smeltzer, Jacob (born c1820, Pennsylvania) (laborer, 7th District), married Henrietta Galt (born c1822, born Pennsylvania) circa 7 Feb 1845 (date of license); son William Smeltzer born c1848, Maryland, and other children were all born in Maryland (Cecil County Marriage License Book; 1860 Cecil County Census)

Smeltzer, Philip (1820-1898), married Lydia Jane Logan (1828-1905) circa 16 Feb 1847 (date of license) (Cecil County Marriage License Book; Asbury Methodist Church Cemetery tombstone inscriptions)

Smeltzer, William, see Jacob Smeltzer

SMITH

Smith, Ann, see Francis Rock and William Williams

Smith, Anna J., see Samuel Smith

Smith, Anna M., see Samuel Jefferson Smith

Smith, Annie S., see Robert H. Smith

Smith, Caroline, see Stephen Davis

Smith, Catherine, see Christian Baker

Smith, Deborah, see Samuel Marshall

Smith, Ebenezer, married Nancy A. Gilmore circa 6 May 1825 (date of license) by Rev. Magraw (Cecil County Marriage License Book)

Smith, Elihu J., see Richard Smith

Smith, Eliza, see Samuel Buckwith

Smith, Eliza Jane, see Robert Kennedy Strickland

Smith, Elizabeth, see Benjamin T. Alexander

Smith, Elizabeth T. Scarborough, see Sutton Scarborough

Smith, Francis P., see Samuel Marshall

Smith, George I., son of William Smith of Chester Co., Pennsylvania, later of Cecil Co., and Mary DeHaven, also of Chester Co., married Miss Anna E. Riddell, of New Castle Co., DE in 1849 (*Portrait and Biographical Record of Harford and Cecil Counties, Maryland* (1897, repr. 1989), p. 393, did not give the exact date of their marriage)

Smith, George J., see John Ross Smith

Smith, George P., see Samuel Smith

Smith, George W. (1794-1879) (esquire), married Isabella Reynolds (1808-1871) probably circa 1828 (Zion Presbyterian Church Cemetery tombstone inscriptions; *Cecil Whig*, 29 Apr 1871)

Smith, Hugh E., see Robert H. Smith

Smith, James, see Samuel Smith

Smith, James, married Mary Griffee circa 12 May 1827 (date of license) (Cecil County Marr. License Book)

Smith, James (born c1819, Maryland) (farmer near Blue Ball in the 9th District), married Mary Jane Gregg (born c1824, Maryland) circa 22 Feb 1847 (date of license) (Cecil County Marriage License Book; 1860 Cecil County Census)

Smith, James E., see Robert H. Smith

Smith, James H. (born c1814) (carpenter at Elkton), married Eveline (N) (born c1816) probably circa 1843; son Thomas W. Smith born c1845 (1860 Cecil County Census)

Smith, James K., see Samuel Jefferson Smith

Smith, James R. (1821-1864) (proprietor of the Railroad Hotel in Elkton), married Caroline Mahoney (born c1822) circa 3 May 1846 (date of license) (Cecil County Marriage License Book; 1860 Cecil County Census; *Cecil Whig*, 13 Feb 1864)

Smith, Jane, see Caleb Steel and William H. Way

Smith, John (b. c1804, Maryland) (African American) (laborer, 7th District), married Mary (N) (b. c1810, Maryland) (African American) prob. circa 1829; daughter Ruth born c1830 (1860 Cecil County Census)

Smith, John, married Sarah W. (N) (1807-1868) probably circa 1825 (Union Methodist Church Cemetery tombstone inscription for Sarah W. Smith)

Smith, John (1810-1879), married Julia A. (N) (1812-1883) probably circa 1831 (Cherry Hill Methodist Church Cemetery tombstone inscriptions)

Smith, John G., see Samuel Marshall

Smith, John R., see Robert H. Smith

Smith, John Ross (born c1822, Scotland) (wheelwright at Cecilton), married Elizabeth C. Walmsley (born c1824, Maryland) circa 13 Jul 1849 (date of license); son George J. Smith born c1850, Maryland (Cecil County Marriage License Book; 1860 Cecil County Census)

Smith, Joseph V., of Centreville, married Henrietta W. Briscoe, daughter of John Briscoe, of Kent Co., on 13 Jun 1850, after obtaining a license on 12 Jun 1850, by Rev. Lybrand (*Cecil Democrat and Farmer's Journal*, 22 Jun 1850; Kent County Marriage License Book gave his middle initial as E.)

Smith, Joseph W., married Miss Sarah Ann Guthrie circa 28 Mar 1837 (date of license) by Rev. Wilson (Cecil County Marriage License Book)

Smith, Laura O., see R. M. Russell

Smith, Letitia, see Peregrine F. Lloyd

Smith, Levi G. (1813-1895, born Pennsylvania) (millwright near Elkton), married Isabella Burnite (1810-1898, born Maryland) circa 27 Jul 1835 (date of license) by Rev. Barratt (Cecil County Marriage License Book; Cherry Hill Methodist Church Cemetery tombstone inscriptions; 1860 Cecil County Census)

Smith, Margaret R., married James A. Davis

Smith, Margaret Jane, see Samuel Jefferson Smith

Smith, Mary, see David M. Sherer, Samuel Marshall, George Davis, Richard Griffee and William Phillips

Smith, Mary Ann, see Daniel Stull

Smith, Mary H., see Robert H. Smith

Smith, Mary Jane, see William Armstrong

Smith, Nicholas, married Ann Dougherty on 23 Apr 1826, after obtaining a license on 20 Apr 1826, by Rev. Epinette (Cecil County Marriage License Book; *History of Saint Francis Xavier Church and Bohemia Plantation Now Known as Old Bohemia, Warwick, Maryland*, by Joseph C. Cann (1976), p. 47)

Smith, Olympblus Gregory, see Joseph Stebbing

Smith, Phebe Ann, see Ebenezer W. Nowland

Smith, Rachel, see Rouce Coe and William H. Gilpin

Smith, Rebecca, see Thomas Hayes and Samuel Jefferson Smith

Smith, Rebecca Ann, see William Slagle

Smith, Richard (born c1814, New Jersey) (farmer at Cecilton), married Martha (N) (born c1825, Maryland) circa 1848; son Elihu J. Smith born c1849, Delaware (1860 Cecil County Census)

Smith, Robert (1811-1884) (reverend), married Eliza J. (N) (1817-1865) probably circa 1835 (St. John's Church Cemetery, at Lewisville, tombstone inscriptions)

Smith, Robert H. (1818-1861, born Maryland) (blacksmith, 7th District), married Cassandra Butler (1824-1904, born Maryland) on 3 Sep 1845 after obtaining a license on 1 Sep 1845 (Cecil County Marriage License Book; 1860 Cecil County Census; *Maryland Bible Records, Volume 4: Eastern Shore*, by Henry C. Peden, Jr. (2004), pp. 213-214, listed the births of their nine children: Sarah E., born 15 May 1846; James E., born 19 Sep 1847, died 8 Jun 1848; Truman, born 24 Jul 1849, died 23 May 1885; William, born 23 Apr 1851, died 4 Jul 1851; Mary H., born 10 Jun 1852; Robert H., born 29 Mar 1854; Hugh E., born 16 Apr 1856; John R., born 9 Feb 1858, died 24 Mar 1860; and, Annie S., born 8 Apr 1861)

Smith, Ruth, see John Smith

Smith, Samuel (1804-1862) (railroad builder and farmer at Elkton), son of Rev. James Smith, married Sarah J. Batton (1819-1891), of Newcastle, DE, daughter of William Batton, circa 1838, had six children and all except Thaddeus S. Smith (1839-1877) were living in 1897, namely, Samuel C. Smith (born c1845), Mary A. Brown (born c1847), William J. Smith (born 26 Jun 1850), Rev. George P. Smith (born c1853) and Anna J. Smith (born c1855) (*Portrait and Biographical Record of Harford and Cecil Counties, Maryland* (1897, repr. 1989), p. 295; 1860 Cecil County Census)

Smith, Samuel, married Amelia Barratt circa 26 May 1828 (date of license) by Rev. Goforth (Cecil County Marriage License Book)

Smith, Samuel A. (1802-1885), married Mary Nunns (1799-1883) probably circa 1825 (Zion Presbyterian Church Cemetery tombstone inscriptions)

Smith, Samuel C., see Samuel Smith

Smith, Samuel Jefferson (born 1811), married Mary Eliza McIntire (1817-1875) on 4 Sep 1838 (*Bible Records, Genealogical Society of Cecil County*, by Gary L. Burns (1990), p. 79 listed the births and deaths of their four children: Rebecca, born 31 May 1839; James K., born 10 Dec 1840, died 30 Apr 1873; Anna M., born 29 Jan 1842; and, Margaret Jane, born 31 Dec 1844, died – Jul 1845)

Smith, Sarah E., see Robert H. Smith

Smith, Stephen, married Jane Ella Gordon circa 17 Sep 1834 (date of license) by Rev. Hammill (Cecil County Marriage License Book)

Smith, Thaddeus S., see Samuel Smith

Smith, Thomas (born c1822) (laborer at Charlestown), married Miss Louisa Grant (born c1827), also of Charlestown, on 5 Mar 1846, after obtaining a license on 4 Mar 1846, by Rev. Humphries (*Cecil Whig*, 28 Mar 1846; Cecil County Marriage License Book; 1860 Cecil County Census)

Smith, Thomas, married Emily Carter circa 19 May 1846 (date of license) (Cecil Co. Marr. License Book)

Smith, Thomas (1814-1866), son of Thomas Smith (1777-1866), married Hannah (N) (1826-1851) probably before 1850 (St. Mark's Episcopal Church tombstone inscriptions)

Smith, Thomas W., see James H. Smith

Smith, Truman, see Robert H. Smith

Smith, William, see William Armstrong, George I. Smith and Robert H. Smith

Smith, William J., see Samuel Smith

SMITHERS, SMYTHERS

Smithers, Sarah, see Henry Templeman

Smythers, Ruth Ann, see John Ash

SMITHSON

Smithson, Cassandra G., see Gerard Gover

Smithson, Catherine C., see Henry Dorsey Smithson

Smithson, Henry Dorsey (1813-1885) (farmer, 7th District), son of William Smithson and Margaret Hall Lee, married Catherine Cassandra Archer (1810-1903), daughter of Dr. John Archer and Ann Stump, of Rock Run, on 12 Jul 1836, after obtaining a license on 11 Jul 1836, and lived near Port Deposit in Cecil Co. (Harford County Marriage License Book; John Archer, Jr. Family Bible; *Thomas Smitbson (1675-1732) of Baltimore County, Maryland and His Descendants*, by Diane Dieterle (1993), p. 63; *Substantial Copy of Genealogical Record of the Stump Family of Maryland*, by Albert P. Silver and Henry W. Archer (1891), p. 3; *Descendants of the Signers of the Bush Declaration of March 22, 1775, Harford County, Maryland*, by Christopher T. Smithson and Henry C. Peden, Jr. (2010), p. 36; Archer Genealogy on file at the Historical Society of Harford County; 1860 Cecil County Census; *The Aegis and Intelligencer*, 6 Oct 1893, reported that Mrs. Catherine C. Smithson died at her home *Beechwood* near Perryville)

Smithson, William, see Henry Dorsey Smithson

Smithson, William Jr., see Gerard Gover

SMYTH

Smyth, Sarah E., see William H. Curtis

SNOW

Snow, Israel, married Ann Craig circa 12 Jan 1835 (date of license) by Rev. Griffith (Cecil County Marriage License Book)

SNOWDEN

Snowden, John, of Cecil Co., married Mary (N) and their marriage was annulled and they were divorced on 13 Feb 1827; her name was changed to Mary Bailey and she was to have custody of their children (*Divorces and Names Changed in Maryland by Act of the Legislature, 1634-1867*, by Mary Keysor Meyer (1991), p. 83)

Snowden, Sophia Jane, see James McKowen

Snowden, Washington, married Martha Jane Brown circa 31 May 1845 (date of license) (Cecil County Marriage License Book)

Snowden, William, married Lydia Ann Carter, daughter of Robert Carter, Esq., on 29 Jan 1839, after obtaining a license on 25 Jan 1839, by Rev. Miller at Cecil Paper Mills (*Cecil Gazette*, 2 Feb 1839; Cecil County Marriage License Book)

SOULNIER

Soulnier, Matilda, see Benjamin B. Price

SPENCE

Spence, Ann, see William P. Mahan

Spence, Elizabeth E., see Enos T. Scarborough

Spence, Ephraim (born c1817) (laborer at Elkton), married Zeppora (N) (born c1825) probably circa 1844; son William Spence born c1845 (1860 Cecil County Census)

Spence, Frances S., see Hugh F. Scarborough

Spence, James (1820-1894), of Cherry Hill, married Miss Mary Ann Short (1828-1911) on 16 Mar 1848, after obtaining a license that day, by Rev. McIntire (*Cecil Whig*, 18 Mar 1848; Cecil County Marriage License Book; *Easton Gazette*, 31 Mar 1894; Cecil County Burial Permit states Mary Ann Spence died at age 83 years, 10 months, of arteriosclerosis and was buried at Cherry Hill by undertaker A. T. Abernathy)

Spence, Jane, see Benjamin Scott

Spence, Maria, see James H. Lemon Drummond

Spence, Mary Ann, see James Spence

Spence, Ruth Ann, see John Garrett

Spence, Susan Ann, see Walter Register

Spence, William, see Ephraim Spence

Spence, William, married Jane Gilpin circa 3 Oct 1838 (date of license) by Rev. Greenbank (Cecil County Marriage License Book)

Spence, William D. (born c1802) (farmer near Cherry Hill), married Eliza J. Dunn (c1815-1868) circa 15 Sep 1835 (date of license) by Rev. Wilson (Cecil County Marriage License Book; *Cecil Democrat and Farmer's Journal*, 21 Mar 1868, obituary did not give her age; 1860 Cecil County Census)

SPENCER

Spencer, Caroline, see John Shafer

Spencer, Ellen, see Joseph Spencer

Spencer, Joseph (born c1815) (African American) (farmer at Cecilton), married Sarah (N) (born c1815) (African American) by 1844; daughter Ellen born c1845 (African American) (1860 Cecil County Census)

Spencer, Martha, see William Scotten

Spencer, Sarah E., see John Frazier, Jr.

Spencer, Thomas K., married Jessie Haswell circa 28 Sep 1840 (date of license) (Cecil Co. Marr. Lic. Book)

SPROSTON

Sproston, John T. and Mary B., see Stephen Armour

STAATS

Staats, David (born c1817, Delaware) (farmer), of Cecil Co., married 1st to Sarah Boots, of Kent Co., circa 18 Mar 1840 (date of license, Kent Co.) by Rev. Houston and married 2nd to Hannah Price (born c1826, Maryland) circa 18 Sep 1847 (date of license) (Cecil Co. Marr. License Book; 1860 Cecil County Census)

Staats, James R., of Delaware, married Mary A. Caulk, daughter of Jacob Caulk, of Middle Neck, Cecil Co., on 7 Feb 1850, after obtaining a license on 29 Jan 1850, by Rev. Henry (*Cecil Democrat and Farmer's Journal*, 9 Feb 1850; *Cecil Whig*, 9 Feb 1850; Cecil County Marriage License Book; DAR transcript copied in 1955 mistakenly spelled her name Carrier)

STACKHOUSE

Stackhouse, G. W. (born c1821, Pennsylvania) (store clerk, 7th District), married Rebecca (N) (born c1822, Pennsylvania) probably circa 1847; daughter Elizabeth born c1848, Maryland (1860 Cecil Co. Census)

Stackhouse, Mary M., of Cecil Co., divorced from John Stackhouse on 19 Mar 1840 (*Divorces and Names Changed in Maryland by Act of the Legislature, 1634-1867*, by Mary Keysor Meyer (1991), p. 83)

STALCUP

Stalcup, Ann, see John Stalcup

Stalcup, James, married Rebecca Matthews on 26 May 1839, after obtaining a license on 24 May 1839, by Rev. Hagany (Cecil County Marriage License Book; DAR transcript copied in 1928 misspelled his name Stalcap; Elkton Methodist Church Register, p. 139)

Stalcup, John (born c1825, Maryland) (laborer, 7th District), married Hester (N) (born c1830, Maryland) probably circa 1849; daughter Ann born c1850 (1860 Cecil County Census spelled the name Stalkup)

Stalcup, William, married Eliza Ann Hitchcock on 14 Jun 1839, after obtaining a license on 7 May 1839, by Rev. Hagany (Cecil County Marriage License Book; Elkton Methodist Church Register, p. 139)

Stalcup, William H., married Elizabeth Ann Lewis on 26 Dec 1843, after obtaining a license on 25 Dec 1843, by Rev. Shields (Cecil County Marriage License Book; Elkton Methodist Church Register, p. 140)

Stalcup, Zapola, see John M. Terry

STANERT

Stanert, Sarah Ann, see George Flintham

STANLEY, STANDLEY

Stanley, James, married Ann Etherington (1809-1872), daughter of James and Sarah E. Etherington, circa 1830 (St. Stephen's Episcopal Church Cemetery tombstone inscription for Ann Etherington Stanley)

Standley, Sarah, see Jacob James Howell

STANTON

Stanton, Elizabeth, see George W. Thompson

Stanton, William, married Mary Evans circa 5 Jan 1825 (date of license) by Rev. Russell (Cecil County Marriage License Book)

STAPLEFORD

Stapleford, Elizabeth, see John H. Pearce

Stapleford, Sarah, see David Townsend

STAPLER

Stapler, Mary, Sarah and Stephen, see Stephen Woodrow

STAPLES

Staples, Samuel W., of New York State, married Louisa H. Nowland, of Cecil Co., circa 26 Nov 1831 (date of license) by Rev. Rees (Cecil County Marriage License Book)

STARR

Starr, John Thomas, married Grizzelda Boyd circa 30 Sep 1845 (date of license) (Cecil County Marriage License Book)

STAYTON

Stayton, David H. (esquire), married Eliza Ann (N) (1804-1864) probably circa 1822-1825 and she died at Camden, Delaware in 1864 (*Cecil Whig*, 16 Apr 1864)

STEBBING

Stebbing, Joseph (1823-1901, born Maryland) (shoemaker, 7th District), married Francina Kerr (1828-1885, born Maryland) on 18 Nov 1847, after obtaining a license on 15 Nov 1847, by Rev. Elliott (Cecil County Marriage License Book; *Maryland Bible Records, Volume 4: Eastern Shore*, by Henry C. Peden, Jr. (2004), pp. 216-217, listed the births and marriages of their seven children as follows: Sarah Patton, born 11 Sep 1848, married John Whyte, died – Jan 1889; James Andrew, born 16 Feb 1850, married Cornelia Stevens, died 14 Oct 1914; Joseph Francis "Frank," born 7 Sep 1852, married Georgeanna Poplar, died 4 May 1889; (N), twin, born 7 Sep 1852; Mary Georgeanna, born 22 Sep 1856, died 16 Sep 1942, married Clinton L. Thompson; Martha Indiana, born 22 Sep 1856, married Olympblus Gregory Smith; and, Emma Elizabeth, born 2 Sep 1862, married John Sterrett Beaven; 1860 Cecil County Census)

STEEL, STEELE

Steele, Anna E., see George Bush

Steel, Caleb, married Jane Smith circa 2 Apr 1829 (date of license) by Rev. Barratt (Cecil County Marriage License Book)

Steel, David (born c1824, Maryland) (cooper, 9th District), son of David and Sarah Steel, married Catherine White (born 1828, Maryland), daughter of John White and Jane Hall, on 4 Jun 1846 after obtaining a license on 2 Jun 1846 (Cecil County Marriage License Book spelled his name Steele; *Maryland Bible Records, Volume 4: Eastern Shore*, by Henry C. Peden, Jr. (2004), p. 250, spelled his name Steel; 1860 Cecil County Census also spelled his name Steel)

Steel, Esther, see John Patterson Evans

Steele, George A. (carpenter), of Chesapeake City, son of Joseph Steele, married Rebecca R. Sharp circa 1835 (son Joseph H. Steele born 13 Dec 1836) (*Portrait and Biographical Record of Harford and Cecil Counties, Maryland* (1897, repr. 1989), p. 247)

Steele, Henry, see George Bush

Steel, Hugh (1810-1878, born Maryland) (farmer, 7th District), married Hannah Jane Rowland (1816-1881, born Maryland) circa 5 Nov 1842 (date of license); son John Steel born c1847 (Cecil County Marriage License Book; West Nottingham Cemetery tombstone inscriptions; 1860 Cecil County Census)

Steel, Hugh, see John Patterson Evans

Steel, James M., married Martha S. Evans circa 2 Jan 1847 (date of license) (Cecil Co. Marr. License Book)

Steel, Jeremiah, married Eliza Wright circa 16 Jun 1828 (date of license) by Rev. Barratt (Cecil County Marriage License Book)

Steel, John (1799-1868), married Sarah Patton (1806-1854) circa 16 Nov 1831 (date of license) by Rev. Magraw (Cecil County Marriage License Book; West Nottingham Cemetery tombstone inscriptions)

Steel, John, see Hugh Steel

Steele, Joseph, see George A. Steele

Steele, Joseph H., see George A. Steele

Steel, Margaret, see William Moore

Steel, Mary, see Amos Ewing

Steel, Rebecca, see John Patterson Evans

Steel, Sarah, see David Steel and Elisha Alexander

STEPHENS

Stephens, Caroline, see Zebdial W. Potter

Stephens, Catharine, see Nicholas Lloyd

Stephens, Eliza, see William H. Nowland

Stephens, Elizabeth, see William B. Price

Stephens, Frances E., see Sylvester H. Stephens

Stephens, John, see John Bozman Kerr

Stephens, Lucy Hamilton, see John Bozman Kerr

Stephens, Samuel H., see Zebdial W. Potter

Stephens, Sylvester H. (born c1816) (master carpenter at Cecilton), married Marion (N) (born c1824) circa 1846; daughter Frances E. Stephens born c1847 (1860 Cecil County Census)

Stephens, Thomas K., married Juliana Virginia Wilson circa 16 Jul 1834 (date of license) by Rev. James McKenney, a Protestant Episcopal minister in North Sassafras (Cecil County Marriage License Book)

Stephens, also see Stevens

STEPHENSON

Stephenson, James, see Corbin Cooley and Robert Stephenson

Stephenson, Mary Douglas, see Corbin Cooley

Stephenson, Robert (1806-1861, born Maryland) (lumber inspector, 7th District), son of James Stephenson and Priscilla Hopkins, married Agnes M. Kerr (born c1820, Maryland) circa 6 Dec 1842 (date of license), and Robert murdered by Union soldiers at Port Deposit on 21 Sep 1861 (Cecil County Marriage License Book; *Portrait and Biographical Record of Harford and Cecil Counties, Maryland* (1897, repr. 1989), p. 275; 1860 Cecil County Census)

STERN

Stern, Thomas (1811-1853), married Mary N. (N) (1811-1895) probably circa 1831-1832 (St. John's Church Cemetery, at Lewisville, tombstone inscriptions)

Stern, William (1807-1865), married Eleanor (N) (1809-1896) probably circa 1828-1829 (St. John's Church Cemetery, at Lewisville, tombstone inscriptions)

STEVENS

Stevens, Ann H., see John L. Hague

Stevens, Cornelia, see Joseph Stebbing

Stevens, John, see John C. Eccleston

Stevens, M. Almira, see John C. Eccleston

Stevens, William (merchant), of Centreville, married Miss Louisa Massey, daughter of Major J. Massey, of Queen Anne's Co., on 10 Feb 1829 by Rev. Thompson (*Elkton Press*, 21 Feb 1829)

Stevens, also see Stephens

STEWART

Stewart, Joseph Henry, married Arrietta Craddock circa 25 Jan 1825 (date of license) by Rev. Stephenson (Cecil County Marriage License Book)

Stewart, Mary, see John McGee

Stewart, Naomi, see Abraham Clark

Stewart, Samuel, married Mary Bratton circa 14 Sep 1843 (date of license) (Cecil Co. Marr. License Book)

Stewart, Sarah Ann, see George Flintham

Stewart, Seth (born c1820, Delaware) (laborer at Elkton), married Hannah Johnson (born c1822, Maryland) on 20 Mar 1834, after obtaining a license that same day, by Rev. Hagany (Cecil County Marriage License Book; DAR transcript copied in 1928 mistakenly listed the license date as 29 Mar 1834; Elkton Methodist Church Register, p. 5, listed the marriage date as 20 Mar 1834; 1860 Cecil County Census)

STIDHAM

Stidham, Eliza S., see William Asay

STITES

Stites, Ann, see James T. Taylor

Stites, Henry S. (1797-1870, born Pennsylvania) (major, of Port Deposit, later general and farmer), married Harriett Stump (c1799-1876), daughter of John Stump, deceased, all of Cecil Co., on 5 Apr 1831, after obtaining a license that same day, by Rev. Finney at Perry Farm in Cecil Co.; son Richard Stites died on 14 Aug 1847 in his 12th year (Cecil County Marriage License Book; *Independent Citizen*, 9 Apr 1831; *Baltimore American and Commercial Daily Advertiser*, 14 Apr 1831; 1860 Cecil County Census; *Kent News*, 2 Apr 1870; *Cecil Whig*, 21 Aug 1847 (included a short poem) and 19 Feb 1876)

Stites, Richard, see Henry S. Stites

STOKES

Stokes, Henry (born c1809, Maryland) (African American) (laborer, 7th District), married Angeline (N) (born c1815, Maryland) (African American) probably circa 1839; son James Stokes born circa 1840, Maryland (1860 Cecil County Census)

Stokes, William Axon, of Philadelphia, married Mary Scanlin, daughter of the late Dr. James Scanlin, of Cecil Co., on 5 Jan 1842 by the Rt. Rev. Bishop Kendrick at St. John's Church in Philadelphia (*Cecil Gazette*, 15 Jan 1842)

STOOPS

Stoops, Benjamin, married Mary Ann Simpers circa 23 Mar 1841 (date of license) (Cecil County Marriage License Book)

Stoops, Catherine Ann, see William Bristow, Jr.

Stoops, Joseph T., married Ann Maria Law circa 17 Feb 1829 (date of license) by Rev. Woolford (Cecil County Marriage License Book)

Stoops, Rachel, see Benjamin Croucer(?)

STOREY

Storey, James (esquire), of Penn Township, Chester Co., PA, married Miss Eliza Ann Wright, of New Garden Township, Chester Co., PA, on 28 Mar 1849 by Rev. Plummer at Mt. Olivet, New London Township, Chester Co., PA (*Cecil Democrat and Farmer's Journal*, 14 Apr 1849)

STOUT

Stout, Joseph T. (1810-1898) (merchant at North East), son of Edward Stout (1786-1859) and Claressa Mulford (1789-1870), of New Jersey, married Mary Mauldin Simpers (1819-1864), only daughter of Johnson Simpers and Millicent Ford or Foard, of Cecil Co., on 8 Mar 1842 after obtaining a license that same day (Cecil County Marriage License Book; North East Methodist Church Cemetery tombstone inscriptions; *Maryland Bible Records, Volume 4: Eastern Shore*, by Henry C. Peden, Jr. (2004), pp. 217-219, listed the births of their three children, namely, Ellen Herbert, born 13 Nov 1843, Salem, NJ, Mary Millicent, born 23 Mar 1847, Salem, NJ, and Clara Virginia, born 5 Apr 1857, North East, MD; 1860 Cecil County Census; *Cecil Whig*, 2 Apr 1864)

STRADLEY

Stradley, John W. (born c1816, Maryland) (laborer at Cecilton), married 1st to Mary Walmsley circa 31 Jan 1839 (date of license) by Rev. Piggot, a Protestant Episcopal minister in North Sassafras, and married 2nd to Sarah A. Anderson (born c1824, Maryland) circa 27 Dec 1851 (date of license) (Cecil County Marriage License Book; 1860 Cecil County Census)

Stradley, Lucretia, see Samuel Stradley

Stradley, Rebecca, see Isaac B. Jester

Stradley, Samuel, married Lucretia Stradley circa 22 Jan 1834 (date of license) by Rev. Duke (Cecil County Marriage License Book)

Stradley, Thomas (born c1812, Maryland) (farmer at Cecilton), married Penina or Penanah Ruley (born c1819, Maryland) circa 6 Jan 1835 (date of license) by Rev. Duke (Cecil County Marriage License Book spelled her name Penanah and the DAR transcript copied in 1928 misspelled it Penance; 1860 Cecil County Census listed her name as Penina Stradley and his name as Thomas V. Stradley)

Stradley, William, married Frances Carroll circa 10 Nov 1838 (date of license) by Rev. Piggot, a Protestant Episcopal minister in North Sassafras (Cecil County Marriage License Book)

STRAWBRIDGE

Strawbridge, Ann, see Evan Morgan

Strawbridge, Joseph, married Eliza Oldham circa 11 Oct 1825 (date of license) by Rev. Graham (Cecil County Marriage License Book)

STRICKLAND

Strickland, John S., married 1st to Deborah A. Davidson, both of Cecil Co., on 12 Oct 1848, after obtaining a license on 10 Oct 1848, by Rev. McIntire, and married 2nd to Ann R. Shockley circa 26 May 1852 (date of license) (Cecil County Marriage License Book; *Cecil Democrat and Farmer's Journal*, 14 Oct 1848, listed his name as John A. Strickland)

Strickland, Margaret, see Edward Berry

Strickland, Palmer C. (1818-1890), married Miss Margaret E. Scott (1824-1890), both of Elkton, on 31 Oct 1850, after obtaining a license in 30 Oct 1850, by Rev. Fernley (*Cecil Whig*, 2 Nov 1850; Cecil County Marriage License Book; Elkton Methodist Church Register, p. 141; Elkton Presbyterian Church Cemetery tombstone inscriptions; *Midland Journal*, 25 Apr 1890; *Cecil Democrat and Farmer's Journal*, 2 Nov 1850, noting that "The happy pair will accept our thanks for the very delicious cake which we received. We give them the old Spanish blessing, which is: – 'May they live a thousand years, and their shadows never grow less.'")

Strickland, Robert Kennedy, of Cecil Co., married Miss Eliza Jane Smith, of East Nottingham Township, Chester Co., PA, on 20 Jun 1850 at the residence of J. Pusey Smith near Lewisville, PA (*Cecil Democrat and Farmer's Journal*, 20 Jul 1850)

Strickland, William P. (1811-1864) (master carpenter), of Chester Co., PA, later of Elkton, married Miss Martha Ann Gallaher (1824-1880), of Cecil Co., on 14 Oct 1845, after obtaining a license that same day, by Rev. McIntire (*Cecil Whig*, 15 Nov 1845; Cecil County Marriage License Book; 1860 Cecil County Census; Elkton Presbyterian Church Cemetery tombstone inscriptions; *Cecil Whig*, 16 Apr 1864)

STRONG

Strong, Mary, see John F. Crouch

STROUD

Stroud, James, of Mount Airy, married Hannah F. Hedges (1811-1864), daughter of John Hedges, probably circa 1830 (*Cecil Whig*, 9 Jan 1864)

STROUT

Strout, Arthur M. (born c1810, Maine) (stone cutter, 7th District), married Susanna W. Thompson (born c1818, Maryland) circa 1 Nov 1834 (date of license) by Rev. Griffith (Cecil County Marriage License Book; 1860 Cecil County Census)

STUART

Stuart, Margaret, see William McClelland

STUBBINS

Stubbins, Annjaline, see William Jackson

Stubbins, William, married Harriet Todd circa 10 Feb 1849 (date of license) (Cecil Co. Marr. License Book)

STUBBS

Stubbs, Daniel (1812-1869), son of Isaac and Hannah Stubbs, married Rachel Ann Kirk (1818-1871), daughter of Josiah Kirk and Phebe Passmore, circa 1846 (oldest child Theodore Kirk Stubbs born 8th day of the 6th month 1847) (*Births, Deaths and Marriages of the Nottingham Quakers, 1680-1899*, by Alice L. Beard (1989), pp. 60, 105; Brick Meeting House, at Calvert, tombstone inscriptions)

Stubbs, Isaac, see Daniel Stubbs

Stubbs, James, son of Daniel and Ruth Stubbs, of Little Britain Township, Lancaster Co., PA, married Sarah (N), of East Nottingham Hundred, Cecil Co., circa 1830 [information illegible] (*Births, Deaths and Marriages of the Nottingham Quakers, 1680-1899*, by Alice L. Beard (1989), p. 222)

Stubbs, Joseph I. (1816-1884), married Martha (N) (1827-1912) probably circa 1850 (Rosebank Cemetery, at Calvert, tombstone inscriptions)

Stubbs, Mary, see Jesse Tatman

Stubbs, Sarah A., see Job Eldridge

Stubbs, Theodore Kirk, see Daniel Stubbs

STUCHERST

Stucherst, William M., married Olivia Ann Cazier, daughter of John Cazier, Esq., of New Castle Co., DE, on 24 Jan 1850 by Rev. Elliott (*Cecil Whig*, 26 Jan 1850, and *Cecil Democrat and Farmer's Journal*, 26 Jan 1850, both noted, Delaware papers please copy; *Delaware Gazette*, 29 Jan 1850)

STUCKERT

Stuckert, Susan M. and William, see Lewis P. Ellison

STULL

Stull, Daniel, married Mary Ann Smith circa 26 Mar 1839 (date of license) by Rev. Kennard (Cecil County Marriage License Book)

Stull, Mary, see Joseph C. Cloud

STUMP

Stump, Ann, see Henry Wilson Archer and Henry Dorsey Smithson

Stump, Harriet, see Henry S. Stites

Stump, John (1804-1896) (esquire), of Perry Point, married Miss Mary Alicia Mitchell (1817-1894), eldest daughter of the late Col. George Edward Mitchell and Mary Hooper, on 18 Dec 1834, after obtaining a license on 17 Dec 1834, by Rev. Russell (Cecil County Marriage License Book; *Cecil Gazette*, 20 Dec 1834; Elkton Presbyterian Church Cemetery tombstone inscriptions; *History of Cecil County*, by George Johnston (1881, repr. 1989), p. 507)

Stump, John, see Henry S. Stites

Stump, Mary, see John Archer

STURDEVANT

Sturdevant, Catharine J., see John Thomas Calvert

Sturdevant, Nancy, see Evy S. Adams

Sturdevant, Susanna Elizabeth, see Thomas Williams

STURGEON

Sturgeon, Mary Ann, see Enoch Johnson and Jonathan Gillespie

Sturgeon, Thomas (born c1820), of North East, married Martha Ann Redgraves (born c1821) circa 7 May 1840 (date of license) (Cecil County Marriage License Book; 1860 Cecil County Census)

SULLIVAN
Sullivan, Angeline Caroline, see Thomas Williams
Sullivan, Timothy, married Jane Cannon circa 16 Jan 1843 (date of license) (Cecil Co. Marr. License Book)

SUMPTION
Sumption, Joseph, married Mary Kilpatrick circa 23 Sep 1825 (date of license) by Rev. Sharpley (Cecil County Marriage License Book)

SUTOR
Sutor, Susanna, see Bennett Charshee

SUTTON
Sutton, Ann, see John Scott
Sutton, Ellen, see John Scott
Sutton, Hannah Ann, see Daniel Willis

SWEENY, SWENEY
Sweeny (Sweney), James, married Miss Margaret Alexander, daughter of Joseph Alexander, all of Cecil Co., on 11 Jan 1838, after obtaining a license on 8 Jan 1838, by Rev. Russel (Cecil County Marriage License Book spelled his name Sweeny; *Cecil Gazette*, 3 Feb 1838, spelled his name Sweney)

SWEET
Sweet, Benjamin B., married Hetty Ann Humphreys circa 14 Jun 1839 (date of license) by Rev. Pierson (Cecil County Marriage License Book)

SWIFT
Swift, Mayor, see Francis Vincent

SWISHER
Swisher, Jeremiah (1820-1876, born Maryland) (farmer, 6th District), son of John Swisher (1790-1871) and Rebecca (N) (1788-1859), of Pennsylvania, married Rebecca R. (N) (1825-1901) probably circa 1843; daughter Gemima Swisher born c1844, Maryland (West Nottingham Cemetery tombstone inscriptions; 1860 Cecil County Census)
Swisher, John, see Jeremiah Swisher
Swisher, Rachel Maria, see Robert N. Hindman
Swisher, Rebecca, see Jeremiah Swisher

TAGART, TAGGART
Tagart, Louisa, see Robert Gilmore
Taggart, William, married Eliza Jane Wright circa 20 Dec 1850 (date of license) (Cecil County Marriage License Book)

TALLEY
Talley, Jane, see John Wilson

TAMBLIN
Tamblin, Martha, see James McNit

TAMMANY

Tammany, William, married Rachel M. Griffee (1803-1874) circa 9 Dec 1831 (date of license) by Rev. McCarrol, a Methodist Episcopal minister in Port Deposit (Cecil County Marriage License Book; DAR transcript copied in 1928 misspelled his name Tamnay and her name Griffie; West Nottingham Cemetery tombstone inscription for Rachel M. Tammany)

TARMAN, TARNAN

Tarman (Tarnan?), James, married Eleanor Slaven circa 3 Oct 1825 (date of license) by Rev. Duke (James' name in the original Cecil County Marriage License Book was unclearly written and it looked more like Tarman or Tarnan, even though the DAR transcript copied in 1928 had listed it as "Forman?")

TARBURTON

Tarburton, John W., married Elizabeth S. Vandegrift circa 15 Dec 1836 (date of license) by Rev. Potts (Cecil County Marriage License Book; DAR transcript copied in 1928 listed her name as "Eliz. Van Digrift")

TARRING

Tarring, Edward, see George W. Thompson

Tarring, Edward H. (born c1827, Maryland) (lumber inspector, 7th District), son of Edward T. Tarring, Esq., of Port Deposit, married Sarah Childs (born c1830, Pennsylvania), daughter of John Childs, Esq., of West Philadelphia, on 24 Jan 1850 by Rev. Roth (*Cecil Whig*, 16 Feb 1850; 1860 Cecil County Census)

Tarring, Edward T., see Edward H. Tarring

Tarring, Elizabeth H., see James Coulson

Tarring, Sara, see Edward H. Tarring

Tarring, Sarah Ann, see George W. Thompson

TATMAN

Tatman, Bayard, married Eleanor Cunningham circa 29 Jan 1833 (date of license) by Rev. Torbert (Cecil County Marriage License Book)

Tatman, Jesse, married Mary Stubbs circa 17 Dec 1834 (date of license) by Rev. Smith (Cecil County Marriage License Book)

TAYLOR

Taylor, Abram, married Miss Mary Sophia Pearce, both of Elkton, on 18 Apr 1833, after obtaining a license that same day, by Rev. Morris (*Cecil Republican*, 20 Apr 1833; Cecil County Marriage License Book; DAR transcript copied in 1928 mistakenly listed their names as Abraham Taylor and Mary L. Pearce)

Taylor, Ann (Annie), see David A. McCrea, James Girvin, Levi Taylor and William C. Clark

Taylor, Anna, see James Taylor

Taylor, Benjamin, married Miss Mary Hemphill on 31 Oct 1844, after obtaining a license that same day, by Rev. Shields (Cecil County Marriage License Book; Elkton Methodist Church Register, p. 140; *Cecil Whig*, 2 Nov 1844)

Taylor, Caroline, see (N) Jackson

Taylor, David, see James Taylor

Taylor, David, married Elizabeth Gorrell circa 6 Jan 1831 (date of license) by Rev. Goforth (Cecil County Marriage License Book)

Taylor, Deborah, see Jacob Markee

Taylor, Eliza, see William Green and Joel Reynolds

Taylor, Elizabeth, see Jacob Woollehan

Taylor, Emily, see Joseph Gurlie

Taylor, Emma J., see John Taylor

Taylor, Frances, see Jonathan McVey

Taylor, George W. (1814-1864), of Perryville, married (N) probably circa 1835 (*Cecil Whig*, 9 Apr 1864, obituary included a poem by his wife, but her name was not given)

Taylor, Harriet M., see William H. Taylor

Taylor, Helen, see John Keithley

Taylor, Isaac, see John Taylor

Taylor, Isaac R. (born 1821, Maryland) (cabinet maker and undertaker, Rising Sun), married Miss M. Harlan in 1846, according to *Portrait and Biographical Record of Harford and Cecil Counties, Maryland* (1897, rpr. 1989), p. 265, but the1860 Cecil County Census listed his wife as Lucetta, born c1827, Pennsylvania)

Taylor, Isabella (Isabelle), see James Taylor and Elisha England Kirk

Taylor, James (1810-1901, born Ireland), married Jane or Jennie (N) (1815-1892, born Ireland) probably circa 1840 and children born in Ireland were William c1841, James c1843, John c1845, Isabella c1847, David c1849, Thomas c1851, Jane c1754; and, daughter Anna was born c1858 in Maryland (Rosebank Cemetery, at Calvert, tombstone inscriptions; 1860 Cecil County Census)

Taylor, James, see Elisha England Kirk

Taylor, James T., married Ann Stites circa 20 Jun 1848 (date of license) (Cecil County Marr. License Book)

Taylor, Jane, see Benjamin C. Cowan

Taylor, Jesse (1821-1895), married Hannah B. (N) (1812-1883) probably circa 1842 (Cherry Hill Methodist Church Cemetery tombstone inscriptions)

Taylor, John, see John Keithley

Taylor, John, married Eleanor Navy on 9 Oct 1841 after obtaining a license that same day (Cecil County Marriage License Book; Elkton Methodist Church Register)

Taylor, John (born c1822, Delaware), married Elizabeth (N) (born c1824, Maryland) circa 1842; son Isaac Taylor born c1843 (1860 Cecil County Census)

Taylor, John, married Sarah Ann Knight circa 5 Oct 1846 (date of license) (Cecil Co. Marr. License Book)

Taylor, John (born c1824, Delaware) (forgeman at Elkton), married Emma (N) (born c1824, Maryland) probably circa 1848; son William F. Taylor born c1849, Delaware, daughter Emma J. Taylor born c1851, Maryland, daughter Mary A. Taylor born c1854, Maryland, son John W. Taylor born c1856, Maryland (1860 Cecil County Census)

Taylor, John Wesley, married Mary Black circa 10 Jul 1835 (date of license) by Rev. Coleman (Cecil County Marriage License Book)

Taylor, Joseph (1802-1866, born Pennsylvania) (hotel keeper at Elkton), probably married 1st to (N) circa 1825 and married 2nd to Mrs. Jane Henry (born c1805, Delaware), of Elkton, on 24 Jan 1843, after obtaining a license that same day, by Rev. McIntire; daughter Josephine Taylor born c1846, Maryland (Cecil County Marriage License Book; 1860 Cecil County Census; *Cecil Whig*, 28 Jan 1843 and 21 Apr 1866); see David A. McCrea, *q.v.*

Taylor, Joseph James (captain), of Baltimore, married Miss Sidney A. Creswell, of Port Deposit, on 12 Nov 1850, after obtaining a license on 8 Nov 1850, by Rev. Lacy in Port Deposit (*Cecil Whig*, 16 Nov 1850; Cecil County Marriage License Book; *Cecil Democrat and Farmer's Journal*, 23 Nov 1850; *Baltimore Sun*, 18 Nov 1850)

Taylor, Levi (1820-1902, born Maryland) (farmer, 8th District), married Rebecca J. (N) (1825-1892, born Pennsylvania) probably circa 1850; daughter Annie Taylor, born c1851, born Pennsylvania; their other children were also born in Pennsylvania and the family moved to Cecil County circa 1859-1860 (Friends Cemetery, at Harrisville, tombstone inscriptions; 1860 Cecil County Census)

Taylor, Lydia, see George Winchester

Taylor, Margaret, see Edwin W. Aston

Taylor, Maria, see Silas Evans Carter and James Lyon

Taylor, Mary A., see John Taylor

Taylor, Mary A. E., see John W. Oldham

Taylor, Rachael Ann, see Elias B. Glenn

Taylor, Reuben, married Rachel Ward circa 28 May 1831 (date of license) by Rev. Barnes (Cecil County Marriage License Book)

Taylor, Samuel, married Janetta Cunnay circa 28 Sep 1825 (date of license) by Rev. Magraw (Cecil County Marriage License Book)

Taylor, Sarah, see Evan, Joseph, Thomas T. and William Benjamin, and John W. Alexander

Taylor, Susan, see Samuel Buenes

Taylor, Thomas, see James Taylor

Taylor, Thomas (born c1805) (blacksmith at Cecilton), married Margaret Saw (born c1805) circa 8 Mar 1828 (date of license) (Cecil County Marriage License Book; 1860 Cecil County Census)

Taylor, William, see James Taylor

Taylor, William F., see John Taylor

Taylor, William H., of Baltimore City, married Harriet M. Taylor, of Cecil Co., daughter of Jeremy Taylor, on 5 Sep 1848, after obtaining a license on 4 Sep 1848, at St. Francis Xavier Church in Bohemia by Rev. King (Cecil County Marriage License Book; *Baltimore Sun*, 7 Sep 1848; *Cecil Democrat and Farmer's Journal*, 9 Sep 1848; *Cecil Whig*, 9 Sep 1848; *Directory of Ministers and the Maryland Churches They Served, 1634-1990*, by Edna A. Kanely, Volume I, p. 386)

Taylor, Zimri (1812-1888), married Julia A. (N) (1809-1885) probably circa 1833 (Rosebank Cemetery, at Calvert, tombstone inscriptions)

TEAGUE
Teague, Albert R., married Eliza M. Williamson circa 15 May 1832 (date of license) by Rev. Griffith (Cecil County Marriage License Book)

TEMPLE
Temple, Simon J., of New Castle Co., DE, married Sarah Jane Cooley, of Harford Co., MD, circa 18 Mar 1845 (date of license) (Cecil County Marriage License Book)

TEMPLEMAN
Templeman, Henry, married Sarah Smithers circa 11 Jun 1827 (date of license) (Cecil County Marriage License Book)

TENNANT
Tennant, Thomas, married Caroline Davis, daughter of the late Richard Davis, Esq., of Cecil Co., on 3 Mar 1835 (*Baltimore American and Commercial Daily Advertiser*, 5 Mar 1835)

TERBIT
Terbit, William D., married Hannah Lynch circa 9 Jun 1835 (date of license) by Rev. Houston (Cecil County Marriage License Book)

TERHUNE
Terhune, Anna, see Abraham DeWitt

TERRELL
Terrell, Joseph T. (1816, Delaware) (stone mason at Elkton), married Lydia Ann McCauley (born c1818, Maryland) circa 28 Dec 1839 (date of license) by Rev. Miller (Cecil County Marriage License Book; 1860 Cecil County Census spelled his name Terl)

Terrell, Timothy N., married Harriet C. Andrews circa 12 Sep 1832 (date of license) by Rev. Rees (Cecil County Marriage License Book)

TERRY
Terry, John M., married Miss Zapola Stalcup, both of Cecil Co., on 28 Jan 1845, after obtaining a license on 25 Jan 1845, by Rev. Shields (Cecil County Marriage License Book; Elkton Methodist Church Register, page 140; *Cecil Whig*, 1 Feb 1845)

Terry, Margaret, see Upton Terry

Terry, Mary Ellen, see Charles F. Merritt

Terry, Thomas (1811-1878), of near Bay View, married Margaret Armstrong (1824-1907) circa 6 Nov 1850 (date of license) (Cecil County Marriage License Book; St. Mary Anne's Episcopal Church Cemetery tombstone inscriptions; *Cecil Whig*, 20 Apr 1878)

Terry, Upton (1797-1855), married Margaret Gamble (1804-1883, born Maryland) circa 18 Feb 1826 (date of license) by Rev. Sharpley (Cecil County Marriage License Book; DAR transcript copied in 1928 mistakenly listed his name as Myron Perry (Terry?); Zion Methodist Cemetery tombstone inscriptions; 1860 Cecil County Census listed Margaret Terry, aged about 55, as head of household near Bay View)

THACKERY

Thackery, Rachel, see Arthur Clark

Thackery, Robert H. (1804-1872, born Maryland) (farmer at North East), married Sarah Ann Knotts (1804-1887, born Delaware) circa 1 Jun 1835 (date of license) by Rev. Houston (Cecil County Marriage License Book; 1860 Cecil County Census; Hart's Methodist Church Cemetery tombstone inscriptions; *Cecil Whig*, 21 Sep 1872, reported Robert Thackery, of Elk Neck, died in his 79th year and left a widow and five grown children)

Thackery, Thomas (1810-1872), married Miss Sarah Matthews (born c1818) on 29 Mar 1838, after obtaining a license that same day, by Rev. McFarland (*Cecil Gazette*, 31 Mar 1838; Cecil County Marriage License Book; DAR transcript copied in 1928 mistakenly listed the minister's name as Farland; James McFarland was a Methodist minister in Elkton at that time; Elkton Methodist Church Register, p. 138; 1860 Cecil County Census; *Cecil Whig*, 2 Nov 1872)

THOMAS

Thomas, Alfred B., married 1st to Alice O'Donald circa 15 Jun 1829 (date of license) by Rev. Epinette (Cecil County Marriage License Book listed her name as O'Donal; DAR transcript copied in 1928 mistakenly listed her name as Alice O. Donald and misspelled the minister's name as Effenie (Peter Epinette was a Catholic priest in the Bohemia area at that time); Alfred married 2nd to Jane A. Shields circa 14 Oct 1839 (date of license) by Rev. King (Cecil County Marriage License Book)

Thomas, Ann, see Thomas Boulden and George Davidson

Thomas, Ann Eliza, see John T. Alexander and Thomas Poe

Thomas, Benjamin, see Samuel Thomas

Thomas, Bryan M., formerly of Cecil Co., married Miss Mary J. Logie, daughter of John Logie, of Baltimore, on 3 Jul 1849 by Rev. Sargeant in Baltimore (*Cecil Democrat and Farmer's Journal*, 7 Jul 1849; *Baltimore Sun*, 6 Jul 1849, spelled his first name Bryant)

Thomas, David (free African American), married Catherine Gibbons (free African American) circa 19 Sep 1842 (date of license) (Cecil County Marriage License Book)

Thomas, Elizabeth, see Joseph Thomas

Thomas, Emily, see Thomas Wilson

Thomas, Francis (honorable), of Maryland, married Sally McDowell, daughter of James McDowell, of Virginia, on 8 Jun 1841 by Rev. Skinner at *Colralta* in Lexington, Virginia (*Cecil Gazette*, 19 Jun 1841)

Thomas, George, married Louisa Little, daughter of Christopher Little, Esq., all of Charlestown, on 5 Dec 1843, after obtaining a license on 4 Dec 1843, by Rev. Goentner at Charlestown (Cecil County Marriage License Book; *Cecil Whig*, 9 Dec 1843)

Thomas, Hannah, see Richard L. Thomas

Thomas, Harriet, see Samuel H. Freeman

Thomas, John, see William Thomas

Thomas, John E. (born c1810, Maryland) (carpenter at Elkton), married Matilda Jones (born c1820, Delaware) circa 8 Feb 1837 (date of license) by Rev. Potts (Cecil County Marriage License Book; 1860 Cecil County Census)

Thomas, John H., of Cecil Co., married Miss Susan Lindsey, of New Castle Co., DE, on 31 Mar 1829 by Rev. Russel near Newark, DE (*Delaware Gazette*, 3 Apr 1829; *Elkton Press*, 4 Apr 1829)

Thomas, Joseph, son of Joseph and Elizabeth Thomas, the former deceased, of Wilmington, DE, married Adrianna Moore (born 1807), daughter of Joseph Moore and Mercy Cutler, the latter died in 1822, of Cecil Co., on the – day of the 3rd month 1826 at ---- (*Births, Deaths and Marriages of the Nottingham Quakers, 1680-1899*, by Alice L. Beard (1989), pp. 66, 221)

Thomas, Joseph R., married Susan J. (N) (1815-1877) and died in Baltimore at the residence of her son-in-law W. C. Barnes, her husband having pre-deceased her (*Cecil Whig*, 2 Jun 1877)

Thomas, Lewis W. (born c1824) (merchant at North East), married Frances Ann Lum (born c1825) circa 29 Dec 1845 (date of license) (Cecil County Marriage License Book; 1860 Cecil County Census)

Thomas, Lydia, see Richard Thomas

Thomas, Mary, see William Thomas

Thomas, Mary Ann, see Philip Thomas

Thomas, Mary H., see Charles Boulden

Thomas, Philip, married Mary Ann Thomas circa 21 Oct 1842 (date of license) (Cecil County Marriage License Book)

Thomas, Philip Jr., of Cecil Co., married Emily Ann Seegar, of Queen Anne's Co., circa 30 Jan 1837 (date of license) by Rev. Humphreys (Queen Anne's County Marriage License Book)

Thomas, Richard, see Susanna Thomas

Thomas, Richard (1817-1892, born Wales) (lumber inspector, 7th District), married Elizabeth (N) (1825-1901, born Maryland) probably circa 1850; daughter Lydia Thomas born c1851, Maryland (Elkton Cemetery tombstone inscriptions; 1860 Cecil County Census)

Thomas, Richard L. (1809-1888) (merchant), son of Samuel and Hannah Thomas, married 1st to Sarah Johnson, daughter of Charles and Mary Johnson, circa 21 Oct 1830 (date of license) by Rev. Hodgson and she died childless in 1838; Richard married 2nd to Ruth Ann McCracken (1830-1867), daughter of John and Martha Jane McCracken, circa 5 Feb 1845 (date of license) (Cecil County Marriage License Book; DAR transcript copied in 1928 misspelled the minister's name as Hodson (Francis Hodgson was a Methodist Episcopal minister in Elkton at that time); *Portrait and Biographical Record of Harford and Cecil Counties, Maryland* (1897, repr. 1989), pp. 577-578, mistakenly stated his second marriage was in 1854; *Cecil Democrat and Farmer's Journal*, 19 Oct 1867, stated Ruth Anna *(sic)* Thomas, wife of Richard L. Thomas, died in her 38th year at North East)

Thomas, Samuel (born c1829, Maryland) (laborer, 7th District), married Nancy (N) (born c1830, Maryland) probably circa 1850; son Benjamin Thomas born c1851 (1860 Cecil County Census)

Thomas, Samuel, see Richard L. Thomas

Thomas, Sarah, see Thomas R. Sewall and William Thompson

Thomas, Sarah H., see Jeremiah B. Haines

Thomas, Susan, see Samuel Phillips

Thomas, Susan Jane, see George Jenkins

Thomas, Susanna, of Cecil Co., divorced from Richard Thomas on 8 Mar 1848 (*Divorces and Names Changed in Maryland by Act of the Legislature, 1634-1867*, by Mary Keysor Meyer (1991), p. 89)

Thomas, William (born c1815, Maryland) (farmer at North East), married Sarah (N) (born c1821, Maryland) probably circa 1839; daughter Mary Thomas born c1840 (1860 Cecil County Census)

Thomas, William (born c1830, Maryland) (African American) (laborer, 7th District), married Mary (N) (born c1824, Maryland) (African American) probably circa 1848; son William Thomas born c1849 and son John Thomas born c1853 (1860 Cecil County Census)

THOMPSON

Thompson, Amelia, see John Cameron

Thompson, Andrew, of Cecil Co., married Mary Greenwood, of Kent Co., circa 17 Nov 1827 by Rev. Smith (Kent County Marriage License Book)

Thompson, Ann, see John Hackett

Thompson, Benjamin, married Miss Mary Sophia Alexander, both of Cecil Co., on 24 Jun 1841, after obtaining a license on 23 Jun 1841, by Rev. Maddux (*Cecil Gazette*, 3 Jul 1841; Cecil County Marriage License Book)

Thompson, Benjamin B., married Sarah Graham circa 2 Jul or 20 Jul 1841 (date of license) (Cecil County Marriage License Book; date unclear)

Thompson, Catharine, see William Cosgrove and Thomas Williams

Thompson, Clinton L., see Joseph Stebbing

Thompson, David, married Elizabeth Ann McJilton circa 25 Jul 1832 (date of license) by Rev. McCarrol, a Methodist Episcopal minister in Port Deposit (Cecil County Marriage License Book)

Thompson, Edward J. (1804-1885) (farmer near Principio), son of William Thompson and Amelia Jones, married Hester Harlan (1814-1903) on 30 Dec 1841 after obtaining a license on 25 Dec 1841 (Cecil County Marriage License Book; *Ancestral Charts, Volume 4*, pp. 178-179, Harford County Genealogical Society Publication, 1988; *Maryland Bible Records, Volume 4: Eastern Shore*, by Henry C. Peden, Jr. (2004), pp. 234-235, listed the births of their four children: George H., born 18 Oct 1843; (N) [page torn] Thomas, born 27 Dec 1848; Mary Agnes, born 19 Mar 1853; and, Sovilla E., born 10 Feb 1858)

Thompson, Edward T., see George W. Thompson

Thompson, Elizabeth, see John Vannort

Thompson, Emma, see Joshua Thompson

Thompson, Ezekiel, married Elizabeth Aiken circa 7 Jan 1835 (date of their license) by Rev. Griffith (Cecil County Marriage License Book)

Thompson, Fanny, see James Thompson

Thompson, George Ann W., see George W. Thompson

Thompson, George H., see Edward J. Thompson

Thompson, George W. (1816-1848), married Sarah Ann Tarring (1820-1886), daughter of Edward Tarring and Elizabeth Stanton, on 8 Aug 1839, after obtaining a license on 7 Aug 1839, by Rev. Wiggins; Sarah Ann Thompson married 2nd to John W. Barry circa 3 Nov 1859 (date of license) (*Ancestral Charts, Volume 4*, pp. 178-179, Harford County Genealogical Society Publication, 1988; Cecil County Marriage License Book; DAR transcript copied in 1928 mistakenly listed the minister's name as Diggins (William W. Wiggins was a Methodist Protestant minister in Port Deposit at that time); 1860 Cecil County Census; *Maryland Bible Records, Volume 4: Eastern Shore*, by Henry C. Peden, Jr. (2004), pp. 225-226; p. 235 listed the births of their five children: James Columbus, born 19 Mar 1840; Edward T., born 29 Jul 1842; Maria Virginia, born 6 Mar 1844; Mary Letitia, born 13 Apr 1846; George Ann W., born 15 Apr 1848)

Thompson, Green M., married Mary A. Veazey on 3 Nov 1835 (*Baltimore American and Commercial Daily Advertiser*, 7 Nov 1835)

Thompson, Hannah R., see Jacob Hyland

Thompson, Hugh A. (1822-1882), of Port Deposit, married Mary Jane Bell (1826-1885) circa 25 Nov 1846 (date of license) (Cecil County Marriage License Book; Hopewell United Methodist Church Cemetery tombstone inscriptions; *Cecil Democrat and Farmer's Journal*, 14 Oct 1882)

Thompson, James (born c1822, Pennsylvania) (African American), married Alice (N) (born c1824, Pennsylvania) (African American) circa 1847; daughter Fanny born c1848 (1860 Cecil County Census)

Thompson, James Columbus, see George W. Thompson

Thompson, John, see Thomas Williams

Thompson, John (1809-1875), married Elizabeth J. (N) (1811-1885) probably circa 1830-1832 (North East Methodist Church Cemetery tombstone inscriptions)

Thompson, John, married Jane Lum circa 19 Jan 1831 (date of license) by Rev. Barratt (Cecil County Marriage License Book)

Thompson, John (1818-1883) (cooper at Elkton), married Miss Prudence Jane Anderson (1828-1904, Pennsylvania), both now of Cecil Co., on 21 Dec 1848, after obtaining a license on 20 Dec 1848, by Rev. DeWitt (Cecil County Marriage License Book; *Cecil Democrat and Farmer's Journal*, 23 Dec 1848; Sharp's Cemetery tombstone inscriptions; 1860 Cecil County Census)

Thompson, John A. (born c1817, Maryland) (innkeeper, 8th District), married Ann (N) (born c1821, born Maryland) probably circa 1841; daughter Rachel Thompson born c1842 (1860 Cecil County Census)

Thompson, John D., married Catherine Reynolds, daughter of Benjamin Reynolds, late of Cecil Co., on 8 Oct 1835 (*Baltimore American and Commercial Daily Advertiser*, 10 Oct 1835)

Thompson, Joshua (born c1820, Maryland) (mason, 6th District), married Eliza (N) (born c1828, Maryland) probably circa 1849; daughter Emma Thompson born c1850 (1860 Cecil County Census)

Thompson, Letitia, see James Wilson

Thompson, Maria Virginia, see George W. Thompson

Thompson, Martha E., see William Benjamin

Thompson, Mary, see Andrew Ramsey, John Brickley and Uphrey Riddle

Thompson, Mary Agnes, see Edward J. Thompson

Thompson, Mary Ellen, see Aaron Keech

Thompson, Mary Letitia, see George W. Thompson

Thompson, Phoebe Ann, see James Cooper

Thompson, Rachel, see John A. Thompson

Thompson, Rebecca, see Noah Frieze

Thompson, Robert, married Jane Orr circa 11 Apr 1837 (date of license) by Rev. Burrows (Cecil County Marriage License Book)

Thompson, Samuel (born c1808) (African American) (farm hand at Cecilton), married Jane (N) (born c1806) (African American) circa 1830; son Samuel born c1831 (1860 Cecil County Census)

Thompson, Samuel (born c1806, Maryland) (cooper near Bay View), married Alice Calvert (born c1808, Maryland) circa 24 Jan 1832 (date of license) by Rev. Griffith (Cecil County Marriage License Book; 1860 Cecil County Census)

Thompson, Samuel, married Miss Isabella Crothers, both of Cecil Co., on 28 Nov 1844, after obtaining a license on 27 Nov 1844, by Rev. Goldsborough at Trinity Church (Cecil County Marriage License Book; *Cecil Whig*, 30 Nov 1844; *Cecil Whig*, 21 Jan 1865, reported Isabella M. Crothers died at the residence of Samuel Thompson, near College Green, in her 37th year)

Thompson, Sarah E., see George W. Hyland

Thompson, Sophia, see James Morrow

Thompson, Sovilla E., see Edward J. Thompson

Thompson, Susan, see William Ferguson

Thompson, Susanna W., see Arthur M. Strout

Thompson, Thomas, married Mary Ann Graham circa 28 Feb 1849 (date of license) (Cecil County Marriage License Book; DAR transcript copied in 1955 spelled his name Thomson)

Thompson, William, see Edward J. Thompson

Thompson, William, married Catharine Blake circa 13 Feb 1828 (date of license) (Cecil County Marriage License Book)

Thompson, William (1809-1886), married 1st to Rachel S. Lackland (1821-1857) circa 24 Dec 1850 (date of license) and married 2nd to Hannah (N) (1825-1893) after 1857 (Cecil County Marriage License Book; Ebenezer Church Cemetery tombstone inscriptions)

Thompson, William (1819-1870), of Scotland, later of Washington, DC, married Sarah Thomas (1820-1858) probably circa 1840 (West Nottingham Cemetery tombstone inscriptions)

Thompson, (N) Thomas, see Edward J. Thompson

THORNTON

Thornton, Benjamin F., married Rachel Layton circa 13 May 1834 (date of license) by Rev. Goforth (Cecil County Marriage License Book; DAR transcript copied in 1928 mistakenly gave his middle initial as W.)

Thornton, Mary Ann, see William Moore

TIBBITT

Tibbitt, Mary Ann, see George Deal

TIFFANY

Tiffany, Henry, of Baltimore City, married Sally Jones McLane, daughter of Louis McLane, on 28 Jul 1840 after obtaining a license on 25 Jul 1840 (Cecil County Marr. License Book; *Baltimore Sun*, 1 Aug 1840)

TIGNOR

Tignor, John (born 1810, Maryland) (laborer, 7th District, married Deborah Ann "Annie" Jones (born 1814, Maryland) circa 18 Oct 1831 (date of license) by Rev. McCarrol, a Methodist Episcopal minister in Port Deposit (Cecil County Marriage License Book; DAR transcript copied in 1928 misspelled his name Tigna; 1860 Cecil County Census)

TILAMAN

Tilaman, Amanda F., see Levi R. Mearns

TILDEN

Tilden, Ann Maria, see George B. Westcott
Tilden, Catharine, see William P. Worrell

TILLERSON

Tillerson, Roseanna, see William Trusty

TIMMONS

Timmons, Ellen, see Samuel Tyson

TIMMS

Timms, William (born c1806, Maryland) (farmer, Cecilton), married Ann (N) (1812-1878, born Maryland) probably circa 1832 and Ann Timms died at the residence of her son-in-law Daniel Husfelt on Sassafras Neck in 1878, her husband having pre-deceased her (1860 Cecil County Census; *Cecil Whig*, 1 Jun 1878)

TIPPETT

Tippett, Samuel, married Sarah Moore circa 16 Jan 1838 (date of their license) by Rev. Piggot, a Protestant Episcopal minister in North Sassafras (Cecil County Marriage License Book; DAR transcript copied in 1928 misspelled the minister's name Pickett)

TIPTON

Tipton, William W., married Harriet Ramsey circa 3 Mar 1838 (date of their license) by Rev. Parkins (Cecil County Marriage License Book)

TITUS

Titus, Effa and Frank, see Howard Titus
Titus, Howard (1817, Pennsylvania - 1871, Maryland) (farmer and blacksmith at North East), married Mary Euphemia (N) (1825, Pennsylvania - 1912, Maryland) probably circa 1843; first child Frank Titus was born c1844, Pennsylvania, and sixth child Effa Titus was born c1854, Maryland (Elkton Presbyterian Church Cemetery tombstone inscriptions; 1860 Cecil County Census; *Cecil Whig*, 5 Aug 1871)
Titus, Mary and Seruch, see Henry Harding Kimble

TODD

Todd, Agnes Ann, see Robert Love
Todd, Eliza Jane, see John Riddle
Todd, Harriet, see William Stubbins
Todd, James, married Margaret Harris circa 28 Mar 1850 (date of license) (Cecil Co. Marr. License Book)

Todd, Levi, married 1st to Miss Mary Ann Reynolds circa 18 Jun 1828 (date of license) by Rev. Barratt and married 2nd to Miss Sophia C. Scott, both of Cecil Co., on 23 Dec 1847, after obtaining a license on 21 Dec 1847, by Rev. Burrows (Cecil County Marriage License Book; *Cecil Whig*, 1 Jan 1848, noted: "The printers acknowledge the receipt of a slice of excellent cake with the above notice, and in return wish (the wishes of printers effect much) the happy couple a long life and abundant prosperity.")

Todd, Robert (1806-1876) (farm manager, 7th District), married Elizabeth J. (N) (1818-1871) probably circa 1838 (Hopewell United Methodist Church Cemetery tombstone inscriptions; 1860 Cecil County Census)

TOME

Tome, Christian, see Peter Tome

Tome, Jacob (1810-1898) (tinner, teacher, merchant, banker, legislator, founder of Jacob Tome Institute), of Hanover, York Co., PA, later of Port Deposit, Cecil Co., married Miss Caroline M. Webb (1813-1874) on 6 Dec 1841 after obtaining a license on 4 Dec 1841 (Cecil County Marriage License Book; Hopewell United Methodist Church Cemetery tombstone inscriptions; *The Monumental City, Its Past History and Present Resources*, by George W. Howard (1873), pp. 674-676, did not mention his parents nor his marriage; *Cecil Whig*, 1 Apr 1876, contains an image of Jacob Tome and a lengthy front page article about his lifetime achievements up to that point in time)

Tome, Peter (1825-1909), son of Christian and Christina Tome, married Mary Jane Oberlander (1830-1926), daughter of Michael and Catherine Oberlander, on 26 Mar 1850 (*Bible Records, Genealogical Society of Cecil County*, by Gary L. Burns (1990), pp. 36-37, stated this family was from York Co., PA and Cecil Co., MD and listed the births and deaths of their children: Charles Wesley, born 4 Jul 1852, died 12 Sep 1852; Sarah Catherine, born 10 Jun 1853, died 11 Aug 1854; Jacob Eli, born 29 Feb 1856, died 20 Mar 1903; Peter Elias, born 24 Oct 1858, died 19 Apr 1939; Mary Jane, born 20 Jun 1861, married a Kimble, died 19 Nov 1954; Christian Cornelius, born 3 May 1863, died 11 Sep 1954; William Harvey, born 28 Nov 1864; and, Eliza Anna Tome, born 10 Sep 1868, married Charles H. Martindale, died 9 Mar 1941; Hopewell United Methodist Church Cemetery tombstone inscriptions)

TOMLINSON

Tomlinson, Catherine, see Thomas Neal

Tomlinson, Elizabeth, see William C. Blackiston

Tomlinson, John, see Thomas Neal

Tomlinson, John Wesley, of Cecil Co., married Jane G. Owen, daughter of Thomas G. Owen, of Baltimore, on 15 Jun 1841 by Rev. Musgrave in Baltimore (*Cecil Gazette*, 19 Jun 1841; *Baltimore Sun*, 18 Jun 1841)

TOMPKINS

Tompkins, William, of Cecil Co., married Ann Tompkins (date not given) and divorced on 23 Mar 1833; she was "not to remarry and to have custody of their child" (*Divorces and Names Changed in Maryland by Act of the Legislature, 1634-1867*, by Mary Keysor Meyer (1991), p. 90)

TORBERT

Torbert, Elizabeth, see William W. Torbert

Torbert, William (1805-1884, born Delaware) (merchant at Elkton), married Adeline Matilda Silver (1813-1890, born Delaware), granddaughter of William Silver, of Christiana, DE, in June 1832 and had a daughter (N) who died in infancy and four sons: Henry Robinson Torbert (1834-1911, editor of the *Cecil Whig*), W. F. Asbury Torbert (1837-1874, paymaster, U. S. Navy), John Torbert (1839-1885), and Edwin James Torbert (1842-1886) (*Portrait and Biographical Record of Harford and Cecil Counties, Maryland* (1897, repr. 1989), pp. 444-445; 1860 Cecil County Census; Elkton Cemetery tombstone inscriptions; *Midland Journal*, 28 Feb 1890)

Torbert, William W., married Elizabeth Torbert circa 5 Oct 1843 (date of license) (Cecil County Marriage License Book)

TOSH

Tosh, Ellen M., see John S. Everist

Tosh, James, married Eliza Hindman circa 24 Mar 1838 (date of license) by Rev. Burris (Cecil County Marriage License Book)

Tosh, Jane Eleanor, see Samuel Hindman

Tosh, John (1808-1878), married 1st to Jemima McCormick (1811-1855) circa 2 Feb 1839 (date of license) by Rev. Burrows and married 2nd to Catharine A. Love (1810-1877) circa 2 Nov 1862 (date of license) (Cecil County Marriage License Book; West Nottingham Cemetery tombstones; *Cecil Whig*, 1 Jun 1878)

Tosh, Margaret, see John T. Coulson

Tosh, Mary E., see William Wallace Wiley

Tosh, Rachel Maria, see Joseph Brown

Tosh, Samuel (1818-1885), married Mary Jane Wiley (1815-1900) circa 26 Sep 1835 (date of license) by Rev. Magraw (Cecil County Marriage License Book)

TOUCHSTONE

Touchstone, Cornelia, see James Touchstone

Touchstone, Empson (born c1811, Maryland) (plasterer near Brick Meeting House), married Ann (N) (born c1825, Maryland) probably circa 1844; son Joseph born c1845, Maryland (1860 Cecil County Census spelled his name Touchton)

Touchstone, James (1821-1872, born Maryland) (blacksmith in 7th District), married Virginia A. (N) (1828-1905, born Maryland) probably circa 1846; daughter Cornelia Touchstone born 1847 (Hopewell United Methodist Church Cemetery tombstone inscriptions; 1860 Cecil County Census spelled name Touchtone)

Touchstone, Joseph, see Empson Touchstone

Touchstone, Martha J., see Henry B. McCauley

Touchstone, Rachel, see Ambrose Knapp

Touchstone, Thomas M., married Martha A. Holt circa 17 Nov 1841 (date of their license) (Cecil County Marriage License Book; DAR transcript copied in 1955 listed his name without the middle initial)

TOWNSEND

Townsend, David, married Sarah Stapleford circa 3 Jan 1846 (date of license) (Cecil County Marriage License Book; DAR transcript copied in 1955 mistakenly listed the marriage license date as 1 Jan 1846)

Townsend, James, of Cecil Co., married Elizabeth Silcox, of Kent Co., circa 12 Dec 1844 by Rev. Pearson (Kent County Marriage License Book)

Townsend, Mary E., see George T. Megee

Townsend, Silas (born c1820) (laborer at Charlestown), married Miss Mary Ann Gordon (born c1825), both of Cecil Co., on 23 Jan 1845, after obtaining a license on 20 Jan 1845, by Rev. Shields (Cecil County Marriage License Book; Elkton Methodist Church Register, p. 140; *Cecil Whig*, 25 Jan 1845; 1860 Cecil County Census abstract mistakenly listed his name as Lilas Townson)

Townsend, William M., married Sarah E. Galbraith, both of Cecil Co., on 7 Feb 1832, after obtaining a license on 4 Feb 1832, by Rev. Magraw (Cecil County Marriage License Book; *Baltimore American and Commercial Daily Advertiser*, 16 Feb 1832)

TOWSON

Towson, William O., of Baltimore, married Elmira S. Reynolds, daughter of Leonard Reynolds, of Cecil Co., on 25 Jan 1849 by Rev. Barton (*Cecil Democrat and Farmer's Journal*, 3 Feb 1849; *Baltimore Sun*, 27 Jan 1849)

TOYER

Toyer, Gilbert S., married Isabella E. Nickel (1811-1849), daughter of William Nickel (1774-1842) and Ruth (N) (1778-1853) circa 8 Aug 1846 (date of license) (Cecil County Marriage License Book; West Nottingham Cemetery tombstone inscription for Isabella Toyer)

TREDAWAY

Tredaway, Sarah Ann, see Isaac G. Reynolds

TRIDIN

Tridin, Rachel, see James Crow

TRIMBLE

Trimble, David Brown (born 1813), son of John and Elizabeth Trimble, of Baltimore, married Elizabeth Askew, daughter of Peter Askew and Hannah Wilkinson, on the 17th day of the 7th month 1840, or on the 5th day of the 11th month 1840, at East Nottingham *Births, Deaths and Marriages of the Nottingham Quakers, 1680-1899*, by Alice L. Beard (1989), p. 109 stated they married on the 5th day of the 11th month 1840, but p. 224 stated it was on the 17th day of the 7th month 1840)

Trimble, Elizabeth, see David Brown Trimble

Trimble, Isaac, married Rebecca Blair Moore circa 19 Mar 1828 (date of license) (Cecil County Marriage License Book; West Nottingham Cemetery tombstone inscription for Rebecca Blair Trimble (1808-1885), wife of Isaac Trimble, but no marker for him)

Trimble, James, married Eliza H. (N) (1817-1883) probably circa 1835 (Zion Presbyterian Cemetery tombstone inscription for Eliza H. Trimble)

Trimble, James, son of James and Sarah Trimble, of East Nottingham, Cecil Co., married Hannah Mendenhall, daughter of ---ion(?) and Sarah Mendenhall, of the same place, on the 31st day of the 10th month 1838 at East Nottingham (*Births, Deaths and Marriages of the Nottingham Quakers, 1680-1899*, by Alice L. Beard (1989), p. 223)

Trimble, James B., see James R. Trimble

Trimble, James R. (born c1824, Maryland) (carpenter, 6th District), married Cordelia E. Barnes (born c1830, Maryland) circa 18 Aug 1847 (date of license); son James B. Trimble born c1848 (Cecil County Marriage License Book; 1860 Cecil County Census)

Trimble, John, see David Brown Trimble

Trimble, Sarah, see James Trimble

TRIPPE

Trippe, Joseph E. (captain), of Baltimore, married Sarah Patterson Cross (c1817-1853), only daughter of the late Andrew Cross, both of Baltimore, on 29 or 30 May 1837 by Rev. Backus at the First Presbyterian Church (*Cecil Gazette*, 3 Jun 1837, and *Baltimore Sun*, 2 Jun 1837, both stated they married on 30 May 1837; *Presbyterian Records of Baltimore City, Maryland, 1765-1840*, by Henry C. Peden, Jr. (1995), pp. 96, 198; page 250 in the microfilm copy of the church marriage register stated they married 29 May 1837)

TRUIT

Truit, Hester J., see John Biggs

TRUMP

Trump, Levina, see Robert Archibald

Trump, (N), see Ezekiel Moore

TRUSTY

Trusty, William, married Roseanna Tillerson on 15 Mar 1843 (Elkton Methodist Church Register; Cecil County Marriage License Book did not list this marriage)

TUCKER

Tucker, David (1817-1889) (carpenter), of Harford Co., removed to Perryville c1835 and married Grizzella Lynch (1821-1901, born Maryland) circa 13 May 1840 by Rev. Torbert (Cecil County Marriage License Book; *Bel Air Times*, 26 Jul 1889; Principio Cemetery tombstone inscriptions; 1860 Cecil Co. Census)

Tucker, James, married Gracella or Grasella Whitelock circa 8 Dec 1847 (date of license) (Cecil County Marriage License Book)

TUFFREE

Tuffree (Puffree?), John, married Mary Ann Maria Cropper circa 26 Sep 1835 (date of license) by Rev. Wilson (Cecil County Marriage License Book)

Tuffree (Puffree?), Joseph, married Mary Ann Woolston circa 4 Jul 1835 (date of license) by Rev. Smith (Cecil County Marriage License Book)

TUITE

Tuite, Aaron G., of Cincinnati, Ohio, married Mary Elizabeth Howard, daughter of Jacob C. Howard, of Elkton, on 21 Feb 1848 (*Cecil Whig*, 11 Mar 1848, citing *Cincinnati Gazette*); see Jacob C. Howard, *q.v.*

TULL

Tull, Elizabeth, see Jethro Johnson McCullough

Tull, Frisby (1814-1891) (millwright), of North East, married Charlotte Carter Brown (1817-1879), widow of William Brown and daughter of Robert and Lydia Carter, on 9 Jan 1838, after obtaining a license on 8 Jan 1838, by Rev. McFarland (Elkton Methodist Church Register, p. 138; Cecil County Marriage License Book; DAR transcript copied in 1928 listed his name twice, once as Tull and once mistakenly as True, with same bride named Charlotte Brown and same license date, and also mistakenly listed the minister's name as Farland (James McFarland was a Methodist minister in Elkton at that time); 1840 Cecil Census correctly listed Frisby's name as Frisby Tull, not Frisby True; Cherry Hill Methodist Church Cemetery tombstone inscriptions inscribed her name as Charlotte Carter; *Midland Journal*, 17 Apr 1891, stated Frisby was born in 1809, worked for McCullough Iron Company, died at the residence of his daughter-in-law Mrs. Mary C. Tull in Elkton and his wife was the sister of I. Day Carter; see William Brown, *q.v.*)

Tull, John, see Jethro Johnson McCullough

Tull, Mary C., see Frisby Tull

TURNER

Turner, Elizabeth G., see James J. Davids

Turner, George, married Caroline N. Devor or Devon circa 14 Sep 1833 (date of license) by Rev. Duke (Cecil County Marriage License Book)

Turner, George (1826-1904), married Mary Ann (N) (1819-1901) probably circa 1848 (Elkton Cemetery tombstone inscriptions)

Turner, J. M., see James J. Davids

Turner, James (doctor) (1820-1879), married Cornelia M. (N) (1828-1916) probably circa 1850 (Rosebank Cemetery, at Calvert, tombstone inscriptions)

Turner, Janette R., see Edward F. Rasin

Turner, John D., of New Castle, Delaware, married Amelia Margaret Pearce circa 22 Oct 1831 (date of license) by Rev. Duke (Cecil County Marriage License Book)

Turner, Mary Ann, see George Edward Woolley

Turner, Sarah Ann, see James Cormer

TWEED

Tweed, Elizabeth A., see Alexander Scott

TYRREL

Tyrrel, Olivia Ann, see Absalom McCauley

TYSON

Tyson, Abel, see Thomas Tyson

Tyson, Adam (born c1813, Maryland) (African American) (laborer at Elkton), married Ruth (N) (born c1816) (African American) before 1840; son William Tyson born c1841 (1860 Cecil County Census)

Tyson, Amelia, see Samuel Tyson and Daniel McJilton

Tyson, Anna, see Joseph M. Eldridge

Tyson, Beulah Ann, see Jesse Pierson

Tyson, Deborah, see William Benjamin

Tyson, Dollie Ann, see John Lockard

Tyson, Elijah J., married Miss Martha Ann Barnes, both of Cecil Co., on 10 Aug 1843, after obtaining a license on 9 Aug 1843, by Rev. Kennard (*Cecil Whig*, 19 Aug 1843; Cecil County Marriage License Book; DAR transcript copied in 1955 misspelled his name as Elizah)

Tyson, Eliza, see Samuel Hall

Tyson, Eliza Jane, see Diedrich H. Black

Tyson, Emily C., see John W. Tyson

Tyson, George M. (born c1816, Pennsylvania) (master plasterer at Warwick), married Sarah E. (N) (born c1815, Maryland) circa 1840 (1860 Cecil County Census)

Tyson, I. B., see John W. Tyson

Tyson, James, see (N) Tyson

Tyson, Jesse (1819-1908, born Pennsylvania) (farmer near Brick Meeting House), married Hannah R. (N) (1828-1891, born Maryland) probably circa 1850; daughter Mary born c1851 (Rosebank Cemetery, at Calvert, tombstone inscriptions; 1860 Cecil County Census)

Tyson, John (born c1810, Maryland) (farmer near Bay View), married Mary McDowell (born c1810, Maryland) circa 20 Oct 1834 (date of license) by Rev. Hammill (Cecil County Marriage License Book; 1860 Cecil County Census)

Tyson, John P., see John W. Tyson

Tyson, John W. (1821-1896), married Sarah Jane Carter (1823-1891), daughter of Cloud Carter, on 5 Jan 1843, after obtaining a license on 4 Jan 1843, by Rev. Thomas (Cecil County Marriage License Book; *Cecil Whig*, 7 Jan 1843; *Portrait and Biographical Record of Harford and Cecil Counties, Maryland* (1897, repr. 1989), p. 573, stated they had twelve children of whom six were living in 1897, namely, Thomas M. (born 27 Oct 1843), Emily C. (married), Margaret J. (widow) Sarah K. (married), John P., and I. B. Tyson, most of whom lived in Pennsylvania by 1897 (Shelemiah Methodist Church Cemetery tombstone inscriptions for John W. Tyson who is buried beside Rawlings A. Tyson (1846-1929) who was not mentioned above; Union Methodist Church Cemetery tombstone inscription for Sarah J. C. Tyson)

Tyson, Joseph, married 1st to Mary (N) before 1827 and she divorced him on 2 Mar 1836; he married 2nd to Miss Mary Abrams, both of Cecil Co., on 4 Feb 1838, after obtaining a license on 1 Jan 1838, by Rev. Woolley (*Cecil Gazette*, 3 Mar 1838; Cecil County Marriage License Book; DAR transcript copied in 1928 spelled her name Abrahams; *Elkton Press*, 11 Jul 1828, reported Mary Tyson advertised that Joseph Tyson, in the fall of 1827, eloped from her bed and board without just cause and forewarned persons from paying him any debts due her; *Divorces and Names Changed in Maryland by Act of the Legislature, 1634-1867*, by Mary Keysor Meyer (1991), p. 92)

Tyson, Joseph, see Mary Tyson

Tyson, Margaret J., see John W. Tyson

Tyson, Mary, see Jesse Tyson

Tyson, Matthias, see Alexander Curry

Tyson, Prudence Amelia, see Alexander Curry

Tyson, Rachel, see (N) Tyson

Tyson, Samuel (1818-1894), married Harriet Gorrell (1818-1881) circa 1 Jan 1839 (date of license) by Rev. Wooley (Cecil Co. Marr. License Book; North East Methodist Church Cemetery tombstone inscriptions)

Tyson, Samuel (born c1805, Maryland) (miller at Elkton), married Ellen Timmons (born c1818, Delaware) circa 18 Jun 1840 (date of license); daughter Amelia Tyson born c1841 (Cecil County Marriage License Book; 1860 Cecil County Census)

Tyson, Sarah K., see John W. Tyson

Tyson, Thomas (born c1812, Maryland) (farmer near Bay View), married Dorothy A. (N) (born c1810, Maryland) probably circa 1834; son Abel Tyson born c1835, Maryland (1860 Cecil County Census)

Tyson, Thomas M., see John W. Tyson

Tyson, Thomas W., married Miss Mary Jane McCauley, both of Cecil Co., on 27 Jul 1843, after obtaining a license on 26 Jul 1843, by Rev. Barratt (Cecil County Marriage License Book; *Cecil Whig*, 29 Jul 1843)

Tyson, William, see Adam Tyson

Tyson, William, married Eliza Poe circa 18 Feb 1835 (date of license) by Rev. Griffith (Cecil County Marriage License Book)

Tyson, William, married Elizabeth Boulden circa 1 Jun 1842 (date of license) (Cecil County Marriage License Book)

Tyson, (N), son of James and Rachel Tyson, of Cecil Co., married Ann Johnson, daughter of Charles and Mary Johnson, of the same place, on the 6th day of the 11th month 1828 at East Nottingham (*Births, Deaths and Marriages of the Nottingham Quakers, 1680-1899*, by Alice L. Beard (1989), p. 222)

UNDERWOOD

Underwood, Ann, see Joseph Underwood

Underwood, Charles (born c1825) (farmhand near Elkton), married Hannah (N) (born c1827) probably circa 1847; daughter Rebecca Underwood born c1848 (1860 Cecil County Census)

Underwood, George W., of Chester Co., PA, married Miss Susannah Bayard, of Cecil Co., on 13 Apr 1841 by Rev. McCullough in Wilmington, DE (*Delaware Gazette*, 16 Apr 1841)

Underwood, Jane, see John Price

Underwood, John E. (1806-1878), married Margaret (N) (1808-1900) circa 1827; buried beside daughter Margaret Underwood, 1828-1888 (Rosebank Cemetery, at Calvert, tombstone inscriptions)

Underwood, Joseph (born c1814) (iron roller near Elkton), married Alice (N) (born c1812) probably circa 1837; daughter Ann Underwood born c1838 (1860 Cecil County Census)

Underwood, Margaret, see John E. Underwood

Underwood, Rebecca, see Charles Underwood

UNKNOWN, UNDETERMINED NAMES (N)

(N), see Henry H. Aldrich, Richard Boyer, Daniel Carter, John R. Conoly, Washington Cowen, William H. Emerson, Daniel F. Ewell, John G. Hanna, Robert McCoy, John C. Murray, George W. Taylor, Joseph Taylor, John Weir and William T. West

(N), A. C., see Samuel S. Maffitt

(N), A. W., see Henry R. Walker

(N), Abigail, see John H. Krauss and John B. Arrison

(N), Adeline, see John Berry

(N), Agnes G., see James J. Ewing

(N), Albinah, see John Moore

(N), Alice, see Timothy O'Rourke, Joseph Underwood and James Thompson

(N), Amanda, see Washington Hill

(N), Amelia, see Reuben Reynolds, Gilbert L. Crisfield, Thomas Fulton and L. Biddle

(N), Angeline, see H. Vanderford, Jr. and Henry Stokes

(N), Ann (Anne), see Amassa Churchman, John G. Jenness, James O. McCormick, Samuel L. Burlin, John Husfelt, John T. Morgan, Henry Nindson, Hyland Marcus, Jonathan Drennan, William Timms, J. Van

Horn, John Maher, John Halman, J. P. Lockwood, Robert Jackson, John Boyd, William Harris, William Cochran, John A. Thompson, George Chambers, William Slack, Empson Touchstone, Benonia Nowland

(N), Ann B., see John R. Hogg

(N), Ann C., see Thomas P. Jones

(N), Ann Catherine, see James Mercer

(N), Ann E., see John Watson and Ellis G. Chandlee

(N), Ann H., see Samuel D. Moffitt

(N), Ann J., see Andrew Alexander

(N), Ann P., see James A. Massey

(N), Ann Maria, see Nathaniel Cox

(N), Ann R., see Stephen Gilbert

(N), Ann S., see James L. Hickey

(N), Anna, see William Lindsey, John McCullough and Nicholas Voloker

(N), Anna B., see William C. Moore

(N), Anna E., see Samuel Estes

(N), Anna M, see Thomas J. Janney, Thomas A. Lackland, Isaac Pass and Solomon Barrett

(N), Anna S., see Sidney George Bradford

(N), Annie A., see William L. Packer

(N), Annie E., see Haines England

(N), Arabella A., see William Knight

(N), Araminta, see Thomas Keatley

(N), Augusta, see Thomas Pearce

(N), Augustena, see (N) Richardson

(N), Barbara, see James Adams

(N), Barbara Ann, see Joseph Booth

(N), Bridget, see Joseph Walker and Martin Maloney

(N), Caroline, see Thestty (Westly?) Roach, Daniel Collins, Thomas M. Krauss, Thomas Larue, John Lamm

(N), Caroline H., see Edwin J. Brown

(N), Catharina P., see John McCafferty

(N), Catherine (Catharine), see Thomas Berry, James K. McVey, William Budd, Joseph Hutchinson, John W. Brown, John Shure, James McKinsey, Thomas M. Krauss, Frederick Pensel, Peter Mariner, William Brints, John Baker, Holland Hardgraves, William Johnson and John Moore

(N), Charlotte, see David Cather, Henry Hopkins, David Cather and James Alexander

(N), Christiana, see Enoch Crouch

(N), Cornelia, see James Turner

(N), Deborah (Debora), see Robert McMullen, George Johnston and J. Lum

(N), Delia A., see George H. Peterson

(N), Dinah, see William Gibson

(N), Dorothy A., see Thomas Tyson

(N), Eleanor, see William Shroff and William Stern

(N), Elinor M., see Benjamin F. Pickering

(N), Eliza, see Joel Reynolds, Samuel Krewson, George Haden, (N) Love, William Lilley, Joseph Hellinger, Joseph Reben, Benjamin Bateman, John Buckworth, Joshua Thompson, Jeremiah Gatchell, James Caldwell, John Sheridan, Henry Bowser, George Ferguson and Edward Bradley

(N), Eliza A., see Abraham Brumfield and John Campbell

(N), Eliza Ann, see George P. Whitaker and David H. Stayton

(N), Eliza C., see Amos Moore and William McNamee

(N), Eliza H., see James Trimble

(N), Eliza J., see (N) Lukens, Arad B. Newton, Charles Lowman, R. M. Hayes, Robert Smith, James A. Hall

(N), Eliza M., see Davidson D. Pearce

(N), Eliza Y., see John Peach, Jr.

(N), Elizabeth, see Joshua Durborow, John Algard, Sylvester Coulson, Thomas Way, Frederick McNamee, Anton Hohn, Elam Brickley, John Keithley, James McCall, William Watkins, James Elliott, Charles Hall, James Morris, Isaac Walker, Thomas Savin, George R. Pearce, Thomas C. Crookshanks, Edward Kernan, Daniel Pennington, Charles Buckley, David Archibald, Richard Thomas, Solomon Wooden, William A. Musgrove, Lewis Brints, Levy Price, Joshua Johnson, David A. Roberts, Hiram Gilbert, Eli Mendenhall, John Lilley, David Johnson, R. Donaldson, Job Haines, Nathan McVey, Job Gatchell, P. T. Kirk, John Hammersmith, John Kelly, Hamilton Morrison, Jacob Morrison, John B. Knight, William G. Hall, Freedom Bond, Henry Whitelock, Jacob Dean, Eli Cosgrove, Chaulkley B. Culler, Charles Ritchie, John Jones and Humphrey E. Watson

(N), Elizabeth A., see Otto Haarhans and George W. Janney

(N), Elizabeth B., see Eli Hurford

(N), Elizabeth E., see William G. Hall

(N), Elizabeth H., see R. J. Milburn (Millburn)

(N), Elizabeth J., see Josiah Reeder, John Thompson and Robert Todd

(N), Elizabeth L., see Elisha Brown

(N), Elizabeth R., see John Egan

(N), Elizabeth S., see Thomas J. Jones

(N), Elizabeth W., see John T. Reynolds

(N), Ellen, see Samuel Gillespie, Samuel Barratt, Elisha Harris, George Chandler and Joseph H. Roberts

(N), Ellen J., see James Hall

(N), Ellen M., see William Dorsey

(N), Elmira, see Marshall Hunt

(N), Emaline (Emeline), see And. Brown, Robert Quein and John Cavender

(N), Emily, see Edward F. Keithley, James Frazer and William H. Clayton

(N), Emma, see Justus Dunott, John Taylor and Mark Manlove

(N), Emma J., see Charles Gamble

(N), Emma K., see Janes S. Rea

(N), Esther, see John P. Patten, William J. Marshbank and Joseph Gracy

(N), Esther E., see Jesse R. Coulson

(N), Esther J., see John McCauley

(N), Eveline, see Jacob Fulton and James H. Smith

(N), Fanny, see Samuel Carhart and Henry Purnell

(N), Frances, see George W. Benjamin and John Gardener

(N), Francina M., see Noble Biddle

(N), Gertrude, see E. H. Roberson

(N), Hannah, see (N) Cook, Isaac Hill, William Thompson, John Barr, John D. McCreary, Thomas Dixson, Thomas McNeal, Isaac Evans, William Crookham, David Cornish, Isaac Clark, Isaac Hill, Thomas Smith

(N), Hannah A., see Patrick Boyle and John Coleman

(N), Hannah B., see Jesse Taylor

(N), Hannah E., see Joseph Founds, William Coale, Thomas C. Hopkins and John W. Brown

(N), Hannah H., see William W. Moore

(N), Hannah J., see Joseph S. Riale and John Anderson

(N), Hannah R., see Jesse Tyson

(N), Harriet, see Joseph Haines, John Green, Joshua Green, Alexander McDole, Leven Owl, Abner Allison and L. H. Purnell

(N), Harriet N., see N. J. Atkinson

(N), Harriet T., see John P. Vanneman

(N), Helena R., see George Burrowes

(N), Henrietta Mary, see Cyrus Huntington

(N), Hester, see James McCane, John Stalcup and Richard Goven

(N), Hester E., see Jacob Berriker

(N), Hulden (Huldeh?) W., see Timothy W. Brown

(N), Isabella, see John McFarlove, William Jackson, John W. Buckley and Peter Carngy

(N), Isabella M., see Henry J. Lofland

(N), Ischell, see James Hawkins

(N), James, married Rebecca (N) on 6 Apr 1825 by Rev. Epinette (*History of Saint Francis Xavier Church and Bohemia Plantation Now Known as Old Bohemia, Warwick, MD*, by Joseph C. Cann (1976), p. 47)

(N), Jane, see William Morrow, John Perry, Samuel Thompson, John Coppin, Hugh Armstrong, James Ham, William R. Marnes, John Conway, Westley Wiley, James Simpson, Alfred Bell, Benjamin Allen, James Grey, Hanson Jones, James Taylor and Joseph Baird

(N), Jane B., see John B. Cathers

(N), Jane E., see John Burroughs and John L. Biles

(N), Jemima, see Levy Enals

(N), Jennie, see James Taylor

(N), Joanna, see James Boyd

(N), Josephine, see Joseph McGill (Megill)

(N), Julia, see T. Rohalski

(N), Julia A., see Cornelius Barrett, (N) Garrett, Zimri Taylor and John Smith

(N), Kesiah, see Charles Husfelt

(N), Laura, see Hyland Benson

(N), Laura E., see George A. Ford

(N), Lavenia, see James Mearns

(N), Letitia, see John B. Baker and John Chandler

(N), Letitia A., see Stephen Johnson

(N), Levinia, see W. Sidwell, George Scott and Gibson Valentine

(N), Louisa, see Elisha R. Ewing, James Hasson, William Bell, John Elderdice, Joshua Mercer, Wakeman Richardson, Samuel Reed and Perry Sewall

(N), Louisa A., see Samuel Haddock

(N), Lucetta, see Isaac R. Taylor

(N), Lydia, see Stephen P. Norman, James Lambert, Samuel Baren, George Booth, William Minker, L. Lynch, Bazil Haines, John Grey and William Waring

(N), Lydia A., see William Parker

(N), Lydia C., see Charles Harris and William B. Woodrow

(N), Mahala, see Thomas Keithley

(N), Malissa, see James McCowan

(N), Margaret, see Dennis Mahoney, John Smith Hilaman, Samuel E. Gillespie, William McClenan, Joseph Cochran, Ebenezer Perry, Nelson McDowell, William Cornish, Alpheus Crothers, Nelson Carter, Nathaniel Brickley, Ambrose B. Owens and Jacob Kidd

(N), Margaret E., see Jonathan Currier and William H. Reeder

(N), Margaret H., see William J. Gillespie

(N), Margaret J., see Enoch M. Ferguson and Jacob Boulden

(N), Margaretta, see Robert J. Cameron

(N), Margery H., see Rudolph Bennett

(N), Maria, see George Coale, Samuel Harris and John H. Mahoney

(N), Maria Elizabeth, see James Egan

(N), Maria J., see Reuben Reynolds

(N), Marion, see Sylvester H. Stephens and Jefferson Ramsey

(N), Martha, see Henry Hathaway, Joseph I. Stubbs, William Peoples, John Shelley, Richard Smith, Josiah Blackway, Isaac Bayard, John Mattix, Henry Krauss, Samuel Glenn and John Burke

(N), Martha A., see John Richards

(N), Martha C., see Christian V. Reeder

(N), Martha Ellen, see William Dorsey

(N), Martha J., see Montillion Brown, William Fay and Elijah Kirk

(N), Martha Jane, see Matthew Morrison

(N), Martha R., see John Scott

(N), Mary, see John Snowden, John Astle, John Kirk, Joseph Hambleton, George Haines, Enoch Gallaher, James H. McCullough, Thomas Bond, William Griffee, Emory Cates, John H. Morgan, Stephen Lofland, William H. Price, James Biggs, John T. Heath, Robert Butler, William Howitt, Andrew M. Watts, William D. Morris, David D. Davis, Samuel Watts, Francis Denny, John T. Jones, Samuel King, James Biddle, Bryan Fields, John Partridge, Francis Maloney, Richard Barnett Keithley, John Gregg, Joseph M. Eldridge, Thomas McCrery, (N) Ferry, D. W. Farra, Samuel Powell, Joshua B. Pearce, William Bayard, John Boyds, Samuel Boyer, William Curry, J. Collier, Levy Riddle, W. W. Potts, James Halmon, William G. Harvey, Asael Jackson, John Nickel, Moses R. Pierson, Robert Williams, Samuel Hopkins, Henry Nelson, Thomas Ringold, Frank Burlin, William Thomas, Lloyd Bond, John Smith, James Graham, Samuel Hines, James McClintock, Jacob Cunningham, James Hill, Wilson Marshall, John Emmons and David W. Sharpless

(N), Mary A., see James Murray, John V. Price, John T. Ward, James Marcus, Samuel McDaniel, Joshua Biddle and William Griffee

(N), Mary Ann, see (N) Chapman, (N) Basketter, George Turner, Robert Boyer, Edward J. Emmons and James T. Bond

(N), Mary C., see George Earle

(N), Mary E., see Hugh Armour, Boulden N. Biddle, John A. McAllister, William R. Bayer, Henry C. McCall and James Gillespie

(N), Mary E. M., see James B. Finley

(N), Mary Euphemia, see Howard Titus

(N), Mary F., see P. Washington Webb

(N), Mary H., see Jeremiah Brown and Samuel Brickley

(N), Mary J., see Benjamin R. Lair, Hamilton Morton, John Pierce, (N) Groves and Moses Nesbitt

(N), Mary Jane, see John Wood Beaven

(N), Mary M., see Sewall Boggs and Benjamin F. Peterman

(N), Mary Matilda, see Burton P. Morris

(N), Mary N., see Thomas Stern

(N), Mary S., see Daniel Arbuckle

(N), Mary Susanne, see Richard Boucher

(N), Mary T., see John Webb Niblock and Andrew J. McVey

(N), Mary V., see John S. Crossmore

(N), Mary Y., see Nicholas H. Gillespie

(N), Matilda, see (N) Hogan, William Grant, William T. Grant and John W. Egner

(N), Matilda E., see Samuel Cann

(N), Matilda J., see William S. White

(N), Melinda, see Jacob Dawson

(N), Menamy, see James Fulton

(N), Merium N., see Anson Griffith

(N), Milcah E., see Joseph H. Pyle

(N), Minta (Minty), see Anthony Brooks, Edward Bond and William Ivory

(N), Miranda E., see Sheldon Beach

(N), N. J. Elizabeth, see William A. Musgrove

(N), Nancy, see James Magaw and Samuel Thomas

(N), Nancy A., see Robert J. Cameron

(N), Nancy O., see George Boddy

(N), Nancy S., see Ellis C. Phillips

(N), Naomi P., see Thomas L. Bonsal

(N), Nehetta, see John Hopkins

(N), Susanna E., see James Yates
(N), Susanna G., see Richard Warner
(N), Virginia A., see James Touchstone
(N), William, see Ephraim Buffington
(N), Zeppora, see Ephraim Spence

UPDEGROVE
Updegrove, Hannah, see John Jester
Updegrove, Jesse (born 1787), married 1st to Margaret Tyson circa 16 Mar 1813 (date of license) and married 2nd to Lancy or Laney Miller circa 7 Oct 1835 (date of license) by Rev. Woodley (Cecil County Marriage License Book; DAR transcript copied in 1928 misspelled his name as Jose Updegrave; 1840 Cecil County Census Index spelled his name Jesse Updegrove; 1860 Cecil County Census misspelled his name Jesse Uptegrove, age 72, but his wife was not mentioned; War of 1812 Bounty Land Warrant No. 55-160-738)

VALENTINE
Valentine, Gibson (born c1820) (teamster at Elkton), married Levinia (N) (born c1830) probably circa 1848; son Jesse Valentine born c1849 (1860 Cecil County Census)

VAN ANTWERP
Van Antwerp, Eliza and Thomas, see H. B. Bascom

VAN BUREN
Van Buren, Abraham (major), eldest son of President Martin Van Buren, married Sarah Angelica Singleton, youngest daughter of Richard Singleton, at her father's home in Sumpter (sic) District, South Carolina,, on 27 Nov 1838 by Rev. Converse (Cecil Gazette, 22 Dec 1838)

VANCE
Vance, Amanda, see Joseph Hedrick
Vance, Rachel, see David P. Claypool

VANDEGRIFT
Vandegrift, Andrew Jackson, married Miss Ann Price, both of New Castle Co., DE, on 1 Feb 1838 at Port Penn, Delaware, by Rev. Brown (Cecil Gazette, 10 Feb 1838)
Vandegrift, Elizabeth S., see John W. Tarburton
Vandegrift, Nicholas, married Elizabeth Fillingame circa 12 Apr 1830 (date of license) by Rev. Duke (Cecil County Marriage License Book)
Vandegrift, Peregrine, married Mary Simmons circa 12 Sep 1840 (date of license) (Cecil County Marriage License Book)

VANDERFORD
Vanderford, H. Jr. (born c1812) (editor at Elkton), son of H. Vanderford Sr. (born c1792), married Angeline (N) (born c1821) circa 1840; son Julien Vanderford born c1841, printer (1860 Cecil County Census)

VANDIVER
Vandiver, Benjamin (1803-1860), married Margaret S. Lynn (1806-1888) circa 16 Jul 1828 (date of license) by Rev. Goforth (Cecil County Marriage License Book; DAR transcript copied in 1928 misspelled his name Vandever; West Nottingham Cemetery tombstone inscriptions)
Vandiver, Robert R., married Miss Mary Russell, of North East, on 25 Jan 1838 by Rev. Goldsborough (Cecil Gazette, 10 Feb 1838)

VAN DYKE

Van Dyke, Thomas L. (born c1818, Maryland) (farmer at Cecilton), married Elizabeth Cochran (1818-1867, Maryland) circa 13 Dec 1836 (date of license) by Rev. Duke; son John born c1838, Maryland (Cecil Co. Marriage License Book; 1860 Cecil Co. Census; *Cecil Democrat and Farmer's Journal*, 30 Mar 1867)

VAN GESEL

Van Gesel, Angelina and John, see Matthew J. Clarke

VAN HORN (VANHORN)

Van Horn (VanHorn), Elizabeth, see Elisha Hughes England, Samuel England and William Kirk

Van Horn (VanHorn), J. (born c1823, Pennsylvania) (farmer at Port Herman, Cecil Co.), married Anne (N) (born c1822, Pennsylvania) probably circa 1844; son Dallas born c1845, Pennsylvania; daughter Mary born c1848, Maryland (1860 Cecil County Census)

VANNEMAN

Vanneman, John P. (1806-1875), of Port Deposit, married Harriet T. (N) (1807-1893) probably circa 1827 (Hopewell United Methodist Church Cemetery tombstone inscriptions; *Cecil Whig*, 23 Jan 1875)

VANNORT

Vannort, John (1805-1886), married Elizabeth Thompson (1805-1880) circa 20 May 1826 (date of license) by Rev. Goforth (Cecil County Marriage License Book spelled his name Vanort; DAR transcript copied in 1928 misspelled it Venort; Hopewell United Methodist Church Cemetery tombstone inscriptions)

Vannort, John, see David U. Norris

Vannort, Sarah E., see John A. Atkinson

VANSANT

Vansant, Eliza, see Samuel Davis

Vansant, Louisa, see Alexander Anderson

Vansant, William H. (born c1822, Pennsylvania) (farmer near Elkton), married Caroline (N) (born c1827, Pennsylvania) probably circa 1849; son Silas Vansant born c1850, Pennsylvania; moved to Maryland circa 1851 and daughter Mary Vansant born c1852 (1860 Cecil County Census)

VAN WINKLE

Van Winkle, James (esquire), of Paterson, NJ, married Miss Martha McNutt, of Newark, DE, on 30 April 1850 by Rev. H. D. Moore in Philadelphia (*Cecil Whig*, 11 May 1850)

VAUX

Vaux, George and Hannah S., see William Penn Chandler

VEACH

Veach, Ann, see Roger Mayner

Veach, Joseph, married Emily Morgan circa 31 May 1841 (date of license) (Cecil Co. Marr. License Book)

Veach, Margaret, see Jacob Woollehan

Veach, Zadock, married Mary Ann Evans on 25 May 1838, after obtaining a license that same day, by Rev. Hagany (Cecil County Marriage License Book; DAR transcript copied in 1928 mistakenly spelled his first name Yadock; Elkton Methodist Church Register, p. 139)

VEAL

Veal, James, married Elizabeth Biddle circa 28 Nov 1833 (date of license) by Rev. Duke (Cecil County Marriage License Book)

VEAZEY, VEASEY

Veazey, Anna W., see James Ward

Veazey, Augusta, see Thomas A. Roberts

Veazey, Caleb (born c1820, born Maryland), of North East, married Miss Harriet Jackson (born c1822, Maryland), also of Cecil Co., on 14 Jan 1845, after obtaining a license on 13 Jan 1845, by the Rev. J. Humphries (Cecil County Marriage License Book; 1860 Cecil County Census; *Cecil Whig*, 18 Jan 1845, mistakenly reported they were married "on Tuesday 4ᵗʰ instant," but it was actually on Tuesday the 14th)

Veazey, George Clinton, son of Col. Veazey, of Cecil Co., married Lydia Gilpin Hirons, daughter of John Hirons, of Wilmington, DE, on 21 Jan 1834 by Rev. Pardee in Wilmington (*Delaware Gazette*, 24 Jan 1834, spelled his name Veasey)

Veazey, George Ross (esquire), married Eliza Duncan, daughter of Rev. Dr. Duncan of Baltimore, on 16 May 1850 in Baltimore (*Cecil Whig*, 1 Jun 1850; *Cecil Democrat and Farmer's Journal*, 8 Jun 1850, spelled his name Veazy)

Veazey, Harriet, see Morgan Price

Veazey, John T. (born c1813, Maryland) (farmer at North East), married Miss Ellenora Cole (born c1818, born Maryland), both of Cecil Co., on 1 Apr 1845, after obtaining a license on 29 Mar 1845, by Rev. Humphries (Cecil County Marriage License Book; *Cecil Whig*, 5 Apr 1845; 1860 Cecil County Census)

Veazey, Joseph W., married Margaret S. Manly, daughter of Capt. John Manly, all of Cecil Co., on 29 Jan 1838, after obtaining a license that same day, by Rev. McFarland (*Cecil Gazette*, 3 Feb 1838; Cecil County Marriage License Book; DAR transcript copied in 1928 mistakenly listed the minister's name as Farland (James McFarland was a Methodist minister in Elkton at that time); Elkton Methodist Church Register, p. 138, misspelled Veazey's name as Vasy)

Veazey, Letitia, see James Burk

Veazey, Margaret, see James Mulholland

Veazey, Mary A., see Green M. Thompson

Veazey, Rebecca, see Joshua Ward

Veazey, Sarah, see Joseph Wallace

Veazey, Thomas Brockus, see Henry Nindson

Veazey, Thomas W., see Matthew C. Pearce

Veazey, William (born c1825, Maryland) (laborer at Bay View), married Eliza Ann Mercer (born c1827, Maryland) circa 20 Jul 1844 (date of license) (Cecil Co. Marr. License Book; 1860 Cecil County Census)

VERNON

Vernon, Ann Maria, see William H. Hendrickson

VINCENT

Vincent, Francis, of the Blue Hen's Chicken, married Miss Harriet F. Farra, daughter of the late John Farra, Esq., of Brandywine Hundred, on 1 Jun 1848 by Mayor Swift at the Morris House in Philadelphia (*Cecil Democrat and Farmer's Journal*, 10 Jun 1848)

VINCINGER

Vincinger, William, married Miss Lavinia Ann Hill, both of Cecil Co., on 24 Dec 1835, after obtaining a license on 19 Dec 1835, by Rev. Russel (Cecil County Marriage License; *Delaware Gazette*, 1 Jan 1836)

VIRTUE

Virtue, John, married Maria R. Coale circa 4 Jan 1825 (date of license) by Rev. Grace (Cecil County Marriage License Book)

Virtue, Robert (cabinet maker), married Rebecca Roach circa 19 Apr 1827 (date of license) (Cecil County Marriage License Book; *Elkton Press*, 18 Aug 1828)

VOGLESONG

Voglesong, William, of York, PA, married Margaret C. Cloud, daughter of Col. E. Cloud, on 23 May 1850 by Rev. Hitchcock at the Second Presbyterian Church (*Cecil Democrat and Farmer's Journal*, 8 Jun 1850, reported a double wedding ceremony with her sister Julia M. Cloud who married Albert M. Long, as did the *Cecil Whig*, 1 Jun 1850, which latter newspaper also stated that they had found "the following notice [the aforesaid dual marriages] in the *Ohio State Journal* of Friday last"); see Albert M. Long, *q.v.*

VOLOKER

Voloker, Nicholas (1811-1881), married Anna (N) (1805-1879) probably circa 1832 (Hart's Methodist Church Cemetery tombstone inscriptions)

WAITE

Waite, Joseph T., married Miss Elizabeth Butler, of Wilmington, DE, on 20 Sep 1849 by Rev. Dubose at New London, Chester Co., PA (*Cecil Democrat and Farmer's Journal*, 22 Sep 1849; *Delaware Gazette*, 25 Sep 1849; *Cecil Whig*, 22 Sep 1849)

WAKEMAN

Wakeman, Roswell or Rosewell (born c1810, New York) (dentist, Port Deposit), married Mary Slicer (born c1822, Maryland) circa 22 Jun 1842 (date of license) (Cecil County Marriage License Book and the 1850 Cecil County Census spelled his name Roswell; DAR transcript copied in 1955 and 1860 Cecil County Census both spelled his name Rosewell)

WALKER

Walker, Eliza Ann, see Arthur Dykes

Walker, George W., married 1st to Eliza Ann (N) (1815-1849) probably circa 1835; Mrs. Eliza Ann Walker died in her 34th year in Pencader Hundred, New Castle Co., DE, and George married 2nd to Miss Mary E. Hutton, both of New Castle Co., DE, on 1 Nov 1849 by Rev. Ashton in Philadelphia (*Cecil Democrat and Farmer's Journal*, 10 Nov 1849; *Cecil Whig*, 10 Nov 1849, and 17 Mar 1849, the latter newspaper noted "Wilmington and Philadelphia papers please copy")

Walker, Henry R. (born c1812, Delaware) (farmer at Cecilton), married A. W. (N) (born c1816, Delaware) circa 1835; son J. H. Walker born c1836 (1860 Cecil County Census)

Walker, Isaac, married Sarah Ann Reed circa 11 Jan 1843 (date of license) (Cecil Co. Marr. License Book)

Walker, Isaac (born c1825, Delaware) (farmer at Cecilton), married Elizabeth (N) (born c1830, Pennsylvania) circa 1846; daughter Rebecca Walker born c1847 (1860 Cecil County Census)

Walker, J. H., see Henry R. Walker

Walker, John, married Eliza Noble circa 28 Oct 1834 (date of their license) by Rev. Griffith (Cecil County Marriage License Book)

Walker, John G. (1822-1860), married Abbey Francina Ham (1825-1864) circa 23 Jan 1844 (date of license) (Cecil County Marriage License Book listed his name without the middle initial and spelled her name Abby; Hopewell United Methodist Church Cemetery tombstone inscriptions)

Walker, John W., see Henry Wilson Archer

Walker, Joseph (1805-1892), married Bridget (N) (1816-1895) probably circa 1834-1836 (West Nottingham Cemetery tombstone inscriptions)

Walker, Margaret, see Josiah McClenahan

Walker, Mary, see Alexander Brown

Walker, Mary Elizabeth, see Henry Wilson Archer

Walker, Rebecca, see Isaac Walker

WALLACE

Wallace, Elizabeth, see William Hutchinson

Wallace, Elizabeth Black, see John C. Groome and Matthew Carroll Pearce

Wallace, George, see Joseph Wallace

Wallace, Hannah, see William I. Brown

Wallace, Joseph (1791-1872) (doctor), of Elkton, son of Dr. George Wallace (1752-1796) and Elizabeth Black (1797-1876), married Elizabeth Ward, daughter of Joshua Ward and Sarah Veazey, on 17 Jun 1825 while stationed at Fort McHenry in Baltimore (*Portrait and Biographical Record of Harford and Cecil Counties, Maryland* (1897, repr. 1989), pp. 237-238; *Easton Journal*, 19 Sep 1872)

Wallace, Leah, see Thomas Bryan

Wallace, Mary, see James Walton

Wallace, Mary Ann, see Jonathan Knotts

Wallace, Rachael, see Abel C. Davis

Wallace, Rebecca, see Joshua Ash

Wallace, Sarah, see John A. Wallace

Wallace, Thomas, see William Hutchinson

WALLEN, WALLING

Wallen, Henry, married Julia McDaniel circa 19 Feb 1828 (date of license) (Cecil Co. Marr. License Book)

Walling, Martha A., see William E. Maffitt

WALLIS

Wallis, Margaret, see John E. Davis

WALMSLEY

Walmsley, Ann, see Alexander Patterson

Walmsley, Araminta, see Joseph Benton

Walmsley, Benjamin, married Cornelia Ford circa 18 Feb 1830 (date of license) by Rev. Griffith (Cecil County Marriage License Book)

Walmsley, Benjamin, married Sarah Ann Ward circa 24 Mar 1835 (date of license) by Rev. Smith (Cecil County Marriage License Book)

Walmsley, Elizabeth C., see John Ross Smith

Walmsley, George W. married Ann E. Wroth circa 13 Sep 1843 (date of license) (Cecil County Marriage License Book)

Walmsley, James T., of Cecil Co., married Miss Mary E. Ellis, of Anne Arundel Co., on 30 May 1850 in Baltimore by Rev. Slicer (*Baltimore Sun*, 1 Jun 1850, and *Cecil Democrat and Farmer's Journal*, 8 Jun 1850, both misspelled his name Wamsley)

Walmsley, John, married Araminta Dowling circa 19 Sep 1835 (date of license) by Rev. Coleman (Cecil County Marriage License Book)

Walmsley, John K., married Sarah Dalster circa 27 Jan 1834 (date of license) by Rev. McKenney, a Protestant Episcopal minister in the North Sassafras (Cecil County Marriage License Book)

Walmsley, Mary, see John W. Stradley

Walmsley, Rachel R., see John R. Price

Walmsley, Rebecca, see John Moore

Walmsley, Robert, married Mary Lister circa 27 Jun 1835 (date of license) by Rev. Coleman (Cecil County Marriage License Book; DAR transcript copied in 1928 transcribed her name as Sister)

Walmsley, Robert M. (1803-1879), married Margaret G. Beard (1809-1879) circa 12 Feb 1827 (date of license) by Rev. Wilson (Cecil County Marriage License Book; Elkton Cemetery tombstone inscriptions)

Walmsley, Sophia, see Alexander Patterson

Walmsley, William H., married Sarah M. Glanden circa 21 Dec 1846 (date of license) (Cecil County Marriage License Book)

WALSH

Walsh, Mary, see Thomas Beers

WALTER

Walter, William, of Chester Co., PA, married Miss Catharine E. Mousely, of Cecil Co., on 20 Apr 1848 by George W. Bartram, Esq., at Chester, PA (*Cecil Whig*, 29 Apr 1848)

WALTON

Walton, James, married Mary Wallace circa 11 Jun 1827 (date of license) (Cecil Co. Marr. License Book)

Walton, Margaretta E., see Joseph Merritt

WAPLES

Waples, Gideon (merchant), of Milton, Delaware, married Mrs. Sarah Cottingham, daughter of Miers Burton (merchant), of Millsboro, Delaware, on 24 Mar 1829 by Rev. Higbee (*Elkton Press*, 4 Apr 1829)

WARBURTON

Warburton, Eliza, see Otto Nowland

Warburton, Hannah, see William T. Warburton

Warburton, James, married Miss Mary S. Maffitt, both of Cecil Co., on 13 Jul 1847, after obtaining a license on 11 Jul 1847, by the Rev. Dr. J. P. Durben, of Philadelphia (*Cecil Whig*, 31 Jul 1847; Cecil County Marriage License Book)

Warburton, Margaret, see Joseph Miller

Warburton, Mary, see John Nowland and William T. Warburton

Warburton, Thomas, see William T. Warburton

Warburton, William T. (1809-1885), son of Thomas Warburton, married Elizabeth McCauley (1816-1899), daughter of John and Elizabeth McCauley, circa 1846 and had five children, namely, Hannah Warburton, Elizabeth Ruley, William T. Warburton, Jr. (born 16 Jul 1852), Thomas H. Warburton, and Mary Warburton (*Portrait and Biographical Record of Harford and Cecil Counties, Maryland* (1897, repr. 1989), pp. 369-370; Shelemiah Methodist Church Cemetery tombstone inscriptions)

WARD

Ward, Adda, see Levi Ward

Ward, Catharine M., see Levi Ward

Ward, David (born c1817) (farmer at Elkton), married Sarah Biddle (born c1825) on 10 Aug 1843, after obtaining a license on 9 Aug 1843, by Rev. McIntire; eldest daughter Martha Ward born c1845 (*Cecil Whig*, 19 Aug 1843; Cecil County Marriage License Book; 1860 Cecil County Census)

Ward, Eliza, see Thomas V. Ward

Ward, Elizabeth, see William W. Foster and Joseph Wallace

Ward, Ellen J., see Levi Ward

Ward, Henry, see Thomas McCrery

Ward, James, married Anna W. Vesey (Veazey?), of Baltimore, on 27 May 1850 by Rev. Bates of the Methodist Protestant Church in Baltimore (*Baltimore Sun*, 1 Jun 1850, and *Cecil Democrat and Farmer's Journal*, 8 Jun 1850, both spelled her name Vesey)

Ward, John, married Mary Richardson circa 20 Jun 1839 (date of license) by Rev. McIntire (Cecil County Marriage License Book)

Ward, John T. (born c1814) (farmer at Elkton), married Mary A. (N) (born c1810) circa 1842; daughter Rachel Ward born c1843 (1860 Cecil County Census)

Ward, Joshua, see Joseph Wallace

Ward, Joshua, married Rebecca Veazey circa 30 Jan 1828 (date of license) (Cecil Co. Marr. License Book)

Ward, Julia Ann, see George R. Pearce

Ward, Levi (born c1821, Maryland) (farmer near Elkton), married Mary H. (N) (born c1829, Maryland) probably circa 1848; daughter Ellen J. born c1849, Pennsylvania, daughter Susan F. born c1851,

Pennsylvania, daughter Catharine M. born c1854, Pennsylvania, daughter Adda born c1857, Maryland (1860 Cecil County Census)

Ward, Lydia, see George R. Ewing

Ward, Maria F., see Thomas C. Cazier

Ward, Martha, see David Ward

Ward, Rachel, see Reuben Taylor and John T. Ward

Ward, Sarah Ann, see Benjamin Walmsley

Ward, Susan F., see Levi Ward

Ward, Thomas V. (born c1809) (farmer at Cecilton), son of (N) and Eliza Ward (born 1787), married Mary McLane (born c1822), daughter of Dr. Allan McLane, of Wilmington, DE, on 18 Dec 1838 by Rev. McCullough (*Cecil Gazette*, 22 Dec 1838; 1860 Cecil County Census; *Midland Journal*, 28 Aug 1891)

Ward, William, see William W. Foster

WARDELL

Wardell, Isaac, married Ann Logan circa 9 Dec 1834 (date of their license) by Rev. Griffith (Cecil County Marriage License Book)

WARDEN

Warden, William, married Mary Ann Gibson circa 12 Sep 1839 (date of license) by Rev. Pierson (Cecil County Marriage License Book)

WARING

Waring, John, married Rachel Saunders circa 11 Dec 1841 (date of license) (Cecil County Marriage License Book spelled his name Warring)

Waring, William (1808-1884), married Lydia (N) (1812-1890) probably circa 1830 (Friends Cemetery, at Colora, tombstone inscriptions; *Midland Journal*, 30 May 1890, stated Lidia Waring, aged about 80, relict of William, died at the residence of her son Wilson Waring at Colora)

Waring, Wilson, see William Waring

WARNER

Warner, James, married Ann G. Wirt circa 13 Nov 1845 (date of license) (Cecil County Marr. License Book)

Warner, Richard (1801-1878), married Susanna G. (N) (1803-1875) probably circa 1821-1825 and she died at Pilot Town (Bethesda Cemetery tombstone inscriptions; *Cecil Whig*, 27 Nov 1875, obituary stated Susan Warner, wife of Richard, died at age 71; *Cecil Whig*, 30 Mar 1877, stated he died in his 77th year)

WARTER

Warter, James, married Suzanne Shiffley on 29 May 1825 by Rev. Epinette (*History of Saint Francis Xavier Church and Bohemia Plantation Now Known as Old Bohemia, Warwick, Maryland*, by Joseph C. Cann (1976), p. 47)

WASON

Wason, James (1825-1898), married 1st to Margaret Elizabeth McKinney (1828-1861), youngest daughter of John S. and Elizabeth M. McKinney, probably circa 1846-1850 and married 2nd to Mary A. Brown (1834-1881), daughter of Joshua and Mary Brown (West Nottingham Cemetery tombstone inscriptions)

WATERS

Waters, Adeline, see Charles H. Brown

Waters, Elizabeth A., see Oliver Perry Killingsworth

WATERSON

Waterson, Margaret, see William Moarn (Mourn)

WATKINS

Watkins, Harriet, see John T. Diffenderfer

Watkins, Mary, see Frederick H. Michael

Watkins, Samuel, married Harriet McMullin circa 2 Aug 1836 (date of license) by Rev. Megredy, and Mrs. Harriet Watkins married 2nd to John T. Diffenderfer, both of Port Deposit, on 13 Apr 1843 (*Cecil Whig*, 29 Apr 1843; Cecil County Marriage License Book)

Watkins, William (1818-1879), married Elizabeth (N) (1818-1886) probably circa 1840 (Mount Pleasant United Methodist Church Cemetery tombstone inscriptions)

WATSON

Watson, Abraham, married Miss Letitia Lee, both of Carpenters Point Neck, Cecil Co., on 28 Nov 1843, after obtaining a license on 27 Nov 1843, by Rev. Goentner at North East (Cecil County Marriage License Book; *Cecil Whig*, 9 Dec 1843)

Watson, Caroline, see Edward Jackson

Watson, Elizabeth W., see James H. Morgan

Watson, Humphrey E. (1820-1887), married Elizabeth (N) (1819-1896) before 1846; buried beside son J. Calvin Watson (1847-1920) and his wife Annie R. Wherry (1857-1927) (Rosebank Cemetery, at Calvert, tombstone inscriptions)

Watson, Isaac, see Jeremiah Watson

Watson, J. Calvin, see Humphrey E. Watson

Watson, Jeremiah (born c1810, Maryland) (farmer near Charlestown), married Elizabeth White (born c1817, Maryland) circa 18 Mar 1841 (date of license) (Cecil County Marriage License Book; 1860 Cecil County Census also listed Susan Watson age 21, and Isaac age 17, Sarah age 11, Mary age 8, and John age 7)

Watson, John (1825-1904), married Ann E. (N) (1818-1883) probably before 1850 (Rosebank Cemetery, at Calvert, tombstone inscriptions)

Watson, John, see Jeremiah Watson

Watson, Mary, see Jeremiah Watson

Watson, Millicent, see William Johnson

Watson, Sarah, see John C. Anderson and Jeremiah Watson

Watson, Sarah Ann, see Joseph Coale

Watson, Silas H., of Chester Co., Pennsylvania, married Ruth Ann Alden, of Cecil Co, circa 25 Aug 1832 (date of license) by Rev. Duke (Cecil County Marriage License Book)

Watson, Susan, see Benjamin Gifford and Jeremiah Watson

Watson, Susan L., see John T. Ricketts

Watson, Thomas, see John T. Ricketts

Watson, Thomas, married Delilah Ryan circa 20 Mar 1849 (date of license) (Cecil Co. Marr. License Book)

Watson, William, married Maria McClenahan circa 15 Feb 1831 (date of license) by Rev. Mahan (Cecil County Marriage License Book)

WATTS

Watts, Andrew M. (born c1819, Maryland), married Mary (N) (born c1810, Delaware) circa 1844; son John Watts born c1845, Delaware (1860 Cecil County Census)

Watts, Samuel (born c1812, Delaware) (farmer at Cecilton), married Mary (N) (born c1816, New Jersey) circa 1845; daughter Mary born c1846, Delaware, daughter Elizabeth born c1850, Delaware, son Samuel born c1853, Maryland, and son John born c1869, Maryland (1860 Cecil County Census)

Watts, William, married Margaret Andrews on 24 Aug 1843, after obtaining a license that same day, by Rev. Shields (Cecil County Marriage License Book; Elkton Methodist Church Register, p. 140)

WAUGH

Waugh, Mary and Robert, see John Mearns

WAY

Way, Francis, see Thomas Way

Way, Samuel F., married Elizabeth M. Nesbitt circa 17 Aug 1846 (date of license) (Cecil County Marriage License Book; DAR transcript copied in 1955 mistakenly spelled his surname May)

Way, Thomas (1815-1890, born Delaware) (blacksmith near Colora), married Elizabeth (N) (1823-1879, born Pennsylvania) circa 1848; son Francis Way born c1850, Maryland (Friends Cemetery, at Harrisville, tombstone inscriptions; 1860 Cecil County Census; *Midland Journal*, 25 Apr 1890)

Way, Thomas H., see William H. Way

Way, William H., son of Thomas H. Way, of Kennett Township, Chester Co., PA, married Mary Elma Moore (born 1821), daughter of Joseph Moore and Jane Smith, both deceased, of West Nottingham Hundred, Cecil Co., on the 18th day of the 3rd month 1847 at a public meeting of Friends at the home of Amos Moore of West Nottingham. Among the witnesses were Richard B. Moore, Amos Moore and Timothy Moore. (*Births, Deaths and Marriages of the Nottingham Quakers, 1680-1899*, by Alice L. Beard (1989), pp. 67, 226)

WEAVER

Weaver, George C. (born c1811) (cooper at Elkton), married Martha Gill (born c1812) circa 4 Sep 1832 (date of license) by Rev. Mahan; daughter Sarah Weaver born c1834 (Cecil County Marriage License Book; 1860 Cecil County Census)

Weaver, Margaret Ann, see Thomas G. McKinney

Weaver, Mary, see James Matthews

Weaver, Rebecca Ann, see Elisha Mahoney

Weaver, Samuel H. (1823-1871), of Elkton, married Sarah Fulton circa 31 Mar 1847 (date of license) (Cecil County Marriage License Book; *Cecil Whig*, 22 Jul 1871)

Weaver, Sarah, see George C. Weaver

WEBB

Webb, Abner, see Samuel W. T. Hopper

Webb, Caroline M., see Jacob Tome

Webb, Edward, married Martha Alexander circa 14 Nov 1826 (date of license) by Rev. Magraw (Cecil County Marriage License Book)

Webb, Emeline Virginia, see Samuel W. T. Hopper

Webb, Esther An, see Samuel Howard

Webb, James (born c1824) (farmer at Cecilton), married Sarah Jane Woodell (born c1829) circa 24 Jul 1848 (date of license) (Cecil County Marriage License Book; 1860 Cecil County Census)

Webb, P. Washington (1807-1887), married Mary F. (N) (1811-1877) probably circa 1830 (Hopewell United Methodist Church Cemetery tombstone inscriptions)

Webb, Sarah, see William D. Bristow

WEIR

Weir, Andrew, married Mary Murphy circa 5 Jan 1826 (date of license) by Rev. Goforth (Cecil County Marriage License Book mistakenly spelled his name Were)

Weir, John (born c1807, Maryland) (farmer, 7th District), married 1st to (N) before 1840 (son John Weir born c1842) and married 2nd to Martha Rutter (born c1820, Maryland) circa 11 Feb 1850 (date of license); son William Weir born c1851 (Cecil County Marriage License Book; 1860 Cecil County Census)

Weir, Nancy, see William Campbell

Weir, William, see John Weir

WELCH

Welch, Catharine, see Sylvester McGee

Welch, Thomas S., of Elkton, married Miss Mary Rosetta Briscoe, of Kent Co., on 23 Apr 1833, after obtaining a license on 22 Apr 1833, by Rev. Smith (Kent County Marriage License Book; *Cecil Republican*, 27 Apr 1833)

WELLS

Wells, Benjamin (1814-1894) (Pennsylvania Railroad station agent at Elkton), married Rebecca Jane Alexander (1823-1897), daughter of Henry Alexander, circa 2 Feb 1841 (date of license) (Cecil County Marriage License Book; *Portrait and Biographical Record of Harford and Cecil Counties, Maryland* (1897, repr. 1989), p. 449, listed their four children in 1897 as H. [Henry] A. Wells [born c1848], Mary A. Aldrich, Benjamin M. Wells (born 6 Jan 1855) and Charles G. Wells; 1860 Cecil County Census; Elkton Cemetery tombstone inscriptions)

Wells, Charles G., see Benjamin Wells

Wells, David M., married Hannah Mahan on 16 Dec 1841 after obtaining a license on 15 Dec 1841 (Cecil County Marriage License Book; Elkton Methodist Church Register)

Wells, Edwin E., see Joseph Wells

Wells, George W. (1820-1896), married 1st to Elizabeth Hutton circa 4 May 1840 (date of license) by Rev. McIntire and married 2nd to Miss Elizabeth "Eliza" Krauss (1818-1851) on 20 Jun 1844, after obtaining a license on 18 Jun 1844, by Rev. McIntire (Cecil County Marriage License Book and Elkton Cemetery tombstone inscriptions gave his middle initial as W., but the *Cecil Whig*, 22 Jun 1844, gave it as M.; the newspaper stated "With the above we received a splendid slice of cake for which we tender our thanks and our best wishes for the success of the happy couple" and followed this with a poem of twelve lines.)

Wells, H. A., see Benjamin Wells

Wells, John C., see Joseph Wells

Wells, Joseph L. (1818-1897) (mail carrier, storekeeper and a Civil War veteran), married Miss Cornelia Crouch (1822-1897), of Elk Neck Creek, on 8 Apr 1845, after obtaining a license that same day, by Rev. McIntire (Cecil County Marriage License Book; *Portrait and Biographical Record of Harford and Cecil Counties, Maryland* (1897, repr. 1989), p. 398, listed three children, namely, John C. Wells [born c1846], Edwin E. Wells [born c1851] and Anna R. Cooper [born c1856], but the 1860 Cecil County Census also listed a son Joseph L. Wells born c1853; Elkton Cemetery tombstone inscriptions; *Cecil Whig*, 12 Apr 1845, included an eight line poem by Tom Moore)

Wells, Lydia, see George Mahan

Wells, Mary, see William B. Giles

Wells, Orin, see William B. Giles

Wells, Sarah Ann, see William C. Woods

WESSELLY

Wesselly, Sarah, see Thomas Jefferson Potts

WEST

West, Isabel, see William T. West

West, John T., married Araminta Boyce (c1813-1864) circa 22 Aug 1833 (date of license) by Rev. Barratt and she died at Pivot Bridge in her 51st year (Cecil Co. Marr. License Book; *Cecil Whig*, 27 Aug 1864)

West, Mahlon H., see Joseph Roman, Jr.

West, Mary T., see Joseph Roman, Jr.

West, Philip, see William T. West

West, Rebecca T., see Joseph Roman, Jr.

West, Ruth, see William T. West

West, Samuel A., of Port Deposit, married Martha C. Simpers, of North East, on 25 Oct 1842, after obtaining a license that same day, by Rev. Cunningham (Cecil Co. Marr. License Book; *Cecil Whig*, 29 Oct 1842)

West, Thomas, married Ann McCullough circa 5 Jan 1836 (date of license) by Rev. Potts (Cecil County Marriage License Book)

West, William T. (born c1814, Maryland) (farmer, 8th District), married (N) probably circa 1837 and she died between 1854 and 1860; daughter Isabel West born c1838, Maryland, and their other children were born in Maryland, the youngest being twins Philip and Ruth West, born c1854 (1860 Cecil County Census)

WESTCOTT
Westcott, George B., of Cecil Co., later of Kent Co., married 1st to Mary Ann Hynson, of Kent Co., circa 14 Jun 1831 by Rev. Smith and married 2nd to Ann Maria Tilden circa 17 Oct 1843 by Rev. Jones (Kent County Marriage License Book)

WHANN
Whann, Hannah Ann, see George Grant
Whann, Martha, see Joseph W. Miller

WHEELER
Wheeler, Helen M., see Thomas Ford

WHERRY
Wherry, Annie R., see Hunphrey E. Watson
Wherry, David, married Sarah Ann Alexander circa 15 Apr 1835 (date of license) by Rev. Duke (Cecil County Marriage License Book)
Wherry, John D., married Ann Eliza Biles circa 6 Mar 1832 (date of license) by Rev. Duke (Cecil County Marriage License Book)

WHITAKER
Whitaker, Abraham (b. c1820, Maryland) (carpenter, 7th District), married Rebecca M. Harlan (b. c1823, Maryland) circa 25 Jul 1846 (date of license) (Cecil Co. Marr. License Book; 1860 Cecil County Census)
Whitaker, Emeline, see Samuel B. Irwin
Whitaker, Francis A., see Samuel B. Irwin
Whitaker, George P. (1803-1890) (esquire and member of the legislature in 1867), of Berks Co., PA, later of Cecil Co., married Eliza Ann (N) (1808-1875) probably circa 1828 and died on his birthday, 13 Dec 1890, at Principio Furnace (St. Mark's Episcopal Church tombstone inscriptions; *Midland Journal*, 2 Jan 1891, stated his wife had also died on her birthday, which was 16 Nov 1875)
Whitaker, James Jr. (1816-1877), married Ann Maria Jones (1819-1900) circ 25 Nov 1839 (date of license) by Rev. Mason (Cecil County Marriage License Book listed his name as James Whitaker, Jr.; DAR transcript copied in 1928 listed it as James Whittaker; *Cecil Whig*, 7 Apr 1877)
Whitaker, Mary Ann, see George W. Hasson
Whitaker Sarah B., see Benjamin F. Heath

WHITCRAFT
Whitcraft, Richard Kennedy, of London Britain Township, Chester Co., PA, married Eliza Jane Gregg, of Cecil Co., on 29 Sep 1850 (*Cecil Democrat and Farmer's Journal*, 26 Oct 1850)

WHITE
White, Adaline, see Robert M. Gilmore
White, Adaliza, see Theodore Osborne
White, Cassandra, see Benjamin Mercer
White, Catharine (Catherine), see David Steel and Joseph Keetley
White, Clinton J. (1810-1882, Maryland) (carpenter, 7th District), married Barbara H. Dennison (1815-1892, born Maryland) circa 14 Oct 1833 (date of license) by Rev. Goforth (Cecil County Marriage License Book; Hopewell United Methodist Church Cemetery tombstone inscriptions; *Cecil Republican*, 19 Oct 1833, listed their marriage, but did not give the date; 1860 Cecil County Census)

White, David (born c1810, Maryland) (steamboat captain, 7th District), married Miss Millicent A. Cazier (born c1816, Maryland), both of Cecil Co., on 8 Jan 1835, after obtaining a license on 2 Jan 1835, by Rev. Spry (Cecil County Marriage License Book; DAR transcript copied in 1928 misspelled her name Cozier; *Cecil Gazette*, 10 Jan 1835; 1860 Cecil County Census)

White, Edward, married Sophia Rutter circa 13 Jun 1843 (date of license) (Cecil County Marriage License Book; DAR transcript copied in 1955 mistakenly listed the marriage license date as 18 Jun 1843)

White, Eli, married Sarah Megredy circa 10 May 1836 (date of license) by Rev. Crouch (Cecil County Marriage License Book)

White, Eliza Ann, see Walter Moore

White, Eliza Jane, see William Conley

White, Elizabeth, see David Gilmore and Jeremiah Watson

White, Elmira C., see Joseph C. Gilmore

White, Emaline, see William J. Donahoo

White, Hannah Maria, see Evan Benjamin

White, Harriet B., see Samuel Hitchcock

White, Isabella S., see Peter M. Coulter

White, James, married Ann R. Cameron circa 23 Sep 1835 (date of license) (Cecil Co. Marr. License Book)

White, Jefferson M., married Grizzell "Grizzy" Currier circa 15 Oct 1825 (date of license) by Rev. Magraw (Cecil County Marriage License Book)

White, John, married Miss Rachel Phillips, both of Cecil Co., on 8 Mar 1838, after obtaining a license on 1 Mar 1838, by Rev. Kennard (*Cecil Gazette*, 17 Mar 1838; Cecil County Marriage License Book)

White, John (1809-1865), married Mary Ann Brown (1823-1906), daughter of Isaac Brown and Elizabeth England, on the 28th day of the 3rd month 1843; Mary Ann White married 2nd to John Rawlings Abrams in 1859; buried in Rosebank Cemetery (*Joseph England and his Descendants*, by C. Walter England, Ph.D., 1975, p. 194)

White, John, see David Steel, John Rawlings Abrams and Evan Benjamin

White, Laura, see Henry Purnell

White, Margaret, see Elisha Hitchcock and John T. Mitchell

White, Maria E., see William Edmondson

White, Mary, see William Reed

White, Mary F., see John Whitelock

White, Robert (1814-1889), married Mary Ann McVey (1819-1918) on 1 Oct 1838, after obtaining a license that same day, by Rev. Hagany (Cecil County Marriage License Book; Elkton Methodist Church Register, p. 139; Shelemiah Methodist Church Cemetery tombstone inscriptions)

White, Sarah, see Hugh Kelly

White, Sarah A., see William Boyd

White, Sarah A. C., see Robert E. Oldham

White, Susan E., see Thomas White

White, Thomas, see Robert E. Oldham

White, Thomas, married Susan E. White circa 28 Jan 1833 (date of license) by Rev. Goforth (Cecil County Marriage License Book)

White, William S. (1817-1905), married Matilda J. (N) (1810-1880) probably circa 1840 (Rosebank Cemetery, at Calvert, tombstone inscriptions)

WHITELOCK

Whitelock, Charles (born c1810, Maryland) (mason in the 7th District), married Catherine (N) (born c1820, Maryland) probably circa 1840; son Sylvester Whitelock born c1841 (1860 Cecil County Census)

Whitelock, Elizabeth, see James Ruley

Whitelock, Gracella or Grasella, see James Tucker

Whitelock, Henry, married Grace Jackson circa 6 Jan 1829 (date of license) by Rev. Magraw (Cecil County Marriage License Book)

Whitelock, Henry (born c1819, Maryland) (laborer in the 7th District), married Elizabeth (N) (born c1825, Maryland) probably circa 1841; son James Whitelock born c1842 (1860 Cecil County Census)

Whitelock, James, married Susan Price circa 15 Dec 1836 (date of license) by Rev. Potts (Cecil County Marriage License Book)

Whitelock, James (born 1822) (miller at Perryville, later of Lapidum, Harford Co.), son of John Whitelock (1785-1858) and wife Ann Gorrell, married Miss Caroline Bowman circa 2 Nov 1842 (date of license) in Harford County (*Portrait and Biographical Record of Harford and Cecil Counties, Maryland* (1897, repr. 1989), pp. 267 and 522 mistakenly stated they were married in 1846)

Whitelock, James (born c1826, Maryland) (miller at Perryville), married Mary Jane Calvert (born c1824, Maryland) circa 7 Feb 1849 (date of license); son Thomas Whitelock born 1850 (Cecil County Marriage License Book; 1860 Cecil County Census)

Whitelock, James, see Henry Whitelock

Whitelock, John (1815-1855), married Mary F. White (1819-1856) circa 7 Feb 1843 (date of license) (Cecil County Marriage License Book; DAR transcript copied in 1955 mistakenly listed the marriage license date as 6 Feb 1843; Principio Cemetery tombstone inscriptions)

Whitelock, John Charles Jr. (1819-1896), of Cecil Co. and Harford Co., MD and later New Castle Co., DE (died in Philadelphia, PA), son of John Charles Whitelock and Ann (Agnes) Hamilton Gorrell, married Ann Eliza Wilson (1819-1893), daughter of William Kenly Wilson and Sarah Miller, circa 22 Dec 1846 (Harford County license; *Family Record of John Albert Whitelock*, by Amy Burton Moore (2013), p. 18)

Whitelock, Joseph, married Mary Hodge circa 10 Aug 1826 (date of license) by Rev. Barratt (Cecil County Marriage License Book)

Whitelock, John, see James Whitelock

Whitelock, Louisa, see William Norris

Whitelock, Margaret, see John Cunningham

Whitelock, Martha, see James Jackson

Whitelock, Rebecca, see William Physick

Whitelock, Samuel, married Elizabeth Bell circa 15 Jun 1837 (date of license) by Rev. Grace (Cecil County Marriage License Book)

Whitelock, Thomas, see James Whitelock

WHITELY

Whitely, Elizabeth, see Sidney George Bradford

WHITLOCK

Whitlock, Samuel, married Elizabeth Loftis circa 13 Apr 1825 (date of license) by Rev. Duke (Cecil County Marriage License Book)

WHITNEY

Whitney, Myra Clark, see E. P. Gaines

WHITSON

Whitson, Annie, see William T. Miller

WHITTALL

Whittall, Ann Maria, see William Rutter

WHITTINGHAM

Whittingham, Richard Jr. (reverend), of New York, married Sarah Rebecca "Sally" Chamberlaine, daughter of Henry Chamberlaine, Esq., and Henrietta Elizabeth Gale (1787-1850) of Richmond Hill, Cecil Co., on 19 Nov 1849, after obtaining a license on 14 Nov 1849, by Rev. Goldsborough in St. Mark's Catholic Chapel (Cecil County Marriage License Book; DAR transcript copied in 1955 misspelled his name

Wittingham and her name Chamberlin; *Cecil Democrat and Farmer's Journal*, 24 Nov 1849, listed his name without the Jr.; *Cecil Democrat and Farmer's Journal*, 6 Jul 1850)

WHYTE
Whyte, John, see Joseph Stebbing

WICKS, WICKES
Wicks, Elizabeth, see Jonathan M. Rowland
Wickes, Joseph, see B. Franklin Green
Wickes, Mary E., see B. Franklin Green

WICKWORTH
Wickworth, Mary A., see David Fulton

WILCOX
Wilcox, Charles H., of Baltimore, married Harriet A. P. Brown, eldest daughter of Isaac Brown, Esq., formerly of Port Deposit, on 29 Dec 1850 by Rev. Sargent (*Cecil Democrat and Farmer's Journal*, 4 Jan 1851; *Baltimore Sun*, 31 Dec 1850)

WILEY
Wiley, Elizabeth, see Peter Ross
Wiley, Hugh, see James Wiley
Wiley, James (born c1820, Ireland) (farmer in the 6th District), married Rebecca (N) (born c1820, Maryland) probably in the 1840s (1860 Cecil County Census did not list any children, but did list Hugh Wiley born c1822, Ireland, laborer, and John Alexander born c1840, Maryland, teamster, living in this household)
Wiley, Mary Jane, see Samuel Tosh
Wiley, Westley (born c1820, Maryland) (merchant, 7th District), married Jane (N) (born c1831, Maryland) probably circa 1850; son William Wiley born c1851 (1860 Cecil County Census)
Wiley, William, see Westley Wiley
Wiley, William Wallace (1811-1895), married Mary E. Tosh (1820-1899) circa 10 Feb 1846 (date of license) (Cecil County Marriage License Book; West Nottingham Cemetery tombstone inscriptions)

WILKINS
Wilkins, Edward, of Kent Co., MD, married Miss Deborah Jones, of North East, Cecil Co., on 27 Feb 1838, after obtaining a license on 26 Feb 1838, by Rev. Kennard at *Green Hill*, the residence of Mary Ann Russell (*Cecil Gazette*, 10 Mar 1838; Cecil County Marriage License Book)
Wilkins, John, married Miss Rebecca Paynter, both of Wilmington, DE, on 3 Apr 1846 by Rev. William Urie of Philadelphia (*Cecil Whig*, 11 Apr 1846)
Wilkins, Milcah, see William McDaniel

WILKINSON
Wilkinson, Hannah, see David Brown Trimble
Wilkinson, John W. (1820-1891), married Sarah (N) (1826-1902) probably circa 1845 (Rosebank Cemetery, at Calvert, tombstone inscriptions)
Wilkinson, Nathan, married Miss Sarah Ann Garrett, daughter of the late William Garrett, on 20 Aug 1844, after obtaining a license that same day, by Rev. Wilson at Elk Mills (Cecil County Marriage License Book; *Cecil Whig*, 24 Aug 1844; *Delaware Gazette*, 27 Aug 1844, spelled her surname Garret)

WILLARD
Willard, James H., married Mary Bryan circa 20 Mar 1837 (date of license) by Rev. Morris (Cecil County Marriage License Book)

WILLEY

Willey, Charles, married Elizabeth Bond circa 18 Feb 1828 (date of license) (Cecil Co. Marr. License Book)

WILLIAMS

Williams, Alexander (c1820-1859), of Pennsylvania, married Rebecca M. (N) (1824-1916) probably circa 1845 and Rebecca M. Williams married 2nd to Edwin Barnes in 1861 (Cecil County Marriage License Book; Hopewell United Methodist Church Cemetery tombstone inscriptions; Rebecca M. Williams Barnes is buried beside her first husband Alexander)

Williams, Andrew Jackson, see Thomas Williams

Williams, Angeline Caroline, see Thomas Williams

Williams, Ann Eliza, see Robert Robertson

Williams, Charles S., see Thomas Williams

Williams, Deborah, see Robert McMullen

Williams, Elizah Ann, see Thomas Williams

Williams, Emma, see Robert Williams

Williams, George Whitaker, see Thomas Williams

Williams, Green, married Sarah Edmondson circa 19 Nov 1833 (date of license) by Rev. Duke (Cecil County Marriage License Book; DAR transcript copied in 1928 spelled her name Edmundson)

Williams, James Henry, see Thomas Williams

Williams, Jane, see William Kirk

Williams, Jesse, see Thomas Williams

Williams, John, see James Brown and Joseph Scarborough

Williams, John (born c1816, Maryland) (farmer near Principio), married Rebecca Ann Irwin (born c1818, Maryland) circa 7 Feb 1838 (date of license) by Rev. Dunn (Cecil County Marriage License Book; 1860 Cecil County Census)

Williams, John C., married Susanna Riddle circa 17 Mar 1825 (date of license) by Rev. Magraw (Cecil County Marriage License Book; DAR transcript copied in 1928 spelled her name Biddle)

Williams, Joseph, married Charlotte Pearce, of Elkton, on 6 Mar 1832 (*Baltimore American and Commercial Daily Advertiser*, 13 Mar 1832)

Williams, Joseph, married Miss Rebecca Jeanes, both of New Castle Co., DE, on 31 Jan 1843 by Rev. Janes (*Cecil Whig*, 4 Feb 1843; Elkton Methodist Church Register)

Williams, L. J. (doctor) (U. S. Navy), married Harriet H. Archer, youngest daughter of the late Chief Justice Archer, on 19 Jun 1850 by Rev. Finney (*Cecil Democrat and Farmer's Journal*, 22 Jun 1850; *Baltimore Sun*, 20 Jun 1850)

Williams, Leah G., see Thomas Williams

Williams, Margaret, see James Brown

Williams, Mary Ann, see Thomas Williams

Williams, Mary E. M., see Samuel Campbell

Williams, Melinde Alice, see Thomas Williams

Williams, Rachel, see David Moon

Williams, Rebecca M., see Alexander Williams

Williams, Robert (born c1825, Maryland) (farmer, 6th District), married Mary (N) (born c1822, Maryland) probably circa 1847; daughter Emma Williams born c1848 (1860 Cecil County Census)

Williams, Samuel, married Rebecca McVey circa 22 Jun 1826 (date of license) by Rev. Barratt (Cecil County Marriage License Book)

Williams, Samuel Reeve, married Sarah Harding (1825-1861), of Elkton, later of Cincinnati, OH, daughter of Philip Harding (1797-1825) and Amelia Giles (1787-1864), probably circa 1845 (*Thomas Giles, Born 1752 – Birmingham, England, Died 1812 – Elkton, Maryland, U.S.A., A Genealogical History of His Descendants*, by Alexander W. Giles, Jr. (1986, updated 1996), p. 14)

Williams, Sarah, see James Brown and Joseph Scarborough

Williams, Sylvester, married Miss Rebecca Ash on 29 Jan 1839, after obtaining a license that same day, by Rev. Duke (Cecil County Marriage License Book; Elkton Methodist Church Register, p. 139; *Cecil Gazette*, 2 Feb 1839)

Williams, Thomas (1811-1892), married 1st to Susanna Elizabeth Sturdevant (1819-1839) on 20 Oct 1836 and married 2nd to Sarah Ann Barton (1822-1891) on 26 Nov 1840 (*Bible Records, Genealogical Society of Cecil County*, by Gary L. Burns (1990), p. 15, stated this family was from Maryland and Delaware and listed the births of his nine children, one by his 1st wife and eight by his 2nd wife: Charles S., born 19 Sep 1837; Andrew Jackson, born 22 Nov 1843, died 12 Feb 1844; James Henry, born 30 Dec 1844; Angeline Caroline, born 14 Oct 1847, married ---- Sullivan, died 19 Aug 1918; Mary Ann, born 29 Jun 1852; Melinde Alice, born 30 Jun 1855; Leah Green (Geren?), born 30 Dec 1857; George Whitaker, born 2 Aug 1860, died 12 Dec 1902; and, Elizah Ann, born 31 May 1863)

Williams, Thomas, married Margery H. Robinson circa 30 Jun 1847 (date of license) (Cecil County Marriage License Book)

Williams, Thomas (1818-1891) (farmer near Principio), son of Jesse Williams, of Cecil Co. and of Welsh descent, married Catharine Thompson (1826-1906), daughter of John Thompson, all of Cecil Co., on 3 Feb 1848, after obtaining a license on 1 Feb 1848, by Rev. A. Milby at Elkton (*Cecil Whig*, 19 Feb 1848; Cecil County Marriage License Book; *Portrait and Biographical Record of Harford and Cecil Counties, Maryland* (1897, repr. 1989), p. 428; West Nottingham Cemetery tombstone inscriptions; 1860 Cecil County Census)

Williams, William (1798-1876), married Ann Smith (1809-1882) circa 30 Mar 1837 (date of license) by Rev. Wilson (Cecil County Marr. License Book; Union Methodist Church Cemetery tombstone inscriptions)

WILLIAMSON

Williamson, Eliza M., see Albert R. Teague

Williamson, James, see James H. Finley

Williamson, James A., married Sarah M. Williamson circa 13 Jun 1825 (date of license) by Rev. Miller (Cecil County Marriage License Book)

Williamson, Sarah Lydia, see James H. Finley

Williamson, Sarah M., see James A. Williamson

WILLIS

Willis, Daniel, married Hannah Ann Sutton circa 15 Apr 1847 (date of license) (Cecil County Marriage License Book)

Willis, James (born c1820) (carpenter near Elkton), married Mary Segars (born c1830) circa 10 Feb 1846 (date of license); son Joseph born 1837 (Cecil County Marriage License Book; 1860 Cecil Co. Census)

WILLIX

Willix, Hannah, see Jethro Johnson

WILMER

Wilmer, Edwin (1819-1888), of Baltimore, married Hannah E. Megredy (1819-1907), daughter of Daniel Megredy, of Port Deposit, on 11 Apr 1839 by Rev. Coombe at Port Deposit (*Cecil Gazette*, 20 Apr 1839; *Baltimore Sun*, 13 Apr 1839; Hopewell United Methodist Church Cemetery tombstone inscriptions also inscribed their marriage date)

Wilmer, L. A, married Miss Sydney Ann Bayless on 28 Sep 1834 (*Cecil Gazette*, 11 Oct 1834)

WILSON

Wilson, Alexander, married Catharine Mauldin circa 12 Feb 1834 (date of license) by Rev. Barratt (Cecil County Marriage License Book; *Cecil Democrat and Farmer's Journal*, 4 Feb 1882, reported that a Catharine A. Wilson died at age 67 in Baltimore)

Wilson, Alexander, married Miss Milcah Ann Crouch, both of Elk Neck, on 21 Mar 1850, after obtaining a license on 20 Mar 1850, by Rev. Arthur (*Cecil Whig*, 23 Mar 1850; Cecil County Marriage License Book; *Cecil Democrat and Farmer's Journal*, 30 Mar 1850)

Wilson, Alexander H., married Sarah Wingate circa 21 Aug 1844 (date of license) (Cecil County Marriage License Book)

Wilson, Andrew (1797-1870), married Susan or Susanna Gray (1814-1896) circa 18 Feb 1842 (date of license) (Cecil County Marriage License Book listed her name as Susanna; North East Methodist Church Cemetery tombstone inscription spelled her name Susan)

Wilson, Ann Eliza, see John Charles Whitelock, Jr.

Wilson, Catharine, see Alexander Wilson and David Garrett

Wilson, David, see Samuel Wilson

Wilson, Eliza, see John Wilson

Wilson, Eliza Jane, see William Henry Baker

Wilson, Fanny, see Stephen Bayard

Wilson, Hannah E., see John Wilson

Wilson, Isaac, married Letitia W. Jones on 13 Mar 1834, after obtaining a license on 12 Mar 1834, (date of license) by Rev. Davis (Cecil County Marriage License Book; Elkton Methodist Church Register, p. 5)

Wilson, James, see Joseph Barnaby

Wilson, James, married Lavinia Green on 12 Sep 1833, after obtaining a license that same day, by Rev. Hagany (Cecil County Marriage License Book; Elkton Methodist Church Register, p. 5)

Wilson, James, married Letitia Thompson circa 9 Apr 1836 (date of license) by Rev. Megredy (Cecil County Marriage License Book)

Wilson, James, married Henrietta Maria Nesbitt, second daughter of the late Samuel Nesbitt, Jr., Esq., all of Port Deposit, on 22 Feb 1849, after obtaining a license on 15 Feb 1849, by Rev. Taft (*Cecil Whig*, 3 Mar 1849; Cecil County Marriage License Book)

Wilson, James M., married Sophia Logan circa 19 Nov 1846 (date of license) (Cecil County Marriage License Book)

Wilson, Jane, see John Savin

Wilson, John, see John H. Gilmore

Wilson, John, married Jane Talley, both of New Castle Co., DE, on 11 Dec 1828 by John Cosgrove, Justice of the Peace for Chester Co., PA (*Elkton Press*, 13 Dec 1828)

Wilson, John (1811-1863, born Maryland) (sea captain, 7th District), married 1st to Adaline Gilmore circa 8 Oct 1838 (date of license) by Rev. Greenbank and married 2nd to Eliza Gilmore (1818-1886), widow of Capt. John H. Gilmore, circa 10 Sep 1858 (date of license) (Cecil County Marriage License Books; Hopewell United Methodist Church Cemetery tombstone inscriptions for Capt. John Wilson and Eliza Wilson, who are buried next to Capt. J. H. Gilmore (1813-1855), but there is no marker for Adaline Gilmore Wilson; 1860 Cecil County Census)

Wilson, John, married Hannah Gooding Baker (born 1816) circa 15 Nov 1845 (date of license) (Cecil County Marriage License Book; *Maryland Bible Records, Volume 4: Eastern Shore*, by Henry C. Peden, Jr. (2004), pp. 18-19, and p. 263 listed the births of their five children: John Henry, born 22 Jan 1847; Stephen Z., born 27 Sep 1848; Sarah Louise, born 19 Nov 1850; Hannah E., born 23 Feb 1854; and, William J., born 20 Nov 1859)

Wilson, John (captain), of Port Deposit, married Caroline M. Andrews, of Dorchester Co., on 14 Oct 1849 in Baltimore City by Rev. Martin (*Cecil Democrat and Farmer's Journal*, 27 Oct 1849; *Baltimore Sun*, 16 Oct 1849)

Wilson, John B. (1812-1880, born Pennsylvania) (shoemaker, 7th District), married Miss Sarah Ann Grubb (1821-1893, born Maryland) circa 27 Apr 1842 (date of license) (Cecil County Marriage License Book; Hopewell United Methodist Church Cemetery tombstone inscriptions; 1860 Cecil County Census)

Wilson, John Henry, see John Wilson

Wilson, John S., married Mary A. Irvin circa 8 Feb 1848 (date of license) (Cecil Co. Marr. License Book)

Wilson, Judith, see Enoch Mortimer Bye

Wilson, Julia Ann, see George H. Moore

Wilson, Juliana Virginia, see Thomas K. Stephens

Wilson, Lydia, see Job H. Kirk

Wilson, Margery, see James W. Rutter and John Rarick

Wilson, Martha, see Jacob Price

Wilson, Mary Jane, see David Scott

Wilson, Phebe, see Job H. Kirk

Wilson, Rosanna, see Joseph Barnaby

Wilson, Samuel, see Job H. Kirk

Wilson, Samuel (born c1820) (laborer at Chesapeake City), married Rachel (N) (born c1830) probably circa 1850; son David Wilson born c1851 (1860 Cecil County Census)

Wilson, Sarah Ann, see Franklin Beatty

Wilson, Sarah Louise, see John Wilson

Wilson, Stephen Z., see John Wilson

Wilson, Thomas, married Susan Mingling circa 6 Jan 1829 (date of license) by Rev. Duke (Cecil County Marriage License Book)

Wilson, Thomas, married Emily Thomas, both of Cecil Co., on 21 Sep 1837, after obtaining a license that same day, by Rev. Barratt (*Cecil Gazette*, 23 Sep 1837; Cecil County Marriage License Book)

Wilson, William, see William H. Gilpin

Wilson, William (born c1824, Maryland) (steamboat captain, 7th District), married Miss Sarah Ann Slicer (born c1822, Maryland) on 12 Jun 1845, after obtaining a license on 4 Jun 1845, by Rev. Townsend near Perryville (*Cecil Whig*, 21 Jun 1845; Cecil County Marriage License Book; 1860 Cecil County Census)

Wilson, William H., married Catharine Foster circa 8 Nov 1830 (date of license) by Rev. Rider (Cecil County Marriage License Book)

Wilson, William H., married Miss Mary E. Murphy, both of Cecil Co., on 10 Jan 1850, after obtaining a license on 9 Jan 1850, by Rev. Arthur at North East (*Cecil Whig*, 19 Jan 1850; Cecil County Marriage License Book spelled her name Murphey; *Cecil Democrat and Farmer's Journal*, 19 Jan 1850)

Wilson, William J., see John Wilson

Wilson, William Kenly, see John Charles Whitelock, Jr.

Wilson, William W., married Eliza Ann Price circa 6 Mar 1832 (date of license) by Rev. Duke (Cecil County Marriage License Book)

WINCHESTER

Winchester, George (born c1815) (farmer near Charlestown), married Lydia Taylor (born c1822) circa 20 Sep 1841 (date of license) (Cecil County Marriage License Book; 1860 Cecil County Census)

Winchester, Sophia, see William A. Hotchkiss

WINDLE

Windle, Lydia A., see George B. Kinkead

WINGATE

Wingate, James (editor of the *Maryland Free Press*), of Annapolis, married Jane Maria Eddy, daughter of O. T. Eddy, Esq., of Baltimore, on 27 Aug 1850 by Rev. Killin in Baltimore (*Cecil Democrat and Farmer's Journal*, 31 Aug 1850)

Wingate, Joseph S. (born c1806, Maryland) (farmer at North East), married Mary Ann Little (born c1808, Maryland) circa 22 Dec 1835 (date of license) (Cecil Co. Marr. License Book; 1860 Cecil Co. Census)

Wingate, Millicent, see Henry L. Gaw and Nicholas George

Wingate, Rebecca, see Francis B. Gottier

Wingate, Richard, married Sarah Robinson circa 1 Apr 1839 (date of license) by Rev. McFarland (Cecil County Marriage License Book; DAR transcript copied in 1928 mistakenly listed the minister's name as Farland; James McFarland was a Methodist minister in Elkton at that time)

Wingate, Sarah, see Alexander H. Wilson

Wingate, Thomas, married Millicent Hyland circa 25 May 1826 (date of license) by Rev. Barratt (Cecil County Marriage License Book)

WIRT

Wirt, Ann G., see James Warner

Wirt, Francina B., see Henry Kibler

Wirt, Henry Biddle, see John W. Wirt

Wirt, John Sluyter, see John W. Wirt

Wirt, John T., see Henry Kibler

Wirt, John W. (1808-1855) (doctor), of Bohemia Manor, Cecil Co., son of Samuel Wirt and wife Francina Bayard, of Delaware, married Mrs. Margaret Savin Biddle Mercer (7 Apr 1818 – 15 Feb 1896), widow of William D. Mercer and daughter of Peregrine Biddle, of Cecil Co., on 1 Aug 1848 in Wilmington by Rev. Wiley, and had three sons: William Bayard Wirt (27 Jul 1849 – 4 Mar 1896); John Sluyter Wirt (16 Nov 1851 – 17 May 1904) and Henry Biddle Wirt (30 Apr 1854 – 8 Feb 1881) (Elkton Cemetery tombstone inscriptions for Margaret Savin Wirt and three sons; *Portrait and Biographical Record of Harford and Cecil Counties, Maryland* (1897, repr. 1989), p. 211-212, 226-228; *Cecil Whig*, 12 Aug 1848, noted "Delaware Papers please copy.")

Wirt, Samuel, see John W. Wirt

Wirt, William Bayard, see John W. Wirt

WISER

Wiser, William M., married Miss Elizabeth Dunlap, both of London Brittain Township, Chester Co., PA, on 21 Jun 1849 by Rev. Plummer at Mt. Olivet, New London Township, Chester Co., PA (*Cecil Democrat and Farmer's Journal*, 7 Jul 1849)

WITTER

Witter, Mary, see Elisha Reynolds

WOELPER

Woelper, Mary, see Walter Elias Harding

WOLCOTT

Wolcott, Jane L., see Thomas A. Biddle

WOOD

Wood, Elizabeth, see George Mahan

Wood, Enos D., married Francina McCauley (born c1815) circa 11 Oct 1834 (date of license) by Rev. Wilson (Cecil County Marriage License Book; DAR transcript copied in 1928 listed his name as Enos T. Wood; 1860 Cecil County Census listed Francina Wood as head of household in Elkton; Cecil County Administration Account in 1845 gave his name as Enos D. Wood)

Wood, Mary A., see Jonathan Zane

Wood, Rachel, see Richard L. Simpers

Wood, Thomas, married Temperance Ann Shivery circa 20 Apr 1839 (date of license) by Rev. Hagany (Cecil County Marriage License Book)

Wood, William Simmons, married Amelia Pennington (c1800-1864) circa 24 Oct 1829 (date of license) by Rev. Duke and she died at Urieville, Kent Co., MD in her 64th year (Cecil County Marriage License Book; *Cecil Whig*, 24 Sep 1864)

WOODELL

Woodell, Sarah Jane, see James Webb

WOODEN, WOODDEN

Wooden, Solomon (1797-1875), married Elizabeth (N) (1807-1897), both of Baltimore Co. probably circa 1827 (North East Methodist Church Cemetery tombstone inscriptions)

Woodden, Ann, see James Gorrell

Woodden, Emily J., see John E. Grant

WOODFORD

Woodford, Julia, see Thomas W. Simmons

WOODLAND

Woodland, Mary Emma, see Edward T. Bailey

WOODROW

Woodrow, Eliza, see John H. McCartney

Woodrow, Henry, married Margaret Hindman circa 5 Dec 1832 (date of license) by Rev. (Cecil County Marriage License Book)

Woodrow, Jeremiah, married Clarissa Everett circa 26 Dec 1831 (date of license) by Rev. Duke (Cecil County Marriage License Book)

Woodrow, Jane, see William B. Woodrow

Woodrow, Judith, see William B. Woodrow and Stephen Woodrow

Woodrow, Prudence, see Samuel Hindman

Woodrow, Rachel, see Stephen Woodrow

Woodrow, Rebecca, see Stephen Woodrow

Woodrow, Samuel, married Miss Margaret E. Rafe circa 25 Dec 1848 (date of license) by Rev. Burroughs (Cecil County Marriage License Book; *Cecil Democrat and Farmer's Journal*, 6 Jan 1849)

Woodrow, Simeon, see Stephen Woodrow and William B. Woodrow

Woodrow, Stephen, married Alice Cook circa 24 Sep 1833 (date of license) by Rev. Guiber (Cecil County Marriage License Book)

Woodrow, Stephen, son of Simeon and Judith Woodrow, the latter deceased, married Sarah Stapler, daughter of Stephen and Sarah Stapler, the former deceased, on the 18th day of the – month 1835 at West Nottingham. Among the witnesses were Simeon Woodrow, Rebecca Woodrow, Stephen Woodrow, Rachel Woodrow and Mary Stapler. (*Births, Deaths and Marriages of the Nottingham Quakers, 1680-1899*, by Alice L. Beard (1989), pp. 222-223)

Woodrow, William B. (1806-1897) (farmer in the 6th District), son of Simeon and Judith Woodrow, married Lydia C. (N) (1809-1874, born Pennsylvania) probably circa 1833; daughter Jane born c1834, Maryland (Friends Cemetery, at Harrisville, tombstone inscriptions; 1860 Cecil County Census)

WOODS

Woods, Elizabeth, see John Reynolds

Woods, Thomas, see John Reynolds

Woods, William C., of Wilmington, DE, married Miss Sarah Ann Wells, of Elkton, on 10 Feb 1846, after obtaining a license that day, by Rev. McIntyre (Cecil County Marriage License Book; DAR transcript copied in 1955 listed his name as Wood; *Delaware Gazette*, 20 Feb 1846; *Cecil Whig*, 14 Feb 1846, partly illegible: "With the above notice we received an excellent slice of cake – We trust the happy couple may realize a large slice of ---- life as they pass through it and that ---- may ever attend on their path.")

WOODWARD

Woodward, Joseph Janvier, see Edward J. Emmons

WOOLLEHAN
Woollehan, Jacob, married Elizabeth Taylor circa 5 Feb 1833 (date of license) by Rev. Duke (Cecil County Marriage License Book; DAR transcript copied in 1928 spelled his name Woolehand)

Woollehan, Jacob, married Margaret Veach circa 2 Aug 1828 (date of license) by Rev. Cooper (Cecil County Marriage License Book)

WOOLLEY
Woolley, George Edward (1810-1855), married Mary Ann Turner (1810-1889) circa 16 Oct 1832 (date of license) by Rev. McCarrol, a Methodist Episcopal minister in Port Deposit (Cecil County Marriage License Book; Zion Methodist Cemetery tombstone inscriptions)

WOOLSTON
Woolston, Mary Ann, see Joseph Tuffree (Puffree?)

Woolston, Rachel, see Lewis McKey

Woolston, Susannah Q., see William Broadwell

WORRELL
Worrell, William P., married Miss Catharine Tilden, both of Kent Co., on 27 Jan 1829 by Rev. Clowes (*Elkton Press*, 7 Feb 1829)

WORTH
Worth, Ann V., see Jacob Gilbert

Worth, Joseph, married Margaret Grant circa 13 Jan 1830 (date of license) by Rev. Barratt (Cecil County Marriage License Book)

Worth, Sarah, see Seborn Grant

WORTHINGTON
Worthington, John Y., married Margaret Coale, second daughter of Skipwith Coale, on 8 May 1832 at West Nottingham, Cecil Co. (*Baltimore American and Commercial Daily Advertiser*, 1 May 1832)

Worthington, Margaret, see William H. Davis

WRIGHT
Wright, Cornelia, see Charles Hall

Wright, Eli, married Millicent Biddle on 5 Jan 1843 (Elkton Methodist Church Register; Cecil County Marriage License Book did not list this marriage)

Wright, Eliza, see Jeremiah Steel

Wright, Eliza Ann, see James Storey

Wright, Eliza Jane, see William Taggart

Wright, Jane, see Watson Scarborough

Wright, John, married Carlotta Ralston circa 14 Sep 1835 (date of license) by Rev. Houston (Cecil County Marriage License Book)

Wright, John, married Mary Ann Clifton circa 28 Jul 1832 (date of license) by Rev. Torbert (Cecil County Marriage License Book)

Wright, Joseph (born c1812) (African American) (farmer at Cecilton), married Rebecca (N) (born c1816) (African American) circa 1837; son Solomon born c1838 (1860 Cecil Co. Census spelled his name Write)

Wright, Lewis, married Eliza Jane Brown circa 19 Sep 1832 (date of license) by Rev. Duke (Cecil County Marriage License Book)

Wright, Margaret J., see Jacob Boulden

Wright, Martha, see John D. Miller

Wright, Mary S., see Joseph Scarborough

Wright, Peter R. (born c1818) (farmer near Elkton), married Miss Susan Ann Plummer (born c1816), both of Cecil Co., on 24 Nov 1844, after obtaining a license on 21 Nov 1844, by Rev. Shields (Cecil County Marriage License Book; Elkton Methodist Church Register, p. 140; *Cecil Whig*, 30 Nov 1844; 1860 Cecil County Census)

Wright, Solomon, see Joseph Wright

Wright, William, see Jacob Boulden

WROTH

Wroth, Ann E., see George W. Walmsley

Wroth, John, married Miss Araminta M. Morgan, both of Cecil Co., married on 7 Sep 1834, after obtaining a license on 5 Sep 1834, by Rev. McKenney, a Protestant Episcopal minister in the North Sassafras (*Cecil Gazette*, 13 Sep 1834; Cecil County Marriage License Book)

YARNALL

Yarnall, John B. (esquire), of Port Deposit, married Mary Cropper, daughter of Ebenezer Cropper, Esq., of Elk Neck, on 17 Nov 1847, after obtaining a license that same day, by Rev. Barrett (*Cecil Whig*, 4 Dec 1847; Cecil County Marriage License Book)

YATES

Yates, Hannah Louise, see James McCauley

Yates, James (1814-1885), married Susanna E. (N) (1819-1887) probably circa 1838-1840 (Elkton Cemetery tombstone inscriptions)

YEAGER

Yeager, Elizabeth, see Nicholas Lottman

YEAMANS

Yeamans, Caroline, see Andrew Fisher

Yeamans, John (1794-1878), of Cecil Co., married 1st to Sarah (N) and their marriage was annulled and they divorced on 2 Mar 1827; he married 2nd to Mary Grant (1807-1868) circa 8 Mar 1827 (date of license) (Cecil County Marriage License Book; *Divorces and Names Changed in Maryland by Act of the Legislature, 1634-1867*, by Mary Keysor Meyer (1991), p. 102; Charlestown Cemetery tombstones)

YEARSLEY

Yearsley, Joseph (1813-1879), married Esther (N) (1810-1880) before 1844; buried beside daughter Hannah Yearsley, 1845-1877 (St. John's Church Cemetery, at Lewisville, tombstone inscriptions)

YELLOTT

Yellott, John (esquire), of Baltimore Co., married Sarah Jane Maulsby, daughter of Gen. I. D. Maulsby, on 1 Feb 1838, after obtaining a license on 31 Jan 1838, by Rev. Keech (Pastoral Records of Rev. John R. Keech at Christ Church and St. John's Parish; Harford Co. Marriage License Book; *Cecil Gazette*, 10 Feb 1838, stated they married "on Thursday morning at the seat of Gen. Maulsby, near Bel Air, Harford Co.")

YORKMAN

Yorkman, Nancy, see Jacob Sewall

YOUNG

Young, Ann Eliza, see Caleb Parker Johnson

Young, Hannah, see Isaac Freeman

Young, Mary, see George Davis

Young, John (born c1821, Ohio) (vessel captain at Chesapeake City), married Rebecca (N) (born c1818, New Jersey) probably circa 1849; daughter Mary born c1850, Maryland (1860 Cecil County Census)

Young, Martha B., see Caleb Parker Johnson

Young, Mary, see John Young

Young, Mary Sophia, see John England

Young, Peter, see John England

Young, Sophia, see John England

Young, Thomas H., of Elkton, married Miss Rebecca Ricketts (1807-1891), sister of William H. Ricketts, probably circa 1828 (Elkton Cemetery tombstone inscription; *Midland Journal*, 6 Mar 1891)

Young, William S. (lieut., U. S. Navy), married Sarah S. Black, daughter of the late Hon. James R. Black, of New Castle, DE, on 12 May 1841 by Rev. Presstman at New Castle (*Cecil Gazette*, 29 May 1841)

ZANE

Zane, Ann, see Nicholas Lum

Zane, Jonathan (1817-1866), of New Leeds, married Mary A. Wood (1816-1854) circa 20 Apr 1840 (date of license) by Rev. Kennard (Cecil County Marr. License Book; DAR transcript copied in 1928 spelled his name Zanes; Cherry Hill Methodist Church Cemetery tombstone inscriptions; *Cecil Whig*, 24 Mar 1866)